THE SOCIAL DESIGN READER

THE SOCIAL DESIGN READER

Edited by

Elizabeth Resnick

BLOOMSBURY VISUAL ARTS
LONDON • NEW YORK • OXFORD • NEW DELHI • SYDNEY

BLOOMSBURY VISUAL ARTS
Bloomsbury Publishing Plc
50 Bedford Square, London, WC1B 3DP, UK
1385 Broadway, New York City, 10018, USA

BLOOMSBURY, BLOOMSBURY VISUAL ARTS and the Diana logo are trademarks of Bloomsbury Publishing Plc

First published in Great Britain 2019

A catalogue record for this book is available from the British Library.

A catalog record for this book is available from the Library of Congress.

ISBN: HB: 978-1-3500-2606-3
PB: 978-1-3500-2605-6
ePub: 978-1-3500-2603-2
ePDF: 978-1-3500-2602-5

Typeset by Newgen KnowledgeWorks Pvt. Ltd., Chennai, India
Printed and bound in India

To find out more about our authors and books visit www.bloomsbury.com
and sign up for our newsletter.

This book is dedicated to the memory of my colleague, mentor, and friend

Albert J. Gowan *(1934–2017)*

Professor Emeritus, Massachusetts College of Art and Design, Boston
Author of "Victor Papanek: Path of a Design Prophet"

CONTENTS

ACKNOWLEDGMENTS   x

LIST OF ILLUSTRATIONS   xi

PREFACE   xiii

SECTION 1 MAKING A STAND: A NEW SOCIAL AGENDA FOR DESIGN

1   Introduction   3
    Elizabeth Resnick

2   Is Social Design a Thing?   9
    Cameron Tonkinwise

3   Social Design: From Utopia to the Good Society   17
    Victor Margolin

4   Émigré Culture and the Origins of Social Design   31
    Alison J. Clarke

SECTION 2 CREATING THE FUTURE: DEFINING THE SOCIALLY RESPONSIBLE DESIGNER 1964–99

5   Introduction   39
    Elizabeth Resnick

6   First Things First Manifesto   47
    Ken Garland

7   Here Are Some Things We Must Do   49
    Ken Garland

8 Edugraphology—The Myths of Design and the Design of Myths   57
   Victor Papanek

9 Design as a Socially Significant Activity   63
   Clive Dilnot

10 Designerly Ways of Knowing   73
   Nigel Cross

11 The Future Isn't What It Used to Be   87
   Victor Papanek

12 Commerce or Culture: Industrialization and Design   101
   John Heskett

13 Wicked Problems in Design Thinking   117
   Richard Buchanan

14 Good Citizenship: Design as a Social and Political Force   137
   Katherine McCoy

15 Feminist Perspectives (Design for Society)   145
   Nigel Whitely

16 There Is Such a Thing as Society   167
   Andrew Howard

17 Design and Reflexivity   175
   Jan van Toorn

18 Design Noir   179
   Anthony Dunne

SECTION 3 A SEA CHANGE: THE PARADIGM SHIFT FROM OBJECTS TO SYSTEMS 2000–20

19 Introduction   185
   Elizabeth Resnick

20 First Things First 2000 Manifesto   199

21 A "Social Model" of Design: Issues of Practice and Research   201
   Victor Margolin and Sylvia Margolin

22 The Dematerialization of Design   209
   Jorge Frascara

23 Why Being "Less Bad" Is No Good (Cradle to Cradle)   217
   William McDonough and Michael Braungart

24 Clothes That Connect   229
   Kate Fletcher

25 Design's Role in Sustainable Consumption   241
    Ann Thorpe

26 Transformative Services and Transformation Design   257
    Daniela Sangiorgi

27 Rethinking Design Thinking: Part I   277
    Lucy Kimbell

28 Rethinking Design Thinking: Part II   295
    Lucy Kimbell

29 Design Things and Design Thinking: Contemporary Participatory
    Design Challenges   311
    Erling Bjögvinsson, Pelle Ehn, and Per-Anders Hillgren

30 From Design Culture to Design Activism   327
    Guy Julier

31 Decolonizing Design Innovation: Design Anthropology, Critical Anthropology,
    and Indigenous Knowledge   345
    Elizabeth (Dori) Tunstall

32 Social Design and Neocolonialism   361
    Cinnamon Janzer and Lauren Weinstein

33 Futuristic Gizmos, Conservative Ideals: On Speculative Anachronistic Design   375
    Pedro J. S. Vieira de Oliveira and Luiza Prado de O. Martins

34 Privilege and Oppression: Towards a Feminist Speculative Design   381
    Luiza Prado de O. Martins

35 Is Sustainable Innovation an Oxymoron?   393
    Elizabeth B.-N. Sanders

36 Social Innovation and Design: Enabling, Replicating and Synergizing   403
    Ezio Manzini

37 Global Methods, Local Designs   417
    Ahmed Ansari

38 The Emerging Transition Design Approach   431
    Terry Irwin

List of Contributors   455

Further Readings   461

Index   465

ACKNOWLEDGMENTS

This collection of seminal texts simply could not have been possible without the very generous support of *all* the contributors to this effort: Ahmed Ansari, Erling Björgvinsson, Gui Bonsiepe, Scott Boylston, Max Bruinsma, Michael Braungart, Richard Buchanan, Sharon Burdett, Valerie Casey, Jonanthan Chapman, Alison J. Clarke, Nigel Cross, Sheila Levrant de Bretteville, Decolonising Design, Clive Dilnot, Carl DiSalvo, Kees Dorst, Anthony Dunne, Pelle Ehn, Joost Elffers, David Evans, Terence Fenn, Kate Fletcher, Jorge Frascara, Alastair Fuad-Luke, Nick Gant, Ken Garland, John Heskett, Per-Anders Hillgren, Jason Hobbs, Stefan Holmlid, Andrew Howard, Gordon Hush, Terry Irwin, Tim Jackson, Cinnamon Janzer, Guy Julier, Lucy Kimbell, Ilpo Koskinen, Diana Krabbendam, Klaus Krippendorff, Kalle Lasn, Ezio Manzini, Victor Margolin, Katherine McCoy, William McDonough, Ivica Mitrovic, Chantal Mouffe, David Oswald, Rev. Nicolette Papanek/Victor Papanek, Luiza Prado de O. Martins, Elizabeth B.-N. Sanders, Daniela Sangiorgi, Michiel Schwarz, Ann Thorpe, Cameron Tonkinwise, Elizabeth (Dori) Tunstall, Jan van Toorn, Pedro Vieira de Oliveira, Lauren Weinstein, and Nigel Whitely.

There are a few individuals who deserve special thanks for their encouragement and advice during the book project: Lisa Abendroth, Fatima Cassim, Audra Buck Coleman, Annelys de Vet, Ariel Guersenzvaig, Terry Irwin, Jackie Malcolm, Massimo Santanicchia, and Victor Margolin for his patience with my questions and frequent requests for advice.

I am indebted to my editor, Rebecca Barden, for giving me this unique opportunity to create *The Social Design Reader*. I wish to thank her editorial assistant, Claire Constable for keeping me on track and for all the small things she helped me with during the course of this project.

And, I am very grateful and thankful to my husband, Victor Cockburn, and my adult children, Alex and Elana, who all endured my distraction and frequent spells of anxiety with encouragement and grace.

ILLUSTRATIONS

FIGURES

32.1 A Social Design Action Matrix. © Cinnamon Janzer and Lauren Weinstein 2014   365

35.1 The shape of the design development process has changed with the growth of a large front end   394

35.2 The roles that designers play (in the left column) and the roles that people play (in the right-column) have been changing over time   396

35.3 A framework for navigating the fuzzy front end of the design development process where the problems are wicked and the landscape is fuzzy   397

35.4 The fuzzy front end of design sits in the intentional design space   398

35.5 The participatory prototyping cycle (PPC) is a framework for action and a model for co-creation in design   399

35.6 The participatory prototyping cycle in action   400

35.7 Making, telling and enacting take on different forms in the fuzzy front end, the gap and in the design development process   401

38.1 The Transition Design Framework brings together a body of practices in four key areas useful in designing for systems-level change   435

38.2 The emerging Transition Design approach suggests three phases comprised of reframing the problem and its context in the present and future, designing interventions, then observing how the system responds. These broad phases accommodate a variety of practices and processes tailored to specific problems and contexts   436

38.3 Backcasting from a co-created future vision creates a "transition pathway" along which new and existing projects can be connected and situated as "steps" in a long transition toward the desired future 440

38.4 Transition Design draws upon the concept of the Multi-Level Perspective (Geels, 2006) to situate both the wicked problem and a future, lifestyle-based vision in a large, spatio-temporal context. This large context is explored in order to identify the most promising points of "intervention" lie within this large context 441

38.5 Specific questions can be asked at each level in the past, present and future in order to guide research and bring a higher level of fidelity to the future vision 442

38.6 The practices above are listed in the Transition Framework and can be especially useful in designing systems interventions within large, spatio-temporal contexts 443

38.7 (A–C) An overview of the emerging Transition Design approach is presented using several of the practices included in the Framework. These can be configured differently and appropriately for different problems and situations 446

TABLES

27.1 Different Ways of Describing Design Thinking 281

32.1 Selected Appropriate Research Methods Organized by Matrix Quadrant 367

PREFACE

The Social Design Reader is an anthology[1] of key writings written over the past fifty-five years by leading proponents, researchers, and practitioners shaping the emergence of socially responsible design as a concept, as a nascent field of study, and as a developing discipline within professional design practice.

During the past thirty-five years, there has been a tsunami of books published on the subject of design—expounding on its critical nature, its history, its technology, and its continuously evolving culture of professional practice and significant practitioners. Art and design libraries (typically housed in colleges and universities) have archived many of the important international design magazines and academic journals from the early twentieth century to the present day. With the rise of the internet and the demand for easily accessible research materials to build a history of design culture and activity, there has been a vigorous movement toward anthologizing historically significant texts and articles previously published in design magazines and academic journals that are simply not accessible to the public, as many such publications are either out-of-print or housed in private libraries or collections that are very expensive to access.

An anthology is above all, a collaborative work. My aim with this compilation is to bring together a group of authentic voices—theorists, scholars, writers, and designers—who are building a canon of informed literature that documents the genesis and rapid development within this field of study. In concert, these texts build upon the notion that *social design is design with a conscience*, and, as such, can help the reader understand how design can be employed as a catalyst for social change. Editing an anthology of this nature can be quite a daunting task, especially for someone without experience in this genre and format.

There are many restrictions when framing a compilation of this kind: contracted word count; the stringency of academic permission fee budgets; the availability of key texts; and the ensuing economic and physical challenge to gain permission to republish them. Another contributing factor to the framing of this anthology is its bias for language preference—the decision to collect texts written (or translated) in English (the editor's sole language)—which impedes a wider variety of writing from alterative economic, cultural, or political perspectives.[2] All pivotal criteria that contributed to the selection of what texts to publish.

The crucial advantage to this type of anthology is its ability to feature texts emphasizing the theoretical and discursive dialogue threads from multiple perspectives current within mainstream academic and professional discourse, and those from the margins of the status quo. The texts were reproduced as they had been first published—written in either British English or American English.[3] A unique aspect that emerges from such a diversity of voices is the different and distinctive writing styles that should be embraced by the reader.

STRUCTURE OF THE READER

The Social Design Reader is divided into three sections:

Section 1: Making a Stand: A New Social Agenda for Design includes the introduction to the term *social design* and papers that explore its historical underpinnings to build a foundation to support the expanding dialogue and embody the social design movement.

Section 2: Creating the Future: Defining the Socially Responsible Designer 1964–99 feature papers that document the emergence of *social design* as a concept, as a nascent field of study, and as a rapidly developing professional discipline.

Section 3: A Sea Change: The Paradigm Shift from Objects to Systems 2000–20 feature papers that acknowledge *design* as a firmly established professional discipline. As such, there is an increased need for both quantitative and qualitative research that utilizes strategic and critical thinking as designers are now being challenged to tackle complex social problems during the first two decades of the twenty-first century.

Contextualizing section introductions are provided to assist readers in understanding the nature of the material discussed along with summary messages that articulate how each text fits within the larger milieu of social design theory, methods, and practice.

KEY FEATURES

- *The Social Design Reader* brings together *previously published* seminal papers, essays, articles, and excerpts with a laser focus on the social nature of design to provide the reader with a solid overview of the trajectory and key advancements toward a more human-centered profession.

- *The Social Design Reader* draws from a wide range of writing published in academic journals—publications that are not easily accessed by students and working practitioners and are often behind a pay wall.

- *The Social Design Reader* assists the reader in comprehending the ever changing nature of design practice while encouraging an active understanding of social design thinking and its role in preparing more empathetic, creative leaders for society's challenges.

- *The Social Design Reader* is the first anthology on this topic to be produced by an editor who has experience—both professional communication design practice and university-level teaching—in organizing meaningful social design interactions with local community groups within the university classroom environment.[4] The goal is to encourage the reader to think about design as an agent of social change.

NOTES

1. An anthology is a book or other collection of selected writings by various authors, usually in the same literary form, of the same period, or on the same subject. https://www.dictionary.com/browse/anthology.
2. "Within the current landscape of design academia, non-Western epistemologies and practices have not been taken seriously, and this has a history going all the way back to the need to develop design methods as a reaction to what was seen as craft-based design—incidentally associated with pre-industrial, non-European cultures." Ahmed Ansari, *What a Decolonisation of Design Involves: Two Programmes for Emancipation*, April 12, 2018. At http://www.decolonisingdesign.com/topics/actions-and-interventions/publications/ (accessed August 28, 2018).
3. British and American people often spell the same word differently. A good example would be "colour" in British English and "color" in American English. Both "dialects" of English often feature different terms to describe the same thing. A good example would be "mobile phone" in British English and "cell phone" in American English. A good read on the history of these differences can be found at http://www.bbc.com/culture/story/20150715-why-isnt-american-a-language (accessed August 28, 2018).
4. *Developing Citizen Designers* (2016) by Elizabeth Resnick is a book containing international university-level case study assignments and pedagogical texts aimed at students, educators, and designers in the early stages of their careers, to learn and practice design in a socially responsible manner. It responds to the rise of academic debate and teaching in the areas of social design, sustainable design, ethical design, and design futures.

Making a Stand: A New Social Agenda for Design

Social design … with its growing range of genres and practices, has seen an exponential expansion in the last decade. Design is no longer a twentieth-century studio-based practice confined to the authorship of given individuals, or the strictures of a purely profit-driven design management team working to a fixed brief and a crude consumer profile. Models of the autocratic design guru behind his drawing board appear today as anachronistic as the notoriously misogynistic advertising industry of the 1950s. As user groups, co-design and participatory methods increasingly shape the practice, and as a renewed focus on people, their relations, beliefs and practices comes to the fore, we are witnessing a seismic shift to the "social."

—Alison J. Clarke, *Émigré Culture and the Origins of Social Design*, 2015

CHAPTER ONE

Introduction

ELIZABETH RESNICK

Social Design is the practice of design where the primary motivation is to promote positive social change within society. As both a discipline and a professional practice that has experienced dramatic growth in recent years, Social Design remains nascent in its teaching, research, and community-oriented practices. Initially inspired by the writings of Victor Papanek and many others, social design's "social" agenda is to encourage designers and creative professionals to adopt a proactive role and effect tangible change to make life better for others—rather than to sell them products and services they neither need nor want, which has been the primary motivation for commercial design practice in the twentieth century.

The term "social design" has continued to gain momentum within academia, business, and governmental organizations over the past twenty years. But what does this term actually mean? When linked together, the two words social design seem to simulate a state of ambiguity. It is no wonder that there seems to be no consensus on the meaning of this term! If we separate the words "social" and "design," we discover that both words are nouns.[1] As a noun, the word social is defined as "an informal social gathering, especially one organized by the members of a particular club or group." As a noun, the word design is defined as a "purpose or planning that exists behind an action, fact, or object."[2] The word social is also an adjective which is "a word naming an attribute of a noun"; and the word design is also a verb which is "a word used to describe an action, state, or occurrence, and forming the main part of the predicate of a sentence, such as hear, become, happen."[3] For example: "Everyone designs who devises courses of action aimed at changing existing situation into preferred ones."[4]

A *term* is a "word or phrase used to describe a thing or to express a concept, especially in a particular kind of language or branch of study."[5] In the *term* social design, the use of the word social functions as an adjective naming a particular attribute of design or "a synonym for 'highly problematic condition', which poses the need for urgent intervention, outside normal market or public service modalities" as suggested by eminent researcher and educator

Ezio Manzini.[6] However, what do we have in mind when we use the term social design? Isn't all design understood as social by nature? "Design is the enactment of human instinct and a construct that facilitates the materialization of our world."[7] I would agree with this statement. Design gives shape and form to the material and immaterial products and services that can address problems and contribute to the well-being of humankind. *Wikipedia* defines the term social design in this way: "Social design is design that is mindful of the designer's role and responsibility in society; and the use of the design process to bring about social change. Within the design world, social design is sometimes defined as a design process that contributes to improving human well-being and livelihood."[8]

And on the use of the term itself:

> The term social design is also increasingly used to describe design of the social world. This definition implicates a perception of a man-made reality, which consequently can only be changed by humans, and *is* changed by humans all the time. In this view social design is inescapable, it is there whether people are aware of it or not. The social reality is created as a result of the sum of all our individual actions. There is an emerging discussion of this concept of social design, which encompasses all other definitions of the term.[9]

In 2010, the Winterhouse First Symposium on Design Education and Social Change was convened to form the basis for a collaborative network with the goal of providing students with the tools and training to explore and address social-design problems:

> The diffuseness of social-design educational efforts can be partly attributed to vagueness in definition. The phrases "social change," "social innovation" and "social design" appear frequently in academic and journalistic discourse, but rarely with precision. At the same time, the meaning of "design" has expanded beyond the creation or arrangement of objects and communications to describe such conceptual approaches as systems design, service design and design thinking ... The concept of "social design" is still in its infancy. Social design needs to be defined more clearly in relation to social enterprise, social entrepreneurship and social innovation.[10]

In 2012, the Social Impact Design Summit was convened at the Rockefeller Foundation headquarters in New York to address the challenges and opportunities within the field today. A white paper based on the summit titled "Design and Social Impact: A Cross-Sectoral Agenda for Design Education" was published and widely disseminated. One of the major stumbling blocks that emerged was that "summit participants singled out the lack of a clear understanding of what the term means. Greater clarity, they proposed, would lead to better-defined goals and would boost appreciation of the value of the field."[11]

They identified socially responsible design [as] an overarching term for design that is socially, environmentally, and economically sustainable—three quality-of-life pillars defined and addressed by an international community. The field is also known as public-interest design, social design, social impact design, socially responsive design, transformation design, and humanitarian design. In this report, the terms social impact design and socially responsible design will be used interchangeably.[12] Laura Kurgan, one of the thirty-four summit participants offered:

> Socially responsible is often the wrong term to define what it is trying to address. Often, socially responsible design implies a) solving the problem of poverty, or b) prioritizing people and use in a design problem rather than design itself, or c) sustainable design, which is equally hard to define. Being socially responsible—or solving urban problems through design—means addressing politics, globalization, health, education, criminal justice, or economics among others.[13]

In 2014, a report was commissioned by the UK-based Arts and Humanities Research Council (AHRC) and published by the University of Brighton that presented the findings of a nine-month study of opportunities and challenges for research in the social design arena. This report offered a cogent description of the term social design:

> The term "social design" highlights the concepts and activities enacted within participatory approaches to researching, generating and realising new ways to make change happen towards collective and social ends, rather than predominantly commercial objectives. Social design can therefore be understood to encompass a broad set of motivations, approaches, audiences and impacts. For instance, these may be embedded within government policies or public services extremely critical of and divergent from these. Social design may be carried out by people who think of themselves as designers or who studied at design schools, or it might be an activity of designing that takes place involving people who are not professional designers.[14]

IS SOCIAL DESIGN A THING?

To continue the exploration of the meaning of the term social design, design academic Cameron Tonkinwise posits important questions we should all consider and contributes a "schema of the different meanings of the 'social' in Social Design" in his 2015 rumination "Is Social Design a Thing?" He concludes (thankfully) that Social Design is indeed a "thing" in its own right.

SOCIAL DESIGN: FROM UTOPIA TO THE GOOD SOCIETY

"I believe we are at a global turning point. Design now has to be for social good and I'm shaping a vision of what a 'good society' could be and how design and designers could help to bring it about."[15] Eminent design historian and scholar Victor Margolin shapes his vision of the "good society" in his 2015 paper "Social Design: From Utopia to the Good Society." Design has a long history of commitment to addressing social issues in the design movements of the late nineteenth century that sought to improve working conditions to the mid-twentieth-century designers critical of consumerist society. Surveying social design's historical roots, Margolin connects its origins by examining influential utopian visionaries such as designers William Morris, Walter Gropius, and Richard Buckminster-Fuller. Margolin concludes that such a study of their foresight, ethos, and values could be very beneficial in visioning the future of social design—"utopian thought is a particular kind of proactive thought that is removed from the constraints of the real world. It provides an opportunity to imagine an ideal place that can serve as a beacon towards which to strive." While Margolin does recognize the aspirational value of utopian ideals, he argues that the "good society" project[16] should move beyond these ideals to address real world situations realized by real world actions.

In evaluating the importance of Victor Papanek's 1971 book *Design for the Real World*, Margolin acknowledges that Papanek "was one of the first designers to call attention to ways that design could be practiced outside the market." But Margolin is also critical that Papanek did not "recognize the problems he identified as part of a dysfunctional social and political system that itself was badly in need of redesign" when he argues that "when the mechanisms to engender change from within the 'real-world' are flawed, we need to address these mechanisms themselves and develop an alternative 'action frame.'" To this end, Margolin advocates that designers should come up with a new "action frame" for the world: "We need to rethink the way we organize our lives at every level from the local to the global." He concludes by asking "whether the international community of design educators and designers can recognize its own power as a collective agent of change and undertake a radical rethinking of how we could live, a rethinking that this community, better than anyone, can translate into propositions for projects that inspire people to carry them out."

ÉMIGRÉ CULTURE AND THE ORIGINS OF SOCIAL DESIGN

In her influential paper "Émigré Culture and the Origins of Social Design," design historian and social anthropologist Alison J. Clarke explores the genesis of social design through the focused lens of the Austrian and Central European émigrés and exiled designers who established influential networks within the United States—to promote a more progressive humanist culture encompassing new strategies—for a socially inclusive design culture that continues to influence contemporary design practice. Clarke examines the significance of the 1970s political activism and also cites (as Margolin does) the important contribution of American-Austrian émigré Victor Papanek as "the best known and pioneering proponent of social design" whose ground-breaking and best-selling 1971 book *Design for the Real World: Human Ecology and Social Change* coincided with "the revolutionary spirit of the 1960s and 1970s [which] gave rise to counter design and anti-design movements pitted against the hierarchies, environmental negligence and technological determinism of the design industry."

NOTES

1. A noun is a word (other than a pronoun) used to identify any of a class of people, places, or things (common noun), or to name a particular one of these (proper noun). https://en.oxforddictionaries.com/definition/noun.

2. https://en.oxforddictionaries.com/definition/design.

3. https://en.oxforddictionaries.com/definition/social.

4. H. A. Simon, "The Science of Design: Creating the Artificial," *Design Issues* 4, nos. 1 and 2 (1988), pp. 67–82.

5. https://en.oxforddictionaries.com/definition/term.

6. Mapping Social Design Research & Practice, *Social Design Rant 4—Ezio Manzini*, 2014, https://mappingsocialdesign.wordpress.com/2014/06/16/social-design-rant-4-ezio-manzini/ (accessed August 26, 2018).

7. A. Fuad-Luke, *Design Activism Beautiful Strangeness for a Sustainable World* (London: Earthscan, 2009), 152.

8. *Wikipedia*, "Social Design," 2018, http://en.wikipedia.org/wiki/Social_design.

9. Ibid.

10. In 2006, graphic designers William Drenttel and Jessica Helfand established The Winterhouse Institute to explore the value of design education for Social Impact (http://www.winterhouseinstitute.org/). William Drenttel and Julie Lasky, *Winterhouse Symposium on Design Education and Social Change: Final Reports*. https://designobserver.com/feature/winterhouse-first-symposium-on-design-education-and-social-change-final-report/22578.

11. *Design and Social Impact*, 2013, 1st ed. (New York: The Smithsonian's Cooper-Hewitt, National Design Museum, 2014), 6.

12. Ibid., 8.

13. Ibid., 20.

14. Leah Armstrong, Jocelyn Bailey, Guy Julier, and Lucy Kimbell, *Social Design Futures: HEI Research and the AHRC. Project Report* (Brighton/London: University of Brighton/Victoria and Albert Museum, 2014).

15. Victor Margolin quoted in the interview with Don Ryun Chang in 2015, https://www.linkedin.com/pulse/special-interview-5-victor-margolin-idc-gwangju/ (accessed August 28, 2018).

16. "Design's entitlement is grounded in its contribution to the creation of 'the good society.' A society that ensures that everyone has access to the goods and services needed for a decent existence. 'The good society' is a dream of a world that is fair and just, a utopian concept, which provides direction and enables us to join forces. By virtue of their powers of imagination and expertise, designers are well placed for expressing this dream of 'the good society' in an appealing way and to help translate it into practice." From the Utrecht Manifesto 2015, http://www.utrechtmanifest.nl/files/doc/026/utrechtmanifesto.pdf (accessed August 28, 2018).

CHAPTER TWO

Is Social Design a Thing?

CAMERON TONKINWISE

© Cameron Tonkinwise, 2015

During a workshop that was part of the UK AHRC funded Mapping Social Design Practice and Research project (http://mappingsocialdesign.org/), Ezio Manzini cogently insisted that there is no such thing as 'social design,' nor should there be. At best, argued Manzini, there is designing—the more or less conventional forms of (material) designing with which (modern[ist]) design schools and design professionals are already familiar—applied to contexts that you might characterize as 'social.'

If we take for granted that our societies today face complex social challenges that demand new kinds of responses, is the task merely to lend the existing practices of designing, which have hitherto served mostly commercial clients, to these 'social' contexts? Or are we in need of a different kind of designing when it comes to these contexts? To what does the 'social' in 'social design' refer? Is it just the context for designing or is it a qualifier for distinct forms of design?

I want to try to defend the idea that Social Design, if not yet a 'thing,' should be a thing, something that entails a different, though still related, kind of designing than that with which we are familiar. To do this, I would like to contribute something like a schema of the different meanings of the 'social' in Social Design.

1. SOCIAL DESIGN = DESIGNING AS A SOCIAL ACTIVITY

Talk of design frequently has recourse to the modernist myth of the genius individual artist, alone in his [sic] studio with his (asocial) things. The adjective 'social' is therefore an important corrective, insisting that all designing is collaborative. In addition to almost always involving a team, designing is inseparable from negotiations between sponsoring clients, representative users or their mediating researchers, material and component suppliers, manufacturers and coders, marketers and retailers, sometimes regulatory agencies and legal counsel, etc.

This socially collaborative quality to designing is not merely pragmatic. Since designing involves making decisions about preferred futures, its validity lies only in the social, in people sharing a commitment to materialize those kinds of futures. Design, especially Design Thinking, is often feted for its ability to have insights into creative breakthrough ideas. But these are worth nothing unless supported by diverse social networks that enable them to become real—and this is the real work of Design.

Given this, you might expect that designers are highly accomplished persuaders or politicians, and that facilitation and negotiation are core to design education. To some extent, this is the role of 'crit' in designing—where ideas are comprehensively stress-tested—an aspect of the process that often makes non-designers uncomfortable. However, it is nevertheless true that designers frequently try to let their designs argue for themselves. Material things, like prototypes, are powerful rhetorical devices. But then the question becomes, what is a persuasive prototype of a social design?

As such, design in the context of complex societal challenges requires quantitatively greater and perhaps qualitatively new forms of 'design as a social activity.'

2. SOCIAL DESIGN = DESIGN WORKS WITH THE SOCIOMATERIAL

Design emerged out of craft and is usually characterized as the skilful material practice of making things. The icons of design are seemingly timeless physical forms. However, the real aim of the designed products are to be 'of use.' A successful design enables new ways of doing things and so becomes a habitual part of how we live. Rather than standing out like museum pieces, designs become part of the dynamic fabric of our built environments supporting our everyday activities.

Counter intuitively, designed things enable everyday activities not being inert tools, but being 'alive' to the everyday needs and desires of their users. Designing involves the development of forms and mechanisms that can activate material products to people's tasks. The essence of a design are its affordances, the ways in which a product or system actively offers uses to people whose attention is focused on accomplishing a goal rather than searching for a means. These sociomaterial forces are most evident in digital devices which can literally 'call out' to someone how they might be helpful; but they are also present in the way analogue devices indicate how they should be handled without needing instruction manuals.

Designers have always worked with this kind of socio-materiality. What is perhaps new to 'social designers' is the obverse implication. All that we value and do, what we normally call the social, is structurally dependent on those material products that make up our built environments. To paraphrase, Bruno Latour (1990), 'Design is Society made Durable.' The argument here is not a materialistically determinist one; merely that designs are a force promoting certain ways of living and working, by making them more efficient or effective or pleasurable to do.

The conclusion should be, as Allan Chochinov (http://www.manifestoproject.it/allanchochinov/) is fond of saying, 'designers are not in the artifact business, but the consequence business.' All design is the design of lifestyles and work practices.

And this is even more apparent when designing in the contexts of complex societal challenges. Designers bring to the social a focus on materiality, the ways in which things can promote, sustain or obstruct certain types of social life. To do this responsibly, designers need to be much more critically articulate about their role in making social affordances.

3. SOCIAL DESIGN = ALL INNOVATION IS SOCIOTECHNICAL

If designers are often portrayed as lone creatives, designs are often thought of as lone artifacts. However, every product functions only within particular environments and systems. This is most apparent with products that require power to operate. They must not only be near to a power source (which in turn is connected to entire energy infrastructure), but must be designed to fit, literally, in with that power supply. This is also evident for any aspect of information and communication technology whose functionality depends on being successfully networked. However, this locationality and connectivity is also the case for any designed product, even static ones. To function as designed, products must be situated within an appropriate milieu analogous to species adapted to particular niches. An office chair does not work with a kitchen table; an electric kettle is of little use when camping; without paper and something to lean on, pens are hard to use. Successful design is always contextually sensitive design.

This presents a challenge for design innovation. It is not enough to innovate a disruptive design: you must also design how that design connects to existing infrastructures and/or establishes its own new environments. The Segway promised to be a breakthrough transport technology but did not fit either on the sidewalk or in the street; in the end, its appropriate ecosystems seem only to be the private 'roads' of shopping malls, airports and industrial parks. By contrast, iPad appears to have successfully changed the couch into a workspace, at least insofar as working has also become more a practice of browsing-reading with only brief amounts of writing.

Designers have always thought about these sociotechnical systems, often citing Eero Saarinen's maxim to always design something with respect to its next larger context—the chair in a room, the room in a building, the building in a street, etc. At the other extreme is the way modernist designing strived for 'total design,' that is, the attempt to control the design of every single thing in a particular environment: furniture, flatware and light fixtures.

Social design would therefore signal this kind of contextual design directed at the creation of systems and places that support particular kinds of social activities. We take for granted that social practices are similarly place- and context-based. Laws can only be enacted in a parliament; sports require particular sets of equipment and marked fields; good restaurants are rarely designed purely for calorific intake but instead for enabling conversations, whether casual or intimate. The challenge of online learning for instance is not merely technological, but the creation of the right kinds of sociotechnical ensembles in which learning can take place.

A contemporary challenge for social designers is securing times and spaces for social innovations in a world of increasingly overlapping and competing networks and activities.

4. SOCIAL DESIGN = DESIGN OF SYSTEMS WITH SIGNIFICANT SOCIAL MEDIA ASPECTS

The term 'social' is frequently these days a metonym for 'social software.' 'Social Business' for example tends to mean the value propositions derived from online service delivery, or digital platforms for peer-to-peer interactions, or the social media aspects of a business' marketing and public relations.

There are arguments as to whether these kinds of digital sociality displace or enhance what is sometimes characterized as more authentic face-to-face sociality. More likely is that these digital platforms afford different forms of sociality, new ways of interacting with people, some of whom you would have been unlikely to find, or find value in interacting with, in off-line everyday life. Certainly, the way in which online exchanges have developed their own terminology—flame, friend, like, snark, sext, etc.—suggests that there are distinct forms of communication and collaboration occurring.

Interaction design of these social platforms—what could be called 'social design'—remains a nascent field. The rapid evolution of, and frequent missteps by digital social systems, evidence the fact that patterns let alone principles are yet to be found for these kinds of designing.

A complexifying factor is that digital platforms are not just neutral media for social exchanges but increasingly agents participating in those exchanges. The design of these systems structure how people are able to present themselves—the database and form design behind a profile page for example. It is increasingly apparent that the algorithms serving the business models underwriting some platforms are used to curate what aspects of other people's online contributions you get to see. Contributions are prompted rather than spontaneously arising in people. In each of these cases, the digital domain, as designed, has a sociomaterial force, affording, scripting and prohibiting particular kinds of social interaction.

Therefore, while social (media-based) design presents social (change-oriented) design with powerful opportunities, the interrelations between the two are worryingly larger than the current 'build an app for that' mentality that is predominant. For instance, the always-on-anywhere notifications trend in mobile and now wearable device design runs counter to the place-based tendencies discussed in 3 above.

5. SOCIAL DESIGN = SOCIAL SCIENCE BASED PROJECTS CONDUCTED AS/WITH/BY DESIGNERS

As design has established itself as a discipline, with an increasing research output, and as the profession of design has expanded its remit through strategic design thinking, designers are being asked to be on transdisciplinary teams tackling complex social challenges that are not directly design-related.

There seem to be three ways in which this happens. The first is when a designer is merely one other member of a team, offering a distinct perspective. It might be a designer's disposition toward sociomateriality that makes them relevant, but the project remains led by its original non-design professional domain. The second is when the designer is more prominent on the team, but as a process enabler rather than a content expert. By this I mean when designers are brought in to do facilitation or brainstorming. The project remains a non-design project, but design skills are used as a means of coordinating the team's response to a situation in ways that are not normally available to the other experts involved. The third is when the project is done in designerly ways with or without designers on the team, as when there was a recognition that management could be conducted 'as a kind of designing.' [Boland & Collopy, 2004]

In any of these cases, there tends to be an important motivating assumption: that existing professional expertises, on their own, are proving incapable of negotiating current social challenges. Social design often represents merely an optimistically creative alternative, valued precisely for its lack of expertise, its amateuristic ability to ask naïve questions and approach problems from unconventional perspectives.

But it is important to note that design also signals a challenge to existing professions. Its attentiveness to the sociomaterial and sociotechnical structure of activities and their contexts foreground things—i.e., material products—that disciplines of social research have overlooked. As Bruno Latour (1992) argues, the exclusive focus on the social by anthropology, philosophy and sociology to date resulted in inadequate accounts of our societies, missing the ways in which we depend on a range of physical things for maintaining civility—alarms that prompt us to wake and work; traffic lights that orchestrate turn-taking for us; phones that bring us news of our community's decisions and events.

This suggests that social design is not merely a helpful partner to other social professions, but could, if it took itself seriously a distinct new (trans)discipline, perhaps even be a replacement.

6. SOCIAL DESIGN = DESIGN OF/FOR SERVICES

Design is a recent profession birthed by industrialization. Mass producing identical items as part of the project of modernization demanded a new art and science that could interface between the needs of manufacturing and the needs of the consumer class.

For at least 50 years, design thinkers have spoken about post-industrial design. What might designing be if it is no longer merely outputting more material stuff? Service design is one of the most explicit examples. As indicated in 2, design's objective has always been social even if its direct object has been material. Service design shifts the emphasis more directly toward designing people, though as a practice it still does so through existing material design disciplines—scripting the activities of service providers and recipients through interior design, communication design, web design, etc.

However, it is important to register what has motivated the recent emergence of Service Designing. Services were 'designed' prior to the creation of the discourse of service design; they were 'engineered' by managers with an emphasis on back-office logistic efficiency. The introduction of design to service management comes with a prioritization of the front-line service experience, especially on enabling customization. This means that what is being designed by service design are people in all their tricky variability. This makes service design quite distinct from more material design practices. To put it crudely: it is hard to steam-bend wood into a chair, but this is nothing compared to sculpting customizable-yet-not-anarchic service interactions between people.

7. SOCIAL DESIGN = DESIGNING FOR/OF GOVERNMENTS

Governments can be understood as sociotechnical systems/places (3) that collaboratively design (1) the structures of our society (2). However because governments are normally considered a sector unto themselves (as opposed to the commercial private sector and the voluntary/informal third sector of nongovernmental civic society), thinking of government as designing appears to be an example of 5. An example is initiatives in the areas of Policy Design, bringing designers' optimistic creativity based on quick empathetic social research to the process of creating policies. These days, designers often have a seat at the table of governmental projects, such as policy making, because governments are keen to make use of the sociality afforded by digital platforms (4).

Another driver for social design in relation to governments is the reconception of government as service provision (6). Lending design to government services is often seen as a creative opportunity to increase their efficiency and effectiveness. However, the service design of government agencies meets many obstacles as a process that was created to generate commercial value is applied to a deliberately non-market organization. These difficulties suggest that service design in government contexts be a quite distinct expertise.

8. SOCIAL DESIGN = DESIGNING FOR/WITH
NON-COMMERCIAL CONTEXTS

Though design is the child of industrial commerce, it has always been focused on enabling wider social change. The products of design afford not just enhanced effectiveness in relation to this or that task, but allow consumers to buy into the wider universalizing modernization of humanity, accelerating progress toward ideal ways of living and working. However, these wider effects of design have mostly depended upon such products being more or less affordable to individual consumers.

Victor Papanek (1971) famously argued that designers have an obligation to lend their skills to segments of the population who normally cannot afford to be design clients. This call created the most widely accepted understanding of 'social design:' design to improve the quality of life of those without the financial capital to buy quality products.

For Papanek, these projects deployed the same design processes as those in commercial design, just now redirected at the challenges faced by those outside the consumer class. However, the resulting products tended not to look like those generated for market-based clients. This was often not just because of budgetary constraints, but because of what was considered 'appropriate' to such contexts. When Papanek was writing, the 'alternative technology' movement explicitly developed less sophisticated versions of existing products so that they might be better suited to what was thought to be the 'intermediate' sociotechnical contexts of developing nations. The organizing assumption then was that is only one inevitable development path.

By contrast, social design, if authentically serving the challenges of groups of people not large enough to constitute markets worth commercial investment, should result very different kinds of products (and services), not just less sophisticated ones. The outcomes of such social designing challenge one of the fundamental tenets of the modernist social value of design: universalism. Social design products demonstrate that different kinds of people demand different kinds of products. If these are to be more than customizations, then the process of designing for non-commercial contexts must be different too.

9. SOCIAL DESIGN = DESIGN IN THE CONTEXT OF UNMET NEEDS

When pressed to define the 'social' of social design, Manzini (2015) talks of situations with 'unmet needs,' that is, services and resources that communities need for their well-being but which are not and will not be provided by commercial markets or government services. In Manzini's 'Theory of Change,' some in a few communities will feel so compelled that they will heroically innovate ways of meeting their needs themselves, making use of the alternative economies and organizations of social capital, volunteer labor and perhaps local under-utilized resources. The task of the designer is not to innovate in response to social needs, as in 8 above, but instead to find these already existing social innovations, and lend them design expertise (6, perhaps 7) so that those innovations become more robust over the longer term. By collaborating (1) with those unmet-need-fulfilling pioneers, designers will also learn models for community need fulfilment that might be translatable to other sociotechnical contexts.

Increasing numbers of community needs are becoming 'unmet' as austerity agendas cause governments to wind-back welfare provisions. According to neoliberalism, the free market will step in where needed, such as when government services are withdrawn. The work of social designers such as Manzini makes clear that there are limits to commerce's capacity or willingness to meet all needs; there are significant gaps into which communities and then social designers must step. In servicing unmet needs, social designers can appear to be validating the politics of small government, demonstrating that something will step up. As with 7 above, is design merely an agent of marketization? How can social designers' processes be distinct enough from conventional commercial designing to guarantee that social design is not an apologist for, if not agent of, neoliberalism?

10. SOCIAL DESIGN = DESIGN-ENABLED SOCIAL CHANGE

Social Designing with respect to unmet needs (9) that is more than remedial (8), that resists the danger of being a kind of marketizing service design (6) of government (7) and non-government sectors, must afford significant social change. Its outcomes must be substantial sociotechnical innovations (3). These are political acts (1), but ones that make use of design's particular transdisciplinary research-led (5) expertise with respect to the socio-material (2), even and especially in social media contexts (4). The scale of this challenge, precisely in its negotiation of design's commercial genealogy, demands that Social Design be undertaken as a thing in its own right.

REFERENCES

Boland, Richard, & Fred Collopy, eds. 2004. *Managing as Designing*. Stanford University Press.
Latour, Bruno. 1990. "Technology is society made durable." *The Sociological Review* 38.S1: 103–131.
Latour, Bruno. 1992. "Where are the missing masses, the sociology of mundane artefacts." Bijerker, WE & Law, J. 1992. Eds., *Shaping Technology/Building Society: Studies in Sociotechnical Change*. MIT Press: 255–258.
Manzini, Ezio. 2015. *Design, When Everyone Designs*. MIT Press.
Papanek, Victor. 1971. *Design for the Real World: Human Ecology and Social Change*. Pantheon Books.

CHAPTER THREE

Social Design: From Utopia to the Good Society

VICTOR MARGOLIN

© Victor Margolin, 2015

INTRODUCTION

In the August 2002 edition of *Design Issues*, my wife, Sylvia, and I published an article entitled "A 'Social Model' of Design: Issues of Practice and Research." In that article, we posited social work intervention as a model and discussed product design within that framework, limiting our focus to "people with low incomes or special needs due to age, health, or disability."[1] In developing our model, we looked at various domains within what social workers call the ecological perspective—biological, psychological, cultural, social, natural, and physical/ spatial.[2] Of these domains, we identified the physical/spatial as the one where designers could make the most significant interventions. This domain as we conceived it "is comprised of all things created by humans such as objects, buildings, streets, and transportation systems." We recognized that "Inadequate or inferior physical surroundings and products can affect the safety, social opportunity, stress level, sense of belonging, self-esteem, or even physical health of a person or community."[3]

While I still believe in the validity of the social work intervention model, in the years since we published the *Design Issues* article, I have expanded my thinking to recognize a far broader terrain for social design. This has been prompted not only by the worsening of large-scale ecological and social problems such as climate change and the grossly unequal distribution of wealth but also by the recognition that a time of crisis provides a stellar opportunity to think about change at the largest possible level. The latter is an alternative to confining social change strategies to situations that systemic disorders and injustices will perpetuate despite well-meaning interventions. For the sake of this essay I will focus on this issue of large-scale change. With reference to various precedents for envisioning a new world based on fairness, justice, and equality, I suggest a way forward that can involve large numbers of people, particularly designers as well as design educators and their students, in imagining a world that could be. I begin by recognizing that what designers do and what they might do are absolutely crucial to making the world as it is and as it could be. Here I would like to use design in its widest possible sense to include non-material things such as institutions and social systems.[4] Such a broad definition is entirely consistent with the way many people are thinking about design's possibilities today. A definition of this magnitude helps us to recognize the wide range of designed products—whether material or non-material—among which we live: objects, graphics, systems, services, and even political and legal structures. The latter were shaped for particular purposes and constitute frames for how we may be inspired to act and what we are actually able to do. When all these entities function well, design is a productive activity that enables positive action. When they do not and design leaves the fundamental reasons for this dysfunction untouched, it becomes an obstacle to meaningful change.

In recent years, the interest in design for social good or social change has been growing within the design professions and the design education community. A recent article by Cinnamon Janzer and Lauren Weinstein foregrounds "situation-centered design" as a way to expand the idea of social design practice. "In designing social situations as social design aims to do," they write, "a different set of processes and research methodologies must be used than those employed in designing objects."[5] Complementing the article by Janzer and Weinstein is a far more extensive survey of social design examples and possibilities. Funded by several British government agencies including the Arts & Humanities Research Council, the survey, which focuses on Britain, presents different approaches to social design including design for social innovation, socially responsive design, and design activism, while also addressing issues of research, funding, and professional opportunities.[6]

Design for social good is not actually a new idea but its definition as a distinct form of practice is. Victor Papanek was one of the first designers to call attention to ways that design could be practiced outside the market. In his book *Design for the Real World*, published first in English in 1971, he discussed opportunities for designers to work in the developing world and also to design for people in need, essentially the same population that the social work intervention model recognizes. Papanek's book made a great impact and led many designers and design students to think about populations with needs that design could address beyond the standard consumerist model. What Papanek did not do, however, was to recognize the problems he identified as part of a dysfunctional social and political system that itself was badly in need of redesign.

Over the past decade, a number of exhibitions have called attention to the social needs that design might address. Perhaps the highest profile of these shows in recent years is *Massive Change*, organized by the Vancouver Art Gallery in 2004. Graphic designer

Bruce Mau curated it with Jennifer Leonard and the Institute without Boundaries, whose efforts were directed by Greg Van Alstyne. *Massive Change* had the virtue of looking at design from a global perspective that consisted of large systems but its espousal of the market economy as the framework for change, especially through the agencies of many corporations who would be seen by progressives as part of the problem, prevented the arguments in the exhibition from being translated into a program that would radically challenge the status quo.[7]

Another approach to exhibitions about social need emphasizes design for developing countries. *Design for the Other 90%*, shown at the Cooper-Hewitt National Design Museum in New York, in 2007, exemplifies this type.[8] Victor Papanek was a leader in promoting such a practice in *Design for the Real World* as well as in his work with the International Council of Societies of Industrial Design (ICSID). He inspired designers like Reinder van Tijen, who founded 'Demotech' to provide low-tech DIY designs to be constructed locally by inhabitants of developing countries. Van Tijen's 1976 *Rope Pump for Burkina Faso* is a case in point.[9] In the discussion that ensues, I will consider design within what I call an 'action frame'—a set of assumptions of how the world is or could be that animates our human activity. The action frame is the source of the values that guide our actions as well as the source of the worldviews that justify our behavior. The way design contributes to the action frame is crucial because it is that frame that provides both the opportunities and constraints for the activities of everyone.

Thus, existing political and economic systems and institutions, rules and laws, and also customs and habits are all part of an action frame that makes them possible, while rendering alternatives less possible or even not possible at all. The question before us is whether the action frame that has produced the world we live in is adequate to meet the challenges of the twenty-first century. I don't believe it is. Consequently we need to rethink the way we organize our lives at every level from the local to the global. I claim that the ultimate purpose of design is to contribute to the creation of a good society. By a good society, I mean one that is fair and just. It insures that all citizens can receive the goods and services they need to survive with dignity. I use the good society as a construct or prototype of a society that could be and in fact one whose contours are already being shaped by myriad activities around the world. The purpose of envisioning such a prototype is to help make sense of the many forces of positive change that are currently in motion and to aid in imagining how they could contribute to forms of shared social life at a large scale.

In this essay, I aim to demonstrate that the desire to think about the world in an entirely new way is not strange for designers and therefore my proposal to take it up again is not such a radical proposition. After tracing a relatively brief history of global worldviews to show both the potential and limitation of building on those views to pursue the good society project, I explain why I believe the existing action frame is inadequate. Then I describe the specific challenges that a new action frame has to meet, and I mention some initiatives that are already underway. Finally, I consider the implications of the good society project for designers and for design education, emphasizing in the latter both curriculum development and a collaborative research effort to move a prototyping process forward.

DESIGNERS ENVISION THE FUTURE: UTOPIAN THOUGHT

Utopian thought is a particular kind of proactive thought that is removed from the constraints of the real world. It provides an opportunity to imagine an ideal place that can serve as a beacon towards which to strive. Some utopian visions have been formulated in such detail that we can even envision what the home furnishings look like, while others are more abstract, crystallizing urges for a better world in statements that express values rather than pictures of how that world might appear. Within design there has been a trajectory of 'utopian thought' that extends at least as far back as the Greeks. As Frank and Fritzie Manuel note in their monumental history of utopia in the Western world:

> "The Greek philosophical utopia was concretely embodied in the architectural design of ideal city plans from the classical through the Hellenistic periods of which only cursory notices survive..."[10]

I could follow this utopian strain through the *città ideale* of the Renaissance and beyond but instead I will pick up the discussion in the late nineteenth century with William Morris, a prodigious designer and thinker whose vision of how the world might be is still relevant today.

For some years Morris was deeply engaged in socialist politics in Britain. He was a member of the Socialist Democratic Federation and a founder of the breakaway Socialist League. In a speech entitled 'The Society of the Future,' that he gave to the Hammersmith (London) branch of the Socialist League in 1887, he referred to 'dreams for the future' that "make many a man a Socialist whom sober reason deduced from science and political economy and the selection of the fittest would not move at all."[11] For many utopian architects and designers on the European continent after World War I, Morris was a strong influence because of his interest in an ideal society that was set in an earlier time when craftsmanship was more important than technology and the devastation of the environment seemed less than the Industrial Revolution and a harsh factory system had brought about. Henry van de Velde's residence, Bloemenwerf, may well have been inspired by Morris's residence, the Red House, while the various workshops in Vienna, Munich, and elsewhere were surely influenced by the practices of Morris's firm, Morris & Co. A nostalgia for the past such as Morris enunciated in his novel *News from Nowhere* was evident in Bruno Taut's visionary book *Alpine Architecture* as it was in Walter Gropius's *Bauhaus manifesto of 1919*. That year Gropius became the director of the Bauhaus, then an experimental design school in Weimar that continues to exert an influence on design education today.[12]

For the founding manifesto of the school, Gropius chose the image of a cathedral, which he called the 'Cathedral of Socialism'.[13] Like William Morris, he envisioned a return to the cooperative work practices of the Middle Ages that characterized the construction of the great European cathedrals. Apart from representing the 'unified work of art' in which Gropius strongly believed, we can be reasonably sure that the cathedral image, created as a woodcut by the artist Lyonel Feininger, was also a metaphor, perhaps for a good society based on cooperative practices. At the same time we see that Gropius imagined the Bauhaus itself as a utopian community grounded in curricular organization and social relations that were radical departures from the other schools of applied arts in Germany. Though Morris's distaste for industrial culture was likely a precedent for Gropius's choice of the cathedral as a metaphor for the Bauhaus goals, within several years, Gropius had, like Taut, moved beyond Morris's vision of a utopian past and began to advocate a relation between art and industry, which resulted in some important designs such as Marcel Breuer's chromed steel Wassily chair, his modular nesting tables, and Marianne Brandt's Kandem table lamps. Although these objects are now icons of elite taste, they arose from a vision that posited modernity as a socially progressive condition, fostered by large-scale industrial production. Similarly inspiring was an event of a very different sort, the Russian Revolution, which began in 1917 and was completed by 1920. Whereas Morris and other visionary thinkers of his day had to inject their idealistic visions into a society that was for the most part resistant to them, the Russian artists, designers, and architects who created new building types, furniture, graphics, textiles, and fashion after the Revolution did so in the belief that they were designing for a new society that had never before existed and would therefore adopt their ideas. Hence, they were free to embody the imagined revolutionary values of this new society in artistic forms that likewise were totally new.

After World War I, when artists, designers, and architects in Europe were imagining ways to rebuild a battered continent, the Russian Revolution was an inspiration to the Workers' Council on Art in Berlin and to architects in the Netherlands like Mart Stam and in Germany like Ernst May and Hannes Meyer, who went to Russia to help build entire new cities. Some members of the Workers' Council on Art such as Bruno Taut moved beyond their nostalgic visions and went on to build Socialist-inspired housing developments like the horseshoe-shaped Britz apartments in Berlin.

The utopian impulse was marginalized during the late 1930s and it remained dormant in the early postwar years when European nations were concentrating on rebuilding after the devastation of World War II, while some Americans were busily consuming all the new houses, cars, and appliances that postwar industry in the United States could offer. The impulse surged again in the 1960s, taking several forms. One was the struggles for human rights and environmental justice and the other embraced new ways of living and celebrating such as communes, music festivals, and experimentation with design and architecture by such "counter-design" groups as Archigram in Britain, Ant Farm in the United States, the Utopie group in France, and Superstudio, Archizoom, and Global Tools in Italy. All of these groups shared a focus on design as a driving force behind social change from large-scale urban innovation to rethinking the very relationship between humans and technology. During this decade, Ken Garland and a group of designers in Britain issued the *First Things First Manifesto*, which reacted against British consumerist culture of that time and urged a more humanist and socially-oriented practice of graphic design.[14]

Since the 1920s and particularly in the 1960s, Richard Buckminster Fuller was a major force in rethinking the potential of design for creating a better world. A brilliant American engineer and inventor, he was the opposite of William Morris. He believed in technology that was rationally and democratically applied and he actually produced a spate of technological inventions, the most widely adopted of which is the geodesic dome. Another was his Dymaxion World Map, which was created in 1943, patented in 1946, and reissued in 1954. Fuller attracted many adherents to his project of a World Resources Inventory and his inauguration of a World Design Science Decade. His legacy to designers was to think in large systemic terms unencumbered by the political and social obstacles that might prevent such big thoughts from turning into realized projects.[15]

THE DEVELOPMENT OF SPACESHIP EARTH

Just as the end of World War I spawned a movement of utopian visionaries who produced designs for worlds or places that were free of political constraints, so did the termination of World War II result in seeds that sprouted in the form of reflections on how diverse peoples could live together on earth in a world of justice and peace. Among these initial postwar globalists was the British economist Barbara Ward who began to think about global issues by first considering the problems of what were called in the 1950s and 1960s underdeveloped countries. Her 1962 book *The Rich Nations and the Poor Nations* was an early attempt to connect the problems of these underdeveloped countries with the economic power of their wealthier counterparts and consider how changes in the economic policies and practices of wealthy nations could affect policies that would benefit countries in less developed parts of the world.[16]

Ward's 1966 book, *Spaceship Earth*, was among the first to describe the impact of new global problems such as pollution, urbanization, and resource consumption on what she called the 'planetary economy.' Her title also preceded Buckminster Fuller's use of the term in his short book *Operating Manual for Spaceship Earth*, which was published in 1969. Ward was realistic in creating her inventory of problems that had a global dimension and she had no recommendations for easy solutions. Nonetheless her book was useful in providing a rudimentary example of a global problem statement that others would address after her.[17] This 'problematique' was addressed when the Italian industrialist, Aurelio Peccei, convened a group of international colleagues from different disciplines, who shared a recognition that the world was heading for a crisis. As a response, they created a Project on the Predicament of Mankind. At a conference in Cambridge, Massachusetts in 1970, MIT professor Jay Forrester, who had been a pioneer of methods for analyzing technical systems during World War II, presented a model that would enable an analysis of global factors that limit growth. These included population, agricultural production, natural resources, industrial production, and pollution. When completed and published in 1972, the ensuing report titled *Limits to Growth* challenged previous visions in the developed countries of limitless resources and argued that a series of trade-offs would henceforth be required if the planet were to survive.

The growing catalog of problems coupled with the Club of Rome's claim that resources were finite, began to generate a new mindset among a few politicians and scholars who realized that new ways to think about managing the planet were drastically needed. Such concern prompted the United Nations to create the World Commission on Environment and Development in 1983. It was intended on the one hand to produce a thorough survey of environmental resources and issues, while on the other to add a new factor, social well-being, to the definition of *sustainability*. The now oft repeated definition was enunciated in the introduction to the Commission's report, *Our Common Future*:

> "Humanity has the ability to make development sustainable—to ensure that it meets the needs of the present without compromising the ability of future generations to meet their own needs."[18]

Though its report was filled with helpful analyses of different factors that contributed to the dire situation it recognized—population, industry, energy, food security, urban affairs—the Commission did not make any recommendations that would have seriously challenged the world's most powerful industries. Nor did it confront the idea that economic growth might have to be limited in order to insure the availability of resources for the future generations that it purported to safeguard.

In the trajectory of United Nations conferences on environmental issues, the United Nations Conference on Environment and Development, also known as the Rio Summit, held in Rio de Janeiro in 1992, produced a compelling report, *Agenda 21: The Earth Summit Strategy to Save Our Planet*, replete with optimistic though non-enforceable resolutions for environmental improvement.[19] One outcome of the conference, the Earth Charter, has codified a set of environmentally and socially sustainable principles, yet translates none of them into policies that could result in concrete actions. Consequently, it enunciates a 16-point code of conduct that any well-intentioned and reasonable person would agree with but stops short of confronting any obstacles to the massive and necessary environmental and social changes it advocates.[20] Among its principles are a respect for the diverse life on earth, caring for the global 'community of life' with compassion and love, building just democratic societies that are participatory, sustainable, and peaceful, and protecting the integrity of the Earth's environmental systems. In its own way, the Earth Charter is as idealistic as the avant-garde manifestoes of the early twentieth century and consequently makes its greatest impact as a statement of ideals rather than a blueprint for action. By the time of the Rio Summit in 1992, global politics had begun to harden into opposing camps such that subsequent summits on climate change and environmental issues ceased to reach any conclusions that were uniformly endorsed by all the delegates, despite the fact that environmental conditions have worsened considerably. Likewise, neo-liberal policies that the World Bank and the International Monetary Fund have imposed on developing countries have stifled many valuable initiatives and facilitated the entry of large global corporations into countries that should have been given the means to ameliorate their own situations first. The United Nations continues to hold meetings on the Millennium Development Goals, but it has been unable to garner sufficient support to reach them nor has it shown any capacity to stem the tide of corporate privatization that is spreading around the globe.

A NEW ACTION FRAME

The mountain of crises that the world faces today is a clear indication that the action frame that has shaped the world's development for the past six hundred years is no longer adequate to address them. While the frame was in place, many positive results were achieved. The middle class was created and large numbers of people entered it. Models of entrepreneurship were created and these delivered new goods and services that have enriched the lives of millions of people. Diseases have been cured and overall the health of the world population has improved immensely. Within this frame, whose primary actors are nations, and more recently international and transnational entities like the United Nations and global corporations, capitalism has been the dominant economic system, having weathered a brief challenge from the command economies of the Soviet Union and its former Eastern bloc satellites and China, all of whom have by now embraced variants of capitalist economics and production. The tide has now turned and a new set of conditions calls for a very different action frame that would not only better enable the thousands of small to medium scale initiatives that are challenging the values of the old frame but also provide a new set of global and national institutions to counter the sharp divide between rich and poor individuals and nations that capitalism has fostered. We need to recapture the utopian impulse that was so strongly present in the thought and feelings of such great designers and visionaries as William Morris, Walter Gropius, and Buckminster Fuller, while also reviving the perspective of Spaceship Earth, which established a clear set of global problems that need to be addressed.

To invent a new action frame is not only a matter of changing values. It is necessary to change strategies as well. I would like to mention here eight conditions that call for a new strategy of action on a global scale.

> *First*: Population growth. More people on the planet require more resources and a different
>   means of distributing them.
> *Second*: More older people who require care and financial support.
> *Third*: Climate change.
> *Fourth*: Increased consumption of natural resources.
> *Fifth*: A global financial system that is out of control.
> *Sixth*: An unacceptable gap between the rich and the poor worldwide.
> *Seventh*: A reduction of jobs due to new robotic and expert systems technology.
> *Eighth*: Fundamentalist religious beliefs that divide the world's peoples.

Even in the midst of the current crises, millions of people are actively seeking alternatives to unsustainable lifestyles and institutions. Projects range from food production, to banking, skills bartering, altering patterns of land ownership, and new means of energy production and means of transport. Some of these projects are microcosms of what larger sustainable systems might look like, while others isolate sustainable practices within systems that are difficult to change. The projects cut across many disciplines and institutions, raising fundamental questions about how we organize our life on earth.

Designers have been involved in quite a number of them. A particularly forceful organization is the DESIS Network, originated by Ezio Manzini, who has led the charge for many years to promote social sustainability through citizen action. DESIS is working across numerous areas around the world including aging, transport, food production and distribution and strengthening relations between urban and rural populations. In general, DESIS works through laboratories that have been established at more than thirty design schools and new labs are continually being proposed.[21] The lab network is closely affiliated with Cumulus, the international association of design schools, and lab representatives meet regularly at Cumulus gatherings. In September 2014, Cumulus held a major conference, 'Design with the Other 90%: Changing the World by Design' in Capetown, South Africa, as part of Capetown's designation by the International Council of Design Associations (ICSID) as the 2014 World Capital of Design.

Besides the design activism of DESIS, Cumulus, and many other organizations including Designers Without Borders, Architects for Humanity, and the Rural Studio at Auburn University, numerous economists and social theorists have been writing about new options for social organization. The American political scientist Gar Alperovitz has introduced a concept called The Pluralist Commonwealth, by which he means a new system of wealth production made up of diverse components, many of which are already in place. He describes the Commonwealth as a model that "projects the development over time of new ownership institutions including locally anchored worker-owned and other community benefitting firms, on the one hand, and various national wealth-holding, asset-based strategies, on the other. These ultimately would take the place of current elite and corporate ownership of the preponderance of large-scale capital."[22] Alperovitz is one of many people doing research on the 'New Economy.' Their ideas range from radical to reformist but all agree that the prevailing model of capitalism has failed.[23]

Pursuing some of the ideas that have arisen in the 'New Economy' movement would lead to a complete rethinking of the money system and its place in the distribution of goods and services. Even a simple analysis will make clear, for example, how much wealth is squandered in the casino sector of the Wall Street economy or else on cleaning up the messes engendered by unsustainable financial and environmental practices. It should be no surprise that various writers on the 'New Economy' describe the monetary system as something that is designed, making clear that it is the product of strategic thought and conscious construction and can be changed if there is sufficient rationale.

I could go on to discuss other sectors such as food production, health care, or transport where the results of small to medium sized projects could easily lead to deeper reflection on how to change large-scale systems that address such issues. There is also a relatively recent impulse by governments and municipalities to employ designers to develop policies, programs, and products that address social problems. MindLab in Copenhagen is one example. Funded jointly by several Danish ministries, the group has addressed a number of social issues and problems. Beginning in September 2011, MindLab sponsored several conferences entitled 'How Public Design?,' which brought together participants now working in this emerging sector to compare experiences and ideas. The major emphasis of the 2013 conference was on how design can address the kinds of problems that governments face today. The challenge that some participants saw was to introduce significant changes in how governments operate by creating new institutions that, as one of the participants put it, are "more experimental and hybrid."[24]

The emphasis on governments as objects of design represents a considerable advance in what some designers believe they are capable of doing. As progressive as the ambitions of the MindLab conference participants may appear, however, they do not in my own view go far enough to lay the groundwork for a radical rethinking of how human beings can organize themselves in a global society to insure a fair distribution of wealth and the delivery of rights such as education, food, and housing to insure the well-being of everyone. What I am calling for is an investigation of the contours that would shape an innovative action frame. Such a frame could help to conceptualize a common denominator for many positive change initiatives that are currently underway and it could create an opportunity for prototyping new large-scale systems that might successfully address some of the crises I have outlined above. While economics is a central discipline for the construction of a new action frame, numerous other disciplines and fields such as environmental science, energy production, and housing design can and are making changes that represent new modes of social organization that would make sense within such a frame. Consider the many projects that involve sharing. These include the sharing of rides, facilities, tools, and food production. Consider also projects that reduce the need for ownership such as bicycle and car rental systems; projects that distribute profits more equitably such as cooperatives and reduce excessive banking fees such as credit unions and micro-lending; and new forms of distributing goods through the internet that allow more people to sell their products directly to their customers, while Airbnb has enabled individuals throughout the world to earn extra income by renting out rooms to travelers. One could criticize many of these initiatives—and especially their online facilitators—for merging capitalist economics with ancient bartering models, but at the very least they represent a departure from the corporate one-to-many model of production and distribution. For the distribution of waste, there is also the Zero Waste initiative that has been adopted by communities and cities in different parts of the world. Some of these projects are still in the early stage but others are fully developed and are being widely adopted. Many have been taken up by established enterprises, which have created new models of positive but gradual change without, however, challenging the economic premise of capitalism. As one example, I can cite the American grocery chain Whole Foods, which is teaming up with Gotham Green to build a new store in Brooklyn, N.Y. with a greenhouse farm on the roof. The farm will produce vegetables that will be sold in the store. This project is one of the many initiatives of 'urban farming' that flourish in New York City.

STRATEGIES FOR CHANGE

Today, we often hear the word *design* being used to characterize the thought processes behind the conception and planning of not only manufactured products and graphic communication but also far less tangible entities like commercial services, corporate organizations, social activities, government policies, and even systems of laws. In short, design for many people, has come to mean a process of envisioning an activity—rather than a product—that leads to a specific outcome which is useful to many. While this broad definition is confusing for some, it is an opportunity for others to expand what was once a discipline limited to market commodities and branded public communication. There is a chance to develop many new ways to think about designing as a way to organize what Sir Geoffrey Vickers has called 'human social systems.'[25] The network of design schools around the world, as one source of ideas and activities, could be the site of a noble experiment to see whether a group of project-oriented research centers could generate a new social vision for the twenty-first century—a Good Society that makes use of all forms of design activity, both established and new. Another site would be the local, national, and international organizations of designers in connection with active citizens worldwide.

To address the question of why a global network of design schools and design organizations would be the appropriate place to launch a sustained reflection on a new global action frame, I offer four thoughts:

First: design is a propositional activity—its thought can proceed unhampered by disciplinary rules that restrict its content.
Second: designers are good at analyzing situations and extracting from them projects that can lead to improvements.
Third: designers are skilled at integrating the knowledge of others as numerous examples of managing multidisciplinary or even transdisciplinary design teams show.
Fourth: design is changing radically as it expands to include many new forms of activity.

The Good Society as a project could also provide a framework for putting into practice some of the new forms of design. If students and practicing designers were simultaneously working to understand the characteristics of a good society, there could also be a valuable confluence of methodology and values. In May, 2013, Virginia Tassinari and I taught a workshop at the Milan Politecnico on Design for the Good Society. Participants were service design students who were eager to work on a project they perceived to be a valuable social contribution. The workshop was conducted with only a few lectures as a prior research base but the students were extremely resourceful in imaging how a different way of thinking about social possibilities could be converted into design projects.[26] Each of the ten teams created a project related to a different sector such as transportation, education, care of the elderly, food distribution, and lodging.

What was particularly noteworthy about the projects is that the students looked in a thoughtful way at the potential of unused human capital to help deliver much needed services. In one project for an urban education exchange, students envisioned a role for immigrants to teach something about their cultures of origin or a skill such as playing a musical instrument. Another project focusing on elder care identified people in communities who might be willing to spend time with older people. Since the students were from many different countries, the plight of immigrants was a theme that surfaced for some and one project in particular explored ways that the immigration experience could be made much easier through helping to guide immigrants through the morass of bureaucracy that they have to face in establishing themselves in a new country.

Both design practice and design education are in a situation today that calls for bold new initiatives. On the one hand, many of the activities for which designers were traditionally trained have disappeared or at have at least vanished from the high wage industrialized societies, having been outsourced to countries where designers with comparable skills work for a fraction of the cost. Or else, the activities themselves have been automated and human skills are no longer required, even if those skills were once a guarantee of better quality than can be achieved with automated services.[27]

On the other hand, there are many initiatives underway that are becoming established as alternatives to prevailing capitalist market models. Some of these are detailed in a recent book by Jeremy Rifkin, *The Zero Marginal Cost Society*, where the author posits the emergence of the Creative Commons, which he characterizes as exemplary of a Third Industrial Revolution. For Rifkin, such phenomena as 3D-printing, open source software, and free internet access are democratizing consumption and creating a society where the market is undermined by the availability of goods or services free or at a low cost.[28] Rifkin is correct in the catalog of trends he provides but he skirts the issues of how a new form of social organization will address issues of income inequality, financial speculation, and the equation of wealth with political influence, which are still inherent qualities of capitalism even if some aspects of its market model are undermined.

CONCLUSION: FROM UTOPIA AND SPACESHIP EARTH TO THE GOOD SOCIETY

As I have demonstrated, the history of design is no stranger to utopian projects. I argued that the value of such visionary projects has been to provide a space for aspirations that have no other locus for expression. While recognizing the aspirational value of utopian ideals, the Good Society project should move beyond them. Though energized and animated by utopian thought, it addresses real world situations and could be realized by real world actions. However unlike the image of Spaceship Earth, which is one of a closed entity, the Good Society is open and is being shaped by thousands of people and not just a group of experts who are piloting the spaceship. The question I pose is whether the international community of design educators and designers can recognize its own power as a collective agent of change and undertake a radical rethinking of how we could live, a rethinking that this community, better than anyone, can translate into propositions for projects that inspire people to carry them out.

© Victor Margolin 2015. Republished with kind permission from M. Bruinsma and I. van Zijl (Eds.), *Design for the Good Society—Utrecht Manifest 2005–2015*. Rotterdam, the Netherlands: NAI010, 2015. Republished with kind permission from Victor Margolin.

NOTES

1. Victor Margolin and Sylvia Margolin, "A 'Social Model' of Design: Issues of Practice and Research," *Design Issues* 18 no. 4 (Autumn 2002): 25.
2. Ibid. 25–26.
3. Ibid. 26.
4. For a discussion of the latter see Sir Geoffrey Vickers, *Human Systems Are Different* (London: Harper & Row, 1983).

5. Cinnamon L. Janzer and Lauren S. Weinstein, "Social Design and Neocolonialism," *Design and Culture* 6 no. 3 (2014): 328.

6. Leah Armstrong, Jocelyn Bailey, Guy Julier, and Lucie Kimbell, *Social Design Futures; HEI Research and the AHRC* (n.p.: University of Brighton and the Victoria and Albert Museum, 2014). http://www.mappingsocialdesign.org/2014/10/09/social-design-futures-report (accessed December 18, 2014).

7. See the exhibition catalog, *Massive Change* (London and New York: Phaidon, 2004). For a critical review of the exhibition see Lauren Weinberg, "Massive Change: the Future of Global Design," *Design Issues* 23 no. 4 (Autumn 2007): 86–92.

8. See the catalog *Design for the Other 90%* (New York: Cooper-Hewitt National Design Museum, Smithsonian Institution, 2007. See also my article, "Design for Development: Towards a History," *Design Studies* 28 no. 2 (March 2007). Other publications that address the issue include Tim Coward, James Fathers, and Angharad Thomas, eds. *Design & Development: Seminar Proceedings*, Cardiff 11–12 July 2001 (Cardiff: UWIC Press, 2002), and Åse Kari Haugeto and Sarah Alice Knutslien, eds. *Design Without Borders: Experiences from Incorporating Industrial Design into Projects for Development and Humanitarian Aid* (Oslo: Norsk Form, 2004). Most recently, Cumulus the international association of art, design and media schools, published the proceedings of a 2014 conference entitled *Design with the other 90%*. Available from http://www.cumulusjohannesburg.co.za/index.php/conference-theme-2/ (accessed December 18, 2014).

9. See http://www.demotech.org/d-design/presentation.php?p=14. Accessed January 20, 2015.

10. Frank E. Manuel and Fritzie P. Manuel, *Utopian Thought in the Western World* (Cambridge, MA: The Belknap Press of Harvard University Press, 1979), 65.

11. William Morris, "The Society of the Future," in *Political Writings of William Morris*, edited and with an Introduction by A.L. Morton (New York: International Publishers, 1973), 189.

12. I have discussed these and other utopian avant-garde movements in my essay "The Utopian Impulse," in the exhibition catalogue edited by Vivien Greene, *Utopia: Matters: From Brotherhoods to Bauhaus* (New York: Guggenheim Museum Publications, 2010), 24–32.

13. "Walter Gropius, Programme of the Staatliches Bauhaus in Weimar," in Ulrich Conrads, ed. *Programs and Manifestoes on 20th-Century Architecture*. Translated by Michael Bullock (Cambridge, MA: The MIT Press, 1975, c. 1970), 49–53.

14. The original manifesto and a brief description of it can be found at http://www. designishistory.com/1960/first-things-first. Accessed January 20, 2014. A new version of *First Things First* entitled *First Things First 2000* was drafted in 1999 and published the following year in *Adbusters* as well as other magazines. Matt Soar discusses the relation between the two manifestoes in his article, "The First Things First Manifesto and the Politics of Culture Jamming: Towards a Cultural Economy of Graphic Design and Advertising," *Cultural Studies* 16 no. 4 (2002); 570–592.

15. Fuller's writings are numerous. Among them are *Nine Chains to the Moon* (Garden City, N.Y.: Anchor Books, 1971, c. 1938, 1963), *Operating Manual for Spaceship Earth* (Carbondale: Southern Illinois University Press, 1969), *Utopia or Oblivion; The Prospects for Humanity* (Toronto, New York, London: Bantam Books, 1969), and *No More Secondhand God and Other Writings* (Garden City, N.Y.: Anchor Books, 1971, c. 1963).

16. Barbara Ward was more than likely guided by the work of the Swedish economist Gunnar Myrdal who addressed the disparity between rich and poor nations in his 1956 book, *An International Economy: Problems and Prospects* (New York: Harper & Row, 1956).

17. Barbara Ward, *Spaceship Earth* (New York: Columbia University Press, 1966).

18. "From One Earth to One World: An Overview by the World Commission on Environment and Development," in *Our Common Future: World Commission on Environment and Development* (Oxford and New York: Oxford University Press, 1987), 8.

19. Daniel Sitarz, ed, *Agenda 21: The Earth Summit Strategy to Save Our Planet.* Introduction by U.S. Senator Paul Simon (Boulder: Earth Press, 1993).

20. The Earth Charter can be downloaded in any one of multiple languages on the website of The Earth Charter Initiative, http://www.earthcharterinaction.org. Accessed May 29, 2014.

21. For more information on DESIS, see http://www.desis-network.org/. Accessed October 16, 2014.

22. Gar Alperovitz, *America Beyond Capitalism: Reclaiming Our Wealth, Our Liberty, & Our Democracy*, 2nd ed. Takoma Park MD: Democracy Collaborative Press and Boston: Dollars and Sense, 2011, c. 2005), 71.

23. There is a rich literature on the "New Economy." Books on the subject include James Robertson, *Future Wealth; A New Economics for the 21st Century* (London and New York: Cassell Publishers, 1990), Lester R. Brown, *Eco-Economy: Building an Economy for the Earth* (New York; W.W. Norton, 2001), Peter G. Brown and Geoffrey Garver with Keith Helmuth, Robert Howell, and Steve Szeghi, *Right Relationship: Building a Whole Earth Economy*. Foreword by Thomas E. Lovejoy (San Francisco: Berrett-Koehler Publishers, 2009), David C. Korten, *Agenda for a New Economy: From Phantom Wealth to Real Wealth*, 2nd ed. (San Francisco; Berrett-Koehler Publishers, 2010), and James Gustave Speth, *America the Possible; Manifesto for a New Economy* (New Haven and London; Yale University Press, 2012). A pioneer in this field is the economist Herman E. Daly, whose numerous books and articles include *Beyond Growth: The Economics of Sustainable Development* (Boston; Beacon Press, 1996).

24. A brief summary of the first conference was published on the Internet at http://www.issuu.com/ copenhagendesignweek/docs/howpublicdesign. Accessed on November 7, 2014. Comments on the second conference by Joeri van den Steenhoven, one of the participants can be found at http://www.marsdd.com/systems-change/mars-solutions-lab/news/design-innovation-government. Accessed January 11, 2014.

25. Geoffrey Vickers, *Human Systems Are Different*.

26. The final student projects were documented but unfortunately no report of the workshop was published.

27. Concerns that a point will come when automation will not create new ancillary jobs are emerging. See Claire Cain Miller, "Rise of Robot Work Force Stokes Human Fears," *The New York Times* (December 16, 2014), A1, A3.

28. Jeremy Rifkin, *The Zero Marginal Cost Society; The Internet of Things, The Collaborative Commons,* and *The Eclipse of Capitalism* (New York; Palgrave Macmillan, 2014).

CHAPTER FOUR

Émigré Culture and the Origins of Social Design

ALISON J. CLARKE

© Alison J. Clarke, 2015

In recent years the concept of design has extended its ubiquity to the point of provoking some critics into questioning the utility of the term altogether. Contemporary design practice has transmuted into multitudinous sub-disciplinary branches (design anthropology, design thinking, design studies, design culture, etc.). Once a transformative practice, design seems to have devolved to such an extent that its hyper-inflation may render it impotent: it is simultaneously everywhere and nowhere. So has current design become so amorphous as to have lost its critical capacity? Taking a more optimistic stance, is design's contemporary lean to pluralism and its shift to social inclusion just an inevitable outcome of its original humanist vision? As design becomes ever more deeply inculcated into a neo-liberal and free-market expansionism, the need for a sharpened critical perspective regarding its capacity for dissent is surely intensifying.

Social design in particular, with its growing range of genres and practices, has seen an exponential expansion in the last decade. Design is no longer a twentieth-century studio-based practice confined to the authorship of given individuals, or the strictures of a purely profit-driven design management team working to a fixed brief and a crude consumer profile. Models of the autocratic design guru behind his drawing-board appear today as anachronistic as the notoriously misogynistic advertising industry of the 1950s. As user groups, co-design and participatory methods increasingly shape the practice, and as a renewed focus on people, their relations, beliefs and practices comes to the fore, we are witnessing a seismic shift to the 'social'.

Arguably design, by nature, is inherently social. At its best it is a practice of empathy, whose main task is to imagine and facilitate the 'other' (the user). Some critics have even gone so far as to suggest design matches the classical anthropological definition of the 'the gift' in the sense of its acting as a non-obligatory expression of an ideal reciprocal social relation; the perfect counterpoise to the rational, asocial, form of the commodity.

> [The design] object, no matter what its mundanity, is like a collective gift: it is issued for all of us, and its function or work is giftlike in that its form embodies recognition of our concrete needs and desires ... the designer-maker knows, and has understood, recognized, affirmed, and sought to concretely meet our most intimate and human needs and desires. (Dilnot 2003: 58)

Theoretical definitions of the discrete nature of 'the gift' and 'the commodity', originally derived from nineteenth-century models of political economy, have shifted dramatically since design theorist Clive Dilnot's commentary on the role of design. In neo-liberal economy in which even barefaced selling takes on the mantle of the social, should this shift be treated with cautious cynicism? What to think, for example, of the US university, which recently promoted a Positive Marketing Centre 'dedicated to upholding market as a force for satisfying the interdependent needs of organizational stakeholders, individual citizens and society at large'?[1] How does this turn to 'the social', and the blossoming of social design as a specific area of expertise, actually affect change in the real world?

The commonsensical notion of the designer as envisaging and 'making' the future is at once clichéd and pertinent. The history of design, and most significantly its social agenda for the transformation of lives, has generally relied on this preposition. What is less discussed, and conspicuous by its absence, is any sense of the historiographical origins of the various rubrics of the social in design.

The best known and pioneering proponent of social design was the American-Austrian émigré Victor Papanek, who put socially responsible design firmly on the mainstream design agenda in the 1970s with his best-selling book *Design for the Real World: Human Ecology and Social Change*, published in English in 1971. Papanek's populist polemic acted as a manifesto for design activism; advocating co-design, anthropologically inspired models of non-professional design, 'social' object that undermined the logic of commodity capitalism and defied commercialism. *Design for the Real World* has remained in print consistently for over four decades, initially spawning uprisings and dissent in design institutions across Europe during the 1970s by calling to account a profession that stymied grassroots change and boosted corporate profit-making. 'Design', declared Papanek in one of the opening pages of *Design for the Real World*, 'is a luxury enjoyed by small clique who form the technological moneyed, and cultural "elite" of each nation.'

By the early 1960s design had already been identified as a principle mechanism in the perpetuation of material inequality and social elitism, its collusion with capitalist machinations placing it on a par with the much reviled advertising industry. In 1964, British graphic designer Ken Garland with twenty-two colleagues launched *First Things First,* a manifesto calling on their counterparts in the advertising and communication industry to devote their skill and imagination to better causes than 'cat food, stomach powders, detergent, hair restorer, striped toothpaste, aftershave lotion, beforeshave lotion, slimming diets, fattening diets, deodorants, fizzy water, cigarettes, roll-ons, pull-ons and slip-ons.'[2] And in 1968, the May opening of the 14th Milan Design Triennale, titled 'The Greater Number' in clumsy gesture to political correctness, was ransacked by students protesting against its apolitical attitude and unembarrassed display of rampant first-world materialism. On the back of the a group-swell of international student activism, the humanitarian horrors of Vietnam and the Biafra-Nigerian civil war, the notion of 'design for need' emerged as an ever more potent theme completely at odds with the extravagant design exposition world of the Triennale. Tapping into this unrest, Victor Papanek critiqued a design culture that celebrated unbridled consumer culture with its endless expos, society meetings and international congresses, provoking fellow designers with barbed taunts aimed directly at the design establishment; 'Watching the children of Biafra dying in living color while sipping frost-beaded martini can be kicks for lots of people, but only until *their* town starts burning down.'

Design for the Real World depended on a broader context of critique, in which the societal and environmental impact of late-industrial development brought into question the role of design as part of a broader network of indices including neo-colonialism, labor rights, feminism, development and user-centered technologies. The book sat alongside titles and genres including Rachel Carson's environmental treatise *Silent Spring* (1962), Teresa Hyter's critical *Aid as Imperialism* (1971), and E.F. Schumacher's highly influential *Small is Beautiful: A Study of Economics as If People Mattered* (1973), in which design had taken on a new prescience in addressing social inequality and challenging 'top-down' solutions. Significantly, the upsurge in design activism was not confined to the art school—it was directly linked to Worker's Unions, ecological groups, pedagogic reform, NGOs, the social landscape movement, ergonomics, alternative and appropriate technology, community activism, disability rights, alternative transport activists, health design, occupational therapy and humanitarian relief.

Neo-Marxist sociologist and philosopher Wolfgang Haug has castigated design as the 'hand-maiden of capitalism' in his *Kritik der Warenästhetik* published the same year as *Design for the Real World*. But by the mid-1970s students in design schools, inspired by Papanek's easily quoted polemic, were engaging in overtly social projects: corn mills for Africa; toys for disabled pre-school children; medical apparatus; appropriate technologies for 'developing countries'. By 1976, the 'design for need' agenda had penetrated the upper echelons of the design establishment it had originally set out to dismantle when London's Royal College of Art hosted an international conference on the social contribution of design, featuring leading figures of the manufacturing industry and government policy-making.

The revolutionary spirit of the 1960s and 1970s gave rise to counter design and anti-design movements pitted against the hierarchies, environmental negligence and technological determinism of the design industry. Most recently dubbed 'Hippie Modernism' (invoking an alternative utopianism built on the socialist modernism of the previous design generation) this loosely networked movement of design counter-cultures experimented with alternative configurations of contemporary material life.[3] In 1972, radical Italian architecture design group Superstudio famously posited a vision of a 'life without objects' in their installation *Italy: The New Domestic Landscape* at the MoMA in New York. In the UK, architecture group Archigram honed a neofuturist, pro-technological vision unpicking conventional ideas of architecture as mere building with interventionist and speculative projects such as the 'Plug-In City' (1964).

Counter culture even influenced industrial designers famed for the styling of desirable contemporary consumer goods. Legendary Italian designer Ettore Sottsass, creator of the ultimate pop-design icon (the Olivetti scarlet red 'Valentine' typewriter, 1969) turned his back on the profession that had made him and joined the rebels of Memphis and Alchymia—heralds of post-modernism's all-out war on the aesthetic standards of the International Style of design and architecture. Sottsass, by his own account, 'felt a need to visit deserted places, mountains, to re-establish a physical tie with the cosmos as the only real environment, precisely because it is not measurable, nor predictable, nor controllable, not knowable…'[4]

The various mutations of the counter design culture drew on similar sources and shared generally similar intentions. However, a brand of social design rhetoric emerged specifically from an émigré discourse. Victor Papanek himself drew on a progressive liberal politics that arose from his experience as a refugee having escaped the Nazi *Anschluss* of 1938. And like many of his contemporaries, his turn to the newly emerging profession of design upon arrival in New York in 1939 stemmed from a desire to engage with a new brand of humanism that stretched beyond the rationalist utopia of the International Style. Historically émigrés have played a crucial role within design, not just as accomplished individual design figures, but in forging a vision of alternative lives, quickened by interdisciplinary networks and a dual status as 'outsider-insiders'.

Much has been written of the Austrian and German 'Cultural Exodus' and the formative role of Central European émigrés in exporting an identifiably progressive approach to architecture and design that underpinned key aspects of Modernism. Émigré designers and architects in the twentieth century, from Walter Gropius to Richard Neutra, formulated a specific critical approach grounded less in concrete references but more specifically in a modern consciousness that, coupled with the experience of displacement, equipped émigré networks of individuals with a distinctive visionary capacity.

The social design movement was built, in part, on a broader legacy of émigré ideas. Curator and design critic (and émigré) Bernard Rudofsky pre-empted Papanek's social design agenda with major post-war exhibitions at the New York institution MoMA, arguing for a humane design agenda. In ground-breaking initiatives like *Are Clothes Modern* (1944) and the MoMA exhibit *Architecture without Architects* (1964) he encapsulated a design approach that suspended formal aesthetic judgments in favor of a cross-cultural emphasis on the vernacular, indigenous and cosmopolitan. A humanist theorist of architecture and material culture, Rudofsky developed a highly accessible form of criticism based on his detailed, often provocative, nuanced observations of the lived aspects of human environments, clothing and buildings. Papanek followed this émigré 'tradition' in formulating an 'agent provocateur' model of dissemination, appropriating Rudofsky's rhetorical style rather than the conservative discourse and didacticism of design reform movements.

During the same period the theories of a specific brand of cultural critique emanating from the Frankfurt School émigrés and their neo-Marxist discourse around consumption and the objects of consumer culture gained influence in academia. Theodor W. Adorno and Max Horkheimer, exiled from Nazi Germany and situated in Los Angeles in the heart of the Hollywood film industry, famously critiqued the detrimental effects of mass culture in *The Culture Industry: Enlightenment as Mass Deception* (1944). Like figures including Papanek and Rudofsky, the Frankfurt School émigrés were profoundly aware of a paradoxical relation to a culture of modernity that proffered democracy while seemingly engendering passivity and homogeneity. The historical specificity of this paradoxical relation has been identified by some historians as a defining feature of the liberal bourgeois European émigré experience: an experience that would go on to define the progressive liberalism that informed a late twentieth-century social design agenda.[5]

Papanek effectively mediated and translated this high-brow European critical theory and cultural politics into popular design discourse. As the chief protagonist of social design, he extended his role as an anti-consumption intellectual within a broadly liberal and socialist perspective, by authoring theoretical writings that appeared alongside those of fellow Viennese émigré and political economist, Karl Polyani, in a cutting-edge journal edited by Marshall McLuhan.[6] Papanek belonged to a network of émigrés that included architectural theorist Christopher Alexander, pedagogic theorist Ivan Illich and political economist and philosopher André Gorz, all of whom generated a rebellious rhetoric of aesthetics and ethics. Much of contemporary design discourse, and its humanism, was effectively formulated on the back of this émigré experience, which rejected Eurocentrism in favor of an open international cosmopolitanism that thrived in US institutions such as the New School for Social Research, NYC and the Black Mountain College, North Carolina. While the counter-design initiatives of Superstudio and their ilk dominate exhibitions and design and architectural history of the 1960s and 1970s, their impact outside the parameters of formal design is perhaps over-stated. While the influence of design émigrés from the Bauhaus, from Walter Gropius to Mies Van der Rohe, is well documented, what is less thoroughly examined is the legacy of the émigré experience in the making of socially responsible design.

Design moves ever and ever further into multiple aspects of decision-making under the mantle of 'the social' within the globalized context. There is an urgent need for critical reassessment of the discipline of design to prevent it from declining into a perfunctory, tokenistic, 'tick-box' practice used for suggesting social inclusion, rather than actually facilitating it. Design, with its empathetic core of envisioning the other, has always thrived on exceptional insights offered by 'outsiders'—it's humanist agenda is formed in part from the unique histories of displacement, emigration and exclusion. Design's focus beyond the product, to a culture of co-design, open course and interdisciplinarity follows the trajectory of the progressive political and practical humanism pioneered by Papanek and fellow émigrés. As current globalized design practice expands its remit ever further, moving into the realm of policy-making and beyond, the seismic shift to the social must be critically fostered in a newly honed version of the progressive, inclusive humanism its early protagonists envisaged. Design must, in other words, be left with the capacity for dissent.

NOTES

1. Significantly, the Center for Positive Marketing at Fordham University, NYC hosted the international EPIC (Ethnographic Praxis in Industry Conference) 2014, recognized as the major annual event involving transdisciplinary designers using social research in the commercial sector. See epiconference.com/2014, accessed February 2015.
2. See: http://maxbruinsma.nl/ftf1964.htm.
3. See the exhibition *Hippie Modernism: The Struggle for Utopia*, curated by Andrew Blauvelt, October 2015–February 2016, Walker Art Center, Minneapolis, USA.
4. Quotes in Barbara Radice & Ettore Sottsass, *Design Metaphors*, 1988, 9.
5. Bessner, Daniel, 2012, '"Rather More than One-Third Had No Jewish Blood": *American Progressivism and German-Jewish Cosmopolitanism at the New School for Social Research, 1933–1939*.' Religions 3: 99–129.
6. Victor J. Papanek 1967. 'A Bridge in Time' in *Verbi-Voco-Visual Explorations* ed. McLuhan, M. (Something Else Press: New York).

Creating the Future: Defining the Socially Responsible Designer 1964–99

Design has always played a social and political role. Directly or indirectly and whether consciously or not, it has assumed all kinds of stances towards dominant social, cultural and economic systems: ranging from enthusiastic support to radical criticism and alternative propositions. Nowadays, in view of the pervasiveness of neoliberal thinking and practices, and the numerous catastrophes they are leading to, a growing number of designers are deciding to oppose majority tendencies and work for a cultural and social change towards resilience and sustainability. That is, towards a new civilization.

—Ezio Manzini, *Design as Everyday Life Politics*

CHAPTER FIVE

Introduction

ELIZABETH RESNICK

The chapters featured in this section document the emergence of *social design* as a concept, as a nascent field of study, and as a developing professional discipline. Social design is the practice of design where the primary motivation is to promote positive social change within society. Initially inspired by the writings of William Morris, R. Buckminster Fuller, Victor Papanek, and others, the "social" in social design's agenda is to encourage designers and creative professionals to adopt a more proactive role to effect tangible change to make life better for others rather than to sell them products and services they neither need nor want, which has been the primary motivation for commercial design practice in the twentieth century. Yet, one of the fundamental tenets of the modernist era was the social value of design—designing for the masses. The chapters included in this section address this mid-twentieth-century irony, while calling for a wider definition of designing to improve the quality of life for the betterment of society.

FIRST THINGS FIRST MANIFESTO

Design journalist Rick Poynor recounts the birth of Ken Garland's 1964 *First Things First* Manifesto—how it came to be published, disseminated—and how it "struck a nerve" at a time when "design was taking off as a confident, professionalized activity" in support of an affluent Western consumerist culture:

> Garland penned his historic statement on 29 November 1963, during a crowded meeting of the Society of Industrial Artists at London's Institute of Contemporary Arts. At the end he asked the chairman whether he could read it out. "As I warmed to the task I found I wasn't so much reading it as declaiming it," he recalled later; "it had become,

we all realized simultaneously, that totally unfashionable device, a Manifesto." There was prolonged applause and many people volunteered their signatures there and then. The manifesto received immediate backing from an unexpected quarter. One of the signatories passed it to Caroline Wedgwood Benn, wife of the Labour Member of Parliament, Anthony Wedgwood Benn (now Tony Benn). On 24 January, Benn reprinted the manifesto in its entirety in his weekly *Guardian* newspaper column. "The responsibility for the waste of talent which they have denounced so vehemently is one we must all share," he wrote. "The evidence for it is all around us in the ugliness with which we have to live. It could so easily be replaced if only we consciously decided as a community to engage some of the skill which now goes into the frills of an affluent society." That evening, as a result of the *Guardian* article, Garland was invited onto a BBC TV news program to read out a section of *First Things First* and discuss the manifesto. It was subsequently reprinted in *Design*, the *SIA Journal* (which built an issue round it), The Royal College of Art magazine *Ark* and the yearbook *Modern Publicity* 1964/65, where it was also translated into French and German. This publicity meant that many people, not just in Britain but abroad, heard about and read *First Things First*.

That *First Things First* struck a nerve is clear. It arrived at a moment when design was taking off as a confident, professionalized activity. The rapid growth of the affluent consumer society meant there were many opportunities for talented visual communicators in advertising, promotion and packaging. The advertising business itself had experienced a so-called creative revolution in New York, and several influential American exponents of the new ideas-based graphic design were working for London agencies in the early 1960s. A sense of glamour and excitement surrounded this well-paid line of work. From the late 1950s onwards, a few skeptical designers began to ask publicly what this nonstop tide of froth had to do with the wider needs and problems of society ... For Garland and the other concerned signatories of *First Things First*, design was in danger of forgetting its responsibility to struggle for a better life for all.[1]

HERE ARE SOME THINGS WE MUST DO

Four years later at the Vision 67 *Design for Survival Conference* held at New York University, Ken Garland's contribution was the critical paper "Here Are Some Things We Must Do." Garland took the opportunity to push against mass media's tendency to blatantly disregard content when he stated: "The implication of the misleading slogan 'The medium is the message' is that those of us working in the communications media may now treat with lofty condescension the initial content presented to us knowing that however trivial it may be we shall transform it into something significant." Garland also enumerated four "survival tasks" essential to the both the survival of design and the health of society, the fourth task being "that we make some attempt to identify, and to identify *with*, our real clients: the public. They may not be the ones who pay us, nor the ones who give us diplomas and degrees, but if they are to be the final recipients of the results of our work, they're the ones who matter."

EDUGRAPHOLOGY—THE MYTHS OF DESIGN
AND THE DESIGN OF MYTHS

Victor Papanek was an early proponent of human-centered, sustainable, and socially responsible design. He was a controversial yet highly influential figure who recognized the potential of design as a vehicle to address the needs of the poor, disabled, elderly, and underserved communities in developing countries. Proselytizing through his writing, lecturing, practice, and teaching, Papanek challenged designers—in his scathing criticism of widespread unsustainable development—to embrace their social and ethical responsibilities by producing more ethical products that were not harmful to our increasingly fragile environments.

Victor Papanek's denunciatory paper "Edugraphology—The Myths of Design and the Design of Myths" was penned in 1975, four years after the publication of his book *Design for the Real World*. In it, he synopsizes and negates ten design myths—created and perpetuated by Western design education—each with the aim to foster elitism between professional designers and design education and the public at large. In concert with enumerating these "myths," Papanek offers ten "remedies" concluding with his criticism that "design is a basic human ability to help autonomous self-realization. Designers and design educators are engaged in withdrawing this ability from all but a carefully screened group of people, through mythologizing who we are and what we do."

DESIGN AS A SOCIALLY SIGNIFICANT ACTIVITY

The meaning and the responsibility of design within society is the subject of Clive Dilnot's influential 1982 paper "Design as a Socially Significant Activity." Design, he argues, must be acknowledged as a unique form of activity with value beyond the commodification of goods and services. He positions his paper "to uncover and resolve confusions which occur in the use of 'design' as a term; to delineate the significance, philosophically, socially, politically ... of the design activity ... and to outline some particular benefits of this in problems to do with understanding the social benefits of design ..." For Dilnot, design can be viewed as a distinctive mode of thinking and communicating that is concerned with how "design" relates to or is indistinguishable to "society" in our present time. His underlying premise is that design embodies the potential for wider social significance (than previously explored at that time), and that any discussion of design should include design's social relevance to humanity as a whole.

DESIGNERLY WAYS OF KNOWING

The concept of *designerly ways of knowing* emerged in the late 1970s in association with the development of new approaches in design education articulated in a report on the Royal College of Art's research project on "Design in general education": that "there are things to know, ways of knowing them, and ways of finding about them" at the core of the design area of education. "Designerly Ways of Knowing" written by design academic Nigel Cross—as one of a series of articles published in the *Design Studies* journal in 1982—strove to build a theoretical rationale to position design as a cogent field of study.

In his paper, Cross ultimately challenges our perception of, and makes an argument for, a neglected third area of education, namely Design. He acknowledges that Science and the Humanities are the two dominant areas of education. His underlying argument is there are "ways of knowing" embedded in the process of design and that is different from that of science. For Cross, science relates to a process of a linear analysis to find a solution, while a *designerly way of knowing* is a process of synthesis and iteration. Here the designerly way of knowing is embodied in the process of designing, and the products of designing are also imbued with this knowledge. Cross argues that "design in general education is *not* primarily a preparation for a career, nor is it primarily a training in useful productive skills for 'doing and making' in industry. It must be defined in terms of the *intrinsic* values of education … the arguments for, and defence of, design in general education must rest on identifying the intrinsic values of design that make it justifiably a part of everyone's education."

THE FUTURE ISN'T WHAT IT USED TO BE

In *Design for the Real World: Human Ecology and Social Change,* his highly polemic 1971 book, Victor Papanek calls for a revisionary design culture based on social responsibility. He is merciless as he exhorts designers to counter the rampant consumerism taking hold of our societies: "There are professions more harmful than industrial design, but only a few of them. And possibly only one profession is phonier. Advertising design, in persuading people to buy things they don't need, with money they don't have, in order to impress others who don't care, is probably the phoniest field in existence today. Industrial design, by concocting the tawdry idiocies hawked by advertisers, comes a close second. Never before in history have grown men [and women] sat down and seriously designed electric hairbrushes, rhinestone-covered shoehorns, and mink carpeting for bathrooms, and then drawn up elaborate plans to make and sell these gadgets to millions of people."[2] Of course, at the time he wrote this text fifty years ago, this notion of ethical and sustainable design practice would have required a radical readjustment in a designer's process—to encompass the wider repercussion—of their capricious consumer-driven work.

In "The Future Isn't What It Used To Be," Papanek's 1988 paper, he once again takes critical aim at designers on what he considers their failed adaptation of the design process to the new digital age. He argues that designers are fashioning unsuitable products by systematizing the design process to become more scientific to better meet the requirements of digital technologies. He states:

Many designers are trying to make the design process more systematic, scientific, and predictable, as well as computer-compatible. Their attempts to rationalize design by developing rules, taxonomies, classifications, and procedural design systems are extreme examples of trying to provide design with a respectable scientific-sounding theoretical background or, at least, a theory-like structure that smacks of science. Their approach stands for reason, logic, and intellect, but such a method leads to reductionism and frequently results in sterility and the sort of high-tech functionalism that disregards human psychic needs at the expense of clarity.

COMMERCE OR CULTURE: INDUSTRIALIZATION AND DESIGN

Eminent design academic John Heskett taps into his deep knowledge of economics, politics, and history to describe the economic and social upheaval caused by early industrialization in Britain which opened up both new challenges and new opportunities in his paper, "Commerce or Culture: Industrialization and Design." Heskett also describes the unique role design played in the Industrial Revolution with its commercialization of production and the tensions that created a wider debate about art, culture, industry, and the quality of life that ensued: " ... industrialization has wrought massive change across the globe, not just in patterns of life and work, but also in consciousness of ourselves and our world."

WICKED PROBLEMS IN DESIGN THINKING

In this seminal paper "Wicked Problems in Design Thinking" published in 1992, design theorist and academic Richard Buchanan elucidates the importance of the emergence of design thinking in contemporary society while linking it directly to *wicked problems—* design problems are characterized as "wicked" because "design has no specific subject matter apart from what a designer conceives it to be." This notion would thus enable designers to continuously position and reposition problems or issues based on the "tools by which a designer intuitively or deliberately shapes a design situation, identifying the views of all participants, the issues which concern them and the invention that will serve as a working hypothesis for exploration and development."

To this end, Buchanan identifies "four broad areas in which design is explored throughout the world by professional designers and by many others who may not regard themselves as designers." They are signs (symbolic and visual communications), things (material objects), actions (activities and organized services), and thoughts (complex systems or environments for living, working, playing, and learning). He argues that these areas should not be viewed within the context of traditional practices but instead as four broad areas of design thinking that share a commonality of practice in all the design professions: " ... *signs, things, actions, and thoughts* ... interpenetrate and merge in contemporary design thinking with surprising consequences for innovation." Buchanan's argument for this expanded design practice is based on his belief that design is "a new liberal art of technological culture" that has the capacity "to connect and integrate useful knowledge from the arts and sciences alike, but in ways that are suited to the problems and purposes of the present."

GOOD CITIZENSHIP:
DESIGN AS A SOCIAL AND POLITICAL FORCE

Design academic Katherine McCoy fashions a stirring call to action for all designers—to rediscover the purpose of design as a social, cultural, and political force and to truly become responsible advocates for the messages they put out into the world—in her paper "Good Citizenship: Design as a Social and Political Force": "We cannot afford to be passive anymore. Designers must be good citizens and participate in the shaping of our government and society." What is important about McCoy's argument is the notion that "design is not a neutral value-free process" as it inherits political and social ideals that are rooted within its content. Designers must consider the moral implications of the work they take on: "A design has no more integrity than its purpose or subject matter. Garbage in, garbage out. The most rarefied design solution can never surpass the quality of its content."

FEMINIST PERSPECTIVES

In 1993, design historian Nigel Whitely published *Design for Society*, an influential book that examines the value of design and its implications. In the book, Whitely expresses his angst over the state of the design profession in a society that ignores such significant issues as sustainability, population growth, and rampant global development. Within the book's five chapters—Consumer-led design, Green Design, Responsible Design and Ethical Consuming, Feminist Perspectives, and The Way Forward?—Whitely provides crucial insights into the fields of sustainable design and eco-friendly "green" design, while advocating for the need to rethink consumerist practices. He raises the issue of a lack of ethics in the design profession when he emphatically states: "Designers can no longer take refuge from responsibility for their own actions and continually repackage the same old type of consumer goods at a time when issues about consuming and its relationship to the world's resources and energy need urgently to be acted upon."

In chapter 4 "Feminist Perspectives," Whiteley details the plight of women in their "gendered" roles—as both user and consumer—including the contemporary feminist critiques of stereotyped sexist consumerist design that translate into poorly designed products for women's use. In our Western patriarchal societies where a women's status is considered inferior to men, most consumer products are designed and created by men for women, or by men for men. Whitely correctly predicts that any change within the gender makeup of the design profession will only result from what he considers promising advancements in society at large.

THERE IS SUCH A THING AS SOCIETY

In titling his article "There Is Such a Thing as Society," Andrew Howard challenges the shocking assertion made by Britain's former prime minister Margaret Thatcher (in a published interview) that "there is no such thing as society":

I think we've been through a period where too many people have been given to understand that if they have a problem, it's the government's job to cope with it. "I have a problem, I'll get a grant." "I'm homeless, the government must house me." They're casting their problem on society. And, you know, there is no such thing as society. There are individual men and women, and there are families. And no government can do anything except through people, and people must look to themselves first. It is our duty to look after ourselves and then, also, to look after our neighbours.[3]

Howard uses this opportunity to reintroduce "First Things First," the 1964 manifesto penned by British designer, Ken Garland and twenty-one of his colleagues, as "a succinct and gutsy appeal to reject the 'high pitched scream of consumer selling' and omnipotent lure of the advertising industry in favor of what was defined as socially useful graphic design work." Howard posits that graphic design "has a part to play in creating a visual culture that empowers and enlightens, that makes ideas and information accessible and memorable," an encouraging affirmation of graphic design's political and cultural agency. "We cannot separate our work" Howard argues, "from the social context in which it is received and from the purpose it serves." This article not only served to renew interest in the thirty-year-old manifesto but also the harbinger of its rebirth as the "First Things First Manifesto 2000."

DESIGN AND REFLEXIVITY

One of the most significant and influential postwar Dutch graphic designers to have emerged since the early 1960s, Jan van Toorn has written extensively on both the social and cultural responsibility of designers and on the need for designers to develop what he termed an "oppositional form of practice." In his 1994 paper "Design and Reflexivity," van Toorn muses that "every professional practice operates in a state of schizophrenia, in a situation full of inescapable contradictions. So too communicative design, which traditionally views its own action as serving the public interest, but which is engaged at the same time in the private interests of clients and media." Here the design practice is described as "imprisoned in a fiction which does not respond to factual reality beyond the representation of the culture industry and its communicative monopoly." He asserts that designers must oppose this monopoly through critical practice. If designers were more involved in the initial planning of projects rather than just the production then there would be more opportunities to serve the greater good.

DESIGN NOIR

In this short article titled "Design Noir" published in UK's *Blueprint* magazine, Anthony Dunne postulates "that product designers could become more like authors" by drawing "from the narrative potential of electronic product misuse and abuse to create alternative notions of use and need" proposing new products that challenge preconceived and prevailing notions on how electronics define our lives. He critically cites that product designers can only see the social value of their work when it is directly linked to marketplace success and therefore reinforcing rampant consumerist ideology. "The challenge," Dunne argues, "is to blur the boundaries between the real and the fictional, so that the conceptual becomes more real and the real is seen as just one limited possibility."

The term "critical design" is credited to Anthony Dunne and was first used in Dunne's book *Hertzian Tales* (1999), and later in *Design Noir: The Secret Life of Electronic Objects* (2001). The notion of "conceptual design" made it easier for noncommercial forms of design like critical design to develop. It describes a form of practice developed by Dunne and Fiona Raby during their time as research fellows at the Royal College of Art (RCA) London in the early 1990s. "Critical Design uses speculative design proposals to challenge narrow assumptions, preconceptions and givens about the role products play in everyday life. It is more of an attitude than anything else, a position rather than a method."[4]

NOTES

1. This excerpt is from "First Things First, A Brief History" published in *Adbusters* No. 27 (Fall 1999). Reprinted with kind permission from Kalle Lasn/*Adbusters*.
2. Quoted from the preface of *Design for the Real World: Human Ecology and Social Change* by Victor Papanek, 1963–71.
3. Quoted from the interview with Margaret Thatcher and accessed on June 28, 2018 https://www.margaretthatcher.org/document/106689.
4. Quote accessed on June 28, 2018 from http://www.dunneandraby.co.uk/content/bydandr/13/0.%20.

CHAPTER SIX

First Things First Manifesto

KEN GARLAND

© Ken Garland, 1964

We, the undersigned, are graphic designers, photographers and students who have been brought up in a world in which the techniques and apparatus of advertising have persistently been presented to us as the most lucrative, effective and desirable means of using our talents. We have been bombarded with publications devoted to this belief, applauding the work of those who have flogged their skill and imagination to sell such things as: cat food, stomach powders, detergent, hair restorer, striped toothpaste, aftershave lotion, before shave lotion, slimming diets, fattening diets, deodorants, fizzy water, cigarettes, roll-ons, pull-ons and slip-ons.

By far the greatest effort of those working in the advertising industry are wasted on these trivial purposes, which contribute little or nothing to our national prosperity.

In common with an increasing number of the general public, we have reached a saturation point at which the high pitched scream of consumer selling is no more than sheer noise. We think that there are other things more worth using our skill and experience on. There are signs for streets and buildings, books and periodicals, catalogues, instructional manuals, industrial photography, educational aids, films, television features, scientific and industrial publications and all the other media through which we promote our trade, our education, our culture and our greater awareness of the world.

We do not advocate the abolition of high pressure consumer advertising: this is not feasible. Nor do we want to take any of the fun out of life. But we are proposing a reversal of priorities in favour of the more useful and more lasting forms of communication. We hope that our society will tire of gimmick merchants, status salesmen and hidden persuaders, and that the prior call on our skills will be for worthwhile purposes. With this in mind we propose to share our experience and opinions, and to make them available to colleagues, students and others who may be interested.

Signed: Edward Wright, Geoffrey White, William Slack, Caroline Rawlence, Ian McLaren, Sam Lambert, Ivor Kamlish, Gerald Jones, Bernard Higton, Brian Grimbly, John Garner, Ken Garland, Anthony Froshaug, Robin Fior, Germano Facetti, Ivan Dodd, Harriet Crowder, Anthony Clift, Gerry Cinamon, Robert Chapman, Ray Carpenter, Ken Briggs.

Republished with kind permission from Ken Garland.

CHAPTER SEVEN

Here Are Some Things We Must Do

KEN GARLAND

© Ken Garland 1967

Before offering any general proposals for future action it is necessary to attempt a definition of the existing situation as it appears to me.

As a graphic designer working in Britain in 1967, I have to operate within the limits set by the capitalist system functioning not only in my country but also in the rest of western Europe, in North and South America, in Australia and in some parts of Asia. The tasks which my clients pay me for are either (a) directly related to the purpose of making profitable business; (b) indirectly related to it as a form of commercial prestige-seeking or commercial goodwill; or (c) as part of a public service which is financed by an economy founded on the conduct of profitable business.

So when I think about my work in the short term I always have in mind this fact: that financial profit is the spur to industrial initiative, the reward for commercial achievement, the balm for battered professional consciences; and the lack of financial profit is a sign of failure, no matter what.

Of course it's possible to push the profit motive thing into the background as many of us do, and to concentrate on the job in hand as being a useful information task in its own right, or a means of experimenting with new graphic forms, or simply as a piece of fun that may give people pleasure. And of course a task may contain any or all of these qualities. But however enlightened the patronage and however open the brief may be, there is no getting away from the fact that in our society a business must show a healthy profit before it can indulge in such patronage; nor is it likely that any results of that patronage which prove hostile to business profitability will continue to be sponsored for very long.

For myself, I wish neither to remain outside the commercial world which forms the focus of capitalist society, nor to try and ignore the profit seeking which motivates it. It seems to me ridiculous to make apologies, as do so many business people in my country, for profit motive. On the whole I'm much happier doing a specific selling task such as the design of a catalogue than when I'm working on a prestigious promotion piece loaded with cultural overtones. I've no quarrel with any client who points out that my work is valueless to him because, although it looks pretty, it doesn't help his sales figures. This is the vital factor to him, and so it is to me.

But I *do* quarrel with the artist, scientist, butcher, baker or candlestick-maker who claims that in his daily work he is unaffected by the dominant forces in capitalist society. Most especially will I take issue with those of my colleagues working in the communication field who minimize this influence. A prominent 19th century author wrote that:

> ...the class which is the ruling material force of society, is that the same time its ruling intellectual force...Insofar, therefore, as they rule as a class and determine the extent and compass of an epoch, it is self-evident that they do this in their whole range, hence among other things rule also as thinkers, as producers of ideas, and regulate the production and distribution of the ideas of their age...[1]

It follows that there is no real difference between work done in the communication arts and science which is an integral part of the commercial system, and work which is done outside the immediate requirements of that system but nevertheless financed by it and so subject to its sanctions. Perhaps there is a marginal area of artistic and professional freedom in the latter situation; but both are utterly dependent on the health and resilience of a profit based economy, in which the real power, as Estes Kefauver demonstrated, is increasingly concentrated in the hands of a few people.[2]

Since I don't believe that there is any appreciable future in a so-called free enterprise system, there is no point in discussing its growth potential. But there are certain limited targets such as increased efficiency in social services, improved housing standards, better public transport system and so on, which can be described as survival operations.

I suppose you could say, 'If you're so damn unhappy about the present condition and future prospects of our capitalist society why do you come on with this "survival" bit? Why not let it die of its own accord?' Well, I can't accept this notion of opting out of the system; nor can I agree with the revolutionary who claims that the whole setup is so rotten that we must kick it all to pieces before we can start on a new one. In a country plunged into a state of advanced social decay on the one hand, or of the revolutionary chaos on the other, too many innocent people would suffer. A sudden dislocation of our delicately balanced society would result in the breakdown of our communication, transport, and distribution networks which alone could cause the death by disease and starvation of hundreds of thousands, maybe millions.

So until the majority of people in the western world become convinced (as they will) that they are victims of a self-perpetuating elite system, and find ways to get rid of it (as they will), what short- and medium-term survival tasks can we attempt?

First, let those of us who are employed in the information business get shot of any cockeyed nonsense that may have accumulated to the effect that the media we serve have any significant value in themselves apart from the messages transmitted through them. It seems to have become an occupational disease in our business, this urge to turn its operations into art forms and its devices into art objects in their own right. Eagerly we seize our camera, caressing its sensitive controls as we bring the searching lens to bear on—another equally skillful photographer aiming his equally superb camera on us! Yet another feature about trendy photographers, by trendy photographers, for whom? Or, darting into an art gallery, our straining eyeballs reach maximum blink-rate as their gaze fixes on our own exhibit: the advertisement for baked beans we designed last year, now transmogrified into this year's design award winner. No longer just a message about the unbeatable value of baked beans, it is now recognized for what it truly is: a prized gem in our environmental setting, a pacemaker in the race for new cultural symbols; which is more than can be said for baked beans, however tasty.

Flattering of course, for us in the business of processing information to be assured that the clever ways we have found to handle the media are very likely more important than the messages which we are commissioned to convey through them. Frequently, it is argued, the initial content of a film, or play, or TV program, or advertisement or what have you is of little or no value in itself, but that value accrues to it as a result of its processing for the medium, so that the content becomes something more, or something other than that at first intended.

But whether this observation has any grain of truth or not, it is surely no basis for a program of action. The implication of the misleading slogan 'The medium is the message' is that those of us working in the communications media may now treat with lofty condescension the initial content presented to us knowing that however trivial it may be we shall transform it into something significant; we can, in fact, welcome the triviality as being a fit challenge for our talents.

This is eyewash. Respect for the content is an absolute requirement in our business, whether it is about baked beans, or the future of mankind, or what you will.

Secondly—and this leads on from the first point—we must attempt a cure for the galloping elephantiasis from which the information media are now suffering. In 1955 Lewis Mumford wrote:

> Why should we gratuitously assume, as we so constantly do, that the mere existence of a mechanism for manifolding or mass production carries with it an obligation to use it to the fullest capacity?...to achieve control, we shall even, I suspect, have to reconsider and perhaps abandon the whole notion of periodical publication...as a needless incitement to premature or superfluous publication...we cannot continue inertly to accept a burdensome technique of overpopulation without inventing a social discipline for handling it.[3]

I'm reminded of an occasion when I was the newly appointed art editor of a trade magazine. The editor thrust a few photographs into my hand and said, 'Lay out a six page feature using these.' Asked what was to be the text he told me to let him know how many column inches I would like, and they would write to fill. When I pointed out that even the maximum conceivable amount of text there weren't anything like enough illustrations to fill six pages he said, 'Well, use your head—pick out some details and blow 'em up—give us a large fancy heading—that sort of thing.' 'That sort of thing' is now so familiar an operation to me that I have continually to remind myself that it isn't an integral part of the method by which information is handled, but rather the unhappy result of the way we abuse it.

Of course the main reason for the staggering over-population of broadcast and printed materials is the stimulus of intensely competitive advertising. A well-known British press tycoon, when asked if he ever interfered in editorial policies of the newspapers and periodicals he controlled, stated that as far as he was concerned the editorial content was just the thing that kept the advertisements apart, and that he left journalism to the journalist. We shouldn't be fooled by such disingenuous claims to impartiality: the very concept of news and comment as a purely quantifiable product like jam or toilet paper is itself a partial one. An increase in the volume of advertising booked requires an increase in the number of editorial pages—to keep the ads apart—regardless of whether there is any news to fill them, and vice-versa.

The cure? Well, until we get rid of the conditions that favor the production of news and comment as though it were a species of plastic extrusion there can be no complete cure; but *something* can be done by the editorial staffs in publishing, radio, and TV. They surely can't be happy at being called on to engage in the tatty business of padding out their work in this way, whatever their political attitudes may be. If they can achieve enough solidarity in their unions and professional association, they will be strong enough to refuse to collaborate in the degradation of journalism into an aid to advertising.

Thirdly, we will not survive if we ignore the warning signs of dislocation in our *essential* information networks. Those signs are already becoming urgent. On 21 October 1966 a coal tip swept down a Welsh mountainside and killed 144 people, 116 of them children. The official report on the causes of the disaster said that the authority responsible 'should forthwith examine afresh its lines of communication to ensure that essential knowledge passes easily and automatically to those whose business is to become possessed of it and to eliminate those breakdowns and omissions with undoubtedly played a big part in bringing about the disaster.'[4]

Dare we hope that the kind of communication failure that contributed to the Aberfan disaster will not recur? I don't think we should. The responsible executives in this case were hard working, intelligent people; but they lacked an effective system of collecting, classifying, assessing, and acting upon information about the coal tips in the area, and about coal tips in general. Perhaps if some part of the vast amount of money spent on urging the British public to use gas as a domestic fuel rather than coal, or coal rather than gas, or electricity rather than either, had been diverted to the implementation of such a system, this disaster wouldn't have happened.

We must devote more energy and give higher priority to survival tasks of this kind. They may well demand the close cooperation of such unaccustomed colleagues as industrial psychologists, site workers, telecommunications engineers, specialist librarians, industrial and graphic designers, technical writers, politicians, and assorted civil servants. And those of us in the communications business who may be involved in such tasks need to know how to tackle them.

It is only a matter of bringing together hitherto unfamiliar skills; a change of attitude is needed as well. To take a small example: like many graphic designers I'm familiar with the problem of arranging lettering and symbols on commercial vehicles as part of a corporate identity program, in order to achieve the greatest possible impact on the travelling public. But if I were asked to assess road safety factors relating to the design of vehicle livery of this kind and to ensure that they were fully taken into account, I would hardly know how to begin because the concept behind such a consideration is at such variance with any previous considerations involved.

But it is no excuse to say that no one has ever before asked me to think about this problem. We should be able to *anticipate* incipient social needs in our sphere of activity, in the same way as some far-sighted architects have done in theirs; then we won't be so badly thrown by them when they arise. So often, I believe, it is the minor factors that matter because they build up to a serious total problem. To continue the example of road safety: what about such problems as the effective (as against merely flashy) design of vehicle dashboards; the consideration of the conflicting effect of store and street lighting on traffic sign systems; the presentation of vehicle operation and maintenance manuals; and the measurement of visibility requirements in design of vehicle windows and rear view mirrors?

Are not these some of the components in what is literally a major survival task? Yet how much effect have we in the visual communications field spent on this task in contrast to the time we have spent on designing detergent packs or advertisements for deodorants?

Fourthly, we of all people must see the danger in the urge to form in-groups and join exclusive elites. It can be one of our especial functions in society not only to help in devising new communication techniques, but also to keep open lines of communication which are threatened with extinction or which are becoming dangerously one-way-only. Speaking of the trend in western society (and there is every reason to believe that the same thing has happened in the U.S.S.R.), C. Wright Mills pointed to the following development:

(1) Far fewer people express opinions than receive them…(2) The communications that prevail are so organized that it is difficult or impossible for the individual to answer back immediately or with any effort. (3) The realization of opinion in action is controlled by authorities who organize and control the channels of such action. (4) The mass has no autonomy from institutions; on the contrary, agents of authorized institutions penetrate this mass, reducing any autonomy it may have in the formation of opinion by discussion.[5]

There is no reason why we have to connive at these authoritarian trends; our skills can be equally useful to those voluntary bodies and local associations that stand outside the operations of mass communication media and their controlling elites. In particular, we can find ways in which hitherto unvoiced yet deeply felt opinion may be made clear. The great success in Britain of the Consumers Association, based on pioneer American organizations of the same kind, shows the urgent need of effective feedback in the producer-consumer link.

In so far as we cut ourselves off from the feelings and hopes of those not in authority or positions of privilege, we reduce our usefulness to society. It is a bitter irony that many creative people who feel strongly about the threat to our social life caused by authoritarian pressures are unable to give expression to their feelings in any but esoteric forms. In stylish films like *The Red Desert* Antonioni attempts to describe the plight of human beings isolated and estranged in a world where machines are more at home than they are; but the films are littered with in-group symbols, fashionable illusions and smart visual tricks, to such an extent that they are only understandable (if at all) to a resolutely sophisticated middle class audience. Yet more than thirty years before, in *Modern Times*, Charlie Chaplin dealt with the same vital theme in a clear, unpretentious and universally understood form. And even the best of filmmakers may find that in their work they have lost touch with common experience; for example, the vivid simplicity of Fellini's *La Strada* has turned into the weird, self-indulgent nonsense of his 8½. In my own sphere of graphic design we often find ourselves trapped in a similar kind of closed circuit, so that we are designing for, and seeking the approval of, our fellow designers to the exclusion of any consideration for those to whom the work is ostensibly directed. But the trap is mostly of our own making, and the relief when we escape it is enormous. It is not that our work is thus free from hard criticism; quite the reverse. The in-group of professionals and professional critics can often be too indulgent over those aspects of work about which laymen would be ruthless in their judgment. The toughest design critics I have ever come across were the children who live in my street, whom I consulted about a toy I was designing. But they were also by far the most helpful critics I know, unimpeded by consideration of taste and current trend, scornful of irrelevant detail and delighted by any evidence of careful thought for the wishes of *them*, the destined users of the toy.

What I am suggesting as the fourth survival task in my list is that we make some attempt to identity, and to identify *with*, our real clients: the public. They may not be the ones who pay us, nor the ones who give us diplomas and degrees. But if they are to be the final recipients of the results of our work, they're the ones who matter.

If you don't detect a common attitude running through these proposals, and feel sympathetic towards it, you will no doubt add your own items to the list. What I must say in conclusion, though, is this. These tasks operate in the short and middle-term. They might play some part in preventing the disintegration of our society which will surely take place if it hardens into its present unhappy mold. In the long term there must be vast, probably painful changes. And I cannot agree with Buckminster Fuller when he says: 'All politics are obsolete as fundamental problem solvers. Politics are only adequate for secondary housekeeping tasks.'[6]

We cannot hope, nor should we try, to effect fundamental changes in our society by side stepping the issues of government. Political change is the inevitable outcome of economic pressures; Those of us who believe in an egalitarian society will not bring it nearer by scorning the political instruments by which it will be attained.

On one historic dictum I think we at this Vision 67 Congress will all agree: 'The philosophers have only interpreted the world in various ways: the point, however, is to change it.'[7]

© Ken Garland 1967. Previously published in Ken Garland's book, *A Word in Your Eye*. Reading: University of Reading, 1996. Republished with kind permission from Ken Garland.

NOTES

1. Marx, Karl, *The German Ideology* (1846).
2. Kefauver, Estes, *In a Few Hands* (1965).
3. Mumford, Lewis, 'Technics and the future of Western Civilization,' *Perspectives* II, New York (1955).
4. *Report of the Tribunal Appointed to Inquire into the Disaster of Aberfan on October 21, 1966* (1967).
5. Mills, C. Wright, *The Power Elite* (1956).
6. Fuller, R. Buckminster, Final summary at Vision 65 Congress on 'New challenges to human communications' (1966).
7. Marx, Karl, *The German Ideology* (1846).

CHAPTER EIGHT

Edugraphology— The Myths of Design and the Design of Myths

VICTOR PAPANEK

They want production to be limited to "useful things," but forget that the production of too many "useful" things results in too many "useless" people.

—Karl Marx

Design philosophy and the designer's self-image have been victim to a series of shocks. Some twenty years ago designers saw themselves primarily as artists, able to close the gap between technology and marketing through their concern with form, function, color, texture, harmony, and proportion. For an industrial designer or architect, a further concern was with cost, convenience, and "taste." Within ten years the designer's role had broadened into a systems approach, showing greater interest in production, distribution, market-testing, and sales. This opened the door to team-design, although with the team largely made up of the technocrats, sales specialists, and modish "persuaders."

More recently a very few designers have attempted to create a new design coalition in which users of tools and makers of tools (read: consumers and workers) participate in the shaping of the design process together with social anthropologists, ecologists, and others.

Elitist circles in design have even more recently given rise to such gimmicks as the "Nostalgia wave," "Kitsch Nouveau," "New Brutalism," and other fashions carefully manipulated to increase hedonistic ethnocentricity.

In the Western world the concept that "designing things" and "making things" are different is only about 250 years old. From then on the idea of design was increasingly connected to the appreciation of things deemed "beautiful" by an upper-class culture that created a moral and ethical basis for the concept of beauty.

Louis Sullivan's "Form-follows-Function," Frank Lloyd Wright's "Form-and-Function-are-one" and "Truth-to-Material," like the Bauhaus' "Fitness-for-Purpose" and "Unity-in-Diversity" were all basically ethical and moral imperatives. Often the moral imperatives ousted the practical reality, as anyone who ever sat on a Frank Lloyd Wright chair or read by a Bauhaus *Kugellicht* can testify.

Our future job in design education is made easier, not harder, by these changes design has experienced. For now the nexus between autonomous man and the benign environment has emerged as our new moral imperative.

Now the whole formal concept of design is under attack. Increasing numbers of people feel that design no longer serves them: that modern planning and architecture are alienating (they are); industrial design class-oriented (it is); and graphic design trivial and boring (it is). Design is further and further removed from people and the real world and it seems that "they up there" are out of touch with "us down here" (and all that is all too true).

Design education and the design establishment have responded to this in two ways:

1. Relabeling: a frenzied search for new words or labels to cloak an essentially unchanged activity. "Commercial Art" has become "Advertising Design," then "Graphic Design," and more recently "Visual Design," "Communication Design," more absurdly "Environmental Graphic Communications," etc., *ad absurdum*.

   "Industrial Design" has been relabeled "Product Design," "Product Development," or "Form-giving" and, in an increasingly frantic attempt to make it acceptable to new constituencies: "Alternative Design," "Appropriate Technology," "Social Design," "Intermediate Technology," or "Advocacy Design," *ad nauseam*.

   It can be said that relabeling doesn't work: you can call a Crematorium the "Final Departure Lounge," or an idiot: "educationally under-advantaged" but nothing changes except for exposing the manipulative character of language.

2. "Business-as-usual" on one level, with increasing preoccupation by small design sectors with artificially invented "Third World" design, playground planning, aids for the handicapped, or other minority groups.

   About concentrating on an invented Third World and other "needs," one can say that this has to do with what Freud called *Verdinglichung* and when I translate as "Objectification." It involved the change from knowing one's real needs into a demand for consumer goods. It makes survival of marginal or oppressed groups or countries dependent on the knowledge-monopoly of a professional elite and on the production-monopoly of specialists.

   "Basic needs" thus are redefined as those that can be solved only by internationalized professions. (Since *local* production of internationalized products is highly profitable to native, highly trained elites, such groups will defend this as a "legitimate struggle against foreign domination.")

Finally, by flipping out into *only* designing for real or invented minorities, the mainstream of design is left to the mercy of establishments and their valuation.

Graphic design and graphic design education seem generally dedicated to six discernible directions:

1. To persuade people to buy things they don't need with money they don't have to impress others who don't care.

2. To persuasively inform about the class-merits or an artifact, service, or experience.

3. To package in a wasteful and ecologically indefensible way, artifacts, services, or experiences. (Look at any undertaker's coffin!)

4. To provide visual delight or visual catharsis to those classes taught to respond "properly."

5. To undo with one hand what the other had done. (Anti-pollution posters, anti-cigarette commercials).

6. To systematically research the history, present, and future practices in the five fields listed above.

In design education we have accepted myths that exist in the public about design, as well as invented new ones about ourselves.
I now plan to list ten of these myths and propose also ten remedies:

1. THE MYTH THAT DESIGN IS A PROFESSION. Design fails to satisfy people to the degree to which it is professionalized and it can satisfy people only to the extent to which it can again be made participatory. This particular myth is most propagated by Professional Design Societies that often turn out to be geriatric clubs, dedicated to legal tax-evasion and similar self-help schemes.

2. THE MYTH THAT DESIGNERS HAVE TASTE. On record, designers do seem to have taste (whatever that means) but only for the work of a few other designers. Students are exposed to "function formalism," "radical software," "romantic primitivism," or "socialist (-imperialist) realism."

   In all these cases people and designers drift apart, since "taste" is always manipulative in the end.

3. THE MYTH THAT DESIGN IS A COMMODITY. A commodity exists to be consumed. The more we make design into a commodity, the more it will be consumed, measured, divided, eaten, eaten-up.

   Styles, fashions, fads, and eccentricities will follow one another at an ever-increasing pace, subject to the same market-manipulations that govern other commodities.

4. THE MYTH THAT DESIGN IS FOR PRODUCTION. With some of the balance having gone awry we may now well ask: Mass Production or Production by the Masses?

   The industrialized countries, containing one third of the population of Earth, threaten the economy of the entire planet. Mainly the threat is to people: through noncreative work; through making people subservient to technology; and by making believe that "Growth" can solve problems. In terms of the environment; production (as we have come to know it) harms the environment by concentrating people in cities; and treating nonrenewable (capital) resources as if they were renewable (income resources).

5. THE MYTH THAT DESIGN IS FOR PEOPLE. Design is mainly for designers. All designers know how hard it is to persuade marketing people to accept their designs. Marketing people in turn know how hard it is to get people to buy the goods. Right now millions carry expensive fountain pens that must be softly sandpapered from time to time to be kept "good-looking," just so that its designer might win a prize in Milano or a magazine page in Britain or a Museum of Modern Art award in New York.

   If Design were really for people it would enable people to participate in design and production; help conserve scarce resources; and minimize environmental damage.

6. THE MYTH THAT DESIGN SOLVES PROBLEMS. It does, but only problems that are self-generated. A graphic designer "solves the problem" of advertising rail-travel as ecologically saner than automobile-travel, but at the cost of neglecting walking or bicycling, *and in so doing diminishes the choices people can make.*

7. THE MYTH THAT DESIGNERS HAVE SPECIAL SKILLS AND THAT THESE SKILLS ARE DEVELOPED THROUGH SIX YEARS OF HIGHLY SPECIALIZED EDUCATION. What we *do* have is the ability to tell things (via poster, film, technical drawing, rendering, printed page, spoken word, or prototype model); and to organize parts not a meaningful whole.

   But these are innate human potentials. On the other hand: "trick-of-the-trade" skills are taught by many vocational schools in one year.

8. THE MYTH THAT DESIGN IS CREATIVE. In reality design schools (teaching such subjects as "Creativity 101") direct students into analytical and judicial modes of thought and permit creativity only with narrow institutional limits. ("How do you spell: Cat?" or "What is the square root of minus one?" are analytical questions; "Who is right?" a judicial one; whereas creativity involves synthesis rather than cloning). Education tends to turn out competent and competitive consumers rather than creative and autonomous individuals.

9. THE MYTH THAT DESIGN SATISFIED NEEDS. It does, but at great social cost; furthermore the needs satisfied are invented ones. An airbrush, for instance, is an expensive, specialized, and hierarchical tool. It takes months to really master it (or to be mastered by it). It makes its user into a professional specialist whereas a plain sable brush is cheap, easy to use, open to all, and has infinitely more creative scope for the user.

10. THE MYTH THAT DESIGN IS TIME-RELATED. Much design is concerned with creating artificial obsolescence. But obsolescence always creates devaluation, leading to alienation, and finally existential *Angst.*

When design is for permanence, permanence is interpreted as five to ten years, whereas in reality a good tool (say: a bicycle, a motorized pushcart, a community freezer, or an axe) should minimally last a lifetime. Design is a basic human ability to help autonomous self-realization. Designers and design educators are engaged in withdrawing this ability from all but a carefully screened group of people, through mythologizing who we are and what we do. We must de-mythologize and de-professionalize our work and our training.

I would like to list ten ways of bringing design back into the mainstream of life:

1. Some designers will be able to connect themselves differently in the future: why do thousands of us work for industry, but almost none of us for trade unions? Why do we work *directly* for cigarette companies or carmakers, but almost never for cancer clinics or autonomous groups or pedestrians or bicyclists?

2. Designers will have to concern themselves consistently with the important differences between non-renewable and renewable resources, as mentioned earlier.

3. Design must enable people to participate directly both in the design development and the production stages of objects. Cross-disciplinary teams must contain makers and users.

4. Designers will form new coalitions with makers and users; new coalitions between users and reusers.

5. A well-designed technology must be one of self-reliance. That is a technology that is capital saving (the word "capital" is used here to denote nonrenewable resources). It will further be a technology that is simple, small in scale, and aware of ecological, social, and political consequences of the design act.

6. Design must cure people of product addiction. This can only be done by demythologizing not only design, but also the object itself.

7. Some of us can, through schools, bring our students into direct and continuous contact with real people's real needs in a real world instead of manufacturing needs for them.

8. Design will still be concerned with tools. But they will be as unlike most of today's products as feasible: products and tools that only create the very demands they are specialized to satisfy and thus eliminate or diminish human labor, participation, and ability.

9. As I have said somewhere else: all men are designers. All that healthy men do is design. We must take note of that and through our own work enable more and more people to design their own experiences, services, tools, and artifacts. *The poor countries need to do this to find work for their people, the rich countries in order to survive.*

10. Technology as such need not be feared; the alphabet, Arabic numbers, moveable type, typewriter, photocopier, tape-recorder, and camera have given us the "open-ended" tools to move design from myth to participation, from participation to a joyous, autonomous way of personal fulfillment.

Let me close by quoting a proverb from China that sums up why design and design education must be directly tied to meaningful work and participatory life:

I hear and I forget,
I see and I remember,
I do and I understand.

First published in Icongraphic no. 9 (Croydon, England: 1975). Republished with kind permission from Nicolette Papanek.

CHAPTER NINE

Design as a Socially Significant Activity

CLIVE DILNOT

© *Clive Dilnot, 1982*

In understanding design-society relationships it is crucial that we understand what we are talking about when we use the word 'design'. Too often the term is used not to denote a specific (designing) but rather to denote either, or both, the results of that activity (designed products) or the problems which initiate design activity.

This paper seeks to uncover and resolve confusions which occur in the use of 'design' as a term; to delineate the significance, philosophically, socially, politically, and so on, of the design activity (considered both as an 'ideal' activity and in its empirical reality); and to outline some particular benefits of this in problems to do with understanding the social benefits of design, design evaluation, technological control, education and social futures.

The paper also seeks to show the importance of design in epistemological terms: how it provides a model of rationality which, properly developed, challenges one-dimensional rationalities. Thus the social and political implications of design, it is suggested, are wider than is usually supposed.

PREAMBLE

Re-reading the paper[1] which formed the background to this presentation, I am struck most of all by the difficulties there are in moving from statement in critique—containing arguments about the weaknesses in our current models of design understanding, such as our failure to be able to define satisfactorily either design phenomena or design activity or to assert powerfully enough, and at the right levels, design's wider social significance—to positive statements; to being able to say *this* is the phenomena with which design is concerned, *this* is the nature of design activity, *this*, therefore, is the significance of design—epistemologically, socially, and practically.

There are two points here. First, clearly, this is not a problem unique to me. It is a general problem within design studies. But it has particular force when attempting to understand design-and-society relations. For it, as has recently been persuasively argued, design practice should not become too involved in the search for general design principles, design theory, by its very nature, has no choice. If the former involves drawing on a richness of tacit knowledge the latter is necessarily concerned with reversing this process, i.e. with making *explicit* the tacit richness of design activity.

So we can come to the second point. If we are to argue design's social significance or to model its social relations this must be based on our understanding, our explicit, sharable and imperfect understanding as to what' design' *is* and what design *does*. Only then can we model 'design-and-society' relations (beginning of course by replacing this wholly misleading formula...design, of course, is *in* society). Note that we are here trying to derive models for designing—or at least not in the first instance. This task is prior to such work. It defines, from a point 'outside' designing, the context in which design operates and 'lives'. It tries to make evident, to say what in these complex relations remains unsaid and therefore unthought, in design practice as much as in design policy or social thinking.

But of course this in itself has implications for method. Precisely because we are forced, in order to model these relations, into defining design activity as it takes place in its real context—that of the social—and do not attempt to abstract it, to isolate it from these relations, we find we build a model of designing that has surprising efficacy in application to questions of design method. Questions of design—society relations then appear of major significance—not only for society or for questions of 'design-and-society' but for design itself. If we think about it this is hardly surprising.

DESIGN AND SOCIETY

The antithetical models of design's significance that we possess today, all of which contain implicitly or explicitly a view that sees design as merely the activity of commodity shaping, or the view that sees design as the activity which allows us to organize consciously the meeting of material human needs—which 'involve things or usable products'—in forms consonant with and conducive to particular kinds of social relations or ways of life...) contain also, naturally, a view of what design is. The two are in internal relation to one another: views of design imply notions as to what design is socially and vice versa. Debates as to the 'nature of design' thus have social implications. Equally revelations as to the form of design-society interactions have consequences for 'pure' design theory and for design method. In a context where design debate, narrowly conceived, seems to be meeting with little success in evaluating design's social import, the questions raised—is design the means whereby we can shape future socio- technological systems?—become a means to general design understanding. The key to the latter now appears to be in understanding, both structurally and historically, the relations involved in what is misleadingly termed 'design-and-society'.

No statement in the whole of design is more peculiar than this one. It is peculiar on the one hand because a moment's reflection reveals design as a human activity taking place within, and not without, human societies. Yet on the other hand it is frighteningly indicative of our real position. It models precisely the position of alienation vis-a-vis design and society felt on the one hand by designers—who in general express profound unease at even thinking about the social sphere—and who embody this alienation in the very fabric of design practice (mass housing is the obvious example)—and on the other by society in general which remains both deeply suspicious of designers and their possible beneficial work and, paradoxically, deeply uncertain about objects—or, more precisely, about the significance of their form.

The most characteristic version of this alienation lies here in the responses we have both to objects in general and their forms in particular instances. In relation to the former as I indicated in the first paper, our relation to the former, as I indicated in the first paper, our capacity to invent commodity vocabulary is not paralleled by levels of commodity understanding. The 'Worlds of Goods', as Douglas and Isherwood have made clear,[2] is still a world closed to our understanding above all in relation to the communicative function, the language functions, which goods perform. Since communication through goods depends on our abilities to read form, and since designing is that activity which 'gives' forms to things, (c.f. Abel: design "lends concrete form to the cultural processes of human individuation and identity formation")[3] it is scarcely surprising that, while we 'know how' to read designed form (form as the mediation between technical and communicative [i.e. social] requirements) crucially inhibits the understanding of design in general and 'design-and-society' relations in particular.

What is lost here is the sense of form as integral element, as the mean, in fact, whereby a particular human need is meet—i.e. is materially realized—in a way consonant at once with the levels of provision and 'list of requirements' and with a certain way of life. Forms embody and enable not only technical functions (utility) but 'ways of life'. The form in which a need is met (say, the need or the production of very basic goods or services) opens up some human possibilities and closes down others. Forms do not then merely passively reflect or represent 'ways of life' (though they do this too); crucially they *enable* or curtail forms of living (producing, reproducing). 'Ways of life' then are not simply characterized by forms, rather, 'ways of life' are structured by forms of organization, by material forms which themselves, 'habitus'-like, structure activities…).

But design then is not socially peripheral. Design is the activity which produces the form, which mediates the complex of inputs and shapes these into a form. The ends of design activity are social and not (merely) technical: "the architect empathizes with a people and a place in order to *give form* to that identity…."

But supposing this sense of design is lost?… "What many feel, touch upon, but hardly articulate… 'design' as a term which is a noun and a verb, and also one which denotes a form of representation, an activity, a practice, a product etc etc at one and the same time"[4]… i.e. design as a *priori* a social activity unable to be undertaken without having social implications. In that case design loses its context. In relation to our 'design-and-society' problem, design, in rending itself from the social fabric and attempting to construct itself as an independent discipline—and having constructed its own pantheon of values and principles with only tangential relation to the social becomes, quite literally, socially unintelligible. It values now those of a specialist activity, design severs the communicative link which formerly bound it to society.

These values and this separation of course react back on to design practice itself; after all practice models itself on conceptions of what then, knowledge of design then, knowledge which merely describes attempts to objectify or to naturalize this kind of practice does so in asocial terms.

At the same time if design in both practice and theory cannot be 'read' as belonging to the social, the latter turns its back on it. Design's effective denial of a social formative or linguistic-representational function further isolates itself from the academies traditionally orientated towards understanding and valuing these. In this situation neither the academy nor design itself can any longer be aware of design's actual social content (designed without explicit social formative function, such functions are 'achieved despite design's comprehension').

But worse at this point, design can no longer be aware of itself, for to separate the social formative and communicative-representational functions is to reduce itself, to make its activity into a variation of technical activity, unimportant in itself, important only in so far as a problem can be solved through it, a product constructed.

Socially, at this point the significance of design as such, is more or less lost: significance can only be seen in terms of problems solved or products produced. *But then design too disappears*. For design cannot be identified wholly with either 'products' or 'problems'. As I discussed in the first paper[1], design has to be characterized in terms of *activity*. It is design activity which gives designed products significance, which finds solutions to the problems. In turn both solutions (products) and problems, and the activity itself receive their 'value' socially. Denial of the social reduces the felt value of design at the same time as activity is devalued. Devaluing activity, assimilating it in analogous models (art, science, technology), design makes of itself models of its practice which deny design (in the sense we have been working towards here) both in process and in end.

RETHINKING 'DESIGN'

We can best begin to sketch the positive characteristics of this activity by reversing the usual procedures. As I hinted in the first paper, traditional design understanding has tried, in effect, to simplify design to make it conform to an already existent model of what an (scientific, technological, artistic) activity should look like. Such approaches have always seen the complexity of design with its range of apparently contradictory impulses and antithesis; is the emphasis to be on questions of form or of function or on solving technical or aesthetic desires and needs? Are we to consider it an activity in itself or as an instrumental activity significant only in terms of ends? We should ask if it is product (end) or problems (origin) that should be seen as the generic base of 'what design is'—not as a challenge to construct a dialectical, interactionist model of design activity, which takes each of these moments seriously as a necessary moment or characteristic of 'what design is', but as an affront to rationalism. The dialectic of apparent antithesis has been suppressed in favor of a one-dimensional model of what design is; depending on the format of precise models, one of the antithesis has been subsumed or repressed under the aegis of the other. Activity has been made to conform to rational pattern.

This simplification of what design has also extended until very recently to pictures of the design activity itself. Seeing the latter in one-dimensional terms, and characterizing it as a weak version of the more prestigious intellectual analogues used (design as weak art or weak science), such models never explored design-cognitive activity from its own standpoint or in respect of its own efficacy. The idea that design was a form of knowing in its own right and one moreover significantly different from and possibly, in certain respects, superior to, the analogous 'prestige' model—was never explored; indeed given the processes of false rationalism noted above, *could* never have been since the prerequisites of a truly rational model of design activity—comprehension of all of design's moments as a prelude to modeling what whole they constituted in interaction—were never realized.

The challenge now is to reverse these standpoints. To read design first socially, second in its full complexity and richness (and, bearing in mind injunctions concerning the significance of the tacit dimension and tacit knowing in design, to try to incorporate these levels in this complex model), and third, as a cognitive—*practice* in its own right, with its own levels and spheres of operation both mental and praxiological, irreducible to metaphoric models.

If we take the social as a 'given'—bearing in mind everything we have said above in regard to this—then we can approach the second of these injunctions by modeling the 'antitheses' of design activity as internal relations, aspects of a totality (design) which embraces, and theoretically transcends, any single pole of the matrix. How can we consider this matrix? Very crudely we can base it on those elements which albeit often apparently antithetical or contradictory as they seem to be, have figured more or less constantly in discussions on 'what design is'. *Very roughly* we can characterize perhaps four main axes to this debate. *Firstly*, there is the tension between *product* and *activity*, between design as embodied in products (objects, buildings, systems) and design as an activity in its own right. Secondly, the tension surrounding the questions of 'form'—the sense that what design is or does is embodied in form i.e. the material form of objects, yet also the sense that form, once considered as important is yet not enough, that design id' more than' a matter of merely forming things. This is closely linked, possibly indivisibly, to the debate between form (aesthetics) and function. Finally, there is the tension in the design process between the sense of design as a transformative activity, a positing activity, transcendent of the givens of a problem (in the sense of both breaking with context and with the form of the immediately perceived requirements—design as defining needs as well as solutions) and design as a posited activity, that which works from the given which deals with what is real not with what is merely planned or speculated or imagined.

If we approach these tensions from the perspective of assuming that these represent the dialectical poles, or at least some of them (for of course others could be discussed here had we the space: for example the tension between 'knowing how' and 'knowing that' in design activity) of a design activity which encompasses *all* of these in a vertical moment of synthesis, a synthesis that is counter posed horizontally (i.e. over time) by the changing movements of the activity itself (from product critique through to problem definition to cognitive modeling of potential solutions etc.) a movement of understanding and practice which parallels in its sphere the circle of historical understanding and historical praxis (and just as the latter is the 'way' in which history itself moves' so the former is the 'way praxis itself moves') so design can be seen as embodying that movement in its movement from across actuality it in its activity of transformation from one set of 'givens' to another; in its movement from problem to product. The total process is a double synthesis of moments of cognition and practice. Taken together we have a unity of knowing and doing, of 'actuality' and 'the human interest in self perfection and fulfillment': design, in this theoretical sense, as the model of human culture.[5]

Perhaps the easiest way to begin to explain this is to consider design as a model *in practice* of human culture in general. Design models, in its transformative activity, both action and consciousness, both 'work' (purposeful instrumental activity) and 'speech' (all that is involved in communication from attribution of meaning-both on things and ourselves, to systems of classification and symbolism, to modes of communication) and models these not merely theoretically but in reality, in form. Bhaskar has defined 'the ontological structure of human activity or praxis... as consisting in the transformation by efficient (intentional) agency of pre-given material (natural and social) causes'.[6] Design mirrors (represents and directly embodies) this transformative reality by uniting, in vertical direction, in the 'moment' of designing, complex human abilities both cognitive and practical and in the horizontal (over time but in interaction with the vertical moment), the movement from critique through the various moments of problem resolution and definition to the realization of the solution but of a different order).

This unity of abilities and moments movement between the theoretical and the practical within the context of transformation has special significance in terms of social ontology. As the philosopher Gillian Rose has pointed out, 'recognizing our transformative or productive activity has a special claim as a mode of acknowledging actuality which transcends the dichotomies between theoretical and practical reason... transformative activity acknowledges actuality in the act and does not oppose act to non-act.'[7] As far as I can read her argument, it is precisely this which allows recognition of it to model our human position as suspended between, as she says at another point, 'unconditioned actor... and conditioned agent'—ie transformative activity, above all design activity, allows and recognizes actuality in its equation, understanding and transcending the usually antithetical worlds of the given (the positing). Because design necessarily sees this relation (albeit tacitly) then its thinking (whether it recognizes it or not) has social import.

Design then, 'cognitive-modeling'—'an action-based 'form of knowledge' for thinking, reasoning and operating' which is not tied to concrete-operational levels of thinking' but deals also with 'formal operational thought and hypothetical- deductive reasoning'—returns these levels of thought to the concrete through the medium of form and the activity of forming.

The concept of forming should be seen as an extension of the notion of 'cognitive modeling' as developed by Archer describes this as 'imaging'—the ability 'to conjure up in the mind's eye an image of something or system... rotate and transform it... make shrewd judgments about its construction, practicability and worth'. But clearly designing involves more than this rather technical definition: we are talking about the ability to shape and unite, to being together complexes of factors.

Consider for a minute the tenacity that the concept of 'form' has held in design even amongst those most determined to eradicate the idea of aesthetics'. Clearly 'form' even in its most denuded days had a necessary content for design. That content too has always been felt to be linked to the aesthetic in some way—though again as of late, in theoretical studies this has not been examined. But if we consider for example the kind of idea about 'aesthetic experience' held by Adorno we can begin to understand this persistence. Adorno, says Susan Buck-Morss, argued that 'aesthetic experience was in subject and object, idea and nature, reason and sensual experience were interrelated without either pole getting the upper hand-in short, it provided a structural model for "dialectical", "materialist" cognition'.[8]

This is a long way from traditional ideas regarding 'good form'. But the latter were clearly hopelessly reductionist in relation to a concept such as this which at once opens up the possible significances of what was once merely seen as the aesthetic.

The connection between this and the concept of form as sketched much earlier in this paper—the notion of form as enabling ways of life, or form as a part of 'processes of human individuation'—is contained within the concept. The dialectic of subject and object (human, social and technical-economic factors) is part of the concept in both senses (it is absent only from current asocial concepts of what 'form' or aesthetics are). But what we have here is a model of cognitive experience which privileges synthesis as its active principle and whose particular cognitive ability is that of interrelating the interconnections between phenomena or 'opposed' moments of experience. Like this it is at once a moment of knowledge ('to understand reality is to see and understand things in their connectedness and their interpretation, one to the other') and moment of praxis (synthesis) whose material embodiment is the process of modeling (forming: here both terms of cognitive modeling, including the modeling of *meaning* and the extension of this modeling, with all its reciprocal interactions). Modeling/forming in this sense models double patterns of interconnections: both that of relations between 'objects', and between minds (and of course, in the synthesized representation which is the process of 'bringing to form' in design, the interaction between these two worlds).

Even the briefest of sketches we can begin to glimpse the wider significances of design activity considered the wider significances of design activity considered in this manner. The cognitive-epistemic implication is clear. Design as a complex, multi-dimensional activity achieves through forming at once a mode of knowing the world which is at the same time also a mode of acting in the world. This acting knowing unifies the purposive-instrumental and communicative-symbolic impulses in praxis (in that it is unique). This models, too, the complex interactive relation of subject and object privileging neither pole. Discursively design unites two discursive worlds (that of technique—science and that of communication—understanding) normally held apart in the alienated world. In relation to, for example, technological systems, design posits a means of overcoming control problems since it posits a means of knowing-practice which incorporates the technical *as a moment* and which can itself thus *internally* incorporate social requirements (no other mode of knowledge practice can do this). Politically this has clear significance. Design becomes the means for ordering the socio-technical world in a manner compatible with both socio-cultural and technical-economic ends; the means for forming, literally, future society in a manner at once desired and yet internally dialectically related to actuality requirements. Socially, design models as a practical transformative. Practically, design becomes the means whereby we can change (transform) society in accordance simultaneously with what is desired and the reality principle.

It is proper to end this presentation by returning to the equation we began with. That premised the understanding design-and-society relations as a means to reconciling the rupture that was evident between design as is and it's public position and design as felt, or intuited, or could be—or as was necessitated by the possible changes in social structure occurring, in accelerating form, in the new configurations of late capitalism. Implicit in this argument, though not explored, was the idea that current models of design understanding, with all their weaknesses, were not accidental—that in fact they grew out of the present configuration may well give rise to new forms of designing...Except that to say this like this negates some of the significance of what has been said earlier.

For the import of the 'new' sense of design which I have hypothesized could be developed from these sketches is its interaction with social forces—literally its forming of them. Design, which has had poor record in not exercising choice, in not challenging what is 'given', in eschewing the social, is faced in these propositions with a 'new' operative role. If forming is social, forming organizes the future. Moreover, extrapolated outside design—into society, politics, education, living- design in this sense becomes the means by which more of us begin to determine and to form our own lives. Design is, for example, the means by which we regain control of technological processes by assimilating their one dimensionality into the overarching and multi dimensional (higher cover-set) model of design. (Which is, if you think about it, precisely what the Lucas Aerospace shop-stewards have done in their Alternative Corporate Plan.)

Design then is more than design. Certainly more than Design (capitalized). Probably more than design (verb; lowercase 'd') in the sense that we understand at the moment; paradoxically, not only does design become the only possible means of saving the human species (and I mean this very seriously; I can think of no other approach which could enable us to transcend the dichotomies—between reason and emotion, technique and meaning, power of technical systems against impotence of ethical systems, and so on-built into our dominant culture) but it 'finds itself' at just this moment; at this point the contradictions that run through present forms of design practice, contradictions which we can now read as the 'distortions' of the holistic and embracing matrix of design, cease to exist. Design then becomes truly social; and the social becomes a matter of what is designed and formed socially. At that point the phrase design-and-society will finally become redundant.

© Clive Dilnot 1982. Previously published in *Design and Society: Vol. I of the Proceedings of the International Conference on Design Policy* (Design Council, London, 1982) pp. 101–5. Republished with kind permission from Clive Dilnot.

NOTES

1. This paper is an extension and development of that published in the Design Policy Conference edition of *Design Studies*, Vol. 3, July 1982.
2. Penguin, Harmondsworth, 1980.

3. 'Vico and Herder. The origins of a methodological pluralism', in *Design: Science: Method*, Proceedings of 1980 Design Research Society Conference, Westbury House, Guildford, 1981.

4. The quote is by Necdet Teymur from 'The Materiality of Design', in *Block 5*, 1981, p 19.

5. On this see Bauman, Z. *Culture as Praxis*, Routledge, 1973.

6. Clearly, this is the briefest of sketches. The issues presented here (in much too abstract a fashion—though as J.C. jones says, the 'abstract... can be release from the status quo') require more careful exploration. It may be worth reminding readers though of the significance of concepts and conceptual explorations. As Roy Bhaskar says: 'To explain something is to resolve some agent's perplexity about it: it is to render the unintelligible—by the elucidation, extension, modification or replacement of that agent's existing conceptual field. In particular scientific explanations do not resolve problems by subsuming some particular problem under a more general one but by locating such (normally already generalized) problems in the context of a new cognitive setting; it is (new) concepts, not (universal) *quantifiers* which accomplish explanatory problem resolution in science'. (From, 'Scientific explanation and human emancipation', in *Radical Philosophy*, 26, Autumn 1980, p 16–28).

7. *Hegel Contra Sociology*, Athlone Press, London, 1981. See especially the final chapter, 'With What Must the Science End?'

8. *Origins of Negative Dialectics*, Harvester, Brighton, 1977, p 124.

CHAPTER TEN

Designerly Ways of Knowing

NIGEL CROSS

ABSTRACT

This is the third paper in a series being published in *Design Studies*, which aims to establish the theoretical bases for treating design as a coherent discipline of study. The first contribution in the series was from Bruce Archer, in the very first issue of *Design Studies*, and the second was from Gerald Nadler, in Vol. 1, No 5. Here, Nigel Cross takes up the arguments for a 'third area' of education—design—that were outlined by Archer. He further defines this area by contrasting it with the other two—sciences and humanities—and goes on to consider the criteria which design must satisfy to be acceptable must imply a reorientation from the instrumental aims of conventional design education, towards intrinsic values. These values derive from the 'designerly ways of knowing'. Because of a common concern with these fundamental 'ways of knowing', both design research and design education are contributing to the development of design as a discipline.

Keywords: education, 'third area', design criteria.

A principal outcome of the Royal College of Art's research project on 'Design in general education' was the restatement of a belief in a missing 'third area' of education.[1] The two already-established areas can be broadly classified as education in the sciences and education in the arts, or humanities. These 'two cultures' have long been recognised as dominating our social, cultural and educational systems. In the English educational system, especially, children have been forced to choose one or other of these two cultures to specialise in at an early age—about 13.

The 'third culture' is not so easily recognised, simply because it has been neglected, and has not been adequately named or articulated. Archer[2] and his RCA colleagues were prepared to call it 'Design with a capital D' and to articulate it as 'the collected experience of the material culture, and the collected body of experience, skill and understanding embodied in the arts of planning, inventing, making and doing'.

From the RCA report, the following conclusions can be drawn on the nature of 'Design with a capital D':

- The central concern of Design is 'the conception and realisation of new things'.
- It encompasses the appreciation of 'material culture' and the application of 'the arts of planning, inventing, making and doing'.
- At its core is the 'language' of 'modelling'; it is possible to develop students' aptitudes in this 'language', equivalent to aptitudes in the 'language' of the sciences (numeracy) and the 'language' of humanities (literacy).
- Design has its own distinct 'things to know, ways of knowing them, and ways of finding out about them'.

Even a 'three cultures' view of human knowledge and ability is a simple model. However, contrasting design with the sciences and the humanities is a useful, if crude, way of beginning to be more articulate about it. Education in any of these 'cultures' entails the following three aspects:

- the transmission of knowledge about a phenomenon of study
- a training in the appropriate methods of enquiry
- an initiation into the belief systems and values of the 'culture'

If we contrast the sciences, the humanities, and design under each aspect, we may become clearer of what we mean by design, and what is particular to it.

- The phenomenon of study in each culture is
  - in the sciences: the natural world
  - in the humanities: human experience
  - in design: the artificial world

- The appropriate methods in each culture are
  - in the sciences: controlled experiment, classification, analysis
  - in the humanities: analogy, metaphor, criticism, evaluation
  - in design: modelling, pattern-formation, synthesis

- The values of each culture are
  - in the sciences: objectivity, rationality, neutrality, and a concern for 'truth'
  - in the humanities: subjectivity, imagination, commitment, and a concern for 'justice'
  - in design: practicality, ingenuity, empathy, and a concern for 'appropriateness'

In most cases, it is easier to contrast the sciences and the humanities (e.g. objectivity *versus* subjectivity, experiment *versus* analogy) than it is to identify the relevant comparable concepts in design. This is perhaps an indication of the paucity of our language and concepts in the 'third culture', rather than any acknowledgement that it does not really exist in its own right. But we are certainly faced with the problem of being more articulate about what it means to be 'designerly' rather than to be 'scientific' or 'artistic'.

Perhaps it would be better to regard the 'third culture' as technology, rather than design. This 'material culture' of design is, after all, the culture of the technologist—of the designer, doer and maker. Technology involves a synthesis of knowledge and skills from both the sciences and the humanities, in the pursuit of practical tasks; it is not simply 'applied science', but 'the application of scientific and *other organised knowledge* to practical tasks...[3]

The 'third culture' has traditionally been identified with technology. For example, A. N. Whitehead[4] suggested that: 'There are three main roads along which we can proceed with good hope of advancing towards the best balance of intellect and character: these are the way of literary culture, the way of scientific culture, the way of technical culture. No one of these methods can be exclusively followed without grave loss of intellectual activity and of character.'

DESIGN IN GENERAL EDUCATION

I think it is no accident that a fundamental reconceptualising of design emerged from a project, such as the Royal College of Art's, related to the development of design in general education. Our established concepts of design have always been related to specialist education: design education has been preparation of students for a professional, technical role. But now we are exploring the ways and the implications of design being a part of everyone's education, in the same ways that the sciences and the humanities are parts of everyone's education.[5]

Traditionally, design teachers have been practising designers who pass on their knowledge, skills and values through a process of apprenticeship. Design students 'act out' the role of designer in small projects,[6] and are tutored in the process by more experienced designers. These design teachers are firstly designers, and only secondly and incidentally teachers. This model may be defensible for specialist education,[7] but in general education all teachers are (or should be) firstly teachers, and only secondly, if at all, specialists in any field.

To understand this distinction we must understand the differences between specialist education and general education. The main distinction lies in the difference between the instrumental, or *extrinsic*, aims that specialist education usually has, and the *intrinsic* aims that general education must have. It is perfectly acceptable for architectural education, say, to have the instrumental aim of providing competent designers of buildings, but this cannot be an aim of general education. Anita Cross[8] has pointed out that, 'Since general education is *in principle* non-technical and nonvocational, design can only achieve parity with other disciplines in general education if it is organized as an area of study which contributes as much to the individual's self-realisation as to preparation for social roles.'

Whatever government ministers or industrialists may think, the aim of general education is not the preparation of people for social work roles. In a sense there is no 'aim' to general education. Peters[9] claims that:

It is as absurd to ask what the aim of education is as it is to ask what the aim of morality is... The only answer that can be given is to point to something intrinsic to education that is regarded as valuable such as the training of intellect or character. For to call something 'educational' is to intimate that the processes and activities themselves contribute to or involve something that is worthwhile... People think that education must be for the sake of something extrinsic that is worthwhile, whereas the truth is that being worthwhile is part of what is meant by calling it 'education'.

EDUCATIONAL CRITERIA

According to Peters the concept of education is one which only suggests *criteria* by which various activities and processes can be judged to see if they can be classified as 'educational'. Thus, giving a lecture *may* be educational, but it might not be if it does not satisfy the criteria; a student design project *may* be educational, but also might not be.

Peters suggests three principal criteria for education, the first of which is that worthwhile knowledge of some value must be transmitted. This first criterion seems straightforward, but actually raises problems of defining what is 'worthwhile'. The example offered by Peters is simplistic: 'We may be educating someone while we are training him: but we need not be. For we may be training him in the art of torture.' Deciding what is worthwhile is obviously value-laden and problematic. We might all agree that 'the art of torture' hardly counts as worthwhile, but what about, say, 'the art of pugilistics'? However, 'the arts of planning, inventing, making and doing' (to draw on Archer's definition of design again) are presumably clearly recognised as 'worthwhile'.

Peters' second criterion derives from his concern with the processes by which students are educated. He stresses that the *manner* in which people are educated is just as important as the matter which is transmitted[9]:

Although 'education' picks out no specific processes it does imply criteria which processes involved must satisfy in addition to the demand that something valuable must be passed on. It implies, first of all, that the individual who is educated shall come to care about the valuable things involved, that he shall want to achieve the relevant standards. We would not call a man 'educated' who knew about science but cared nothing for truth or who regarded it merely as a means to getting hot water and hot dogs. Furthermore it implies that he is initiated into the content of the activity or forms of knowledge in a meaningful way, so that he knows what he is doing. A man might be conditioned to avoid dogs or induced to do something by hypnotic suggestion. But we could not describe this as 'education' if he did not know what he was learning while he learned it.

This second criterion of 'education' therefore stresses the need for the student to be both self aware and aware of what and why he is learning. It is a process neither of imposing patterns on the student's mind, nor of assuming that free growth towards a desirable end will somehow occur without guidance. Education must be designed deliberately to enhance and to develop students' intrinsic cognitive processes and abilities.

Peters' third criterion derives from the consideration that: 'We often say of a man that he is highly trained, but not educated. What lies behind this condemnation?... It is...that he has a very limited conception of what he is doing. He does not see its connection with anything else, its place in a coherent pattern of life. It is, for him, an activity which is cognitively adrift.'

Peters concludes from this consideration that 'education' is related to 'cognitive perspective', which 'explains why it is that some activities rather than others seem so obviously to be of educational importance. There is very little to know about riding bicycles, swimming, or golf. It is largely a matter of "knowing how" rather than of "knowing that"[10]—of knack rather than understanding. Furthermore what there is to know throws very little light on much else.'

This is therefore a challenging criterion for design education, since design is often regarded as a skill, perhaps something like bicycle-riding, swimming, or playing golf. Indeed, elsewhere we have used Ryle's distinction between 'knowing how' and 'knowing that' to emphasise the role of 'know how' in design. However, I would now accept Peters' suggestion that:

An 'educated man' is distinguished not as much by what he does as by what he 'sees' or 'grasps'. If he does something very well, in which he has to be trained, he must see this in perspective, as related to other things. It is difficult to conceive of a training that would result in an 'educated' man in which a modicum of instruction has no place. For being educated involves 'knowing that' as well as 'knowing how'.

So to satisfy this third criterion of 'education', simple training in a skill is not enough. One *is* 'trained' as a designer, or doctor, or philosopher, but that alone does not make one 'educated'.

I have considered Peters' three criteria for 'education' at some length because it is important for the proponents of design in general education to be able to meet such criteria. It entails a fundamental change of perspective from that of a vocational training for a design profession, which is the only kind of 'design education' we have had previously. Design in general education is *not* primarily a preparation for a career, nor is it primarily a training in useful productive skills for 'doing and making' in industry. It must be defined in terms of the *intrinsic* values of education.

The interpretation of 'education' that Peters has developed, then, stresses its intrinsic merits. To be educated is of value in and of itself, not because of any extrinsic motivating factors or advantages it might be considered to offer, such as getting a job. In order to justify design as a part of general education, therefore, it is necessary to ensure that what is learned in design classes, and the way it is learned, can meet these criteria. We have to be able to identify that which is intrinsically valuable in the field of design, such that it is justifiably a part of everyone's education and contributes to the development of an 'educated' person.

DESIGNERLY WAYS OF KNOWING

The claim from the Royal College of Art study of 'Design in general education' was that 'there are things to know, ways of knowing them, and ways of finding out about them' that are specific to the design area. The authors imply that there are designerly ways of knowing, distinct from the more usually-recognised scientific and scholarly ways of knowing. However, the Royal College of Art authors do little to explicate this designerly ways of knowing. They do point out that 'it would not do to accept design as a sort of ragbag of all the things that science and the humanities happen to leave out,' but they are less than precise about what design should include. Design must have its own inner coherence, in the ways that science and the humanities do, if it is to be established in comparable intellectual and educational terms. But the world of design has been badly served by its intellectual leaders, who have failed to develop their subject *in its own terms*. Too often, they have been seduced by the lure of *Wissenschaft*, and turned away from the lore of *Technik*; they have defected to the cultures of scientific and scholarly enquiry, instead of developing the culture of designerly enquiry.

So what can be said about these ill-defined 'designerly ways of knowing'? There has, in fact, been a small and very slowly-growing field of enquiry in design research over the last 20 years or so, from which it is possible to begin to draw some conclusions.

Design Processes

For example, a number of observational studies has been made of how designers work. These studies tend to support the view that there is a distinct 'designerly' form of activity that separates it from typical scientific and scholarly activities. Lawson's studies of design behaviour, in particular, have compared the problem-solving strategies of designers with those of scientists.[11] He devised problems which required the arrangement of 3D coloured blocks so as to satisfy certain rules (some of which were not initially disclosed), and set the same problems to both postgraduate architectural students and postgraduate science students. The two groups showed dissimilar problem-solving strategies, according to Lawson. The scientists generally adopted a strategy of systematically exploring the possible combinations of blocks, in order to discover the fundamental rule which would allow a permissible combination. The architects were more inclined to propose a series of solutions, and to have these solutions eliminated, until they found an acceptable one. Lawson has commented:

> The essential difference between these two strategies is that while the scientists focused their attention on discovering the rule, the architects were obsessed with achieving the desired result. The scientists adopted a generally problem-focused strategy and the architects a solution-focused strategy. Although it would be quite possible using the architect's approach to achieve the best solution without actually discovering the complete range of acceptable solutions, in fact most architects discovered something about the rule governing the allowed combination of blocks. In other words, they learn about the nature of the problem largely as a result of trying out solutions, whereas the scientists set out specifically to study the problem.[12]

These experiments suggest that scientists problem-solve by analysis, whereas designers problem-solve by synthesis. Lawson repeated his experiments with younger students and found that first-year students and sixth-form school students could not be distinguished as 'architects' and 'nonarchitects' by their problem-solving strategies: there were no consistent differences. This suggests that architects learn to adopt their solution-focused strategy during, and presumably as a result of, their education. Presumably, they learn, are taught, or discover, that this is the more effective way of tackling the problems they are set.

A central feature of design activity, then, is its reliance on generating fairly quickly a satisfactory solution, rather than on any prolonged analysis of the problem. In Simon's[13] inelegant term, it is a process of 'satisficing' rather than optimising; producing any one of what might well be a large range of satisfactory solutions rather than attempting to generate the one hypothetically-optimum solution. This strategy has been observed in other studies of design behaviour, including architects,[14] urban designers,[15] and engineers.[16]

Why it should be such a recognisably 'designerly' way of proceeding is probably not just an embodiment of any intrinsic inadequacies of designers and their education, but is more likely to be a reflection of the nature of the design task and of the nature of the kinds of problems designers tackle. The designer is constrained to produce a practicable result within a specific time limit, whereas the scientist and scholar are both able, and often required, to suspend their judgements and decisions until more is known—'further research is needed' is always a justifiable conclusion for them.

It is also now widely recognised that design problems are ill-defined, ill-structured, or 'wicked'.[17] They are not the same as the 'puzzles' that scientists, mathematicians and other scholars set themselves. They are not problems for which all the necessary information is, or ever can be, available to the problem-solver. They are therefore not susceptible to exhaustive analysis, and there can never be a guarantee that 'correct' solutions can be found for them. In this context a solution focused strategy is clearly preferable to a problem-focused one: it will always be possible to go on analysing 'the problem', but the designer's task is to produce 'the solution'. It is only in terms of a conjectured solution that the problem can be contained within manageable bounds.[18] What designers tend to do, therefore, is to seek, or impose a 'primary generator'[19] which both defines the limits of the problem and suggests the nature of its possible solution.

In order to cope with ill-defined problems, designers have to learn to have the self-confidence to define, redefine and change the problem-as-given in the light of the solution that emerges from their minds and hands. People who seek the certainty of externally structured, well-defined problems will never appreciate the delight of being a designer. Jones has commented that 'changing the problem in order to find a solution is the most challenging and difficult part of designing'.[20] He also points out that 'designing should not be confused with art, with science, or with mathematics.'

Such warnings about failing to recognise the particular nature of designing are now common in design theory. Many people have especially warned against confusing design with science.

The scientific method is a pattern of problem-solving behaviour employed in finding out the nature of what exists, whereas the design method is a pattern of behaviour employed in inventing things of value which do not yet exist. Science is analytic; design is constructive. (Gregory[21])

The natural sciences are concerned with how things are...design, on the other hand, is concerned with how things ought to be. (Simon[13])

To base design theory on inappropriate paradigms of logic and science is to make a bad mistake. Logic has interests in abstract forms. Science investigates extant forms. Design initiates novel forms. (March[22])

The emphasis in these admonitions is on the constructive, normative, creative nature of designing. Designing is a process of pattern synthesis, rather than pattern recognition. The solution is not simply lying there among the data, like the dog among the spots in the well known perceptual puzzle; it has to be actively constructed by the designer's own efforts. Reflecting on his observations of urban designers, Levin[15] commented that:

The designer knows (consciously or unconsciously) that some ingredient must be added to the information that he already has in order that he may arrive at an unique solution. This knowledge is in itself not enough in design problems, of course. He has to look for the extra ingredient, and he uses his powers of conjecture and original thought to do so. What then is this extra ingredient? In many if not most cases it is an 'ordering principle'. The preoccupation with geometrical patterns that is revealed in many town plans and many writings on the subject demonstrates this very clearly.

And of course it is not only in town planning, but in all fields of design, that one finds this preoccupation with geometrical patterns; a pattern (or some other ordering principle) seemingly *has* to be imposed in order to make a solution possible.

This pattern-constructing feature has been recognised as lying at the core of design activity by Alexander, in his 'constructive diagrams'[23] and 'pattern language'[24]. The designer learns to think in this sketch-like form, in which the abstract patterns of user requirements are turned into the concrete patterns of an actual object. It is like learning an artificial 'language', a kind of code which transforms 'thoughts' into 'words':

Those who have been trained as designers will be using just such a code...which enables the designer to effect a translation from individual, organisational and social needs to physical artefacts. This code which has been learned is supposed to express and contain actual connections which exist between human needs and their artificial environment. In effect, the designer learns to 'speak' a language—to make a useful transaction between domains which are unlike each other (sounds and meanings in language, artefacts and needs in design) by means of a code or system of codes which structure that connection. (Hillier and Leaman[25])

Designerly ways of knowing are embodied in these 'codes'. The details of the codes will vary from one design profession to another, but perhaps there is a 'deep structure' to design codes. We shall not know this until more effort has been made in externalising the codes.

What designers know about their own problem-solving processes remains largely tacit knowledge—i.e. they know it in the same way that a skilled person 'knows' how to perform that skill. They find it difficult to externalise their knowledge, and hence design education is forced to rely so heavily on an apprenticeship system of learning. It may be satisfactory, or at least understandable, for practising designers to be inarticulate about their skills, but teachers of design have a responsibility to be as articulate as they possibly can about what it is they are trying to teach, or else they can have no basis for choosing the content and methods of their teaching.

Design Products

So far, I have concentrated on designerly ways of knowing that are embodied in the *processes* of designing. But there is an equally important area of knowledge embodied in the *products* of designing.

There is a great wealth of knowledge carried in the objects of our material culture. If you want to know how an object should be designed—e.g. what shapes and sizes it should have, what material it should be made from—go and look at existing examples of that kind of object, and simply copy (i.e. learn!) from the past. This, of course, was the 'design process' that was so successful in generating the material culture of craft society: the craftsperson simply copied the design of an object from its previous examples. Both Jones[20] and Alexander[23] have emphasised how the 'unselfconscious' processes of craft design led to extremely subtle, beautiful and appropriate objects. A very simple process can actually generate very complex products.

Objects are a form of knowledge about how to satisfy certain requirements, about how to perform certain tasks. And they are a form of knowledge that is available to everyone; one does not have to understand mechanics, nor metallurgy, nor the molecular structure of timber, to know that an axe offers (or 'explains') a very effective way of splitting wood. Of course, explicit knowledge about objects and about how they function *has* become available, and has sometimes led to significant improvements in the design of the objects. But in general, 'invention comes before theory'[26]; the world of 'doing and making' is usually ahead of the world of understanding—technology leads to science, not *vice versa* as is often believed.

A significant branch of designerly ways of knowing, then, is the knowledge that resides in objects. Designers are immersed in this material culture, and draw upon it as the primary source of their thinking. Designers have the ability both to 'read' and 'write' in this culture: they understand what messages objects communicate, and they can create new objects which embody new messages. The importance of this two-way communication between people and 'the world of goods' has been recognised by Douglas and Isherwood.[27] In a passage that has strong connections to the arguments for a 'third area' of human knowledge in design, as distinct from the sciences and the humanities, they say:

For too long a narrow idea of human reasoning has prevailed which only accepts simple induction and deduction as worthy of the name of thinking. But there is a prior and pervasive kind of reasoning that scans a scene and sizes it up, packing into one instant's survey a process of matching, classifying and comparing. This is not to invoke a mysterious faculty of intuition or mental association. Metaphoric appreciation, as all the words we have used suggest, is a work of approximate measurement, scaling and comparison between like and unlike elements in a pattern.

'Metaphoric appreciation' is an apt name for what it is that designers are particularly skilled in, in 'reading' the world of goods, in translating back from concrete objects to abstract requirements, through their design codes. 'Forget that commodities are good for eating, clothing, and shelter', Douglas and Isherwood say; 'forget their usefulness and try instead the idea that commodities are good for thinking; treat them as a nonverbal medium for the human relative faculty.'

INTRINSIC VALUE OF DESIGN EDUCATION

The arguments for, and defence of, design in general education must rest on identifying the intrinsic values of design that make it justifiably a part of everyone's education. Above, I have tried to set out the field of 'designerly ways of knowing', as it relates to both the processes and the products of designing, in the hope that it will lead into an understanding of what these intrinsic values might be. Essentially, we can say that designerly ways of knowing rest on the manipulation of non-verbal codes in the material culture; these codes translate 'messages' either way between concrete objects and abstract requirements; they facilitate the constructive, solution-focused thinking of the designer, in the same way that other (e.g. verbal and numerical) codes facilitate analytic, problem-focused thinking; they are probably the most effective means of tackling the characteristically ill-defined problems of planning, designing and inventing new things.

From even a sketchy analysis, such as this, of designerly ways of knowing, we can indeed begin to identify features that can be justified in education as having intrinsic value. Firstly, we can say that design develops students' abilities in tackling a particular kind of problem. This kind of problem is characterised as ill-defined, or ill-structured, and is quite distinct from the kinds of well structured problems that lie in the educational domains of the sciences and the humanities. We might even claim that our design problems are more 'real' than theirs, in that they are like the problems or issues or decisions that people are more usually faced with in everyday life.

There is therefore a strong educational justification for design as an introduction to, and the development of cognitive skills and abilities in, real-world problem solving.[28] We must be careful not to interpret this justification in instrumental terms, as a training in problem-solving skills, but in terms that satisfy the more rigorous criteria for education. As far as problem-solving is concerned, design in general education must be justified in terms of helping to develop an 'educated' person, able to understand the nature of ill-defined problems, how to tackle them, and how they differ from other kinds of problems. This kind of justification has been developed by McPeck in terms of the educational value of 'critical thinking'.[29] A related justification is given by Harrison, particularly in the context of practical design work, in terms of the radical connections between 'making and thinking'.[30]

This leads us into a second area of justification for design in general education, based on the kind of thinking that is peculiar to design. This characteristically 'constructive' thinking is distinct from the more commonly acknowledged inductive and deductive kinds of reasoning. (March[22] has related it to what C. S. Peirce called 'abductive' reasoning.)

In educational terms, the development of constructive thinking must be seen as a neglected aspect of cognitive development in the individual. This neglect can be traced to the dominance of the cultures of the sciences and the humanities, and the dominance of the 'stage' theories of cognitive development. These theories, especially Piaget's, tend to suggest that the concrete, constructive, synthetic kinds of reasoning occur relatively early in child development, and that they are passed through to reach the higher states of abstract, analytical reasoning (i.e. the kinds of reasoning that predominate in the sciences, especially). There are other theories (for example, Bruner's) that suggest that cognitive development is a continuous process of interaction between different modes of cognition, all of which can be developed to high levels. That is, the qualitatively different types of cognition (e.g. 'concrete' and 'formal' types in Piaget's terms, 'iconic' and 'symbolic' in Bruner's terms) are not simply characteristic of different 'stages' of development, but are different kinds of innate human cognitive abilities, *all* of which can be developed from lower to higher levels.

The concrete/iconic modes of cognition are particularly relevant in design, whereas the formal/symbolic modes are more relevant in the sciences. If the 'continuous' rather than the 'stage' theories of cognitive development are adopted, it is clear that there is a strong justification for design education in that it provides opportunities particularly for the development of the concrete/iconic modes.

From this, we can move on to a third area of justification for design in general education, based on the recognition that there are large areas of human cognitive ability that have been systematically ignored in our educational system. Because the theorists of cognitive development are themselves thoroughly immersed in the scientific-academic cultures where numeracy and literacy prevail, they have overlooked the third culture of design. This culture relies not so much on verbal, numerical and literary modes of thinking and communicating, but on nonverbal modes.[31] This is particularly evident in the designer's use of models and 'codes' that rely so heavily on graphic images—i.e. drawings, diagrams and sketches that are aids to internal thinking as well as aids to communicating ideas and instructions to others.

As well as these graphic models, there is also in design a significant use of mental imagery in 'the mind's eye'.[32] The field of nonverbal thought and communication as it relates to design includes a wide range of elements, from 'graphicacy' to 'object languages', 'action languages' and 'cognitive mapping'.[33] Most of these cognitive modes are strongest in the right hemisphere of the brain, rather than the left.[34] So on this view the 'neglected area' of design in education is not merely one-third of human experience and ability, but nearer to one-half!

French[35] has recognised nonverbal thinking as perhaps the principal justification for design in general education: 'It is in strengthening and uniting the entire nonverbal education of the child, and in its improvement of the range of acuity of his thinking, that the prime justification of the teaching of design in schools should be sought, not in preparing for a career or leisure, nor in training knowledgeable consumers, valuable as these aspects may be.'

DESIGN AS A DISCIPLINE

In this paper I have taken up the argument put forward in the Royal College of Art report on 'Design in general education' that there are 'designerly ways of knowing' that are at the core of the design area of education. First, I have stressed that we must seek to interpret this core of knowledge in terms of its intrinsic educational value, and not in the instrumental terms that are associated with traditional, vocational design education. Second, I have drawn upon the field of design research for what it has to say about the way designers work and think, and the kinds of problems they tackle. And third, I have tried to develop from this the justification that can be made for design as a part of general education in terms of intrinsic educational values.

I identified five aspects of designerly ways of knowing:

- Designers tackle 'ill-defined' problems.
- Their mode of problem-solving is 'solution-focused'.
- Their mode of thinking is 'constructive'.
- They use 'codes' that translate abstract requirements into concrete objects.
- They use these codes to both 'read' and 'write' in 'object languages'.

From these ways of knowing I drew three main areas of justification for design in general education:

- Design develops innate abilities in solving real-world, ill-defined problems.
- Design sustains cognitive development in the concrete/iconic modes of cognition.
- Design offers opportunities for development of a wide range of abilities in nonverbal thought and communication.

For me, something else also begins to emerge from these lines of argument. It seems to me that the design research movement of the last 20 years and the design education movement of the last 10 years are beginning to converge on what is, after all, their common concern—the discipline of design. The research path to design as a discipline has concentrated on understanding those general features of design activity that are common to all the design professions: it has been concerned with 'design in general' and it now allows us to generalise at least a little about the designerly ways of knowing. The education path to design as a discipline has also been concerned with 'design in general', and it has led us to consider what it is that can be generalised as of intrinsic value in learning to design. Both the research and the education paths, then, have been concerned with developing the general subject of design.

However, there is still a long way to go before we can begin to have much sense of having achieved a real understanding of design as a discipline—we have only begun to make rough maps of the territory. Following on from his comments on nonverbal education as the prime justification for design in general education, French also points out that there are certain implications arising from this:

If design teaching is to have this role it must meet certain requirements. It must 'stretch the mind', and ideally this involves a progression from step to step, some discipline of thought to be acquired in more or less specifiable components, reflected in a growing achievement of the pupil that both he and his teacher can recognise with some confidence. At present, there does not seem to be enough understanding, enough scholarly work on design, enough material of a suitable nature to make such teaching possible. I believe we should strive to remedy this state of affairs.

The education path to design as a discipline forces us to consider the nature of this general subject of design, what it is that we are seeking to develop in the individual student, and how this development can be structured for learning. Like our colleagues in the sciences and the humanities we can at this point legitimately conclude that further research is needed! We need more research and enquiry: first into the designerly ways of knowing; second into the scope, limits and nature of innate cognitive abilities relevant to design; and third into the ways of enhancing and developing these abilities through education.

We need a 'research programme', in the sense in which Lakatos[36] has described the research programmes of science. At its core is a 'touch-stone theory' or idea—in our case the view that 'there are designerly ways of knowing'. Around this core is built a 'defensive' network of related theories, ideas and knowledge—and I have tried to sketch in some of these in this paper. In this way both design research and design education can develop a common approach to design as a discipline.

© 1982 Elsevier Ltd. Previously published in *Design Studies*, 3(4) pp. 221–227.

REFERENCES

1. Royal College of Art. *Design in general education*, Royal College of Art, London (1979).
2. Archer, B. "The Three Rs" *Design Studies*, Vol. 1, No. 1 (July 1979) pp. 18–20.
3. Cross, N., Naughton, J. and Walker, D. "Design method and scientific method", *Design Studies*, Vol. 2, No. 4 (October 1981) pp. 195–201.
4. Whitehead, A. N. "Technical education and its relation to science and literature" in Whitehead, A. N. *The aims of education*, Williams and Norgate, London (1932). Second edition: Ernest Benn, Ltd, London (1950).
5. Cross, N. "Design education for laypeople" in Evans, B., Powell, J. and Talbot, R. (eds) *Changing Design*. Wiley, Chichester, UK (1982).
6. Simmonds, R. "Limitations in the decision strategies of design students". *Design Studies*, Vol. 1, No. 6 (October 1980) pp. 358–384.
7. Abel, C. "Function of tacit knowing in learning to design", *Design Studies*, Vol. 2, No. 4 (October 1981) pp. 209–214.
8. Cross, A. "Design and general education," *Design Studies*, Vol. 1, No. 4 (April 1980) pp. 202–206.
9. Peters, R. S. "Education as initiation", in Archambault, R. D. (ed) *Philosophical Analysis and Education*, Routledge and Kegan Paul, London (1965).
10. Ryle, G. *The Concept of Mind,* Hutchinson, London (1949).

11. Lawson, B. "Cognitive Strategies in Architectural Design," *Ergonomics* Vol. 22, No. 1 (1979) pp. 59–68.

12. Lawson, B. *How Designers Think*, Architectural Press, London (1980).

13. Simon, H. A. *The Sciences of the Artificial*, MIT Press, Cambridge, MA, USA (1969).

14. Eastman, C. M. 'On the analysis of intuitive design processes' in Moore, G. T. (ed), *Emerging Methods in Environmental Design and Planning*, MIT Press, Cambridge, MA, USA (1970).

15. Levin, P. H. 'Decision making in urban design' *Building Research Station Note EN51/66*, Building Research Station, Garston, Herts, UK (1966).

16. Marples, D. *The Decisions of Engineering Design*, Institute of Engineering Designers, London (1960).

17. Rittel, H. and Webber, M. 'Dilemmas in a General Theory of Planning' *Policy Science*, Vol. 4, (1973) pp. 155–169.

18. Hillier, B. and Leaman, A. 'How is design possible?' *J. Archit. Res* Vol. 3, No. 1 (1974) pp. 4–11.

19. Darke, J. 'The primary generator and the design process' *Design Studies*, Vol. 1, No. 1 (July 1979) pp. 36–44.

20. Jones, J. C. *Design Methods*, Wiley, Chichester, UK (1970).

21. Gregory, S. A. 'Design and the design method' in Gregory, S. A. (ed) *The Design Method*, Butterworths, London (1966).

22. March, L. J. 'The logic of design and the question of value' in March, L. J. (ed) *The Architecture of Form*, Cambridge University Press, UK (1976).

23. Alexander, C. *Notes on the Synthesis of Form*, Harvard University Press, Cambridge, MA, USA (1964).

24. Alexander, C. et al. *A Pattern Language*, Oxford University Press, New York (1979).

25. Hillier, B. and Leaman, A. 'Architecture as a discipline' J. Archit. Res. Vol. 5, No. 1 (1976) 28–32.

26. Pye, D. *The Nature and Aesthetics of Design*, Barrie and Jenkins, London (1978).

27. Douglas, M. and Isherwood, B. *The World of Goods*, Allen Lane, London (1979).

28. Fox, R. 'Design-based studies: an action-based "form of knowledge" or thinking, reasoning, and operating', *Design Studies*, Vol. 2, No. 1 (January 1981) pp. 33–40.

29. McPeck, J. E. *Critical Thinking and Education*, Martin Robertson, Oxford, UK (1981).

30. Harrison, A. *Making and Thinking*, Harvester Press, Hassocks, Sussex, UK (1978).

31. Ferguson, E. S. 'The mind's eye: non-verbal thought in technology' *Science*, Vol. 197, No. 4306 (1977).

32. Archer, B. 'The mind's eye': not so much seeing as thinking', *Designer* (January 1980) pp. 8–9.

33. Cross, A. 'An introduction to non-verbal aspects of thought' *Design Educ. Res. Note 5*, Design Discipline, The Open University, Milton Keynes, Bucks, UK (1980)

34. Ornstein, R. E. *The Psychology of Consciousness*, Jonathan Cape, London; Penguin Books, Harmondsworth, Middx, UK (1975).

35. French, M. J. 'A justification for design teaching in schools' *Engineering* (design education supplement) (May 1979) p. 25.

36. Lakatos, I. 'Falsification and the methodology of scientific research programmes in Lakatos, I. and Musgrave, A. (eds) *Criticism and the Growth of Knowledge*, Cambridge University Press (1970).

CHAPTER ELEVEN

The Future Isn't What It Used to Be

VICTOR PAPANEK

© *Victor Papanek* / Design Issues / *MIT Press*

Many designers are trying to make the design process more systematic, scientific, and predictable, as well as computer-compatible. Their attempts to rationalize design by developing rules, taxonomies, classifications, and procedural design systems are extreme examples of trying to provide design with a respectable scientific-sounding theoretical background or, at least, a theory-like structure that smacks of science. Their approach stands for reason, logic, and intellect, but such a method leads to reductionism and frequently results in sterility and the sort of high-tech functionalism that disregards human psychic needs at the expense of clarity.

Other designers follow feeling, sensation, revelation, and intuition. This is often called "seat-of-the-pants" design. Their work is not reductionist but is stifling in its rich romanticism, substituting sentimental passion for responses to human needs.

Rather than attempting a synthesis between such divergent views, this article will show that both groups neglect important new insights that are being developed in other domains and will demonstrate that there is an enormous amount of data available about how people relate to their environment esthetically and psycho-physiologically. Much of these data are still unknown to designers, architects, and planners as the data come from such diverse fields as ergonomics, ecology, archeology, psychiatry, cultural history, anthropology, biology, ethology, and human geography.

The first part of this paper, "The Microbes in the Tower," describes some of this information that leads to new conclusions about human responses to an increasingly technological environment. The second part, "Toward a Biotechnology of Communities," presents several observations on community planning, arranged in a somewhat kaleidoscopic manner.

THE MICROBES IN THE TOWER

Many overlapping sorts of evidence—mainly research findings by public health and public safety researchers; discoveries about how the human mind, emotions, and thinking functions; and personal experiences in many different settings—have recently enlarged the understanding of the rich and subtle ways in which people interact with their everyday surroundings. The offices, roadways, parks, train stations, airports, and other places (manufactured or natural) that people work or live in, move through, seek out for play or relaxation, are not just a given: a backdrop that can be ignored.

The kind of sunlight (compare a July morning in Greece to the autumnal sun setting over Stockholm), the chemical composition of the air (contrast the birch-scented breeze on an island in the Finnish archipelago with the heady aroma of Frangipani and jungle vines on Bali or the plastic air in a shopping mall); and colors, spaces, shapes, materials, views, sounds, and odors affect everyone's physical well being, mental ability and cognitive grasp, sense of self, humanity, and, by extension, understanding of humanity's pressing problems and unfinished business.

Some examples may serve. Experiments in psychology and psychiatry at Yale University have demonstrated that some smells cause blood pressure changes similar to those achieved through meditation: the scent of spiced apple reduces blood pressure drastically. Biometeorologists and microbiologists have found that unscented air containing a certain amount of small-air ions (clusters of molecules with a negative electrical charge) lower the quantity of serotonin in the midbrain. Serotonin is a hormone associated with anxiety. The response of another brain-body system to the environment has been followed: some of the light entering the eyes in bright sunlight bypasses the cortex entirely and directly acts upon the hypothalamus, the spinal cord, and the pineal gland. There it suppresses the production of a hormone called melatonin, which affects moods, fertility, and many other body functions. For decades there has been awareness that a certain red-orange color will kick several psychophysiological systems dealing with aggression and sexuality into high gear. Recent studies in color therapy and photobiology, however, seem to show that "passive pink" (the bubble-gum color) has an almost immediate effect on aggressive behavior. A berserk teenager, when placed in a two by three-meter passive-pink cell will calm down within minutes and may, after a quarter hour or so, be lying on the floor, ready to go to sleep.[1]

Inasmuch as humans have always responded to air, smells, light, and colors, why have we only now managed to get significant data on these responses? Only since the war has a majority of people in the western world moved indoors, protected from bright sunshine and sealed off hermetically from the waterfalls, forests, rivers, and mountains that carry large amounts of small-air ions. In technologically developed countries, most people spend much of their time inside buildings under artificial lighting, with fixed windows, breathing recycled air. Especially in Canada and the United States, once-a-week shopping patterns and speculative land use have resulted in enormous, enclosed shopping malls. These malls are finding an increasing secondary use as jogging and walking spaces year-round, gossiping places for the elderly, and ideal hangouts for teenagers—all in a climate-controlled environment. Dr. Richard Wurtman, a professor of brain and cognitive sciences at Massachusetts Institute of Technology, says, "We are all unwitting subjects of a long-term experiment on the effects of artificial lighting on our health." Therefore, we must take conscious responsibility for creating manufactured environments that won't damage the performance of our brain-body systems even more.

Without going into more detail, certain facts about how humans relate to their environments have emerged. Dr. John H. Falk, a biologist and ecologist is an expert on human responses to grass. He spent approximately 20 years researching landscape preferences with people of all ages from Africa, India, Europe, and America. The subjects' backgrounds included every kind of human habitat from savannah to montane terrain, from desert to rain forest.

Photographs of different landscapes were shown to Falk's subjects. Not surprisingly, they liked best the environments they were used to—a reaction that might be explained as a purely cultural phenomenon. But unexpectedly, Falk also found a deep, innate preference for a grass landscape, even among people who had never experienced a grassland setting in their lives. Dr. Falk theorizes that, because the most extensive grasslands in the world are the savannahs of East Africa where human beings first evolved, we may have a genetically transmitted predisposition for the milieu of our species' birth and early development. Habitat preference may be tied to anatomy: walking upright, using hands to carry tools, the opposable thumb, binocular vision. Evolving to walk across the spongy texture of grass may even explain why— although we have the technology to make any floor surface—many people prefer the grass analog of rugs. Carpets from Persia and Pakistan are actually hand-knotted representations of formal gardens done in silk.

This innate and imprinted preference for grasslands may also help by providing an internal guide to our optimal nouveau of environmental stimulus, the kind of complexity we need—in the things we touch, sniff, listen to, look at, feel against our skin or underfoot—to be our best. "Any reduced or raised level of stimulus may impair our functioning."

Dr. Falk's ideas are directly related to other fairly recent research fields. The development of the mammalian brain's shape, size, structure, and function is intimately linked to early sensory experience. (The negative effects of this are now all too well-known from the performance of black children from slums and ghettos in the United States and the United Kingdom.) Furthermore, the beauty of human surroundings has been demonstrated to have a profound influence on human behavior and job performance.[2]

Without giving in to reductionist reasoning, neuroanatomical experiments with rats at the University of California at Berkeley have shown that when a young rat is put in an enriched environment (one with more playmates and toys) its cerebral cortex begins thickening within a few days; whereas, the cortex of a young rat in an impoverished milieu actually shrinks. Even old rats with an equivalent human's age of 75 to 90 years old grow bigger brains in an enriched environment. The brains of rats raised in a semi-natural outdoor environment grow bigger still and, moreover, raise the animal's general intelligence. "The ambient lighting, noise, and odor, all appear to influence behavior positively," one researcher remarks.[3]

But Dr. Falk and others think that humans may have other unborn predispositions to parts of the natural landscape other than grasslands. A preference for water in the landscape seems innate in all people. Dr. Stephen Kaplan and Dr. Rachel Kaplan, psychologists at Michigan University believe that humans may have an imprinted preference for winding paths that provide "mystery" and "give the impression that one could acquire new information if one were to travel deeper into the scene."[4] This liking for winding paths, mystery, wishing to "travel deeper into the scene," has been used successfully for millennia in Japanese gardens and, more recently, in English landscape architecture. An argument could be made that it also informs *haptic* satisfaction we derive from viewing a painting or a boxing match.

In their book, the Kaplans write: "Mystery ... is somewhat unexpected in the context of psychology. Perhaps for this reason there has been an inclination to translate it into a more familiar concept, such as 'surprise.' A critical difference between mystery and surprise, however, is that in a surprise the new information is present and it is sudden. In the case of mystery, the new information is not present; it is only suggested or implied. Rather than being sudden, there is a strong element of continuity. The bend in the road, the brightly lighted field seen through a screen of foliage—these settings imply that the new information will be continuous with, and related to, that which has gone before. Given this continuity one can usually think of several alternative hypotheses as to what one might discover."[5]

Jay Appleton, a geographer at Hull University in England, has used the words *prospect* and *refuge* to describe two more human desiderata in landscapes: both are enablers to survival and functioning. *Prospect* means a broad, sweeping vista, an outlook point from which we can take in visual information from many miles around without hindrance. *Refuge* means a hiding place where, secure in concealment, we can observe without being seen, gaining information in safety. Our concepts of *snug* in English, *cosy* in American, *gemütlich* in German, or *hyggelig* in Danish relate to this feeling.

We also seek environments that are easy to read, that is, landscapes that look as if they could be explored extensively without getting lost. The Kaplans consider such open landscapes with distinctive natural landmarks to provide legibility.

To summarize, environments speak to us in a number of ways, which can be listed in order of magnitude. These universal environmental elements consist first of those that are inborn, innate—the archetypal elements that apparently rise from the collective unconscious of humanity. These include a clear preference for grasslands, water, winding paths that embody mystery, places of refuge, and lookout points forming prospects. Add to these legibility, because, as the landscape architect William M. C. Lam has pointed out, we look to the environment for information regarding survival, sustenance, orientation, defense, and stimulation.

Then there are culturally conditioned elements. These are tied to specific cultures, yet change slowly with time. In his early books *The Silent Language* and *The Hidden Dimension*, Dr. Edward Hall established the science of proxemics. People walk through life within an invisible proxemic bubble. The shape and size of the bubble is culturally determined. The simplest example is the distances individuals maintain between each other during conversations. Northern Europeans tend to face one another at a distance of about three feet, Southern Europeans narrow this distance by a third, whereas some North Africans face each other at only ten inches. Another example: in Chad or the Cameroons, a conversation partner will bathe you in clouds of cigarette smoke because it is considered friendly. Such actions would be considered thoughtless in Europe, whereas in the United States smoking is now considered an antisocial act by many.[6]

Locally conditioned elements in the environment, distinct from cultural elements, may depend on climate and life-styles. These too may change in time. As a small boy in Austria, I would go to school on skis; I was delighted when, years later, I could commute on skis in Oslo. The flat landscapes of Holland and Denmark lend themselves to bicycling, just as the extensive canals and freezing temperatures of Ottawa provide an environment that delighted us when we were able to skate to and from work.

Personal elements are signifiers in the environment of events that have individual or familiar meaning. Someone looks out the window and says, "My great great grandfather planted that oak tree in 1790, when he was a boy." Or, "This is where I first kissed a girl," or, "My uncle once worked for that newspaper."

There is also the question of beauty in the environment. Approximately 30 years ago, Dr. Abraham Maslow, one of the founders of humanistic psychology, conducted some of the first experiments on the effects that a beautiful environment have on human functioning. He built three rooms: a "beautiful," an "average," and an "ugly" room. The ugly one was designed to look somewhat like a janitor's room, with a naked, hanging light bulb, an old mattress on the floor, battleship-grey walls, ripped window shades, trash, brooms, mops, and a good deal of dust and litter. The beautiful room had large windows, a superbly woven Navajo rug on the floor, off-white walls, paintings and sculpture, indirect lighting, a bookcase, a soft armchair, and a wooden desk. The average room had, according to the experimenters, "the appearance of a clean, neat, 'worked-in' office, in no way outstanding enough to elicit any comments."

Volunteers were handed photographs of people and asked to report if the faces displayed energy and well-being. The volunteers were supervised by three examiners (who were themselves unaware of the real objective of the experiment). The true purpose was to study people's reactions to their environments. The results showed that the volunteers found energy and well-being in faces when seeing them in the beautiful room, but found fatigue and sickness in the same faces viewed in the ugly room. The behavior of the examiners (unaware of the intent of the test) also varied: they brusquely rushed through interviews in the ugly room, exhibiting "gross behavioral changes" while working there and complaining of monotony, fatigue, headache, hostility, and irritability. Strangely, even though their job performance and work satisfaction were over and over again influenced by where they worked, they failed to notice this fact even once. *They were completely unaware that their activities were in such a close relationship to the appearance of the rooms*, although they realized that they preferred not to work in the ugly room. Reactions by both volunteers and examiners to the average room were closer to the ugly than to the beautiful room.[7]

Often a cure for a problem has to begin before the sickness is recognized or proper diagnosis is possible. Beginning around 1830, doctors studying urban diseases realized that, as more and more people lived together in cities, local springs and wells could no longer be clean and pure. First, they noticed that people got sick more in the new cities than in villages. Next, they realized that in certain city areas, people got sick more often. Finally, doctors discovered that bacteria that had entered specific wells could cause cholera in those who drank from those wells. Eventually, such discoveries led to today's protected reservoirs and water filtration systems. These nineteenth century public health officials started research methods still being used: finding correlations between two kinds of unintended changes: fluctuations in people's health or mental functions that point back to specific changes in the environment.

What makes this search important is the understanding that changing the environment—carelessly or in good faith—can catastrophically damage some as yet unsuspecting internal mechanism. Now that the need for clean water is self-evident, the fact that it took nearly 100 years to find this out should be remembered. Much of the public health changes were made *before the actual causes were fully understood.*[8]

One can only wish that we would stop the lethal effects of acid rain on forests, and the hole in the ozone layer over the Antarctic, without the plunderers that run most governments arguing endlessly about the precise percentages of damage done by industry vis-a-vis motorcars.

Recently, public health researchers have found that a relatively new use of water—in the central air conditioning systems of tall buildings—causes infections and may contribute to the sick-building syndrome. Symptoms range from headache to sore throat, wheezing, and shortness of breath. This is transmitted simultaneously in airborne and waterborne ways and can also be contracted on lengthy flights in aircraft.

Contemporary office and residential buildings are tightly sealed structures, usually with fixed windows. The integrated heating, ventilating, and air-conditioning systems reduce heating and cooling expenses (and energy use) by using the same recycled air over and over. Soon this stable air in sealed buildings will contain fungi, bacteria, and gases produced by most of the manufactured materials. Textiles for carpets and upholstery are increasingly made of plastics. These materials and the adhesives used to apply them release what a medical epidemiologist calls "a variety of volatile organic compounds" that cause eye irritations and infections of the upper respiratory tract. (Fluorescent lighting also causes irritations of the respiratory tract in ways not yet fully understood.)[9]

The problems of sealed buildings are compounded by "cooling-tower drift," the presence in the air of water droplets so tiny they can penetrate, unnoticed, deep in a person's lungs. Sometimes the fresh air intake of one high-rise building is so close to the cooling tower of another sealed building that drift will transmit bacteria growing in the cooling tower water more efficiently than breathing outdoor air. One such infection is already well known, Legionnaires' Disease. According to the Third International Conference on Indoor Air Quality and Climate, Stockholm, 1986, most sealed buildings are in a sick condition at least part of the time and should be written off as failures.

Although many of the connections among places, experiences, and health have yet to be discovered, some designers, architects, and planners have begun treating their own experiences to places in the same manner as mid-nineteenth-century clean water activists. They fight to prevent the demolition of buildings and communities, knowing that the destruction of an historic section will lead to psychological damage and even death of older people, *even though the exact mechanisms are not yet understood.*

This has not just to do with beauty of design, but the character of a place, the quality of life, its flavor, and ambience. It deals with human scale rather than metropolitan scale. "There is abundant evidence to show that high buildings can actually damage people's minds and feelings," says Christopher Alexander.[10]

TOWARD A BIOTECHNOLOGY OF COMMUNITIES

On Centering Communities

André Gide, a world-renowned author and a communist most of his life, visited Leningrad some years ago. Afterward, he deeply offended his Russian hosts by saying, "What I loved most in Leningrad was St. Petersburg."[11] Gide was not trying to insult his Russian friends. The reason he loved the St. Petersburg in Leningrad was that it was not built by modern planners and designers.

Cities, towns, villages, and groups of communities that were designed hundreds of years ago obviously are based upon some basic purpose of living that eludes current designers. Previous ages possessed one great advantage, a precise moral aim that gave meaning and direction to all planning and design. Classical antiquity pursued harmony; the middle ages strove for mystic fulfillment; the Renaissance, the elegance of proportions; more recent times, the enlightenment of humanism. The people of each period knew exactly what they wanted.

What then is the purpose of contemporary planners? Earlier builders knew what they were doing, because they executed the cultural imperatives of their society as their minds conceived them. In contrast, modern designers nourish public taste and have tried desperately to find out what that taste is. To help in this quandary designers use research staffs and questionnaires. What do they discover when at last their work is complete? That those for whom they have built, after one look, move back toward those parts of cities built hundreds of years ago.

There has (until very recently) been no such thing as a changing purpose in planning settlements. That old towns are charming and new ones are not is because city planners of former times—ancient Greece, medieval city states, the heart of Amsterdam, London, Paris, or Vienna—did not pursue *different* aims as their age changed, but instinctively always worked toward the one unchanging purpose that has always made people desire to live in urban centers in all human communities.

Aristotle expressed this purpose, saying that men form communities not for justice, peace, defense, or traffic, but for the sake of the good life, the *Summum Bonum*. This good life has always meant the satisfaction of four basic social desires, desires to which earlier designers have always given material and structural shape. These desires are *conviviality*, *religiosity*, *intellectual growth*, and *politics*. Therefore, the nucleus of cities, with all the variations in styles, consisted always of the same basic structures. Taverns, sports arenas, and theaters were built to satisfy conviviality; churches or temples, to facilitate religiosity; museums, zoos, libraries, and schools, to help intellectual growth; and city halls, political temperament. And because the satisfaction of these four community-shaping desires required an economic base, these structures were naturally and organically grouped around the marketplace, creating and serving the fifth communal activity: trade and commerce.

If a new region is to be successfully developed, decentralized, and open-ended to many different possibilities, some interventions are simple. What will be needed is the construction of focal points at primitive crossroads: a sidewalk cafe, a restaurant serving excellent meals, a little concert hall or theater, a charming church, a well-designed meeting hall.

To sum up the success of old and the failure of modern community design in one sentence: ancient planners, recognizing the invariable Aristotelian purpose of why people live in communities, put all their talent into the building of the communal nucleus: inns, churches, and city halls. The rest of the settlement then followed naturally. In contrast, modern designers are forever building the rest of the city. But without a nucleus nothing can be held together. There are difficulties now in conceptualizing a nucleus, since we have become convinced—falsely—that every age has a different purpose; but, by the time we might discover our own, it will have run through our hands like sand.

On Traffic

Modern civilization lives with traffic jams everywhere. The only question is what causes them? Too narrow streets? Streets have been widened, and jams have become worse. Too few traffic arteries? Traffic arteries have multiplied, and tie-ups have become more frequent. Urban density? Cities have exploded outward into suburbs and exurbs, *reducing* density, yet the gridlock has increased in proportion. Bad planning? International experts have made plans, and when implemented, jams have grown. Too little thought? Actually, the reverse is true: *too much thought*. Modern planners are so concerned about traffic that they have stopped thinking about anything but the fastest movement of cars and the attendant problems, as if the only function of the city is to serve as a racetrack for drivers between petrol pumps and hamburger stands. Los Angeles is at present the ultimate example of too much thought about traffic dislodging common sense. The result? What might have become an elegant city has instead become the first city that incorporates rural distances into its tormented, traffic-choked *urban* sprawl.

What most planners have overlooked in their rush to eliminate all obstacles to traffic is that they are removing the most precious obstacle to traffic: the community itself. The function of a community, unlike that of a petrol station or a snack bar in the countryside, is to act as a goal, not as a passage point; an end, not a means; a stop, not a flow; a place to get out, not for driving through. This is why most good cities exist where the flow of traffic was bound to stop: at the base of mountains or at their top, on the bend of rivers, on the shores of lakes or oceans, or—in the case of some of the most spectacular, such as Venice, Stockholm, Amsterdam, Bangkok, San Francisco, or Manhattan—in the midst of canals and lagoons, or on the tips of thin islands where any movement beyond is restricted in all directions.

What designers must do if they want to improve the quality of modern life is to follow two guidelines: first, they must reverse their current hierarchy of values and give less, not more, thought to traffic planning and, instead, concentrate on trade and community planning. Second, designers must turn to a new set of experts. Inasmuch as the foremost city planners are responsible for the most glaring obscenities (Brasilia, Canberra, Ottawa, and the new towns of post-war England, to mention a few), the "new" experts will be found in the genius of the past. The field must look back in humility to study not what is the latest in Los Angeles or Milano, but what is oldest in Boston or Siena.

On Site and Beauty

One tried-and-true method to keep a community from turning into a speedway is the inclusion of squares into the road network. These squares act as traffic obstacles, and, at the same time, become enhanced by parks, statues, sculpture, music pavilions, seating, water fountains, and venerable trees.

Yet such is the paradoxical nature of communities that once a town attains both commercial desirability and esthetic attractiveness, it begins to act like a magnet and drains people from other communities. This drift toward centralization has to be fought, because even the most beautiful community, once involved in this cumulative process, will attract so much trade and attendant traffic that it will head toward perpetual decay.

Received wisdom explains site selection through the interplay of four determinants: distance from markets, raw material sources, transport, and labor pool. The esthetic factor, distance from a convivial center appealing to the senses, is ignored.

This fifth location determinant, the esthetic modifier, is not just equal in strength to any of the other four, but can be stronger than all others combined. This can be demonstrated positively whenever a new factory opens in the countryside. A sort of magnet begins to operate; instead of firmly anchoring the new plant to the ground, it draws people back to the city. The manager usually starts by deciding to subject himself to hour-long commuting daily, rather than face the meaningless idleness of the countryside. The workers usually follow as soon as they can afford to do so. Some, indeed, prefer unemployment and a richly convivial existence against a background of exciting architecture, theaters, galleries, inns, and a sparkling nightlife.

This esthetics of site has been overlooked, because modern location theory originated at a time during the nineteenth century when virtually all cities, towns, and villages possessed it to such an extent that the esthetic assets of each were cancelled out by the almost equal beauty of the others. Even the most remote western villages in Colorado boasted an opera house 100 years ago, as well as museums and decent inns. Austria-Hungary had so many glamorous small capital cities—most of them with their own operas, palaces, theaters, courts, and universities—that each had enough central force to hold beauty in balance across the land.

Location

Just as birds choose the ideal location for their nests with their strongly developed siting instincts and without the help of design consultants, so do certain human groups. Living and working in barrios in Brazil, Colombia, and Venezuela, one is struck by the paradox that the rich have luxury flats in high-rise towers at the base of a valley that is frequently choked by pollution, noise, and traffic, whereas the poor live in slums on mountainsides overlooking the city, the ocean, or the mountains. Even the large barrio just north of Guadalajara in Mexico is more pleasantly situated than the city. At Boroka in Papua, New Guinea, the slums are individual homes set on stilts in one of the most beautifully sheltered ocean bays just outside Port Moresby. The high level of social happiness that exists in these slums often surprises visitors. They are medically unhealthy and poverty is great, yet their inhabitants have solved many social and urban problems. There is no loneliness for the old, no lack of supervision for children. But, the high degree of social happiness aside, what slum dwellers demonstrate from a design viewpoint is that they are one of the five lucky categories of people endowed with a wonderful sense of location. The other four categories are, or were, the aristocrats, the innkeepers, the military, and the church. And a direct result of their well-developed "bump of location" is that where these favored groups pitch their tents, it is good to live. And where it is good to live, it is also beautiful to live.

On Certain Magic Numbers

Beginning to do anticipatory design for an entirely new region that does not even exist as yet, designers instinctively look for some guideposts on which to base assumptions. Nothing is as frustrating to a designer than to begin with a complete *tabula rasa*, without any constraints or limitations. Reassuringly, there are many guideposts dealing with the ergonomics of communities. If architects, designers, and planners have neglected to use these facts in their work, it is because they are unaware that there is an emerging body of knowledge that deals primarily with human scale. These magic numbers are based on physical, psychological, and species abilities.

Our biogenetic heritage governs expectations of size, weight, distance, speed, and time. Old measurements, such as mile, pound, yard, foot, and stone, reflect what persons can lift or carry easily and how they use their bodies as templates for measure. The *eidetic image* that people carry with them through life provides another system for judging harmonious relationships and scale. Invented measuring systems, such as the meter, are as meaningless as is time shown by a digital watch. Le Corbusier published two books of incredibly sloppy and inaccurate mathematics, trying to fit the meter system to human perceptions, and failed.

Perception and *gestalt* mechanisms provide still more of a basis for magic numbers: all we have seen growing in nature since we were born reflects the Fibonacci series and thus deeply affects our concept of esthetics.

Eye-rotation and distance recognition yield ideal distances for houses from the street, house heights, and so forth. Experienced spaces, that is, our familiar and personal experiences, help determine what size a bedroom, a kitchen, or a restaurant should be. This is modified by cultural constraints: rooms in traditional Japanese farmhouses tend to be larger than in England, yet the Japanese rooms are multifunctional. Single-function bathrooms in the United States are palpably bigger than in the Scandinavian countries, but much space is wasted.

Terrain and climate influence distance measurements, as do driving, walking, and riding distance: the distances between villages reflect how far a man could walk in a day carrying a load (obviously in mountainous countries such as Switzerland, Papua, New Guinea, or Colombia, towns are closer together). How far a horse could be ridden or a cart driven in a day also affects spacing.

As far as the size of communities is concerned, here, too, some natural, magic numbers exist. They are determined by human's collective unconscious regarding group size, which in turn is affected by tribal life-styles, climate, even incest taboos in tribal societies that limit the number of people within an area.[12]

What are some of these magic numbers? Ideally, a private house should be half as tall as it is set back from the street, perhaps 32 feet tall and 60 feet from the road. Assuming a height of 32 feet, then 60 feet would give us a satisfyingly wide building, speaking esthetically. Physiological optics tell us that in looking at others, 50 feet is the limit to the distance at which facial expressions can be recognized; gender, outlines, gait, and basic contours can be identified at circa 450 feet. At 1,000 feet we can no longer make *any* identifications.[13]

These numbers may seem pedantic and completely useless, unless they are applied to real-world situations. For example, in plazas of many different periods, styles, and cultures, nearly everywhere the major axis of the square is the same length. Thus, the major axis of the square at the Acropolis is 480 feet long, St. Peter's in Rome is 435, *place* Vendome is 430, Amalienborg is 450, and Piazza San Marco is 422 feet in length. Although the large square at the imperial city in Beijing measures 9,000 feet, each unbroken segment is just 470 feet long. There is some inherently pleasing and esthetically appealing scale at work here, especially if other squares, piazzas, and plazas are added only to find that almost without exception, they measure between 420 and 580 feet.

To this we can relate numbers of commuter distances; that is, how far office workers will walk to sit in a public plaza at lunchtime or how far residents will walk willingly to reach a park. In the United States, these distances are about three city blocks, or a three-minute walk. This not only suggests that office neighborhoods function much as residential areas do, but also something about ideal size again. If people will walk three minutes to reach a central gathering point, then a neighborhood is, in effect, about six minutes' walking time wide; or, in linear terms, five or six blocks, which is between 1,500 and 1,625 feet. Europeans and Asians will walk a little farther, resulting in Doxiades' "kinetic field," with a ten minute or 2,500-foot radius (twice the length of a typical plaza).[14]

Magic Numbers and Community Size[15]

Professor George Murdoch of Yale University has studied more than 250 societies of different kinds and found that magic numbers operate here, as well. Aboriginal dialectical tribes, Amazonian Indian groups, and Peruvian and Tupi-Guarani hunting bands usually number between 400 and 600 individuals. Iroquois Indian longhouses accommodated 500, and excavated villages from Mesopotamia and Anatolia numbered 400 to 600 residents. So-called intentional religious communities in the United States during the eighteenth and nineteenth centuries usually had about 500 members, as did hippie communes 20 years ago. The average-size elementary school in several countries has 500 students in some 40,000 school systems.

These numbers hold steady even among primates: a tribe of Gelada baboons in Ethiopia will number 500 members, as will the snow monkeys of Japan. When groups of Langur monkeys in India exceed 500 in number, the tribe splits up.

Thus, a community size averages 450 to 600 individuals. However, in business groups working closely together some minor stresses appear only when the group exceeds 750; the "trouble threshold" appears at 1,200.

Behavioral scientists consider 250 people to constitute a small neighborhood, 1,500 a large one, and 450 to 1,000 constitute a social neighborhood.

From these numbers we can go further: with the objective being a benign, neighborly way of life, rich in interconnections and cultural stimuli, we can say that communities will consist of 400 to 1,000 people (the ideal is 500), common neighborhoods will accommodate roughly 5,000 to 10,000 residents (or 10 to 20 face-to-face communities), and the ideal city will house 50,000 souls (or 10 to 20 common neighborhoods). Special functional reasons may decrease city size to 20,000 or increase it to 120,000, beyond that lies social chaos.

We can provide some historical underpinnings for this. The major cathedral towns of Europe—Chartres, Avignon, Koln, Canterbury, Siena, Padua, Rheims, and Salisbury—each housed approximately 10,000 inhabitants at the height of their flowering. At the time of the Renaissance, the major universities, located in Bologna, Paris, Oxford, and Cambridge, had a faculty and student population of 20,000 to 35,000. The Florence of Leonardo and Botticelli built cathedrals, theaters, palaces, and public gardens with a population of 40,000. Michelangelo's Rome held 50,000. The musically, artistically, and architecturally exciting Germany of Durer, Cranach, and Holbein during the fifteenth century listed its 150 large cities. In the first census, each had about 35,000 residents.

There is much more knowledge becoming available than would be suspected. It comes from many different disciplines, yet designers are the logical people to use and apply it. Whatever other definitions may come to mind, basically designers, planners, or architects work best as synthesists.

© MIT 1988. Previously published in *Design Issues* Vol. 5, No. 1, Fall 1988, pg 4–17.

NOTES

1. Robert Ornstein, *The Healing Brain* (New York: Simon & Schuster, 1987).
2. Some of the material about Dr. Falk's findings are cited in two articles by Tony Hiss in *The New Yorker*: "Reflections," Part I (June 22, 1987): 45–68, and Part II (June 29, 1987): 73–86.
3. Ornstein, *The Healing Brain*.
4. Stephen Kaplan and Rachel Kaplan, *Cognition and Environment: Functioning in an Uncertain World* (New York: Praeger, 1982).
5. Kaplan, *Cognition and Environment*.
6. In addition to my own observations, I refer the reader to O. Michael Watson's *Proxemic Behavior* (The Hague: Mouton, 1970), as well as Edward T. Hall's *The Silent Language* (Garden City, NY: Doubleday, 1959) and *The Hidden Dimension* (Garden City, NY: Doubleday, 1966).
7. Abraham H. Maslow, *Toward a Psychology of Being* (Princeton: Van Nostrand Reinhold Company, 1968), especially Part V: "Values."
8. Hiss, *The New Yorker*.
9. For this and the following observations, see also Robert A. Levine, *Culture, Behaviour and Personality* (Chicago: Aldine Publishing Company, 1973), as well as Irenäus Eibl-Eibesfelt, *Stadt und Lebensqualität* (Stuttgart: Deutsche Verlags-Anstalt, 1985), especially Parts I & II, written with Harry Glück.
10. Christopher Alexander, *A Timeless Way of Building* (New York: Oxford University Press, 1979).

11. Cited by Leopold Kohr in *The Overdeveloped Nations: The Diseconomies of Scale* (New York: Schocken Books, 1977).

12. The foregoing material is also explored in Victor Papanek, *Design for Human Scale* (New York: Van Nostrand Reinhold Company, 1983), and in *Seeing the World Whole: Interaction Between Ecology and Design* (University of Kansas, Fifth Inaugural Lecture, 1982).

13. The following material is largely developed from H. Maertens, *Der Optische Maasstab oder die Theorie und Praxis des Aesthetischen Sehen* (Berlin: Ernst Wasmuth, 1884).

14. Many of these figures are cited in Kirkpatrick Sale's, *Human Scale* (New York: Coward, McCann & Geoghegan, 1980).

15. Most of the material in this section rests on Konrad Lorenz, *Der Abbau des Menschlichen* (München: R. Piper, 1983), and Leopold Kohr, *Die Kranken Riesen: Krise des Zentralismus* (Wien: F. Deuticke, 1981).

Much of the material in this paper is based on my own experiences in many countries, interviews with people and researchers, reading, and observation. Besides the sources cited in the text, I should mention:

Christopher Alexander, et al., *A Pattern Language: Towns, Buildings, Construction* (New York: Oxford University Press, 1977).

Christopher Alexander, et al. *The Production of Houses* (New York: Oxford University Press, 1985).

Kevin Lynch, *The Image of the City* (Cambridge: MIT Press, 1960).

Yi-Fu Tuan, *Landscapes of Fear* (New York: Pantheon Books, 1979).

William H. Whyte, *The Social Life of Small Urban Spaces* (Washington, DC: Conservation Foundation, 1980).

These writers are in no way responsible for any conclusions I have reached.

CHAPTER TWELVE

Commerce or Culture: Industrialization and Design

JOHN HESKETT

Text by John Heskett, now copyright of Ingrid Heskett

INTRODUCTION

In an age of change, there are problems in understanding the nature of what is afoot and what the consequences are. For most people, change is resented as a disruption, challenging the rhythms, beliefs and practices of everyday life. To be accepted, change needs to be presented as 'improvement' or 'betterment,' or disguised, slipped into our life by small, incremental stages, using forms and metaphors of what is already familiar—'the iron horse' to describe the locomotive, or the trashcan symbol on a Macintosh computer.

Over the last two centuries, industrialization has wrought massive change across the globe, not just in patterns of life and work, but also in consciousness of ourselves and our world. In its origins, it aroused a deep, instinctive opposition as time-hallowed beliefs and practices were supplanted or marginalized. Today, similar reactions continue to be generated, from the cosmic sweep of Islamic fundamentalism, to the remnants of Australian aboriginal tribes protesting the desecration of traditional ritual sites for mineral extraction.

While echoes of the Industrial Revolution still reverberate, layered upon them is another level of complexity. The technological changes of our own time represent yet another step-change into a further dimension of possibility. In this situation, looking to the past is, paradoxically, the only means available of understanding what this future might be like. It will not help us accurately predict, there are too many unknown and independent variables for that, but it can help us understand some of the problems and dilemmas involved and define the critical issues of human values at stake.

As a comparison with the potential scale of change we face today, this paper will examine examples of change from the historically recent past. Firstly, it will consider the period of early industrialization in Britain and how positive responses to its potential opened up new opportunities. Secondly, it will discuss the reaction to industrialization in Britain in the nineteenth century, which set the agenda for debate in many countries. Thirdly, the different emphases of the second phase of industrialization in the United States will be discussed.

On a superficial level, two main attitudes to industrialization are evident. It has been welcomed, associated with concepts of progress, and seen as an opportunity for social or individual improvement or advancement. In contrast, it has also been resented, regarded as destructive of time-honoured values and social relationships, leading to attempts to restore or recreate these values. Digging even a short depth below that surface, however, reveals complications that reflect the reality and ambivalence of the human situation. For example, the paradox that industrialization might have diffused material benefits, but at the price of concentrating knowledge, power and wealth in a diminishing sector of the population who recognize no other need but their own ambition. On the other hand, another paradox, that the reaction against industrialization, although often reactionary and riddled with nostalgia, has an important message about human and social needs and our relationship with the natural environment.

A short account cannot cover the range of possible permutations and variations opened here, but it can consider, in broad strokes, some key reactions to the changes, and their effects upon design and how design is understood to function in an industrial world.

I

Great Britain was the cradle of the Industrial Revolution, a process that began to take-off around the decade 1770–80. By the mid-nineteenth century this resulted in a degree of trading supremacy and economic power that was feared, resented and emulated across the world, in a way mirrored by similar reactions to the U.S.A. in the early and mid-twentieth century, and by present-day attitudes to Japan.

The price paid in Britain to achieve that world status as a result of industrialization was revealed in 1851. A government census of population revealed that for the first time in any civilization, the number of people living in towns exceeded those living in the countryside. Behind that bland statistic was a wrenching process of upheaval. Within one generation, patterns of life that in essentials had changed but little over the centuries and then for most part imperceptibly, were totally and irrevocably changed.

Until the Industrial Revolution, most of the population of Britain lived their lives in a small radius from the place they were born, a world circumscribed by how far they could walk, there and back, in one day—a radius of some 13–15 miles. What they lacked in broad worldview, however, they compensated for in depth, by the detail in which they understood their immediate locality. Within that radius, what was needed was produced and made in the locality, by hand, or using simple machinery and tools powered by human, animal or natural sources, using local materials. George Sturt's famous book *The Wheelwright's Shop* gives a vivid insight into craft practices and values. Another English wheelwright, Jubal Merton of Suffolk, also illustrates this relationship with the immediate environment, when he writes of how timber was selected for shafts and felloes, the curved sections that when fitted together, made up a wheel rim:

"... the wheelwright always chose roadside trees for his fellies. He'd never touch a low-meadow ash because that wouldn't do at all. Of course, ash that grew down by the river was lovely timber to use, but a wheelwright would never use it. He went to the hedges, where the wood was tough and hard. He'd walk through the lanes and note the ashes and when he saw a good one, he'd buy it, cut it down and let it lie in the ditch for a couple of years until the bark fell off. Then it was ready. He also looked for shaft wood. If you look at the ash trees you'll find that many of their boughs grow in the shape of shafts. When my father saw a good shaft shape a-growing, he'd keep his eye on it until it was just the right size to cut and plane. Then he'd have it."[1]

Spotting a shape of the right timber on the bough and patiently waiting for it to grow to the desired size and maturity—the anecdote reveals a balance with the natural environment that we would do well to recreate.

The forms and techniques used by craftsmen were traditional, handed down through generations. Learning was by following accepted practice and absorbing its values by experience, rather than by precept.

"... sometimes I was allowed to cut out shafts for the tumbrils. ... Heaps of times I did a shaft and I'd think, "That's lovely!" Then my father would rub his hand up it and say, "Why, boy, it aint half done!" He was a first-class wheelwright and was known all over Suffolk, and my grandfather and greatgrandfather were the same. They all worked in this same shop and the wagons they made lie about in the farmyards. They ain't used but they can't wear out."[2]

Although change took place slowly, making and shaping were part of the everyday fabric of life. Access to craft skill was, of course, limited to whoever had the wealth to pay, or the time and ability to shape artefacts themselves. Nevertheless, even with that caveat, products and processes were capable of infinite adaptation to individual people and their needs, in a process they intimately understood, and artefacts were made to last. Like the accumulated wisdom of how to make them, they too were often handed down and used by succeeding generations.

Tradition was respected, because it embodied the accumulated experience of those who had faced the difficult task of survival. Craft culture can be easily romanticized, overlooking the fact that most people lived a short, deprived existence, submitting to the vagaries of nature and brutally oppressive social structures. Famine, plague, natural disaster and human injustice were constant threats. In our prosperous modernity, we forget that for most people throughout history, survival has been a constant fight against precarious circumstances. The crafts embodied practices that had been tried, tested and proven in that struggle, and therefore were not lightly abandoned.

With industrialization, all that began to change. The term, 'revolution' is in some respects a misnomer for this process. In many areas of production there was gradual change and adaptation, utilizing old skills in a new context. Increasingly, however, mechanized production, using artificial power, coal and later electricity, concentrated production into factories, producing standardized goods, distributed over ever larger geographical areas, at costs accessible to greater numbers of people.

There were undoubted benefits from this huge change. Health and life expectancy increased, opportunities for talent and fulfillment were multiplied, and new materials, processes and products brought undreamt-of prosperity to great numbers and opened up new worlds to the imagination. There were also disadvantages. Business became increasingly detached from any other values than those it defined as important to its survival. Responsibility to its workers, to society, to the environment generally, did not come within that compass. Those involved in the processes of making became increasingly specialized in function, lacking knowledge of or involvement in the whole process of manufacture, ignorant of how a product was determined or who it was destined for.

As the gulf between maker and user increased and became more abstract, expressed in terms of producer and consumer, so the relationship of people and the objects of everyday life changed. Under industrialization, workers lost any holistic knowledge of processes, and users lost intimate contact with how things were made. As a result, both workers and users were deskilled. People adapted to products and processes that treated them as a mass, and rarely in terms of unique individual or social entities.

A formative figure in providing a framework of ideas that profoundly influenced concepts of modern economics and provided a rationale for the processes of industrialization, was the Scotsman, Adam Smith. His philosophy had three main points: man's basic economic drive was self-interest; the sum total of individual self-interest combined together, represented the social good; and maximum benefit for all would result from governments refraining from interfering in economic processes. The free market place was the arena in which products would be judged by the enlightened self-interest of purchasers. His basic ideas still have many adherents.

In his major work, *The Wealth of Nations*, Smith gave a seminal example of pin production that illustrated the productive power of the new system of manufacture. A worker untrained in the trade and its machines "could scarce, perhaps, with his utmost industry, make one pin in a day, and certainly could not make twenty."[3] In contrast, a small manufactory equipped with simple machinery and operating on the basis of the division of labour and specialization of task was capable of producing at a level of four thousand, eight hundred pins a day per workman involved in the process. "The division of labour," he concluded, "… occasions, in every art, a proportionable increase of the productive powers of labour."[4]

Several British entrepreneurs in Adam Smith's time provided illustrations of his philosophy. Matthew Boulton of Soho, near Birmingham, commenced construction in 1761 of a water-powered plant to produce buckles and buttons for the fashionable market known then as the 'toy' trade, later venturing into a wide range of metal products for domestic use, such as Sheffield plate tableware and clocks.

Boulton understood that mechanized production enabled manufacture on a larger scale and more cheaply than competitors. He wrote in a letter to the Earl of Warwick: "it is from the extreme cheapness that we are enabled to send them to every corner of Europe, although in many places they have as good and as cheap Materials as we have, and have Labour Cent P. Cent [100%] cheaper and yet nevertheless by the Super activity of our people and by the many mechanical contrivances, and extensive apparatus which we are possess'd of, our men are enabled to do from twice to ten times the Work that can be done without the help of such Contrivances, and even Women and children to do more than Men can do without them... ."[5]

Boulton illustrates some enduring lessons, however, in his understanding that cheapness was not the sole criterion for competiveness. Catering for the various tastes in the markets he supplied, meant he had to adapt to different circumstances, rather than attempting to impose a uniform taste. "Fashion hath much to do in these things, and that of the present age distinguishes itself by adopting the most Elegant ornaments of the most refined Grecian artists, I am satisfied in conforming thereto, and humbly copying their style, and making new combinations of old ornaments without presuming to invent new ones...."[6] Frequent reports from friends and travelers abroad about articles in demand supplied valuable information. Models were borrowed from aristocratic friends, and leading artists of the day providing him with drawings and engravings. To provide the necessary range and variations in products, "he set up his own drawing school at Soho and regularly employ some of the leading engravers of the period such as John and Francis Eginton, Peter Rouw and W. Pidgeon. He was from the first essentially design-conscious."[7] He was also convinced that a small, consistent profit on a large quantity of goods for large markets was the only way to sustain a large manufactory.

In his later career, Boulton was involved in two other developments that were critical to the accelerating trajectory of the Industrial Revolution. He joined with the inventor James Watt to begin the serial production of steam engines that provided the motive power for new industrial methods of production across the globe. Secondly, his experience in the metal trades enabled him to develop methods of producing fine, standard coins in large quantities, which was necessary for the rapidly developing monetary economy that was a corollary of industrialization.

His contemporary Josiah Wedgwood, who similarly transformed ceramics production in the late eighteenth century, shared Boulton's belief in an expanding market in which steady profits could be obtained from good quality products made available to a large number of people. He too paid close attention to both form and decoration. In the Experiment Book that catalogued his constant striving for improvement, he wrote of the products of his native Staffordshire: "White Stone Ware was the principal article of manufacture. But this had been made a long time, and the prices were now reduced so low that the potters could not afford to bestow much expense upon it or to make it so good in any respect as the ware would otherwise admit of. And with regard to elegance of form, that was an object very little attended to."[8]

In modern terms, Wedgwood wanted to break out of the downward spiral of poor products and price competition and create value added products. To achieve the necessary elegance of form required good modellers and designers to produce prototypes for quantity production. William Hackwood, one of the most skilled in the trade, was engaged in 1769 and other employees were trained in drawing skills, but difficulty in obtaining sufficient competent designers led Wedgwood to lament that he could do with half-a-dozen Hackwoods. From 1776, he began to turn to well-known artists such as John Flaxman and later Joseph Wright and George Stubbs.[9]

Boulton, Wedgwood and other pioneering entrepreneurs of the late 18th century faced a dilemma. They understood the potential of mechanized methods of production and the role of design in creating new markets. However, new skills were required. Traditional craftsmen were generally unable to adapt to mechanized methods. The need for improved design in products required specialists within the division of labour, capable of adapting to the demands of mass-production. Since no established system of training existed, demand far exceeded the competent people available. Entrepreneurs therefore turned to artists of repute, the only people well-trained in visual techniques, to fill the gap with drawings, sketches and models that could be freely adapted by the draughtsmen and modellers employed in the factories.

It is possible, though it would stretch the facts, to see in this a precursor of modern design consultancies. The point is rather that if, in a time of change, a suitable competency is needed but is in short supply, other skills will be brought into play and adapted for the purpose in hand. The lesson from that early phase of industrialization for designers in the present is that if, like traditional craftsmen, they are unable to adapt and anticipate the competences needed in the current processes of change, they too may find themselves superceded.

II

The application of art to industry originated as a marriage of convenience, the path of which has hardly run smooth. Like an embattled married pair in a D.H. Lawrence novel, desire and loathing have been inextricably mixed. Even advocates of the alliance have had reservations. A writer in the journal Art-Union stated in 1848: '...we do not wish artists to become the servants of manufacturers; we do wish them to be their friends and allies; their partners in educating the people; in improving the tastes, and consequently, the morals, of the community; in developing the intellectual strength and the intellectual resources of the United Empire.'[10] Imperial sentimentality has had its day, but the idea that art, diffused by industry, could improve morality and quality of life, has many forms and still endures.

The optimism of the new age in Britain was revealed with stunning impact in The Great Exhibition of All the Nations in London's Hyde Park, which opened in Joseph Paxton's magnificent Crystal Palace in May, 1851. Half the space was devoted to British products, the other half allocated to the rest of the world—a proportion representing a judicious, if generous, division of influence in British eyes. The exhibition was open until October for 141 days, with the total visitors numbering 6,039,195. The average daily attendance was almost 43,000.[11] Such throngs were only possible with the new railway lines that had proliferated in the 1840s. A tenfold increase of the radius of travel to 150 miles in one day was not uncommon. Day trips to the Great Exhibition were a significant stage in the development of mass travel in Britain.

The products shown at the Great Exhibition are often cited as typical of the age, yet many informed observers such as Richard Redgrave were at pains to point out the contrary: "… such exhibitions… hardly represent the normal state of manufacture… The goods are like the gilded cakes in the booths of our country fairs, no longer for use, but to attract customers."[12] In fact, reaction to overwhelming decoration gave new impetus in Britain to measures of reform in design practice, theory and education.

A leading figure in attempting to harness mechanized methods of production to improvements in design was Henry Cole, a civil servant and a prime mover in organizing the 1851 exhibition. Using the pseudonym Felix Summerley, he designed a tea service for a Society of Arts competition in 1846, winning a silver medal, and in 1847, went on to establish a firm to produce domestic wares, such as ceramics and cutlery, under the title of Summerley's Art Manufactures. The purpose of the firm, according to Cole was:

> "… to revive the good old practice of connecting the best art with familiar objects in daily use. In doing this, Art manufacturers aim to produce in each article superior utility, which is not to be sacrificed to ornament; to select pure forms; to decorate each article with appropriate details relating to its use, and to obtain these details as directly as possible from nature."[13]

The emphasis on the primacy of utility as the basic consideration in a product was echoed by Richard Redgrave, who, like Cole, was heavily involved in government efforts to improve standards of design, and was one of the most consistent advocates of the need to rethink the relationship between art and industry.

If there is one rule more than another which may lead us to a style characteristic of our own age, it is that of making the purpose and utility of our buildings or furniture, and every object and utensil the first consideration; then of selecting the proper materials, by the use of which that utility may be most completely obtained; and, thirdly, ornamenting consistently with the nature of the material chosen, the leading forms arising out of such construction, irrespective of the mere reproduction of the bygone elements and ornamental details of any style.[14]

Cole and Redgrave were influential figures, occupying high positions in the administration of art and design education and major museums. Their belief that industry could produce better products for much of the population had practical influence, as witness the work of Christopher Dresser. His metalware, ceramic and furniture designs for leading manufacturers were of a consistently high standard in concept, utility and aesthetics. He exemplified the possibilities of what could be achieved on the basis of close cooperation between designer and manufacturer.

Yet despite these efforts, ultimately, the impetus for reform petered out. The reasons are complex, but two immediate explanations present themselves. Firstly, the emphasis on art became precious, tending to lofty preaching that industrialists ignored, if they bothered to listen. The South Kensington Museum (now the Victoria and Albert) founded from the proceeds of the Great Exhibition to promote the relationship between art and industry, was a treasure-house of decorative arts from across the globe, and the source of learned treatises of value to the antique trade, but, generally, a world apart from the needs of industry. Only recently has the museum's administration sought to revive a sense of the institution's original purpose.

Another reason for the failure of the reformers efforts, however, was the unwillingness of industrialists to acknowledge their arguments. The prevailing economic philosophy of the age was Utilitarianism, and the overwhelming value it engendered, was profit. "The satirist did not exaggerate much when he made the Utilitarian ask, 'What is the use of a nightingale unless roasted? What profit is there in the fragrance of the rose, unless you can distil from it an otto at ten shillings a drop.'"[15]

This arithmetical approach was not confined to business, but became instead applied to every aspect of life—politics, society and culture—all of which could be conveniently regarded as a mirror image of business attitudes and procedures. Theories of industry as an instrument of moral improvement were indeed advocated by some industrialists such as Robert Owen and Titus Salt, but in general played little role in the pursuit of commercial success. For most industrialists, investment in mechanization was to increase personal assets or corporate dividends. Particularly in the production of domestic articles, there was a scramble for greater profit by generating a constant impression of novelty. This led to precisely the indiscriminate combination of decorative forms lifted from all ages and cultures across the world with cheapness and crudeness of execution, that Cole and Redgrave so vehemently criticized. The endemic incapacity to look beyond the tunnel vision perspective of short term profit is often seen as a peculiarly modern affliction of American industry, but it can also be seen as a root explanation for the failure of so many vain attempts, by a succession of governmental bodies, to achieve a fundamental improvement in British design over the last 150 years. The economic philosophy common to both countries, which separates out business concerns from any other concerns in society, and refuses to acknowledge certain values and approaches, may be the problem here, rather than the 'nature' of industrial production or the 'culture' of either society.

There is a great contrast, and also a profound irony, in the way in which nineteenth century opponents of art in industry were far more successful than Cole and his followers in gaining public attention and commitment, but they began with an enormous advantage. Their's was a world of the ideal, in which a conviction of total moral superiority was possible, untrammeled by problems of coming to terms with industry. They were not simply moved by a concern for art, but outraged by the impact of industrialization on the social values of Britain and the physical fabric of the land.

The outcome was a powerful philosophy. Under the banner of art, ideas of joy in work, involving the whole human being through handwork, of the influence of objects and environment on people, were linked to a programme of reform to fundamentally change the direction of how life and work would be organized. The moral potency of art was a central tenet, but only outside the compass of modern industry. The movement proposed changing the whole economic and social basis of society, but had its greatest success in tapping the fears of those British middle class people who regarded industry as a vulgar intrusion and a threat to the social order.

In formulating this critique, the influence of John Ruskin was paramount. In speeches and prose whose Old Testament tones echoed the religious temper of his age, Ruskin indicted economic theory and practice that separated action for personal benefit from consideration of its social consequences. One of his most memorable essays, *"Unto this Last"*, opens:

"Among the delusions which at different periods have possessed themselves of the minds of large masses of the human race, perhaps the most curious—certainly the least creditable—is the modern soi-disant science of political economy, based on the idea that an advantageous code of social action may be determined irrespectively of the influence of social affection."[16]

Unto this Last was acknowledged by Mahatma Gandhi as a work that transformed his life. Gandhi subsequently advocated the crafts, and especially spinning, as a personal discipline and as a non-violent means of subverting the British Raj in India by countering imports of British mass-produced textiles that undermined the traditional Indian economy. To this day, the Congress Party founded by Gandhi has the symbol of a spinning wheel on its flag and emblems.

Rather than subordinating morality to its ends, Ruskin argued that moral values must be the foundation and justification of social organisms and actions:

"Political economy (the economy of a state, or of citizens) consists simply in the production, preservation and distribution, at fittest time and place, of useful or pleasurable things. The fanner who cuts his hay at the right time; the shipwright who drives his bolts well home in sound wood; the builder who lays good bricks in well-tempered mortar, the housewife who takes care of her furniture in the parlour, and guards against all waste in the kitchen; and the singer who rightly disciplines, and never overstrains her voice: all are political economists in the true and final sense; adding continually to the riches and well-being of the nation to which they belong. But mercantile economy, the economy of "merces" or of "pay," signifies the accumulation, in the hands of individuals, of legal or moral claim upon, or power over, the labour of others; every such claim implying precisely as much poverty or debt on one side, as it implies riches or right on the other. It does not, therefore, necessarily involve an addition to the actual property, or well being, of the State in which it exists."[17]

Virtue lay in right-doing. Ruskin's condemnation of a system that not only separated cause from effect, but denied responsibility for it, had powerful appeal. Although forceful, however, his social critique never coalesced into a programme for political action. Moreover, his detestation of the forces changing the world around him led him to ignore many positive aspects. Instead, he relied upon romantic visions of the past and the power of art to transform life.

William Morris, who derived many core beliefs from Ruskin, went this further stage and became politically active as a socialist. However, he had little in common with Karl Marx. Rather than looking to the Communist Manifesto and its certainties, he turned instead to the tradition of indigenous, English socialism summed up in the utopian radicalism stemming from John Bunyan and expressed in William Blake's poem, Jerusalem, that became the battle hymn of the British labour movement:

I will not cease from mental fight,
Nor shall my sword sleep in my hand,
Till we have built Jerusalem,
In England's green and pleasant land.

The influence of work on those who produce, the nature of the products, and their influence on those who use them, is a broad seam throughout Morris' life and work.

"… the chief source of art is man's pleasure in his daily necessary work, which expresses itself and is embodied in that work itself; nothing else can make the common surroundings of life beautiful, and whenever they are beautiful it is a sign that men's work has pleasure in it, however they may suffer otherwise. It is the lack of this pleasure in daily work which has made our towns and habitations sordid and hideous, insults to the beauty to the earth which they disfigure, and all the accessories of life mean, trivial, ugly—in a word, vulgar."[18]

And in another essay:

"It is right and necessary that all men should have work to do which shall be worth doing, and be of itself pleasant to do; and which should be done under such conditions as would make it neither over-wearisome nor over-anxious."[19]

On the plethora of meretricious articles commonly available and the effect on all who produced, sold and used them, he wrote:

"It would be an instructive day's work for any one of us who is strong enough to walk through two or three of the principal streets of London on a week-day, and take accurate note of everything in the shop windows which is embarrassing or superfluous to the daily life of a serious man."

He continues:

"But I beg you to think of the enormous mass of men who are occupied with all this miserable trumpery, from the engineers who have had to make the machines for making them, down to the hapless clerks who sit daylong year after year in the horrible dens wherein the wholesale exchange of them is transacted, and the shopmen who, not daring to call the soul their own, retail them amidst numberless insults which they must not resent, to the idle public which doesn't want them, but buys them to be bored by them and sick to death of them. I am talking of the merely useless things; but there are other matters not merely useless, but actively destructive and poisonous, which command a good price in the market; for instance, adulterated food and drink. Vast is the number of slaves whom competitive Commerce employs in turning out infamies such as these."[20]

Morris' critique is at times still devastatingly relevant. The solution he proposes, however, is less convincing, essentially a romanticized re-creation of the assumed virtues of the medieval period. In his Utopian vision of the future, *News from Nowhere*, he depicted the economic organization of a society founded upon Banded Workshops. A character in the story describes them as places where 'folk collect... to do hand-work in which working together is necessary or convenient; such work is often very pleasant.'[21] His reaction to the worst features of his own time are matched with this vision in the opening lines of his poem, "The Earthly Paradise":

> Forget six counties overhung with smoke,
> Forget the snorting steam and piston stroke,
> Forget the spreading of the hideous town;
> Think rather of the packhorse on the down,
> And the dream of London, small, and white, and clean,
> The clear Thames bordered by its gardens green.[22]

In another irony, the debate on art and industry in Britain reached its peak at the time when Britain was losing its dominance in world trade to the rapidly growing economies of Germany and the United States. In the subsequent, lingering decline, the genteel beliefs of the Arts and Crafts movement could play little role other than that of a personal consolation.

The influence of Ruskin, Morris and their followers of the Arts and Crafts movement was particularly strong, however, in Germany, where it split into two trends. On one hand it became part of a mainstream influence in that country that saw industrialization as a positive force for change. Stripped of the insistence on handwork, it allowed machinery to be incorporated into its thinking, as just another tool capable of being used well for quality production. In organizations such as the German Werkbund and many leading companies it thus became transformed into a concept of industrial quality that was an expression of contemporary German culture. Joy in work became translated into a recognition that taking care of workers could be a means of bridging divisions in the workplace, countering union influence, and valuable in achieving quality products. Such attitudes do much to explain the continuing success of German products in international trade. The second trend continued the emphasis on rural nostalgia and eventually became one of the resentments exploited for political purposes in the rise of the Nazi party to power in the 1920s.

Arts and Crafts ideas were also popular in the United States.[23] Despite differences in the course of development, they also expressed a deep sense of disquiet and doubt about the nature of changes that were fundamentally transforming old certainties for a predominantly middle class following. In the U.S., however, as in Britain, it failed to have any sustained impact on the thrust of change. The reasons are similar: in general it found small response in industrial attitudes that recognized no values but its own. Beyond that similarity, however, the contexts cannot be compared, for a new phase of industrial technology and organization was opening in the United States.

III

The tempo of American industrialization rapidly increased in the late 19th century, but took a significantly different course to Britain. There, most industry remained small-to-medium-scale into the twentieth century, with family ownership or partnerships still widespread. Economic power in the U.S.A., in contrast, was falling into the hands of large enterprises on a scale previously unknown in human history, with ownership separated from management. This dominance fundamentally changed every aspect of life and culture in America and has been a significant influence across the globe in the twentieth century.

The changes in America were greater in scale than in Britain and more compressed in time. In 1790, according to Alfred Chandler, 'only 202,000 of 3,930,000 Americans lived in towns and villages of more than 2,500, and of 2,881,000 workers, 2,069,000 labored on farms.' Manufacturing was a small-scale activity carried on in artisan shops, owned by a master who was typically assisted by one or two journeymen or apprentices who often lived in with the family. As Sam Bass Walker wrote of Philadelphia on the eve of the American Revolution: "The core element of the town economy was the one-man shop. Most Philadelphians labored alone, some with a helper or two."[24] It was in this context that the tradition of Yankee ingenuity evolved and flourished.

In 1900 the rural population of the U.S.A. still outnumbered those living in towns and cities with over 2,500 inhabitants, although increasingly farming was for commercial crops. Spearheaded by the expanding railroad system across the continent, the economy rapidly grew and changed in nature, further accelerating in the early twentieth century with the development of electrical technology.[25] In 1914, 30% of US industry was electrified, by 1920 the figure reached 70%.[26] Also in 1920, the urban population of the United States exceeded the rural population for the first time.

Technological change was significant, but so too were changes in business organization. On every level of society, large institutions were imposing their procedures and values, which were very different to those found in a small business economy.

> "By 1904, …about three hundred industrial corporations had won control over more than two fifths of all manufacturing in the country, affecting the operation of about four fifths of the nation's industries… By 1929, the two hundred largest corporations held 48 per cent of all corporate assets (excluding banks and insurance companies) and 58 per cent of net capital assets such as land, buildings, and machinery."[27]

Thus by 1930, large business units were firmly established as the dominant form in the American economy, with mass-production redefining the "manufacturing sector, and a professional management cadre to operate these large organizations supplanting other disciplines. The effects, however, were not only confined to economic organization. As with the Utilitarians in nineteenth century Britain, the new industrial system, its methods, its calculation of value, were justified as a natural evolution on the path of progress and a model for the whole of society. The difference in twentieth century America lay in the power and scale of the mass media, the natural adjuncts of mass production, with a symbiotic relationship of interest and ownership linking the two. The role of the mass media, newspapers and journals, radio, film and television, in conditioning and altering the nature of perception and experience, not in the direction of greater awareness, but to align it with the needs of business is difficult to underestimate. "The advertisement," writes Alan Trachtenberg, "is unique among artworks in that its cardinal premise is falsehood, deceit, its purpose being to conceal the connection between labor and its product in order to persuade consumers to buy this brand. The advertisement suggests the fictive powers of that product, its ability to stand for what it is not."[28]

This was a far cry from belief in the moral power of art to improve life through industry. The idea of the artist as designer decisively influencing modern business organizations has remained a hope of many designers, but has had little credence among businessmen. Instead, at the precise point in the late 1920s when large businesses established control of the economy with new managerial methods, the industrial designer as stylist emerged into the light of day.

Interestingly, the first designer/stylists were also drawn from other spheres of work, those that emphasized spectacle and image, such as advertising and the theatre. The role of designers in this new guise was generally to provide the constant superficial visual changes needed to give an impression of innovation and stimulate sales, with the underlying technology remaining virtually unchanged.

Alfred P. Sloan, the man who built General Motors into one of the most formidable firms in the world, and a prime mover in establishing modern practices of management, was also important in evolving the concept and practice of styling. In his autobiography, he wrote:

"The degree to which styling changes should be made in any one model run presents a particularly delicate problem. The changes in the new model should be so novel and attractive as to create demand for the new value and, so to speak, create a certain amount of dissatisfaction with past models as compared with the new one, and yet the current and old models must still be capable of giving satisfaction to the vast used-car market. ...The design must be competitive in its market. Great skill and artistry are needed to fulfill these complex styling requirements."[29]

Artistry was acknowledged, but in a role that was utterly subordinate to marketing needs and the stimulation of sales. In terms of the Art-Union article of 1848 cited earlier, artists had indeed 'become the servants of manufacturers.' For a time, it could be justified by the years of market dominance and great success enjoyed by GM and its numerous imitators. Today, when that dominance has buckled under the combined effect of foreign competition and its own inflexibility in the face of contemporary change, the benefits of hindsight reveal the flaws of the system that Sloan inaugurated.

Despite the material benefits it has undoubtedly provided, acceptance of the mass-production paradigm has never been total. There have always been voices raised against the pattern of work and life it demands. Thoreau, Walt Whitman, Frank Lloyd Wright and Lewis Mumford, the beliefs and practices of the Amish and Shaker communities, are just a few whose contribution has been enduring and influential beyond the boundaries of their own country.

A contemporary example is Wendell Berry, who expresses a sensibility linking him directly with the tradition of opposing a holistic view to mechanization and its values:

"The industrial economy requires the extreme specialization of work—the separation of work from its results—because it subsists upon divisions of interest and must deny the fundamental kinships of producer and consumer; seller and buyer; owner and worker; worker, work, and product; parent material and product; nature and artifice; thoughts, words and deeds. Divided from those kinships, specialized artists and scientists identify themselves as "observers" or "objective observers"—that is, as outsiders without responsibility or involvement. But the industrialized arts and sciences are false, their division is a lie, for there is no division of results."[30]

Berry's alternative emphasizes human values rather than economic imperatives. His vision essentially rests upon reviving ownership of family farms and a property owning democracy, which in his view has been sacrificed to 'specious notions of efficiency or the economics of the so-called free market... Like a small craft shop, it 'gives work a quality and a dignity that it is dangerous, both to the worker and the nation, for human work to go without.'[31] Ruskin and Morris would recognize a fellow spirit in such statements.

Berry gives renewed force to several generations of protest against alienation and abstraction from both sides of the Atlantic, and takes it a stage further to apply it to present day ecological concern:

"No one can make ecological good sense for the planet. Everyone can make ecological good sense locally, if the affection, the scale, the knowledge, the tools, and the skills are right.

   The right scale in work gives power to affection. When one works beyond the reach of one's love for the place one is working in, and for the things and creatures one is working with and among, then destruction inevitably results. An adequate local culture, among other things, keeps work within the reach of love."[32]

In the decades in which mass-production has been so dominant, and self-justifyingly depicted as inevitable, such views could perhaps be dismissed as a quaint irrelevance in the onward march of progress. Large organizations and mass concepts applied across the whole spectrum from production to use, however, increasingly seem neither so inevitable, all-powerful or beneficial. The evolution of flexible technology means that E.F. Schumacher's advocacy of 'small is beautiful' becomes realizable and economic. Small-scale, user-oriented production opens up new possibilities for the nature of work, its role and value in our society. Above all it raises questions of human values and how designers can adapt to creatively realize them.

Ruskin, Morris, Berry and the whole tradition they represent are, at one and the same time, so right and so wrong. They are right to emphasize such ideas as the need for creative work and respect for the natural world. They are wrong, I believe, because they specifically identify their philosophy with particular forms of production and organization stemming from the pre-industrial period. They fail to understand or adequately acknowledge that from the beginning of industrialization, men have gained deep pleasure and fulfillment from mastering machines and their processes, sometimes creating out of mechanization forms that are as beautiful as any in history, sometimes creating industrial companies that are successful both in business terms and as a social/cultural expression of all who are a part of them. It would be possible to argue, for example, that the success of many outstanding Japanese companies is founded precisely on applying these values in an industrial context.

In attempting to assess the nature and potential of the changes all around us, we need to avoid nostalgia for a past that has gone, and in some respects, probably never was. We cannot turn the clock back. We can, however, be clear about our philosophy and values and seek opportunities in the process of change to give them new directions, new forms and expression. As Hiroshi Shinohara, design director of Canon said in a personal conversation in 1982, when speaking of the future, "First we must think with the heart, and try to understand what kind of life people want and need, then we must think with the head to provide it." The human concerns of the critique of industrialization survive the particularity of their origins, and their views of the role and responsibility that design has in improving life still has much to offer in shaping our vision of the future.

First published as "Commerce or Culture: Industrialization and Design," in *American Center for Design Journal*, Vol. 6, no. 1, 1991, Chicago, pp. 14–33. Republished in "*A John Heskett Reader: Design, History, Economics*" edited by Clive Dilnot, Bloomsbury 2016, pp. 24–41.

NOTES

1. Jubal Merton quoted in Blythe, Ronald, *Akenfield,* Harmondsworth, Penguin, 1969, pp. 146–8. George Sturt's famous text is *The Wheelwright's Shop* (Cambridge, Cambridge University, 1963).
2. Blythe, *Akenfield*, pp. 146–8.
3. Smith, Adam, *The Wealth of Nations*. Original 1776. This edition, edited by Edwin Canaan, New York, The Modern Library, 1937, p. 4.
4. Smith, *The Wealth of Nations*, p. 5.
5. Robinson E. 'Eighteenth-Century Commerce and Fashion: Matthew Boulton's Marketing Techniques', *The Economic History Review*, Vol. xvi, No. 1, 1963, p. 43.
6. Robinson, 'Eighteenth-Century Commerce and Fashion,' p. 46.
7. Robinson, 'Eighteenth-Century Commerce and Fashion,' p. 46.
8. Kelly, Alison, *The Story of Wedgwood*, London, Faber & Faber, 1930, revised 1975, p. 15.
9. Kelly, *The Story of Wedgwood*, p. 34.
10. Taylor, W. Cooke, 'Art and Manufacture,' *Art-Union*, 1 March, 1848, quoted in Harvie, C. et al, (eds.), *Industrialization &. Culture 1830–1914*, London, Macmillan for the Open University Press, 1970.
11. Gibbs-Smith C.H. *The Great Exhibition of 1851*. London, HMSO, 1964.
12. Redgrave, Richard. *The Manual of Design*, London, Chapman & Hall, 1876, p. 7.
13. Cole, Henry, quoted in Naylor, Gillian, *The Arts and Crafts Movement*, Studio Vista, London, 1971, p. 17.
14. Redgrave, *The Manual of Design*, p. 35.
15. Saunders J. J. *The Age of Revolution*, London, Hutchison & Son, n.d. p. 73.

16. Ruskin, John. *Unto This Last,* Original 1862. This edition, London, Dent Everyman's Library, 1968, p. 115.

17. Ruskin, *Unto This Last,* p. 133.

18. Morris, William. 'The Worker's Share of Art,' in Briggs, Asa (ed.), *William Morris: Selected Writings and Designs.* Harmondsworth, Penguin, 1962, pp. 140–1.

19. Morris, William. 'Art and Socialism: the Aims and Ideals of the English Socialists of Today,' in Harvie, *Industrialization & Culture,* p. 341.

20. Morris, 'Art and Socialism,' p. 342.

21. Morris, William. 'News from Nowhere,' in Briggs, Asa (ed.), *William Morris: Selected Writings and Designs.* Harmondsworth, Penguin, 1962, p. 221.

22. Excerpted in Briggs, Asa (ed.), *William Morris: Selected Writings and Designs.* Harmondsworth, Penguin, 1962, p. 68.

23. See Kaplan, Wendy. *The Art that is Life: The Arts & Crafts Movement in America, 1875–1920.* Boston, Museum of Fine Arts, 1987.

24. Chandler, Alfred P., Jr. *The Visible Hand: The Managerial Revolution in American Business.* Cambridge, Mass.: The Belknapp Press, 1977, p. 17.

25. Chandler, *The Visible Hand,* p. 230.

26. Hirschhorn, Larry. *Beyond Mechanization: Work and Technology in a Postindustrial Age.* Cambridge, MA: MIT Press, 1986.

27. Trachtenberg, Alan. *The Incorporation of America: Culture and Society in the Gilded Age.* New York, McGraw Hill, 1982, p. 4.

28. Trachtenberg, *The Incorporation of America,* p. 138.

29. Sloan, Alfred, P. *My Years with General Motors.* New York, Doubleday. Original 1963, this edition 1990, p. 265.

30. Berry, Wendell. *Home Economics.* San Francisco, North Point Press, 1987, p. 74.

31. Berry, *Home Economics,* pp. 164–5.

32. Berry, Wendell. 'Out of your Car, Off your Horse,' *The Atlantic Monthly,* February, 1991, p. 63.

CHAPTER THIRTEEN

Wicked Problems in Design Thinking

RICHARD BUCHANAN

© Richard Buchanan, 1992

INTRODUCTION

Despite efforts to discover the foundations of design thinking in the fine arts, the natural sciences, or most recently, the social sciences, design eludes reduction and remains a surprisingly flexible activity. No single definition of design, or branches of professionalized practice such as industrial or graphic design, adequately covers the diversity of ideas and methods gathered together under the label. Indeed, the variety of research reported in conference papers, journal articles, and books suggests that design continues to expand in its meanings and connections, revealing unexpected dimensions in practice as well as understanding. This follows the trend of design thinking in the twentieth century, for we have seen design grow from a *trade activity* to a *segmented profession* to a *field for technical research* and to what now should be recognized as a new *liberal art of technological culture*.

It may seem unusual to talk about design as a liberal art, particularly when many people are accustomed to identifying the liberal arts with the traditional "arts and science" that are institutionalized in colleges and universities. But the liberal arts are undergoing a revolutionary transformation in twentieth-century culture, and design is one of the areas in which this transformation is strikingly evident.

To understand the change that is now underway, it is important to recognize that what are commonly regarded as the liberal arts today are not outside of history. They originated in the Renaissance and underwent prolonged development that culminated in the nineteenth century as a vision of an encyclopedic education of *beaux arts, belles lettres,* history, various natural sciences and mathematics, philosophy, and the fledgling social sciences. This circle of learning was divided into particular subject matters, each with a proper method or set of methods suitable to its exploration. At their peak as liberal arts, these subject matters provided an integrated understanding of human experience and the array of available knowledge. By the end of the nineteenth century, however, existing subjects were explored with progressively more refined methods, and new subjects were added to accord with advances in knowledge. As a result, the circle of learning was further divided and subdivided, until all that remained was a patchwork quilt of specializations.

Today, these subject matters retain an echo of their old status as liberal arts, but they flourish as specialized studies, leading to the perception of an ever more rich and detailed array of facts and values. Although these subjects contribute to the advance of knowledge, they also contribute to its fragmentation, as they have become progressively narrow in scope, more numerous, and have lost "connection with each other and the common problems and daily life from which they select aspects for precise methodological analysis."[1] The search for new integrative disciplines to complement the arts and sciences has become one of the central themes of intellectual and practical life in the twentieth century. Without integrative disciplines of understanding, communities, and action, there is little hope of sensibly extending knowledge beyond the library or laboratory in order to serve the purpose of enriching human life.

The emergence of design thinking in the twentieth century is important in this context. The significance of seeking a scientific basis for design does not lie in the likelihood of reducing design to one or another of the sciences—an extension of the neo-positivist project and still presented in these terms by some design theorists.[2] Rather, it lies in a concern to connect and integrate useful knowledge from the arts and sciences alike, but in ways that are suited to the problems and purposes of the present. Designers, are exploring concrete integrations of knowledge that will combine theory with practice for new productive purposes, and this is the reason why we turn to design thinking for insight into the new liberal arts of technological culture.[3]

DESIGN AND INTENTIONAL OPERATIONS

The beginning of the study of design as a liberal art can be traced to the cultural upheaval that occurred in the early part of the twentieth century. The key feature of this upheaval was described by John Dewey in *The Quest for Certainty* as the perception of a new center of the universe.

> "The old center of the universe was the mind knowing by means of an equipment of powers complete within itself, and merely exercised upon an antecedent external material equally complete within itself. The new center is indefinite interactions taking place within a course of nature which is not fixed and complete, but which is capable of direction to new and different results through the mediation of intentional operations."[4]

What Dewey describes here is the root of the difference between the old and new liberal arts, between specialization in the facts of the subject matter and the use of new disciplines of integrative thinking.

Dewey observes, however, that the meaning and implications of the new direction are still not fully understood.

"Nowadays we have a messy conjunction of notions that are consistent neither with one another nor with the tenor of our actual life. Knowledge is still regarded by most thinkers as direct grasp of ultimate reality, although the practice of knowing has been assimilated to the procedure of the useful arts;—involving, that is to say, doing that manipulates and arranges natural energies. Again while science is said to lay hold of reality, yet "art" instead of being assigned a lower rank is equally esteemed and honored "[5]

Carrying these observations further, Dewey explores the new relationship between science, art, and practice. He suggests in *Experience and Nature* that knowledge is no longer achieved by direct conformity of ideas with the fixed orders of nature; knowledge is achieved by a new kind of art directed toward orders of change.

"But if modern tendencies are justified in putting art and creation first, then the implications of this position should be avowed and carried through. It would then be seen that science is an art, that art is practice, and that the only distinction worth drawing is not between practice and theory, but between those modes of practice that are not intelligent, not inherently and immediately enjoyable, and those which are full of enjoyed meanings."[6]

Although the neo-positivists courted Dewey for a time, it was apparent that his understanding of the development of science in the twentieth century was quite different from their understanding.[7] Instead of treating science as primary and art as secondary, Dewey pointed toward science as art.

"The consideration that completes the ground for assimilating science to art is the fact that assignment of scientific status in any given case rests upon facts which are experimentally produced. Science is now the product of operations deliberately undertaken in conformity with a plan or project that has the properties of a working hypothesis."[8]

What Dewey means by "art" in this context is crucial to understanding the new role of design and technology in contemporary culture.

"After a period in which natural knowledge progressed by *borrowing* from the industrial crafts, science entered upon a period of steady and ever-accelerated growth by means of deliberate invention of such appliances on its own account. In order to mark this differential feature of the art which is science, I shall now use the word "technology."... Because of technologies, a circular relationship between the arts of production and science has been established."[9]

What Dewey defines as technology is not what is commonly understood in today's philosophy of technology. Instead of meaning knowledge of how to make and use artifacts or the artifacts themselves, technology for Dewey is an art of experimental thinking. It is, in fact, intentional operations themselves carried out in the sciences, the arts of production,[10] or social and political action. We mistakenly identify technology with one particular type of product—hardware—that may result from experimental thinking, but overlook the art that lies behind and provides the basis for creating other types of products.

From this perspective, it is easy to understand why design and design thinking continue to expand their meanings and connections in contemporary culture. There is no area of contemporary life where design—the plan, project, or working hypothesis which constitutes the "intention" in intentional operations—is not a significant factor in shaping human experience. Design even extends into the core of traditional scientific activities, where it is employed to cultivate the subject matters that are the focus of scientific curiosity. But perceiving the existence of such an art only opens the door to further inquiry, to explain what that art is, how it operates, and why it succeeds or fails in particular situations. The challenge is to gain a deeper understanding of design thinking so that more cooperation and mutual benefit is possible between those who apply design thinking to remarkably different problems and subject matters. This will help to make the practical exploration of design, particularly in the arts of production, more intelligent and meaningful.

However, a persistent problem in this regard is that discussions between designers and members of the scientific community tend to leave little room for reflection on the broader nature of design and its relation to the arts and sciences, industry and manufacturing, marketing and distribution, and the general public that ultimately uses the results of design thinking. Instead of yielding productive integrations, the result is often confusion and a breakdown of communication, with a lack of intelligent practice to carry innovative ideas into objective, concrete embodiment. In turn, this undermines efforts to reach a clearer understanding of design itself, sometimes driving designers back into a defense of their work in the context of traditional arts and crafts. Without appropriate reflection to help clarify the basis of communication among all the participants, there is little hope of understanding the foundations and value of design thinking in an increasingly complex technological culture.

THE DOCTRINE OF PLACEMENTS

By "liberal art" I mean a discipline of thinking that may be shared to some degree by all men and women in their daily lives and is, in turn, mastered by a few people who practice the discipline with distinctive insight and sometimes advance it to new areas of innovative application. Perhaps this is what Herbert Simon meant in *The Sciences of the Artificial*, one of the major works of design theory in the twentieth century, when he wrote: "the proper study of mankind is the science of design, not only as the professional component of a technical education but as a core discipline for every liberally educated man."[11] One may reasonably disagree with aspects of Simon's positivist and empiricist view of design as a science[12] (as one may disagree with the pragmatic principles that stand behind Dewey's observation of the importance of intentional operations in modern culture),[13] but there is little reason to disagree with the idea that all men and women may benefit from an early understanding of the disciplines of design in the contemporary world. The beginning of such an understanding has already turned the study of the traditional arts and sciences toward a new engagement with the problems of everyday experience, evident in the development of diverse new products which incorporate knowledge from many fields of specialized inquiry.

To gain some idea of how extensively design affects contemporary life, consider the four broad areas in which design is explored throughout the world by professional designers and by many others who may not regard themselves as designers. The first of these areas is the design of *symbolic and visual communications*. This includes the traditional work of graphic design, such as typography and advertising, book and magazine production, and scientific illustration, but has expanded into communication through photography, film, television, and computer display. The area of communications design is rapidly evolving into a broad exploration of the problems of communicating information, ideas, and arguments through a new synthesis of words and images that is transforming the "bookish culture" of the past.[14]

The second area is the design of *material objects*. This includes traditional concern for the form and visual appearance of everyday products—clothing, domestic objects, tools, instruments, machinery, and vehicles—but has expanded into a more thorough and diverse interpretation of the physical, psychological, social, and cultural relationships between products and human beings. This area is rapidly evolving into an exploration of the problems of construction in which form and visual appearance must carry a deeper, more integrative argument that unites aspects of art, engineering and natural science, and the human sciences.[15]

The third area is the design of *activities and organized services*, which includes the traditional management concern for logistics, combining physical resources, instrumentalities, and human beings in efficient sequences and schedules to reach specified objectives. However, this area has expanded into a concern for logical decision making and strategic planning and is rapidly evolving into an exploration of how better design thinking can contribute to bring an organic flow of experience in concrete situations, making such experiences more intelligent, meaningful, and satisfying. The central theme of this area is connections and consequences. Designers are exploring a progressively wider range of connections in everyday experience and how different types of connections affect the structure of action.[16]

The fourth area is the design of *complex systems or environments for living, working, playing, and learning*. This includes the traditional concerns of systems engineering, architecture, and urban planning or the functional analysis of the parts of complex wholes and their subsequent integration in hierarchies. But this area has also expanded and reflects more consciousness of the central idea, thought, or value that expresses the unity of any balanced and functioning whole. This area is more and more concerned with exploring the role of design in sustaining, developing, and integrating human beings into broader ecological and cultural environments, shaping these environments when desirable and possible or adapting to them when necessary.[17]

Reflecting on this list of the areas of design thinking, it is tempting to identify and limit specific design professions within each area—graphic designers with communication, industrial designers and engineers with material objects, designers-cum-managers with activities and services, and architects and urban planners with systems and environments. But this would not be adequate, because these areas are not simply categories of objects that reflect the results of design. Properly understood and used, they are also *places of invention* shared by all designers, places where one discovers the dimensions of design thinking by a reconsideration of problems and solutions.

True, these four areas point toward certain kinds of objectivity in human experience, and the work of designers in each of these areas has created a framework for human experience in contemporary culture. But these areas are also interconnected, with no priority given to any single one. For example, the sequence of signs, things, actions, and thought could be regarded as an ascent from confusing parts to orderly wholes. Signs and images are fragments of experience that reflect our perception of material objects. Material objects, in turn, become instruments of action. Signs, things, and actions are organized in complex environments by a unifying idea or thought. But there is no reason to believe that parts and wholes must be treated in ascending rather than descending order. Parts and whole are of many types and may be defined in many ways.[18] Depending on how a designer wishes to explore and organize experience, the sequence could just as reasonably be regarded as a descent from chaotic environments to the unity provided by symbols and images. In fact, *signs, things, actions,* and *thoughts* are not only interconnected, they also interpenetrate and merge in contemporary design thinking with surprising consequences for innovation. These areas suggest the lineage of design's past and present, as well as point to where design is headed in the future.

It is easy to understand that industrial designers are primarily concerned with material objects. But the research reported in design literature shows that industrial designers have found new avenues of exploration by thinking about material objects in the context of signs, actions, and thoughts. For example, some have considered material objects communicative, yielding reflections on the semantic and rhetorical aspects of products. Others have placed material objects in the context of experience and action, asking new questions about how products function in situations of use and how they may contribute to or inhibit the flow of activities. (Of course, this is a significant shift from questions about the internal functioning of products and how the visual form of a product expresses such functioning.) Finally, others are exploring material objects as part of larger systems, cycles, and environments, opening up a wide range of new questions and practical concerns or reenergizing old debates. Issues include conservation and recycling, alternative technologies, elaborate simulation environments, "smart" products, virtual reality, artificial life, and the ethical, political, and legal dimensions of design.

Comparable movements are evident in each of the design professions: their primary concern begins in one area, but innovation comes when the initial selection is repositioned at another point in the framework, raising new questions and ideas. Examples of this repositioning abound. For example, architecture has traditionally been concerned with buildings as large systems or environments. For nearly twenty years, however, a group of architects have aggressively sought to reposition architecture in the context of signs, symbols, and visual communication, yielding the postmodern experiment and trends such as deconstructionist architecture. Oxymorons such as "deconstructionist architecture" are often the result of attempts at innovative repositioning. They indicate a desire to break old categories, as in the now familiar and accepted "constructivist art" and "action painting." The test, of course, is whether experiments in innovation yield productive results, judged by individuals and by society as a whole.[19] Some experiments have fallen like dead leaves at the first frost, swept away to merciful oblivion. At present, the results of deconstructionist architecture are mixed, but the experiment will continue until individuals or groups reposition the problems of architecture and shift general attention toward new questions.[20]

A strikingly different repositioning is now beginning in the profession of graphic design and visual communication. In the late nineteenth and early twentieth centuries, graphic design was oriented toward personal expression through image making. It was an extension of the expressiveness of the fine arts, pressed into commercial or scientific service. This was modified under the influence of "communication theory" and semiotics when the role of the graphic designer was shifted toward that of an interpreter of messages. For example, the graphic designer introduced emotional colorings of corporate or public "messages" or, in technical terms, the graphic designer "coded" the corporate message. As a result, the products of graphic design were viewed as "things" or "entities" (material texts) to be "decoded" by spectators.[21] Recently, however, a new approach in graphic design thinking has begun to question the essentially linguistic or grammatical approach of communications theory and semiotics by regarding visual communication as persuasive argumentation. As this work unfolds, it will likely seek to reposition graphic design within the dynamic flow of experience and communication, emphasizing rhetorical relationships among graphic designers, audiences, and the content of communication. In this situation, designers would no longer be viewed as individuals who decorate messages, but as communicators who seek to discover convincing arguments by means of a new synthesis of images and words.[22] In turn, this will shift attention toward audiences as active participants in reaching conclusions rather than passive recipients of preformed messages.

What works for movements within a design profession also works for individual designers and their clients in addressing specific problems. Managers of a large retail chain were puzzled that customers had difficulty navigating through their stores to find merchandise. Traditional graphic design yielded larger signs but no apparent improvement in navigation—the larger the sign, the more likely people were to ignore it. Finally, a design consultant suggested that the problem should be studied from the perspective of the flow of customer experience. After a period of observing shoppers walking through stores, the consultant concluded that people often navigate among different sections of a store by looking for the most familiar and representative examples of a particular type of product. This led to a change in display strategy, placing those products that people are most likely to identify in prominent positions. Although this is a minor example, it does illustrate a double repositioning of the design problem: first, from *signs to action,* with an insight that people look for familiar products to guide their movements; second, from *action to signs,* a redesign of display strategy to employ products themselves as signs or clues to the organization of a store.

There are so many examples of conceptual repositioning in design that it is surprising no one has recognized the systematic pattern of invention that lies behind design thinking in the twentieth century. The pattern is found not in a set of *categories* but in a rich, diverse, and changing set of *placements,* such as those identified by signs, things, actions, and thoughts.

Understanding the difference between a category and a placement is essential if design thinking is to be regarded as more than a series of creative accidents. Categories have fixed meanings that are accepted within the framework of a theory or a philosophy, and serve as the basis for analyzing what already exists. Placements have boundaries to shape and constrain meaning, but are not rigidly fixed and determinate. The boundary of a placement gives a context or orientation to thinking, but the application to a specific situation can generate a new perception of that situation and, hence, a new possibility to be tested. Therefore, placements are sources of new ideas and possibilities when applied to problems in concrete circumstances.[23]

As an ordered or systematic approach to the invention of possibilities, the doctrine of placements provides a useful means of understanding what many designers describe as the intuitive or serendipitous quality of their work. Individual designers often possess a personal set of placements, developed and tested by experience.[24] The inventiveness of the designer lies in a natural or cultivated and artful ability to return to those placements and apply them to a new situation, discovering aspects of the situation that affect the final design. What is regarded as the designer's style, then, is sometimes more than just a personal preference for certain types of visual forms, materials, or techniques; it is a characteristic way of seeing possibilities through conceptual placements. However, when a designer's conceptual placements become categories of thinking, the result can be mannered imitations of an earlier invention that are no longer relevant to the discovery of specific possibilities in a new situation. Ideas are then forced onto a situation rather than discovered in the particularities and novel possibilities of that situation.[25]

For the practicing designer, placements are primary and categories are secondary. The reverse holds true for design history, theory, and criticism, except at those moments when a new direction for inquiry is opened. At such times, a repositioning of the problems of design, such as a change in the subject matter to be addressed, the methods to be employed, or the principles to be explored, occurs by means of placements. Then, history, theory, or criticism are "redesigned" for the individual investigator and sometimes for groups of investigators.[26] As the discipline of design studies adds a reflective and philosophic dimension to design history, theory, and criticism, positive consequences are possible. Historians, for example, may reconsider the placement of design history as it has been practiced throughout most of the twentieth century and work to discover other innovative possibilities. Discontent with the results of current design history suggests that new repositionings are called for if the discipline is to retain vitality and relevance to contemporary problems.[27]

The doctrine of placements will require further development if it is to be recognized as a tool in design studies and design thinking, but it can also be a surprisingly precise way of addressing conceptual space and the non-dimensional images from which concrete possibilities emerge for testing in objective circumstances.[28] The natural and spontaneous use of placements by designers is already evident; an explicit understanding of the doctrine of placements will make it an important element of design as a liberal art.

All men and women require a liberal art of design to live well in the complexity of the framework based in signs, things, actions, and thoughts. On one hand, such an art will enable individuals to participate more directly in this framework and contribute to its development. On the other, professional designers could be regarded as masters in its exploration. The ability of designers to discover new relationships among signs, things, actions, and thoughts is one indication that design is not merely a technical specialization but a new liberal art.

THE WICKED PROBLEMS THEORY OF DESIGN

Recent conferences on design are evidence of a coherent, if not always systematic, effort to reach a clearer understanding of design as an integrative discipline. However, the participants, who increasingly come from diverse professions and academic disciplines, are not drawn together because they share a common definition of design; a common methodology, a common philosophy, or even a common set of objects to which everyone agrees that the term "design" should be applied. They are drawn together because they share a mutual interest in a common theme: *the conception and planning of the artificial*. Different definitions of design and different specifications of the methodology of design are variations of this broad theme, each a concrete exploration of what is possible in the development of its meanings and implications. Communication is possible at such meetings because the results of research and discussion, despite wide differences in intellectual and practical perspectives, are always connected by this theme and, therefore, supplemental. This is only possible, of course, if individuals have the wit to discover what is useful in each other's work and can cast the material in terms of their own vision of design thinking.

Members of the scientific community, however, must be puzzled by the types of problems addressed by professional designers and by the patterns of reasoning they employ. While scientists share in the new liberal art of design thinking, they are also masters of specialized subject matters and their related methods, as found in physics, chemistry, biology, mathematics, the social sciences, or one of the many subfields into which these sciences have been divided.[29] This creates one of the central problems of communication between scientists and designers, because the problems addressed by designers seldom fall solely within the boundaries of any one of these subject matters.

The problem of communication between scientists and designers was evident in a special conference on design theory held in New York in 1974.[30] This conference was interesting for several reasons, the most significant directly related to the content of the meeting itself. Reviewed in one of the initial papers,[31] the "wicked problems" approach to design proved to be one of the central themes to which the participants often returned when seeking a connection between their remarkably diverse and seemingly incommensurate applications of design.[32] Also significant was the difficulty that most of the participants had in understanding each other. Although an observation of an outsider on the dynamics of the meeting, it is an excellent example of a "wicked problem" of design thinking.

The *wicked problems* approach was formulated by Horst Rittel in the 1960s, when design methodology was a subject of intense interest.[33] A mathematician, designer, and former teacher at the Hochschule für Gestaltung (HfG) Ulm, Rittel sought an alternative to the linear, step-by-step model of the design process being explored by many designers and design theorists.[34] Although there are many variations of the linear model, its proponents hold that the design process is divided into two distinct phases: *problem definition* and *problem solution*. *Problem definition* is an *analytic* sequence in which the designer determines all of the elements of the problem and specifies all of the requirements that a successful design solution must have. *Problem solution* is a *synthetic* sequence in which the various requirements are combined and balanced against each other, yielding a final plan to be carried into production.

In the abstract, such a model may appear attractive because it suggests a methodological precision that is, in its key features, independent from the perspective of the individual designer. In fact, many scientists and business professionals, as well as some designers, continue to find the idea of a linear model attractive, believing that it represents the only hope for a "logical" understanding of the design process. However, some critics were quick to point out two obvious points of weakness: one, the actual sequence of design thinking and decision making is not a simple linear process; and two, the problems addressed by designers do not, in actual practice, yield to any linear analysis and synthesis yet proposed.[35]

Rittel argued that most of the problems addressed by designers are *wicked problems*.[36] As described in the first published report of Rittel's idea, *wicked problems* are a "class of social system problems which are ill-formulated, where the information is confusing, where there are many clients and decision makers with conflicting values, and where the ramifications in the whole system are thoroughly confusing."[37] This is an amusing description of what confronts designers in every new situation. But most important, it points toward a fundamental issue that lies behind practice: the relationship between *determinacy* and *indeterminacy* in design thinking. The linear model of design thinking is based on *determinate* problems which have definite conditions. The designer's task is to identify those conditions precisely and then calculate a solution. In contrast, the *wicked-problems* approach suggests that there is a fundamental *indeterminacy* in all but the most trivial design problems—problems where, as Rittel suggests, the "wickedness" has already been taken out to yield determinate or analytic problems.

To understand what this means, it is important to recognize that *indeterminacy* is quite different from *undetermined*. *Indeterminacy* implies that there are no definitive conditions or limits to design problems. This is evident, for example, in the ten properties of *wicked problems* that Rittel initially identified in 1972.[38]

1. *Wicked problems* have no definitive formulation, but every formulation of a *wicked problem* corresponds to the formulation of a solution.

2. *Wicked problems* have no stopping rules.

3. Solutions to *wicked problems* cannot be true or false, only good or bad.

4. In solving *wicked problems* there is no exhaustive list of admissible operations.

5. For every *wicked problem* there is always more than one possible explanation, with explanations depending on the *Weltanschauung* of the designer.[39]

6. Every *wicked problem* is a symptom of another, "higher level," problem.[40]

7. No formulation and solution of a *wicked problem* has a definitive test.

8. Solving a *wicked problem* is a "one shot" operation, with no room for trial and error.[41]

9. Every *wicked problem* is unique.

10. The *wicked problem* solver has no right to be wrong—they are fully responsible for their actions.

This is a remarkable list, and it is tempting to go no further than elaborate the meaning of each property, providing concrete examples drawn from every area of design thinking.

But to do so would leave a fundamental question unanswered. *Why are design problems indeterminate and, therefore, wicked?* Neither Rittel nor any of those studying *wicked problems* has attempted to answer this question, so the *wicked-problems* approach has remained only a description of the social reality of designing rather than the beginnings of a well-grounded theory of design.

However, the answer to the question lies in something rarely considered: the peculiar nature of the subject matter of design. Design problems are "indeterminate" and "wicked" because design has no special subject matter of its own apart from what a designer conceives it to be. The subject matter of design is potentially *universal* in scope, because design thinking may be applied to any area of human experience. But in the process of application, the designer must discover or invent a *particular* subject out of the problems and issues of specific circumstances. This sharply contrasts with the disciplines of science, which are concerned with understanding the principles, laws, rules, or structures that are necessarily embodied in existing subject matters. Such subject matters are undetermined or under-determined, requiring further investigation to make them more fully determinate. But they are not radically indeterminate in a way directly comparable to that of design.[42]

Designers conceive their subject matter in two ways on two levels: general and particular. On a *general level,* a designer forms an idea or a working hypothesis about the nature of products or the nature of the humanmade in the world. This is the designer's view of what is meant, for example, by the "artificial" in relation to the "natural." In this sense, the designer holds a broad view of the nature of design and the proper scope of its application. Indeed, most designers, to the degree that they have reflected on their discipline, will gladly, if not insistently, explain on a general level what the subject matter of design is. When developed and well presented, these explanations are philosophies or proto-philosophies of design that exist within a plurality of alternative views.[43] They provide an essential framework for each designer to understand and explore the materials, methods, and principles of design thinking. But such philosophies do not and cannot constitute sciences of design in the sense of any natural, social, or humanistic science. The reason for this is simple: design is fundamentally concerned with the particular, *and there is no science of the particular.*

In actual practice, the designer begins with what should be called a *quasi-subject matter,* tenuously existing within the problems and issues of specific circumstances. Out of the specific possibilities of a concrete situation, the designer must conceive a design that will lead to *this* or *that* particular product. A *quasi-subject matter* is not an undetermined subject waiting to be made determinate. It is an indeterminate subject waiting to be made specific and concrete. For example, a client's brief does not present a definition of the subject matter of a particular design application. It presents a problem and a set of issues to be considered in resolving that problem. In situations where a brief specifies in great detail the particular features of the product to be planned, it often does so because an owner, corporate executive, or manager has attempted to perform the critical task of transforming problems and issues into a working hypothesis about the particular features of the product to be designed. In effect, someone has attempted to take the "wickedness" out. Even in this situation, however, the conception of particular features remains only a possibility that may be subject to change through discussion and argument.[44]

This is where placements take on special significance as tools of design thinking. They allow the designer to position and reposition the problems and issues at hand. Placements are the tools by which a designer intuitively or deliberately shapes a design situation, identifying the views of all participants, the issues which concern them, and the invention that will serve as a working hypothesis for exploration and development. In this sense, the placements selected by a designer are the same as what determine subject matters are for the scientist. They are the *quasi-subject matter* of design thinking, from which the designer fashions a working hypothesis suited to special circumstances.

This helps to explain how design functions as an integrative discipline. By using placements to discover or invent a working hypothesis, the designer establishes a *principle of relevance* for knowledge from the arts and sciences, determining how such knowledge may be useful to design thinking in a particular circumstance without immediately reducing design to one or another of these disciplines. In effect, the working hypothesis that will lead to a particular product is the principle of relevance, guiding the efforts of designers to gather all available knowledge bearing on how a product is finally planned.

But does the designer's working hypothesis or principle of relevance suggest that the product itself is a determinate subject matter? The answer involves a critical but often blurred distinction between design thinking and the activity of production or making. Once a product is conceived, planned, and produced, it may indeed become an object for study by any of the arts and sciences—history, economics, psychology, sociology, or anthropology. It may even become an object for study by a new humanistic science of production that we could call the "science of the artificial," directed toward understanding the nature, form, and uses of humanmade products in all of their generic kinds.[45] But in all such studies, the activities of design thinking are easily forgotten or are reduced to the kind of product that is finally produced. The problem for designers is to conceive and plan what does not yet exist, and this occurs in the context of the indeterminacy of *wicked problems,* before the final result is known.

This is the creative or inventive activity that Herbert Simon has in mind when he speaks of design as a science of the artificial. What he means is "devising artifacts to attain goals" or, more broadly, "doctrine about the design process."[46] In this sense, Simon's science of the artificial is perhaps closer to what Dewey means by technology as a systematic discipline of experimental thinking. However, Simon has little to say about the difference between designing a product and making it. Consequently, the "search" procedures and decision-making protocols that he proposes for design are largely analytic, shaped by his philosophic view of the determinacies that follow from the natural laws that surround artifacts.[47]

For all of the insight Simon has in distinguishing the artificial as a domain of humanmade products different from objects created by natural processes, he does not capture the radical sense in which designers explore the essence of what the artificial may be in human experience.[48] This is a synthetic activity related to indeterminacy, not an activity of making what is undetermined in natural laws more determinate in artifacts. In short, Simon appears to have conflated two sciences of the artificial: an inventive science of design thinking which has no subject matter aside from what the designer conceives it to be, and a science of existing humanmade products whose nature Simon happens to believe is a manipulation of material and behavioral laws of nature.[49]

Design is a remarkably supple discipline, amenable to radically different interpretations in philosophy as well as in practice. But the flexibility of design often leads to popular misunderstanding and clouds efforts to understand its nature. The history of design is not merely a history of objects. It is a history of the changing views of subject matter held by designers and the concrete objects conceived, planned, and produced as expressions of those views. *One could go further and say that the history of design history is a record of the design historians' views regarding what they conceive to be the subject matter of design.*

We have been slow to recognize the peculiar indeterminacy of subject matter in design and its impact on the nature of design thinking. As a consequence, each of the sciences that have come into contact with design has tended to regard design as an "applied" version of its own knowledge, methods, and principles. They see in design: an instance of their own subject matter and treat design as a *practical demonstration* of the scientific principles of that subject matter. Thus, we have the odd, recurring situation in which design is alternately regarded as "applied" natural science, "applied" social science, or "applied" fine art. No wonder designers and members of the scientific community often have difficulty communicating.

DESIGN AND TECHNOLOGY

Many problems remain to be explored in establishing design as a liberal art of technological culture. But as it continues to unfold in the work of individual designers and in reflection on the nature of their work,[50] design is slowly restoring the richer meaning of the term "technology" that was all but lost with the rise of the Industrial Revolution. Most people continue to think of technology in terms of its *product* rather than its form as a *discipline of systematic thinking*. They regard technology as things and machines, observing with concern that the machines of our culture often appear out of human control, threatening to trap and enslave rather than liberate. But there was a time in an earlier period of Western culture when technology was a human activity operating throughout the liberal arts.[51] Every liberal art had its own *technologia* or systematic discipline. To possess that technology or discipline of thinking was to possess the liberal art, to be human, and to be free in seeking one's place in the world.

Design also has a *technologia,* and it is manifested in the plan for every new product. The plan is an argument, reflecting the deliberations of designers and their efforts to integrate knowledge in new ways, suited to specific circumstances and needs. In this sense, design is emerging as a new discipline of practical reasoning and argumentation, directed by individual designers toward one or another of its major thematic variations in the twentieth century: *design as communication, construction, strategic planning, or systemic integration.*[52] The power of design as deliberation and argument lies in overcoming the limitations of mere verbal or symbolic argument—the separation of words and things, or theory and practice that remains a source of disruption and confusion in contemporary culture. Argument in design thinking moves toward the concrete interplay and interconnection of signs, things, actions, and thoughts. Every designer's sketch, blueprint, flow chart, graph, three-dimensional model, or other product proposal is an example of such argumentation.

However, there is persistent confusion about the different modes of argumentation employed by the various design professions. For example, industrial design, engineering, and marketing each employ the discipline of design thinking, yet their arguments are often framed in sharply different logical modalities. Industrial design tends to stress what is *possible* in the conception and planning of products; engineering tends to stress what is *necessary* in considering materials, mechanisms, structures, and systems;[53] while marketing tends to stress what is *contingent* in the changing attitudes and preferences of potential users. Because of these modal differences in approaching design problems, three of the most important professions of design thinking are often regarded as bitter opponents in the design enterprise, irreconcilably distant from each other.[54]

What design as a liberal art contributes to this situation is a new awareness of how argument is the central theme that cuts across the many technical methodologies employed in each design profession. Differences of modality may be complementary ways of arguing—reciprocal expressions of what conditions and shapes the "useful" in human experience. As a liberal art of technological culture, design points toward a new attitude about the appearance of products. Appearance must carry a deeper, integrative argument about the nature of the artificial in human experience. This argument is a synthesis of three lines of reasoning: the ideas of designers and manufacturers about their products; the internal operational logic of products; and the desire and ability of human beings to use products in everyday life in ways that reflect personal and social values. Effective design depends on the ability of designers to integrate all three lines of reasoning. But not as isolated factors that can be added together in a simple mathematical total, or as isolated subject matters that can be studied separately and joined late in the product development process.

The new liberal art of design thinking is turning to the modality of *impossibility*. It points, for example, toward the impossibility of rigid boundaries between industrial design, engineering, and marketing. It points toward the impossibility of relying on any one of the sciences (natural, social, or humanistic) for adequate solutions to what are the inherently *wicked problems* of design thinking. Finally it points toward something that is often forgotten, that what many people call "impossible" may actually only be a limitation of imagination that can be overcome by better design thinking. This is not thinking directed toward a technological "quick fix" in hardware but toward new integrations of signs, things, actions, and environments that address the concrete needs and values of human beings in diverse circumstances.

Individuals trained in the traditional arts and sciences may continue to be puzzled by the neoteric art of design.[55] But the masters of this new liberal art are practical men and women, and the discipline of thinking that they employ is gradually becoming accessible to all individuals in everyday life. A common discipline of design thinking—more than the particular products created by that discipline today—is changing our culture, not only in its external manifestations but in its internal character.

© Richard Buchanan 1992. Previously published in *Design Issues*, Vol. 8, No. 2 (Spring, 1992), pp. 5–21.

This essay is based on a paper presented at "Collogue Recherches sur le Design: Incitations, Implications, Interactions," the first French university symposium on design research held October 1990 at l'Université de Technologie de Compiègne, Compiègne, France.

NOTES

1. From Richard McKeon, "The Transformation of the Liberal Arts in the Renaissance," *Developments in the Early Renaissance*, ed. Bernard S. Levy (Albany: State University of New York Press, 1972), 168–69.

2. Neo-positivism, pragmatism, and various forms of phenomenology have strongly influenced design education and practice in the twentieth century. If design theory has often tended toward neo-positivism, design practice has tended toward pragmatism and pluralism, with phenomenologists in both areas. Such philosophical differences are illustrated in the split that developed between the theoretical and studio courses at the Hochschule für Gestaltung (HfG) Ulm before its closing. The split between theory and practice in design is an echo of the difference between the predominantly neo-positivist philosophy of science and the exceptionally diverse philosophies of practicing scientists. Design history, theory, and criticism could benefit from closer attention to the pluralism of views that guide actual design practice.

3. Walter Gropius was one of the first to recognize the beginnings of a new liberal art in design. In an essay written in 1937, he reflected on the founding of the Bauhaus as an institution grounded on the idea of an architectonic art: "Thus the Bauhaus was inaugurated in 1919 with the specific object of realizing a modern architectonic art, which like human nature was meant to be all-embracing in its scope… Our guiding principle was that design is neither an intellectual nor a material affair, but simply an integral part of the stuff of life, necessary for everyone in a civilized society." *Scope of Total Architecture* (New York: Collier Books, 1970), 19–20. The term "architectonic," in this case, transcends the derivative term "architecture" as it is commonly used in the modern world. Throughout Western culture, the liberal arts have similarly been described as "architectonic", because of their integrative capacity. Gropius appeared to understand that architecture, regarded as a liberal art in its own right in the ancient world, was only one manifestation of the architectonic art of design in the twentieth century.

4. John Dewey, *The Quest for Certainty: A Study of the Relation of Knowledge and Action* (1929; rpt. New York: Capricorn Books, 1960), 290–91.

5. John Dewey, *Experience and Nature* (1929; rpt. New York: Dover Publications, Inc., 1958), 357.

6. Dewey, *Experience and Nature*, 357–58.

7. The neo-positivist *International Encyclopedia of Unified Science*, which included Charles Morris's Foundations of the Theory of Signs, also included Dewey's Theory of Valuation. However, Dewey's Logic was ignored or ridiculed by neo-positivist logicians and grammarians.

8. John Dewey, "By Nature and By Art," *Philosophy of Education (Problems of Men)* (1946; rpt. Totowa, New Jersey: Littlefield, Adams, 1958), 288.

9. Dewey, "By Nature and By Art," 291–92.

10. For Dewey, the arts of production, include the fine arts. He makes no sharp distinction between fine and useful arts.

11. Herbert A. Simon, *The Sciences of the Artificial* (Cambridge: M.I.T. Press, 1968), 83.

12. Although Simon's *The Sciences of the Artificial* is cited repeatedly in design literature because of its definition of design, it is often read with little attention given to the full argument. A careful analysis from the standpoint of industrial design would be a useful contribution to the literature. Such a reading

would reveal the positivist features of Simon's approach and help to explain why many designers are somewhat disenchanted with the book. Nonetheless, it remains an exceptionally useful work.

13. See Richard Buchanan, "Design and Technology in the Second Copernican Revolution" *Revue des sciences et techniques de la conception (The Journal of Design Sciences and Technology)*, 1.1 (January, 1992).

14. The phrase "bookish culture" is used by literary critic George Steiner and is a theme in a forthcoming book by Ivan Illich, *In the Vineyard of the Text*.

15. The design of material objects includes, of course, new work in materials science, where a highly focused form of design thinking is evident.

16. Some of the psychological and social dimensions of this area are illustrated in works as diverse as George A. Miller, Eugene Galanter, and Karl H. Pribram, *Plans and the Structure of Behavior* (New York: Holt, Rinehart and Winston, 1960); Lucy Suchman, *Plans and Situated Actions: The Problem of Human Machine Communication* (Cambridge: Cambridge University Press, 1987); and Mihaly Csikszentmihalyi, *Flow: The Psychology of Optimal Experience* (New York: Harper & Row, 1990).

17. One of the early works of systems engineering that influenced design thinking is Arthur D. Hall, *A Methodology for Systems Engineering* (Princeton, New Jersey: D. Van Nostrand Company, 1962). For more recent developments in systems thinking, see Ron Levy, "Critical Systems Thinking: Edgar Morin and the French School of Thought," *Systems Practice*, vol. 4 (1990). Regarding the new "systemics," see Robert L. Flood and Werner Ulrich, "Testament to Conversations on Critical Systems Thinking Between Two Systems Practitioners," *Systems Practice*, vol. 3 (1990), and M. C. Jackson, "The Critical Kernel in Modern Systems Thinking," *Systems Practice*, vol. 3 (1990). For an anthropological approach to systems, see James Holston, *The Modernist City: An Anthropological Critique of Brasilia* (Chicago: University of Chicago Press, 1989).

18. Compare the Platonic, Aristotelian, and classic materialist treatments of parts and wholes. These three approaches to the organization of experience are well represented in twentieth century design thinking. For example, see Christopher Alexander, *Notes on the Synthesis of Form* (Cambridge: Harvard University Press, 1973).

19. Such judgments are the measure of objectivity in contemporary design thinking. Without objectivity to ground the possibilities discovered in design, design thinking becomes design sophistry.

20. Architect Richard Rogers seeks to reposition the problems of architecture in a new perception of multiple overlapping systems, rejecting the notion of a system as "linear, static, hierarchical and mechanical order." According to Rogers: "Today we know that design based on linear reasoning must be superseded by an open-ended architecture of overlapping systems. This 'systems' approach allows us to appreciate the world as an indivisible whole; we are, in architecture, as in other fields, approaching a holistic ecological view of the globe and the way we live on it." *Architecture: A Modern View* (New York: Thames and Hudson Inc., 1991), 58. Rogers's notion of "indeterminate form" derives not from the ideas of literary deconstruction but from his innovative view of multiple systems. For more on Rogers's pointed criticism of postmodern architecture from the perspective of multiple systems, *see Architecture: A Modern View*, 26.

21. Although still a common and useful way of studying visual communication, this approach has lost some of its initial force in actual design practice because it has moved into personal idiosyncrasy and a search for novelty, which often distracts one from the central tasks of effective communication. This is evident, for example, among those graphic designers who have made pedestrian readings of deconstructionist literary theory the rationale for their work. Visual experimentation is an important part of graphic design thinking, but experimentation must finally be judged by relevance

and effectiveness of communication. For a discussion of the limits of semiotics and design, see Seppo Vakeva, "What Do We Need Semiotics For?," *Semantic Visions in Design*, ed. Susann Vihma (Helsinki: University of Industrial Arts UIAH, 1990), g-2.

22. Swiss graphic designer Ruedi Ruegg has recently spoken of the need for more fantasy and freedom in graphic design thinking. Based on his approach, one might argue that efforts to introduce deconstructionist literary theory into graphic design have often led to a loss of freedom and imagination in effective communication, contrary to the claims of its proponents.

23. The concept of placements will remain difficult to grasp as long as individuals are trained to believe that the only path of reasoning begins with categories and proceeds in deductive chains of propositions. Designers are concerned with invention as well as judgment, and their reasoning is practical because it takes place in situations where the results are influenced by diverse opinions.

24. Some placements have become so common in twentieth-century design that they hardly attract attention. Nonetheless, such placements are classic features of design thinking, and in the hands of a skilled designer retain their inventive potential. Designer Jay Doblin sometimes employed a cascade of placements stemming from the basic placement "intrinsic/extrinsic." Doblin's placements serve as a heuristic device to reveal the factors in design thinking and product development. Other placements are described by Doblin in *Innovation, A Cook Book Approach*, n.d. (typewritten.) With different intent, Ezio Manzini recently argued that the designer needs two mental instruments with opposite qualities to examine a design situation: a microscope and a macroscope. The mental microscope is for examining "how things work, down to the smallest details," particularly in regard to advances in materials science. A further series of placements fill out the microscope to give it efficacy. See Ezio Manzini, *The Materials of Invention: Materials and Design* (Cambridge: M.I.T. Press, 1989), 58.

25. The ease with which placements are converted into categories should make any designer or design educator cautious in how they share the conceptual tools of their work. The placements that might shape an innovative approach for the founder of a school of design thinking often become categories of truth in the hands of disciples or descendants.

26. Thomas Kuhn was interested in the repositionings that mark revolutions in scientific theory. His study of this phenomenon, perhaps contrary to his initial expectations, has helped to alter the neo-positivist interpretation of the history of science. But Kuhn's "paradigm shifts" were never developed to their fullest intellectual roots in rhetorical and dialectical invention, which are based on the theory of topics. Chaim Perelman has developed an important contemporary approach to what is called here the doctrine of placements. See Chaim Perelman and L. Olbrechts-Tyteca, *The New Rhetoric: A Treatise on Argumentation* (Notre Dame: University of Notre Dame Press, 1969). See also, Stephen E. Toulmin, *The Uses of Argument* (Cambridge: Cambridge University Press, 1958) for a modern discovery of dialectical topics. Although remote from the immediate interests of designers, these works are cited because they deal with practical reasoning and have important bearing on aspects of design theory, including the logic of decision making discussed in Simon's *The Sciences of the Artificial*.

27. In order to solve such problems, more attention should be given to the various conceptions of design held by designers in the past. This would reposition design history from material objects or "things" to thought and action. In other words, what designers say and do, the history of their art as philosophy and practice. For a discussion of the subject matter of design history, see Victor Margolin's "Design History or Design Studies: Subject Matter and Methods," *Design Studies*, vol. 13, no. 2 (April 1992): 104–16.

28. The phrase "non-dimensional images" refers to all images created in the mind as part of design thinking and, in particular, to the various schematizations of conceptual placements (e.g. hierarchical, horizontal, or in matrix and table form) that may aid invention.

29. This list could also include the humanistic disciplines and the fine arts, because there is as much difficulty in communicating between some traditional humanists and designers as between designers and scientists. This is evident in the persistent view that design is simply a decorative art, adapting the principles of the fine arts to utilitarian ends, held by many humanists.

30. William R. Spillers, ed., *Basic Questions of Design Theory* (Amsterdam: North Holland Publishing Company, 1974). The conference, funded by the National Science Foundation, was held at Columbia University.

31. Vladimer Bazjanac, "Architectural Design Theory: Models of the Design Process," *Basic Questions of Design Theory*, 3–20.

32. Graph theory, developed by the mathematician Frank Harary, also served to connect the work of researchers in many areas. It was reported by the organizers that Harary, who attended this conference and delivered the paper "Graphs as Designs," suggested that the basic structure of design theory could be found in his work on structural models. Whether or not Harary made such a suggestion, it is possible to see in graph theory, and, notably, the theory of directed graphs, a mathematical expression of the doctrine of placements. Comparison may establish a surprising connection between the arts of words and the mathematical arts of things, with further significance for the view of design as a new liberal art. "Schemata" are the connecting link, for placements may be schematized as figures of thought, and schemata are forms of graphs, directed or otherwise. For more on graph theory see F. Harary, R. Norman, and D. Cartwright, *Structural Models: An Introduction to the Theory of Directed Graphs* (New York: Wiley, 1965).

33. A series of conferences on Design Methods held in the United Kingdom in 1962, 1965, and 1967, led to the formation of the Design Research Society in 1967, that today continues to publish the journal *Design Studies*. Parallel interest in the United States led to the establishment of the Design Methods Group in 1966, which published the *DMG Newsletter* (1966–71), renamed the *DMG-DRS Journal: Design Research and Methods*, and then renamed in 1976 and published to the present as *Design Methods and Theories*. For one attempt to describe and integrate a set of methods used in design thinking, see J. Christopher Jones, *Design Methods: Seeds of Human Futures* (1970; rpt New York: John Wiley & Sons, 1981). Many of the methods Jones presents are consciously transposed from other disciplines. However, they all can be interpreted as techniques for repositioning design problems, using placements to discover new possibilities.

34. Rittel, who died in 1990, completed his career by teaching at the University of California at Berkeley and the University of Stuttgart. For a brief biographical sketch, see Herbert Lindinger, *Ulm Design: The Morality of Objects* (Cambridge: M.I.T. Press, 1990), 274.

35. Bazjanac presents an interesting comparison of linear models and the wicked problems approach.

36. The phrase wicked problems was borrowed from philosopher Karl Popper. However, Rittel developed the idea in a different direction. Rittel is another example of someone initially influenced by neo-positivist ideas who, when confronted with the actual processes of practical reasoning in concrete circumstances, sought to develop a new approach related to rhetoric.

37. The first published report of Rittel's concept of wicked problems was presented by C. West Churchman, "Wicked Problems," *Management Science*, (December 1967), vol. 4, no. 14, B-141–42. His editorial is particularly interesting for its discussion of the moral problems of design and planning that can occur when individuals mistakenly believe that they have effectively taken the "wickedness" out of design problems.

38. See Horst W. J. Rittel and Melvin M. Webber, "Dilemmas in a General Theory of Planning," working paper presented at the Institute of Urban and Regional Development, University of California, Berkeley, November 1972. See also an interview with Rittel, "Son of Rittelthink,"

Design Methods Group 5th Anniversary Report (January 1972), 5–10; and Horst Rittel, "On the Planning Crisis: Systems Analysis of the First and Second Generations," *Bedriftsokonomen*, no. 8: 390–96. Rittel gradually added more properties to his initial list.

39. Weltanschauung identifies the intellectual perspective of the designer as an integral part of the design process.

40. This property suggests the systems aspect of Rittel's approach.

41. Rittel's example is drawn from architecture, where it is not feasible to rebuild a flawed building. Perhaps the general property should be described as "entrapment" in a line of design thinking. Designers as well as their clients or managers are often "entrapped" during the development phase of a new product and are unable, for good or bad reasons, to terminate a weak design. For a brief illustration of entrapment in the product development process of a small midwestern company, see Richard Buchanan, "Wicked Problems: Managing the Entrapment Trap," *Innovation*, 10.3 (Summer, 1991).

42. There is one case in which even the subject matters of the sciences are indeterminate. The working hypotheses of scientists invariably reflect distinctive philosophic perspectives on and interpretations of what constitutes nature and natural processes. This is a factor in accounting for the surprising pluralism of philosophies among practicing scientists and suggests that even science is shaped by an application of design thinking, developed along the lines of Dewey's notion of "intentional operations." Even from this perspective, however, scientists are concerned with understanding the universal properties of what is, while designers are concerned with conceiving and planning a particular that does not yet exist. Indeterminacy for the scientist is on the level of second-intention, while the subject matter remains, at the level of first-intention, determinate in the manner described. For the designer, indeterminacy belongs to both first and second-intention.

43. For a brief discussion of different conceptions of subject matter on this level held by three contemporary designers, Ezio Manzini, Gaetano Pesce, and Emilio Ambaz, see Richard Buchanan, "Metaphors, Narratives, and Fables in New Design Thinking," *Design Issues,* vol. 8, no. 1 (Fall, 1990): 78–84. Without understanding a designer's view of subject matter on the general level, there is little intelligibility in the shifts that occur when a designer moves, for example, from designing domestic products to graphic design or architecture. Such shifts are usually described in terms of the designer's "personality" or "circumstances" rather than the continued development of a coherent intellectual perspective on the artificial.

44. Failure to include professional designers as early as possible in the product development process is one of the sources of entrapment in corporate culture. Professional designers should be recognized for their ability to conceive products as well as plan them.

45. The earliest example of this science is Aristotle's *Poetics*. Although this work is directed toward the analysis of literary productions and tragedy in particular, Aristotle frequently discusses useful objects in terms of the principles of poetic analysis. "Poetics," from the Greek word for "making," is used by Aristotle to refer to productive science or the science of the artificial, which he distinguishes both from theoretic and practical sciences. Few investigators have recognized that poetic analysis can be extended to the study of making "useful" objects. When designer and architect Emilio Ambaz refers to the "poetics of the pragmatic," he means not only esthetic or elegant features of everyday objects, but also a method or discipline of analysis that may contribute to design thinking.

46. Simon, *The Sciences of the Artificial*, 52–53.

47. For Simon, the "artificial" is an "interface" created within a materialist reality: "I have shown that a science of artificial phenomena is always in imminent danger of dissolving and vanishing. The peculiar properties of the artifact lie on the thin interface between the natural laws within it and

the natural laws without." Simon, *The Sciences of the Artificial*, 57. This is one expression of the positivist or empiricist philosophy that guides Simon's theory of design.

48. For Simon, the equivalent of a wicked problem is an "ill-structured problem." For Simon's views on how ill-structured problems may be addressed, see "The Structure of Ill Structured Problems," *Models of Discovery* (Boston: D. Reidel, 1977), 305–25. This paper has interesting connections with the doctrine of placements because placements may be used to organize and store memories, and Simon is particularly concerned with the role of long-term memory in solving ill-structured problems. But Simon's methods are still analytic, directed toward the discovery of solutions in some sense already known rather than the invention of solutions yet unknown.

49. Although Simon's title, *The Sciences of the Artificial*, is a perfectly adequate translation of what we have come to know in Western culture as Aristotle's Poetics, Simon seems unaware of the humanistic tradition of poetic and rhetorical analysis of the artificial that followed from Aristotle. This is not an antiquarian issue, because the study of literary production—the artificial formed in words—prefigures the issues that surround the study of the artificial in all other types of useful objects. Aristotle carefully distinguished the science of the artificial from the art of rhetoric. When Aristotle comes to discuss the thought that is presented in an artificial object such as a tragedy, he pointedly refers the reader to his treatise on the inventive art of rhetoric for the fullest elaboration of the issue. However, Simon deserves less criticism for overlooking this connection than humanists who have been amazingly neglectful, if not scornful, of the rise of design and technology in the twentieth century.

50. One example of such reflection is the interdisciplinary conference "Discovering Design," organized by R. Buchanan and V. Margolin and held at the University of Illinois at Chicago in 1990. The collected papers from this conference have been published as *Discovering Design: Explorations in Design Studies* (Chicago: University of Chicago Press, 1995).

51. Richard McKeon, "Logos: Technology, Philology, and History," in *Proceedings of the XVth World Congress of Philosophy: Varna, Bulgaria, September 17–22, 1973* (Sofia: Sofia Press Production Center, 1974), 3: 481–84.

52. For Rittel's view of argumentation in design, see Rittel and Webber, *Dilemmas*, 19. Also discussed in Bazjanac, "Architectural Design Theory: Models of the Design Process," *Basic Questions of Design Theory*. Students report that late in his career Rittel came to recognize the affinity between his approach and rhetoric.

53. The necessary is sometimes referred to as "capacity" or "capability" in engineering. For a useful introduction to engineering design, see M. J. French, *Invention and Evolution: Design in Nature and Engineering* (Cambridge: Cambridge University Press, 1988).

54. Philip Kotler, the internationally recognized expert on marketing, has suggested that what many industrial designers object to in marketing should not be regarded as marketing itself, but as bad marketing. For new developments in marketing, see Philip Kotler, "Humanistic Marketing: Beyond the Marketing Concept," *Philosophical and Radical Thought in Marketing*, eds. A. Fuat Firat, N. Dholakia, and R.P. Bagozzi (Lexington, Massachusetts: Lexington Books, 1987).

55. "Neoteric" is a term often associated in Western culture with the emergence of new liberal arts. Neoteric arts are arts of "new learning." For a discussion of neoteric and paleoteric liberal arts, see Richard Buchanan, "Design as a Liberal Art," *Papers: The 1990 Conference on Design Education, Education Committee of the Industrial Designers Society of America* (Pasadena, CA, 1990).

CHAPTER FOURTEEN

Good Citizenship: Design as a Social and Political Force

KATHERINE MCCOY

© Katherine McCoy, 1993

This decade finds us in a crisis of values in the United States. Our increasingly multicultural society is experiencing a breakdown in shared values—national values, tribal values, personal values, even family values—consensual motivating values that create a common sense of purpose in a community.

The question is: How can a heterogeneous society develop shared values and yet encourage cultural diversity and personal freedom? Designers and design education are part of the problem, and can be part of the answer. We cannot afford to be passive anymore. Designers must be good citizens and participate in the shaping of our government and society. As designers we can use our particular talents and skills to encourage others to wake up and participate as well.

Before the U.S. congratulates itself too much on the demise of Communism, we must remember that our American capitalist democracy is not what it used to be either. Much of our stagnation comes from this breakdown of values. Entrepreneurial energy and an optimistic work ethic have deteriorated into individual self-interest, complacency, corporate greed, and resentment between ethnic groups and economic classes. Our traditional common American purpose is fading—that sense of building something new where individuals could progress through participating in a system that provided opportunity. Consumerism and materialism now seem to be the only ties that bind. The one group that seems to be bound by more than this is the Far Right; but their bond is regressive, a desire to force fundamentalist prescriptive values on the rest of us.

In the Reagan–Bush era we were told it was all O.K., that we could spend and consume with no price tag attached. During this period, graphic designers enjoyed the spoils of artificial prosperity with the same passive hedonism as the rest of the country. Now we are beginning to realize it was not all O.K. The earth is being poisoned, its resources depleted, and the US has gone from a creditor to a debtor nation. Our self–absorption and lack of activism has left a void filled by minority single-issue groups aggressively pushing their concerns.

There are serious threats to our civil liberties in the United States from both fundamentalist censorship of the Right and political correctness from the Left. We have seen the dismemberment of artistic freedom at the National Endowment for the Arts in recent years, and aggressive attempts to censor public schools' teaching—from Darwin to Hemingway to safe sex. A conservative Congress continues to push for content restrictions on Internet discourse. And as graphic designers specializing in visual communications, the content of our communications could be seriously curtailed if we do not defend our freedom of expression.

But even more troubling is our field's own self-censorship. How many graphic designers today would feel a loss if their freedom of expression was handcuffed? Most of our colleagues never exercise their right to communicate on public issues or potentially controversial content. Remove our freedom of speech and graphic designers might never notice. We have trained a profession that feels political or social concerns are either extraneous to our work, or inappropriate.

Thinking back to 1968, the atmosphere at Unimark International during my first year of work typified this problem. Unimark (an idealistic international design office with Massimo Vignelli and Jay Doblin as vice presidents and Herbert Bayer on the Board) was dedicated to the ideal of the rationally objective professional. The graphic designer was to be the neutral transmitter of the client's messages. Clarity and objectivity were the goal. During that year, the designers I worked with, save one notable exception, were all remarkably disinterested in the social and political upheavals taking place around us. Vietnam was escalating with body counts touted on every evening newscast; the New Left rioted before the Democratic National Convention in Chicago, Martin Luther King and Robert Kennedy were assassinated; and Detroit was still smoking from its riots just down the street from our office. Yet hardly a word was spoken on these subjects. We were encouraged to wear white lab coats, perhaps so the messy external environment would not contaminate our surgically clean detachment.

These white lab coats make an excellent metaphor for the apolitical designer, cherishing the myth of universal value—free design—that design is a clinical process akin to chemistry, scientifically pure and neutral, conducted in a sterile laboratory environment with precisely predictable results. Yet Lawrence and Oppenheimer and a thousand other examples teach us that even chemists and physicists must have a contextual view of their work in the social/political world around them.

During that time, I became increasingly interested in the social idealism of the times: the Civil Rights movement, the anti-Vietnam peace movement, the anti-materialism and social experimentation of the New Left, and radical feminism. Yet it was very difficult to relate these new ideas to the design that I was practicing and the communication process that I loved so much. Or perhaps the difficulty was not the values of design so much as the values of design community. About all I could connect with was designing and sending (to appalled family members) an anti-Vietnam feminist Christmas card and silk-screening t-shirts with a geometricized "Swiss" version of the feminist symbol. Meanwhile, we continued to serve the corporate and advertising worlds with highly "professional" design solutions.

The implication of the word "professional" as we use it is indicative of the problem here. How often do we hear, "Act like a professional" or "I'm a professional, I can handle it." Being a professional means to put aside one's personal reactions regardless of the situation and to carry on. Prostitutes, practitioners of the so-called oldest profession, must maintain an extreme of cool objectivity about this most intimate of human activities, highly disciplining their personal responses to deliver an impartial and consistent product to their clients.

This ideal of the dispassionate professional distances us from ethical and political values. Think of the words used to describe the disciplined objective professional, whether it be scientist, doctor or lawyer: impartial, dispassionate, disinterested. These become pejorative terms in a difficult world crying for compassion, interest, concern, commitment and involvement. Disinterest is appropriate for a neutral arbitrator but not for an advocate. In fact, most often design education trains students to think of themselves as passive arbitrators of the message between the client/sender and audience/receiver, rather than as advocates for the message content or the audience. Here is the challenge: how to achieve the objectivity and consistency of professionalism without stripping oneself of personal convictions.

Our concept of graphic design professionalism has been largely shaped, and generally for the better, by the legacy of 20th century Modernism as it has come to us through the Bauhaus and Swiss lineages. However, there are several dominant aspects of this Modernist ethic that have done much to distance designers from their cultural milieu. The ideals, forms, methods and mythology of Modernism are a large part of this problem of detachment, including the paradigms of universal form, abstraction, self-referentialism, value free design, rationality and objectivity.

Objective rationalism, particularly that of the Bauhaus, provided a much needed antidote to the sentimentality and gratuitous eclecticism found in nineteenth century mass production, visual communications and architecture. Linked to functionalism, objective analysis formed the basis of problem-solving methods to generate functional design solutions to improve the quality of daily life. Expanded more recently to include systems design, this attitude has done much to elevate the quality of design thinking.

Linked to the ideal of the objective clear-sighted designer is the ideal of value-free universal forms. Perhaps a reaction to the frequent political upheavals between European nations, especially World War I, early Modern designers hoped to find internationalist design forms and attitudes that would cross those national, ethnic and class barriers that had caused such strife. In addition, a universal design—one design for all—would be appropriate for the classless mass society of industrial workers envisioned by early 20th century social reformers.

But passing years and different national contexts have brought different results from the application of these Modernist design paradigms. The myth of objectivity unfortunately does much to disengage the designer from compassionate concerns. Strongly held personal convictions would seem to be inappropriate for the cool-headed objective professional. Functionalism is narrowly defined in measurable utilitarian terms. Too often this means serving the client's definition of function—generally profits—over other concerns, including safety, the environment, and social/cultural/political/environmental impacts. Universalism has brought us the homogenized proper corporate style based mainly on Helvetica and the grid, ignoring the power and potential of regional, idiosyncratic, personal or culturally specific stylistic vocabularies. And the ideal of value-free design is a dangerous myth. In fact all design solutions carry a bias, either explicit or implicit. The more honest designs acknowledge their biases openly rather than manipulate their audiences with assurances of universal "truth" and purity.

Abstraction, Modernism's revolutionary contribution to the visual language of art and design, further distances both designer and audience from involvement. Stripped of imagery, self-referential abstraction is largely devoid of symbols and disconnected from experience in the surrounding world, cool and low on emotion. Abstraction is predictable in application—polite, inoffensive and not too meaningful—thereby providing a safe vocabulary for corporate materials. Imagery, on the other hand, is richly loaded with symbolic encoded meaning, often ambiguous and capable of arousing the entire range of human emotions. Imagery is difficult to control, even dangerous or controversial—often leading to unintended personal interpretations on the part of the audience—but also poetic, powerful and potentially eloquent.

The Modernist agenda has conspired to promote an attitude of apoliticism among American designers, design educators and students, building on the pragmatic American tendency to avoid political dialectics. American designers consistently take European theories and strip them of their political content. Of the various strains of Modernism, many of which were socially concerned or politically revolutionary, American design either chose those most devoid of political content or stripped the theories of their original political idealism.

More recently we have seen a strong interest in French literary theory. But its original element of French contemporary Marxism has been largely ignored in the U.S., perhaps rightly so. The American political environment is far different from the European; European political dialectics may not be appropriate to us. Yet we cannot assume that no political theory is needed to ground our work—all designers need an appropriate framework to evaluate and assess the impacts of their work within its social/ethical/political milieu. Perhaps this evaluative framework is different for each individual, dependent on the values of each, reflecting our strong tradition of American individualism.

Designers must break out of the obedient neutral servant-to-industry mentality, an orientation that was particularly strong in the Reagan–Thatcher–Bush years, and continues to dominate design management and strategic design. Yes, we are problem-solvers responding to the needs of clients. But we must consider the problems we take on. Should one help sell tobacco and alcohol, or design a Presidential memorial library for a man who reads only pulp cowboy novels? Does society really benefit from a strategic plan for plastic housewares or fast food? The answers may be more subtle than a yes or no. But one thing is clear: design is not a neutral value-free process. A design has no more integrity than its purpose or subject matter. Garbage in, garbage out. The most rarefied design solution can never surpass the quality of its content.

A dangerous assumption is that corporate work of innocuous content is devoid of political bias. The vast majority of student design projects deal with corporate needs, placing a heavy priority on the corporate economic sector of our society. Commerce is where we are investing our assets of time, budgets, skills and creativity. This is a decisive vote for economics over other potential concerns, including social, educational, cultural, spiritual and political needs. This is a political statement in itself both in education and practice.

Postwar American art has greatly ignored societal issues as well. The self-reference of abstract expressionism and minimalism has been largely divorced from external conditions. Pop art embraced materialism more than it critiqued it. The more recent postmodernist ironic parodies have been full of duplicity and offer no program as antidote to the appalling paradigms they deconstruct. But the past several years have brought a new involvement by artists in the social-political environment round them. A recent book, *The Reenchantment of Art*, advocates a second postmodernism, a reconstruction that moves beyond the detachment of Modernism and deconstruction. Suzi Gablik, the author, wants an end to the alienation of artists and aesthetics from social values in a new interrelational audience-oriented art.

There are signs that this is happening. Issue-oriented art has been spreading like wildfire among graduate students in the fine arts. At Cranbrook and a number of other design programs, fine arts students are attending graphic design critiques, eager to learn design methods for reaching their audiences. Fashion advertising is beginning to occasionally embrace issues— perhaps humanistic content is good for sales. Witness Esprit, Benetton, Moschino. That these clients are prepared to make social advocacy part of their message is evidence of a need and receptivity in their audiences. But are many graphic designers prepared to deal with this type of content? Graphic design is a powerful tool, capable of informing, publicizing, and propagandizing social, environmental and political messages as well as commercial ones.

How does the compassionate design shape a practice? The occasional pro bono piece as a relief from business as usual is not the answer here. The choice of clients or content is crucial. The most fortunate can find a worthy cause in need of a designer with the funds to pay for professional design services. Unfortunately, good causes often seem to have the least resources in our present economic system. Is it possible to shape a practice around non-business clients or introduce social content into commercial work? The compassionate designer must strategize an ethical practice and be an informed, involved citizen in a Jeffersonian participatory democracy, agile and flexible, prepared to turn the tools of visual communications to a broad spectrum of needs.

How does one educate graphic design students with an understanding of design as a social and political force? Can a political consciousness be trained? Can an educator teach values? The answer is probably no in the simplistic sense. However, the field of education has a well-developed area referred to as values clarification that offers many possibilities for graphic design educators. Too often we take individuals with eighteen years of experience and strip them of their values, rather than cultivate them for effective application in design practice.

In teaching, these issues must be raised from the beginning for the design student. This is not something to spring on the advanced student after their attitudes have been fixed on neutrality. At the core of this issue is the content of the projects we assign from the very first introductory exercise. Most introductory graphic design courses are based on abstract formal exercises inherited from the Bauhaus and the classic Basel school projects. The detachment problem begins here. These projects either deal with completely abstract form—point, line and plane, for instance—or they remove imagery from context. The graphic translation projects, so effective in training a keen formal sense, unfortunately use a process of abstractional analysis, thereby stripping imagery of its encoded symbolism. (I have to admit to being guilty of this in my assignments in past years.) Divorcing design form from content or context is a lesson in passivity, implying that graphic form is something separate and unrelated to subjective values or even ideas. The first principle is that all graphic projects must have content.

The type of content in each assignment is crucial. It is disheartening to see the vast number of undergraduate projects dedicated to selling goods and services in the marketplace devoid of any mission beyond business success. Undoubtedly all students need experience in this type of message and purpose. But cannot projects cover a broad mix of content, including issues beyond business? Cultural, social and political subjects make excellent communications challenges for student designers.

Project assignments can require content developed by the student dealing with public and personal social, political and economic issues and current events. The responsibility for developing content is a crucial one; it counteracts the passive design role in which one unquestioningly accepts client-dictated copy. On a practical level, we know how frequently all designers modify and improve client copywriting; many graphic designers become quite good writers and editors, so closely is our function allied to writing. In a larger sense, however, self-developed content and copy promotes two important attitudes in a design student. One is the ability to develop personal content and subject matter, executed independently of client assignments, where the reward is the expression of personal concerns. Secondly, the challenge to develop subject matter stimulates the design student to determine what matters on a personal level. A process of values clarification must go on in the student before a subject or subject-matter position can be chosen. And the breadth of concerns chosen as subjects by fellow students exposes each student to a wider range of possibilities.

The critique process for issue-oriented work can be a very effective forum for values clarification. This is particularly true of group critiques in which all students are encouraged to participate, rather than the authoritarian traditionalist crit in which the faculty do all the speaking. In evaluating the success or failure of a piece of graphic communications, each critic must address the subject matter and understand the design student's stated intentions before weighing a piece's success. This expands the critique discussion beyond the usual and necessary topics of graphic method, form and technique. Tolerance, as well as objectivity, are required of each critique participant, in that they must accept and understand the student's intended message before evaluating the piece.

For instance recently two fundamentalist Christian students brought their religiously oriented work to Cranbrook graphic design crits during a two-semester period. It was a challenge—and a lesson in tolerance—for the other students to put aside their personal religious (or non-religious) convictions in order to give these students and their work a fair critique from a level playing field. It was quite remarkable—and refreshing—to find us all discussing spirituality as legitimate subject matter. This has held true for many other subjects from the universe of issues facing our culture today, including local and global environmental issues, animal rights, homelessness, feminism and reproductive choice.

The point here is content. As design educators, we cast projects almost as a scientist designs a laboratory experiment. The formula and the variables conspire to slant the results in one direction or another. The project assignment and the project critique are powerful tools that teach far more than explicit goals, and carry strong implicit messages about design and designer's roles.

Design history also offers a rich resource for understanding the relationship of form and content to socio-political contexts. We all know how often works from art and design history are venerated (and imitated) in an atmosphere divorced from their original context. By exploring the accompanying cultural/social/political histories, students can see the contextual interdependencies and make analogies to their present time.

Am I advocating the production of a generation of designers preoccupied with political activism, a kind of reborn 60s mentality? I think rather what I have in mind is nurturing a crop of active citizens—informed, concerned participants in society who happen to be graphic designers. We must stop inadvertently training our students to ignore their convictions and be passive economic servants. Instead we must help them to clarify their personal values and to give them the tools to recognize when it is appropriate to act on them. I do think this is possible. We still need objectivity, but this includes the objectivity to know when to invoke personal biases and when to set them aside. Too often our graduates and their work emerge as charming mannequins, voiceless mouthpieces for the messages of ventriloquist clients. Let us instead give designers their voices so they may participate and contribute more fully in the world around them.

CHAPTER FIFTEEN

Feminist Perspectives (Design for Society)

NIGEL WHITELY

CRITIQUES OF PATRIARCHY

As contemporary feminism began to gather momentum following the radical political and social questioning of the late 1960s, it seemed inevitable that consumerist design would be confronted head-on in feminist critiques. For, if design was an expression of society, and society was patriarchal, design would reflect male domination.[1] Following on from the more general critiques published in the late 1960s and early 1970s—such as Kate Millett's *Sexual Politics* (1969), Eva Figes' *Patriarchal Attitudes* (1970), and Germaine Greer's *The Female Eunuch* (1970)—which concentrated on society's social and political construction of femininity, a strand of feminist criticism focused on the contexts and ideologies in which consumerist design operated. The use of gender stereotyping in advertising—as discussed, for example, in Judith Williamson's *Decoding Advertisements* (1978)—was relatively easy prey because it was so blatant; a more complex subject was the various forms of 'women's work' in the home. Books such as Ann Oakley's *Housewife* (1974), and Ellen Malos's book of extracts dealing with *The Politics of Housework* (1980) exposed the underlying patriarchal assumptions about housework and the role of women.

Two keyworks of this strand of feminism in the early 1980s—one American, one British—were Ruth Schwartz Cowan's *More Work for Mother: The Ironies of Household Technology from the Open Hearth to the Microwave* (1983) and Caroline Davidson's *A Woman's Work is Never Done: A History of Housework in the British Isles 1650–1950* (1982). Both brought into focus the relationship between housework and the development of domestic technological items such as washing machines, irons and microwaves. Also from the United States was Dolores Hayden's *The Grand Domestic Revolution: A History of Feminist Designs for American Houses, Neighbourhoods and Cities* (1981), while in Britain, Leonore Davidoff and Catherine Hall's essay on "The Architecture of Public and Private Life" (1982) informed the feminist debate. Marion Roberts's *Living in a Man-Made World* (1991) has added a highly valuable British perspective to this earlier work.

Paralleling these studies, feminist design histories attempted to redress some of the bias that had resulted from a patriarchal view of history. One of the first books, Isabelle Anscombe's *A Woman's Touch: Women in Design from 1860 to the Present Day* (1984) was critically berated by most feminist design historians because it failed to question the underlying male values and assumptions about design practice and history. A similar reception greeted Liz McQuiston's *Women in Design—A Contemporary View* (1988), which merely profiled a number of female designers without questioning the foundation of femaleness in relation to design and the design profession. The various conferences and discussion groups on the theme of women in design gave rise to the more recent *A View from the Interior: Feminism, Women and Design* (1989), edited by Judy Attfield and Pat Kirkham, which presents a series of essays that map out the issues that are pertinent to feminist design and history.

The 1980s also saw the development of specialist feminist architecture and design groups. The Feminist Design Collective, started in London in 1978, was formed with the aim of understanding and developing a feminist approach to architecture through discussion and practice. The group transmogrified into the Matrix collective in 1980, continuing the aim of providing advice, information and designs for, among others, women's community groups. Their *Making Space: Women and the Man-Made Environment* was published in 1984. Matrix were able to offer free advice while they were funded by the Greater London Council, whose Women's Committee also addressed a range of issues directly that affected women in the built environment. The Women's Design Service (WDS), an information and resource centre on women and the built environment, publishes a magazine, WEB, subtitled "Women and the Built Environment", which deals with such issues as housing, leisure, children's play spaces and crèches facilities. The Women's Environmental Network (WEN) is a pressure and campaign group that was formed in 1988 "to give ordinary women clear information about the environmental problems that affect them specifically—like consumer goods, pregnancy and radiation, things you eat and buy every day, the transport system and development plans."

In spite of the enormous importance of feminist critiques of design, and in spite of the wealth of books on various aspects of feminism in the last decade, depressingly little has been published specifically about feminist design. Some major contributions to an understanding of feminism and design, including Phil Goodall's "Design and Gender" essay (1983), have been tucked away in relatively esoteric, small-circulation journals such as *Block*. *Feminist Arts News (FAN)* devoted an issue to design in 1985 but, again, its circulation is small. One could argue that this relative paucity of material is healthy, in that feminism should not be packaged into discrete areas of activity such as 'design': to attempt to do so is to fall into the male academic practice of separation through specialization. Because the major feminist issues are all embracing and holistic, design should not be discussed in isolation.

The counter-argument is more convincing: design should be directly discussed because, according to the editors of *FAN's* issue on design:

"...design is so pervasive in our lives. We sit on it, live in it, eat off it, work with it, read it, see through it, wear it. As a branch of professional expertise design works on environments, objects and images. It's also an everyday activity that most of us engage in. Design has an economic role and social effects. Since the processes that lead to the formation of commodities are crucial to material culture, design as a terrain needs to be understood. Particularly by women, as we live in a material world largely not of our making (though with consent) and our role is predominantly to respond or consume rather than one of initiation and production."[2]

Furthermore, design tells us about the society in which we live. It should be studied, in the words of the design historian Cheryl Buckley, because it "is a process of representation. It represents political, economic, and cultural power and values ... Designs, as cultural products, have meanings encoded within them which are decoded by producers, advertisers and consumers according to their own cultural codes."[3] Nor, in Buckley's view, is it the case that work on feminism and design is not being undertaken, it's just that it "rarely seems to get published."[4]

Books about design, as any cursory visit to a bookshop will reveal, almost invariably deal with 'star' designers (usually male), historical design movements (which show a male bias in their conventional, patriarchal approach), or professional, male-determined organizations and activities. This is even true of fashion design, which is traditionally associated with women and which is certainly more actively practised by women designers than industrial product design. Until the publication of feminist books on fashion, such as Elizabeth Wilson's *Adorned in Dreams: Fashion and Modernity* (1985), fashion books upheld and promoted *femininity* (with its connotations of decorativeness and triviality), as opposed to *femaleness,* as the essence of female clothing.

Buckley's advice to design historians is equally valid to those writing about contemporary design: "one of the main issues for historians to tackle ... is patriarchy and its value systems."[5] This includes the terms and processes by which inferior status is assigned to certain design activities. The ideological nature and implications of terms such as 'feminine', 'delicate' and 'decorative' within the context of women's design need to be understood and challenged. Second, it is crucial that design historians recognize the patriarchal bias of the sexual division of labour which attributes to women certain design skills on the basis of biology. Third, in Buckley's words, design historians must acknowledge that women and their designs fulfil a "critical structuring role in design history in that they provide the negative to the male positive—they occupy the space left by men." And finally, historians should take note of the value system which gives privilege to exchange-value over use-value, because at a very simple level, as Elizabeth Bird has pointed out, "the objects women produce have been consumed by being used, rather than preserved as a store of exchange-value. Pots get broken and textiles wear out."[6] If we examine consumerist design from a feminist perspective, then both inadequacies in its functional performance, and certain implicit values and meanings, become ever more apparent.

GENDER STEREOTYPING

The two major feminist criticisms of marketing-led design are that it stereotypes women in a sexist way, and that it disregards women as endusers. The two criticisms are interrelated because both result from a patriarchal society, in which women are granted an inferior status to men.

Gender stereotyping, as mentioned above, has always been most readily observable in advertising. Women are usually depicted as mothers, cleaners, cooks or beautiful appendages; that is, in a serving and/or servile role. They represent the general carer or dutiful servant who maintains order so that others (men and children) can get on with their lives; the provider of sustenance and primary needs; or the sex object who underlines a man's status, power or attractiveness. Women in advertising act as if the latest washing powder, floor cleaner or deodorant is the ultimate answer to their existential problems on Planet Earth. They provide *meaning* for a product both in terms of its supposed necessity and its apparent level of success: "advertising creates both an ideal use for a product and an ideal user."[7] And if the ecstasy does not derive directly from a product, it is implicitly suggested by means of a woman's sexual attractiveness and availability, that it will be unleashed by the man who buys the new car or aftershave. A product's meaning is determined by its social, cultural and political context. Advertisers are well aware of this: advertising is an attempt to create or enhance meaning via association or evocation. It is a way of making the product more desirable because of its 'added value'.

It has always been a limiting view to think of design as a straightforward problem-solving activity. Products are not—and, in consumerist society, certainly not—bought just to fulfil primary functions or use-value. They are also bought to confirm status, confer prestige and, in a general sense, to satisfy longing (if only temporarily). It might be argued that many products—such as washing powder—are not intrinsically stereotyped. This is true but, in a consumerist society, it is not possible neatly to separate out a product's function from its image, or its use-value from its exchange-value. Unless you have somehow contrived to cocoon yourself from the media and advertising, when you buy a product you are consuming a total mix of the product and its meaning. And it is the advertisers' and marketers' hope that—as in the case of a lifestyle product like Coca Cola—*they* have fixed the meaning so that it will have the maximum effect in the marketplace. This may all, of course, be obvious to the reader, but it is necessary to make the point that the meaning of a product cannot be derived solely from an analysis of its particular form and decoration. Most contemporary cultural critics would deny that we can enter an art gallery—let alone the marketplace—with a disinterested aesthetic faculty attuned to abstract form, as Formalist critics might have supposed. We take to an analysis of any consumerist product external societal and cultural factors that shape our perception and understanding.

Washing powder may not be intrinsically stereotyped—even its packaging and graphics may be gender-free—but many products wear their stereotyping as blazenly as a sloganized T-shirt. Any shop or catalogue with a range of product lines will almost certainly offer 'feminine' versions of a product. Mugs with delicate and detailed pictures of flowers or sentimentalized cuddly animals, and casserole dishes and saucepans with romantic images of nature in contrived patterns or vistas, are all aimed at the conventional 'feminine' woman. Products associated with cooking or the kitchen—the 'woman's realm'—are often treated in this unsubtle way. The situation is more complex when it comes to technological products. If the product is located in the kitchen, such as a toaster, it is likely to receive the same 'feminine' graphic treatment, especially as kitchen accessories are increasingly graphically co-ordinated.

Personal technological products utilize form and colour to denote femininity or 'difference'. The woman's electric or battery-operated shaver, for example, is a relatively recent product development compared to its male counterpart. Male shavers are almost invariably 'masculine': matt black and/or silver, sometimes with red-line highlighting like a sports car; monolithic and chunky; and sometimes with a 'rugged' texture, supposedly to improve handling. Apart from the different location and different coarseness of body hair, shaving is essentially a common activity and the electric shaver could be a unisex product— the extra power that the male shaver needs for facial hair would not damage female skin, and the ergonomic differences of design resulting from body location are minor (some female shavers are ergonomically identical to male shavers). Yet most female shavers are clearly gendered through colour (white for purity or hygiene; or colour for fashionability) and form (less monolithic, more curved, and more 'elegant'). So whereas male electric or battery shavers signify technology and powerfulness (and so masculinity), female shavers connote hygiene, prettiness and fashionability (and thus femininity). The norm is, needless to say, the male shaver: the female shaver, in departing from the norm, reinforces women as 'different'. Beyond mere product design and styling, the whole question of female shavers raises the feminist issue of depilation. Women are indoctrinated to remove visible body hair because of its direct confirmation of body processes, and because the smooth- and silky-skinned female body, associated with the pre-independent female child, constitutes the 'feminine' ideal. This time-consuming and, for many feminists, pointless and reactionary activity adds to the burden of women's labours. Manufacturers would argue that they were only responding to consumers' demands, but this misses the point that these 'demands' are socially constructed and developed. The rise of the female shaver, a marketing and economic triumph, demonstrates the anti-feminist tendencies of consumerist design: upholding gender stereotyping and maintaining social pressures.

The comments about the design and styling of the female shaver show that to stereotype femininity as simply images of flowers and furry animals is inadequate. Marketing theory now recognizes socio-psychological categories of consumers rather than categories based on type of work and income. 'Mainstreamers' may read romantic novels, show considerable loyalty to 'big name' brands, companies and retailers, and be attracted to conforming and confirming imagery such as flowers. Other groups have other tastes which are equally 'feminine'. 'Aspirers', for example, will seek the fashionable and socially prestigious and so may, in the case of shavers, purchase a Braun-like design of pure form and simplicity which is less overtly feminine, but ultimately still strongly gendered. 'Reformers' constitute the group most likely to reject marketingled design and its stereotyping, but 'reformers' are still consumers and, like 'Green consumers', seldom reject consumerism as a system.

Gender stereotyping in clothing is the most fully researched and welldocumented area of feminist critiques of design. Clothing is probably the most visible means of giving form to gender construction and femininity. Feminine clothes are 'pretty', 'delicate', 'decorative' or 'sexy'; they are designed for the satisfaction of the (male) viewer rather than the comfort of the (female) wearer. Laura Ashley clothing, for example, has endorsed femininity, albeit a slightly shifting vision of femininity, throughout the 1980s, from images of rural simplicity, through the 'romance [and] understated femininity' of patterns with 'the most delicate mix of lace and flowers', to 'Edwardian-inspired' formal ball-gowns which are "well-mannered, elegant, sensual and flattering ... happy at the smartest cocktail party, the finest restaurant, or the most intimate dinner for two."

Clothing does not only signify femininity visually, but also helps to determine it physically: many clothes are designed not only to look feminine, but also to consolidate feminine body movement and language. Elaborate garments may restrict movement or bring about discomfort or exposure if a woman moves in anything but a careful or demure way. Shoes are often neither ergonomic nor comfortable and subvert natural balance. They are also often flimsy and would fall apart easily if used for much more than standing in. Generally, feminine fashions constrict and inhibit movement while male fashions facilitate movement and activity. The feminine woman poses silently and statically; the masculine man is boisterously active. And fashionableness usually means a series of absurd manifestations of femininity. Some feminist writers argue that to reject fashion in favour of purely sensible and functional clothing (even if the functions—which implies particular activities and roles—are determined by women rather than men) is a puritanical denial of a creative expression. The fact that men have become less ashamed of admitting their participation in fashion and, more importantly, the rise of 'female' fashions which do not conform to feminine models—such as comfortable but inelegant shoes, and clothes which do not restrict or impede—show that femaleness is not necessarily incompatible with fashion.

Predictably enough, gender stereotyping percolates down to children's clothing; indeed, it is in this arena that it is most marked, in spite of the fact that children's bodies are less differentiated than adults. One interesting recent example is from one of the slightly more enlightened firms associated with 'aspirers'. The front of their catalogue illustrates the post-macho 'new man' caringly and lovingly protecting his baby. While the cover image may have broken with the stereotypes associated with children's clothing catalogues, the inside pages showed that the change was little more than cosmetic. Images of girls in decorative or over elaborate costumes, passive and coy, contrasted with boys in workaday clothes or activity outfits running, jumping or role playing at explorers or—in one case—mechanics, complete with smeared axle grease on their foreheads!

Toys are a crude and blunt microcosm of the adult world and its stereotypes. Girls' toys frequently promote patience (embroidery kits), grooming expertise ('My Little Pony') and care (nurses' outfits); they can be played with quietly and with little physical movement. Boys' toys are based on war and action; they encourage physical activity and noise. The activities related to boys' toys suggest a spreading area of space, while girls' toys are contained within an enclosing space: 'Action Man' (and his contemporary derivatives) take off in helicopters and space ships; 'Barbie' (and her friends) keep their spotless home in order awaiting the return of Ken. Her extended space is nothing more than the glittering ball, either at Ken's side or as a venue for meeting the Ken of her dreams.

Companies producing stereotyping marketing-led design would no doubt argue that they are providing what the public demands; this demand provides the meaning and validation of consumer- and marketing-led design. This may well be true, and it could be argued that the profitability of many such companies demonstrates it to be so. If the public demanded non-stereotyping design, then the companies would happily provide it. But, because of its patriarchal nature, society is hardly likely to demand it, and so marketing-led design plays a major role in upholding the socially and culturally reactionary status quo.

WOMEN AS USERS

The second feminist criticism of marketing-led design is that many products are badly designed in relation to women as users. In some cases products are so badly designed that they cause long-term injuries. Nurses, the feminist architect and designer Rosy Martin points out, "suffer from back injuries—it is the major reason for leaving the profession—yet where is the work on efficient patient-lifting machines?"[8] In a paper written for a conference on the 'Organisation and Control of the Labour Process', Margaret Bruce rightly complains that:

> "… irons are uncomfortable and heavy to use for sustained periods of time, tools for putting up shelves and mending cars are often heavy and are designed with the 'macho' man in mind, food mixers are clumsy, awkward to clean and clutter up work-tops, and fridge door and seals perish long before the useful life of the appliance has ended."[9]

The reason is, as Bruce goes on to demonstrate, that the vast majority of products are designed either *by* men (producers) *for* women (consumers), or by men for men. When consistent and regular, the effect on women can be as damaging psychologically as physically: "Women may be put off using power tools, such as drills, because they are heavy, unwieldy," writes Goodall:

> "[we] tend to assume that if we can't use them properly it is our fault, rather than a design feature that does not accommodate to our physical needs…Far from being designed in the light of scientific investigation into differentiated use, much familiar machinery originated in an industrial context or by rule of thumb, based on masculine experience. All too often men are content to let us go on thinking it is our incompetence rather than divulging their knowledge of tools in use which makes their capacities visible."[10]

This kind of experience confirms the negative attitude to machinery, equipment and technology that many women form during childhood and school, and which is reinforced by advertising and design in consumerist, patriarchal society. Cynthia Cockburn, in an essay about technological processes and productive machinery, questions whether the bias of male designers is conscious or 'planned':

This need not be conspiracy, it is merely the outcome of a pre-existing pattern of power. It is a complex point. Women vary in bodily strength and size; they also vary in orientation, some having learned more confidence and more capability than others. Many processes could be carried out with machines designed to suit smaller or less muscular operators or reorganised so as to come within the reach of the "average" woman.[11]

Cockburn's general point about machinery and industrial technology can be directly applied to Bruce's complaint about domestic technology. Men can be insensitive designers for women as users in two ways: first, by disregarding the physical characteristics of women; and second, by assuming that women feel as 'at home' with advanced technology as men— some do, but the majority will have developed less confidence through negative socialization processes.

The result of this, according to Cockburn, is that "the appropriation of muscle, capability, tools and machinery by men is an important source of women's subordination, indeed it is part of the process by which females are constituted as women."[12] It is not insignificant that it is almost always the male who controls the remote control unit of a television (power through technology); and who learns how to programme a video recorder (control through technology). Male familiarity with technology partly accounts for the relative expertise of men with videos, but the fact that women can master—it is interesting to note how ludicrous the word *mistress* sounds in this context—a sewing machine (which men usually find unfathomable) shows that machine expertise is not absolute but gendered (sewing machine = 'fiddly'= female/ 'women's work'). Furthermore, in the case of the video recorder, the male is likely to have had time to learn the operations while the female was busy with cooking, washing up, or getting the children ready for bed. The example of the video also raises a related design and women issue: with the advent of videos, entertainment and leisure has shifted to the home, so further 'imprisoning' many women.

WOMEN AS PROVIDERS

A product's implications and meaning cannot, therefore, be isolated from its social context. In no area of design is this more apparent than in the design of 'labour-saving' equipment. It is now a well-rehearsed argument that, since the advent of equipment and products marketed as cutting down the housewife's workload, the number of hours worked by most housewives on household and family chores has not only not decreased, but has actually risen.[13] This is not surprising in relation to the inter-war period, when the 'servantless home' was becoming the norm in comfortable middle-class circles, but it is a less predictable phenomenon for the post-war, consumerist period when the catch-phrase 'labour-saving' was employed with almost monotonous regularity in the marketing of household equipment. In fact, the housewife's workload climbed from 70 hours a week in 1950 to 77 hours twenty years later.[14] Ann Oakley in her research concludes that "the amount of time housework takes shows no tendency to decrease with the increasing availability of domestic appliances, or with the expansion of women's opportunities outside the home."[15] Nor is there any evidence to suggest that this trend has reversed in the last twenty years.

The increase is partly related to expectations: the *qualitative* demands of 'women's work' have increased. Cowan describes the change from house work as a chore to:

"... something quite different—an emotional 'trip'. Laundering was not just laundering, but an expression of love; the housewife who truly loved her family would protect them from the embarrassment of tattletale grey. Feeding the family was not just feeding the family, but a way to express the housewife's artistic inclinations and a way to encourage feelings of family loyalty and affection. Diapering the baby was not just diapering, but a time to build the baby's sense of security and love for the mother. Cleaning the bathroom sink was not just cleaning, but an exercise of protective maternal instincts, providing a way for the housewife to keep her family safe from disease."[16]

Housework acquired psycho-social meaning for the housewife through consumerist marketing and advertising.

In particular, expectations about meals changed in keeping with social mobility and consumerist values. Holidays abroad became more common from the 1960s; different types of restaurants based on national cuisine or specialist diets—for example, vegetarian—expanded the palette; and magazines and colour supplements bombarded their readers with mouthwatering but time-consuming suggestions to break away from the monotony of 'meat-and-two-veg'. Not only did a new vocabulary and grammar of cooking have to be learned, but a new range of equipment was necessary to grind, shred, liquidize and pulverize. A mixer became an 'essential' kitchen machine because it carried out difficult functions speedily, but it also brought with it fiddly and difficult cleaning needs. Goodall makes a telling point: "The use of mixers to provide omelettes for 200 saves time, and effort. With the same operation for a family of four a proportionally large time is spent preparing the machine for use."[17]

The microwave cooker is another product which can actually increase workload, although it is supposed to increase convenience and lessen time. Instead of the family sitting down to eat the same food together at one time, the microwave is sold as providing 'flexibility', which means, in effect, that different members of the family can eat different meals at different times. If labour is spread across the family, the housewife's workload will be decreased, but if she is expected to take control of all the meals, then her time is eaten into. The advantage and flexibility of the microwave is gained by the consumers (the family) at the expense of the producer's (the housewife's) time. Feminist critiques of labour-saving devices seldom suggest a wholesale ransacking of the kitchen. For Judy Attfield, "It is one thing to discuss how masculine technology which produced household appliances has not really liberated women from the home, but quite another to throw away our automatic washing machine."[18] Technology has clearly brought benefits to the quality of life, but it is certainly not neutral in its effects and implications, especially when it comes to gender roles in a consumerist, patriarchal society.

STYLE AND GENDER

The two major feminist criticisms of consumerist design—that it stereotypes and that it is badly designed for women as users—frequently overlap. The visual appearance of many consumerist items, especially the technological items, compounds gender difference and discourages or alienates potential or actual female users by making the devices look more difficult to use than they actually are. A colleague puts it this way:

"Many products I find alien and therefore inaccessible because of the way they *look*. Cars, stereo-and video-equipment is designed for male customers: shiny, black, hard-edged, machine-like, technological. Women do use machines but they have a less-aggressive look, e.g. vacuum-cleaners, cookers, sewing machines, and some unisex typewriters. Machines used by men are considered 'technology'; whereas women's machines are not."[19]

There is, however, a danger that while men's consumerist technology appears mysterious and technologically advanced, women's consumerist technology could merely be packaged in some other, equally formulated way. Sometimes the ergonomic appearance of men's design indicates that this design is being designed ergonomically; whereas consumerist design for women looks less ergonomic because it is more 'feminine', and is poorly made. My colleague again:

"Men's tools—such as DIY—are taken seriously and designed sturdily; women's tools are not. Vacuum cleaners, brooms and dustpans are plasticy, flimsy and brightly-coloured with 'taste' in mind in spite of the fact that women use these tools much more frequently than, say, a man might use a power drill or hedgetrimmer. These items are not made to the same standard."

The last few years have witnessed a partial reaction against overtly macho styling, and even ergonomic appearances, in favour of what has variously been called 'sensorial'[20] or 'soft',[21] in which sensual qualities have been given greater import. But the arrival of what might be considered a more female attitude to technology has to be treated with caution. Martin claims that:

"This move away from the 'hard' forms and manifestations of technology, the hard-edged black box, towards a consideration of the sensual, comfort response, subjectivity is to be welcomed since it implies a greater understanding of people's psychological and sensory needs. On the other hand, it also highlights the marketing of such desires and pleasures as commodities and this addition of a 'feminine' ingredient to product design is most certainly *not feminist*."[22]

'Soft' styling, in other words, may be just another superficial consumerist aesthetic which ignores all the basic feminist issues—it may be no more than femininity for designer-consumers. 'Soft' styling may indeed utilize an approach to ergonomics that is more inclusive and which deals with psychological and psycho-social factors. However, the commodification of perceived needs or desire, which Martin refers to and which lies at the heart of marketing-led design, may remain unquestioned and unchallenged.

An interesting example of function, form and gender is illustrated by Bruce. She examines a range of prototype irons that were created by male and female industrial design students in response to an identical brief, arguing that the "female student's prototype has taken into account the fiddly bits—ironing sleeves, gathers, tucks—so that the rounded top reaches the places other irons can't."[23] She concludes that the "male designer was much more concerned with 'style', the female with 'user need', namely, the problem of ironing sleeves and making a compact iron."[24] Whether this particular distinction would be upheld by further analysis is less important than the general point that Bruce is making: the different approaches of the students arise out of their respective 'successful' induction into gendered roles in a patriarchal society.

DESIGNING WITH 'TACIT KNOWLEDGE'

What usually happens, because of the paucity of female industrial designers, is that women's 'tacit knowledge' is not drawn upon. Design methodologists acknowledge that 'tacit knowledge' is an essential component of the skills and qualitative decision-making processes of designers. It is the difference between 'knowing what' and 'knowing how': the former refers to the explicitly stated rules of doing something; the latter is the implicitly and internalized knowledge of doing something. 'Tacit knowledge' is knowledge 'we know but cannot tell'; it is intrinsically non-verbal, is derived from experience, and often makes the difference between doing something in a satisfactory manner, and doing it well. Anyone can learn what to do by following the rules or instructions for an activity such as cooking or playing tennis, but it is only once you have internalized the rules and developed a *feeling* for the activity, based on experience and the need for judgements and 'fine tuning', that you are likely to do it well. Of course, the criterion of goodness or success in an activity may vary. This is indeed what happens in design. Male designers applaud other male designers and award prizes for their formalistically breathtaking, but often functionally mind-numbing, objects of desire. An iron, to return to a previous example, may be aesthetically pleasing and visually sophisticated by the standards of a classical aesthetic, but it may still be poor at coping with the 'fiddly' bits of a sleeve. Men's 'tacit knowledge' may be at its best when dealing with the visual discriminations and niceties of abstract form, whereas women's 'tacit knowledge', because of their socialization and experience, may relate more to an object's use and/or 'meaning'. Of course, this is not to say that a female designer can never be as inspired as a male designer in the realm of abstract form: individuals often confound their socialization, or may occasionally even manage to avoid it entirely. At the other extreme, women may be socialized into a male preserve, and thus become 'honorary' members, and play by male rules. This, in effect, is the option open to female industrial designers.

DESIGNING IN A MAN'S WORLD

Industrial design is a man's world—literally. Only about two per cent of British industrial design graduates are women. Women tend to enter the traditionally female/feminine realm of fashion and textiles and, to a lesser extent, graphics and illustration (where there is a balance of genders). Male students heavily outweigh female students in interiors, furniture and ceramic courses. The percentage gets worse when one looks at the design industry, in which less than one per cent of industrial designers are women. The Design Innovation Group's work between 1982 and 1984 on British manufacturing companies employing from twenty-five to two thousand people showed that in a typical sector (office furniture), 72 per cent of firms employed in-house industrial designers, but only one company employed a woman in this capacity. International comparison found that a similar situation obtained in European companies, although 20 per cent of the industrial designers employed by Japanese companies were female. Of the forty-three international female designers in McQuiston's book, *Women in Design,* only a handful identified themselves as industrial designers, and none mentioned or revealed feminist or female concerns in her statement or the designs depicted in the book. (To back up the Design Innovation Group's findings, virtually half the selected designers worked in graphics or animation. Fashion design, where some of the most feminist designers might have been located, was not even included in the book.)

The quantitative situation of women in industrial design may improve in the later 1990s as the competition for jobs slackens, due to demographic changes, and women have more opportunity to resume careers in their middle years. Schools and colleges may also change the way that they approach or market design to make it less technical and masculine. However, there is still little prospect of equal numbers, and females are likely to remain a definite minority, as will female tutors. The unwritten rules of the game are likely to remain masculine and so, as Bruce and Jenny Lewis lament:

"Women working in such male-dominated environments cannot relax and 'be one of the boys', are not privy to the private conversations and networks of the men and so do not have the same support channels as their male colleagues and so on. This is by no means a trivial point, as it determines who gets on and who does not in career terms."[25]

In the Design Innovation Group survey previously cited, industrialists unambiguously voiced their perception of industrial design as being 'a job for the lads': "Consistently, product design was described as 'technical', 'dirty' and 'industrial' with the implication that this profession is not suitable for women. The work requires the ability to liaise with production engineers "who would not take orders from or listen to a woman."[26] Patriarchal attitudes will inevitably change more slowly than material conditions.

The last quotation begins to give some indication of the qualitative situations of women working in industrial design. The professional and organizational structure of marketing-led industrial design consultancies is especially male-dominated, making great use of male networks and male bonding which heighten women's disadvantages. Hours are long and unpredictable and a young aspiring designer has to demonstrate total commitment and boundless energy to meet client and project requirements. A female designer trying to manage both a career and a family in such circumstances will be enormously disadvantaged; as career breaks are unheard of, women tend to find themselves trapped at lower levels of the profession.

THE CULTURE OF DESIGN

But it is the professional ethos of marketing-led industrial design which is so profoundly anti-feminist. "The culture", write Bruce and Lewis, "is entrepreneurial—everyone competing individualistically for more money and more recognition, in terms of write-ups and rewards.[27] Many young designers in the consultancies reflect the naked egotism and brazen ambition of enterprise culture. Feminists reject the value system that underlies this attitude.

Bruce claims that because women are 'invisible' in the industrial design profession, and their 'tacit knowledge' not drawn upon, "designs and markets which meet women's needs and concerns are underdeveloped."[28] Would more women in design mean the growth of feminist design? Or are feminist and marketing-led design incompatible? Can consumerist design serve feminism and provide the goods and services that women believe would create an egalitarian and caring society? The fundamental conflict of values was highlighted in a 'face to face' conversation, transcribed in *Creative Review*, between Rodney Fitch, then managing director of what was once Britain's biggest design consultancy, and Jos Boys, a member of the Matrix group. The conversation focussed on the mid-1980s retail design boom, and whom it benefited. Boys identified the fundamental issue as:

"... the relationship between people and the places they use and live in...A lot of the environment is treated just on the level of appearances. Design becomes a series of events you pass through once. The city becomes a chaotic place, full of random, uncontrollable events, which can either excite you or alienate you depending on your resources. Whether or not you have a car or money affects your relationship with the environment."[29]

Boys's starting point is people, who may or may not desire to consume. Fitch's response, which is a claim that the retail environment responds to "customer needs, and the intelligibility of the design environment"[30] presumes as its starting point the customer or consumer. The difference is significant and resurfaces at other times in the conversation. When Boys complains that his account of design turns 'everyone into consumers', Fitch retorts:

"The problem with turning people into consumers is only a problem if you believe people shouldn't have things. I think people should have better things, lots of things, the more the better. The moment you think they shouldn't then you have a very superior view of what's good for people.[31]

Fitch's simple consumerist populism is premised on the financially autonomous consumer and disregards any questions about the public realm, and goods or services that cannot be consumed by materialistic individuals. In the act of consuming, according to Fitch, people "are expressing their preferences by claiming their individuality" (although one wonders whether his nouns were not meant in the reverse order).[32] In the consumerist value system, a definition of 'good design' is straightforward: "Whether environments or products, something that is well-designed not only looks good and works well but also sells. If it doesn't sell, it isn't good design."[33] In a way that is typical of marketing-led designers, Fitch returns always to the *sine qua non* of consumerism: making money.

The reply from Boys, as one might expect, was to question the very basis of Fitch's value system: "But I don't think designers should always take the priorities of the market as the norm. Some things are obvious to everyone *except* designers. Take lighting in relation to women and safety."[34] Boys could not be accused of naive anti-consumerism, and acknowledged during the conversation that people would always have to go shopping, but "people could be provided with other things in shops besides the opportunity to consume—such as nappy-changing facilities. There's a conflict between social needs in shops and the need to make the space pay."[35] In the end, Boys continued, consumerism always prioritizes profit maximization over social needs or even convenience:

> "Take department stores. In a male-dominated world, the men's department is on the ground-floor because men have the spending power and will only want to slip quickly in and out of a store. Mother with baby in a buggy will probably have to drag herself up several flights of stairs to find what she wants or go to the toy department."[36]

This was not a criticism Fitch had any sympathy with, and in his final statement he asserted that "we should disabuse the view that the female consumer is oppressed, downtrodden, powerless, never listened to." His next remark was perhaps truer than he realized: "I don't know what world you live in but it's not the world I live in."[37] The world of a (then) highly successful male entrepreneur is indeed very different from that of a feminist who often works with unwaged single-parent women on council housing estates!

DESIGN FOR CHILDREN

However, one must never underestimate the ability of consumerism (and, in a more general sense, capitalism) to adapt in order to respond to a changing situation. Sometimes there are products which women are happy to make use of which can be incorporated into the consumerist system. Women's needs and market forces can, so long as the woman is able to afford the products, operate for mutual benefit. In the last decade, such has increasingly been the case with a lot of the design associated with babies. First, it has to be acknowledged that to presume that designs for baby facilities fall within the woman's realm is itself stereotyping. Such designs ought to be unisex, and there is some indication that this is beginning to occur. If they are unisex, it is crucial that ergonomic considerations are based on the female user as much as the male. An 'average' woman must be able to manipulate the product without undue difficulty.

Some of the more recent 'buggy' pushchairs, for example, are now designed for one-hand assembly so that a mother trying to look after her child with one hand will also be able to assemble the pushchair from its collapsed position. Buggies provide an interesting illustration of the need for women's 'tacit knowledge'. In the past, design awards have been given (usually by men) for buggies in fashionable colours and 'go-faster' graphics which *looked* good (to men, because they reminded them of car styling) rather than because they were functionally superior. At one design ceremony that I attended, an award-winning buggy was scathingly criticized by a mother in the audience who claimed with considerable authority that it was extremely difficult to assemble and could trap fingers, that it overbalanced easily, that it had no shopping bag or parcel facility, and that it was not equipped with an easily attachable rain-hood. It transpired that the buggy was designed by a man who had no direct, everyday experience of using such a vehicle. And it is probably significant that it was male designers who orientated the seat so that it pointed forward, thus denying the child any contact with the parent, as well as facing the child toward the road with all its fumes, noise and dangers. Recent designs, making far greater use of women's 'tacit knowledge' have provided buggies and pushchairs with reversible swivel-seat units, integral shopping trays or bags, and adjustable handle heights. Improvements have been made in the lightness/strength ratio, which is of especial relevance to women. The problem of adequate, but easy-to-assemble and convenient to store, rain protection remains a problem.

'Tacit knowledge' is also being used to consider the pushchair in relation to its various ancillary functions. Buggies and pushchairs now have seats which can be removed to make way for a carry-cot. The carry-cot itself is adjustable and can fold away flat. Designs are even being considered for a pushchair seat which can be attached quickly but securely to a car seat. Needless to say, none of the designs mentioned above is cheap, for they retail at around £100. Consumerist design solutions always presuppose a financially viable consumer! Other recent consumerist products have made life easier for women as mothers. A device that plugs into a car lighter-socket to warm a baby's feeding bottle, and bowls and beakers with click-on plastic lids so that food and drink are portable, are useful products which make life less of a struggle.

Pro-consumerist writers argue that market forces are the best mechanism for giving the public what it wants, because they create the financial power to develop desired products. An example of socially useful product development for parents is an improved feeding bottle that is manufactured by Avent. It makes use of Silopren, a rubbery material with advantages of softness, durability, a lack of rubbery smell and taste, stability, and an ability to withstand hot and cold sterilization methods. The teat has a built-in skirt which clamps against the bottle when it is inverted, preventing leaks. When the baby sucks, negative pressure causes a valve to open and air is allowed in through tiny holes behind the skirt. Like a nipple, but unlike conventional teats, the Avent teat has several tiny holes, pierced by laser. The teat is fitted to a short, broad, wide-necked polycarbonate bottle. This shape of bottle makes mixing the infant feed easier than is the case with the more common tall and thin bottle, which has a neck opening the size of a large coin. Avent have also manufactured a breast pump which can be used to express breast milk using only one hand. Both of these products required the kind of painstaking and costly research and development (R&D) which only highly profitable and consumerist-orientated companies are able to afford.

Product development and innovation usually require a considerable R&D budget, and a frequent criticism of state-controlled industries was that in this area, particularly, inertia and poor standards predominated. The performance of manufacturing industries in what was the Eastern bloc countries was generally held up as evidence of this criticism. However, the counter argument is that the number of genuinely improved product developments, such as the infant-feeding equipment described above, constitute a very small proportion of consumerist products, the majority of which are unnecessary and wasteful of resources. There is no inherent reason why some form of non-consumerist structure could not produce socially useful products. The problem is ultimately a political one about the ownership of resources; determining social priorities; and the social ethos of the society.

For example, feminists might argue that the prohibitive price of improved products such as buggy-pushchairs could be circumvented if, say, maternity units at hospitals operated a loan system of equipment in the same way as some social service departments loan wheelchairs. Considering the relatively short period of time a buggy is needed, this would make economic sense to many parents at a time when expenditure increases for essential items like children's clothing. That this does not happen is due to a range of factors: economic (too little funding in the public sector); political (prioritizing private affluence for certain sectors of the population); social (people are encouraged to aspire to ownership); and commercial (consumerist companies would argue that this sort of scheme would undermine their profitability, and thus retard R&D).

ALTERNATIVE CRITERIA

When women design products, they are sometimes radically different from the existing norm. Research undertaken on women's criteria for car design revealed an emphasis on function, ergonomics and safety, which was at odds with the seductively advertised status symbols that massage the male ego.[38] Women claimed that they wanted functional, durable, environmentally friendly, low-speed cars which were easy to clean and maintain, even to the extent of having engine parts labelled to help do-it-yourself repair and maintenance. Seat heights would be adjustable and seat belts would be padded. Many of the health and safety features recommended by women—including rear seat-belts, childproof locks and lead-free petrol—have become more common as manufacturers try to gain a competitive edge by responding to the market. However, a ramp to lift or wheel a buggy or trolley directly into the car without any lifting; privacy for breastfeeding; and built-in entertainment for children do not seem to form part of the manufacturers' planning. Even more unlikely to be fulfilled is the call for a public car transport system, combining high-technology computers and low-energy, and renewable and non-polluting fuels, in which individual needs for convenience are met by numerous 'podlike' vehicles located in community spaces such as housing estates and health centres.[39]

The criteria underlying the community-linked transport system tie in closely with Boys's contention that the relationship between people and the places that they use is the fundamental issue for women in design. Such an approach takes the emphasis away from products and objects, and points it towards relationships and meanings. Other feminists have also attacked the consumerist ambition of identifying, encouraging or creating a desire, and then producing a product to fulfil it. Phil Goodall and Erica Matlow argue that:

"Well-intentioned feminists may still use unexamined assumptions about women's desire and about the nature of design and such a strategy serves to render femininity and female desire into commodity forms and further open-up womanhood to the market—not liberate them."[40]

They resolutely oppose the idea that design should be intrinsically, or even normally, concerned with producing *"things,* rather than social and economic relations or ideas, desires, pleasures, miseries".[41] Martin is in complete agreement: "Feminist design must ask the question of women: Is a product needed at all? Would a service, or a reorganisation of existing social or physical management be better than a product?"[42] This explains why so much feminist design thinking has been given over to considering socio-spatial issues rather than designs for products or commodities.

SOCIO-SPATIAL PERSPECTIVES

An example of a socio-spatial design in relation to retail is the provision of crèches and supervised play areas in shopping centres and some of the more progressive department stores such as Ikea. Crèche provision is of particular significance to women because research on shopping patterns undertaken by the Greater London Council's Women's Committee conclusively established that it is—as one could easily predict—women who bear the main burden of daily and weekly shopping for households. Ten percent of women are accompanied on their shopping trips by young children, and as a result "these expeditions are frequently slowed down or curtailed."[43] Some shops are now beginning to provide facilities, but other stores see social provision as hostile to profit. When questioned about their lack of special provision for children and their parents, Marks and Spencer surprisingly replied: "the provision of a breastfeeding/changing area is not necessarily in all our customers' interests. By introducing this facility we would considerably reduce our selling space."[44] Most women would unreservedly welcome childcare facilities which benefit both the parent or carer and the child,[45] but there remains a suspicion by feminists that the mother is being relieved of her offspring in order to make her a less harassed, more relaxed and therefore a 'better' (more receptive, more co-operative) consumer.

On the other hand, crèche provision means that isolated parents have the opportunity to make contact with other parents, and single parents and childminders can have a break and receive support. Analysis of one inner city crèche revealed the important role that crèches can play in helping parents and children from minority groups to integrate into local communities. In a society in which the public realm is threatened by privatized and profit-maximizing consumerist culture, a crèche in a shopping centre can help to provide a space for social intercourse—especially amongst women. Sue Cavanagh compares new shopping centres with:

"Older town centres [which] offer communities amenities such as clinics, dentists, libraries, etc, which do not only focus on consuming. They also offer more opportunities for informal social meetings and are usually more accessible by public transport or on foot from residential districts than the new shopping developments which tend to favour the more affluent car-owning shoppers."[46]

Out-of-town shopping complexes further disadvantage low-income women, the majority of whom are working-class and/or black, because these women lack private transport. The report published by the Women's Design Service details sixteen categories of design guidelines for crèche design, ranging from space and signposting to floor-surfaces and play equipment. However, the design guidelines cannot be divorced from the broader social and economic issues that relate to gender roles and expectations, financial provision and sources of funding, and the priorities determined by consumerist criteria (including the siting of shopping facilities). It cannot be over-emphasized that designers who deal only with 'solutions' to the perceived needs identified by consumerism, without questioning the social and gender implications of their work, may well produce attractive and appealing 'toys for the boys' which ignore, disregard, manipulate or stereotype women. Nothing can better illustrate a legitimate and urgent 'women's issue' in design.

That crèche provision is necessarily described as a 'women's issue' also illustrates our social and cultural attitude to childcare. As Cavanagh comments: "We look forward to a time when men are equally involved in domestic and caring tasks and see the provision of good public facilities for children and their carers as an important step towards making childcare more socially visible and valued."[47] Motorway services and some of the more progressive stores sometimes now offer a 'childcare room', whereas previously they may have signposted a 'mothers' room'. Some women may, however, regret the loss that a 'mothers' room' provides for privacy, or even just conversation with other women. Women, obviously, vary in their demands and values: ultimately one can no more talk about a singular and unified 'women's design' than one can talk of a 'men's design'—a point acknowledged by feminist writers.[48]

Design in relation to housing and housing estates is a further example of socio-spatial design that is of crucial concern to women. Goodall takes some satisfaction that women:

"...may have been active in tenants' campaigns, damp campaigns, in reclaiming public space for women's use from sexual harrassment and violence. [But women]...have been less active in demanding of planning authorities physical and spatial conditions that would make it possible to break down divisions by gender in personal and public life. Housing types are predicated on a limited number of household forms, the family, single persons, the elderly for example and do not readily allow for larger looser groupings. In their spatial capacity and form, as well as in their relation to workplaces, homes make a reorganisation of paid work and personal life practically impossible."[49]

Historians including Hayden, Roberts, and Davidoff and Hall have demonstrated the integral relationship between gender politics and the material form of domestic environment in both the United States and Europe. Houses have been increasingly designed around the model of the nuclear family, with a father who goes out to work, and a mother that stays at home, even though, nowadays, fewer than half of children come from such homes. Matrix refer to the 'privatization of family life' in which each household becomes more separate from the next; this may conform to the ideal of the 'home as castle', but it also isolates women from one another.[50] Communal wash-facilities or play-areas, ideas in good currency in some 1920s and 1930s public-housing design, for example, are less and less common today. Layout has, feminists would argue, reflected male priorities, with most ground-floor space being given over to entertainment and status, while the work areas for cooking and laundering have been tucked away into ever-smaller kitchens that are designed for one person—with the result that labour is less likely to be shared. Kitchens are usually placed at the rear of the house, where an interesting view is less likely—some houses of the 1950s placed kitchens at the front of the house so that they overlooked the street and the children's communal play areas, and thus acted to reduce the woman's sense of isolation.

Matrix complain that modern society "pays lip service to the importance of mothering but does not cherish its mothers."[51] The presence of a baby or young child reveals how many houses are ill-conceived for children. One mother describes the type of problem caused by an unsuitable spatial organization and layout:

> "Our hall is particularly narrow, so I knew a normal pram was out of the question and I bought one of those pram-buggies…When I wanted to go out I would have to 1) take the bouncing chair down to the hall, 2) come upstairs … and dress Kim in his outdoor clothes and take him down and strap him in the chair, 3) go upstairs and dismantle the pram and take the buggy wheels down to the hall, 4) go upstairs and carry the carrycot and blankets down to the hall (very difficult to manoeuvre this quite heavy object down the narrow stairs), 5) take the buggy wheels down the steep front steps to the pavement and set them up, 6) take the carrycot down to the pavement and fix it to the wheels, shouting through the open front door to Kim so he didn't feel abandoned, 7) rush in and get Kim … and carry him down the front steps and put him in the pram and *at last* set out on our expedition."[52]

This is not to suggest that all houses should be built to a standard pattern based around children, but it would surely make sense if considerably more were. A front door which has a ramp rather than two or three steep steps (or perhaps a combination), and a large, warm hall where a pram and, later, a tricycle can be kept, would be major design innovations. Again, perhaps, the lack of the 'tacit knowledge' of women in the design process—the number of practising women architects is shamefully low—is a cause of the problem.

The design of spaces on estates and in town and cities has also received considerable attention from women. The inconsiderate design of walls, garages and other structures can create unlit corners where intruders may hide. Lighting in and around buildings, particularly near doorways, car parks and alleyways, can make an environment potentially threatening and dangerous for a woman. Underpasses are a haven for muggers. The way spaces interconnect by means of stairs can disregard the needs of a mother with a pram, or disabled users. There are many such examples of poor design which need never have occurred, or which could be rectified by redesign.

SYMPTOMS OR CAUSES?

However, feminists are sometimes suspicious of the 'design fix' approach. One of the recommendations in the WDS's report on "Women's Safety on Housing Estates" expressed significant reservations about the role of design in solving the sorts of problems discussed in the report:

> "Solutions that are based solely on design changes are often inadequate and a waste of money. Design guidelines can sometimes trivialise the problem by appearing to reduce safety issues to a matter of appropriate design."[53]

In other words, an emphasis on treating the symptoms of a problem glosses over what may be its social and cultural causes. By presuming the change has to be with the effect rather than the cause, the design 'solution' can be seen to be accepting the status quo. Harrassment and threatening behaviour by men might be reduced by redesigning the environment and so limiting the opportunities for when it can happen, but the best solution would be a change in men's behaviour. Women rightly object when they are the ones who have to modify their activities and lifestyles ("don't go out alone at night"; "don't hitch a ride") because of men's behaviour. What is often presented as a design problem is really a social and cultural issue.

If the discussion is contained within the conventional design discourse it will miss the point. "Women", writes Martin:

> "...need to gain knowledge of the means to effect the decisions that control their material and social environment. Then designers would be better able to serve them, rather than perpetuating the power imbalances. This requires a political change ... Design in its broadest sense is power, control and defining new possibilities to aim for. So, as women, we need to criticise design from a position of knowledge, as users and as practitioners and to initiate new possibilities ourselves."[54]

One of the main problems, as Martin acknowledges, is that product designers:

> "...have the problem of the means of (mass) production; there are not (m)any feminist manufacturers to work with. There are a few women's Co-ops, however, and if the ideas of ... technology networks can be developed, there is a possibility for feminist industrial design practice to exist. It is also possible to construct the design brief and the design activity in a feminist way, and then try to convince manufacturers of the economic sense of producing an object thus researched."[55]

It would seem that, for the foreseeable future, feminist designers and critics will be able to effect but small changes on marketing-led design; manufacturers will, by and large, continue to respond to short-term, patriarchally determined demands in which perceived needs are quickly commodified. And some of those changes will occur only because they are in the manufacturer's financial interests. Any broader changes in design will only result from positive changes in the culture and politics of society. Consumerist design trades deeply and—in its terms—successfully on gender stereotypes for constructing the meaning of and context for a product, and it will remain fundamentally conservative. The issue of consumerist design and feminism again goes to show that the terms 'market' and 'society' are far from synonymous.

© 1993 Nigel Whitely. "Chapter 4: Feminist Perspectives", *Design for Society*, Reaktion Books, LTD, London, pp. 134–157. Reprinted by permission of the publisher.

NOTES

1. For a definition of patriarchy in relation to design, see Cheryl Buckley, "Made in Patriarchy: Toward a Feminist Analysis of Women and Design", *Design Issues*, Vo. 3, no. 2 (1987), pp. 3–14.
2. Phil Goodall and Erica Matlow, editorial, *Feminist Arts News* (December 1985), p. 3.
3. Buckley, op. cit., p. 10.
4. Ibid., p. 13.
5. Ibid., p. 6.
6. Ibid., p. 6.
7. Ibid., p. 9.
8. Rosy Martin, "Feminist Design: A Contradiction", *Feminist Arts News* (December 1985), p. 25.
9. Margaret Bruce and Jenny Lewis, "Divided By Design?: Gender and the Labour Process in the Design Industry", paper presented at the conference on "The Organisation and Control of the Labour Process", held at UMIST, Manchester, March 1989, p. 14. I am indebted to the author for a copy of her paper.
10. Phil Goodall, "Design and Gender", *Block*, no. 9 (1983), p. 54.
11. Cynthia Cockburn, "The Material of Male Power" in Donald MacKenzie and Judy Wajcman, eds, *The Social Shaping of Technology* (Milton Keynes, 1985), p. 139.
12. Ibid., p. 129.
13. See Ruth Schwartz Cowan, *More Work for Mother: The Ironies of Household Technology from the Open Hearth to the Microwave* (London, 1983), and Caroline Davidson, *A Women's Work is Never Done: A History of Housework in the British Isles, 1650–1950* (London, 1982).
14. See Ann Oakley, *Housework* (London, 1974), p. 7.
15. Ibid., p. 6.
16. Ruth Schwartz Cowan, "The Industrial Revolution in the Home" in MacKenzie and Wajcman, op. cit., p. 194.
17. Goodall, op. cit., p. 53.
18. Judy Attfield, "Feminist Designs on Design History", *Feminist Arts News* (December 1985), p. 23.
19. Karen Lyons in notes to the author, May 1988.
20. See Ettore Sottsass, *A Sensorial Technology*, Pidgeon slide-tape lecture, series 11, no. 8401 (London, 1984).
21. See Julian Gibb, "Soft: An Appeal to Common Senses", *Design* (January 1985), pp. 27–29.
22. Martin, op. cit., p. 24.
23. Margaret Bruce, "The Forgotten Dimension: Women, Design and Manufacture", *Feminist Arts News* (December 1985), p. 7.

24. Margaret Bruce, "A Missing Link: Women and Industrial Design", *Design Studies* (July 1985), p. 155.

25. Bruce and Lewis, op. cit., p. 29.

26. Ibid., p. 30–31.

27. Ibid., p. 35.

28. Bruce, "A Missing Link", op. cit., p. 150.

29. Jos Boys and Rodney Fitch, "Face to Face", *Creative Review* (July 1986), p. 28.

30. Ibid., p. 28.

31. Ibid., p. 29.

32. Ibid., p. 29.

33. Ibid., p. 29.

34. Ibid., p. 29.

35. Ibid., p. 29.

36. Ibid., p. 29.

37. Ibid., p. 29.

38. Bruce, "A Missing Link", op. cit., p. 154.

39. Ibid., p. 154.

40. Goodall and Matlow, op. cit., p. 3.

41. Ibid., p. 3.

42. Martin, op. cit., p. 26.

43. Sue Cavanagh, *Shoppers' Crèches: Guidelines for Childcare in Public Places*, Women's Design Service (London, 1988), p. 5.

44. Julie Jaspert, Sue Cavanagh and June Debono, *Thinking of Small Children: Access, Provision and Play*, Women's Design Service et al. (London 1988), p. 24.

45. Jaspert, Cavanagh and Debono point out that the word 'carer' is inclusive and accommodates relatives, family friends, childminders, nannies and au pairs.

46. Cavanagh, op. cit., p. 26.

47. Ibid., p. 3.

48. See, for example, "Women and the Built Environment", *WEB*, issue II, n.d., p. 3.

49. Goodall, op. cit., p. 60.

50. Matrix, *Making Space: Women and the Man Made Environment* (London, 1984), p. 55.

51. Ibid., p. 135.

52. Ibid., p. 123.

53. Vron Ware, *Women's Safety on Housing Estates*, Women's Design Service (London, 1988), p. 24.

54. Martin, op. cit., p. 26.

55. Ibid., p. 26.

CHAPTER SIXTEEN

There Is Such a Thing as Society

ANDREW HOWARD

© Andrew Howard, 1994

In 1964, British designer Ken Garland and a group of twenty-one colleagues issued a manifesto entitled "First Things First." Aimed at fellow graphic designers, it was a succinct and gutsy appeal to reject the "high pitched scream of consumer selling" and omnipotent lure of the advertising industry in favour of what was defined as socially useful graphic design work. The manifesto was reproduced in the publication *Modern Publicity*, together with an interview in which Garland attempted to defend it to Douglas Haines (described as a creative executive with British agency and marketing specialists Mather and Crowther), who was hostile to the idea that there is anything wrong with the marketplace or that the advertising industry does anything other than a good and necessary job.

What makes the manifesto interesting today is the realisation that its premises appear as radical now as they did thirty years ago. And more significantly, the issue it addresses is as unresolved now as it was then. But the manifesto also touches on a dimension that seems to be missing from current debate: a concern with the social function and purpose of graphic design. Discussion in the profession in the mid-1990s appears to have crystallised into a debate between two schools of thought. On the one hand there is the "new wave" of Macintosh-devoted design, some of which has been produced under the theoretical auspices of poststructuralist analysis and is guided by an exploration of the formal problems of representation and meaning, as in the work of the Cranbrook Academy of Art. Some of its exponents claim that their output represents a new aesthetic; their critics dismiss it as a form of visual pyrotechnics, a lavish aesthetic feast but low on nutritional content. Such critics believe that despite its stated intentions (where there have been intentions to state), this work is aimless and impenetrable.

On the other hand, a trend has emerged more recently that claims to seek a new clarity—of intention as well as aesthetic. Rick Poynor (*Eye* no. 9, vol. 3) suggests that there is a growing reaction by "design students, teachers, and young professionals" against what are seen as the "excesses" of formal experimentation and in favour of a less ambiguous, more message-related program. In the Netherlands, designers Dingeman Kuilman and Neils Meulman are calling for an approach that is not sophisticated, not technological, and not intellectual, just "basic" (*Émigré*, no. 25).

For some designers, and I would include myself and many of those I class as colleagues here, a search for formal solutions has only ever been a part of, not an alternative to, a longer-term socially and politically influenced project. For us (only an "us" in as much as we have histories and influences in common), to interpret much of what is characterised as "new wave" as playfully self-indulgent is not a refusal to "join in the party," nor does it signify lack of interest in new technologies and experimentation. Rather, it springs from a continuing interest that goes beyond a search for parts of the design jigsaw, of which formal visual vocabulary is a piece, to an understanding of how the jigsaw fits together.

It is perhaps understandable that recent debate has centred on conflicting ideas about what contemporary design should look like and what methods it should employ in order to create understanding: how it should function formally. The impact of computer technology has transformed the nature of the design activity, allowing designers to assume control (competently or not) of many stages in the production process that were traditionally shared among a number of people with different skills and expertise. It has also had a profound effect on aesthetics. The computer makes it possible to construct multifaceted compositions with relative ease and at vastly increased speeds. Its capacity for sampling, duplication, and the integrated assembly of all manner of visual elements has given designers the opportunity to view countless variations and to realise more visually complex ideas. Visual, formal possibilities have taken centre stage.

Discussion of content, apart from as formal exploration, has tended to concentrate on the internal subject matter of individual works. But there is another sort of content in graphic design: its social content as a form of social production. The significance of this lies in the ways in which function influences form and purpose informs content. It suggests that the character of our work is determined by more than our intentions alone, since production processes and the social context within which the work is received have a profound impact in directing, respectively, its aesthetic and the kinds of understanding it is capable of generating. These issues touch on the very definition of graphic design.

To see graphic design as a form of social production rather than as individual acts of creativity means recognising that it is subject to the same economic and ideological forces that shape other forms of human social activity. It means that in order to understand the nature of our activity and to think about its possibilities, we must be able to locate it within a historical context that relates it to economic and political forces. This is (strangely) problematic, as Anne Burdick rightly states (*Eye* no. 9, vol. 3), because "it is considered outside our role to analyse the content of our work in relation to politics, theory, economics, morals, and so on." But if the present debate is about creating a body of work that is meaningful to people in general, that plays a part in the development of a stimulating visual culture, then it must involve understanding how our culture functions, how it is shaped, and how it shapes our perceptions of ourselves. It means addressing people's need for a culture in which they can participate actively, for which they can help shape the agenda. It will inevitably involve an analysis of what prevents us from building such a culture.

The economic organisation of our society depends on the promise of ever-expanding production and the building of markets to absorb that production. We have the means to make goods in sufficient quantity and range to satisfy all our basic needs. But, "Goods are no longer sold on the basis that they satisfy a known and voiced human need, but instead demands are developed through 'research' and through marketing in order that commodities may be produced to meet them," explains Owen Kelly (*Community, Art, and the State: Storming the Citadels*, 1984). Goods are only a means to an end: the production of surplus value. Consequently, "there can be no such thing as sufficient production of any commodity, since there is no such thing as sufficient surplus value."

Whether one sees advanced capitalism and the consumer society as good or bad, one cannot ignore the ways they have encroached on previously private areas of consciousness. The building of markets is not a purely economic exercise: it is we, the "citizens" who are the intended markets, and their creation is very much an ideological task. This involves a process, explains Kelly, in which our needs are broken down into smaller and smaller units, "so that they match (and can be met by) the outputs of a profitable production process." "Thus, for example," says Kelly, "the desire to avoid giving off offensive odours is redefined as a positive, and normal, desire to achieve 'personal hygiene', and is pictured as a continuous, and inevitable, struggle in which only the deliberately anti-social would refuse to participate." Convinced of the need to obtain this "personal hygiene," we are offered our bodies divided into separate marketing zones—underarm, mouth, vagina, feet—within each of which, writes Kelly, "the consumer can be educated to make choices (roll-on or stick, fragrant or natural), and within each of which separate innovations are possible."

This fragmentation of our needs and desires does not operate only in relation to areas of industrialised production. It is paralleled in the operations of the state, from health and medicine to education and leisure, where we are taught to consume professionalized services. In this sense there are no areas of our personal lives that are not subject to the social pressures of the marketplace, wherein decisions that might have been made by consenting citizens are reduced to purchasing choices made by passive consumers. Since the 1950s and 1960s, writers have referred to these encroachments as inducing a state of crisis in personal and cultural life.

In addition, the political avenues through which we might expect to control the decisions that govern our lives are severely restricted. Stuart Hall has talked about "a growing gap between where people are politically, and the institutions and organisations which express that in a formal political way." Recent trends reveal a growth in intense pseudo-religious movements, in nationalist and neo-fascist ideas, in young people embracing directly oppositional lifestyles. Few would deny that at the centre of this is a search for something meaningful to believe in, a vision of ourselves as empowered human beings able to act upon our needs and desires as we define them.

It is crucial that we recognise that there is a direct correspondence between the condition of our culture and the ways we organise the production of materials. The form of economic organisation we refer to as capitalism ceased long ago to be simply that, and has become a means of organising the consciousness necessary for that economic system to flourish. As designers whose work is concerned with the expression and exchange of ideas and information and the construction of the visual vocabulary of day-to-day culture, we must establish a perspective on where we fit into this scheme. We must ask in what ways our function helps to organise consciousness. We must also discover to what extent and in what ways the solutions, vocabularies, and dialogues that we are able to conceive and construct are determined for us. The "First Things First" manifesto was an attempt at least to address these issues.

Its conclusions, however, fall short of what seems necessary. Written at a time when the high-intensity market was establishing itself at the heart of the design profession in Britain, it was perhaps a last-ditch attempt to hold back the flood of "gimmick merchants, status salesmen, and hidden persuaders." It starts off in a forcible and radical manner. But at the beginning of the fourth paragraph it extinguishes its own flames when it says, "We don't advocate the abolition of high pressure consumer advertising: this is not feasible"—without making clear whether or not this is perceived as desirable. After its declaration of a rebellion against the techniques and apparatus of high-pressure consumer advertising, there is a trace of retreat here, despite the fact that it would probably be defended as "realism."

Garland echoes this concession in the interview, and the power of his argument is all the less compelling for it. Early on he concurs with Haines that "we are not against advertising as a whole. The techniques of publicity and selling are vital to Western society." But isn't that the problem? This allows Haines's contention that high-pressure advertising and the ideology of the marketplace are healthy and natural to go unchallenged, and leaves an impression that what Garland is arguing for is the same cake, sliced differently. But the logic of the manifesto implies that social and cultural needs are constantly circumvented, if not distorted, by the power of an industry whose primary purpose is to create demand for consumption, regardless of usefulness. Furthermore, that the effect—on young designers in particular—of the absence of an alternative sense of what meaningful work might be is leading to a gradual erosion of enthusiasm and creativity. What is needed is a different cake altogether, but to argue for such a thing is to take a leap into the unknown. The modern advertising industry is the creation of the high-intensity market, and graphic design has always been at the centre of its strategy. Its history forms a large part of the history of design. To question that industry and the ideology of consumerism it promotes is to question our whole economic organisation. It is easier to argue for more of the cake.

The manifesto's concern with purpose and social function should not be confused with a moralising preoccupation with "politically correct" subject matter. It should not be interpreted as a determinist concern with "the message," although it does not exclude a commitment to direct (or indirect) political expression. Devotees of the new wave may well demonstrate little interest in the "message-as-content" approach, perhaps justifiably, when one considers the unbelievably inane work of "cultural ground-breakers" such as Oliviero Toscani and his sponsors, Benetton.

"I want to make people think," says Toscani in an interview in *The Independent* (December 16, 1992), "I want them to remember a name." Thus social criticism is appropriated in the struggle for brand identification. "It [the advertising industry] persuades people that they are respected for what they consume, that they are only worth what they possess," says Toscani, angrily upbraiding the industry for corrupting society. Most advertising, he tells us, is based on the emotions and has nothing to do with the product. One can only wonder what graveyard crosses during the Gulf War, a ship overflowing with refugees, an electric chair, children in Third World slums, and a nun and priest kissing have to do with expensive, multicoloured knitwear? But even these are surpassed by Toscani's idea for a "fun" campaign about wife-beating for Guinness. What makes Toscani's ever-so-radical ideas ever so depressing is that his accurate critique of the advertising industry's effect on our aspirations and self-image appears to be of no help to him in establishing the link between the industry and the economic ideology that spawned it.

Whatever his intentions, Toscani's posters are merely a state-of-the-art marketing device masquerading as social conscience. It is extreme arrogance to throw images at people in the belief that they need to be told what issues are of social importance. Radical work is never a question of presenting correct political opinions, but is concerned instead with the nature of the dialogue that is made possible between the author and the audience.

It is not at all clear, on the other hand, in what sense the approach advocated by Dutch designers Kuilman and Meulman is basic, or what is the meaning and significance of what they have to say. Is this perhaps a private argument between them and the technological, intellectual sophisticates about the most effective formal approach to sell spicy sausage or decorative floor tiles? Or is the liberation from confusion they wish to achieve to be reserved for greater purposes? Appending political messages to work as if forms were empty vessels is simple-minded, and advocacy of "basicness" is meaningless if it is concerned only with the internal logic of design. But does this mean that formal exploration, as content, is the way forward?

Writers such as Roland Barthes are said to have been of seminal influence in the development of the work and ideas of at least one agency of the new wave—the Cranbrook Academy of Art. Jeffery Keedy, a former Cranbrook student, says, "It was the poetic aspect of Roland Barthes which attracted me, not the Marxist analysis. After all, we're designers working in a consumer society, and while social criticism is an interesting idea, I wouldn't want to put it into practice" (*Eye* no. 3, vol. 1). Barthes's work is indeed poetic, which gives it a resonance lacking in much Marxist theory, but to disconnect the critique from the form seems a perverse example of literary raiding. The work of other French writers of the same period, such as the situationist Raoul Vaneigem, is also poetic and also concerned with the decay of personal and cultural life under modern capitalism. His book, *The Revolution of Everyday Life* deals with the subjugation of our potential to be active, independent-minded, and creative. It is a complex description of our condition, which focuses on the corruption of our desires, dreams, values, and aspirations, and a ferocious social critique. If it is not on the Cranbrook reading list, perhaps it should be.

The major artistic movements of this century—the Futurists, Constructivists, Dadaists, Surrealists—all had a theory of society that guided their explorations. The exploration of the formal structure of language—its signs, symbols, and how these construct and carry meaning—should be the staple diet of designers. Language is a means through which we express our consciousness of ourselves and our relationship to the world; it is our attempts to describe our situation and to think about the future that lead us to search for appropriate vocabularies. Language changes when it is no longer able to express what its users require of it, so unless it is to be of academic interest only, an exploration of language must also take into account the changing consciousness of human beings. It is difficult to comprehend the point of exploring form if it is not related to contemporary problems of vocabulary and the search for meaning. The study of visual form and language is limited if it does not consider the forces of cultural production, which involve a set of social relations between producer and audience.

Whether our activity and its products are open and empowering, whether they contribute to the building of a democratic culture, is not dependent only on the content of our work, but also on the productive social relations that affect the nature of the dialogues we are able to construct. A large advertising poster for multicoloured knitwear, for instance, is not a dialogue on equal terms, if it is a dialogue at all. It is designed to make an intervention into our consciousness in ways we cannot ignore; it shouts at us so that we may remember a name that will influence our acts of purchasing. It is a form developed for a social context that the audience cannot control. This is what makes it oppressive. No amount of fiddling with the visual forms it employs or the message it carries will transform it into an open-ended product.

But the ideology of consumerism is not limited to the world of commerce. Our consciousness is fragmented so that we are better able to consume everything: films, music, fashion, diets, healthcare, education, information, even our own history. This problem cannot be avoided simply by choosing between "good" or "bad" products, or between commercial and noncommercial work, since the nature of the problem is not just consumption but the ordering of our consciousness to become consumers in the first place.

Graphic design has a part to play in creating a visual culture that empowers and enlightens, that makes ideas and information accessible and memorable. Many designers may argue that their job is not politics, and they would be right. But this does not prevent us from developing ideas about the relationship between culture and democracy. We cannot separate our work from the social context in which it is received and from the purpose it serves. If we care about the integrity of our design decisions, we should be concerned that the relations implicit in our communications extend active participation in our culture. If what we are looking for is meaning and significance, then the first step is to ask who controls the work, and whose ends does it serve?

The computer revolution that brought us new aesthetic possibilities has given us other opportunities too. The technological condensing of the production process has the potential to alter our notion of authorship, and with it our aspirations. The technical self-sufficiency the computer has allowed may give us the conceptual space to develop a more complete consideration of our work in relation to the way it is received and the purpose it serves. It may encourage us to initiate more often, and in the process to establish partnerships and collaborations in which design is not simply a means to sell and persuade, but also a means of organising ideas and finding forms of expression that suit the interests of a more specific audience.

The work that flows from such a practice cannot be prescribed. It may or may not be sophisticated, technological, and so on. It will in no way preclude an exploration of the formal representation of language. Its content may be concerned with what it is we are able to think about (subjects), or the ways in which we are able to think (forms). It will recognise that how something is produced and distributed socially carries with it specific relations that affect the dialogue that is possible between author and audience and limit the sort of meanings that can be constructed. Above all, it will acknowledge the link between our choices as designers and the sort of culture we wish to contribute to.

CHAPTER SEVENTEEN

Design and Reflexivity

JAN VAN TOORN

© *Jan van Toorn, 1994*

LE PAIN ET LA LIBERTÉ

Every professional practice operates in a state of schizophrenia, in a situation full of inescapable contradictions. So too communicative design, which traditionally views its own action as serving the public interest, but which is engaged at the same time in the private interests of clients and media. To secure its existence, design, like other practical intellectual professions, must constantly strive to neutralize these inherent conflicts of interest by developing a mediating concept aimed at consensus. This always comes down to a reconciliation with the present state of social relations; in other words, to accepting the world image of the established order as the context for its own action.

By continually smoothing over the conflicts in the production relationships, design, in cooperation with other disciplines, has developed a practical and conceptual coherence that has afforded it representational and institutional power in the mass media. In this manner it legitimizes itself in the eyes of the established social order, which, in turn, is confirmed and legitimized by the contributions that design makes to symbolic production. It is this image of reality, in particular of the social world that, pressured by the market economy, no longer has room for emancipatory engagement as a foundation for critical practice.

Design has thus become imprisoned in a fiction that does not respond to factual reality beyond the representations of the culture industry and its communicative monopoly. In principle, this intellectual impotence is still expressed in dualistic, product-oriented action and thought: on the one and there is the individual's attempt to renew the vocabulary—out of resistance to the social integration of the profession; on the other there is the intention to arrive at universal and utilitarian soberness of expression—within the existing symbolic and institutional order. Although the lines separating these two extremes are becoming blurred (as a consequence of postmodernist thinking and ongoing market differentiation), official design continues to be characterized by aesthetic compulsiveness and/or by a patriarchal fixation on reproductive ordering.

The social orientation of our action as designers is no longer as simple as that. We seem happy enough to earn our living in blind freedom, leading to vulgarization and simplification of our reflective and critical traditions. That is why it is time to apply our imaginative power once again to how we deal with communicative reality.

SYMBOLIC FORMS ARE SOCIAL FORMS

Symbolic productions represent the social position and mentality of the elites that create and disseminate them. As ideological instruments, they serve private interests that are preferably presented as universal ones. The dominant culture does not serve to integrate the ruling classes only, however; "*It also contributes,*" as Pierre Bourdieu describes it, "*to the fictitious integration of society as a whole, and thus to the apathy (false consciousness) of the dominated classes; and finally, it contributes to the legitimation of the established order by establishing distinctions (hierarchies) and legitimating these distinctions.*"[1] Consequently, the dominant culture forces all other cultures to define themselves in its symbolism, this being the instrument of knowledge and communication. This communicative dependency is particularly evident in the "solutions" that the dominant culture proposes for the social, economic, and political problems of what is defined as the "periphery"—of those who do not (yet) belong.

By definition, the confrontation between reality and symbolic representation is uncertain. This uncertainty has now become undoubtedly painful, since, as Jean Baudrillard puts it, the experience of reality has disappeared "*behind the mediating hyperreality of the simulacrum.*" A progressive staging of everyday life that gives rise to great tension between ethics and symbolism, because of the dissonance between the moral intentions related to reality and the generalizations and distinctions of established cultural production.

For an independent and oppositional cultural production, another conceptual space must be created that lies beyond the destruction of direct experience by the simulacrum of institutional culture. The point is not to create a specific alternative in the form of a new dogma as opposed to the spiritual space of the institutions. On the contrary, the point is to arrive at a "*mental ecology*"[2] that makes it possible for mediating intellectuals, like designers, to leave the beaten path, to organize their opposition, and to articulate that in the mediated display. This is only possible by adopting a radically different position with respect to the production relationships—by exposing the variety of interests and disciplinary edifices in the message, commented on and held together by the mediator's "*plane of consistency.*"[3]

AND MEDIOCRITY

Opportunities for renewed engagement must be sought in initiatives creating new public polarities, according to Félix Guattari, in "*untying the bonds of language*" and "*[opening] up new social, analytical, and aesthetic practices.*"[4] This will only come about within the context of a political approach that, unlike the dominant neoliberal form of capitalism, is directed at real social problems. If we are to break through the existing communicative order, this *"outside thought"*[5] should also reverberate in the way in which designers interpret the theme and program of the client. In other words, the designer must take on an oppositional stance, implying a departure from the circle of common-sense cultural representation. This is an important notion, because the point is no longer to question whether the message is true, but whether it works as an argument—one that manifests itself more or less explicitly in the message, in relation to the conditions under which it was produced and under which it is disseminated.

Such activity is based on a multidimensional, complementary way of thinking with an essentially different attitude to viewers and readers. It imposes a complementary structure on the work as well, an assemblage that is expressed both in content and in form. The essence of this approach, however, is that, through the critical orientation of its products, the reflexive mentality raises questions among the public that stimulate a more active way of dealing with reality. In this manner it may contribute to a process that allows us to formulate our own needs, interest, and desires and resist the fascination with the endless fragmented and aestheticized varieties created by the corporate culture of commerce, state, media, and "attendant" disciplines.

SUBVERSIVE PLEASURES

Despite the symbolically indeterminable nature of culture, communicative design, as reflexive practice, must be realistic in its social ambitions. In the midst of a multiplicity of factors too numerous to take stock of, all of which influence the product, the aim is to arrive at a working method that produces commentaries rather than confirms self-referential fictions. Design will have to get used to viewing substance, program, and style as ideological constructions, as expressions of restricted choices that only show a small sliver of reality in mediation. The inevitable consequence is that the formulation of messages continues to refer to the fundamental uneasiness between symbolic infinity and the real world.

This mentality demands a major investment in practical discourse in those fields and situations where experience and insight can be acquired through work. This is important not only because it is necessary to struggle against design in the form of design, echoing Rem Koolhaas's statement about architecture, but also because partners are required with the same operational options.[6] It is furthermore of public interest to acquaint a wider audience with forms of communication contributing to more independent and radical democratic shaping of opinion.

Moving from a reproductive order to a commentating one, operative criticism can make use of a long reflexive practice. All cultures have communicative forms of fiction that refer to their own fictitiousness in resistance to the established symbolic order. *"To this end,"* Robert Stam writes, *"they deploy myriad strategies—narrative discontinuities, authorial intrusions, essayistic digressions, stylistic virtuosities. They share a playful, parodic, and disruptive relation to established norms and conventions. They demystify fictions, and our naive faith in fictions, and make of this demystification a source for new fictions!*"[7] This behavior alone constitutes a continuous "ecological" process for qualitative survival in social and natural reality.

© 1994 Jan van Toorn. This article is republished without the additional quotes that were included in Jan van Toorn's graphic composition previously published in *Visible Language Journal* Vol. 28, No. 4, Fall 1994, pgs. 316–325. Republished with the kind permission from Jan van Toorn.

NOTES

1. Bourdieu, Pierre. 1991. *Language and Symbolic Power*. Cambridge, Massachusetts: Harvard University Press, 163–170.
2. Guattari, Félix. 1993. "Postmodernism & Ethical Abdications," in *Profile*, 39. Australia Council for the Arts, 11–13.
3. Gilles Deleuze and Félix Guattari. 1987. *A Thousand Plateaus*. Minneapolis: University of Minnesota Press, 506–508.
4. Guattari, Félix. 1993. "Postmodernisme & Ethical Abdications," in *Profile*, 39. Australia Council for the Arts, 11–13.
5. Michel Foucault. 1987. "Maurice Blanchot: The Thought from Outside," in *Foucault/Blanchot*, trans. Jeffrey Mehiman and Brian Massumi. New York: Zone Books.
6. Koolhaas, Rem. 1994. "De ontplooiing van de architectuur," in *De Architect*, 25. The Hague: ten Haagen en Stam, 16–25.
7. Stam, Robert. 1992. *Reflexivity in Film and Literature: From Don Quixote to Jean-Luc Godard*. New York: Columbia University Press, xi.

CHAPTER EIGHTEEN

Design Noir

ANTHONY DUNNE

When the Sony Walkman was introduced in the early 1980s it offered people a new kind of relationship to urban space. It allowed the wearer to create their own portable micro-environment, and it provided a soundtrack for travel through the city encouraging different readings of familiar settings. It functioned as an urban interface.

Fifteen years on there are hundreds of variations on the appearance of the Walkman but the relationship it created to the city remains the same. This scenario reflects how product designers have responded to the aesthetic challenge of electronic technology. They have accepted a role as a semiotician, a companion of packaging designers and marketeers, creating semiotic skins for incomprehensible technologies. The electronic product accordingly occupies a strange place in the world of material culture, closer to washing powder and cough mixture than furniture and architecture.

But this is just one approach to product design, one genre if you like, which offers a very limited experience. Like a Hollywood movie its emphasis is on easy pleasure and conformist values. It reinforces the status quo rather than challenging it. There could be so many other genres of product: e.g. arthouse, porn, horror, noir even, that exploit the unique and exciting functional and aesthetic potential of electronic technology.

DESIGN GENRES

An occasional glance through almost any tabloid newspaper reveals a view of everyday life where complex emotions, desires and needs are played out through the misuse and abuse of electronic products and systems. A mother shoots her son after an argument over which television channel to watch; the police set a trap for scanner snoopers (people who listen illegally to emergency radio frequencies) by broadcasting a message that an UFO has landed in a local forest (within minutes several cars arrive and their scanners are confiscated); a parent is outraged by a speaking doll, made in China, which sounds like it swears. Yet even though industrial design plays a part in the design of extreme pain (e.g. weapons) and pleasure (e.g. sex aids) the range of emotions offered through most electronic products is pathetically narrow. More diverse design genres could offer more complex and demanding aesthetic experiences by referring to this bizarre world of the 'infra-ordinary', where stories show that truth is indeed stranger than fiction, and that our experience of everyday day life lived through conventional electronic products is aesthetically impoverished.

The Truth Phone by the Counter Spy Shop, a real product, is an example of how a design noir product might work. It combines a voice stress analyser with a telephone, and shows how electronic products have the potential to generate a chain of events which together form a story. If you consider products in this way the design shifts from concerns of physical interaction (passive button pushing), to the potential psychological experiences inherent in the product. The user becomes a protagonist and the designer becomes a coauthor of the experience. Imagine speaking to your mother or a lover while the Truth Phone suggests they are lying: the product creates dilemmas rather than resolving them. By using it the owner explores boundaries between themselves and the paranoid user suggested by the product. They enter into a psychological adventure.

What I'm proposing, is that product designers could become more like authors. They could draw from the narrative potential of electronic product misuse and abuse to create alternative notions of use and need, rather than the official images of how people live with technology. Instead of thinking about appearance, user friendliness or corporate identity, industrial designers could propose new products which are more challenging. The Truth Phone looks like any other slick matt black mainstream phone; but it is through using it, or interacting with its paranoid logic, that its real aesthetic is revealed. You won't become paranoid by using it, but you might experience a routine phone call from a paranoid person's perspective.

AESTHETICS OF MIS-USE

In 1994 the British mobile phone company Cellnet produced a booklet, *Mobile Moments: A Collection of Tales for the '90s*, a chronicle of events which, it felt, demonstrated the crucial part the mobile phone has come to play in our lives. The tales are arranged under headings such as Mating by Mobile, Mobile Heroes, Mobile Marvels and, most interestingly, Mobile Mishaps. Each story is an example of the narrative space entered by misusing a simple electronic product, of how electronic technologies can generate rich experiences that challenge the conformity of everyday life by short-circuiting our emotions and states of mind. I am suggesting not that designers try to predict misuses of electronic products, but rather that they refer, as a wider context of use, to the possibilities of the unofficial and the unexpected, instead of standard behavioural models.

We are surrounded by products that give us an illusion of choice and encourage passivity, yet we could have so much more. Different genres of electronic products could enrich and expand our experience of everyday life rather than closing it down. Industrial design's position at the heart of consumer culture (after all, it is fuelled by the capitalist system), could be subverted for more socially beneficial ends by enriching our experiences. It could provide a unique aesthetic language that engages the viewer in ways a film might, without being utopian or prescribing how things ought to be.

CONCEPTUAL DESIGN

But developing alternative genres of electronic product is made difficult by the fact that industrial designers see the social value of their work as inextricably linked to the marketplace. Design outside this arena is viewed with suspicion as escapist or unreal. At the moment, the only alternatives to the Hollywood genre of design are 'concept designs' from earnest but inexperienced students or design consultancies promoting themselves to corporate clients.

Truly radical alternatives could really only exist outside the marketplace, as a form of 'conceptual design'—meaning not the conceptual stage of a design project, but a product intended to challenge preconceptions about how electronics shape our lives. Designers would need to explore how such design thinking might re-enter everyday life in ways that maintain the design proposal's critical integrity and effectiveness while facing criticism of escapism, utopianism or fantasy. The challenge is to blur the boundaries between the real and the fictional, so that the conceptual becomes more real and the real is seen as just one limited possibility.

So how could alternative genres of product that challenge the Hollywood vision of large corporations be developed?

One way this could happen is if design developed its own independent vision, and worked with the public to demand more from industry. But this would require not only a shift in the way designers view their position, but also how design organisations see their role. They would need, like the Architecture Foundation in London, or the Netherlands Design Institute perhaps, to encourage diverse visions through competitions and workshops for practising designers, and engage the public through more challenging exhibitions and publications. Architecture could also play a part in this debate. It has a well established forum for exploring and communicating alternative visions of how life might be, but despite research in the 1960s by Archigram and others, it still struggles to get to grips with how electronic technology embodied in mass-produced products like mobile phones and Global Positioning Systems impacts on traditional architectural and urban experiences. But it is only a matter of time before a new generation of architects start to formulate new visions that include electronic products.

Or, is this a role best left to 'academic' designers—free from commercial restrictions and based in an educational environment. Rather than writing papers and seeking conventional academic approval, they could exploit their privileged position to explore a subversive role for design as social critique, developing provocative design genres to challenge the simplistic Hollywood vision of the consumer electronics industry?

A Sea Change: The Paradigm Shift from Objects to Systems 2000–20

Design is undergoing a momentous change. Where designers were once known for creating the visual appearance of products, whether coffee pots or posters, today they are becoming recognized for their work on the design of services, organizations (including government agencies), and even social networks. Specializations such as interaction design, experience design, social design, and design for sustainability did not exist a few years ago. The older projects of designing artifacts have not disappeared but the recognition that design can be so much more is growing.

—Victor Margolin, *The Good City: Design for Sustainability*, 2015

CHAPTER NINETEEN

Introduction

ELIZABETH RESNICK

An important dimension of social design is to focus on designing systems and frameworks that connect communication, product, and services development sustainably with the natural environment. As our society in the twenty-first century becomes increasingly more complex, we must understand that all design decisions will result in environmental, ethical, social, and political repercussions. It can be argued that no single area of design is, by itself, sufficient to drive sustainable social development. The chapters in this section will argue that as design has firmly established itself as a field of study and professional discipline, there is an increased need for embracing both quantitative and qualitative research through strategic thinking, systemic thinking, and critical thinking at a time when designers are being tasked with tackling complex social challenges, *wicked problems* of great consequence to our future generations.

FIRST THINGS FIRST 2000 MANIFESTO

First Things First 2000 manifesto is an updated version of the 1964 *First Things First* manifesto written by British designer Ken Garland (see page 47). Kalle Lasn, editor of *Adbusters* magazine, had come across the 1964 manifesto in a back issue of *Eye* magazine, reprinted as an image in Andrew Howard's "There Is Such a Thing as Society" article (*Eye* no. 13 vol. 4). Lasn thought its message was still relevant, perhaps even more so thirty-five years on. He showed it to design provocator Tibor Kalman (1950–1999) and both agreed they should act on it. Ken Garland was consulted and in giving his approval to move forward, he left it to *Adbusters* to revise the wording and find the new signatories. *First Things First 2000* manifesto was published in *Adbusters*, *Émigré* and the *AIGA Journal* in North America, in *Eye* and *Blueprint* in the UK, in *Items* in the Netherlands, and *Form* in Germany. The goal was to stimulate a new international dialogue on the changing relationship of advertising, graphic design, commerce, and culture that encompassed all sectors of visual communication—one that focused less on the consumerism and more on meaningful forms of communication for societal good.

A "SOCIAL MODEL" OF DESIGN:
ISSUES OF PRACTICE AND RESEARCH

"A 'Social Model' of Design: Issues of Practice and Research," written by Victor Margolin and Sylvia Margolin, was published in 2002 at the dawn of a new millennium when design was "most often understood by the public as an artistic practice that produces dazzling lamps, furniture, and automobiles." In this seminal paper, the authors outlined their vision for "social design" inspired by social work theory, that extended beyond the "market model" (servicing industry) to include a "social model" (addressing basic human needs) of design practice. They suggest that the "market model" and the "social model" should not be considered opposites but as "two poles of a continuum" in an effort to shift society toward more sustainable thinking and practices. They also discuss an aspect inherent in social work methodology—of gathering diverse professionals to work as a "team"—in an effort to encourage designers to work with other professionals inside and outside of the design realm to assist in social interventions.

An important component to developing their vision of a "social model" of design would include a broad research agenda that would address the following questions: "What role can a designer play in a collaborative process of social intervention? What is currently being done in this regard and what might be done? How might the public's perception of designers be changed in order to present an image of a socially responsible designer? How can agencies that fund social welfare projects and research gain a stronger perception of a design as a socially responsible activity? What kinds of products meet the needs of vulnerable populations?"

THE DEMATERIALIZATION OF DESIGN

A shift toward *human-centered design*—from the design of objects to the design of situations and experience—transforms the concern with the material reality of a product, as object, toward a focus on the immateriality of the service as experience. This is what design educator and theorist Jorge Frascara calls the "dematerialization of design" where design becomes "more concerned with the contexts in which objects and communications are used by people, and with the consequences that the existence of those design creations have on people in general." Here he argues that designers must understand that objects have a cultural impact on society and that designers "need to develop a more accountable design practice ... for both ethical and effective communications and products to come to exist." As Frascara develops his thesis, he recognizes three areas of design practice in striving toward improving our overall quality of life: "design that works to make life possible, design that works to make life easier, and design that works to make life better."

WHY BEING "LESS BAD" IS NO GOOD

Sustainability is the process of maintaining change in a balanced fashion, in which the exploitation of resources, the direction of investments, the orientation of technological development, and institutional change are all in harmony and enhance both current and future potential to meet human needs and aspirations. Simply put, achieving sustainability will enable the earth to continue supporting human life.[1]

Cradle to Cradle: Remaking the Way We Make Things was published in 2002. Co-authored by American architect William McDonough and German chemist Michael Braungart, this book is, in every sense, a powerfully written manifesto that calls for the development of sustainable societies by rethinking and redesigning how products are made—by switching from a "cradle to grave" mentality to the more sustainable "cradle to cradle" mentality—by implementing eco-effective practices. In chapter 2, "Why Being 'Less Bad' Is No Good," the authors describe early attempts to make industry less destructive. They discuss important written contributions made by early the environmentalists—such as Thomas Malthus, Henry David Thoreau, and Rachel Carson—to bring attention to "declining wilderness and diminishing resources merged with pollution and toxic waste as the major realms of concern." They explore the notion of "eco-efficiency," which is respect for natural ecosystems integrated with efficient manufacturing, but acknowledge that attempts at "eco-efficiency" have only resulted in a "less bad" approach that is simply not good enough for long-term human survival. The authors conclude this chapter by making a plea that "we must shrink our presence, our systems, our activities, and even our population … the goal is zero: zero waste, zero emissions, zero 'ecological footprint.'"

CLOTHES THAT CONNECT

Sustainable design is the philosophy of designing physical objects, the built environment, and services to comply with the principles of social, economic, and ecological sustainability. The intention of sustainable design is to eliminate negative environmental impact completely through skillful, sensitive design. Manifestations of sustainable design require renewable resources, that impact the environment minimally, and connect people with the natural environment.[2]

Kate Fletcher is a researcher, writer, and design activist whose work over the past fifteen years has shaped the field of fashion and sustainable design. In "Clothes That Connect" (published as chapter 6 in *Designers, Visionaries and Other Stories: A Collection of Sustainable Design Essays*), Fletcher's aim is to envision a new, more sustainable way of thinking about fashion that "get's to the heart of fashion's 'problem' (namely) our addiction to consumption." She suggests countering globalization's dominance of the "fast" fashion (low cost and high volume impact) with the notion of "shifting from global to local, from consuming to making, from illusion to imagination, from consumption of natural resources to an appreciation of the natural world." The observable principles and dynamics inherent in nature, Fletcher argues, offer sustainable models of "efficiency, cooperation and symbiosis" to study with "the hope is that society might be sustainable in the same way that ecosystems are." As one possibility of a future thinking, Fletcher describes her collaborative conceptual project titled "5 Ways" consisting of five interconnected approaches to fashion textile design that encouraged creativity and ecological thinking in fabric form.

DESIGN'S ROLE IN SUSTAINABLE CONSUMPTION

Author and collaborative design strategist Ann Thorpe describes the environmental, psychological, and sociological issues of consumption in terms of design in her 2010 paper "Design's Role in Sustainable Consumption." She begins by offering a brief timeline of "consumption" as a field of study by outlining its transition from green design to ecodesign to sustainable design in order to understand how its broadening development in theory and practice affected designers as they became more conscious of environmental issues and how to cope with them. Thorpe examines three main research areas in which she advocates that designers can make relevant and rigorous contributions—environmental policy (can we create and convince people to buy environmentally better products?), psychology (can these things make us happy?), and sociology (what does consumption mean to our personal identity?). Within these three areas, she explores the contemporary paradox that finds us heavily relying on consumerism for our psychological and physical well-being. Here she suggests that "lifestyle and behavior change … suggests consumerism is costly not only in environmental terms, but also possibly in other ways" and could possibly be viewed as a contributing factor in the rising levels of depression, personal debt, and overspending on goods and services. She concludes on a hopeful note "by examining a question implied by mainstream research—can design move from being a cog in the wheel of consumerism to having a substantial role in supporting sustainable consumption?"

TRANSFORMATIVE SERVICES AND
TRANSFORMATION DESIGN

Service design is "the activity of planning and organizing people, infrastructure, communication and material components of a service in order to improve its quality and the interaction between service provider and customers. The purpose of service design methodologies is to design according to the needs of customers or participants, so that the service is user-friendly, competitive and relevant to the customers."[3] Service design is a developing design discipline. "Over the past decade, a profession of service designers has emerged and an interdisciplinary field of service design research has begun to take shape. Accounts of service design vary from those that see it as a new field of design to those that stress its origins in other disciplines and make references to existing approaches within design, management and the social sciences."[4]

Service design researcher and educator Daniela Sangiorgi discusses the recent evolution of service design toward becoming transformational in her 2011 paper "Transformative Services and Transformation Design." As she states in the introduction, her aim is to provide a foundation for clarifying the concept of transformational change while exploring the principles and practices of organizational development and community action research as a potentially useful bridge in investigating the transformative role of design combined with the potential transformative role of services. Sangiorgi cites that service design has now transitioned to be less about "design objects" and to a greater extent, a mode for wider societal transformations in service to "a more collaborative, sustainable and creative society and economy."[5] With this notion comes considerable responsibilities associated with transformative practice, and Sangiorgi urges designers to introduce reflexivity into their work to address potential bias issues with each design engagement.

RETHINKING DESIGN THINKING: PART I

Design thinking is a method for creative problem-solving that designers use during the process of designing. It is also an approach with a repeatable protocol that can be applied to business strategy and social systems problems. The design thinking process has various stages including: defining the problem, researching, forming ideas, prototyping, and testing. It is important to note that there are many definitions and uses for the term "design thinking." There have also been doubts expressed around the notion that design thinking is a panacea for success in fields outside of design.[6] Tim Brown, the CEO of the design consultancy IDEO, defines design thinking as "a human-centered approach to innovation that draws from the designer's toolkit to integrate the needs of people, the possibilities of technology, and the requirements for business success."[7]

"The term 'design thinking' has emerged among some scholars, managers, designers and educators as a way to distinguish between the craft skills of designers, and a way of approaching problems supposedly common to designers that might be adopted by managers and applied to organizational issues."[8] Designer, researcher, and educator Lucy Kimbell offers two excellent papers on design thinking and practice theory. The first paper "Rethinking Design Thinking: Part I," published in 2011, presents an overview of the term's history, its adaptation to management fields and social innovation, as well as its place in the contemporary global economy. She situates design thinking in a wider social, economic, and cultural context while making a persuasive argument for a robust review of how design practices manifest in business and policy: "While the term design thinking originated with academics who conducted research within design disciplines, today the phrase most often situates design thinking in terms of the challenges facing organizations, especially businesses. Concern with design's place in the world and thus with larger social or political questions is lost when design is mobilized within a managerialist framework."

In formulating her notion of *rethinking* design thinking, Kimbell identifies and summarizes three possible aspects in positioning design thinking: "as a cognitive style, as a general theory of design, and as a resource for organizations." Given the diversity inherent in these aspects, the author implies there is still no clear definition of design thinking. She then proceeds to identify three key issues of concern: first, design thinking rests on a dualism between thinking and knowing, and acting in the world; second, generalizing the notion of design thinking while ignoring the diversity within design; and third, theories of design that privilege the designer within design activity. Kimbell concludes by proposing the need for a critical rethinking of the term design thinking, as she states, it remains "undertheorized and understudied."

RETHINKING DESIGN THINKING: PART II

In the sequential paper "Rethinking Design Thinking: Part II" published in 2012, Kimbell states that sources from anthropology, science, and technology studies have entered design research methods and theory, drawing attention to the broader contexts in which designers work and users respond. She introduces a new pair of concepts: "design-as-practice" and "designs-in-practice" in hopes to foster a deeper understanding of design activity and designers' expertise and to "describe and analyse design activity that acknowledges the work done by many actors in constituting designs relationally in practice." Kimbell argues that these concepts can aid in rethinking design thinking while providing tools to help researchers identify the activities and knowledge base of professional designers and other end users/stakeholders involved in designs as well as the materials and objects that are part of these activities, and the discursive practices that inform distinct ways of doing, knowing, and saying. Simply put, "stakeholders are co-designers and designers are another kind of stakeholder" that decenters the designer as the main agent in designing.

DESIGN THINGS AND DESIGN THINKING: CONTEMPORARY PARTICIPATORY DESIGN CHALLENGES

Participatory design is an approach focused on processes and procedures where all stakeholders (e.g., employees, partners, customers, citizens, end users) are involved in the design process as codesigners. Once called "cooperative design" (and now shortened to codesign), participation design had its nascency in the early 1970s as a set of design and research practices rooted in a Scandinavian approach to systems design that focused on designers and users working together in a process aimed at improving the quality of working life (initially with the trade unions). The term is used in a variety of design fields as a way of creating environments that are more responsive and appropriate to their citizenry's cultural, emotional, spiritual, and practical needs. This approach can also encompass a political dimension encouraging user empowerment and democratization.[9]

In their paper "Design Things and Design Thinking: Contemporary Participatory Design Challenges," veteran researchers Erling Bjögvinsson, Pelle Ehn, and Per-Anders Hillgren propose that within the field of Participatory Design there is an essential need to move from the notion of designing "things" (objects) to designing "Things" (sociomaterial assemblies). They argue this new paradigm for the design profession "involves not only the challenges of engaging stakeholders as designers in the design process, as in 'traditional' Participatory Design but also the challenges of designing beyond the specific project and toward future stakeholders as designers" in effect doing "design-after-design." Here design is positioned as an ongoing process rather than a finished process inviting and including participation from users around an open process. Participatory design from this perspective might involve deferring some design until after the participatory encounters: in effect doing "design-after-design." Design then is viewed as a continuing rather than a finished process—the design before design and the design after design—allowing for a process of "infrastructuring" (building and supporting long-term relationships) for continuance of the sociomaterial assembly before and after the design cycle. To illustrate their ongoing research, the authors discuss their "infrastructuring" engagement in Malmö Living Labs as one example in which they design "Things" for social innovation.

FROM DESIGN CULTURE TO DESIGN ACTIVISM

Design activism is generally defined as representing design's central role in (1) promoting social change, (2) raising awareness about values and beliefs (e.g., in relation to climate change, sustainability, etc.), or (3) questioning the constraints that mass production and consumerism place on people's everyday life. Design activism, in this context, is not restricted to a single discipline of design but includes areas such as product design, interaction design, new media, urban design, architecture, and fashion and textiles, among others.[10]

In his paper published in 2013 "From Design Culture to Design Activism," author and educator Guy Julier defines design culture as mainstream commercial design culture consisting of the interrelationships between designers, producers, and consumers. He defines design activism as a movement that critiques the economic practices and ideologies of mainstream design culture. His thesis explores the politics of neoliberalism[11] as the principle link between design activism and mainstream design culture—"the relationship of design culture and design activism to neoliberalism must be understood. This means attempting to grasp how design works within, and takes advantage of neoliberalism's structures, institutions, and resources." Essentially Julier explains that design activism emerged as a movement to "contest" neoliberal processes of change from evolving globalization by giving voice to those who want to distance their professional practice away from commercialization while they "develop new ways of working that coincide with geopolitical, economic, and environmental crises." In the final section of his paper, Julier proposes and elucidates on a conceptual framework of four themes that exist within mainstream design culture and design activism and intervene in the social, political, and environmental arenas: Intensification, coarticulation, temporality, and territorialization.

DECOLONIZING DESIGN INNOVATION: DESIGN ANTHROPOLOGY, CRITICAL ANTHROPOLOGY, AND INDIGENOUS KNOWLEDGE

Design Anthropology is a nascent academic discipline and practice that integrates the strengths of design thinking and anthropological research in a mutually beneficial relationship "that seeks to understand how the processes and artifacts of design help to define what it means to be human and that focuses on how design translates values into tangible experiences."[12] In her paper "Decolonizing Design Innovation: Design Anthropology, Critical Anthropology, and Indigenous Knowledge," Tunstall proposes the development of a methodology for design anthropology that produces decolonized processes of design anthropological engagement; a bridge between the cultural differences among all people and their different ways of being in the world. She is critical of western world innovation initiatives that blindly follow "the hegemonic paradigm of innovation … values of design thinking draw[n] from a progressive narrative of global salvation that ignores non-Western ways of thinking." She cites as an example her personal involvement in the Aboriginal Smart Art project as an example of a decolonized and humane design anthropology driven by values of creating conditions of compassion in among human beings in harmony with their wider environments.

SOCIAL DESIGN AND NEOCOLONIALISM

In their paper "Social Design and Neocolonialism," coauthors Cinnamon Janzer and Lauren Weinstein state "that designers must be sensitive to a variety of complex social and cultural cues and structures or they risk contributing to, or practicing, design neocolonialism." The authors imply that a designer's own cultural aesthetic can be unknowingly or unwittingly imposed when "the agenda of the designer and freedom of creativity" over "end-user empowerment and a deep understanding of the end-user's worldviews" which hints of neocolonialist undercurrents.[13]

In 2010, Bruce Nussbaum sparked a very lively online debate when he questioned if the high-mindedness of self-professed humanitarian designers could be misdirected—"Is the new humanitarian design coming out of the U.S. and Europe being perceived through post-colonial eyes as colonialism? Are the American and European designers presuming too much in their attempt to do good?"[14] Janzer and Weinstein suggest "if social designers want to create social change and solve social issues, they must first understand that solutions cultivated from afar must be considered subordinate to the beliefs, knowledge, and perspectives of the people affected by said issues." To support their thesis, the authors introduce a "matrix to serve as an early iteration of a shared framework." Their matrix splits social design into four sections: Designing a Situation with an Inside Perspective, Designing an Object with an Inside Perspective, Designing an Object with an Outside Perspective, and Designing a Situation with an Outside Perspective, the latter being strongly advised against as it runs the risk of exposing cultural bias and imposing solutions (design neocolonialism).

FUTURISTIC GIZMOS, CONSERVATIVE IDEALS: ON SPECULATIVE ANACHRONISTIC DESIGN

Speculative design is a critical design practice that comprises or is related to a series of similar practices known under the following names: critical design, design fiction, future design, anti-design, radical design, interrogative design, discursive design, adversarial design, futurescape, design art, transitional design, etcetera. Speculative design is a discursive practice, based on critical thinking and dialogue, which questions the practice of design (and its modernist definition). However, the speculative design approach takes the critical practice one step further, toward imagination and visions of possible scenarios. Speculative design is also one of the most representative examples of the new interaction between various disciplines.[15]

In their 2015 paper "Futuristic Gizmos, Conservative Ideals: On Speculative Anachronistic Design," Design researchers Luiza Prado and Pedro Oliveira get to the very heart of their critique when they state that "speculative design is going through a troubled adolescence." They contend that Speculative and Critical Design (SCD)—an emergent strategy developed for product and interaction design enmeshed in contrasting opinions and controversy—has failed to address the political ambitions for which it first instigated debate. They credit Anthony Dunne and Fiona Raby as the first to coin the term "critical design" (now referred to as SCD) but contend that "SCD" as currently practiced has been overly dominated by the concerns of the "Northern-European and/or US-American intellectual middle classes." Their aim is to transform SCD "into a strong political agent" by challenging its shortfalls and by proposing new approaches to "question the hierarchies of privilege" in regards to the pervasive actuality of poverty, colonialism and sexism. "From the moment SCD researchers and practitioners" they argue, "start holding themselves accountable for their political decisions, the field might finally start fulfilling its promises of critique."

PRIVILEGE AND OPPRESSION: TOWARDS A FEMINIST SPECULATIVE DESIGN

In "Privilege and Oppression: Towards a Feminist Speculative Design," design researcher Luiza Prado persists in challenging the underlying notion of SCD by questioning the roots of its intrinsic privilege (as discussed above). She argues the urgency to promote more discussion on how *design*—as a reflection of our society—participates in propagating oppression when it does not confront the prevailing social justice issues concerning race, class, and gender. To this aim and to challenge how issues of gender are framed within SCD, Prado proposes the concept of a "feminist speculative design" as an approach to question the complex relationships between gender, technology, and social and cultural oppression through an intersectional feminist perspective.

IS SUSTAINABLE INNOVATION AN OXYMORON?

"Is Sustainable Innovation an Oxymoron?"[16]—a question Elizabeth Sanders tackles when she argues that innovation from a consumer-led perspective cannot be sustainable but innovation that is driven from a human-centered perspective can be sustainable. She explores the notion that in today's reality, designers face significant economic, environmental, and social challenges that could be met more successfully by working collectively. She describes "collective creativity" as acts of creativity experienced jointly by two or more people employing a human-centered perspective. The real experts are the "future users" who would need to be a part of a shared participatory mindset to "break down the disciplinary and/or cultural boundaries." Sanders argues "design-led innovation needs to be *co-design-led* to address sustainable futures" and utilizing participatory prototyping in "the design development process can result in innovation that is sustainable."

SOCIAL INNOVATION AND DESIGN: ENABLING, REPLICATING AND SYNERGIZING

Social innovation is defined as new strategies, concepts, ideas, and organizations that aim to meet social needs resulting from working conditions, education, community development, and health. These ideas are created with the goal of extending and strengthening civil society. Social innovation includes the social *processes* of innovation, such as open source methods and techniques and also the innovations that have a social purpose.[17]

Design for Social Innovation is the methodology of design applied to the creation of new models, products, and services that address the complex social and environmental challenges facing businesses, governments, society, and humanity. It is really interaction design in the broadest sense; it's interaction between people that takes responsibility for positive, systemic impact. It can take any and every physical or visible form but it inevitably begins with the invisible dynamics and forces that drive human behavior. It takes place within the communities and systems it's working with, not outside them.[18]

"Social design and design for social innovation are converging and areas of objective (and very productive) overlap are created: social design is increasingly oriented towards social innovation, recognizing that this is the only possibility for solving the problems it traditionally deals with. In turn, facing the extension of the economic crisis, design for social innovation is more and more frequently involved in initiatives that invest in socially sensitive issues." Esteemed design researcher and educator, Ezio Manzini elucidates on his concept of design for social innovation[19] in his 2016 paper "Social Innovation and Design: Enabling, Replicating and Synergizing." In the introduction, Manzini proposes "a journey that starting from an introduction to the notion of social innovation, focalizes some strategies *to empower, replicate and synergize*" by outlining, within this framework, what *design* can do to conceive and enhance … new and sustainable ways of living and doing." He talks about the promise of "creative communities"—groups of people "who cooperatively invent, enhance and manage innovative solutions for new ways of living"—who consolidate into "collaborative organizations" that can "operate as social services, responsible enterprises or user associations." He cites existing examples of inventiveness and creativity among everyday people to address their day-to-day life challenges. Manzini considers these examples as "prototypes" for "viable solutions" with the ever-present "possibility to spread and to support sustainable lifestyles for a large number of people."

Ezio Manzini is credited with coining the term "design for social innovation" in a 2013 interview when asked by the interviewer what it meant in practical terms:

Design for social innovation is an "umbrella concept" that includes "whatever design can do to trigger and support social innovation" (here, the term "design" refers to the design community, including whoever is using design knowledge in an expert way: from professional designers to researchers and theorists, from design schools to design journals and publishers). The mainstream way of doing it is, for design experts, to facilitate existing cases of social innovation, helping them to become more effective, accessible, pleasurable and, potentially, replicable. But designers can also act as activists, triggering, or even initiating, new collaborative organizations (replicating good ideas or starting-up brand new ones). Changing of scale, design experts can also promote large systemic changes synergizing a variety of local initiatives and developing specifically conceived framework strategies. Finally, they can feed the social conversations with scenarios and proposals, aiming at building shared visions of the future.[20]

GLOBAL METHODS, LOCAL DESIGNS

In his critical paper "Global Methods, Local Designs," design researcher Ahmed Ansari provides an historical overview of the omnipresent terms "design methods" and "design thinking" now primarily associated with social design. He notes that "it seems that both (terms) ... have undergone a definitional synthesis, enjoying a joint heyday within contemporary professional practice, particularly as design practice moved out of the realm of design agencies and consultancies to become a principal instrument of humanitarian organizations seeking to employ designerly practices in their own repertoire." Through a critical analysis of the *methods toolkit*—a synthesis of design methods and design thinking—Ansari challenges the prevailing notion that toolkits are the *universal* instruments, and that their usage suggests "designing can be reduced to a set of tools, employable by anyone." The use of these toolkits, he argues, can be implicated with inadvertently exporting colonialism to the Global South "as the handmaidens of neoliberal models of development championed by an ascendant technocracy." As Ansari makes clear, there is an emerging tension between the socially engaged design discourses within Western design community (Global North) and the discourses building on postcolonial theory with its critical disentangling and exposing of Anglo-Eurocentrism.[21] There is a great need to diligently question agency, strategy, and politics in order to reveal the biases and politics embedded in design as we move forward.

THE EMERGING TRANSITION DESIGN APPROACH

Transition Design is a new area of design research, practice and study aimed at seeding and catalyzing societal transitions and systems-level change, that argues design and designers have a key role to play in these transitions. Transition Design aspires to (1) develop new tools and approaches that can be used by transdisciplinary teams engaged in this work and (2) educate new generations of designers qualified to join these teams.[22]

Fundamental change at every level of our society is needed to address the issues confronting us in the 21st century. Climate change, loss of biodiversity, depletion of natural resources and the widening gap between rich and poor are just a few of the "wicked problems" that require new approaches to problem solving. Transition Design acknowledges that we are living in "transitional times". It takes as its central premise the need for societal transitions to more sustainable futures and argues that design has a key role to play in these transitions.[23]

Transition Design, which proposes design-led societal transition toward more sustainable futures, was conceived and developed during 2012 at the School of Design at Carnegie Mellon University (USA). In 2013, CMU faculty members Terry Irwin, Cameron Tonkinwise, and Gideon Kossoff developed the Transition Design framework and proposed it as an area of design focus within the newly designed curricula that launched in the fall, 2014. This project became the driving force for subsequent published papers, conference presentations and International symposia. In her 2018 paper "The Emerging Transition Design Approach," Terry Irwin outlines the development of what she describes as an "emerging, design-led approach for addressing complex, wicked problems and catalyzing societal transitions toward more sustainable futures." Irwin argues the need "to engage *all* stakeholders affected by the problem in order to create a shared problem definition and understanding of the oppositions and alignments among them." She proposes the Transition Design Framework (guide) to provide "a logic for bringing together a variety of practices (knowledge and skillsets outside the design disciplines), situated within four mutually-influencing, co-evolving areas" along with a three-part "phased approach" where practices from the framework can be applied that prove useful "to understand root causes and consequences and identify leverage points for interventions aimed at transitioning the system along a transition pathway toward a co-envisioned future."

NOTES

1. Definition of the term "sustainability" accessed on August 26, 2018 from https://en.wikipedia.org/wiki/Sustainability.
2. Definition of the term "sustainable design" accessed on August 26, 2018 from https://en.wikipedia.org/wiki/Sustainable_design.
3. Definition of the term "service design" accessed on August 26, 2018 from https://en.wikipedia.org/wiki/Service_design.
4. L. Kimbell, "Designing for Service as One Way of Designing Services," *International Journal of Design* 5, no. 2 (2011): 41–52.
5. In broad terms, transformation design is a human-centered, interdisciplinary process that seeks to create desirable and sustainable changes in behavior and form—of individuals, systems, and organizations—often for socially progressive ends. Transformation design, like user-centered design, starts from the perspective of the end user. Designers spend a great deal of time not only learning how users currently experience the system and how they want to experience the system, but also cocreating with them the designed solutions. https://en.wikipedia.org/wiki/Transformation_design.
6. Definition of the term "design thinking" accessed on August 26, 2018 from https://en.wikipedia.org/wiki/Design_thinking.
7. Quote by Tim Brown accessed on August 26, 2018 from https://www.ideou.com/pages/design-thinking.
8. L. Kimbell, *Design Practices in Design Thinking* (European Academy of Management, Liverpool, UK, 2009).

9. Definition of the term "participatory design" accessed on August 26, 2018 from https://en.wikipedia.org/wiki/Participatory_design.

10. T. Markussen, "The Disruptive Aesthetics of Design Activism: Enacting Design between Art and Politics," *Design Issues* 29, no. 1 (2013): 38–50.

11. Neoliberalism is an economic ideology centered around the values of a global economy, or globalization: free market, free trade, and the unrestricted flow of capital. Neoliberals advocate minimal government spending, minimal taxation, minimal regulations, and minimal direct involvement in the economy. Definition accessed from https://www.urbandictionary.com/define.php?term=neoliberal.

12. Dr. Elizabeth (Dori) Tunstall situates her definition of design anthropology as coming "directly out of my experiences of being an African American woman who has been trained in critical anthropology and applied that knowledge to the contexts of professional design and design education."

13. Neocolonialism is defined as the economic, cultural, and political policies by which a great power indirectly maintains or extends its influence over other areas or people. https://www.merriam-webster.com/dictionary/neocolonialism.

14. https://www.fastcompany.com/1691553/humanitarian-design-or-neocolonialism.

15. T. Mitrović, M. Golub, and O. Šuran, eds., "Introduction to Speculative Design Practice," *Introduction to Speculative Design Practice—Eutropia, a Case Study* (booklet) (Croatian Designers Association, Arts Academy / University of Split, 2015).

16. "An oxymoron is a figure of speech that combines two contradictory terms. The word *oxymoron* is of Greek origin. It combines the word *oxy* (=sharp) and *moron* (=dull). Thus, oxymoron not only names a contradiction in terms, it is an oxymoron as well. Oxymorons may be used for achieving rhetorical effects, as in *working vacation* and *uninvited guest*. They may also result from conceptual sloppiness, as in *extremely average*, *original copy*, or *same difference*." Klaus Krippendorff, "Design Research, an Oxymoron?" in *Design Research Now: Essays and Selected Projects*, ed. R. Michel (Zürich: Birkhäuser Verlag, 2007), 67–80.

17. Definition of the term "social innovation" accessed on August 26, 2018 from https://en.wikipedia.org/wiki/Social_innovation.

18. Quote from Cheryl Heller, Founding Chair, SVA's MFA Program in Design for Social Innovation. http://www.sva.edu/graduate/mfa-design-for-social-innovation.

19. Concept for 'design for social innovation' articulated https://www.desisnetwork.org/2014/07/25/design-for-social-innovation-vs-social-design/.

20. Quote accessed on August 26, 2018 from http://www.biourbanism.org/interview-with-ezio-manzini/.

21. "To date, mainstream design discourse has been dominated by a focus on Anglocentric/Eurocentric ways of seeing, knowing, and acting in the world, with little attention being paid to alternative and marginalized discourses from the non Anglo-European sphere, or the nature and consequences of design-as-politics today. This narrowness of horizons and deficiency in criticality is a reflection of the limitations of the institutions within which design is studied and practiced, as well as of the larger socio-political systems that design is institutionally integrated into." http://www.decolonisingdesign.com/statements/2016/editorial/.

22. T. Irwin, "Transition Together Symposium Position Papers", June 2018, page 41. Accessed at https://www.academia.edu/37093556/Transition_Together_Symposium_Proceedings_2018.

23. Quote accessed on August 26, 2018 from http://transitiondesign.net/about-transition-design.

CHAPTER TWENTY

First Things First 2000 Manifesto

We, the undersigned, are graphic designers, art directors and visual communicators who have been raised in a world in which the techniques and apparatus of advertising have persistently been presented to us as the most lucrative, effective and desirable use of our talents. Many design teachers and mentors promote this belief; the market rewards it; a tide of books and publications reinforces it.

Encouraged in this direction, designers then apply their skill and imagination to sell dog biscuits, designer coffee, diamonds, detergents, hair gel, cigarettes, credit cards, sneakers, butt toners, light beer and heavy-duty recreational vehicles. Commercial work has always paid the bills, but many graphic designers have now let it become, in large measure, what graphic designers do. This, in turn, is how the world perceives design. The profession's time and energy is used up manufacturing demand for things that are inessential at best.

Many of us have grown increasingly uncomfortable with this view of design. Designers who devote their efforts primarily to advertising, marketing and brand development are supporting, and implicitly endorsing, a mental environment so saturated with commercial messages that it is changing the very way citizen-consumers speak, think, feel, respond and interact. To some extent we are all helping draft a reductive and immeasurably harmful code of public discourse.

There are pursuits more worthy of our problem-solving skills. Unprecedented environmental, social and cultural crises demand our attention. Many cultural interventions, social marketing campaigns, books, magazines, exhibitions, educational tools, television programs, films, charitable causes and other information design projects urgently require our expertise and help.

We propose a reversal of priorities in favor of more useful, lasting and democratic forms of communication—a mindshift away from product marketing and toward the exploration and production of a new kind of meaning. The scope of debate is shrinking; it must expand. Consumerism is running uncontested; it must be challenged by other perspectives expressed, in part, through the visual languages and resources of design.

In 1964, 22 visual communicators signed the original call for our skills to be put to worthwhile use. With the explosive growth of global commercial culture, their message has only grown more urgent. Today, we renew their manifesto in expectation that no more decades will pass before it is taken to heart.

Signed: Jonathan Barnbrook, Nick Bell, Andrew Blauvelt, Hans Bockting, Irma Boom, Sheila Levrant de Bretteville, Max Bruinsma, Sian Cook, Linda van Deursen, Chris Dixon, William Drenttel, Gert Dumbar, Simon Esterson, Vince Frost, Ken Garland, Milton Glaser, Jessica Helfand, Steven Heller, Andrew Howard, Tibor Kalman, Jeffery Keedy, Zuzana Licko, Ellen Lupton, Katherine McCoy, Armand Mevis, J. Abbott Miller, Rick Poynor, Lucienne Roberts, Erik Spiekermann, Jan van Toorn, Teal Triggs, Rudy VanderLans, Bob Wilkinson.

Republished with kind permission from Kalle Lasn, *Adbusters*.

CHAPTER TWENTY ONE

A "Social Model" of Design: Issues of Practice and Research

VICTOR MARGOLIN AND SYLVIA MARGOLIN

© Victor Margolin and Sylvia Margolin / © MIT 2002

INTRODUCTION

When most people think of product design, they envision products for the market, generated by a manufacturer and directed to a consumer. Since the Industrial Revolution, the dominant design paradigm has been one of design for the market, and alternatives have received little attention. In 1972, Victor Papanek, an industrial designer and, at the time, Dean of Design at the California Institute of the Arts, published his polemical book *Design for the Real World* in which he made the famous declaration that "[t]here are professions more harmful than industrial design, but only a very few of them."[1] The book, initially published in Swedish two years earlier, quickly gained worldwide popularity with its call for a new social agenda for designers. Since *Design for the Real World* appeared, others have responded to Papanek's call and sought to develop programs of design for social need ranging from the needs of developing countries to the special needs of the aged, the poor, and the disabled.[2]

These efforts have provided evidence that an alternative to product design for the market is possible, but they have not led to a new model of social practice. Compared to the "market model," there has been little theorizing about a model of product design for social need. Theory about design for the market is extremely well developed. It cuts across many fields from design methods to management studies and the semiotics of marketing. The rich and vast literature of market design has contributed to its continued success and its ability to adapt to new technologies, political and social circumstances, and organizational structures and processes. Conversely, little thought has been given to the structures, methods, and objectives of social design. Concerning design for development, some ideas have been borrowed from the intermediate or alternative technology movement, which has promoted low-cost technological solutions for problems in developing countries, but regarding the broader understanding of how design for social need might be commissioned, supported, and implemented, little has been accomplished.[3] Nor has attention been given to changes in the education of product designers that might prepare them to design for populations in need rather than for the market alone.

The field of environmental psychology has attempted to respond to the environmental needs of the vulnerable. Those working in this field use an interdisciplinary approach to research, and implement solutions that create better living spaces for such populations as the mentally ill, the homeless, and the aged.[4] Architects, psychologists, social workers, occupational therapists, and others have worked together to explore the intersection of people's psychological needs and the landscapes, communities, neighborhoods, housing, and interior space that increase feelings of pleasantness, arousal, excitement, and relaxation, and decrease feelings of fear and stress.[5] There has not been a similar effort in the field of product design.

A "SOCIAL MODEL" OF DESIGN PRACTICE

In this paper, we want to begin a new discussion of design for social need by proposing a "social model" of product design practice and suggesting a research agenda that would examine and develop it in the same way that comparable research has supported design for the market and environmental psychology. Although many design activities can be considered as socially responsible design—sustainable product design, affordable housing, and the redesign of government tax and immigration forms, for example—we will limit this paper to a discussion of product design within a process of social service intervention. Although we base our discussion on the intervention model used by social workers, a similar model could also be applied to collaborations with health care professionals in hospitals and other health care settings, as well as to joint projects with teachers and educational administrators in school settings. The model could work as well with teams of experts engaged in projects in developing countries.

The primary purpose of design for the market is creating products for sale. Conversely, the foremost intent of social design is the satisfaction of human needs. However, we don't propose the "market model" and the "social model" as binary opposites, but instead view them as two poles of a continuum. The difference is defined by the priorities of the commission rather than by a method of production or distribution. Many products designed for the market also meet a social need but we argue that the market does not, and probably cannot, take care of all social needs, as some relate to populations who do not constitute a class of consumers in the market sense. We refer here to people with low incomes or special needs due to age, health, or disability.

To develop a "social model," we will draw on the literature of social work, a practice whose principal objective is to meet the needs of underserved or marginalized populations. Central to social work theory is the ecological perspective.[6] Social workers assess the transaction that occurs between their client system (a person, family, group, organization, or community) and the domains within the environment with which the client system interacts. Various domains that impact human functioning are the biological, psychological, cultural, social, natural, and physical/spatial.[7] The physical/ spatial domain, which concerns us in this paper, is comprised of all things created by humans such as objects, buildings, streets, and transportation systems. Inadequate or inferior physical surroundings and products can affect the safety, social opportunity, stress level, sense of belonging, self-esteem, or even physical health of a person or persons in a community. A poor fit with one or more key domains may be at the root of the client system's problem, thus creating a human need.

For example, some preschool children are misbehaving. An initial diagnosis blames their parents for having poor child-rearing skills. A social worker is asked to organize the parents into a group in order to teach them better child-rearing practices. The assumption here is that the parents will apply these skills, and their children's behavior will improve. When the group meets, the social worker learns that the parents are under tremendous stress due to multiple problems: lack of money because of the inability to find a job; low wages in available jobs; scarce transportation to get to work in distant places; unsafe surroundings; broken playground equipment on a cement lot; and inadequate and unsafe elevators in their apartment buildings. It is clear that the issues with which the parents are dealing go beyond poor child-rearing skills, thus requiring that other factors, including those in the physical/ spatial domain, be addressed.

Social workers tend to follow a model of generalist practice, a six-step problem-solving process that includes engagement, assessment, planning, implementation, evaluation, and termination. The entire process is conducted in a collaborative manner with the client system. Other human service professionals may be brought in as part of the intervention. In the engagement phase, the social worker listens to the client system and gets a sense of the presenting problem. In the next phase, assessment, the social worker looks holistically at the client system's interaction within the various environmental domains. The aim of an assessment is not to take a problem at face value but to look more deeply and more broadly at the client system in the total environment to get at the roots of the problem. The outcome of the assessment phase is a list of different needs to be addressed. In the third phase, planning, the social worker collaborates with the client system to prioritize the needs, trying to determine what is most pressing. Then the social worker and the client system brainstorm in order to devise different solutions. They talk about various ideas and collaboratively decide what will work best. Together, the client system and the social worker make a list of goals and objectives and decide who will do what by when.[8] In the implementation phase, the intervention is guided by the goals and objectives that have already been agreed upon.

In settings such as hospitals or schools, social workers are members of teams that include other professionals. Among these might be psychologists, speech therapists, occupational therapists, and probation officers. The team works collaboratively to assess a problem and different team members intervene as needed. The ways in which product designers could participate in a team process with human service professionals are yet to be explored particularly the designer's involvement in the physical/spatial domain.

Lawton describes a research project for the elderly that sought to learn about the deficiencies in the home environment and the way people cope with them. A social worker, an architect, a psychologist, and an occupational therapist visited the homes of fifty highly impaired older people who were managing to live alone. One of the team's findings was that many of the people they observed had set up "control centers" in an area of their living room that allowed them to view the front door and, through a window, the street. The nearby placement of a telephone, radio, and television also enabled them to have social contact with the outside world. Additionally, on a table within reach were medicine, food, reading material, and other items of use. If a product designer had been on this intervention team, he or she would no doubt have been stimulated to create products that could serve the low-mobility needs of this older population.[9]

To advance the discussion of how the product designer might collaborate with an intervention team, we would like to suggest several options. During the assessment phase, the designer, either as a member of an intervention team or as a consultant, might be able to identify factors that contribute to a problem. In the planning phase, a designer could develop intervention strategies related to the physical environment. During implementation, the designer could create a needed product or work with the client system to design one.

These strategies differ from Papanek's proposals for social action in *Design for the Real World*. Papanek pits socially responsible designers against a commercial market that thrives on the production of excessive and useless products. By harshly criticizing the market economy, he limits the options for a social designer. Papanek argues that socially responsible designers must organize their own interventions outside the mainstream market, yet he gives little guidance as to how this might be done. We believe that many professionals share the goals of designers who want to do socially responsible work, and therefore we propose that both designers and helping professionals find ways to work together. In short, we believe that designers will find many more allies in professions related to health, education, social work, aging, and crime prevention than are evident in Papanek's analysis.

Nonetheless, Papanek's book is extremely helpful in describing the kinds of social products designers might create. Using as a framework a socially-oriented design office, Papanek provides long lists of products that address social needs. Among these are teaching aids of all kinds including aids to transfer knowledge and skills to those with learning difficulties and physical disabilities; training aids for poor people who are trying to move into the work force; medical diagnostic devices, hospital equipment, and dental tools; equipment and furnishings for mental hospitals; safety devices for home and work; and devices that address pollution problems.[10] Some of these products, particularly medical and hospital equipment, are already produced for the market, but there are certainly many that are not manufactured because a market cannot be identified for them.

AN AGENDA FOR SOCIAL DESIGN

Design is most often understood by the public as an artistic practice that produces dazzling lamps, furniture, and automobiles. This is how it is generally presented by the media and the museums.[11] One reason why there is not more support for social design services is the lack of research to demonstrate what a designer can contribute to human welfare.

A broad research agenda for social design must begin by addressing a number of questions. What role can a designer play in a collaborative process of social intervention? What is currently being done in this regard and what might be done? How might the public's perception of designers be changed in order to present an image of a socially responsible designer? How can agencies that fund social welfare projects and research gain a stronger perception of design as a socially responsible activity? What kinds of products meet the needs of vulnerable populations?

A multifaceted approach can be taken to explore these and other questions. Survey research and interviews with human service professionals, designers, and agency administrators can be conducted to gather information on perceptions and attitudes, and to solicit suggestions for change. Content analysis of archival data such as journals, periodicals, and newspapers can be used to gain insight into how the media report on issues of social design.[12]

Another research method is participant observation. This entails designers entering social settings, either as part of a multidisciplinary team or alone, to observe and document social needs that can be satisfied with design interventions. For example, this was done in the research project conducted by Lawton that we described earlier, except that an architect rather than a product designer was on the investigative team.

Research that centers on the development and evaluation of socially responsible products is also important. To create new products, designers have to conduct research on how to translate their ideas into finished designs. They are obligated to evaluate these products in actual situations to test their effectiveness.[13] A good example of socially-oriented product design research is MIT's AgeLab, where Joseph Coughlin, a professor of engineering, and a team of colleagues and graduate students are testing and analyzing new technologies to improve life for the elderly. Although some of the research involves technology that can help the elderly drive more safely and possibly at an older age, much of the investigation relates to the home where such products as an in-home health center and a transit system that would allow people to schedule rides are being considered. Finally, the social design field should have a compendium of case studies such as AgeLab that document examples of relevant practice.

The combined research methods we have outlined are intended to explore questions that range from the broad social context within which designers work to the specifics of developing a product for a particular client system. The scope of research for social design includes public and agency perceptions of designers, the economics of social interventions, the value of design in improving the lives of underserved populations, a taxonomy of new product typologies, the economics of manufacturing socially responsible products, and the way that such products and services are received by populations in need. Until now, the social interventions of designers have been hit-or-miss, with few successes to point the way towards social support for more of the same.

THE EDUCATION OF SOCIAL DESIGNERS

Design skills cut across all situations, but skills in relating to vulnerable or marginalized populations rather than to a brief from a manufacturer need to be developed by future social designers. Students of social design will have to learn more about social needs and how they are currently addressed by helping professionals. They might do an internship with a clinical team in a psychiatric hospital, a community agency, or a residential facility for the elderly. They would also need a stronger background in sociology, psychology, and public policy. As far as we are aware, no university programs specifically train social designers. We can, however, cite as a good beginning the one-year certificate program of Archeworks, a private educational institution in Chicago, founded in 1994 by Stanley Tigerman and Eva L. Maddox, that is dedicated to advancing a socially responsible design agenda. Each year, Archeworks introduces a small interdisciplinary group of students with varied intellectual backgrounds to a process of social design that has resulted in a number of projects and studies including a device for people with Alzheimer's Disease to facilitate their getting into an automobile, a head-pointer designed for people with cerebral palsy, and a new model office environment for the Illinois Department of Human Services. In most cases, projects have been conducted in collaboration with social service organizations or agencies, and many have been funded by grants from public and private sources.[14]

CONCLUSION

Our purpose has been to describe a new "social model" of design practice and to suggest a research agenda through which important questions related to the emergence of such a practice can be addressed. A "social model" of design practice is needed more than ever, and we are hopeful that concerned designers, design researchers, helping professionals, and design educators will find ways to bring it about.

© 2002 MIT. Previously published in *Design Issues*: Volume 18, Number 4, Autumn 2002.

NOTES

1. Victor Papanek, *Design for the Real World: Human Ecology and Social Change*, 2nd ed. (Chicago: Academy Chicago, 1985), ix. We have used Papanek's 1985 revised edition rather than the original one of 1972 because he made a number of changes from one edition to another, and we wanted to draw on his most current thinking. For a discussion of Papanek's concept of socially responsible design, see Nigel Whiteley, *Design for Society* (London: Reaktion Books, 1993), 103–115.
2. See, for example, Julian Bicknell and Liz McQuiston, eds., *Design for Need: The Social Contribution of Design* (Oxford: Pergamon Press, 1977). This volume is a collection of papers from a conference of the same name held at the Royal College of Art in April 1976.
3. There is an extensive literature on appropriate technology. For a critical introduction to the subject, see Witold Rybczynski, *Paper Heroes: A Review of Appropriate Technology* (Garden City, NY: Anchor Press/Doubleday, 1980).
4. The intellectual histories of thirteen first-generation thinkers in environment and behavior studies are presented in *Environment and Behavior Studies: Emergence of Intellectual Traditions*, Irwin Altman and Kathleen Christensen, eds. (New York and London: Plenum Press, 1990).
5. See Jack L. Nasar, "The Evaluative Image of Places" in *Person-Environment Psychology: New Directions and Perspectives*, 2nd ed., W. Bruce Walsh, Kenneth H. Crain, and Richard H. Price, eds. (Mahwah, NJ: Lawrence Erlbaum Associates, 2000).

6. This same perspective is used in environmental psychology.

7. See L. Allen Furr, *Exploring Human Behavior and the Social Environment* (Boston: Allyn and Bacon, 1997), 3–12 and C.B. Germain and A. Gitterman, "The Life Model Approach to Social Work Practice Revisited" in *Social Work Treatment: Interlocking Theoretical Approaches*, Francis J. Turner, ed. (New York: The Free Press, 1986), 618–643.

8. Aspects of the client system/social worker relationship are also evident in *participatory design* but, in this relationship more authority is assigned to the designer whose professional knowledge differentiates his or her ability to conduct a design project from the users or clients, no matter how involved the latter are in the planning process.

9. M. Powell Lawton, "An Environmental Psychologist Ages" in *Environment and Behavior Studies: Emergence of Intellectual Traditions*, 357–358. A research study on the spatial needs of the elderly in Hong Kong was conducted by the Research Group on Urban Space and Culture, School of Design, Hong Kong Polytechnic University, in conjunction with a social service team at St. James Settlement. Using the Wan Chai district as the research site, the group, which was comprised of designers rather than architects, proposed a number of new spatial arrangements to help elderly people function better in cramped apartments. See Kwok Yan-chi Jackie, ed., *Ageing in the Community: A Research on the Designing of Everyday Life Environment for the Elderly* (Hong Kong: Hong Kong Polytechnic University and St. James Settlement, 1999).

10. Papanek, *Design for the Real World*, 63–68.

11. There are some exceptions among museum exhibits such as the Cooper-Hewitt National Design Museum's exhibit on Universal Design, *Unlimited by Design*, held at the museum between November 1998 and March 1999.

12. As an example, the February 2001 issue of *I.D.* magazine edited by Christopher Mount, presented profiles of forty socially conscious designers and architects.

13. In *Design for the Real World*, Papanek provides numerous illustrations of socially responsible projects that students designed under his supervision.

14. For an overview of Archeworks, see the school's website www.archeworks.org.

CHAPTER TWENTY TWO

The Dematerialization of Design

JORGE FRASCARA

© Jorge Frascara, 2003

ABSTRACT

Centering design on human use, positions the task of the designer in a fluid context, in which planning has to make room for self-organization. If design is to facilitate human tasks, increase human performance and assist people in their efforts to achieve their goals, many issues must be faced: what are people's expectations of performance? What is desirable as human goals? In what manner human performance and goals should be contextualized in this increasingly small world? While design has generally been seen as oriented to the satisfaction of people's needs and desires, today we feel it is not that easy to define a boundary between those needs and those desires, nor to see their definition as a way to reach the solution to the problem. We need to look at design as a problem-oriented interdisciplinary activity. We should focus on design itself as a design problem, and seek interdisciplinary input to define its field of competence and action. And we should look at design critically examining the value systems within which it operates.

Keywords: communication, culture, design, human-centered, interdisciplinary

HUMAN CENTERED DESIGN:
COMPLEXITIES AND UNCERTAINTIES

The proposed link between design and the social sciences is the result of two things: the recognition of changes in the design profession in connection with both purposes and methods of operation, and the perception of the way in which these changes require an increased participation of social scientists in the conception and development of consumer products and public services. To elaborate on details, I will discuss a series of headings and brief explanations, regarding those dimensions of design that lead to new understandings of its nature and its practice.

OBJECTS AND PEOPLE

While design has been traditionally concerned with objects and processes, we have to recognize the impact that those objects have on people. We have to stop thinking of design as the construction of graphics, products, services, systems and environments, and think about those as means for people to act, to realize their wishes and satisfy their needs. It is the needs and the wishes that we have to serve; the objects of design must be seen only as means. This requires a better understanding of people, of society, and of the ecosystem, and calls for an interdisciplinary practice.

OPERATIONAL IMPACT VERSUS CULTURAL IMPACT

Every design project has an operational objective: it is supposed to affect the knowledge, the attitudes or the behavior of people in a given and desired way. But any object deployed in the public space, be it communicational or physical, has a cultural impact. This cultural impact affects the way people operate with people and with things, and contributes to the creation of cultural consensus. More has to be done to understand this cultural impact so that designers can operate more responsibly in society.

COMMUNICATION AS PARTNERSHIP AND NEGOTIATION

If visual communication design is concerned with affecting the knowledge, the attitudes and the behavior of people, then it should do this in an ethical way, that is, seeking partnership in the process of change, rather than communicating things to people. The process of communication should be seen as a process of negotiation where the position of the originator of the information and that of the interpreter enter in contact searching for a common terrain. Unidirectional communication is unethical and inefficient, and it promotes a passivity that in the long run will weaken our civilization. In ethical communications, one communicates with someone about something; one does not communicate something to someone. In ethical communications the popular terminology, borrowed from electronics and information science that defines the poles of the communication chain as transmitter and receiver, is untenable.

In a universe of people engaged in communicational exchanges, it is more fitting to talk about producers and interpreters than about transmitters and receivers, terms that do not allow room for context, history, expectations, goals, values, priorities, feelings, preferences, cultural differences and differences of intelligence. In ethical communications, the producer has to speak a language that the audience can understand. If producers really want to communicate, that is, if they want to be understood and not just listened to, they should remember that people can only understand things that relate to things that they already understand, and that it is impossible to communicate, therefore, without using the language and the experience of the audience. This is why the ideal form of human communication is the dialogue, where the interaction allows for exchange and adjustment, and for the building and extending of a shared terrain. Given that in our society a designer fashions communications for mass media, attempting to reach thousands of unknown people, it becomes clear that design needs to liaise with the social sciences to improve our understanding of the audiences and increase the possibilities for both ethical and effective communications and products to come to exist.

ACCOUNTABILITY

There is a need to develop a more accountable design practice, where the judgment of quality should not depend on the coincidence of several subjectivities but where it could be based on actual measurable benefits: human, financial or other, that could be expressed as the return of the design investment. Without attempting to reduce all design activity to only those dimensions that could be measured, it is time to be serious about design as investment, so that it is not seen as expenditure, and a superficial one.

PUBLIC GOOD

Much has been said about doing voluntary work for public service. This is not my point. The public good must be the most important objective of design activity, and it should be sought with the best resources, being understood as an investment with high returns affecting hidden dimensions of the economy. Let's just think about tax return forms, which are filed by some 20 million people in Canada, and about the Australian Communication Research Institute estimate that each error costs about $14 to the administrating agent. Think about the $300,000 that a spinal cord injury in a car crash costs in the first year of treatment to our health care system. Think about the 200,000 Canadians that suffer injuries every year in traffic collisions and the 51 million days of work lost every year in Canada due to injuries in general. Much can be done about this with well-designed communication campaigns, information improvement, public education and concerted programs, but to do this we need the best brains in a variety of fields, centering, of course, on design and the social sciences. And we also need to make substantial investments in these programs. There is experience in this terrain: the traffic safety campaign produced in the state of Victoria, Australia, required $6 million Australian dollars in media, but the government agency that acts as third party liability insurer saved $118 million in payments during the first year of implementation of the campaign. This happened nine years ago, and by now the combination of broad scope police programs and communication campaigns have reduced the injury collision levels to that of the 1950s, about 50% of what it was in 1989.

RELEVANCE

Design has to be relevant so as to rise above fads and fashions and penetrate all dimensions of life with a view to improving it. Irrelevant design is a liability for the profession and the environment. If we are looking at strengthening the position of design among other human activities, we will have to review the relevance of design projects and foster work in those areas where design could actually make a difference for the better.

THE DESIGNER AS A PROBLEM SOLVER VERSUS THE DESIGNER AS A PROBLEM IDENTIFIER

Design is a problem-oriented, interdisciplinary activity. There is a need to identify important problems and develop interdisciplinary strategies to deal with them. It is not sustainable to continue just reacting to clients' requests for design interventions. It is necessary to consider the discovery and definition of physical and cultural problems as an essential part of design. The nature of each problem might suggest the spectrum of disciplines required to confront it. A set of tools to look at the world will have to be developed by inquisitive, critical, interdisciplinary observation, performed by people in love with humanity.

SUSTAINABILITY

Given the state of affairs today, in both environmental and cultural terms, it is not possible to design anything without framing it within the notion of sustainability. The escalation of waste and the generally irresponsible attitude of industry and governments about the use of toxic and damaging products and processes is as bad to the physical environment as the promotion of violence and selfishness by the entertainment industry is to the cultural environment. Cultural and physical sustainability must become part of every design process, and schools will have an important role to play in the formation of the new generations of designers. While internationally there are blatant inequalities, there is a lot to do concerning cultural sustainability in our own backyard.

EFFICIENCY AND DEMOCRACY

These are the two poles between which collective decisions take place. Where to strike the balance, is a matter of judgment. If design decisions, and other decisions that affects us all, are to be collective decisions, then more should be discussed about their nature, and about criteria for appropriate balances between the two poles. Designers at the forefront of the profession are understanding design as the design of interactions between people and objects; now we have to develop a better understanding of the interactions between people and people. To get things done there is no alternative, and many times excellent design ideas do not get realized because the originators lack the necessary ability to interact with people in decision making positions. The more original the design proposal is, the more difficult it will be to implement it, particularly when needing significant investments.

PLANNING AND SELF-ORGANIZATION

It has to be accepted that all design problems involve these two aspects: it is not possible to continue believing that planning can solve it all, or that self-organization can solve it all. Understanding the capacity of things and people to organize themselves when thrown in a given situation puts planning in an interesting perspective. The sport team model or the Panzer Division is not sufficient, and the Calcutta model is not desirable or sustainable. In design we should look more at the way in which things interact with each other, and on the dynamics of large complex systems, such as cities, ecologies or the stock market, and look for better conceptual models to replace old planning strategies. Design is a problem oriented, interdisciplinary activity. There is a need to identify important problems and develop interdisciplinary strategies to deal with them. It is not sustainable to continue just reacting to clients' requests for design interventions. It is necessary to consider the discovery and definition of physical and cultural problems as an essential part of design. The nature of each problem might suggest the spectrum of disciplines required to understand it. A set of tools to look at the world will have to be developed by inquisitive, critical, interdisciplinary observation, performed by people enamored with humanity.

THE COMPLEX AND THE COMPLICATED

I like to make a working distinction between these two terms, for the sake of a clearer use of them. Let's say that a computer network is complicated, since it consists of a great number of parts but it is possible to account for them all. Social relations, instead, are complex. Aspects interact with aspects and constantly change, preventing us ever from developing a perfect description, definition or explanation. Our relations with the complex are always in a state of flux. As soon as we have people in the equation, the problems become complex.

FORM, MATERIALS AND SELF-EXPRESSION VERSUS CONTEXT AND CONTENT

The major preoccupations of the avant-garde/fine-arts based design education of the 1920s were form, materials and self-expression. Materials exploration was added by design education to the self-expression/form exploration approach of the avant-garde fine artists. We now realize that graphic design education today, seventy years later, is in the main concerned with the same issues, to the detriment of a formalized education in content and context, and the way in which these two dimensions condition communication and should, therefore, condition design action. We have now enough collective experience on form and materials; we need to transform self-expression into resourcefulness and inventiveness regarding the visual language in order to be able to speak the language of the public being addressed. We need as well to concentrate on formalizing, codifying the problems of content and context, learning and teaching how to transform them into elements of the design process.

OBJECTS OF THOUGHT AND DIMENSIONS OF JUDGMENT

Public opinions and attitudes are formed on the basis of these two dimensions, that for the purpose of persuasive communications must be distinguished by the designer. Objects of thought are things we have in mind, and these could be concrete objects, such as the Eiffel Tower, my mother or the concept of leisure. Dimensions of judgment are value axes: good-bad, useful-useless, dangerous-safe, attractive-repulsive, etc. The positions of objects of thought on specific points in scales of dimensions of judgment forms the basis of attitude formation and attitude change.

THE SOFTENING OF DESIGN

All the above emphasizes the fact that as designers we have given up our exclusive obsession with products, materials and manufacturing processes, and have become more concerned with the contexts in which objects and communications are used by people, and with the consequences that the existence of those design creations have on people in general. We have moved, for instance, from the design of workstations to the design of work. It is not possible to invent and design the perfect chair on which a person could be sitting for eight hours a day without becoming physically fatigued or handicapped in one way or another. It is wiser to design a work pattern which, including the design of furniture, would be centered on the design of the activities to be performed. We have moved from the design of teaching aids to the design of teaching situations. The success of a learning experience cannot be trusted to the design of a teaching aid. The activity has to be planned so that the teaching aid contributes its best to the experience. Many factors affect this terrain, but certainly the teacher's actions, the student's actions and the environment in which the intervention occurs, all contribute to the learning event and must be seen as part of the design problem. All this, points at areas where the association between design and the social sciences promises to equip us to be able to face a number of complex design problems with a better set of tools.

A WORD OF WARNING

Design, and particularly in its relation to human factors and other aspects of the social sciences, has been connected both in the recent past and in my own words, to the notion of efficiency. Efficiency is central to design discourse. Why to design, otherwise, if not to increase the efficiency of something? To facilitate the satisfaction of needs, to multiply force, to increase comfort, to extend our abilities, design is conceived as the way to bring efficiency to our lives. Efficiency, however, has been excessively emphasized in our culture, and particularly in this continent, and processes of downsizing administrative supports, increasing performance expectations and turning into businesses what used to be public services are destroying our lives. All this puts pressure on people to be efficient, to work harder and to feel guilty when taking a stroll on Saturday instead of dealing with the workload one takes home every weekend. It is imperative to look at the contexts within which design operates, and at the value systems design promotes.

I recognize three areas for the practice of design: design that works to make life possible, design that works to make life easier, and design that works to make life better. I work very much on the first one. My work on traffic safety communications intends to keep more people alive, and to reduce pain and suffering. Like the medical profession, I concentrate on physical survival. It is still a mystery to me why the medical profession is held so high in our culture. They only deal with the animal in us and this is useful, but if we look at design that works to make life better, we look at sensual and intellectual enjoyment, mature feelings, ability to reach high degrees of consciousness about our lives and our actions, and cultural sensitivity to build civilization and relate constructively to others; all those things that make us specifically human.

I see the relation between design and the social sciences as one that will increase the ability of design to deliver efficiency. But I see the need to use that efficiency so that we can increase not only our production of consumer goods, but also our time to reflect about our human condition, our time to interact with others we love, and our time to introduce more significance, enjoyment and consciousness in our daily actions.

I hope this project will promote the possibilities that the formalization of this interdisciplinary connection creates, and that it will also promote a critical look at the contexts within which we operate, ensuring that a humane life is held at the center as the maximum aspiration of any intellectual effort.

CHAPTER TWENTY THREE

Why Being "Less Bad" Is No Good (Cradle to Cradle)

WILLIAM McDONOUGH AND MICHAEL BRAUNGART

© 2002 William McDonough and Michael Braungart

The drive to make industry less destructive goes back to the earliest stages of the Industrial Revolution, when factories were so destructive and polluting that they had to be controlled in order to prevent immediate sickness and death. Since then the typical response to industrial destruction has been to find a less bad approach. This approach has its own vocabulary with which most of us are familiar: *reduce, avoid, minimize, sustain, limit, halt*. These terms have long been central to environmental agendas, and they have become central to most of the environmental agendas taken up by industry today.

One early dark messenger was Thomas Malthus, who warned at the end of the eighteenth century that humans would reproduce exponentially, with devastating consequences for humankind. Malthus's position was unpopular during the explosive excitement of early industry, when much was made of humanity's potential for good, when its increasing ability to mold the earth to its own purposes was seen as largely constructive; and when even population growth was viewed as a boon. Malthus envisioned not great, gleaming advancement but darkness, scarcity, poverty, and famine. His *Population: The First Essay*, published in 1798, was framed as a response to essayist and utopian William Godwin, who often espoused man's "perfectibility." "I have read some of the speculations on the perfectibility of man and of society with great pleasure," Malthus wrote. "I have been warmed and delighted with the enchanting picture which they hold forth." But, he concluded, "The power of population is so superior to the power in the earth to produce subsistence for man, that premature death must in some shape or other visit the human race." Because of his pessimism (and his suggestion that people should have less sex), Malthus became a cultural caricature. Even now his name is equated with a Scrooge-like attitude toward the world.[1]

While Malthus was making his somber predictions about human population and resources, others were noticing changes in nature (and spirit) as industry spread. English Romantic writers such as William Wordsworth and William Blake described the spiritual and imaginative depth that nature could inspire, and they spoke out against an increasingly mechanistic urban society that was turning even more of its attention toward getting and spending. The Americans George Perkins Marsh, Henry David Thoreau, John Muir, Aldo Leopold, and others continued this literary tradition into the nineteenth and twentieth centuries and in the New World. From the Maine woods, Canada, Alaska, the Midwest, and the Southwest, these voices from the wilderness preserved in language the landscape they loved, lamented its destruction, and reaffirmed the belief that, as Thoreau famously put it, "in Wildness is the preservation of the world."[2] Marsh was one of the first to understand man's capacity to wreak lasting destruction on the environment, and Leopold anticipated some of the feelings of guilt that characterize much environmentalism today:

"When I submit these thoughts to a printing press, I am helping cut down the woods. When I pour cream in my coffee, I am helping to drain a marsh for cows to graze, and to exterminate the birds of Brazil. When I go birding or hunting in my Ford, I am devastating an oil field, and re-electing an imperialist to get me rubber. Nay more: when I father more than two children I am creating an insatiable need for more printing presses, more cows, more coffee, more oil, to supply which more birds, more trees, and more flowers will either by killed, or...evicted from their several environments."[3]

Some of these men helped to form conservation societies such as the Sierra Club and the Wilderness Society, to preserve wilderness and keep it untouched by industrial growth. Their writings inspire new generations of environmentalists and nature lovers, and they still do.

But it wasn't until the publication of Rachel Carson's *Silent Spring* in 1962 that this romantic strain of wilderness appreciation merged with a scientific basis for concern. Up until that point, environmentalism meant protesting the obvious damage—deforestation, mining destruction, factory pollution, and other visible changes—and seeking to conserve especially appreciated landscapes, like the White Mountains of New Hampshire or Yosemite in California. Carson pointed out something more insidious; she imagined a landscape in which no birds sang, and moved on to explain that human-made chemicals—particularly pesticides such as DDT—were devastating the natural world.

Although it took almost a decade, *Silent Spring* led to the banning of DDT in the United States and Germany and sparked a continuing controversy about the dangers of industrial chemicals. It influenced scientists and politicians to take up the cause and to form groups such as Environmental Defense, the Natural Resources Defense Council, the World Wildlife Federation, and BUND (the German Federation for Environmental and Nature Conservation). Environmentalists were no longer interested simply in preservation but in monitoring and reducing toxins. Declining wilderness and diminishing resources merged with pollution and toxic waste as the major realms of concern.

Malthus's legacy continued to hold strong. Shortly after *Silent Spring*, in 1968, Paul Ehrlich, a pioneer of modern environmentalism and an eminent biologist working at Stanford, published an alarm of Malthusian proportions, *The Population Bomb*, in which he declared that the 1970s and 1980s would be a dark era of resource shortages and famine, during which "hundreds of millions of people will starve to death." He also pointed out humans' habit of "using the atmosphere as a garbage dump." "Do we want to keep it up and find out what will happen?" he asked. "What do we gain by playing 'environmental roulette'?"[4]

In 1984 Ehrlich and his wife, Anne, followed up the first book with another, *The Population Explosion*. In this second warning to humanity, they asserted, "Then the fuse was burning; now the population bomb has detonated." Primary among "the underlying causes of our planet's unease," the two posited, "is the overgrowth of the human population and its impacts on both ecosystems and human communities." Their first chapter is entitled "Why Isn't Everyone as Scared as We Are?" and their parting suggestion for humanity begins with two urgent suggestions: "Halt human population growth as quickly and humanely as possible," and "Convert the economic system from one of growthism to one of sustainability, lowering per-capita consumption."[5]

The association of growth with negative consequences has become a major theme of environmentalists in the modern age. In 1972, between the publication of the Ehrlich's first and second warnings, Donella and Dennis Meadows and the Club of Rome (a group of international business, state, and scientific leaders) published another serious warning, *The Limits to Growth*. The authors noted that resources were plummeting due to population growth and destructive industry and concluded, "If the present growth trends in world population, industrialization, pollution, food production, and resource depletion continue unchanged, the limits to growth on this planet will be reached sometime within the next one hundred years. The most probable result will be a sudden and uncontrollable decline in both population and industrial capacity."[6] Twenty years later a follow-up, *Beyond the Limit*, concluded with more warnings: "Minimize the use of nonrenewable resources." "Prevent the erosion of renewable resources." "Use all resources with maximum efficiency." "Slow and eventually stop exponential growth of population and physical capital."[7]

In 1973 Fritz Schumacher's *Small Is Beautiful: Economics as If People Mattered* tackled the issue of growth from a philosophical vantage point. "The idea of unlimited economic growth," he wrote, "more and more until everybody is saturated with wealth, needs to be seriously questioned." In addition to advocating small-scale, nonviolent technologies that would "reverse the destructive trends now threatening us all," Schumacher posited that people must make a serious shift in what they consider to be wealth and progress: "Ever-bigger machines, entailing ever-bigger concentrations of economic power and exerting ever-greater violence against the environment, do not represent progress: they are a denial of wisdom." Real wisdom, he claimed, "can be found only inside oneself," enabling one to "see the hollowness and fundamental unsatisfactoriness of a life devoted primarily to the pursuit of material ends."[8]

At the same time that these environmentalists were issuing important warnings, others were suggesting ways consumers could reduce their negative impact on the environment. A recent version of this message is found in Robert Lilienfeld and William Rathje's 1998 *Use Less Stuff: Environmental Solutions for Who We Really Are*. Consumers must take the lead in reducing negative environmental impact, the authors argue: "The simple truth is that all of our major environmental concerns are either caused by, or contribute to, the ever-increasing consumption of goods and services." This devouring impulse in Western culture is comparable, they maintain, to a drug or alcohol addiction: "Recycling is an aspirin, alleviating a rather large collective hangover... overconsumption." Or again, "The best way to reduce any environmental impact is not to recycle more, but to produce and dispose of less."[9]

The tradition of issuing urgent, often moving messages to producers and consumers is rich and long-standing. But it took decades for industries themselves to really listen to them. In fact, it was not until the 1990s that leading industrialists began to recognize causes for concern. "What we thought was boundless has limits," Robert Shapiro, the chairman and chief executive officer of Monsanto, said in a 1997 interview, "and we're beginning to hit them."[10]

The 1992 Rio Earth Summit, co-initiated by Canadian businessman Maurice Strong, was organized in response to this concern. Approximately thirty thousand people from around the world, more than a hundred world leaders, and representatives of 167 countries gathered in Rio de Janeiro to respond to troubling signals of environmental decline. To the sharp disappointment of many, no binding agreements were reached. (Strong is reported to have quipped, "There were many heads of state, but no real leaders.") But one major strategy emerged from the industrial participants: eco-efficiency. The machines of industry would be refitted with cleaner, faster, quieter engines. Industry would redeem its reputation without significantly changing its structures or compromising its drive for profit. Eco-efficiency would transform human industry from a system that takes, makes, and wastes into one that integrates economic, environmental, and ethical concerns. Industries across the globe now consider eco-efficiency to be the choice strategy of change.

What is eco-efficiency? Primarily the term means "doing more with less," a precept that has its roots in early industrialization. Henry Ford himself was adamant about lean and clean operating policies, saving his company millions of dollars by reducing waste and setting new standards with his time-saving assembly line. "You must get the most out of the power, out of the material, and out of the time," he wrote in 1926, a credo that most contemporary CEOs would proudly hang on their office walls.[11] The linkage of efficiency with sustaining the environment was perhaps most famously articulated in *Our Common Future*, a report published in 1987 by the United Nations' World Commission on Environment and Development. *Our Common Future* warned that if pollution control was not intensified, human health, property, and ecosystems would be seriously threatened, and urban existence would become intolerable: "Industries and industrial operations should be encouraged that are more efficient in terms of resource use, that generate less pollution and waste, that are based on the use of renewable rather than non-renewable resources, and that minimize irreversible adverse impacts on human health and the environment," stated the commission in its agenda for change.[12]

The term eco-efficiency was officially coined five years later by the Business Council for Sustainable Development, a group of forty-eight industrial sponsors including Dow, DuPont, Conagra, and Chevron, who had been asked to bring a business perspective to the Earth Summit. The council couched its call for change in practical terms, focusing on what businesses had to gain from a new ecological awareness rather than on what the environment stood to lose if industry continued current patterns. The group's report, *Changing Course*, timed for simultaneous release with the summit, stressed the importance of eco-efficiency for all companies that aimed to be competitive, sustainable, and successful in the long term. "Within a decade," predicted Stephan Schmidheiney, one of the council's founders, "it is going to be next to impossible for a business to be competitive without also being 'eco-efficient'—adding more value to a good or service while using fewer resources and releasing less pollution."[13]

Even more quickly than Schmidheiney predicted, eco-efficiency has wended its way into industry with extraordinary success. The number of corporations adopting it continues to rise, including such big names as Monsanto, 3M (whose 3P—"Pollution Pays Program"—went into effect in 1986, before co-efficiency was a common term), and Johnson & Johnson. The movement's famous three Rs—reduce, reuse, recycle—are steadily gaining popularity in the home as well as in the workplace. The trend stems in part from eco-efficiency's economic benefits, which can be considerable; 3M, for example, announced that by 1997 it had saved more than $750 million through pollution-prevention projects, and other companies too claim to be realizing big savings.[14] Naturally, reducing resource consumption, energy use, emissions, and wastes has a beneficial effect on the environment as well—and on public morale. When you hear that a company like DuPont has cut its emissions of cancer-causing chemicals by almost 70 percent since 1987, you feel better.[15] Eco-efficient industries can do something good for the environment, and people can feel less fearful about the future. Or can they?

THE FOUR R's: REDUCE, REUSE, RECYCLE—AND REGULATE

Whether it is a matter of cutting the amount of toxic waste created or emitted, or the quantity of raw materials used, or the product size itself (known in business circles as "dematerialization"), reduction is a central tenet of eco-efficiency. But reduction in any of these areas does not halt depletion and destruction—it only slows them down, allowing them to take place in smaller increments over a longer period of time.

For example, reducing the amounts of dangerous toxins and emissions released by industry is an important eco-efficient goal. It sounds unassailable, but current studies show that over time even tiny amounts of dangerous emissions can have disastrous effects on the biological systems. This is a particular concern in the case of endocrine disrupters—industrial chemicals found in a variety of modern plastics and other consumer goods that appear to mimic hormones and connect with receptors in humans and other organisms. In *Our Stolen Future*, a groundbreaking report on certain synthetic chemicals and the environment, Theo Colburn, Dianne Dumanoski, and John Peterson Myers assert that "astoundingly small quantities of these hormonally active compounds can wreak all kinds of biological havoc, particularly in those exposed in the womb." Furthermore, according to these authors, many studies on the hazards of industrial chemicals have focused on cancer, while research on other kinds of damage due to exposure has only begun.[16]

On another front, new research on particulates—microscopic particles released during incineration and combustion processes, such as those in power plants and automobiles—show that they can lodge in and damage the lungs. A 1995 Harvard study found that as many as 100,000 people die annually in the United States as a result of these tiny particles. Although regulations for controlling their release are in place, implementation does not have to begin until 2005 (and if legislation only reduces their amounts, small quantities of these particulates will still be a problem).[17]

Another waste reduction strategy is incineration, which is often perceived as healthier than landfilling and is praised by energy efficiency proponents as "waste to energy." But waste in incinerators burns only because valuable materials, like paper and plastic, are flammable. Since these materials were never designed to be safely burned, they can release dioxins and other toxins when incinerated. In Hamburg, Germany, some trees' leaves contain such high concentrations of heavy metals from incinerator fallout that the leaves themselves must be burned, effecting a vicious cycle with a dual effect: valuable materials, such as these metals, bioaccumulate in nature to possible harmful effect and are lost to industries forever.

Air, water, and soil do not safely absorb our wastes unless the wastes themselves are completely healthy and biodegradable. Despite persistent misconceptions, even aquatic ecosystems are unable to purify and distill unsafe waste to safe levels. We have just too little knowledge about industrial pollutants and their effects on natural systems for "slowing down" to be a healthy strategy in the long term.

Finding markets to *reuse* wastes can also make industries and customers feel that something good is being done for the environment, because piles of waste appear to go "away." But in many cases these wastes—and any toxins and contaminants they contain—are simply being transferred to another place. In some developing countries, sewage sludge is recycled into animal food, but the current design and treatment of sewage by conventional sewage systems produces sludge containing chemicals that are not healthy food for any animal. Sewage sludge is also used as fertilizer, which is a well-intended attempt to make use of nutrients, but as currently processed it can contain harmful substances (like dioxins, heavy metals, endocrine disrupters, and antibiotics) that are inappropriate for fertilizing crops. Even residential sewage sludge that contains toilet paper made from recycled paper may carry dioxins. Unless materials are specifically *designed* to ultimately become safe food for nature, composting can present problems as well. When so-called biodegradable municipal wastes, including packaging and paper, are composted, the chemicals and toxins in the materials can be released into the environment. Even if these toxins exist in minute amounts, the practice may not be safe. In some cases it would actually be less dangerous to seal the materials in a landfill.

What about *recycling*? As we have noted, most recycling is actually *downcycling*; it reduces the quality of a material over time. When plastics other than those found in soda and water bottles are recycled, they are mixed with different plastics to produce a hybrid of lower quality, which is then molded into something amorphous and cheap, such as a park bench or a speed bump. Metals are often downcycled. For example, the high-quality steel used in automobiles—high-carbon high-tensile steel—is "recycled" by melting it down with other car parts, including copper from the cables in the car, and the paint and plastic coatings. These materials lower the recycled steel's quality. More high-quality steel may be added to make the hybrid strong enough for its next use, but it will not have the material properties to make new cars again. Meanwhile the rare metals, such as copper, manganese, and chromium, and the paints, plastics, and other components that had value for industry in an unmixed, high-quality state are lost. Currently, there is no technology to separate the polymer and paint coatings from automotive metal before it is processed; therefore, even if a car were designed for disassembly, it is not technically feasible to "close the loop" for its high-quality steel. The production of one ton of copper results in the production of hundreds of tons of waste, but the copper content in some steel alloy is actually higher than it is in mined ore. Also, the presence of copper weakens steel. Imagine how useful it would be if industries had a way to recover that copper instead of constantly losing it.

Aluminum is another valuable but constantly downcycled material. The typical soda can consist of two kinds of aluminum: the walls are composed of aluminum, manganese alloy with some magnesium, plus coatings and paint, while the harder top is aluminum magnesium alloy. In conventional recycling these materials are melted together, resulting in a weaker—and less useful—product.

Lost value and lost materials are not the only concerns. Downcycling can actually increase contamination of the biosphere. The paints and plastics that are melted into recycled steel, for example, contain harmful chemicals. Electric-arc furnaces that recycle secondary steel for building materials are now a large source of dioxin emissions, an odd side effect for a supposedly environmental process. Since downcycled materials of all kinds are materially less rigorous than their predecessors, more chemicals are often added to make the materials useful again. For example, when some plastics are melted and combined, the polymers in the plastic—the chains that make it strong and flexible—shorten. Since the material properties of this recycled plastic are altered (its elasticity, clarity, and tensile strength are diminished), chemical or mineral additives may be added to attain the desired performance quality. As a result, downcycled plastic may have more additives than "virgin" plastic.

Because it was not designed with recycling in mind, paper requires extensive bleaching and other chemical processes to make it blank again for reuse. The result is a mixture of chemicals, pulp, and in some cases toxic inks that are not really appropriate for handling and use. The fibers are shorter and the paper less smooth than virgin paper, allowing an even higher proportion of particles to abrade into the air, where they can be inhaled and can irritate the nasal passages and lungs. Some people have developed allergies to newspapers, which are often made from recycled paper.

The creative use of downcycled materials for new products can be misguided, despite good intentions. For example, people may feel they are making an ecologically sound choice by buying and wearing clothing made of fibers from recycled plastic bottles. But the fibers from plastic bottles contain toxins such as antimony, catalytic residues, ultraviolet stabilizers, plasticizers, and antioxidants, which were never designed to lie next to human skin. Using downcycled paper as insulation is another current trend. But additional chemicals (such as fungicides to prevent mildew) must be added to make downcycled paper suitable for insulation, intensifying the problems already caused by toxic inks and other contaminants. The insulation might then off-gas formaldehyde and other chemicals into the home.

In all of these cases, the agenda to recycle has superseded other design considerations. Just because a material is recycled does not automatically make it ecologically benign, especially if it was not designed specifically for recycling. Blindly adopting superficial environmental approaches without full understanding their effects can be no better—and perhaps even worse—than doing nothing.

Downcycling has one more disadvantage. It can be more expensive for businesses, partly because it tries to force materials into more lifetimes than they were originally designed for, a complicated and messy conversion and one that itself expends energy and resources. Legislation in Europe requires packaging materials that are made of aluminum and polypropylene to be recycled. But because these boxes are not designed to be recycled into new packaging (that is, to be reused by the industry to make its own product again), compliance results in additional operating costs. The components of the old packages are often downcycled into lower-quality products until they are eventually incinerated or landfilled anyway. In this instance as in many others, an ecological agenda becomes a burden for industry instead of a rewarding option.

In *Systems of Survival* the urbanist and economic thinker Jane Jacobs describes two fundamental syndromes of human civilizations: what she calls the *guardian* and *commerce*. The guardian is the government, the agency whose primary purpose is to preserve and protect the public. This syndrome is slow and serious. It reserves the right to kill—that is, it will go to war. It represents the public interest, and it is meant to shun commerce (witness conflicts over capital campaign contributions from vested interests).[18]

Commerce, on the other hand, is the day-to-day, instant exchange of value. The name of its primary tool, currency, denotes its urgency. Commerce is quick, highly creative, inventive, constantly seeking short- and long-term advantage, and inherently honest: you can't do business with people if they aren't trustworthy. Any hybrid of these two syndromes Jacobs characterizes as so riddled with problems as to be "monstrous." Money, the tool of commerce, will corrupt the guardian. Regulation, the tool of the guardian, will slow down commerce. An example: a manufacturer might spend more money to provide an improved product under regulations, but its commercial customers, who want products quickly and cheaply, may be unwilling to absorb the extra costs. They may then find what they need elsewhere, perhaps offshore, where regulations are less stringent. In an unfortunate turnaround, the unregulated and potentially dangerous product is given a competitive edge.

For regulators who are attempting to safeguard whole industries, the readiest solutions are often those that can be applied on a very large scale, such as so-called end-of-pipe solutions, in which regulations are applied to the waste and polluting streams of a process or system. Or regulators may try to dilute or distill emissions to a more acceptable level, requiring businesses to increase ventilation or to pump more fresh air into a building because of poor indoor air quality due to off-gassing materials or processes. But this "solution" to pollution—dilution—is an outdated and ineffective response that does not examine the design that caused the pollution in the first place. The essential flaw remains: badly designed materials and systems that are unsuitable for indoor use.

Jacobs sees other problems with "monstrous hybrids." Regulations force companies to comply under threat of punishment, but they seldom *reward* commerce for taking initiatives. Since regulations often require one-size-fits-all end-of-pipe solutions rather than a deeper design response, they do not directly encourage creative problem-solving. And regulation can pit environmentalists and industries against each other. Because regulations seem like a chastisement, industrialists find them annoying and burdensome. Since environmental goals are typically forced upon business by the guardian—or are simply perceived as an added dimension outside crucial operating methods and goals—industrialists see environmental initiatives as inherently uneconomic.

We do not mean to lambaste those who are working with good intentions to create and enforce laws meant to protect the public good. In a world where designs are unintelligent and destructive, regulations can reduce immediate deleterious effects. But ultimately a regulation is a signal of design failure. In fact, it is what we call a *license to harm*: a permit issued by a government to an industry so that it may dispense sickness, destruction, and death at an "acceptable" rate. But as we shall see, good design can require no regulation at all.

Eco-efficiency is an outwardly admirable, even noble, concept, but it is not a strategy for success over the long term, because it does not reach deep enough. It works within the same system that caused the problem in the first place, merely slowing it down with moral proscriptions and punitive measures. It presents little more than an illusion of change. Relying on eco-efficiency to save the environment will in fact achieve the opposite; it will let industry finish off everything, quietly, persistently, and completely.

Remember the retroactive design assignment that we applied to the Industrial Revolution in Chapter One? If we were to take a similar look at industry under the influence of the eco-efficiency movement, the results might look like this:

Design a system of industry that will:

- release *fewer* pounds of toxic wastes into the air, soil, and water every year

- measure prosperity by *less* activity

- meet the stipulations of thousands of complex regulations to keep people and natural systems from being poisoned too quickly

- produce *fewer* materials that are so dangerous that they require future generations to maintain constant vigilance while living in terror

- result in *smaller* amounts of useless waste

- put *smaller* amounts of valuable materials in holes all over the planet, where they can never be retrieved.

Plainly put, eco-efficiency only works to make the old, destructive system a bit less so. In some cases, it can be more pernicious, because its workings are more subtle and long-term. An ecosystem might actually have more of a chance to become healthy and whole again after a quick collapse that leaves some niches intact than with a slow, deliberate, and efficient destruction of the whole.

EFFICIENT—AT WHAT?

As we have seen, even before the term eco-efficiency was coined, industry generally viewed efficiency as a virtue. We would like to question the general goal of efficiency for a system that is largely destructive.

Consider energy-efficient buildings. Twenty years ago in Germany, the standard rate of oil use for heating and cooling the average house was 30 liters per-square meter per year. Today, with high-efficiency housing, that number has plummeted to 1.5 liters of oil per square meter. Increased efficiency is often achieved through better insulation (such as plastic coatings in potential air-exchange areas so that less air comes into the building from outside) and smaller, leak-proof windows. These strategies are meant to optimize the system and reduce wasted energy. But by reducing air-exchange rates, efficient homeowners are actually strengthening the concentration of indoor air pollution from poorly designed materials and products in the home. If indoor air quality is poor because of crude products and building materials, then people require more fresh air to circulate throughout the building, not less.

Overly efficient buildings can also be dangerous. Several decades ago the Turkish government created inexpensive housing by designing and constructing apartments and houses which were built "efficiently," with a minimum of steel and concrete. During the 1999 earthquakes, however, this housing easily collapsed, while older, "inefficient" buildings held up better. In the short term, people saved money on housing, but in the long term, the efficiency strategy turned out to be dangerous. What social benefit does cheap, efficient housing provide if it also exposes people to more dangers than traditional housing?

Efficient agriculture can perniciously deplete local landscapes and wildlife. The contrast between the former East Germany and West Germany is a good example. Traditionally, the average amount of wheat produced in eastern Germany per acre has been only half that of western Germany, because the agricultural industry in the west is more modern and efficient. The eastern region's "inefficient," more old-fashioned agriculture is actually better for environmental health: it has larger wetland areas that have not been drained and overtaken by monocultural crops, and they contain more rare species—for example, three thousand nesting pairs of storks, compared with 240 pairs in the more developed western lands. These wild marshes and wetland areas provide vital centers for breeding, nutrient cycling, and water absorption and purification. Today agriculture all over Germany is becoming more efficient, destroying wetlands and other habitats, resulting in rising extinction rates.

Eco-efficient factories are held up as models of modern manufacturing. But in truth many of them are only distributing their pollution is less obvious ways. Less efficient factories, instead of sending emissions through high smokestacks into other areas far from the site (or importing them), tend to contaminate local areas. At least local destruction tends to be more visible and comprehensible: if you know what you are dealing with, you may be horrified enough to do something about it. Efficient destruction is harder to detect and thus harder to stop.

In a philosophical sense, efficiency has no independent value: it depends on the value of the larger system of which it is a part. An efficient Nazi, for example, is a terrifying thing. If the aims are questionable, efficiency may even make destruction more insidious.[19]

Last but not least, efficiency isn't much fun. In a world dominated by efficiency, each development would serve only narrow and practical purposes. Beauty, creativity, fantasy, enjoyment, inspiration, and poetry would fall by the wayside, creating an unappealing world indeed. Imagine a fully efficient world: an Italian dinner would be a red pill and glass of water with an artificial aroma. Mozart would hit the piano with a two-by-four. Van Gogh would use one color. Whitman's sprawling "Song of Myself" would fit on a single page. And what about efficient sex? An efficient world is not one we envision as delightful. In contrast to nature, it is downright parsimonious.

This is not to condemn *all* efficiency. When implemented as a tool within a larger, effective system that intends overall positive effects on a wide range of issues—not simply economic ones—efficiency can actually be valuable. It is valuable too when conceived as a transitional strategy to help current systems slow down and turn around. But as long as modern industry is so destructive, attempting only to make it less bad is a fatally limited goal.

The "be less bad" environmental approaches to industry have been crucial in sending important messages of environmental concern—messages that continue to catch the public's attention and to spur important research. At the same time, they forward conclusions that are less useful. Instead of presenting an inspiring and exciting vision of change, conventional environmental approaches focus on what *not* to do. Such proscriptions can be seen as a kind of guilt management for our collective sins, a familiar placebo in Western culture.

In very early societies, repentance, atonement, and sacrifice were typical reactions to complex systems, like nature, over which people felt they had little control. Societies around the world developed belief systems based on myth in which bad weather, famine, or disease meant one had displeased the gods, and sacrifices were a way to appease them. In some cultures, even today, one must sacrifice something of value in order to regain the blessing of the gods (or god) and reestablish stability and harmony.

Environmental destruction is a complex system in its own right—widespread, with deeper causes that are difficult to see and understand. Like our ancestors, we may react automatically, with terror and guilt, and we may look for ways to purge ourselves—which the "eco-efficiency" movement provides in abundance, with its exhortations to consume and produce less by minimizing, avoiding, reducing, and sacrificing. Humans are condemned as the one species on the planet guilty of burdening it beyond what it can withstand; as such, we must shrink our presence, our systems, our activities, and even our population so as to become almost invisible. (Those who believe population is the root of our ills think people should mostly stop having children.) The goal is zero: zero waste, zero emissions, zero "ecological footprint."

As long as human beings are regarded as "bad," zero is a good goal. But to be less bad is to accept things as they are, to believe that poorly designed, dishonorable, destructive systems are the *best* humans can do. This is the ultimate failure of the "be less bad" approach: a failure of the imagination. From our perspective, this is a depressing vision of our species' role in the world.

What about an entirely different model? What would it mean to be 100 percent good?

© 2002 William McDonough and Michael Braungart. The authors have kindly granted permission to republish chapter 2 of *Cradle to Cradle: Remaking the Way We Make Things*, North Point Press, New York.

NOTES

1. Thomas Malthus, *Population: The First Essay* (1798). Ann Arbor: University of Michigan Press, 1959; 3, 49.

2. Henry David Thoreau, "Walking" (1863), in *Walden and Other Writings*, edited by William Howarth, New York: Random House, 1981; 613.

3. Max Oelshaeger, *The Idea of Wilderness: From Prehistory to the Age of Ecology*, New Haven: Yale University Press, 1992; 217.

4. Paul R. Erlich, *The Population Bomb*, New York: Ballantine Books, 1968; xi, 39.

5. Paul R. Erlich and Anne H. Erlich, *The Population Explosion*, New York: Simon & Schuster, 1984; 9, 11, 180–81.

6. Donella H. Meadows, Dennis L. Meadows, and Jorgan Sanders, *Beyond the Limits: Confronting Global Collapse, Envisioning a Sustainable Future*, Post Mills, VT: Chelsea Green, 1992; xviii.

7. Ibid., 214.

8. Fritz Schumacher, *Small Is Beautiful: Economics as if People Mattered*, 1973; rpt. New York: Harper and Row, 1989; 31, 34, 35, 39.

9. R. Lilienfield and W. Rathje, *Use Less Stuff: Environmental Solutions for Who We Really Are*, New York: Ballantine Books, 1998; 26, 74.

10. Joan Magretta, "Growth Through Sustainability: An Interview with Monsanto's CEO, Robert B. Shapiro," *Harvard Business Review* (January–February 1997); 82.

11. Joseph J. Romm, *Lean and Clean Management: How to Boost Profits and Productivity by Reducing Pollution*, New York: Kodansha America, 1994; 21.

12. World Commission on Environment and Development, *Our Common Future*, Oxford and New York: Oxford University Press, 1987; 213.

13. Stephen Schmidheiney, "Eco-Efficiency and Sustainable Development," *Risk Management* 43:7 (1996); 51.

14. 3M, "Pollution Prevention Pays," http://www.3m.com/about3m/environment/policies_about3P. jhtml.

15. Gary Lee, "The Three R's of Manufacturing: Recycle, Reuse, Reduce Waste," *Washington Post*, February 5, 1996; A3.

16. Theo Colborn, Dianne Dumanoski, and John Peterson Myers, *Our Stolen Future*, New York: Penguin Group, 1997; xvi.

17. Mary Beth Regan, "The Dustup Over Dust," *Business Week*, December 2, 1996; 119.

18. Jane Jacobs, *Systems of Survival: A Dialogue on the Moral Foundations of Commerce and Politics*, New York: Vintage Books, 1992.

19. For an interesting discussion of the "value" of efficiency, see James Hillman, *Kinds of Power: A Guide to Its Intelligent Uses*, New York: Doubleday, 1995; 33–44.

CHAPTER TWENTY FOUR

Clothes That Connect

KATE FLETCHER

Fashion is eating itself. It has become so disconnected from reality that many of the key issues of our times—such as climate change, consumption and poverty—barely register their presence on the high street or the catwalk. Its products reinforce inequities, exploit workers, fuel resource use, increase environmental impact and generate waste. Not only that, but the sector places escalating emotional, physical and psychological pressures on everyone involved, from designers and producers to consumers. Pressures such as the drive to consume faster and cheaper, the ever-present demand for newness and the constant reformulation of identity, damage us as individuals and collectively as a society. We are alienated, dissatisfied, depressed, anorexic and more cynical than ever before.

Fashion is transforming itself. Tiny companies are making shareable clothes tuned to alternative models of social activism and aesthetic innovation;[1] giant companies are announcing plans to go carbon neutral and introducing Fairtrade cotton and recycled polyester product lines;[2] individuals are hacking the entire system, producing DIY manuals to help us 're-form' our clothes, and in so doing subvert mainstream fashion with micro-political acts of cutting, sewing and making.[3]

We live in changing times. It is up to us to steer this change towards sustainability and demand a new type of fashion based more on transformative acts and less on consumptive ones. The challenge of sustainability is slowly bringing a shift in the consciousness of consumers, designers and captains of industry. More and more people are realizing that we cannot go on as before: fashion as usual is not an option. However, this shift in consciousness is only skin-deep if it is limited to looking at symptoms of our problems rather than tackling the root causes. This paper gives form to a new vision of fashion that breaks from the past. It gets to the heart of fashion's 'problem'—our addiction to consumption—and envisages solutions that replace quantity with quality. This means shifting from global to local, from consuming to making, from illusion to imagination, from consumption of natural resources to an appreciation of the natural world. This vision is about both big and small. Each small step taken contains a tiny spark of wisdom that adds to the thinking and practice of a new way of doing things, demonstrating an alternative to the current model. The hope is that every small action in turn multiplies into support for big change.

THE FASHION INDUSTRY

The business of producing, selling, wearing and disposal of clothes is deeply problematic. Current evidence suggests that the fashion and textile sector is among the most environmentally damaging, judged on a par with the chemical industry. It consumes vast quantities of resources (most notably water, energy and toxic chemicals); has a dubious history of worker protection; is dominated by consumption-inducing, fast changing trends and low prices that prompt consumers to buy more than they need. Recent figures suggest that in the UK over 35kg of textiles and clothing are consumed per person per year, only 13 per cent of which is re-used or recycled in any way, most of it (74 per cent) going to landfill.[4] The general trend of higher volumes and falling prices, as found at retailers such as Primark, Walmart and Tesco, means that we are consuming more fashion than ever before. In recent years the amount spent on clothing has increased while at the same time prices have dropped; thus over four years the number of garments bought per person in the UK has increased by over a third.[5]

Part of this growth in consumption is linked to an increase in speed, which in turn is only made possible by the exploitation of people and natural resources. A recent report for the international development charity War on Want revealed that some of Britain's best-known high street brands are selling clothes made by Bangladeshi workers earning as little as five pence an hour, despite pledges by these companies to protect basic human rights.[6] Speed is also linked to fashion seasons, which are now not only biannual, but each of the two main seasons contains three mini-collections, opening up new opportunities to consume. High street chains have perfected just-in-time manufacturing, with turnaround for a collection now as little as three weeks. Not only that, but the fashion trends themselves—the escalators of consumption—have repeatedly confused sustainability issues and promoted misconceptions. In the early 1990s for example, the 'eco chic' trend was dominated by natural looking colours and fibres and did not reflect real-world progress. Eco chic was more a stylized reaction against simplistic perceptions of chemicals and industrial pollution than a conversion to sustainability values. The superficial beauty, language and image of fashion trivialized the real debate and skimmed over the deeper 'ugliness' endemic in the sector, typified by a pattern of consumption that reinforces the industry's current power structures and makes fashion's ruling classes rich. Disengaged passive consumers who choose between pre-fabricated goods with no space for personalization boost 'elitist myth production upon the catwalk altar in the urban lifestyle temple'[7] and allow the fashion system to mystify, control and 'professionalize' the knowledge and confidence about the practice of designing and making clothes.

Yet we cannot give up on fashion—it is central to our culture. Fashion is important to our relationships, our aesthetic desires and identity. It has potential to empower individuals and groups, to mediate communication and to fuel creativity. Fashion can be what is set in motion when a designer presents the new collection on a catwalk in Milan. But equally, fashion can be the moment when a teenager crops a pair of jeans, adds a badge to an old sweatshirt and paints her Converse sneakers. Fashion is a magical part of our culture and a celebration of a moment where an individual is in perfect sync with time and place. We cannot give up on fashion—it is part of being human. What we need to do instead is ally it with sustainability.

This alliance involves us acknowledging the difference between fashion and clothes. Fashion and clothing are different concepts and entities. Clothing is material production; fashion is symbolic production. Although their use and looks sometimes coincide, fashion and clothes connect with us in different ways. Fashion links us to time and space and deals with our emotional needs, manifesting us as social beings, as individuals. Clothing, in contrast, is concerned chiefly with physical needs, with sheltering, shielding and adorning. Not all clothes are fashion clothes and not all fashion finds expression in garment form. Yet where the fashion sector and the clothing industry come together (in fashion clothes) our emotional needs are made manifest as garments. This overlaying of emotional needs on physical goods fuels resource consumption, generates waste and promotes short-term thinking as we turn our gaze from one silhouette, hemline and colour palette to the next. It also leaves us dissatisfied and disempowered, as physical goods, no matter how many of them we consume, can never meet our psychological needs. To change this, we need to recognize these differences and design more flexibly and intelligently. We have to celebrate fashion as the beautiful butterfly it is and at the same time divorce it from rampant material consumption. We have to produce clothes that are based on values, on skill, on carefully produced fibres; clothes that are conscientious, sustainable and beautiful.

For many people, 'sustainable' fashion clothes means functional, utilitarian garments. It means buying as few garments as possible and, when clothes are bought, sourcing them second hand, Fair Trade or organic. While this helps reduce the speed and quantity of consumption, it is ultimately a negative vision of the future; it uses yesterday's thinking to cope with the conditions of tomorrow. A new vision for sustainable fashion has to be more than a minimal consumption drive, something more attractive not because we are flippant or fashion junkies but because of the significance of fashion to human culture. A new vision will reconnect us with our clothes, their design concepts, materials and making. It will move away from the needy, destructive relationship that typifies many people's experience of fashion today, to a healthier, more therapeutic one. This view will underline the cultural importance of fashion and will champion choice, transparency and self-reliance. It will encourage a shift from the terms and metrics of quantity to those of quality—ultimately a more positive, forward-looking and creative place to be.

INSPIRED BY NATURE

This healthier, more satisfying and more honest vision of fashion's future needs design tools: tough, reliable concepts and models. Some of the most useful ones are suggested by our study of Nature. By designing around principles observable in Nature, such as efficiency, cooperation and symbiosis, the hope is that society might be sustainable in the same way that ecosystems are. Just as in natural systems, where interdependence and interconnectedness between species dominate, we would look for these same characteristics in human systems and our current culture. We can read Nature's lessons literally; and close loops, naturally recycling almost all materials, and focus on efficient use of materials. We can also interpret Nature more metaphorically and pursue designs that promote flexibility, lightness or a sense of wonder, or those that speak of balance, community values or engagement and playfulness.

Designing clothes around Nature's principles and dynamics demands diversity. There is no single one-size-fits-all solution, but multiple design opportunities working at different scales, levels, time-frames and with many different people. In Nature, diversity means strong, resilient ecosystems, able to withstand a shock or period of crisis. In fashion, it means a wealth of products and producers, different fibres and local jobs. At present, the industry is monolithic, dominated by a large number of similar garments and thematic trends. Though we may think of ourselves as spoiled for choice, most of the world's population swims in a sea of ready-made similarity. Lack of differentiation leads to boredom leads to consumption. Diversity is about not putting all our eggs in one basket. It is about designing with a range of fibres, about avoiding agricultural (and manufacturing) monocultures, spreading risk, decentralizing production, celebrating traditional fibres and giving people creative and productive employment.

Diversity demands that our fibre choices have to change. We need to substitute a variety of more sustainable materials for the socially and ecologically destructive dominant fibres of cotton and polyester (which together account for around 80 per cent of the world fibre market). This portfolio of fibre types includes natural materials like organic cotton and wool, hemp, wild silk and natural 'linen' bamboo; biodegradable synthetics like corn starch and soya bean fibre; and cellulosics manufactured from sustainably harvested eucalyptus. Evidence suggests that together these fibres offer more resource-efficient and people-friendly solutions to cotton and polyester, though they come at a cost—our clothes will get more expensive—and of course the still largely untested question is whether the mass market is prepared to pay more for such change. Designing with a greater number of small volume fibre types encourages farmers to diversify and grow a range of crops. It offers potential for regional and national fibre variation and—perhaps most critically for consumers—a choice in material type. These products could give us work and respect our local environment.

Diverse products sustain our sense of ourselves as human beings; they are heterogeneous and user-specific and recognize a wide range of symbolic and material needs. This ties in with future predictions for business more generally, which will be to find ways of satisfying the precise needs of small markets—the complete opposite of the Fordist way of doing business, where a few generic products are developed and then marketed to all people. Smaller makers with flexible production systems can produce products that are personal and specific and so they are more relevant to our needs. Homogenization and autonomy are eschewed in favour of expressiveness and difference. Diverse fashion grows out of an individual or a particular place.

The vitality of ecosystems depends on relationships and on uses and exchanges of energy and resources. In the same way, the vitality of fashion's future will be secured in the relationships it fosters. We will see beauty and greatness in garments that value process, participation and social integration, in pieces that advance relationships between people and the environment. Friends knitting together is beautiful; compostable garments are beautiful; supporting a disadvantaged community with careful purchasing is beautiful. Relationships can be fostered by designing garments that encourage us to ask deep questions about our sense of place in the natural world. Such garments could accomplish this by supporting our desire to jump on a bike instead of taking the car, or by being shareable between friends. Sustainable fashion is about a strong and nurturing relationship between consumer and producer. It is about producing garments that start a debate, invoke a deep sense of meaning or require the user to 'finish' them with skill, imagination or flair. It is about designing confidence- and capability-inducing pieces that encourage versatility, inventiveness, personalization and individual participation. It is only then that people will be transformed from blind consumers choosing between ready-made 'closed' goods into active and competent citizens making conscious choices as they buy, use and discard their clothes.

Many of these Nature-inspired opportunities lie in the re-conceiving of fashion in an industry context—not out of a philanthropic impulse, but rather because doing so makes money. There is plenty of evidence to show that embracing a social and environmental agenda increases shareholder value, creates brand equity and makes a company a preferred employer, customer and partner. In the case of giant American carpet company Interface,[8] a drive towards a goal of zero waste has saved $290 million, which more than paid for a wide range of environmental initiatives and has led to bigger profits. When companies such as Interface make legitimate returns from being 'green' they become a massive engine for change not just in the world of fashion and textiles but also in society at large. Major clothing companies like Nike[9] are also pushing corporate responsibility forward in specific ways. It has guidelines for its designers regarding materials use including a commitment to use 5 per cent organic cotton in all cotton products by 2010, a ban on PVC and a sustainable product innovation strategy. Other big names, like H&M,[10] are PVC- and fur-free and have agreed codes of conduct with suppliers to guarantee worker protection for those working in low wage economies. The largest T-shirt producer in the US, American Apparel[11] sidesteps criticism often levied at other clothing labels about their ignorance of labour and working conditions in factories in developing countries by making all their clothes in a vertically integrated mill in its own 'backyard': Downtown Los Angeles.

Even though significant momentum for sustainability is building in the fashion business, these big players can still be criticized for 'tinkering around the edges' of environmental and social problems, for making things *less unsustainable* rather than *more sustainable* by focusing on the symptoms rather than tackling a problem at its roots. Creating sustainable fashion requires profound change and radical solutions not limited to the quick fixes favoured by business cycles and profits. Of course, business can also be part of this radical agenda but a different model of business is required, not least one that asks tough questions about consumption and personal satisfaction and is based on entirely different models of individual and social action. This 'back to roots' agenda will in essence mean that sustainable fashion *will reconnect us with Nature* and *with each other*. It will reduce environmental impact, promote our sense of our place in the natural world and foster a new ethic of learning from the Earth. Sustainable fashion will encourage our sense of ourselves as human beings and reconnect us to each other, it will emancipate us and give us the skills to creatively participate with and rework our clothes. We have to become activists, skilful producers and consumers of clothes, our actions exploding some of the mystique, exclusivity and power structures of the fashion system to break the link between fashion and material consumption and to offer alternative visions of fashion's future.

5 WAYS

Applying future visions to the physical reality of today's garments can take a major leap of imagination and creativity. Small signs of our readiness for this leap are all around us; in blogs, fashion magazine features, design school curricula, sustainability reporting on the stock market and Corporate Social Responsibility initiatives; there is an unprecedented interest in sustainable fashion. An important part of this leap involves creating images of and projects about possible futures or, to put it another way, offering glimpses of tomorrow to help orientate ourselves today as we make the transition towards a more sustainable future for fashion.

With that aim in mind a small collaborative research project, 5 Ways,[12] explored what sustainability qualities such as diversity, participation and efficiency might mean for fashion textiles. 5 Ways was a conceptual project producing prototypes or sketches and not fully fledged market ready products. Its aim was not to provide definitive answers to sustainability questions, but rather give some ideas and promising starting points for investigating this complex and shifting territory. 5 Ways began with a team of designers and five simple briefs. From each of the briefs and associated workshop sessions, a prototype product was developed, ranging from a leather bag to a dress. While each of these products works individually, their real value comes more from what they represent together, which is hidden from view—innovative outcomes based on sustainability values and an interconnected approach to design.

The five 5 Ways projects explored:

- things made round the corner from where you live;
- things that you never want to launder;
- things that work with human needs;
- things that have multiple lives pre-ordained;
- things that require you to roll up your sleeves and get involved.

Each of these five projects is described below.

Project 1: Local

Where do you live? What are your roots? The Local project captures the essence of your area and asks you to wear it proudly on your back. It asks you to find the world in your neighbourhood and to know and support what's going on round the corner. Local products inspire and challenge the community while at the same time creating jobs and making use of local resources. The 'best' product is one with a human and material engagement with place. The 'best' product creates work at the local level that is socially enriching and economically viable. The Local project reflected a mix of concerns, some about local aesthetic preferences and others about developing products to sustain communities. These local concerns ran through all of the projects in 5 Ways: all five projects were small, informal and came from the grassroots. All adhered to the biomimicry principle of 'not fouling the nest'; using carefully selected low-impact materials and processing methods so as to keep the local (and de facto global) environment clean. The materials used in the 5 Ways project were organic cotton; Fair Trade wool; recycled polyester; and a hemp/cotton denim. These were dyed with natural indigo, heat transfer pressed or digitally printed.

Local in our case involved the design and development of products for Brick Lane, London, UK. Brick Lane has a very special character, now the centre of London's Bangladeshi community and a curry Mecca; it has a street market, acts as a base for large numbers of designer-makers and artists and is also a thriving textile and leather area. Our product local to Brick Lane evolved out of a mix of these influences. We produced a bag hand-knitted from leather scraps gathered from local workshops. The leather was cut into strips, tied together into a long ribbon and then knitted on chunky needles into a soft, tactile, extendable pouch. The bag is something to carry your fruit and vegetables home from the market stalls (shop local!); something to indicate your community identity (this is where I live!); something made from a local source of waste employing local people in the process (use waste as a resource!).

Project 2: Updatable

Fashion clothes capture a moment in time and are as quickly forgotten. But what if that moment was not one but many moments, a process of transformation? What if that process required you to reach into the sewing kit and update that garment yourself? The Updatable project is all about a switch in emphasis: from one garment to many garments; from passive consumers to active users; from a single snapshot in time to an ongoing movie. This project was concerned with the skills and confidence needed to rework a T-shirt. It was an attempt to make the process of designing and making a garment more transparent; to 'reclaim' it from specialist elite designers and to promote a greater understanding of the many small processes at work in creating a garment and encourage people to 'do-it-yourself'. Layered on top of this capability-inducing agenda was a desire to cut material consumption by recutting, restitching and restyling a piece.

Updatable involved a series of transformations to a T-shirt. Instructions, sent through the post—in our case to our team of designers—suggested modifications which keep the T-shirt at the forefront of fashion and out of the dustbin for another season. We filtered the trends and distilled them into a few smart changes. The design team then interpreted the instructions and produced a singularly stylish piece, which they documented and wore over the next months. In Updatable, the power relationship between original designer and user was changed, so that what developed was a unique collaboration based on change.

Project 3: No Wash

Behind the No Wash project was a concern with designing and wearing a garment that is never laundered. Washing clothes is, quite simply, a chore. We do it without thinking and yet it is an activity closely tied in with social acceptance, personal and romantic success and thus our happiness. Keeping clean used to be about disease prevention, but now the West's obsession with hygiene has led to the startling fact that the energy needed to wash our favourite garments through their life span is about six times that needed to make them. Just by washing clothes half as often, overall product energy consumption is cut by almost 50 per cent (and it is a similar story for air pollution and production of solid waste).

No Wash takes this idea to extremes. Here, a fine knit woollen jumper was transformed into a garment never to be washed. The No Wash top was designed partly to resist or repel dirt but mainly to wear it like a badge. It was developed in response to a six-month laundry diary, which documented majority smell under the arms and majority dirt on cuffs, elbows and front panels. The garment featured wipe-clean surfaces and extra underarm ventilation and has been worn regularly for over three years without washing. With its bold 'decoration' of coffee spills and soap smells, it reminds us of our garment's history as well as our responsibility.

Like all the 5 Ways products, the No Wash top is not a mainstream design solution, but it engages with the issues of sustainability in a new way. The complex, interrelated and constantly changing relationship between design and culture means that novel products or ways of working are not likely to come from the mainstream. Instead we need to start looking to ad hoc projects from the fringes or to alternative lifestyles. Most of us have a durable, never washed item in our wardrobes, but probably have never recognized it as such. One starting point therefore is to identify these garments' features and design to enhance these characteristics. We also need to develop alternative ways of laundering and freshening up items in parallel with designing new garments themselves. Such tricks as hanging a garment in a steamy shower room to remove odour or learning more about how stains and smells diminish, or become more tricky to remove, over time could change practices and usher in alternative models of how to live.

Project 4: Nine Lives

The Nine Lives project trades on the feline analogy and, just like a cat, which 'dies' only to live again, it sees potential in our clothes to be resurrected. We can re-use the thing wholesale; we can re-use key bits; we can rework the fibre into a new yarn; we can use it not as clothes but as stuffing for a mattress. But how can we do this so the act of giving something a new incarnation speaks to us about the cycle of life itself? Eliminating waste is a concept lifted straight from ecosystems and ecosystem-inspired design approaches like permaculture and industrial ecology, where everything is recycled and all waste from one component of the system becomes 'food' for another. Here what appears to be waste is actually exchange. The idea of exchange is a liberating one; it helps to evoke a mindset focused on getting the most out of something; and to emphasize connections, loops, cycles and forward planning.

Cycles connect things and offer opportunity for checks, balances and feedback. Cycles are everywhere in Nature, ensuring resource efficiency and balance between species. Yet to start designing in a way that 'takes a leaf out of Nature's book', a change has to be made; one that rejects the dominant (linear) industrial viewpoint that sees industry, designers and consumers as separate from the natural world; and one which no longer is exclusively focused on making a product and getting it to a customer quickly and cheaply without considering much else.

'Refurbishing' and customizing second-hand garments and fabrics into new, updated products have become some of the best-explored aspects of waste issues in fashion design. A raft of approaches such as restyling, reshaping, embellishing and over-printing give discarded, torn and stained fabrics added value, a new life and divert (or delay) waste from landfill. For example, charitable organizations such as Traid, under the label Traid Remade,[13] employ a team of innovative young designers to rework unwanted garments by transforming them into new one-off fashionable pieces that can be sold and re-used. And London-based outfit Junky Styling[14] deconstructs second-hand traditional men's suits found in jumble sales and charity shops into twisted, tailored garments. The use of vintage garments and fabrics has been a strong element of re-use partially because limited supply guarantees each piece's individuality, something which chimes nicely with the aesthetic of care and hand finishing so prevalent in re-use, but also because vintage fabrics are survivors—old things which have kept their value over time—and as such are easily associated with sustainability values.

The Nine Lives project developed garments with a pre-ordained 'future life' ready installed. The next step is envisaged, planned for and built in and the act of transformation breathes new life into a tired garment. For Nine Lives we produced two pieces that were creatively morphed into one in their next life. A knitted woollen top and simple printed A-line skirt are transformed by embroidery. Using the yarn carefully unwound from the top, and the sewing guide printed on the skirt in its first life, the user stitches into the skirt to produce a new and unique piece. The unravelling of the jumper and the making of the new skirt are deliberate acts of recreation and show us the possibilities of engaging with our garments in a new way.

Project 5: Super Satisfiers

Clothes protect our modesty and keep us warm. We also use them to signal who and what we are, to attract (or repel) others and to put us in a particular frame of mind. These insatiable emotional needs are triggers for dissatisfaction with ourselves and our clothes, and lead to an escalation in how and what we buy. Curbing the quantity of clothes bought and sold would likely have a significant and positive influence on the environmental and social impact caused by the fashion sector. But if we want to avoid depriving people of their need for identity and participation, we cannot just forget about fashion and scrap everything other than the wardrobe basics. There is no point in discouraging the buying of clothes without putting forward alternative ways of signalling who and what we are to others. In other words, we cannot radically cut consumption of clothing until we begin to understand its significance as a satisfier of human needs.

Humans possess specific, identifiable, underlying needs that are the same, regardless of nation, religion or culture. Manfred Max-Neef[15] has identified these as subsistence, protection, affection, understanding, participation, creation, recreation, identity and freedom. Crucially, while these needs stay the same, what changes with time and between individuals is how we go about meeting or satisfying these needs. Different satisfiers have different implications not only for those involved but also for external factors such as the environment. Where these satisfiers are manifest as products or services, they are the traditional (if unconscious) focus of design. The nine needs fall into two broad categories: physical (material) needs and psychological (non-material) needs. As noted earlier, we do not just use materials to satisfy our physical needs, but we also use them to satisfy our psychological and emotional needs too. This means, for example, that many of us relate our individual identity to what and how many materials we consume. Here lies a paradox: psychological needs are not easily satisfied, and in some cases are even inhibited, by consuming materials, a fact long recognized by many religious communities in their guidelines for living materially-simple but spiritually-rich lives. Yet the pressure to consume materials continues to intensify, pushed onwards by marketing, social competition and the driving forces, innate in humans, of emulation and envy.

Super Satisfiers investigated what happens when our need for identity, affection and leisure is the overt rather than covert focus of a garment. Does this begin to break the chain of consumption and dissatisfaction? Does it focus our attention on the futility of trying to meet such emotional needs through clothing or does the act of making hidden needs obvious connect us more with ourselves? The Super Satisfiers project focused on our need for affection and developed the 'caress dress'—one designer's highly personal take on how she attracts attention from others through garments. The dress uses slits and subtle cut-aways to reveal hints of bare skin at the shoulder, the waist and the small of the back. Its purpose is to invite friends to touch and for you to feel the warmth of others' affection for you.

CONCLUSIONS

What sustainable fashion needs is not mass answers but a mass of answers, and 5 Ways, while it has many limitations, is an attempt to glimpse some of this diversity. Central to the success of these ideas, and sustainable fashion more generally, is openness to the qualities and values of sustainability found in Nature, so emphasizing relationships, connectedness and cooperation. It is only then that we will properly acknowledge that ideas of sustainability require more than a focus on environmental issues to make them happen. They also require personal, social and institutional transformation and from this transformation a new way of clothing ourselves will emerge that will speak of a new rhythm and role for fashion, that will engage and empower users and not just cover their bodies, that will release industry from a potentially self-destructive, ever-faster pace of change and will herald the beginning of a way of thinking that champions the creation of a sustainable and satisfying wardrobe.

The future of sustainable fashion lies in being able to see the 'whole' and understand the mosaic of interconnected resource-flows behind a garment while still being able to act insightfully, practically and simply. We need to combine knowledge with instinct and create an industry that provides secure employment, a creative practice for designers and consumers and a staging ground for cutting-edge environmental practices. This industry will have a sense of connection or closeness at its heart; a connection to those who make or use clothes, with the ecological systems that support production and consumption and, critically, with the products themselves.

© 2007 Jonathan Chapman and Nick Gant. Previously published as chapter 6 in Chapman, J. and Gant, N. (eds) *Designers, Visionaries and Other Stories: A Collection of Sustainable Design Essays*. London: Earthscan Taylor & Francis/Routledge 2007. Republished with kind permission from Jonathan Chapman and Nick Gant.

NOTES

1. Keep and Share's alternative luxury knitwear can be found at www.keepandshare.co.uk
2. For more on Marks and Spencer's new sustainability strategy visit www.marksandspencer.com/thecompany/plana/index.shtml
3. Otto von Busch's work can be seen at www.selfpassage.org
4. Allwood, J. M., Laursen, S. E., Malvido de Rodriguez, C. and Bocken, N. M. P. (2006) *Well Dressed?*, University of Cambridge Institute of Manufacturing, Cambridge, p2
5. Allwood, J. M., Laursen, S. E., Malvido de Rodriguez, C. and Bocken, N. M. P. (2006) *Well Dressed?*, University of Cambridge Institute of Manufacturing, Cambridge, p12
6. War on Want (2006), 'Fashion victims: The true cost of cheap clothes at Primark, Asda and Tesco', www.waronwant.org/Fashion+Victims+13593.twl
7. von Busch, O. (2005), 'Re-forming appearance: Subversive strategies in the fashion system—reflections on complementary modes of production', Research Paper, www.selfpassage.org
8. www.interfaceinc.com
9. www.nike.com/nikebiz
10. www.hm.com/us/corporateresponsibility/csrreporting__csrreporting.nhtm
11. www.americanapparel.net
12. 5 Ways ran between June 2002 and May 2003 and was a collaborative project between Kate Fletcher and Becky Earley, funded by AHRB and Chelsea College of Art & Design. For more information see www.5ways.info
13. www.traid.org.uk/custom.html
14. www.junkystyling.co.uk
15. Ekins, P. and Max-Neef, M. (eds) (1992) *Real-Life Economics*, Routledge, London

CHAPTER TWENTY FIVE

Design's Role in Sustainable Consumption

ANN THORPE

Ann Thorpe / © MIT 2010

User consumption has been a long-standing concern for sustainability, stemming from the notion that there are "limits" to global resource capacity and we are consuming beyond those limits. Yet as the field of sustainable consumption has matured, it has moved from largely *technical* concerns about efficient resource consumption and minimizing waste in our existing industrial systems to a more recent focus on the very *social* issue of lifestyle change. The emphasis on lifestyle and behavior change is supported by research that suggests consumerism is costly not only in environmental terms, but also possibly in other ways.

Although design is beginning to struggle with the challenges posed by this move toward lifestyle change, the topic of design is mostly absent from the serious discourse on sustainable consumption. In this article, I will examine the research that underpins recent shifts in the sustainable consumption field and investigate how that broader research resonates with design research and practice.[1]

After a brief timeline, I will look particularly at three main research areas—environmental policy, psychology, and sociology. I will conclude by examining a question implied by mainstream research—can design move from being a cog in the wheel of consumerism to having a substantial role in supporting sustainable consumption?

TIMELINE

Consumption itself is a huge field and here I provide only a brief timeline. Interest in consumption as a field of study is long standing and Tim Jackson suggests that the emerging debates about sustainable consumption must be understood in a broad historical context.[2]

He captures this sweep of work on consumer behavior and society neatly when he notes that these older debates:

> "Have an extraordinary pedigree reaching back to classical philosophy and encompassing the critical social theory of the nineteenth and early twentieth century, the consumer psychology and 'motivation research' of the early post-war years, the 'ecological humanism' of the 1960s and 1970s, the anthropology and social philosophy of the 1970s and 1980s, and the sociology of modernity, popularized in the 1990s."

When environmental concerns emerged in the 1960s and 1970s, with works such as Rachel Carson's *Silent Spring* (1962) or the *Club of Rome's Limits to Growth* (1972) and events such as the 1973 OPEC oil embargo, scholars of both consumption and design incorporated these concerns into studies and practice.[3] On the design side, for example, many of us are familiar with the work of Buckminster Fuller (*Operating Manual for Spaceship Earth*, 1969), Victor Papanek (*Design for the Real World*, 1972), architect Sim Van der Ryn, and "design outlaws" such as Jay Baldwin, among others.[4]

Jackson notes that by the late 1980s, consumption (as part of "sustainable production and consumption") had become a key component of sustainable development. He dates the term "sustainable consumption" to Agenda 21, the main policy document to emerge from the first Earth Summit in Rio in 1992. From that point, sustainable consumption became a more familiar program theme at international policy levels.

On the design side, the 1990s saw a more intense focus on recycled materials, with exhibitions such as "Re-Materialize" (1996) and "Hello Again" (1997–98).[5] Critiques of consumerist design also appeared, notably Nigel Whiteley's *Design for Society* (1993).[6] By the late 1990s, "eco-design" emerged as a recognizable field, exemplified by eco-design principles in *Ecological Design* (1996), and by product lifecycle approaches detailed in works such as *A Guide to EcoReDesign* (1997) and *Ecodesign: A Promising Approach to Sustainable Production and Consumption* (1997).[7]

Throughout the 1990s, for the most part neither policymakers nor designers were typically asking for substantial change in lifestyle, rather they were seeking less resource intensive production and consumption methods to facilitate existing lifestyles, as I detail below. It wasn't until 2003 that the UK government, despite the difficult political and social implications, was among the first to adopt a strategy recognizing that substantial behavior and lifestyle change are essential components for achieving sustainability.[8]

The early 2000s have also seen design work that explores lifestyle change explicitly in terms of sustainable consumption. For example, instead of consuming efficiently (buy two shirts instead of six) one design proposal recognizes laundering as one of clothing's biggest eco-impacts and suggests a "no wash" shirt. (It has ventilation and wipe-able surfaces and otherwise wears dirt or stains like a badge.[9]) We also see other interesting proposals such as: not simply "greening" our houses, but also substantially reducing the size of houses, or sharing a bigger house among several families,[10] relinquishing private car ownership in favor of "city cars,"[11] or reworking existing use patterns, such as putting schools in with other community facilities, art exhibitions in with self-storage, and cultural facilities in with parking garages.[12]

All of these proposals suggest substantial changes to existing lifestyles, not just in terms of technical efficiency but also in socio-cultural terms. The field of sustainable consumption is starting to call for just such a portfolio of diverse lifestyle changes to meet the challenges of sustainability.

In the next section I move into examining broader research in sustainable consumption and the design resonances with that research, beginning with environmental policy.

ENVIRONMENTAL POLICY

Environmental policy has typically asked, "can we make environmentally better products and convince people to buy them?" Research in environmental policy and management traditionally starts with conventional economic notions. For example, researchers assume that consumer desires are basically insatiable and that consumers exercise sovereignty over purchases. Here "sovereignty" is the idea that consumers actually control supply by virtue of allocating their "dollar votes" in a free market—demand controls supply. Most importantly, many researchers have until recently accepted the idea that economic growth is a proxy for growth in well-being, that continuous increases in consumption are equal to continuous increases in well-being.

Given these assumptions, the challenge for environmental policy then becomes meeting consumer demand in a more environmentally friendly way. This task has two sides:

Supply: producing less environmentally damaging goods, and
Demand: educating consumers about these improved goods. The approach, sometimes called "informed choice," hinges on persuading consumers to choose smart/clean/fair/green goods that reduce environmental impacts so that insatiable demand can continue.[13] Since consumers are rational decision makers, the reasoning goes, when they have better information they'll make better choices.

In recent years, "informed choice" has been increasingly criticized. Critics claim the economic view of consumers as "insatiable" is inaccurate as many people choose to live within their means.[14] At the same time, consumers are increasingly distanced from the impacts of consumption (they don't witness firsthand dramatic resource destruction or worker exploitation), so despite being "informed" in an abstract sense, they have relatively little visceral feedback on which to base consumption decisions.[15] Other critiques point out that increases in overall consumption are slated to cancel out any gains made in production efficiency.[16] This reality is made more sobering as increasing numbers of the world's population move from poverty to "middle class" status, for example in India and China.[17]

The consumer sovereignty assumption is also criticized. Michael Maniates suggests that corporations and governments use notions of consumer sovereignty to "individualize" the problem—make individuals responsible for voting with their wallets—and thus avoid making changes either to profitable corporate business practices or convenient patterns of government subsidy (e.g., subsidies for oil drilling).[18] But consumers are not individual sovereigns in a free market, they are heavily influenced by marketing and advertising. Moreover, given tremendous concentrations of wealth, a small number of very rich people have tremendous "voting power" in the market whereas most of us have relatively little.[19]

The fact that we broadly accept the "individualization" of the problem indicates how much we view ourselves primarily as consumers, as opposed to citizens. Are we left with shopping-as political-act, in which our dissent is commodified and sold back to us?[20] A more positive view sees ethical and green consumerism as an emerging social movement, in which individuals take first steps toward further political action, and various organizations mobilize these many first steps into social change campaigns.[21] On the other hand, some critics suggest that many consumer "desires" might be met by means other than consumer goods, but our society is commoditized to such an extent that the "non-purchase" options are rarely explored or supported.[22] For example, we don't invest in alternatives to private automobiles because they don't work well as commodities—they don't make good profits.

A recent counterpoint to "informed choice" is the controversial notion of "choice editing" stemming from the field of behavioral economics. This approach sees a role for government and other organizations in steering individuals into behavior and lifestyle changes. Rather than assuming people always act rationally in their own best interests, behavioral economics incorporates findings from psychology and sociology to account for seemingly irrational behavior. A recent report, "Creatures of Habit? The Art of Behavioral Change," highlights areas where we often knowingly act against our own best interests: not saving for retirement, not losing weight, and not reducing our climate change emissions.[23]

In these areas, the thinking goes, we need outside intervention to motivate new behaviors that we already know are in our best interests for the long term. It's controversial because public intervention (such as a ban on smoking in public places) is usually deemed necessary only when actions cause direct harm to others—where there is a social cost. But forcing people to take action for their own good, such as forced saving for retirement, strikes some as paternalistic. The authors of "Creatures of Habit?" suggest there is a threshold "when individual actions carry consequences for the individual further down the track, *which they themselves recognize*" (emphasis added).[24] In other words, the authors view these as cases where most of us acknowledge we need help.

When it comes to consumption of material goods, choice editing comes up against consumer sovereignty. Rather than consumer "sovereigns" who dictate supply, choice editing sees governments and businesses editing out choices that are less sustainable, while ensuring that sustainable options are the norm—re-setting our "default options." Examples of successful choice editing include the elimination of ozone-depleting chemicals from aerosols and the uptake of efficient fridges and freezers in Europe, where governments banned the low efficiency models and then retailers agreed to remove "middling" rated appliances.[25] Choice editing recognizes that mainstream consumers want to make environmentally "good" choices but are mired in habits, norms, and other factors that limit their ability to do so.

ENVIRONMENTAL POLICY—DESIGN RESONANCES

In an interesting contrast to debates on informed choice that rarely mention design, researchers exploring environmental policy from a design perspective tend to see design as the heart of the problem. This view is often supported by the statistic that as much as 90% of a product's environmental impact is fixed during the design stage.[26]

The predominant design response to the consumption problem has closely followed the informed choice approach. That is, green and eco-designers focus on redesigning products to be more environmentally friendly hoping that better informed consumers will buy them. There has been a great deal of useful work done in this area, resulting in a bundle of principles, toolboxes, and indicators available for designers to use. Examples include: "lifecycle" strategies that assess a product's impact from conception through production, use, and end-of-life, business case studies for sustainability based on savings from efficiency, etc., product and building environmental rating systems such as the US Green Building Council's "LEED" or McDonough and Braungart's "Cradle-to-Cradle."

Eco-design is useful, but seems susceptible to many of the criticisms of informed choice. Eco-design generally accepts the individual, voting-with-your-wallet approach, overlooking public policies and corporate finance systems that significantly weaken an individual's "vote." Although eco-design may sometimes link consumers to *downstream* consequences of products (e.g., by using recognizable recycled material), few eco-design approaches link consumers to *upstream* social and environmental consequences of making products, perhaps because many designers are as distant as consumers from these upstream effects.

"Design for behavior change," an approach that resonates with choice editing policies, has gained ground recently. T. A. Bhamra, D. Lilley, and T. Tang describe a spectrum of design for behavior change.[27] On one end, it is the same as informed choice, where a product displays environmental information—such as the miles per gallon readout on the Prius hybrid automobile—thus better enabling a consumer to act upon it. On the other end of the spectrum, a design solution may actually use technical controls or spatial organization to steer consumer behavior—for example to reduce refrigerator door opening, or prevent consumers from over-filling the tea kettle, and so forth.[28] Bhamra et al. hint at the controversial nature of this approach, pointing out the ethical implications of allocating the power of decision-making between the consumer and the product.

Criticisms of the informed choice model, as well as the evidence supporting the choice editing model, stem from other disciplines. I turn next to psychologists, who have been looking at the connection between the pursuit of material wealth and mental well-being.

PSYCHOLOGY

At a basic level, psychological research on consumption asks, "can things make us happy?" Clearly there is a significant role for material goods in modern life, but recent research indicates that increasing levels of material wealth do not lead to corresponding increases in happiness, and eventually can become detrimental to psychological and even physical health. Tim Kasser has found that people with highly materialistic values report lower levels of mental and physical well-being; his discovery is bolstered by a number of other researchers who found similar results across age groups (young and old), cultures (Eastern and Western), and income groups (rich and poor).[29] The finding suggests that continuous increases in consumption are not a good proxy for increases in well-being.

Underlying these findings is the theory that human beings, in addition to having some universal physical needs (such as for sustenance and shelter) also have universal psychological needs. Needs theory, as it is sometimes known, includes contributions from various scholars on how human needs might be framed. In general, psychological needs tend to fall into the categories of social and personal. Social needs include participation, belonging, and affection, and personal needs include understanding, creativity, authenticity, and freedom.[30]

In social terms, consumer goods have a darker, anxiety producing side, in which they help us avoid shame. Novel or expensive consumer goods gain us a certain position in society, a position lost without relentless striving. This is what's known as "positional" consumption. It's one way that consumerism advances individualism, and suggests that simplistic appeals to "consumeless" won't work.[31]

Kasser notes that individuals who rely primarily on materialism and physical appearances—having the "in" cell phone or the latest hair style—are typically less successful in meeting their psychological needs than people who use a broader range of techniques to develop relationships or pursue inner growth. Perhaps this broadening of techniques gives people alternate ways of gaining or understanding social position.

Studies on how consumption meets psychological needs examine both the act of making a purchase and the state of "happiness." Daniel Miller argues that the act of making a purchase can articulate caring and authenticity in relationships. To the extent that developing meaningful relationships makes us happy, consumption should improve happiness in this regard. He gives examples of a mother's search for children's clothing that balances the child's aesthetic with the family's, as well as the case of a man who can, by himself, purchase a suitable garment or pair of shoes for his woman. These examples demonstrate the love of one for the other and its expression through the process of consumption.[32]

Miller suggests that critics of consumption are making moral judgments on consumers, and he argues that when we appropriate it, consumption is a way to enhance humanism. Miller celebrates consumption and points out that the elimination of poverty worldwide must rely upon more consumption, not less, and upon mass production. Although not commenting on design directly, he dismisses "craft," from which the reader infers "local scale production," as suitable for no more than a hobby.

Mihaly Csikszentmihalyi's studies examine both happiness and the process of making purchases. His research suggests that we are happiest when our consciousness is "tuned," a state he calls "flow" that occurs from active engagement in something such as writing or playing music, but not from passive activities such as watching TV. He found activities that have higher physical resource requirements (in this case BTUs—units of energy) typically correlated to lower happiness levels.[33] He hypothesized that lower BTU activities are "happier" because they require greater *psychic* energy and thus better tune our consciousness. In this view, "psychically" active engagement is key to achieving well-being. He suggests that there is a relatively low threshold beyond which increased material wealth does not add to flow, but more importantly there is an additional threshold beyond which material wealth may start to rob us of flow.

In terms of making purchases, he notes that in contemporary life, shopping is one of the main areas where many people experience a tuned consciousness, in the absence of other opportunities or skills. By contrast, in previous eras people would have experienced a tuned consciousness through activities such as making their own entertainment, making their own goods (e.g., sewing or woodworking), or participating in religion, among other things.

Other research indicates that personal consumption rates are correlated to the quality of an individual's work. If your job makes you feel powerless, you may compensate by shopping, which appears to put you back in control.[34]

It bears repeating that consumption and material goods can and do play a positive role in psychological and physical health. I interpret the psychological research not in terms of whether consumption is good or bad, but rather, in terms of searching for the right intensity of consumerism in our lives.

PSYCHOLOGY—DESIGN RESONANCES

Recent design research and practice reflects the theme of psychological needs, particularly in terms of tuning our consciousness and relationships. Kate Fletcher, Emma Dewberry, and Philip Goggin examine the issue within the context of washing clothes.[35] They suggest that social and cultural ideas about cleanliness go far beyond the basic concern of hygiene, to reflect happiness, success, and even affection. Consider the meaning of a clean white shirt to a successful businessman, schoolchild, or a fashionable young woman. The researchers suggest that in designing both clothes and washing machines, these psychological needs must be considered alongside the "material" needs of production, if we are to reduce the intensity of our reliance on material goods.

"Slow design" also addresses psychological needs, based on the notion that the fast pace of contemporary life tends to reduce our time both for internal reflection and connection with others.[36] Carolyn F. Strauss and Alastair Fuad-Luke suggest that designed objects and architecture can work to slow us down and help us regain temporal stability, partly by enabling us to shift value from material objects to experiences that perhaps help us tune our consciousness.[37] They posit six principles of slow design, ranging from collaborative engagement with end users (as in place-based architecture) to revelation of previously unseen elements of life. Another principle is evolution, a subject also taken up by other designers.

The now defunct Eternally Yours Foundation promoted designing products that would evolve, seeking to strengthen and thus lengthen relationships between people and products.[38] In related work, Stuart Walker suggests that rather than flashy, perfect-looking products, which put too much emphasis on themselves and their constant updating, we need "good enough" looking products that will free us to focus on inner, spiritual development.[39] He attempts to slow the pace of stylistic change by devising "good enough" products built with local, often recycled, materials supplemented by limited globalized components. Walker uses the notion of enduring products to address sustainable consumption through both informed choice (better products to choose) and inner growth (de-emphasis of appearance).

Jonathan Chapman's work also examines lengthening our relationships with our products.[40] He suggests that current relationships with products fail because although we grow and evolve, our products don't. He offers a toolbox of approaches for involving users in empathetic relationships with products, such as making products endearingly unpredictable or giving them "free will." Although Chapman posits these approaches only for a niche market, he appears to encourage using material goods to meet psychological needs. He notes,

"Somewhere during the last 100 years we learned to find refuge outside the species, in the silent embrace of manufactured objects."[41] Rather than question this embrace, Chapman seems to be saying that things can make us happy, as long as designers can create the right kind of empathetic products.

In contrast, Ezio Manzini suggests that design must challenge "product-based" well being, particularly by attending to the quality of our contexts for living.[42] Manzini looks at the services that products provide and for ways to offer these services with fewer physical resources. For example, few people want a drill per se, they want the hole that it creates. Manzini characterizes this as a shift "from products to results" an approach known as "product-service systems."[43] In addition to potentially reducing the material intensity of life, the implication is that reduced ownership duties (shopping for, maintaining, and decommissioning objects) would free up time and attention for other methods of meeting human needs. This approach also tends to have an element of sharing or collectivism, which may provide opportunities for improved relationships.

Manzini suggests that historically, product-based well being stems from the idea of labor-saving technology, which was then extended to a general notion of bundling knowledge and skills into devices, reducing user involvement. He calls these "disabling" solutions. Others have noted this as a process of "de-skilling."[44] Seen in the light of "flow" and other elements of psychological wellbeing (e.g., creativity, participation, understanding), technical approaches that reduce skills do appear to some extent to rob the user of chances to tune their consciousness. Manzini promotes "enabling" solutions that move the user from a passive to an active role as co-designer.

The notion of co-design builds upon a trend (outside the realm of sustainable consumption) toward democratic, representative, or user-enabled design.[45] In the sustainable fashion context, Kate Fletcher (in a publication separate from that cited before) reports on projects that encourage consumers to become co-designers by cutting garments to fit, inventing with mix-n-match or unusually sized garments, or drawing with fabric pens on undergarments.[46] Work by the Design Council (UK) uses "co-creation" in the context of reinventing public services.[47] This research emphasizes the importance of social networks as an aspect of co-creation, repeatedly highlighting the correlation between well-being and the quality of a person's relationships with others. Design's role here involves user research, facilitation, visualizing structures and systems, and inventing a shared language for problem solving.

Kristina Niedderer, a product designer who explores products as mediators of relationships, proposes the idea of "performative objects" which create "mindful interactions" among people.[48] She created "social cups," a group of champagne flutes that only stand up when linked three or more together. In a broader exploration of how objects influence interaction, she observes, "objects are designed to make people independent rather than to make dependency and care acceptable as an integrated part of use."[49] To the extent that her observation is true, it suggests how consumer goods facilitate individualization and potentially minimize relationships.

To summarize, we recall the basic question about how far consumerism can go in meeting our psychological needs. Can things make us happy? Or do material goods rob us of real relationships and render our consciousness out of tune? If material goods make us happy up to a point, then where is that point? We have seen that designers are exploring how to support behaviors and lifestyles that promote psychological well being, both by building relationships and by considering how objects (and their absence) might better contribute to a tuned consciousness. The ideas reviewed here include slow design, good-enough products, co-creation, empathetic products, product-service-systems, and performative objects.

These approaches raise questions about roles and methods of design. For example, what is a designer's role among a group of enabled users who co-create in what Manzini calls "designing communities"? It's also not clear that design methods exist for some of these new approaches. For example, there are elements of services, such as hospitality and customer care, that are not typically captured in a design education. Similarly, few designers are trained in facilitating "flow" for users.

SOCIOLOGY

On a basic level, sociological research on consumption asks, "what does consumption mean?" This research examines the role of material objects and consumption in constructing meaning and identity—how we use goods to make sense of our world and ourselves. For sociologists and other cultural theorists, goods have symbolic meaning, and that meaning is negotiated through social interaction.[50]

In a sense, goods have become our main source of "symbols," in the same way that fossil fuels have become our main source of energy. Goods are "symbolic resources" in the same way the oil is an energy resource. Over time, society has lost many of its older sources of symbols, such as rights of passage, seasonal and ceremonial customs, and personal and community rituals and practices. These used to help people navigate community and identity with less emphasis on material goods. In our fast changing world, we increasingly rely on consumer goods and the process of consumption to continually construct, reconstruct, and project our identities and social relationships.[51]

There are various models for how social relations and consumer goods allow for construction of the self. For example, Csikszentmihalyi (in a separate study from that previously cited) and Eugene Rochberg-Halton suggest a three-layered self that includes the personal self (the individual), the social self (self in relation to community), and the cosmic self (self in the "larger harmony of things"). They see material objects as templates: the possessions one selects to endow with special meaning out of the total environment of artifacts are both models of the self as well as templates for further development. They serve to give a tangible expression and thus a continued existence through signs to one's relationships, experiences and values.[52]

In this model, material objects might express goals or show how they are being achieved, for example professional cookware attests to the goal, and perhaps the achievement, of becoming a gourmet cook. The researchers suggest that this is productive when the psychic energy we put into objects is returned in the form of enjoyment, learning, and creativity—in essence, the form of personal growth. These authors theorize that in recent decades the personal self has dominated and cut us off from wider networks of meaning, leaving the social and especially the "cosmic" self to whither. Without these other selves, it is harder for objects and their meanings to become instruments for personal growth.

Jackson reports on another model for how we construct identity, the "social, symbolic self."[53] Material and symbolic resources make up our daily lives—we operate life with material things—but the social value of the goods and symbols can only be tested and validated in a social milieu. What do you think of my new car? Do my clothes help me gain social status? We must know the social value of our symbolic resources in order to complete the "social, symbolic" self. Seen in the light of identity and meaning, consumer society and material goods are the contemporary response to the need to build a humanly meaningful world—they have become our dominant meaning structure.

Although consumerism arguably fails in environmental terms and to some extent also in psychological terms, to the extent consumerism provides our structure for meaning, the implications for changing lifestyles and behaviors are complex. In this view, the challenge of sustainable consumption lies well beyond the reach of typical informed choice models that environmentalists have tended to pursue.

Jackson concludes that to confront consumerism as the dominant structure for meaning, we must understand it and pose alternatives. He also questions, as few of the cultural theorists seem to do, who *controls* the boundless symbolic resources—the meanings to be found in consumer goods. He notes that goods and their system of symbols are not under any sort of democratic or community control, despite a certain level of "appropriation" of symbols by consumers. Rather, the control of symbols is largely in the hands of business and commercial interests seeking profits.

And here at last, we come back to design. He notes, "Marketers, advertisers, designers, and retailers not only have a vested interest in controlling symbolic resources, they also have a long and rather sophisticated experience in effecting this control to their own best advantage."[54] Business interests typically have more money available to manipulate symbolic resources than public or social sectors that promote sustainable consumption. Perhaps more worryingly, the "vested interest" he mentions is nothing less than continuous economic growth, which implies a goal of continuous growth in consumption.

At a time when consumption and commoditization are steadily increasing, Jackson's analysis suggests that to some degree we need to take the way we construct social meaning and disconnect it from commerce. Although not every aspect of social relations and identity are commoditized, there are an increasing number of social needs that we meet through individual purchases. How much do we rely on appearances of clothes, tools, vehicles, or houses as an essential part of our identity? Commercial services now overtake social relations in areas as diverse as food and cooking, daycare, healthcare, elder care, cleaning, dating, and entertainment. As vested commercial interests mine these profitable services, the "purchase" solutions are the ones that are researched, perfected, and patented. They then begin to appear to "work better" than under-supported alternatives such as providing for ourselves, maintaining social capital (e.g. maintenance and preventative care), or developing cooperatives (such as car sharing).[55]

SOCIOLOGY—DESIGN RESONANCES

The sociology of consumption seems to pose the biggest challenge yet to design. While there is no doubt that consumerism can and should be made much better, through informed choice, choice editing, and other approaches, there is also little doubt that the dominance of commerce and consumerism in social life is problematic. Elsewhere, based on some of Jackson's analysis, I have developed the idea that culturally sustainable design allows for more meaning to be generated among individuals and communities, rather than being globally or even nationally broadcast by commerce.[56] This approach suggests that in parallel with "for profit" design work, we also need design efforts in the nonprofit, social enterprise, and even public sectors.

Seen in this light, solutions that use non-purchase, shared, self-provisioned, or community-provisioned options to meet peoples' needs (either for goods or meaning) are not *non-design* solutions. They are solutions that call upon an alternate economic framework within which to organize design activities. For example, instead of forming a consulting business, designers may need to join public sector efforts or form a non-profit design studio. (Designers would still earn a living as employees—we are not talking about volunteering.)

Yet designers typically view themselves, and others view them, as commercial actors. Designers are trained to respond to clients and consumers, and to add value to businesses. Governments develop policies that position design as a tool of economic growth. Professional design associations largely concern themselves with business practices and responsibilities to clients.[57] Design is a key cog in the wheel of consumerism, so it is no wonder that most designers have trouble conceiving of their work in any other form than commerce and consumerism. Many designers fall back on the idea of making consumerism "better."

MOVING BEYOND A COG

Yet designers are proposing alternatives to "purchased" solutions, though few explicitly recognize how the economic organization of design affects its role. Some of the previously mentioned ideas, such as "designing communities" or local schemes supplemented by global components, suggest a move away from mass production and toward regional production, self-provisioning, or sharing and trading—all activities that would struggle as for profit entities, but thrive as non-profit or social enterprises, perhaps kick started by public investment. Consider a few more examples:

Product service systems. Recent efforts at car sharing have typically been set up and run by nonprofit community organizations.

Design for the elderly. Victor and Sylvia Margolin give an example from the public sector of social interventions in which social workers team with architects to assess how to better meet people's social and physical needs.[58]

Local graphic design. Tremendous global pressure toward a dominant western graphic design can be overcome through awareness of local cultures, via visual traditions and folklore—an awareness best fostered through schools and professional design associations which are typically public institutions or non-profits.[59]

Social self build. In England during the 1970s and 80s, architects employed by the local government (public sector) helped people on housing waiting lists solve their own problems through self build. Government-donated land and simplified building techniques enabled people to design and construct their own housing.[60]

Design strategies that help us meet needs with fewer purchased solutions could lead to more sustainable consumption. Although this approach is not guaranteed to eliminate the development of new products and services—to do away with "stuff"—it could reduce the quantity of stuff and go some way toward changing our lifestyles, potentially by making stuff easier to share, produce locally, repair, or do yourself, which also could have social and psychological benefits.

Even if designers are willing to go in these directions, some might argue that consumers are not. Given the dominance of individualism, consumerism, and private property rights, what is our willingness to share, to be enabled and re-skilled? There is a sense that having lost much of the "civic realm," we now lack the organizational scale with which to engage people.[61] But perhaps design's "project" focus can provide the right scale; its "universal" visual language can provide the basis for conversation and new visions. This leads to additional methods questions for designers. Do designers automatically know how to motivate and build social capital? Do designers understand how to operate in nonprofit groups or public agencies?

The possibilities for enabling users and for building local community meaning are alluring in a digital society, with recent applications of open source methods to the areas of law, biology, and news.[62] Could design be next?[63] Where are the opportunities?

Although the questions are beyond the scope of this paper, they are relevant to further research into design that supports sustainable consumption.

CONCLUSION

This review has captured only a small portion of the work in the enormous fields of design and sustainable consumption. In highlighting important themes in mainstream research and their resonances in design, I have attempted to map out some of the key questions and concerns that now face design research and practice. Answers to these questions about methods and forms of organizing design practice may help move design from a cog in the wheel of consumerism to facilitator of sustainable consumption.

© 2010 MIT. Previously published in *Design Issues*, Vol. 26, Number 2, Spring 2010, pp. 3–16.

NOTES

1. Throughout this article I write mostly of "consumer goods" in terms of products, but there is a case to be made that architecture is becoming a consumer good on some levels and that many of the points made here apply at least partially to architecture.

2. Tim Jackson, "Readings in Sustainable Consumption" in *The Earthscan Reader in Sustainable Consumption*, ed. Tim Jackson (London: Earthscan, 2006). Jackson's *Reader* is a good entry point into the literature on sustainable consumption (and one that I draw upon heavily), because Jackson has assembled a collection largely from pre-existing writings that include many respected consumption scholars from across a range of disciplines and time periods. Another good entry point, particularly for critique of the environmental movement, is the edited volume, *Confronting Consumption*, ed. Thomas Princen, Michael Maniate, and Ken Conca (Cambridge, MA: The MIT Press, 2002).

3. Rachel Carson, *Silent Spring* (New York: Houghton Mifflin, 1962); Donella H. Meadows and Club of Rome, *The Limits to Growth: A Report for the Club of Rome's Project on the Predicament of Mankind* (London: Earth Island, 1972).

4. R. Buckminster Fuller, *Operating Manual for Spaceship Earth* (Carbondale: Southern Illinois University Press, 1969); Victor J. Papanek, *Design for the Real World: Human Ecology and Social Change* (New York: Pantheon Books, 1972); Chris Zelov and Phil Cousineau, *Design Outlaws on the Ecological Frontier* (Philadelphia: Knossus, 1997).

5. Jakki Dehn, "Re-Materialize Exhibition: Materials Made from Waste" (Kingston University, 1996); Susan Subtle Dintenfass, "Hello Again: A New Wave of Recycled Art and Design" (Oakland: Oakland Museum of California, 1997–98).

6. Nigel Whiteley, *Design for Society* (London: Reaktion Books, 1993).

7. Sim Van der Ryn and Stuart Cowan, *Ecological Design.* (Washington D.C.: Island Press, 1996); H. Brezet and C. van Hemel, "Ecodesign: A Promising Approach to Sustainable Production and Consumption" (Paris: United Nations Environment Programme, 1997); J. H. Gertsakis, H. Lewis, and C. Ryan, *A Guide to EcoRedesign* (Melbourne: Centre for Design, Royal Melbourne Institute of Technology, 1997).

8. Jackson, "Readings in Sustainable Consumption."

9. Kate Fletcher, "Use Matters" Chapter 3 in *Sustainable Fashion & Textiles: Design Journeys* (London: Earthscan, 2008).

10. See, for example, Karrie Jacobs, "Revenge of the Small," *Metropolis*, December 2006, and Ingrid Spencer "The Acceleration of Single Speed Design," *Architectural Record*, September 2006.

11. William J. Mitchell, "Going the Extra Mile to Make Mass Transit More Personal" *Architectural Record*, August 2007.

12. See, for example, Thomas de Monchaux "A is for Adaptable" I.D., May 2007, William Weathersby, "Derek Porter Studio elevates the image of FLEX self storage center," Architectural Record, November 2006, and Alec Applebaum "Parking Garages Driven to Good Design" *Architectural Record*, August 2007.

13. Jackson, "Readings in Sustainable Consumption" and Anja Schaefer and Andrew Crane, "Addressing Sustainability and Consumption," *Journal of Macromarketing* 25:1(2005), 76–92.

14. Karl Dake and Michael Thompson, "Making Ends Meet—in the Household and on the Planet," *The Earthscan Reader in Sustainable Consumption* (London: Earthscan, 2006).

15. Ken Conca, "Consumption and Environment in a Global Economy," *Confronting Consumption*, ed. Thomas Princen, Michael Maniates, and Ken Conca (Cambridge, MA: The MIT Press, 2002).

16. Jackson, "Readings in Sustainable Consumption."

17. Conca, "Consumption and Environment in a Global Economy."

18. Michael Maniates, "Individualization: Plant a Tree, Buy a Bike, Save the World?" in *Confronting Consumption*, ed. Thomas Princen, Michael Maniate, and Ken Conca (Cambridge, MA: The MIT Press, 2002).

19. Jeff Gates, *Democracy at Risk* (Cambridge, MA: Perseus Publishing, 2000).

20. For example, see Kersty Hobson, "Competing Discourses of Sustainable Consumption: Does the 'Rationalization of Lifestyles,' Make Sense?," in *The Earthscan Reader in Sustainable Consumption* (London: Earthscan, 2006); Maniates, "Individualization: Plant a Tree, Buy a Bike, Save the World?"; Derrick Jensen, "Forget Shorter Showers: Why Personal Change Does Not Equal Political Change" *Orion* July/August (2009).

21. Nick Clarke et al., "Globalising the Consumer: Doing Politics in an Ethical Register," *Political Geography* 26:3 (2007).

22. Jack Manno, "Consumption and Environment in a Global Economy," in *Confronting Consumption*, ed. Thomas Princen, Michael Maniates, and Ken Conca (Cambridge, MA: The MIT Press, 2002).

23. Jessica Prendergrast, Beth Foley, Verena Menne, and Alex Karalis Isaac, "Creatures of Habit? The Art of Behavioural Change" (London: The Social Market Foundation, 2008).

24. Ibid., 8.

25. Sustainable Consumption Roundtable, "I Will If You Will: Towards Sustainable Consumption" (London: National Consumer Council and Sustainable Development Commission, 2006).

26. Paul Hawken, Amory Lovins, and L. Hunter Lovins, *Natural Capitalism* (New York: Little, Brown and Company, 1999); Helen Lewis and John Gertsakis, *Design + Environment: A Global Guide to Designing Greener Goods* (Sheffield: Greenleaf, 2001).

27. T. A. Bhamra, D. Lilley, and T. Tang, "Sustainable Use: Changing Consumer Behavior through Product Design" in *Changing the Change Conference Proceedings* (Turin, Italy: Allemandi Conference Press, 2008).

28. Some history and a range of examples are reviewed in Dan Lockton, Professor David Harrison and Professor Neville Stanton, "Making the User More Efficient: Design for Sustainable Behaviour" *International Journal of Sustainable Engineering*, preprint (2008). available from http://hdl.handle.net/2438/2137 (accessed 9/23/2008).

29. Tim Kasser, *The High Price of Materialism* (Cambridge, MA: The MIT Press, 2002).

30. Tim Jackson, "Consuming Paradise? Towards a Social and Cultural Psychology of Sustainable Consumption," in *The Earthscan Reader in Sustainable Consumption*, ed. Tim Jackson (London: Earthscan, 2006); Kasser, *The High Price of Materialism*.

31. Tim Jackson, "Prosperity Without Growth: The Transition to a Sustainable Economy" (London: Sustainable Development Commission, 2009), 39, 63–65.

32. Daniel Miller, "The Poverty of Morality," *The Earthscan Reader in Sustainable Consumption*, ed. Tim Jackson (London: Earthscan, 2006).

33. Mihaly Csikszentmihalyi, "The Costs and Benefits of Consuming," *The Earthscan Reader in Sustainable Consumption*, ed. Tim Jackson (London: Earthscan, 2006).

34. Maniates, "Individualization: Plant a Tree, Buy a Bike, Save the World?"

35. Kate Fletcher, Emma Dewberry, and Phillip Goggin, "Sustainable Consumption by Design," *Exploring Sustainable Consumption: Environmental Policy and the Social Sciences*, ed. Maurie J. Cohen and Joseph Murphy (London: Pergamon, 2001).

36. Ann Thorpe. *The Designer's Atlas of Sustainability*, (Washington DC: Island Press, 2007).

37. Carolyn F. Strauss and Alastair Fuad-Luke, "The Slow Design Principles: A New Interrogative and Reflexive Tool for Design Research and Practice," *Changing the Change Conference Proceedings* (Turin, Italy: Allemandi Conference Press, 2008).

38. Ed Van Hinte and Liesbeth Bonekamp, *Eternally Yours* (Rotterdam: 010 Publishers, 1997).

39. Stewart Walker, *Sustainable by Design* (London: Earthscan, 2006).

40. Jonathan Chapman, *Emotionally Durable Design: Objects, Experiences & Empathy* (London: Earthscan, 2005).

41. Ibid., 61.

42. For example, see Eva Heiskanen and Mikko Jalas, "Dematerialization through Services—A Review and Evaluation of the Debate" (Helsinki: Ministry of the Environment, 2000); A. S. Bijma, Brezet, and S. Silvester, "The Design of Eco-Efficient Services: Methods, Tools and Review of the Case Study Based 'Designing Eco-Efficient Services' Project" (Delft: Design for Sustainability Program, Delft University of Technology, 2001); and Ezio Manzini, "Design, Ethics and Sustainability: Guidelines for a Transition Phase" (Milan: Politecnico di Milano, 2006).

43. Ezio Manzini, "Design for Sustainability: How to Design Sustainable Solutions" (Milan: Politecnico di Milano, 2006).

44. Albert Borgmann, "The Depth of Design," in *Discovering Design: Explorations in Design Studies*, ed. Richard Buchanan and Victor Margolin (Chicago: University of Chicago Press, 1995).

45. For example, see Gui Bonsiepe, "Design and Democracy," *Design Issues* 22:2 (Spring 2006), 56–63; Jeff Howard, "Toward Participatory Ecological Design of Technological Systems," *Design Issues* 20:3 (Summer 2004), 40–53; and Peter Blundell Jones, Doina Petrescu, and Jeremy Till, eds., *Architecture and Participation* (New York: Spon Press, 2005).

46. Kate Fletcher, "User Maker," Chapter 8 in *Sustainable Fashion & Textiles: Design Journeys*.

47. Hilary Cottam and Charles Leadbeater, "Health: Co-Creating Services," *Red Papers* (London: Design Council, 2004).

48. Kristina Niedderer, "Designing Mindful Interaction: The Category of Performative Object," *Design Issues* 23:1 (Winter 2007), 3–17.

49. Ibid., 7.

50. Mary Douglas, "Relative Poverty, Relative Communication," *The Earthscan Reader in Sustainable Consumption*, ed. Tim Jackson (London: Earthscan, 2006).

51. See, for example, John Connolly and Andrea Prothero, "Sustainable Consumption: Consumption, Consumers and the Commodity Discourse," *Consumption, Markets and Culture* 6:4 (2003), 275–91; Mary Douglas and Baron Isherwood, *The World of Goods* (London: Routledge, 1979); Tim Jackson, Wander Jager, and Sigrid Stagl, "Beyond Insatiability: Needs Theory, Consumption and Sustainability," *ESRC Sustainable Technologies Programme Working Papers* (Guildford: Centre for Environmental Strategy, University of Surrey, 2004).

52. Mihaly Csikszentmihalyi and Eugene Rochberg-Halton, *The Meaning of Things: Domestic Symbols and the Self* (Cambridge, UK: Cambridge University Press, 1981), 188.

53. Jackson, "Consuming Paradise? Towards a Social and Cultural Psychology of Sustainable Consumption."

54. Ibid., 389.

55. Manno, "Consumption and Environment in a Global Economy."

56. Thorpe, *The Designer's Atlas of Sustainability*.

57. See, for example, Peter Dormer, *Design since 1945* (London: Thames and Hudson, 1993); John Heskett, *Toothpicks and Logos: Design in Everyday Life* (Oxford: Oxford University Press, 2002); Thorpe, *The Designer's Atlas of Sustainability*.

58. Victor Margolin and Sylvia Margolin, "A 'Social Model' of Design: Issues of Practice and Research," *Design Issues* 18:4 (Autumn 2002), 24–30.

59. Sherry Blankenship, "Outside the Center: Defining Who We Are," *Design Issues* 21:1 (Winter 2005), 24–31.

60. Jon Broome, "Technology and Participation Towards Sustainability," *Architecture as Initiative* (London: Architecture Association, 2007).

61. Hobson, "Competing Discourses of Sustainable Consumption: Does the 'Rationalization of Lifestyles' Make Sense?"

62. Geoff Mulgan, Tom Steinberg, and Omar Salem, *Wide Open: Open Source Methods and Their Future Potential* (London: Demos, 2005).

63. See, for example, Bruce Sterling, *Shaping Things* (Cambridge, MA: The MIT Press, 2005); C. Leadbeater, *We Think: Mass Innovation Not Mass Production* (London: Profile Books, 2008); and Alastair Fuad-Luke, *Design Activism: Beautiful Strangeness for a Sustainable World* (London: Earthscan, 2009).

CHAPTER TWENTY SIX

Transformative Services and Transformation Design

DANIELA SANGIORGI

© Daniela Sangiorgi, 2011

ABSTRACT

This article reports on the recent evolution of service design toward becoming transformational. Services are less discussed as design objects and more as means for supporting the emergence of a more collaborative, sustainable and creative society and economy. The transformative role of design is combined with the potential transformative role of services. The term "transformation design" as set forth by Burns, Cottam, Vanstone, and Winhall (2006), has been associated with work within communities for socially progressive ends, but also with work within organisations to introduce a human-centred design culture. The intrinsic element of co-production of services in transformation design necessitates the concomitant development of staff, the public and the organisation. In this way, service design is entering the fields of organisational studies and social change with little background knowledge of their respective theories and principles. This article proposes the adoption and adaptation of principles and practices from organisational development and community action research into service design. Additionally, given the huge responsibilities associated with transformative practices, designers are urged to introduce reflexivity into their work to address power and control issues in each design encounter.

Keywords: Service Design, Transformative Services, Transformation Design, Transformational Change

Relevance to Design Practice—Service design is increasingly oriented toward transformative aims. The concept of transformation design has been proposed, but little research exists on its principles, methodologies and qualities. This article aims to provide some foundations for clarifying the concept of transformational change and suggests a potentially useful bridge with the principles and practices of organisational development and community action research.

INTRODUCTION

Service design has recently been developing by enhancing its capacity to facilitate change within both organisations and communities. Burns, Cottam, Vanstone, and Winhall (2006) defined this area of practice as transformation design. According to their definition, the concept of transformation design suggests that:

> "Because organisations now operate in an environment of constant change, the challenge is not how to design a response to a current issue, but how to design a means of continually responding, adapting and innovating. Transformation design seeks to leave behind not only the shape of a new solution, but the tools, skills and organisational capacity for ongoing change." (p. 21)

The fact that transformation design is aiming at radical change is also emphasized. They suggest that transformation design can be applied to radically change public and community services, working for socially progressive ends, or can, alternatively, trigger change in a private company introducing a human-centred design culture.

Furthermore, service design has recently been considering services less as design objects and more as means for societal transformation. The intrinsic element of co-production of services in transformation design necessitates the concomitant development of staff, the public and the organisation. This is particularly evident in the debate around the reform of public services where both organisations and citizens are asked to evolve and adapt to more collaborative service models thereby changing their roles and interaction patterns (Parker & Parker, 2007). In this way, service design is entering the fields of organisational development and social change, with little background knowledge of their respective theories and principles. In this light, the questions which arise are: How can designers working with communities affect and transform organisations or, vice versa, how can designers working within organisations affect and positively transform user communities? It is also necessary to clarify the form of transformations, why these are desirable and who will particularly benefit from them.

This article aims at providing a first framework for transformation design, in the specific context of public services reform, by suggesting the adoption of key concepts and principles derived from research fields that have focused for decades on the issues of transformational change within organisations and communities, such as organisational development and community action research. Participatory action research has been chosen in particular as a possible integrating methodological framework that characterises both research fields of organisational development and community action research, and which could be adapted to the needs of service design practice.

The following section will clarify the concepts of transformative services, transformation design and transformational change to provide a background knowledge. The article will then introduce a selection of principles from the relevant fields of operational design and community action research and compare them with the principles guiding the transformation of public services and the evolution of participatory design practices within the public sphere.

TRANSFORMATIVE SERVICES

At its onset, service design has focused on services as different kinds of products, exploring modes of dealing with the differentiating service qualities (originally thought of as deficiencies) such as intangibility, heterogeneity, inseparability, and perishability (Zeithaml, Parasuraman, and Berry, 1985).

The design debate then made one step forward when acknowledging the nature of services as complex and relational entities that cannot be fully designed and pre-determined (Sangiorgi, 2004). The focus on service interactions has been broadening to consider interactions within and among organisations, working on the systems and networks therein, while designers have been increasingly approaching issues of organisational and behavioural change (Sangiorgi, 2009). In this evolution, design for services, instead of service design, has gained more credibility, reflecting the interdisciplinary and emergent qualities of this discipline (Kimbell, 2009; Meroni & Sangiorgi, 2011).

In the last few years, a further shift seems to be happening as services are no longer conceived of as an end in themselves, but are increasingly considered as an engine for wider societal transformations. Services are less discussed as a design object, but now more as means for supporting the emergence of a more collaborative, sustainable and creative society and economy. Particular emphasis has been given to collaborative service models and co-creation (Cottam & Leadbeater, 2004; Meroni, 2007).

This evolution is mirrored in the debate around the role of services in developed countries' economies. Together with a growing acknowledgment of the role of services for the development and growth of economy and employment, services have revealed a different model of innovation that is now inspiring manufacturing; as Howells (2007) comments, this model is ill represented by linear positivistic descriptions and is "more likely to be linked to disembodied, non-technological innovative processes, organisational arrangements and markets" (p. 11). The main sources of innovation in service industries are employees and customers (Miles, 2001) and new ideas are often generated through the interaction with users (user-driven innovation) and through the application of tacit knowledge or training rather than through explicit R&D activities (Almega, 2008). Moreover, service innovation is increasingly viewed as an enabler of a "society driven innovation" with policies at national and regional level that are "using service innovation to address societal challenges and as a catalyst of societal and economic change" (European Commission, 2009, p. 70). Tekes, the Finnish Funding Agency for Technology and Innovation, positions service innovation as a core lever for transformative changes in areas such as health and wellbeing, clean energy, built environment, and the knowledge society (Ezell, Ogilvie, & Rae, 2008).

Finally, in a recent study the Arizona State University's Center for Services Leadership collectively identified a set of global, interdisciplinary research priorities focused on the service science (Ostrom et al., 2010). Among ten overarching research priorities, a significant area of present interest emerged titled "Improving Well-being through Transformative Service." Laurel Anderson (a leader in this field from Arizona State University) described the emerging area of transformative service research as "service research that centers on creating uplifting changes and improvements in the well-being of both individuals and communities" (p. 6). She suggested that services, being deeply embedded and diffused in social ecologies, have the potential to impact individuals, families and communities by suggesting new behavioural and interaction models. This area, of particularly contemporary relevance, has been given little attention to date.

TRANSFORMATION DESIGN

Design, additionally, has recently focused increasingly on investigating the transformative role of services as a way to build a more sustainable and equitable society. Main fields of research have been related to the exploration of the role and impact of creative communities and social innovation (Jegou & Manzini, 2008; Meroni, 2007; Thackara, 2007) and the wide debate on the redesign of public services and the welfare state (Bradwell & Marr, 2008; Cottam & Leadbeater, 2004; Parker & Heapy, 2006; Parker & Parker, 2007; Thomas, 2008).

The research on social innovation has been investigating existing examples of inventiveness and creativity among "ordinary people" to solve daily life problems related to housing, food, ageing, transports and work. Such cases represent a way of "living well while at the same time consuming fewer resources and generating new patterns of social cohabitation" (Manzini, 2008, p. 13). Defined as "collaborative services," they have the potential to develop into a new kind of enterprise, a "diffused social enterprise" which needs a supporting environment to grow.

The contemporary debate on the re-design of public services has similarly emphasised the role of co-production and collaborative solutions. With the co-creation model, Cottam and Leadbeater (2004) suggested examining the open source paradigm as the main inspiration, which implies the use of distributed resources (know-how, tools, effort and expertise) collaborative modes of delivery, and the participation of users in "the design and delivery of services, working with professionals and front-line staff to devise effective solutions" (p. 22). This, in turn, requires a significant transformation in both organisations and citizens' behaviors and engrained cultural models.

Simultaneously, design research has recently been exploring design's transformative role in both organisations (Bate & Robert, 2007a, 2007b; Buchanan, 2004; Junginger, 2008; Junginger & Sangiorgi, 2009) and communities (Thackara, 2007). Service design practitioners have been moving from providing solutions to specific problems, to providing organisations with the tools and capacities for human-centred service innovation. Examples of this include the work of Engine Service Design group with Kent City Council to develop a Social Innovation Lab (Kent County Council, 2007) or the work with Buckinghamshire to define a methodology for the engagement of local organisations and citizens (Milton, 2007).

Similarly, the NHS Institute for Innovation and Improvement has developed the Experience-Based-Design (EBD) approach and toolkit in collaboration with *thinkpublic* (a London based service design studio) to co-design more accessible, usable and effective services. They have organised a series of training workshops and pilot projects to support adoption on a wider scale. Since its launch in 2007, the EBD approach, consisting of experience-focused participatory design exercises, has been piloted in various hospitals with the aim of activating a large-scale cultural change in NHS.

This evolution within design has been intuitively defined in its emergence as transformation design by Burns et al. (2006). They summarise the key characteristics of transformation projects as follows: 1) defining and redefining the brief, as designers engage before the definition of the brief and participate in the formulation of the right problem to tackle; 2) collaborating between disciplines, as the complexity of contemporary challenges requires multidisciplinary efforts; 3) employing participatory design techniques, as users and front-line workers can bring in their ideas, expertise and knowledge; 4) building capacity and not dependency, as transformation projects aim to leave the capacities and skills for ongoing change; 5) designing beyond traditional solutions, as designers focus on changing behaviour (and not only forms) and need to tackle issues with a more holistic perspective; 6) creating fundamental change, as projects can initiate a lasting transformation process, leaving a vision and champions to continue the work.

These characteristics bring some challenges as designers are not necessarily trained to work on highly complex issues or to direct their work toward transformational aims. The traditional design consultancy may need to change its practice and relationship with clients and reconsider its identity within design interventions. Also, an understanding of appropriate methodologies and an articulation of key design principles are still missing. When designers engage in transformational projects they have a huge responsibility, especially when engaging with vulnerable communities. In addition, the quality and effectiveness of such interventions are hard to evaluate in the short term and within traditional design parameters. To better understand the modes and outcomes of transformational projects, the first (and most basic) question to ask is: What is a transformational change?

TRANSFORMATIONAL CHANGE

In organisational development, change is discussed and evaluated in terms of degrees or levels. Early studies from Watzlawick, Weakland, and Fisch (1974) identified two levels of change as first-order and second-order change. First-order change was related to adjustments and fluctuations within a given system, while second-order change implied qualitative changes to the system itself. In a similar way, Golembiewski, Billingsley, and Yeager (1989) introduced three levels of change in the context of change measurement: alpha change, related to changes in perceived levels of variables within a given paradigm; beta change, related to changes in standards and perception of value within a given paradigm; and gamma change, related to the change of the paradigm itself. Looking at biology, Smith (1982) suggested comparing the terms *morphostasis* and *morphogenesis*, where the former indicates changes in appearance and maturation processes of an organism, while the latter indicates a change in the genetic code, in the core and essence of it. Organisational development studies in 1960s and 1970s focused on first order changes focusing on improving "the internal working of organisations through the use of role clarification, improved communication, team building, intergroup team building, and the like" (French, Bell, & Zawacki, 2005, p. 7). In 1980s, the external environment changed marked by growing competition with more demanding customers and an instable economy. Companies were asked to change fast to survive. The kind of change required, however, was not incremental, but rather very radical.

Organisational transformation emerged as a specific area of research to better understand the drivers, processes and content of planned, second-order change, defined as transformational change. Levy (1986) claims that second order change is a "paradigmatic change" and that in order to support this transformational change, one has to change the "metarules" (the rules of the rules) of the system. He visualises an integrated model of the perspectives of what is changed in a second-order change, moving from core processes, culture, mission and paradigm. In order to achieve a paradigmatic change that entails change in the core assumptions and worldview of an organisation, companies need to change all the other levels, including the organisational philosophy, mission and purpose, culture and core processes. Changes in the organisational mission or culture do not imply necessarily a paradigmatic transformation. Seen from a service design perspective, projects that improve service interactions and touchpoints (service interaction design) or that help redefining service values, norms or philosophy (service interventions), don't necessarily have a transformational impact. Uncovering and questioning, via design inquiries, core assumptions and organisational worldviews, can have, instead, a far-reaching impact into organisational evolution (Junginger & Sangiorgi, 2009).

How this can happen, however, has not yet been discussed in service design research. Junginger (2006), in her investigations into the role of design for organisational change, suggests a link between human-centred design and organisational learning:

"For an organization, human-centered design offers two key benefits: Firstly, it centers product development on the needs of its customers. Secondly, applying user research methods can reveal the strengths and weaknesses of an organization's interaction with different customers and employees. The findings can serve as a base for an organizational redesign by understanding existing and future relationships within the organization's network from a user perspective." (p. 10)

Nonetheless, as mentioned previously, looking at transformational processes within service organisations is only one side of the coin. Users and communities, that co-produce service activities, might need to go through similar transformational processes. This is particularly true if we look at the deep transformation being advocated in public services, which involves moving from a delivery model that is associated with a paternalistic and top down welfare paradigm, toward an enabling model that is centred on the concept of co-creation and active citizenship. Designers have been adopting two main kinds of transformation strategies with public services (Freire & Sangiorgi, 2010). The first is change from inside-out, working within organisations to instill a human-centred design culture and improve service provisions. The other is change from outside-in, or working with communities and various stakeholders to imagine new systems and service models. Both of these strategies need grounding through understanding change and transformational practices. Working on one side only, without considering potential resistances in both communities and organisations, can lead to failure or achievement of a limited impact. In light of this, designers should learn from studies and projects of organizational development and community action research to provide a more solid foundation on which to build their activities.

TRANSFORMATIVE PRACTICES AND PRINCIPLES

A methodological framework that unifies transformational interventions within organisations and communities is participatory action research. Action research is generally associated with the experimental work of Kurt Lewin in the 1940s on social democracy and organisational change. Kurt Lewin said once that "if you want to understand a phenomenon, try to change it" (French et al., 2005, p. 106). His approach is part of "normative-reeducative strategies of changing" that consider intelligence as social rather than narrowly individual, and consider people as guided by a "normative culture" (Chin & Benne, 2001). As they elucidate:

> "Changes in patterns of action or practice are, therefore, changes, not alone in the rational information equipment of men, but at the personal level, in habits and values as well and, at the sociocultural level, changes are alterations in normative structures and in institutionalized roles and relationships, as well as in cognitive and perceptual orientations." (p. 47)

Action research has been defined as a:

> "Participatory, democratic process concerned with developing practical knowing in the pursuit of worthwhile human purposes... .It seeks to bring together action and reflection, theory and practice, in participation with others, in the pursuit of practical solutions to issues of pressing concern to people. And more generally the flourishing of individual persons and their communities." (Reason & Bradbury, 2001, p. 1)

Action research is about generating practical knowledge that can help improve the wellbeing of individuals and communities. It is based on a postmodern conception of knowledge as a social construct and on the recognition of the intimate relationship between knowledge and power (Reason & Bradbury, 2001). Participatory action research provides a framework, which allows a heterarchical rather than hierarchical approach to research. Doing so, it allows a diversity of opinions and possibilities rather than a forced consensus from a reductionist approach to research. This produces a "power to" effect by empowering those involved in the study, as opposed to a "power over" dominance of the active and knowledgeable researcher over the passive subject of the research (Hosking, 1999).

Action research has been applied and developed in a variety of fields and at different levels, especially in the areas of management, education and development studies. Particularly relevant to the present article is the application of participatory action research with marginalized groups and disadvantaged communities. This application called community action research stated how the researcher neutrality of the traditional scientific approach was inadequate to transform dependency and question inequities. Consciousness-raising or "conscientization" is the central concept of community action research. It is intended as a self-reflection and awareness process that leads from seeing oneself as an object responding to a given system to a subject that can question and transform the system itself (as cited in Ozanne & Saatcioglu, 2008).[1] Also, community action research has been focused particularly on issues of health and wellbeing and is therefore strongly linked to the field of public health research and issues of community empowerment.

Transformation design, with its emphasis on participation and empowerment, can be related to action research, even if it has not developed any particular reflection on its relationship with knowledge generation, power and change. More traditionally concerned with issues of power and control is participatory design, which is mentioned as a key component within transformation design practices. Participatory design has moved from working within organisations (private companies and public service organisations) to emphasizing support for democratic processes of change within communities and public spaces, with the intention of enhancing egalitarian practices of innovation and community empowerment (Ehn, 2008).

Based on these analogies and comparisons of the literature from these different fields, the present research has identified seven key principles that seem to unify transformative practices in design, organisational development and community action research with a particular focus on issues of public service reform and wellbeing. The seven key principles are: 1) Active citizens; 2) Intervention at community scale; 3) Building capacities and project partnerships; 4) Redistributing power; 5) Designing infrastructures and enabling platforms; 6) Enhancing imagination and hope; 7) Evaluating success and impact. What follows is an articulation of the content of the principles to enable reflection on the implications for service design practice within transformative projects.

ACTIVE CITIZENS

The central condition for transformative practices is the understanding of citizens as "agents" and their active role in the creation of wellbeing. As Bentley and Wilson (2003) argue, the key to unlock the potential to offer better and more personalised services is to understand that value is created, and not delivered. At the same time, participation has been promoted as being the basic right of democracy, which is a process leading toward better citizens and a means of generating more efficient and effective programmes and policies (Cornwall, 2008).

In the design debate about public services transformation, participation is seen as a key resource to fundamentally change the traditional hierarchical model of service delivery and the perception of citizens themselves. Cottam and Leadbeater (2004) proposed an alternative approach to the welfare system defined as Open Welfare. The authors suggested an open model to public services delivery based on "mass, participatory models, in which many of the 'users' of a service become its designers and producers, working in new partnerships with professionals" (p. 1).

In line with this perspective, the reform of healthcare services calls for "creating a Patient-Led NHS" (Department of Health, 2005). The claimed aim here is to change the whole system so that "there is more choice, more personalised care, real empowerment of people to improve their health," and to "move from a service that does things to and for its patients to one which is patient-led, where the service works with patients to support them with their health needs" (p. 3).

Participation, however, can have different levels of implementation and motivations at its starting point. When participation is pushed to its extremes it meets other agendas generally named as community or citizen "empowerment" and it is linked with more "transformative" aims. Participation here becomes a mean and an end in itself (White, 1996).

A recent review (Marmot, 2010), combining reflection on health inequalities and community engagement, suggests that to really reduce health inequalities, a strong emphasis must be given to individual and community empowerment, which would create the conditions for people to take control over their lives. This requires, on the local service delivery side, increasing the opportunities for people to participate in the definition of community solutions, thus enabling a real shift of power. Marmot contends that "without citizen participation and community engagement fostered by public service organisations, it will be difficult to improve penetration of interventions and to impact on health inequalities" (p. 151).

Primary care services are required to "develop and adopt inclusive practice that seeks to empower patients and develop their health literacy" (p. 157). Research has shown how moving from a patient information or consultation approach toward more inclusive and participatory methods (supporting a real shift of power and participation in health decisions) may lead to better health outcomes (Attree & French, 2007). An increase in participation can lead to more appropriate and accessible services, while increasing social capital and people's self confidence and health-enhancing attitudes (Popay, 2006).

Within organisational development studies, a strong emphasis is given to participatory research and learning processes within organisations seen as drivers for transformational change. The "reframing" needed to deepen transformations cannot happen without a deep psychological engagement among stakeholders (Chapman, 2002). Also connected to transformational change is the concept of empowerment, where project participants are not only consulted during different phases of the transformation process, but they act as co-creators. In this way, to be empowering, participation needs to become a form of "codetermination" (Elden & Levin, 2001). This level of worker-engagement is defined as "organizational citizenship". Citizenship is seen as both an obligation and as an expectation, given the organizational constraints. In this sense, collaboration in organizational transformation projects is perceived as a top-down process that includes workers' insights, while working within an existing social order. Within community action research, however, citizenship is described as a right, where participation is part of an awakening self-awareness process that questions existing power and societal structures and aims at change as an often conflicting bottom up movement (Ozanne & Saatcioglu, 2008).

INTERVENTION AT COMMUNITY SCALE

Another precondition for transformative practices is the focus on communities as intervention scale. Communities are considered as the right size to activate larger-scale changes. Meroni (2008) promotes the concept of a Community Centred Approach "where the focus of attention shifts from the individual 'user' to the community as the new subject of interest for a design that is more conscious of current social dynamics" (p. 13). Communities, or the dimension of "some", are described as the dimension of change where "elective communities (defined by interest, geography, profession or other criteria) are sufficiently larger than the individual to impose moral restraints that transcend the individual will, but still small enough to be recognised as representative of individual interest" (p. 14).

Within business contexts, community action research is a collaborative process of knowledge creation that engages a wider community of practitioners, consultants and researchers to activate large-scale transformational change (Senge & Scharmer, 2001). It is based on the assumption that the high level of competition that has characterised the industrial era needs now to be tempered with cooperation. Community action research interventions therefore foster relationships and collaborations beyond individual organisations, which create cross-organisational learning communities that, can generate and sustain transformative changes (Senge & Scharmer, 2001). Moreover, in public health, the prevention of lifestyle illnesses, to be effective, requires large-scale community participation and measures (Blumenthal & Yancey, 2004). At the same time, the design of future healthcare services is increasingly connected to integrated and community-based solutions (Department of Health, 2008b).

BUILDING CAPACITIES AND PROJECT PARTNERSHIPS

Participatory and community based interventions have in themselves, if carefully supported, the potential to be transformative. As Cornwall (2008) claims, though, to be effective participation "requires changes in organisational culture, as well as in the attitudes and behaviour of state officials and service providers. It also demands processes and structures through which citizens can claim voice, and gain the means to exercise democratic citizenship, including acquiring the skills to participate effectively" (p. 14).

In public health research, the terms "participation" and "public involvement" are better understood as "building relationships" (Anderson, Florin, Gillam, & Mountford, 2002), and about creating "involved organisations" (Department of Health, 2008a) where patient engagement is integrated into the decision-making processes. The emphasis is therefore not only on developing external "mechanisms of involvement," but also on implementing internal "mechanisms of change" (Anderson, Florin, Gillam, & Mountford, 2002). This comes from the awareness that for any transformation to be sustainable and effective in the long term, there needs to be a change of cultures and attitudes by building trust and on-going dialogues.

One-off interventions in a constantly changing political and socio-technical environment cannot generate significant results in terms of reduction of health inequalities and service improvements (Bauld, Judge, Barnes, Benzeval, & Sullivan, 2005). It is therefore fundamental to create a culture of participation and involvement that can last beyond changes in political objectives and strategies.

Community action research has three guiding principles: 1) to include multiple partners from the community in the research process and generate research partnerships; 2) to be guided by locally-defined priorities and committed to social justice; 3) to aim at community education and empowerment by encouraging people to learn new skills, reflect on their social and economic conditions, and act in their own self interest (Ozanne & Anderson, 2010).

Transformation design has similarly inherited the participatory design principle (Shuler & Namioka, 1991) of learning and transcending, which brings about a reciprocal learning process between designers and project participants leading to transformative understandings. If, however, participatory design focuses on providing tools for an adequate participation to guarantee shared ownership of the final design outcome, the transformational perspective aims also at the final ownership of the process and methods themselves.

When design encounters organisational and behavioral change, pilot projects become vehicles for knowledge exchange within longer transformational processes. An example is *Thinkpublic*, which tackled dementia as part of the DOTT07 programme. The organisers hosted a Skills Share Day with a cameraperson from the BBC providing training for filming and interviewing a user group. As a secondary outcome of this endeavor, key stakeholders participating in the project acknowledged how the communication skills they acquired during the project were transferred into their daily professional lives (Tan & Szebeco, 2009).

As discussed here, building capacities and trusting relationships are fundamental to generate lasting legacy in transformative practices. The next question to consider, however, is when knowledge exchange is conducive to real transformations.

REDISTRIBUTING POWER

Participation in a design process does not depend necessarily on the set of methods used or skills transferred, but on the actual redistribution of power happening in the design decision process. Arnstein (1969), in his famous reflection on citizen participation, talks about eight rungs in the "ladder of participation". The rungs begin at the bottom with *non-participation*, which incorporates actions such as "manipulation" and "therapy". The next rung is *tokenism*, which incorporates such actions as "informing", "consultation" and "placation". The top rung is *citizen power*, articulated as "partnership", "delegated power" and "citizen control". Non-participation is associated with attempts to educate and persuade the population of the benefit of existing plans and programmes, while tokenism gives citizens a voice that lacks power to guarantee its follow-through. Citizen power suggests situations where citizens are actually given the structure, skills and support to really participate in decision processes.

In a similar way, Popay (2006), reporting on the practices of community engagement, suggests four broad approaches that are mainly differentiated by their engagement goal: the provision and/or exchange of information, consultation, co-production, and community control. She highlights that "these approaches are not readily bounded but rather sit on a continuum of engagement approaches with the focus on community empowerment becoming more explicit and having greater priority to the right of the continuum where community development approaches are located" (pp. 6–7).

Bate and Robert (2009) suggest an ideal move in the continuum of patient influence from "complaining" and "giving information" toward "listening & responding", "consulting & advising" and "experience-based co-design". Here, co-design is intended as "more of a partnership and shared leadership, with NHS staff continuing to play a key role in leading service design alongside patients and users" (p. 10). Here, professionals maintain the lead in the change process, while patients are represented as experts of their own experiences.

In this continuum, the roles of researchers and professionals gradually change. A first consideration relates to what each project participant brings to the process; researchers are said to bring their expertise mainly in methods and theories, while people from the community contribute with insights into "theories-in-use", their capacities and needs, and with their implicit understanding of community social and cultural dynamics (Ozanne & Anderson, 2010). Skidmore and Craig (2005), in their celebration of the role of community organisations for citizen activation, talk about "civic intermediaries" as actors that don't have necessarily a predefined aim, but work with "communities of participation" to enhance their skills, willingness and capacities to contribute to whichever public or semi-public spaces they engage with. In the design field there is a growing consent about the role of designers as facilitators of change processes, but there is a division as to who is actually directing the process, moving between design-driven or use-driven (or led) change processes.

In participatory action research, researchers challenge the traditional division of power in research relationships, where few people in academia and industrial laboratories control the production of "scientific knowledge". The transformation process is actually defined as a "cogenerative learning process" where researchers (outsiders) and clients (insiders) are both defined as "colearners" (Elden & Levin, 2001) and not as "experts" or "subjects". This collaborative learning process can lead to the re-formulation of a "local theory" that can help insiders to re-think their work and worldview and outsiders to generate more general (scientific) theory. This is based on the conception of knowledge as socially constructed (Berger & Luckmann, 1966), where both scientific and personal theories of the world are social products that can be investigated, tested and changed if necessary. However, as in design, with participatory action research the "control dilemma" is still present, because even if participants should be in charge of the research process, the researchers can't loose control completely (Elden & Levin, 2005).

BUILDING INFRASTRUCTURES AND ENABLING PLATFORMS

When the final aim is a transformative one, not only the process, but also the outcome needs to better consider people's participation and engagement. Public Services have emphasised the concept of co-production as the key strategy for more effective and personalised services

(Horne & Shirley, 2009). Considering people's role in shaping and contributing to the service delivery and constant redesign requires thinking not only of the role of users in the design "before the use", but also in the design "after the design" (Ehn, 2010). Pelle Ehn, reflecting on the evolution of participatory design practices, suggests that "rather than focusing on involving users in the design process, focus shifts towards seeing every use situation as a potential design situation. So there is design during a project ('at project time'), but there is also design in use ('at use time')" (p. 5).

At project time, the object should then be open to controversies or reiterations that could support the emergence of new products and practices. Using a Leigh Star concept, Ehn talks about "infrastructuring" which he discusses by noting that "an infrastructure, like railroad tracks or the Internet is not reinvented every time, but is 'sunk into' other sociomaterial structures and only accessible by membership in a specific community-of-practice" (p. 5).

In a similar way, when describing the relevance of community organisations to support people's participation and engagement, Skidmore and Craig (2005) recall the capacities of these organisations to build:

"a platform capable of sustaining diverse and sometimes even incoherent sets of activities … The result of taking the platform model seriously is that it can become very difficult to know where the boundaries of organisations start and finish. Embedded in a web of relationships of varying types, it makes more sense to think of organisations in terms of the networks through which they work." (p. 48)

The concept of designing service platforms is also part of the transformation design language. When project participants become co-creators of the service, designers cannot design fixed entities and sequences of actions that allow little adaptation and flexibility. Platforms made up of tools, roles and rules delineate the weak conditions for certain practices and behaviours to emerge (Sangiorgi & Villari, 2005; Winhall, 2004). At the same time, when designers are confronted with the need to diffuse and scale up creative communities' promising solutions, their contributions take the form of "enabling solutions" which are "a system of products, services, communication and whatever is necessary, to improve the accessibility, effectiveness and replicability of a collaborative service" (Manzini, 2008, p. 38).

In community action research, emphasis is on co-creating sustainable locally grown solutions that are based on community strengths and that locals are willing to maintain and further develop. Without this attention, community action research could hardly reach its main aim, which is to conduct research interventions for the benefit of the communities with which researchers work (Ozanne & Saatcioglu, 2008).

ENHANCING IMAGINATION AND HOPE

Part of a process of change is the capacity to imagine a possible and better future. Designers are generally appreciated for their capacity to think out of the box by providing new visions for the future. As Meroni reminds us, mentioning the work of Bateson (Mind & Nature,

1979), evolution is different from "epigenesis" which is "the development of a system from a previous condition using the capabilities it already possesses" (Meroni, 2008, p. 5). If "epigenesis" means predictable repetition, which grows from within, evolution requires instead exploration and change. Designers are considered to act at this second level as they can work from the outside in and guide more systemic interventions if needed. Enhancing the capacity to build new shared and orienting visions is a fundamental quality in transformation processes (Manzini & Jegou, 2003).

In addition to developing a vision, however, communities need to trust their actual capacity and power to implement it in the future. Skidmore and Craig (2005) claim that "without the hope that animates social networks…social capital can go to waste. The networks people have are only as valuable as what they believe they can accomplish through them" (p. 61). This combination of social networks and collective optimism has been called by the American sociologist Robert Sampson "collective efficacy" (as cited in Skidmore & Craig, 2005). Activating collective optimism through shared and orienting visions needs to be supported by the creation of adequate infrastructures and effective power distribution strategies.

Similarly, organisational change is based on radical transformations in the way individuals think and behave. Levy and Merry (1986) talk about two main strategies. The first is "reframing" which aims at changing the way employees perceive reality. The other is "consciousness raising" which aims at increasing the employee's understanding of change processes and the creative methods to achieve them.

EVALUATING SUCCESS AND IMPACT

Finally, one of the key issues when designing for long-term transformation processes is evaluation. How can you measure success and impact in a complex system? What are the dimensions of success? When transformation is related to cultural and worldview change, how do you evaluate it? Or when transformation is related to community empowerment, wellbeing, and social capital, how can you measure it?

Quality in action research is measured looking at five types of validity (Reason & Bradbury, 2001): outcome validity, democratic validity, process validity, catalytic validity, and dialogical validity. Outcome validity is related to an actual improvement of human welfare and relevant problem resolution. Democratic validity depends on the level all the relevant stakeholders potentially affected by the project, participate in the problem definition and solution. Process validity looks at how the project allows for learning and improvement of participants. Catalytic validity looks at how participants have been actually empowered by the process to understand and change reality within and beyond the research study and how the local knowledge could be applied on a wider scale. Finally, dialogical validity refers to the way researchers have engaged in critical discussions about research findings with project participants.

Design, as well, is now starting to consider the importance of measuring long-term impact and legacy when developing transformation projects. As an example, DOTT07[2] has been evaluated in terms of social, economic and educational legacy on the territory (Wood Holmes Group, 2008). On the social aspects, they considered the actual impact of DOTT projects on quality of life (outcome validity), the engagement of disadvantaged communities, the overall level of project participation (democratic and process validity) and any improved capacity to include citizens in processes of service innovation. On the educational side, the focus was on providing inspiring educational initiatives, in particular for young people, and to increase awareness of design capacity and skills (catalytic validity). No particular attention was given to dialogical validity as designers' influence on data interpretation and problem solutions is still mostly unquestioned.

FINAL CONSIDERATIONS

Service designers work increasingly across organisations and communities to enhance transformational processes. Contributing to society transformative aims is extremely valuable, but it also carries with it a huge responsibility. Service design has been attracting, since its onset, enthusiastic young generations of practitioners and researchers that see in designing for services, particularly for the public sector, a more meaningful way to apply their skills and profession. As this societal transformative aim is now becoming increasingly explicit, designers need to become more reflexive as for what concerns their work and interventions. This article compared a selection of literature on the reform of public services with studies on participatory design, organisational development and community action research. Seven key qualifying principles were identified which described the characteristics of and conditions for transformative practices. Service designers need to better understand the dynamics and qualities of transformational change, but also to reflect on designers influence within power dynamics within various kinds of communities. Design literature is generally characterised by a highly positive rhetoric on the role and impact of design in society, while a more critical approach is becoming increasingly necessary.

With different backgrounds, consumer research has been calling for a similar change in their practice as historically their work has been driven by the theoretical and substantive interests of academics. Their new call for a transformative consumer research practice focuses upon making a positive difference in consumers' lives (Bettany & Woodruffe, 2006). A way to do this, it is suggested, relies on introducing reflexivity in their work as a way to address power and control issues in each research encounter, understanding their influence on the research and its results (Bettany & Woodruffe, 2006). Reflexivity is described as a way to reflect on the research process to support the generation of theories and knowledge, touching in this way both issues of ontology and power.

Without deepening the meaning and practice of reflexivity in the scope of this paper, the need to introduce new skills and tools for reflexive practices within projects that hold transformational aims is evident. This might include ways to consciously track and reflect on processes, conflicts, roles, design decision points, mapping multiple perspectives and exploring individual and collaborative interpretations and evaluations of design situations and outcomes. These activities could help to better understand, position, orient, justify and evaluate designers' role within transformational processes. Adding the adjective "transformative" to "service design" requires, therefore, a reflection not only on how designers can conduct transformative processes. There must also include a reflection on which transformations we aspire to, why we do so, and most importantly, on who is benefitted.

ACKNOWLEDGMENTS

The author would like to thank Dr. Valerie Carr and Dr. Sabine Junginger for their critical support in the writing and editing of this article.

NOTES

1. Action research is also at the basis of aforementioned transformative service research or transformative consumer research, which represents a recent effort within the wider field of consumer research to increase the work and research on consumer welfare. David Glen Mick, president of the Association for Consumer Research, defined it as the "investigations that are framed by a fundamental problem or opportunity, and that strive to respect, uphold, and improve life in relation to the myriad conditions, demands, potentialities, and effects of consumption" (2006, p. 2). Even if still framed around the concept of consumption, transformative consumer research calls for research that aims at consumer empowerment and that therefore requires fundamentally different approaches and principles.

2. Dott07 (Designs of the time 2007) is a national initiative of the Design Council and the regional development agency One NorthEast. Dott07 is the first in a 10-year programme of biennial events developed by the Design Council that will take place across the UK. Dott07, a year of community projects, events and exhibitions based in North East England, explored what life in a sustainable region could be like—and how design could help us get there (www.dott07.com).

REFERENCES

Almega. (2008). *Innovativa tjänsteföretag oc forskarsamhället: Omaka par eller perfect match.* Retrieved July 5, 2011, from http://www.s-m-i.net/pdf/Innovativa%20 tjansteforetag.pdf

Anderson, W., Florin, D., Gillam, S., & Mountford, L. (2002). *Every voice counts. Involving patients and the public in primary care.* London: Kings Fund.

Arnstein, S. R. (1969). A ladder of citizen participation. *Journal of the American Planning Association,* 35(4), 216–224.

Attree, P., & French, B. (2007). *Testing theories of change associated with community engagement in health improvement and health inequalities reduction.* Retrieved October 10, 2010, from p.attree@ lancaster.ac.uk

Bate, P., & Robert, G. (2007a). Toward more user-centric OD: Lessons from the field of experience-based design and a case study. *The Journal of Applied Behavioral Science,* 43(42), 41–66.

Bate, P., & Robert, G. (2007b). *Bringing user experience to health care improvement: The concepts, methods and practices of experience-based design.* Oxford: Radcliffe.

Bauld, L., Judge, K., Barnes, M., Benzeval, M., & Sullivan, H. (2005). Promoting social change: The experience of health action zones in England. *Journal of Social Policy,* 34(3), 427–445.

Bentley, T., & Wilsdon, J. (2003). *The adaptive state,* London: Demos.

Berger, P. L., & Luckmann, T. (1966). *The social construction of reality: A treatise in the sociology of knowledge*. New York: Anchor Books.

Bettany, S. M., & Woodruffe-Burton, H. W., (2006). Steps towards transformative consumer research practice: A taxonomy of possible reflexivities. *Advances in Consumer Research, 33*(1), 227–234.

Blumenthal, D. S., & Yancey, E. (2004). Community-based research: An introduction. In D. S. Blumenthal & R. J. DiClemente (Eds.), *Community-based health research* (pp. 3–24). New York: Springer.

Bradwell, P., & Marr, S. (2008). *Making the most of collaboration: An international survey of public service co- design*. London: Demos.

Buchanan, R. (2004). Management and design. Interaction pathways in organizational life. In R. J. Boland & F. Collopy (Eds.), *Managing as designing* (Chap. 4). Stanford, CA: Stanford Business Books.

Burns, C., Cottam, H., Vanstone, C., & Winhall, J. (2006). *RED paper 02: Transformation design*. London: Design Council.

Chapman, J. (2002). A framework for transformational change in organisations. *Leadership & Organisation Development Journal, 23*(1), 16–25.

Chin, R., & Benne, K. D. (2005). General strategies for effecting changes in human systems. In W. L. French, C. Bell, & R. A. Zawacki (Eds.), *Organization development and transformation* (6th ed., pp. 40–62). New York: McGraw- Hill.

Cornwall, A. (2008). *Democratising engagement what the UK can learn from international experience*. London: Demos.

Cottam, H., & Leadbeater, C. (2004). *RED paper 01: Health: Co-creating services*. London: Design Council.

Department of Health. (2005). *Creating a patient-led NHS—Delivering NHS improvement plan*. London: Department of Health.

Department of Health. (2008a). *Real involvement. Working with people to improve health services*. London: Department of Health.

Department of Health. (2008b). *High quality care for all. NHS next stage review final report*. London: Department of Health.

Ehn, P. (2008). Participation in design things. In *Proceedings of the 10th Anniversary Conference on Participatory Design* (pp. 92–101). New York: ACM.

Elden, M., & Levin, M. (2001). Cogenerative learning: Bringing participation into action research. In W. F. White (Ed.), *Participatory action research* (pp. 127–142). London: SAGE.

European Commission. (2009). *Challenges for EU support to innovation in services—Fostering new markets and jobs through innovation* (SEC-1195). Luxembourg: Publications Office of the European Union.

Freire, K., & Sangiorgi, D. (2010, December 3). *Service design and healthcare innovation: From consumption to coproduction and co-creation*. Paper presented at the 2nd Nordic Conference on Service Design and Service Innovation, Linköping, Sweden. Retrieved July 5, 2011, from http://www.servdes.org/pdf/freire-sangiorgi.pdf

French, W. L., Bell, C. H., & Zawacki, R. A. (Eds.). (2005). *Organization development and transformation* (6th ed.). New York: McGraw-Hill.

Golembiewsky, R. T., Billingsley, K., & Yeager, S. (1976). Measuring change and persistence in human affairs: Types of change generated by OD designs. *Journal of Applied Behavioral Science, 12*(2), 133–157.

Horne, M., & Shirley, T. (2009). *Co-production in public services: A new partnership with citizens*. London: Cabinet Office.

Hosking, D. M. (1999). Social construction as process: Some new possibilities for research and development. *Concepts & Transformations, 4*(2), 117–132.

Howells, J. (2007). *Fostering innovation in services*. Manchester, UK: Manchester Institute of
  Innovation Research.

Kent County Council. (2007). *The social innovation lab for Kent—Starting with people*. Retrieved
  June 20, 2010, from http://socialinnovation.typepad.com

Kimbell, L. (2009). The turn to service design. In J. Gulier & L. Moor (Eds.). *Design and
  creativity: Policy, management and practice* (pp. 157–173). Oxford: Berg.

Jégou, F., & Manzini, E. (Eds.). (2008). *Collaborative services. Social innovation and design for
  sustainability*. Milano: Edizioni Polidesign.

Junginger, S. (2006). *Organizational change through human-centered product development*. Pittsburgh,
  PA: Carnegie Mellon University.

Junginger, S. (2008). Product development as a vehicle for organizational change. *Design Issues*,
  24(1), 26–35.

Junginger, S., & Sangiorgi, D. (2009). Service design and organisational change. Bridging the gap
  between rigour and relevance. In *Proceedings of the 3rd IASDR Conference on Design Research* (pp.
  4339–4348), Seoul, South Korea: Korean Society of Design Science.

Levy, A. (1986). Second-order planned change: Definition and conceptualisation. *Organizational
  dynamics*, *15*(1), 5–20.

Manzini, E. (2008). Collaborative organisations and enabling solutions. Social innovation and design
  for sustainability. In F. Jegou & E. Manzini (Eds.), *Collaborative services. Social innovation and
  design for sustainability* (pp. 29–41). Milano: Edizioni Polidesign.

Manzini, E., & Jegou F. (2003). *Sustainable everyday: Scenarios of urban life*. Milano: Edizioni
  Ambiente.

Marmot, M. G. (2004). Tackling health inequalities since the Acheson inquiry. *Journal of
  Epidemiology and Health*, *58*(4), 262–263.

Meroni, A. (Ed.). (2007). *Creative communities. People inventing sustainable ways of living*.
  Milano: Edizioni Polidesign.

Meroni, A. (2008). *Strategic design to take care of the territory. Networking creative communities to
  link people and places in a scenario of sustainable development*. Keynote presented at the P&D
  Design 2008—8° Congresso Brasileiro de Pesquisa e Desenvolvimento em Design, Campus Santo
  Amaro, San Paolo, Brazil.

Meroni, A., & Sangiorgi, D. (2011). *Design for services*. Aldershot, UK: Gower

Mick, D.G. (2006). Meaning and mattering through transformative consumer research. *Advances in
  Consumer Research*, *33*(1), 1–4.

Miles, I. (2001). *Services innovation: A reconfiguration of innovation studies*. Manchester,
  UK: University of Manchester.

Milton, K. (2007). *Shape: Services having all people engaged—A methodology for people-centred
  service innovation*. London: Engine Service Design.

Ostrom, A. L., Bitner, M. J., Brown, S. W., Burkhard, K. A., Goul, M., Smith-Daniels, V., Demirkan,
  H., & Rabinovich, E. (2010). Moving forward and making a difference: Research priorities for the
  science of service. *Journal of Service Research*, *13*(1), 4–36.

Ozanne, J. L., & Saatcioglu, B. (2008). Participatory action research. *Journal of Consumer Research*,
  35(3), 423–439.

Ozanne, J. L., & Anderson, L. (2010). Community action research. *Journal of Public Policy &
  Marketing*, *29*(1), 123–137.

Parker, S., & Heapy, J. (2006). *The journey to the interface. How public service design can connect
  users to reform*. London: Demos.

Parker, S., & Parker S. (2007). *Unlocking innovation. Why citizens hold the key to public service
  reform*. London: Demos.

Popay, J. (2006) *Community engagement and community development and health improvement: A
  background paper for NICE*. London: National Institute for Health and Clinical Excellence.

Reason, P. E., & Bradbury, H. (Eds.). (2001). *Handbook of action research: Participative inquiry and practice*. London: Sage.

Sangiorgi, D. (2004). *Il Design dei servizi come Design dei Sistemi di Attività. La Teoria dell'Attività applicata alla progettazione dei servizi* [Service design as the design of activity systems. Activity theory applied to the design for services]. Milano: Politecnico di Milano.

Sangiorgi, D. (2009). Building a framework for service design research. In *Proceedings of the 8th European Academy of Design International Conference* (pp. 415–420), Aberdeen, Scotland: Robert Gordon University.

Sangiorgi, D., & Villari B. (2006). *Community based services for elderly people. Designing platforms for action and socialisation*. Paper presented at the International Congress on Gerontology, Live Forever, Lisbon, Portugal.

Senge, P., & Schamer, O. (2001). Community action research: Learning as a community of practitioners, consultants and researchers. In P. E. Reason & H. Bradbury (Eds.), *Handbook of action research* (pp. 238–249). London: Sage.

Shuler, D., & Namioka, A. (Eds.). (1993). *Participatory design: Principles and practices*. Hillsdale, NJ: L. Erlbaum Associates.

Skidmore, P., & Craig, J. (2005). *Start with people: How community organisations put citizens in the driving seat*. London: Demos.

Smith, K. K. (1982). Philosophical problems in thinking about organisational change. In P. S. Goodman (Ed.), *Change in organizations*. San Francisco: Jossey-Bass.

Tan, L., & Szebeko, D. (2009). Co-designing for dementia: The Alzheimer 100 project. *Australasian Medical Journal*, *1*(12), 185–198.

Ezell, S., Ogilvie, T., & Rae, J. (2007). *Seizing the white space: Innovative service concepts in the United States*. Helsinki: Tekes.

Thackara, J. (2007). *Wouldn't be great if ...* London: Design Council.

Thomas, E. (Ed.). (2008). *Innovation by design in public services*. London: Solace Foundation Imprint.

Watzlawick, P., Weakland, J. H., & Fisch, R. (1974). *Change: Principles of problem formation and problem resolution*. New York: Norton.

White, S. (1996). Depoliticising development: The uses and abuses of participation. *Development in Practice*, *6*(1), 6–15.

Winhall, J. (2004). *Design notes on open health*. London: Design Council.

Wood Holmes Group. (2008). *Evaluation of design of the times* (Dott 07 Report). London: Design Council.

Zeithamal, A., Parasuraman, A., & Berry, L. (1985). Problems and strategies in services marketing. *Journal of Marketing*, *49*(2), 33–46.

CHAPTER TWENTY SEVEN

Rethinking Design Thinking: Part I

LUCY KIMBELL

ABSTRACT

The term *design thinking* has gained attention over the past decade in a wide range of contexts beyond the traditional preoccupations of designers. The main idea is that the ways professional designers problem-solve is of value to firms trying to innovate and to societies trying to make change happen. This paper reviews the origins of the term *design thinking* in research about designers and its adoption by management educators and consultancies within a dynamic, global mediatized economy. Three main accounts are identified: design thinking as a cognitive style, as a general theory of design, and as a resource for organizations. The paper argues there are several issues that undermine the claims made for design thinking. The first is how many of these accounts rely on a dualism between thinking and knowing, and acting in the world. Second, a generalized design thinking ignores the diversity of designers' practices and institutions which are historically situated. The third is how design thinking rests on theories of design that privilege the designer as the main agent in designing. Instead the paper proposes that attending to the situated, embodied routines of designers and others offers a useful way to rethink design thinking.

Keywords: Design thinking, practices, designers, innovation, organization design

INTRODUCTION

Professional design is now operating within an expanded and increasingly complex field. Some design professionals take solving complex social issues as their domain, often but not always working in close collaboration with specialists in public services from healthcare to those working with disadvantaged families to policing. Other designers and their ways of working are welcomed into business schools to teach the next generation of managers and leaders. Concepts and language that used to be associated with designers now enter other specialist areas: policymakers are told that public services should be more user-centered (Parker and Heapy 2006); businesses engage with customers by offering new meanings for things (Verganti 2009); the US Army is considering the role of design in warfare (School of Advanced Military Studies n.d.). Professional design, in particular design as practiced within the studio-based tradition of many art schools, is taking a new place on the world stage.

For design firms working for global clients in relentless pursuit of new markets, new offerings and new kinds of value creation, design itself is being remade (Tonkinwise 2010). Design as design *thinking* should provide more than mere design. And yet, this re-assembling of some of the approaches, knowledge and practices of professional designers, first within academic design research, and then within business schools and consultancies, has not brought a happy synthesis. Indeed, industry observers are beginning to question its most fundamental assumptions. Working within different contexts and at different speeds, from the slow pace of academia to the fast-moving world of consultancy and blogging, some of its key proponents are beginning to question design thinking, even calling it a "failed experiment" (Nussbaum 2011).

While much of this critical discussion is beginning to take shape outside design circles, this article will examine design thinking from within. Now, at a time when design and designers are working in challenging new contexts, we must engage in discussions about the place of professional design in the world. If we explore design thinking by using theories of practice, we may better understand designers' work within the social worlds in which it takes place. Rather than viewing design thinking as a disembodied and ahistorical cognitive style, we must clarify its function. Design thinking may have failed; instead we should understand design as a situated, contingent set of practices carried by professional designers and those who engage with designers' activities.

ASKING WHAT IF:
THE DESIGNER AS CULTURAL INTERPRETER

When design thinking emerged more than a decade ago, it offered a response to the ebbs and flows of a global, mediatized economy of signs and artifacts; in this context, professional designers play increasingly important roles, less as makers of forms and more as cultural intermediaries (Julier 2008) or as the "glue" in multi-disciplinary teams (Kelley and VanPatter 2005). They are interpreters of changes in culture who then create new kinds of cultural form. Some designers have always seen design as playing important roles socially and politically as well as economically—William Morris, the Arts and Crafts movement, and Italian groups such as Superstudio and Archizoom are examples (Julier 2011)—what is distinctive about the development of design thinking is its adoption within managerialist discourse, in particular business schools, over the past decade.

In just the last five years, the term is more and more ubiquitous. It found its way into conversations at Davos, the annual meeting of politicians and senior executives from global firms (IDEO 2006); at TED (TED 2009), a conference series that attracts leading figures in business, technology and entertainment; and into the pages of the *Harvard Business Review*, an influential (although not peer-reviewed) academic journal (Brown 2008). Design thinking and the designers who say they practice it are associated with having a human-centered approach to problem solving, in contrast to being technology- or organization-centered. They are seen as using an iterative process that moves from generating insights about end users, to idea generation and testing, to implementation. Their visual artifacts and prototypes help multidisciplinary teams work together. They ask "what if?" questions to imagine future scenarios rather than accepting the way things are done now. With their creative ways of solving problems, the argument goes, designers can turn their hands to nearly anything. Design is now central to innovation and since organizations[1] are under pressure to maintain or grow market share, or if in the public sector, increase user satisfaction and effectiveness, then designers and their thinking have something important to offer.[2]

THE CREATIVE CLASS AND THE "NEW SPIRIT" OF CAPITALISM

To understand this move requires attending to wider developments over the last few decades that have been shaping what goes on within and between societies, organizations of different kinds, and political institutions. To address these topics fully would require more space than is available but I want here to highlight particular themes.

The first is a view of capitalism which sees it as unstable, fluid and dynamic (Lash and Urry 1994; Thrift 2005). Boltanski and Chiapello's (2005) description of a "new spirit" of capitalism captures some of the energy in the shift from hierarchies to networks and from bureaucratic discipline to team-work and multi-skilling, as capitalism absorbed its critiques and remade itself as offering managers both autonomy and security. A second theme shaping the product-saturated developed world is the importance of the economy of signs that ignore state borders and in which the value of a commodity cannot be separated from its symbolic value (Lash and Urry 1994). A sophisticated effort to engage diverse audiences or stakeholders in establishing the meaning of these signs marks out those commercial firms which at some level understand this (Verganti 2009). A third theme is the rise of what Florida (2002) calls the creative class, for whom work and professional identities are caught up in creating meaningful new forms. For Florida the word "creative" is not just reserved for designers, musicians and visual artists but also computer programmers and opinion-makers such as columnists. These professionals find meaning in work which is characterized by flexibility, autonomy and creativity and which blurs their professional and personal lives, as they move across national borders without being anchored to industrial modes of production and consumption.

A fourth theme is the ongoing, but recently re-energized questioning about the role of business schools and their place in the world as centers of research and education (Harvard Business Review 2009). As the global financial and economic crisis of 2008 showed, neither MBAS nor their professors have all the answers. On the contrary, some of the practices associated with the world of high finance and its emblematic product, the derivative, carry with them important and yet unanswered questions about governance, accountability and values. Interest within business schools in how designers go about engaging with problems pre-dates the crisis (e.g. Boland and Collopy 2004) but rests on the idea that established ways of thinking about managing and organizing are not adequate to deal with a fluid business environment (Tsoukas and Chia 2002), let alone any number of global challenges from climate change, to resource inequality, to peak oil. What this has meant for managers and policy-makers is that the urgent quest for innovation and novelty has new resources—a creative class who have a privileged place within contemporary capitalism.

UNDERSTANDING DESIGN THINKING

Even on a cursory inspection, just what design thinking is supposed to be is not well understood, either by the public or those who claim to practice it. As Rylander (2009) points out, it's hard enough understanding design and thinking, let alone *design thinking*. So it is not a surprise that those who support its application to business or more broadly to public services or social problems, have trouble articulating what it is, whether all designers can do it, whether it is something new or just a different name for what good designers have always done, and why it might be a good thing that non-designers can learn it and do it too—or perhaps they do it already. Decoupled from any one field or discipline of design, design thinking is meant to encompass everything good about designerly practices. Given the reach and appeal of these claims, it is time to explore the origins of design thinking. Above all, we must examine what it is and understand how it is being mobilized within contemporary conversations about change and innovation.

In this study three things come into view. Firstly that accounts of design thinking often rest on a dualism that makes a distinction between "thinking" and "doing" and between designers and the worlds they do design in, rather than acknowledging the situated, embodied work of design thinking in practice. Secondly, attending to the diversity of designers' practices and the institutions in which they work makes it questionable to generalize about a unified design thinking exhibited across all of them. Thirdly, descriptions of design thinking rest on sometimes contradictory views about the nature of design and, for all the claims about being "user-centered," still emphasize the designer as the main agent within design.

DESIGN AND ITS PROBLEMS

No doubt thinking has always been part of the work that designers do, but the term design thinking that became prominent over the past five years emphasizes the intangible work done by designers. Several recent studies (Bradke-Schaub et al. 2010; Cross 2010; Dorst 2010; Tonkinwise 2010) highlight how recent popular accounts of design thinking ignore the extensive research on designers' ways of working over previous decades since the first Design Thinking Research Symposium in 1991 (Cross et al. 1992), let alone earlier events such as the Conference on Design Methods of 1962 (Jones and Thornley 1963). Although much of the recent public presentation of design thinking is tied to one design consultancy, IDEO (Brown 2008; Brown 2009; Brown and Wyatt 2010), the history of design thinking is more complex. In this section I will outline some of the main contributions and then summarize these into three broad positions (in Table 27.1). Although any such synthesis reduces diverse research into overly simplistic categories, it can advance understanding by making clearer different approaches and their implications.

A stream of research originating in the 1960s focuses on how designers do designing. What began as the design methods movement (Jones 1970; Buchanan and Margolin 1995) gradually shifted towards investigations in design thinking (Cross 1982); researchers sought to understand the processes and methods by which (successful) designers went about design activity. This exploration also lead them to study the nature of design problems in more depth. But to understand how design thinking emerged, we must go back a little earlier to understand how design itself was understood at this time.

Table 27.1 Different Ways of Describing Design Thinking

	Design thinking as a cognitive style	Design thinking as a general theory of design	Design thinking as an organizational resource
Key texts	Cross 1982; Schön 1983; Rowe [1987] 1998; Lawson 1997; Cross 2006; Dorst 2006	Buchanan 1992	Dunne and Martin 2006; Bauer and Eagen 2008; Brown 2009; Martin 2009
Focus	Individual designers, especially experts	Design as a field or discipline	Businesses and other organizations in need of innovation
Design's purpose	Problem solving	Taming wicked problems	Innovation
Key concepts	Design ability as a form of intelligence; reflection-in-action, abductive thinking	Design has no special subject matter of its own	Visualization, prototyping, empathy, integrative thinking, abductive thinking
Nature of design problems	Design problems are ill-structured, problem and solution co-evolve	Design problems are wicked problems	Organizational problems are design problems
Sites of design expertise and activity	Traditional design disciplines	Four orders of design	Any context from healthcare to access to clean water (Brown and Wyatt 2010)

Source: Lucy Kimbell.

DESIGN'S FRAGMENTED CORE

To this day, design remains a fragmented discipline. When in 1971 Christopher Alexander argued that design is about giving form, organization, and order to physical things, he acknowledged an entire school of thought. For Alexander, "the ultimate object of design is form" (1971: 15). The idea that form is a physical arrangement remains a dominant view of what designers do: they make things. Visitors to professional design studios are likely to note a disorderly arrangement of objects on work surfaces, walls and floors. Such clutter reminds us how professional design still involves doing things with and to objects, even for those designers who see their work as designing intangible services or experiences.

Writing contemporaneously with Alexander, Herbert Simon was also trying to understand and describe design. Having already made contributions to economics and organization theory, Simon turned his attention to the organization—or in his terminology—"design"—of human action in the realm of the artificial. In *The Sciences of the Artificial* (1969) Simon identifies design as the knowledge that is in the domain of professions such as engineering, management or medicine.[3] He believed that these fields all concern "what ought to be" and contrast with the sciences, which are concerned with "what is". He saw design as a rational set of procedures that respond to a well-defined problem; solving this problem involves decomposing systems as well as searching for and choosing alternatives. He argued that his approach worked for ill-defined problems too (Simon 1973). Simon assumes that it is possible to determine a desired state of affairs and thus, he writes, "problem solving requires continual translation between the state and process descriptions of the same complex reality" (Simon 1969: 112). Although Simon was also concerned with form in the sense of the boundaries between internal and external worlds, artifacts did not feature strongly in his view.

The tension between these two conceptions of design remains evident today and informs the discussion about design thinking. On the one hand, following Alexander's thesis, designers give form to things; they are privileged makers whose work is centrally concerned with materiality. This is the tradition of craft and professional design fields that create specific kinds of objects, from furniture, to buildings, to clothing. Simon, on the other hand, suggests that designers' work is abstract; their job is to create a desired state of affairs. This way of thinking about design is the core of all professions, not just the work of engineers and designers of artifacts.

Both Alexander and Simon were concerned with describing what design is, and how to do it, but neither emphasized design thinking. Similarly while Jones's (1970) work on design methods emphasized the importance of changing how a problem was thought about in order to develop a new solution, it was only later that the term design thinking emerged. Peter Rowe's *Design Thinking*, originally published in 1987, provides one of the earliest discussions of the concept. Based on Rowe's teaching of architects and urban planners, the book offers both case studies and discussion about the "procedural aspects of design thinking," including descriptions of the design process, and then introducing generalized principles. Two main ideas emerge. Rowe argues that design professionals have an episodic way of approaching their work; they rely on hunches and presuppositions, not just facts. But he also argues that the nature of the problem-solving process itself shapes the solution. For Rowe, discussions of how designers actually design are necessarily shaped by wider conversations about the nature of architecture itself. "We need to move directly into the realm of normative discourse about what constitutes architecture and urban design in order to clarify the inherent nature of the enterprise and the direction in which procedures are inclined" (Rowe [1987] 1998: 37). Although Rowe is rarely cited in more recent texts, these topics frequently reappear in subsequent literature.

Researchers working in several fields, including engineering, architecture and product design, continued to study how designers think and what they know as they solve problems. Key contributors include Nigel Cross, although he generally prefers to use the phrase "designerly ways of knowing."[4] Cross sees designers' mode of problem solving as solution-focused as they tackle ill-defined problems and situates this within a larger argument about design as a coherent discipline of study distinct from the sciences and the humanities (1982; 2001; 2006). Donald Schön introduced the idea of framing and making moves when problem solving during professionals' reflection-in-action (Schön 1983). Bryan Lawson, on the other hand, studied the practice of designing in a context of multiple constraints (Lawson 1997). Nigel Cross and Kees Dorst developed the idea that problems and solutions co-evolve (Dorst and Cross 2001), and Cross suggested that designers treat all problems as ill-defined, even if they are not (Cross 2006). Attempting to explain designers' tendencies to generate new solutions, many researchers have emphasized abductive reasoning (Cross 1982; Dorst 2010). Dorst (2006) noted that since a designer's understanding of a problem shifts during a design process, other concepts might be better employed, suggesting instead that designers construct designs that transcend or connect paradoxes. Burnette (2009) describes different kinds of thinking within a design process. One focus has been to discern different levels of expertise among designers, from novices to visionaries (Lawson and Dorst 2009), although without much reference to sociological work on professions and institutions. In short, while there has been a sustained effort to understand and describe what professional designers do in their design work, this has not yet generated a definitive or historically-informed account of design thinking, nor any explanation for why they might have a particular cognitive style.

While this body of research focused on designers and what they think and do, others continued to take forward work defining the field of design. Buchanan's (1992) paper "Wicked Problems in Design Thinking" shifted design theory away from its legacy in craft and industrial production towards a more generalized "design thinking." This concept, Buchanan argues, could be applied to nearly anything, whether a tangible object or intangible system. Drawing on Pragmatist philosopher John Dewey, Buchanan sees design as a liberal art, uniquely well-placed to serve the needs of a technological culture in which many kinds of things are designed, and human problems are complex. For Buchanan, design problems are indeterminate or wicked problems (Rittel and Webber 1973). The designer brings a unique way of looking at problems and finding solutions. He describes four orders of design which approximate the artifacts that design practitioners tend to work on: signs, things, actions, and thoughts. This version of design thinking is less concerned with individual designers and how they design, but rather seeks to define design's role in the world. Similarly, Rylander (2009) also compares design thinking to a Pragmatist inquiry and concludes that Dewey's work on aesthetic experience provides a useful way to explore designers' special skills and examine the claims made for them in more detail.

DESIGN THINKING:
DE-POLITICIZING MANAGERIAL PRACTICE

The books and papers that have done most to popularize the idea of design thinking mostly ignore this literature. While the term design thinking originated with academics who conducted research within design disciplines, today the phase most often situates design thinking in terms of the challenges facing organizations, especially businesses. Concerned with design's place in the world and thus the larger social or political questions is lost when design is mobilized within a managerialist framework. As Sam Ladner (2009) puts it: "Design is attractive to management because it is a de-politicized version of the well known socio-cultural critique of managerial practices."

Two main proponents have recently reconfigured design thinking. Tim Brown leads one of the world's most influential design consultancies, IDEO, and is the author of *Change by Design: How Design Thinking Transforms Organizations and Inspires Innovation* (2009). The other, Roger Martin, is Dean of the Rotman School of Management in Toronto, with a background in management consulting, whose book is titled *The Design of Business: Why Design Thinking is the Next Competitive Advantage* (2009). Although each describes design thinking somewhat differently, both explore its role within organizations. Their work can be seen as part of growing interest in design in management academia including multiple journal special issues (e.g. Bate 2007; Jelinek et al. 2008), tracks at major conferences (e.g. EURAM 2009; Academy of Management 2010; EGOS 2010), scholarly workshops (e.g. Case Western Reserve 2010) and experiments in teaching design to MBAs and executives including at the Fox School of Business (Temple University 2011); the Rotman School of Management (University of Toronto 2011); Saïd Business School (Kimbell 2011); and the Weatherhead School of Management (Case Western Reserve University 2011).

Presented as a way to balance organizational tensions between exploration and exploitation (Martin 2009) or as a loosely-structured organizational process that stimulates innovation (Brown 2009), these accounts of design thinking do not draw extensively on research in either design studies or management and organization studies. Despite the lack of a wider research base, books by Tim Brown and Roger Martin widely disseminate an idea of design thinking that is gaining legitimacy among designers, organizations and government bodies. In the UK, for example, the government-funded national Design Council argues that design thinking plays a key role in innovation (Design Council 2009). In Denmark, a cross-ministerial innovation unit called MindLab uses a form of design thinking to combine design-centered and social science approaches to create new solutions for society (Mindlab 2009).

Brown's accounts of design thinking present the concept as an answer to challenges facing organizations wanting to innovate but also societies grappling with complex public issues. Brown has published widely. In addition to *Change by Design* (2009), his writings include an essay in the *Harvard Business Review* (2008), and the *Stanford Social Innovation Review*

(Brown and Wyatt 2010), as well as his blog on the topic (Brown 2011). To some extent these echo earlier publications by designers from IDEO such as David Kelley (2001). While Brown never claims that his contributions are academic, he nonetheless rehearses many of the findings from research, for example seeing design thinking as a fundamentally exploratory process (Brown 2009: 17). Design thinkers know there is no right answer to a problem. Rather, he argues, through following the non-linear, iterative design process that he calls inspiration, ideation and implementation, design process can convert problems into opportunities.

Brown places particular emphasis on design thinking as a human-centered activity (Brown, 2009: 115). Underpinning this approach is the idea of empathy: designers are perceived as being willing and able to understand and interpret the perspectives of end users and the problems they face. In doing so, Brown suggests, they more or less feel their way through to a new solution. According to Brown, a successful design outcome exists at the intersection of three concerns: what is desirable from the users' perspective, what is technically feasible, and what is commercially viable for the organization (Brown 2009). In so doing, this approach introduces a key, if often ignored, paradox. On the one hand, designers are positioned as key interpreters of what end users "need." They are expected to do this by using ethnographically-inspired techniques that help them understand the user's perspectives and situated actions. On the other hand, in practice this process shows little of the reflexivity of the social science traditions. In contrast to much contemporary design practice and education, social scientists are trained to question what theoretical, political or other commitments they bring to their work and how these shape their research findings. Construed in this way, design thinking fails to reference wider theories of the social and misses opportunities to illuminate the context into which the designer is intervening.

In *The Design of Business* (2009), Roger Martin presents a different way of thinking about design thinking.[5] Martin argues that design thinking gives business a competitive advantage. In contrast to Brown, who does describe what professional designers do and make and what they are attentive to, Martin focuses on methods used by successful managers he interviewed and examines how firms as a whole function. His version of design thinking deals less with individual cognitive styles and doesn't present sets of material practices; rather, he focuses on systems of organization. In this way he echoes arguments put forward by others teaching and researching in a business school context (e.g. Boland and Collopy 2004). Design thinking as practiced by good designers, Martin says, has something important to offer managers, enabling them to shift from choosing between alternatives to helping them generate entirely new concepts. Martin sees design thinking as combining abductive, as well as inductive and deductive, reasoning. This is particularly of value to businesses tackling the well-established challenge of focusing on either exploitation or exploration (cf. March 1991). Those that have mastered questions of scale and routinization by developing capabilities to produce and distribute lots of the same things, at the right quality and cost, are not so able to innovate. Finding a better balance between exploration and exploitation, and between abductive as well as inductive and deductive reasoning, is what Martin calls design thinking.

Other researchers have begun to study design thinking and are extending this argument further. Robert Bauer and Ward Eagan (2008) also site their discussion of design within a larger critique of what goes on within many organizations. For Bauer and Eagan analytical thinking is part of, and not the opposite of, design thinking. Reviewing and synthesizing much of the research on design thinking, they insist that the subject cannot be reduced to aesthetic judgments or cognitive reasoning; instead, they perceive several epistemic modes that come into play at different points in a design process. Although analytical thinking provides the epistemic underpinning of capital, they believe that design thinking represents the epistemology of creative work. Like Martin and Brown, Bauer and Eagan then offer design thinking as an organizational resource to make up for some of the shortcomings of management and its over-reliance on analysis.

More recent discussions of design thinking have followed this trend, locating designers' knowledge and thinking within the contexts in which they work. For example Robin Adams et al. (2010) study what it means to be a design professional and how designers become professionals. Their analysis avoided dualisms that separate cognition and action; instead they propose a framework in which knowledge and skills are embedded in an embodied understanding of practice. Their findings deflate simplified versions of design thinking and instead highlight differences in knowing, acting and being among designers.

COMPARING APPROACHES TO DESIGN THINKING

To summarize, design thinking has been used to characterize what individual designers know, how they approach and make sense of their own work, as well as how they actually do it. In addition to describing the practices of designers, the term also offers a theory of design that extends Herbert Simon's ideas. In this context, design does not give form to things; instead, it concerns action and the artificial. More recently, the term has been mobilized with some success by design consultancies, management educators, and other scholars. In this context it suggests an approach to business or even social innovation (see Table 27.1).

Given the diversity of these approaches, there is still no clear description of design thinking. On what principles is it based? How different is it to other kinds of professional knowledge? Do all designers exhibit it? What are its effects within the worlds where design takes place? How can it be taught? Further, these descriptions present several issues which need to be addressed by researchers studying professional designers, as well as the managers and educators who apply these practices social innovation or management education. In the next section I identify three such issues and then suggest how design thinking might be reconsidered.

ACKNOWLEDGING THE CULTURES OF DESIGN

Many studies in design thinking replicate a dualism within research fields; they reflect important differences in the underlying ways the world is understood and what can be known about it. Researchers who focus on the individual designer and his or her cognitive style rarely study the world within which the designer works (cf. Bourdieu 1977). Such researchers usually cultivate objective rather than subjective knowledge; moreover, their research assumes there are clear boundaries between the designer and the world s/he is in; further, the researcher is construed as remaining outside this world. These studies describe what designers do and trace how their thinking develops in the course of a project, but they often ignore key aspects of the designer's world. For example, several studies of design thinking as a cognitive style rely on protocol analysis based on recording and then analyzing what designers say about what they are doing. This is usually monitored during an artificial exercise in which the designers are given a problem to solve. While these studies may produce interesting findings, this approach sometimes presents a version of design thinking as a simple form of information processing with inputs and outputs (e.g. Badke-Schaub et al. 2010). Alternately, design thinking can be presented as a process that is supposedly applied to an organization (e.g. Brown 2009), though this approach never clarifies how easy it is to import it from one context to another.

In contrast, some ethnographic accounts of design thinking do not make distinctions between designer and world, or between researcher and object of study and produce "thick description" (Geertz 1973) of what goes on during designing. These accounts attend to the situated, embodied ways that designers go about their work and the artifacts they engage with and make (e.g. Bucciarelli 1994; Henderson 1999). Given extensive research in design fields (e.g. Winograd and Flores 1986; Suchman 1987; Ehn 1988; Ehn 2008), not to mention sociology, anthropology and organization studies, in which embodiment and being in the world are perceived as a condition of knowing and action, it seems reasonable to explore how this approach might describe and explain designers' approaches to their work and the nature of design thinking. Drawing on Dewey, Buchanan (1992) and Rylander (2009) do not rely on this separation between knowing and world; instead, they offer an understanding of the act of designing by studying designers in the world. However, they do not share the close attentiveness paid to the role of artifacts found in material culture approaches influenced by anthropology, nor do they situate their accounts of design within larger historical frameworks. A future direction for research into designers' thinking and knowing, therefore, could take as a starting point practitioners' being in the world and their relation to other social actors including artifacts and other social practices and institutions. To understand what happens in designing, it remains important to explore how political, socio-cultural and economic developments have shaped design practice over time.

Without extensive comparative data, we may wonder how useful it is to generalize across design fields as different as, say, architecture and computer science. Much of the work on design thinking has tried to generalize what designers do, think and know, implying that this is different to what non-designers do (Cross 1982; Buchanan 1992). The recent interest in design within management may destabilize the idea of designerly ways of knowing. Some studies, for example, suggest that medics exhibit qualities associated with design thinking. Such assertions implicitly undermine design's claim to uniqueness (Cross 2010). Although research accounts typically specify what type of design professional has been studied and identify their level of expertise, popular efforts to understand design thinking rarely make clear which design field is being discussed. Much academic research on design thinking ignores the particular context of knowledge-intensive consultancy and its place within a fluid and dynamic economy; this environment demands that designers manage and account for their work in particular ways (e.g. Julier and Moor 2009). But a recent shift in studies of design acknowledges the field's cultural and sociological basis. The move from a visual to a cultural perspective in design history (e.g. Julier 2008) as well as the field's growing focus on practices and consumption (e.g. Shove et al. 2007; Crewe et al. 2009) both recognize this change.

This approach might usefully be introduced in studies of design thinking too. Instead of focusing on individual designers and their cognitive styles, or on a methodology that can be applied in organizations, work on design thinking could attend to the cultures of design. In several professions and disciplines practitioners refer to themselves as designers and they conceive of their work as design. Rooted in distinct educational traditions that legitimize students and practitioners in different ways, these approaches are shaped by national and regional influences over time. In the UK, for example, architecture and engineering have strong professional bodies and authorizing procedures. These can be contrasted with design professions based in art schools. Here, product, communication, and fashion design, for instance, are typically taught without the need for extensive professional accreditation and with limited domain-specific bodies of knowledge (Wang and Ilhan 2009). Engineering is often linked with formal theories of design, but fails to account for the generation of creative ideas (Hatchuel and Weil 2009). Nevertheless, engineering designers have an identifiable visual and material culture (Bucciarelli 1994; Henderson 1999). Emerging fields such as service design (e.g. Meroni and Sangiorgi 2011) often sit uncomfortably between academic and professional boundaries, concerned as they are, not just with the design of objects but also systems, processes and social arrangements. In this context, several different types of professionals do design work, not just "designers". Acknowledging the cultures of designers and understanding the different kinds of practices that have developed within various institutional arrangements would help publics and scholars alike better understand and employ design thinking. Such clarifications would also allow researchers to identify if indeed a particular kind of knowledge practice can be shared across all design fields.

As Rowe points out ([1987] 1998), describing how designers do design, how they think and what they know forces us to examine our assumptions about what constitutes design; it forces us to define design itself. Not surprisingly, many accounts of design thinking identify the designer as the main agent in design; these approaches also explore individual cognitive styles, although some versions also reflect the influence of stakeholders other than the user or customer (e.g. Bauer and Eagan 2008). Even when design thinking involves designers having empathy with users, the designer (or manager practicing design thinking) is presented as an agent of change within an organization or project. This perception starkly contrasts with extensive work in fields such as anthropology, sociology and consumption studies. In the latter context, users, stakeholders and consumers of designed things all act in ways that can challenge or disrupt the intentions of designers. For example, Lucy Suchman (1987) showed how people using photocopiers ignored the plans of designers, by not following instructions displayed on the top of the machine fully and therefore being unable to use the copier, which did not know they had made a mistake. Combining consumption theory with studies of science and technology, Elizabeth Shove et al. (2007) argue that innovation in products often requires innovation in practices. Suchman, Shove and other researchers have rethought design, presenting it as a distributed social accomplishment within which artifacts and other humans play important roles; they help constitute the meaning and effects of a design. In contrast, accounts of design thinking continue to privilege the designer, however empathetic, as the main agent in design. But such ideas may limit research, education or practice. Like anyone else, designers can be attentive to some things, and not others. We must acknowledge that design practice is shaped by designers' own theoretical and political commitments (Fry 2009); we must make such knowledge part of practice and research analysis.

IS DESIGN SPECIAL?

This essay assumes that designs, knowledge and research are constituted in practice. As studies of design practice are gathering pace (e.g. Suchman 1987; Ehn 1988; Julier 2007; Shove et al. 2007; Ehn 2008; Fry 2009; Tonkinwise 2010), the field is increasingly positioned as part of a wider turn within contemporary theory (e.g. Schatzki 2001). But design thinking has captured the imagination of practitioners and educators in a range of fields; this widespread interest leads to a discussion of design based more on anecdotes and claims than theoretically or empirically robust arguments. These accounts of design thinking rely on descriptions of designers' doings and sayings, the things they make, what they know and how they act in the world. By focusing on situated, embodied material practices, rather than a generalized "design thinking", we may shift the conversation away from questions of individual cognition or organizational innovation. Instead, design becomes a set of routines that emerge in context. Such explorations help clarify designers' material practices. They also force us to decide if design is a special way of engaging with and acting on the world, unique to designers, or shared by others such as managers too.[6]

Although this body of research is based on a range of theoretical orientations, it raises important issues. Firstly, accounts of design thinking often make a distinction between thinking and action and between the designer and the context in which they are designing; secondly, they propose that there is something shared by all designers while not acknowledging important differences in how design professions and their institutions have emerged; and thirdly, they emphasize designers as the main agents in design. Instead, an alternative approach is proposed. This alternative draws on extensive work in anthropology, sociology, history, and science and technology studies. Moreover, these attend to the routine practices of those involved in design; they include not just designers, but also known and unknown users and other stakeholders. Design thinking is hardly the "failure" described by commentators like Bruce Nussbaum (2011): the practices of designers play important roles in constituting the contemporary world, whether or not "design thinking" is the right term for this. Design thinking does, however, remain undertheorized and understudied; indeed, the critical rethinking of design thinking has only just begun.

ACKNOWLEDGEMENTS

Versions of this paper were presented at the European Academy of Management conference, Liverpool, May 2009, and at the Centre for Research on Socio-Cultural Change conference, Manchester, September 2009 in a panel I co-organized with Laurene

Vaughan and Nina Wakeford. The paper was improved with feedback from the editor and anonymous reviewers and through discussions with Simon Blyth, Fred Collopy, Anne-Laure Fayard, Tony Fry, Armand Hatchuel, Philip Hill, Guy Julier, Steve New, Ken Starkey, and Cameron Tonkinwise.

© 2011 Berg. Previously published in *Design and Culture*, Vol. 3 Issue 3, pp. 285–306. Reprinted by permission of the publisher Taylor & Francis Ltd, http://www.tandfonline.com, and also by permission of the author.

NOTES

1. The term organization is used here to refer to formally and informally constituted entities that come together to work on a shared purpose, rather than being confined to businesses.
2. It is beyond the scope of the paper to explore claims that designers have an entirely distinct way of working in comparison to other professionals, let alone to assess whether applying a design approach leads to increased effectiveness and efficiency and "more" innovation, and hence to organizational value. Asking such a question is of course already framed by assumptions about how value is thought about and assessed.
3. Simon's views developed over the three editions of *The Sciences of the Artificial* and his work remains open to a diversity of interpretation. A recent paper in the field of management, for example, identified three main approaches to design in Simon's work (Pandza and Thorpe 2010) whereas for Hatchuel (2001), Simon's version of design is best thought of as problem solving.
4. A book with the title *Design Thinking: Understanding How Designers Think and Work* by Nigel Cross is now available from Berg.
5. Although there are closer links to Brown's version of design thinking as discussed in Dunne and Martin's (2006) study of business education.
6. I should draw attention to my own stake in this conversation: I teach in a business school. While it is somewhat overshadowed by the rather older university of which it is a department, as a young school founded in 1996 it has tried to chart a path that offers a vision of management education that draws on several disciplines and on critical discussion, including among its specialisms science and technology studies. Having come from an art and design practice background, I have taught a version of design and design management to MBA students since 2005. My MBA elective is taken by up to 50 students a year, giving them a brief exposure to the material practices of design, opportunities to collaborate with designers, and an orientation to the artifacts and arrangements within organizations as sites for design inquiries, idea generation and intervention. In developing my curriculum, I try to help students make sense for themselves of the claims made for design thinking, while at the same time encouraging them to explore the possibilities and limits of design's material practices and cultures to the projects, organizations and ventures in which they work. See my teaching blog archive at Kimbell (2011).

REFERENCES

Academy of Management. 2010. Annual Meeting Program. Available online: http://program. aomonline.org/2010/pdf/AOM_2010_Annual_Meeting_Program.pdf (accessed May 24, 2011).

Adams, R., S. Daly, L. Mann, and G. Dall'Alba. 2010. "Being a Professional: Three Perspectives on Design Thinking, Acting and Being." *Proceedings of the 8th Design Thinking Research Symposium* (DTRS8) Sydney, October 19–20: 11–24.

Alexander, C. 1971. *Notes on the Synthesis of Form*. Cambridge, MA: Harvard University Press.

Badke-Schaub, P., N. Roozenburg, and C. Cardoso. 2010. "Design Thinking: A Paradigm on Its Way from Dilution to Meaninglessness?" *Proceedings of the 8th Design Thinking Research Symposium* (DTRS8) Sydney, October 19–20: 39–49.

Bate, R. 2007. "Bringing the Design Sciences to Organization Development and Change." *Journal of Applied Behaviorial Science*, 43(8): 8–11.

Bauer, R. and W. Eagan. 2008. "Design Thinking: Epistemic Plurality in Management and Organization." *Aesthesis* 2(3): 64–74.

Boland, R. and F. Collopy. 2004. "Design Matters for Management." In R. Boland and F. Collopy (eds), *Managing as Designing*, pp. 3–18. Stanford, CA: Stanford University Press.

Boltanski, L. and È. Chiapello. [1999] 2005. *The New Spirit of Capitalism*. London: Verso.

Bourdieu, P. 1977. *Outline of a Theory of Practice*. Translated by Richard Nice. Cambridge: Cambridge University Press.

Brown, T. 2008. "Design Thinking." *Harvard Business Review*, June: 84–92.

Brown, T. 2009. *Change by Design: How Design Thinking Transforms Organization and Inspires Innovation*. New York: Harper Collins.

Brown, T. 2011. "Design Thinking." Blog, available online http://designthinking.ideo.com/, (accessed April 13, 2011).

Brown, T. and J. Wyatt. 2010. "Design Thinking and Social Innovation." *Stanford Social Innovation Review*. Winter: 30–35.

Bucciarelli, L. 1994. *Designing Engineers*. Cambridge, MA: MIT Press.

Buchanan, R. 1992. "Wicked Problems in Design Thinking." *Design Issues* 8(2): 5–21.

Buchanan, R. and V. Margolin (eds). 1995. *Discovering Design: Explorations in Design Studies*. Chicago: Chicago University Press.

Burnette, C. 2009. "A Theory of Design Thinking." Paper prepared in response to the Torquay Conference on Design Thinking, Swinburne University of Technology, Melbourne. November 1, 2009. Available online: http://independent.academia.edu/CharlesBurnette/Papers/136254/A_Theory_of_Design_Thinking (accessed March 6, 2011).

Case Western Reserve University. 2010. "Convergence. Managing + Designing," Weatherhead School of Management. June 18 & 19. Available online: http://design.case.edu/convergence/ (accessed April 14, 2011).

Case Western Reserve University. 2011. "Manage by Designing." Available online: http://design.case.edu/ (accessed April 17, 2011).

Crewe, L., N. Gregson and A. Metcalfe. 2009. "The Screen and the Drum: On Form, Function, Fit and Failure in Contemporary Home Consumption." *Design and Culture* 1(3): 307–328.

Cross, N. 1982. "Designerly Ways of Knowing." *Design Studies* 3(4): 221–227.

Cross, N. 2001. "Designerly Ways of Knowing: Design Discipline Versus Design Science." *Design Issues* 17(3): 49–55.

Cross, N. 2006. *Designerly Ways of Knowing*. Berlin: Springer.

Cross, N. 2010. "Design Thinking as a Form of Intelligence." *Proceedings of the 8th Design Thinking Research Symposium* (DTRS8) Sydney, October 19–20, 99–105.

Cross N., K. Dorst and N. Roozenburg (eds). 1992. *Research in Design Thinking*. Delft: Delft University Press.

Design Council. 2009. "Innovation: The Essentials of Innovation." Available online: http://www.designcouncil.org.uk/en/About-Design/Business-Essentials/Innovation/ (accessed August 18, 2009).

Dorst, K. 2006. "Design Problems and Design Paradoxes". *Design Issues* 22(3): 4–14.

Dorst, K. 2010. "The Nature of Design Thinking." *Proceedings of the 8th Design Thinking Research Symposium* (DTRS8) Sydney, October 19–20, 131–139.

Dorst, K. and N. Cross. 2001. "Creativity in the Design Process: Co-evolution of Problem-Solution." *Design Studies* 22(5): 425–437.

Dunne, D. and R. Martin. 2006. "Design Thinking and How It Will Change Management Education: An Interview and Discussion." *Academy of Management Learning & Education* 5(4): 512–523.

EGOS. 2010. Conference of the European Group for Organization Studies. June 28–July 3, Faculdade de Economia, Universidade Nova de Lisboa. Lisbon, Portugal. Sub-theme 32: "Design-Driven Innovation: Linguistic, Semantic and Symbolic Innovations vs. Technological and Functional Innovations." Available online: http://www.egosnet.org (accessed February 18, 2010).

Ehn, P. 1988. *Work-Oriented Design of Computer Artifacts*. Hillsdale, NJ: Lawrence Erlbaum Associates.

Ehn, P. 2008. "Participation in Design Things." *PDC '08 Proceedings of the Tenth Anniversary Conference on Participatory Design*, Bloomington, Indiana, USA, October 1–4.

EURAM. 2009. European Academy of Management annual conference. Available online: http://www.euram2009.org/r/default.asp?iId=MKEFI (accessed March 26, 2009).

Florida, R. 2002. *The Rise of the Creative Class: And How It's Transforming Work, Leisure, Community and Everyday Life*. New York: Basic Books.

Fry, T. 2009. *Design Futuring: Sustainability, Ethics and New Practice*. Oxford: Berg.

Geertz, C. 1973. "Thick Description: Toward an Interpretive Theory of Culture." In C. Geertz *The Interpretation of Cultures: Selected Essays*. New York: Basic Books: 3–30.

Harvard Business Review. 2009. "How to Fix Business Schools." Available online: http://blogs.hbr.org/how-to-fix-business-schools/ (accessed April 13, 2011).

Hatchuel, A. 2001. "Towards Design Theory and Expandable Rationality: The Unfinished Programme of Herbert Simon." *Journal of Management and Governance* 5(3–4): 260–273.

Hatchuel, A. and B. Weil. 2009. "C-K Theory: An Advanced Formulation." *Research in Engineering Design*, 19(4): 181–192.

Henderson, K. 1999. *Online and On paper: Visual Representations, Visual Culture, and Computer Graphics in Design Engineering*. Cambridge, MA: MIT Press.

IDEO. 2006. "Tim Brown and IDEO Visit the Annual Meeting of the World Economic Forum." Available online: http://www.ideo.com/news/archive/2006/01/ (accessed April 13, 2011).

Jelinek, M., G. Romme and R. Boland. 2008. "Introduction to the Special Issue: Organization Studies as a Science for Design: Creating Collaborative Artifacts and Research." *Organization Studies* 29(3): 317–329.

Jones, J.C. 1970. *Design Methods*. Chichester: Wiley.

Jones, J.C. and D. G. Thornley (eds). 1963. *Conference on Design Methods*. Volume 1. Oxford: Pergamon.

Julier, G. 2007. "Design Practice Within a Theory of Practice." *Design Principles and Practices: An International Journal* 1(2): 43–50.

Julier, G. 2008. *The Culture of Design*. 2nd edition. London: Sage.

Julier, G. 2011. "Political Economies of Design Activism and the Public Sector." Paper presented at Nordic Design Research Conference, Helsinki.

Julier, G. and L. Moor (eds). 2009. *Design and Creativity: Policy, Management and Practice*. Oxford: Berg.

Kelley, D. and G. VanPatter. 2005. *Design as Glue: Understanding the Stanford d-school*. NextDesign Leadership Institute.

Kelley, T. 2001. *The Art of Innovation*. London: Profile.

Kimbell, L. 2011. MBA Elective in Designing Better Futures. Available online: http://wwww.designingbetterfutures.wordpress.com/ (accessed April 16, 2011).

Ladner, S. 2009. "Design Thinking's Big Problem." Blog post. Available online: http://copernicusconsulting.net/design-thinkings-big-problem/ (accessed April 13, 2011).

Lash, S. and J. Urry. 1994. *Economies of Signs and Space*. London: Sage.

Lawson, B. 1997. *How Designers Think: The Design Process Demystified*. 3rd edition. London: Architectural Press.

Lawson, B. and K. Dorst. 2009. *Design Expertise*. Oxford: Architectural Press.

March, J. 1991. "Exploration and Exploitation in Organizational Learning." *Organization Science* 2(1): 71–87.

Martin, R. 2009. *The Design of Business: Why Design Thinking is the Next Competitive Advantage*. Cambridge MA: Harvard Business Press.

Meroni, A. and D. Sangiorgi. 2011. *Design for Services*. Aldershot: Gower Publishing.

MindLab. 2009. *About MindLab*. Available online: http://www.mindlab.dk/assets/116/ml_folder_eng.pdf (accessed April 15, 2011).

Nussbaum, B. 2011. "Design Thinking is a Failed Experiment: So What's Next?." Fast Company blog. Available online: http://www.fastcodesign.com/1663558/beyond-design-thinking (accessed April 13, 2011).

Pandza, K. and R. Thorpe. 2010. "Management as Design, but What Kind of Design? An Appraisal of the Design Science Analogy for Management." *British Journal of Management* 21(1): 171–186.

Parker, S. and J. Heapy. 2006. *The Journey to the Interface: How Public Service Design Can Connect Users to Reform*. London: Demos.

Rittel. H. and M. Webber. 1973. "Dilemmas in a General Theory of Planning." *Policy Sciences* 4: 155–169.

Rowe, P. 1998. *Design Thinking*. Cambridge: MIT Press.

Rylander, A. 2009. "Exploring Design Thinking as Pragmatist Inquiry." Paper presented at the 25th EGOS Colloquium, Barcelona, Spain, July 2–4.

Schatzki, T.R. 2001. "Practice Theory." In T.R. Schatzki, K. Knorr Cetina and E. von Savigny (eds), *The Practice Turn in Contemporary Theory*. London: Routledge.

Schön, D. A. 1983. *The Reflective Practitioner*. New York: Basic Books.

School of Advanced Military Studies. n.d. *Art of Design. Student Text. Version 2.0*. Available online: http://usacac.army.mil/cac2/CGSC/events/sams/ArtofDesign_v2.pdf (accessed November 11, 2010).

Shove, E., M. Watson, M. Hand, and J. Ingram. 2007. *The Design of Everyday Life*. Oxford: Berg.

Simon, H. A. 1969. *The Sciences of the Artificial*. Cambridge, MA: MIT Press.

Simon, H. A. 1973. "The Structure of Ill Structured Problems." *Artificial Intelligence*, 4: 181–201.

Suchman, L. 1987. *Plans and Situated Actions*. Cambridge, MA: MIT Press.

TED. 2009. Tim Brown Urges Designers to Think Big. Talk at TED Conference, Oxford, July. Available online http://www.ted.com/talks/tim_brown_urges_designers_to_think_big.html (accessed April 13, 2011).

Temple University. 2011. Center for Design and Innovation. Available online: http://design.temple.edu/ (accessed April 16, 2011).

Thrift, N. 2005. *Knowing Capitalism*. London: Sage.

Tonkinwise, C. 2010. "A Taste for Practices: Unrepressing Style in Design Thinking." *Proceedings of the 8th Design Thinking Research Symposium* (DTRS8) Sydney, October 19–20: 381–388.

Tsoukas, H. and R. Chia. 2002. "On Organizational Becoming: Rethinking Organizational Change." *Organization Science* 13(5): 567–582.

University of Toronto. 2011. "Business Design." Available online: http://www.rotman.utoronto.ca/businessdesign/default.aspx (accessed April 16, 2011).

Verganti. R. 2009. *Design-driven Innovation: Changing the Rules by Radically Innovating What Things Mean*. Cambridge: Harvard Business Press.

Wang, D. and A. Ilhan. 2009. "Holding Creativity Together: A Sociological Theory of the Design Professions." *Design Issues* 25(1): 5–21.

Winograd, T. and F. Flores. 1986. *Understanding Computers and Cognition: A New Foundation for Design*. Norwood, NJ: Ablex.

CHAPTER TWENTY EIGHT

Rethinking Design Thinking: Part II

LUCY KIMBELL

ABSTRACT

This paper uses resources from anthropology and science and technology studies to propose understanding design expertise and activity as constituted materially and discursively in practice. Introducing a pair of concepts—design-as-practice and designs-in-practice—as an analytical device for discussing design solves a number of problems facing researchers working in design studies. First, it helps researchers see design as a situated, local accomplishment involving diverse and multiple actors. Second, it acknowledges the roles of objects in constituting practices. Third, it de-centers the designer as the main agent in designing. This approach moves away from a disembodied, ahistorical design thinking to a situated, contingent set of practices carried by professional designers and those who engage with designs, which recognizes the materiality of designed things and the material and discursive practices through which they come to matter.

Keywords: design thinking, practices, designers, innovation, organization design

INTRODUCTION

Accounts of design *thinking* often hinge on descriptions of the ways designers *do* things. Researchers do not have direct access to what goes on in designers' minds, so they are left with what they believe is going on as they seek to describe and explain designers' thinking. One striking story comes from management researchers Dick Boland and Fred Collopy (2004), reflecting on their experience of working with architects from Frank Gehry's firm designing the new building for their business school. Having spent two days with the architects revising the arrangement of space in the new building, Boland and Collopy describe how the project lead Matt Fineout tears up the plans they have just agreed on. He suggests they start again, now they know they can solve the problem (Boland and Collopy 2004: 5).

Even in this short description, Boland and Collopy draw our attention to practice: the architects' tacit and embodied knowledge, their bodily and mental activities, what structures their professional work and makes particular behaviors possible, and how it feels. These ways of working startle the management professors, since tearing up plans is not part of the routines within their work culture. Boland and Collopy's account draws attention to the embodied, shared experience of working around a table on sheets of onionskin, making marks, and discussing how the building should be designed. Reading it, one can feel the authors' visceral response to seeing the architect destroy what they have all just created together. For this architect, design is not simply problem solving since in this story, he tears up a viable solution. For Boland and Collopy, this experience helps them identify a distinctive "design attitude" to describe how designers do not just choose between alternatives, but generate entirely new concepts. But this account also captures the material and discursive practices in contemporary design professions. It may be possible to identify a distinctive kind of "design thinking." But perhaps more interestingly, we might attend to the material and discursive practices in which designers of particular kinds do, know, and say particular things and how they come to do, know, and say these things but not others. In so doing we might develop a richer understanding of professional design and its effects.

At a time when the term design thinking has become more common outside of professional design, in particular within management fields (Brown 2009; Martin 2009; Kimbell 2011), this paper explores what theories of practice can bring to understanding professional designers and the cultures in which they have expertise. The main contribution is to propose a new analytical device for discussing design based in theories of practice. It conceives of design activity as linking both what designers do, know, and say, with what end-users and other stakeholders do, know, and say, acknowledging the materials and objects involved in practices and at the same time attending to the discursive practices that make possible particular ways of doing, knowing, and saying. A decade after Victor Margolin's (2002) call for studies of design as a cultural practice, the paper's distinctive feature is to propose shifting the level of analysis in research away from individuals to practices, conceived of as a nexus of minds, bodies, things, and the institutional arrangements within which designs and their users are constituted (Reckwitz 2002).

First I review research influenced by anthropology, science and technology studies, and philosophy that views the world in terms of practices. Drawing on the work of Wanda Orlikowski (2000), Theodore Schatzki (Schatzki et al. 2001), Andreas Reckwitz (2002), Mark Hartswood et al. (2002), Lucy Suchman (2003), Elizabeth Shove (Shove 2011; Shove and Pantzar 2005), Karen Barad (2007), Tony Fry (2007, 2009), and others, I identify concepts that help illuminate the material and discursive practices within which professional design is constituted. I then propose a new way of conceiving of design activity. This highlights the practices that constitute designs, designers' work, and their expertise. I introduce a pair of concepts to describe designing: design-as-practice and designs-in-practice.

This pair of concepts solves a number of problems facing researchers analyzing design activity. These include maintaining dualisms between thinking and doing; ignoring the particular contingencies that shape the emergence of design practices; and relying predominantly on the agency of designers to understand design even though other factors, such as non-human actors, are involved in constituting practices (Barad 2007; Harman 2009). I then briefly illustrate the two concepts using research from an ethnographic study of professional designers. The paper concludes with a discussion of the implications for researchers and educators with an interest in design and designers, and limitations of the approach.

Although the term design thinking may be moving on from its time in the spotlight according to some commentators (e.g. Walters 2011), there remains an important task: to describe and explain doing and knowing within design and the particular expertise of design professionals (e.g. Cross 2004, 2006; Lawson and Dorst 2009). We need to understand what effects designers can have within the different projects, organizations, and communities within which they work. The paper's contribution is to use theories of practice in order to advance understanding about designers' work, moving away from a disembodied, ahistorical design thinking to a situated, contingent set of practices carried by professional designers and those who engage with designs, which recognizes the materiality of designed things and how they come to matter.

RECONFIGURING THE WORLD IN PRACTICE

Theories of practice (e.g. Bourdieu 1977; Giddens 1984; Schatzki et al. 2001; Reckwitz 2002; Shove and Pantzar 2005; Warde 2005) draw on the attention paid in anthropology and sociology to what people do in their embodied, often mundane, situated interactions with other people and with things. Practice theories shift the unit of analysis away from a micro level (individuals) or a macro one (organizations or groups and their norms) to an indeterminate level at a nexus of minds, bodies, objects, discourses, knowledge, structures/ processes, and agency, which together constitute practices that are carried by individuals (Reckwitz 2002). Examples of this perspective outside of anthropology and sociology include studying technology use (e.g. Orlikowski 2000; Barley and Kunda 2001); organizational strategy (e.g. Whittington 1996); knowledge in organizations (e.g. Brown and Duguid 2001); product development (e.g. Carlile 2002); service innovation (e.g. Dougherty 2004); and design (e.g. Du Gay et al. 1997; Shove et al. 2007; Balsamo 2011).

Core concepts in theories of practice include bodies, minds, things, knowledge, discourse, structure/process, and agency (Reckwitz 2002). For example, Elizabeth Shove and Mika Pantzar (2005) describe the practice of Nordic walking as an interweaving of competence and skills (how to do Nordic walking), symbolic meaning and images (what it means to do it), and equipment (the material stuff that is part of doing it). While theories of practice may vary, there are, however, two important common ideas. Firstly, practices cannot be considered by taking any one of these elements in isolation (Reckwitz 2002; Shove 2011). Secondly, practices are understood to be produced dynamically through the interplay of these diverse elements in relation to one another (Shove and Pantzar 2005; Barad 2007). Or, as Carsten Østerlund and Paul Carlile (2005: 92) put it, "subjects, social groups, networks, or even artifacts develop their properties only in relation to other subjects, social groups, or networks."

The variety of approaches within this theoretical orientation means that practice perspectives are not necessarily coherent with one another (Reckwitz 2002). For example, Østerlund and Carlile (2005) identify seven distinct attributes within practice theories, including delineating the differences between the entities being studied, or specifying the empirical practices presented by a particular theory. For the purposes of this discussion on design thinking, this paper follows Reckwitz in his definition of an ideal type of practice theory in which practice is understood as "a routinized type of behavior which consists of several elements, interconnected to one another: forms of bodily activities, forms of mental activities, 'things' and their use, a background knowledge in the form of understanding, know-how, states of emotion and motivational knowledge" (Reckwitz 2002: 249). Here I will emphasize four aspects of practice theory.

The first highlights how practices are understood as "(re)configurings of the world through which the determination of boundaries, properties, and meanings is differentially enacted" (Barad 2007: 148). A practice is a dynamic, local accomplishment in which multiple and different kinds of actor are woven together in "artful integrations" (Suchman 1994). For Karen Barad (2007: 152), "the material and the discursive are mutually implicated in the dynamics of intra-activity." This approach avoids established dualisms between subject/object, nature/culture, and body/mind. Instead, for Barad, the primary ontological unit is "phenomena," which she defines as "produced through complex agential intra-actions of multiple, material-discursive practices or apparatuses of bodily production" (Barad 2007: 140). In this way of thinking about what makes up the world (ontology) and how we can know it (epistemology), Barad and others start from a position in which it is *through practice* that the sociomaterial world is constituted. Practice theory offers a way to see design activity as distributed across a number of different people and artifacts that together enact designing and designs.

A second aspect is how structures—such as designs—are constituted in practice, as described in numerous studies of technology design and development (e.g. Suchman 1987; Hutchins 1995; Barley and Kunda 2001) but also media (e.g. Hall [1977] 1992). In her study of the use of Lotus Notes software, for example, Wanda Orlikowski (2000) showed how technologies are constituted in different ways by users' practices. She found that, as they interact with a technology in their ongoing practices, people enact structures which shape the emergent and situated use of that technology. She found that "technology-in-practice" can vary considerably in the ways structures are routinely encoded. "When people use a technology, they draw on the properties comprising the technological artifact, those provided by its constituent materiality, those inscribed by the designers, and those added on through previous interactions" (410). The contribution of this study was to show that structure is not located in organizations, or in technology, but is enacted by users in practice.

The third aspect of practice theory on which I will draw is the attention paid to the role of objects in constituting practices, echoing work by scholars attending to the materiality, matter, and objects in a range of disciplines. Key contributions include anthropology (e.g.

Appadurai 1986; Gell 1998; Miller 2010), studies of science and technology (e.g. Latour 2005; Barad 2007), and philosophy (e.g. Harman 2009). As Reckwitz describes: "For practice theory, objects are necessary components of many practices—just as indispensable as bodily and mental activities. Carrying out a practice very often means using particular things in a certain way" (Reckwitz 2002: 252). Paying attention to objects, be they objects in the natural world, instruments, or objects produced within a knowledge practice is for Karin Knorr Cetina (2001) a way of making a distinction between a definition of practice as rule-based routines or embodied skills, and a notion of practice that is "more dynamic, creative and constructive" (187).

The fourth aspect of practice theory I emphasize is knowledge. The particular contribution of the practice perspective is to avoid the alternatives presented in theories that focus exclusively on what goes on in people's minds, or at the level of social norms, or understood through analysis of language, for example. In theories of practice, knowledge is a social accomplishment situated in the ongoing routines of bodily and mental activities. As Schatzki explains:

"The prioritization of practices over mind brings with it a transformed conception of knowledge. As indicated, knowledge (and truth) are no longer automatically self-transparent possessions of minds. Rather, knowledge and truth, including scientific versions, are mediated both by interactions between people and by arrangements in the world. Often, consequently, knowledge is no longer even the property of individuals, but instead a feature of groups, together with their material setups." (Schatzki 2001: 12)

In this brief overview, I have tried to show that theories of practice offer resources to those studying designers and their work, or what some designers and researchers call design thinking. Understanding the socio-material world as dynamic and constituted in practice enables us to move away from some of the difficulties presented in accounts of design thinking. It may also offer us a way to enrich our understanding of what designers do, know, and say and the effects that designers and designs have in the world.

DESIGN-AS-PRACTICE AND DESIGNS-IN-PRACTICE

The paper now offers an alternative way of conceiving of design activity. I believe the attempt to try to find a new way of thinking about professional design is pressing, at a time when educators, researchers, and professionals within management and other fields are increasingly mobilizing design in their work (Kimbell 2011). I propose a pair of concepts as an analytical device, which draw on literatures in sociology and science and technology studies as well as design studies. To use terminology from design, readers are invited to see this pair of concepts as a sketch. As such, the ideas that follow are understood as tentative, and suggestive, but nonetheless may offer important new ways to change how professional design is conceived of.

The first concept is perhaps an obvious move, to conceive of *design-as-practice*. Descriptions of design thinking often rely on accounts of what designers do in their embodied, situated routines, and cannot be completed without reference to the artifacts they use, make, and work with and which are involved in mutually constituting what design is. So how does it make sense not to explore the resources offered by practice theory? Design-as-practice mobilizes a way of thinking about the work of designing that acknowledges that design practices are habitual, possibly rule-governed, often routinized, conscious or unconscious, and that they are embodied and situated.[1] What designers know, do, and say is constituted by and co-constitutes what is possible for designers to do, know, and say (and what is not possible for them in particular places and at particular times). An attentiveness to practice orients the researcher to how knowing, doing, and saying constitute and are constituted in relation to other elements of a practice. Further, what designers do, know, and say is contingent and has changed over time, nor are the doing, knowing, and saying constituted through practice the same everywhere (Margolin 2002). Design-as-practice cannot conceive of designing (the verb) without the artifacts that are created and used by the bodies and minds of people doing designing. This way of thinking of design sees it as a situated and distributed unfolding in which a number of people, and their knowing, doing, and saying, and a number of things, are implicated.

This moves the unit of analysis away from oppositions between individual skill or knowing (e.g. Schön 1988; Cross 2006), or organizational competence (e.g. Bauer and Egan 2008), to a set of material and discursive practices which are enacted during design activity. Design-as-practice avoids the contradictory accounts of design that see it as a rational problem-solving activity (e.g. Simon 1996) or as something concerned with generating new ideas (e.g. Boland and Collopy 2004) or creating meanings (e.g. Krippendorff 2006; Verganti 2009). It acknowledges the work done by professional designers in these practices, but also opens up design to others, such as managers and employees in organizations, and also customers, end-users and others who, through their practices, also take part in design.

The second concept is *designs-in-practice*. Designing is already understood to be a thoroughly social process (e.g. Schön 1988; Bucciarelli 1994). Like Orlikowski's (2000) technologies-in-practice, this term acknowledges the emergent nature of design outcomes as they are enacted in practice. It takes the plural noun form of "design," which can mean the outputs created during a process of designing, such as blueprints, models, specifications, and what is finally assembled in products and services. The term designs-in-practice draws attention to the impossibility of there being a singular design. But it is not sufficient to study what the designers and others involved in the designing process think and say and do. Drawing on practice-oriented consumption theory (e.g. Shove and Pantzar 2005; Warde 2005; Ingram et al. 2007; Shove et al. 2007), the concept of designs-in-practice foregrounds the incomplete nature of the process and outcomes of designing (Garud et al. 2008). When the designers have finished their work, and the engineers and manufacturers have finished theirs, and the marketers and retailers have finished theirs, and the customer or end-user has bought a product or started using a service artifact, the activity of designing is still not over. Through engagement with a product or service over time and space, the user or stakeholder continues to be involved in constituting what a design is. Designs (the noun) are constituted in relation to professional designers, customers, and identifiable, known end-users as well as other people who are not known, but also to other elements of practice such as knowledge, feelings, and symbolic structures.

There are other examples of a pair of concepts that make a distinction between the designing done primarily by professional designers and that done by end-users or customers. Within the field of Participatory Design, for example, Pelle Ehn has summarized the distinction between "design for use before use" at project time and "design after design" at use time (Ehn 2008). He proposes creating infrastructures that are flexible and open for design after design and unforeseen appropriation. Similarly, writing about digital design, Botero et al. (2010) describe a continuum between creation and design-in-use. They argue that designers can develop strategies that support different kinds of design-in-use, specifically reinterpretation, adaptation, and reinvention.

What the conceptualization offered here does that is different is as follows. Firstly, it is not primarily focused on what designers or others do, but rather conceives of designs, and designers' own working, as constituted relationally through the intra-action (Barad 2007) of several elements. Secondly, it asks how such intra-action results in specific configurations, constituting particular kinds of designs, subjects, and knowledge, and excluding others. Thirdly, it uses these ideas to discuss the design of any designed entity, not just digital configurations where ideas of appropriation are relatively easy to identify, for example in the reuse of digital code or the creation of hashtags in Twitter (cf. Botero et al. 2010).

EXPLORING THE PRACTICE APPROACH

A brief illustration demonstrates how this analytical device might be used. It draws on an ethnography I conducted during a study of professional service designers (Kimbell 2009).[2] The aim of this research was to identify the ways that designers educated in the studio-practice tradition approached designing for service. I studied service designers working for a few days over several months on a short project for a science enterprise offering a service. The designers' goal was to help the organization redesign its smoking cessation support service, then being trialed in UK pharmacies, free to individuals giving up smoking through the National Health Service. The service included genetic testing of the person trying to give up smoking, based on research that showed that genetic factors influence which nicotine replacement therapies are suitable for particular individuals. I describe two scenes from this research, in which I was participant-observer. These activities were also filmed on video to which I had access.

DESIGNS-IN-PRACTICE

I accompanied two of the designers when they visited a pharmacy where the smoking cessation service was being trialed, along with a manager from the science enterprise and a cameraperson. While one designer made notes and sketches and took photographs, the other, a non-smoker, did a "walk-through" of the service—going through various activities with a pharmacy assistant in a similar way to how a user would sign up for the service. The pharmacy assistant took blood and saliva samples from the designer, telling him what she was doing and why this was necessary within the service. The designers wanted to know how she experienced delivering the service as well as how would-be non-smokers engaged with her during the tests and sign-up activities. During this encounter, the designers paid considerable attention to the artifacts and activities within the pharmacy they saw as connected with the service. These included a poster about the service in the pharmacy window, the layout of the small consulting room where the encounter took place, the website where the assistant signed up new service users and entered details, a large file of information about the service trial, and other things such as a hand-written thank-you note stuck on the wall.

One discussion revolved around the design of the test kit used to take samples of saliva and blood. The assistant explained how she found it useful to lay the contents of the kit out on the desk in a particular order. Since the time taken to do the saliva test and obtain a result was around twenty minutes, she had decided to do this activity first when meeting a person in the consulting room. She laid out the kit in a particular way to prompt her to do this. The manager agreed there was a benefit to doing this, since reducing the duration of the encounter reduced costs. Together, the manager and assistant discussed the fact that the pack did not include instructions about which order to do the two tests in. Unprompted, the assistant had analyzed how she could use it to lead to more efficient delivery of the service. Her use of the kit configured it as a more efficient kit in practice than the ways other people might use it. On its own, it would be hard to say if the kit was efficient or inefficient. But within the practices of pharmacy assistants using the kit to conduct tests to constitute a service, it could become efficient or inefficient. The packaging designers' work had been completed. But the assistant's activities as she engaged with the kit in the workplace, within particular reward structures and ways of valuing her expertise, played a role in constituting the design of the kit and potentially the efficiency of the service. An attentiveness to practice orients the researcher to how the assistant's embodied knowledge constituted a particular design of a kit that had been designed by others, resulting in a new configuration of value to the service providers and to potential customers. The designers later built on this reconfiguring with specific suggestions as to how to improve the kit's packaging and information design.

DESIGN-AS-PRACTICE

Some days after the visit to the pharmacy, the designers spent several hours working together in their studio, which was filmed by a cameraperson and in which I was participant-observer. On the wall, the designers assembled photographs, print-outs from the service website, and other materials connected with the service to create a narrative of the customer journey from the perspective of the service user, a technique developed in services marketing. Overlaying this with annotated sticky notes, the two designers who had visited the pharmacy were joined by a colleague. Together, the three designers undertook a critique of the service. Their discussion ranged from considering specific "touchpoints," the name they gave to artifacts connected with the service, such as the poster in the pharmacy window, to the goals and strategy of the firm offering the service, the pharmacies involved in delivering it and their resources, and discussion about how smokers went about giving up smoking. This was an extensive although unstructured conversation drawing on tacit knowledge about what constitutes a good service experience (Bate and Robert 2007), with references to other kinds of consumption and service. Their working was shaped by these designers' long-standing professional relationships and shared background in studio-based education. Using the consultancy's templates, the designers sat around a table and started to draw individually, all of them filling several sheets of paper with their work. They worked quietly, occasionally making comments or showing each other their work. They then presented their sketches to one another. In so doing they brought into view a service that was different to the one they constituted with their explorations in the pharmacy visit described above and other research.

The designers' sketching together resulted in suggestions for improvements to existing service touchpoints such as the test kit; proposals for new artifacts to be part of the service; and in some cases their sketches proposed entirely new services, for example a genetic test data bank. The activities of these three designers involved both explicit and tacit knowledge, with minds and bodies working together, sometimes in silence, with little discussion about what they should do next but rather embodied routines which led them from one activity to another. An attentiveness to practice here orients the researcher to the ways that these activities are made possible and become routinized within the cultures of designers (Julier 2008), while other ways of working are made less possible.

These two illustrations have suggested how a pair of concepts, design-as-practice and designs-in-practice, might be used as an analytical device in research about design. Although not fully developed, this analysis suggests a fruitful way of trying to account for what goes on within design, through the practices which involve professional designers as well as other elements in constituting designs. As a relational pair, design-as-practice and designs-in-practice serve to ground the practices of designers—their knowledge, ways of knowing, ways of doing, and shared routines—within the bodies they use to do their work, their minds, and the institutional arrangements and symbolic structures which make some activities possible and indeed routine in design.

The relationship between the two concepts is not temporal, with one following the other, although in my account here designs-in- practice is followed by design-as-practice. Nor is each concept at one extreme of a continuum. Instead, designs-in-practice and design-as-practice are better thought of as mutually structuring.

The practice perspective connects activities with the objects that are implicated in living and working, and, crucially, to the practices of stakeholders and others co-creating outcomes of design in the world. As an alternative to design thinking, the pairing of design-as-practice and designs-in-practice moves the unit of analysis away from the individual designer or user, or the organization or group and its norms, to a way of thinking about design that is relational, embodied, structured, and structuring. The possible implications of this are now discussed.

DISCUSSION

In an earlier essay (Kimbell 2011), I explored interest in the term design thinking at a time when designers' ways of knowing and working were being adopted within management fields (e.g. Martin 2009). I situated this development in a context of professional designers becoming a creative class (Florida 2002) of privileged cultural intermediaries (Nixon and Du Gay 2002) within a dynamic, mediatized economy in which production, consumption, and distribution have been reconfigured (Lash and Urry 1994). I reviewed several decades of research into design thinking and summarized three strands, although there are significant differences in the research aims, approaches, and methods used in these literatures. The first strand sees design thinking as a cognitive style; the second strand defines design thinking as a general theory of design; and the third sees design thinking as a resource for organizations. I then identified three issues. The first is that many of the descriptions of design thinking rest on a dualism between thinking and knowing and acting in the world. The second issue identified how an idealized design thinking ignores the diversity of designers' ways of doing, knowing, and saying and the specific contexts in which these have come into view. The third is the emphasis on the designer as the main agent in design activity.

In this essay I have summarized theories of practice which I believe help researchers avoid these issues. I have argued that practice theories switch the unit of analysis from individual actors or society and its norms, to a messy, contingent combination of minds, things, bodies, structures, processes, and agencies. Attending to practice offers ways to understand design activity not just as the work of design professionals and what they do or think, but sees designing as constituted in the intra-action (Barad 2007) of these diverse elements. Design thinking can thus be rethought as a set of contingent, embodied routines that reconfigure the sociomaterial world, and which are institutionalized in different ways. This helps us consider what makes it possible for professional designers to do, know, and say particular things, and not others, at particular times and in particular places. This offers a rich way to understand designing that challenges the efforts to describe a generalized (and often celebratory) design thinking.

A practice orientation also opens up the roles that other human and non-human actors play in constituting design activity, including managers, employees, paying customers, end-users, and others, possibly including those who are not yet born, but also sketches, chairs, websites, consultancies, and post-it notes (cf. Ehn 2008; Ravasi and Rindova 2008; Verganti 2009; Botero et al. 2010). Further, by foregrounding the work done by customers, end-users, stakeholders, and other actors in constituting designs-in-practice, this approach suggests that the activity of designing is never complete. With Barad's (2007) emphasis on how practices shape particular possibilities and exclude others, this orientation begs questions about how and where designers locate themselves, echoing research by Lucy Suchman (2003) and Tony Fry (2007, 2009).

I now summarize specific contributions from this approach in relation to the existing literature. Firstly, the practice orientation sees design as a situated, local accomplishment. Instead of dualisms between subject/object, nature/culture, and body/mind, practices are seen as dynamic configurations of minds, bodies, objects, discourses, knowledge, structures/processes, and agency which can be routinized and institutionalized. The implication is that it does not make sense to try to identify specific cognitive styles among designers which ignore how designers' ways of knowing and thinking are structured and structure their wider sociomaterial context. Tony Fry (2007) is one researcher and educator who points to how the education and professional work of many designers within a context of capitalist consumption has resulted in a culture that reproduces a drive towards further unsustainable consumption. A practice orientation enriches understanding of how designers think and what they know by making explicit how their culturally specific expertise can create new possibilities, but exclude others, and how these ways have become established over time in particular places.

The second contribution is the emphasis on objects as involved in constituting practices. In a practice orientation they are not just things designers make or that people buy or use. Instead, objects and materials are crucial to the unfolding of practice. Intuitively this makes sense. It is hard to think about design professionals without considering the emblematic artifacts with which they are associated, whether they are illustrations, models, or prototypes. Ethnographic descriptions of engineering designers (e.g. Bucciarelli 1994; Henderson 1999) and architects (e.g. Yaneva 2005; Ewenstein and Whyte 2009) have shown how designers working within different traditions are entangled with objects, whether they have acquired them in the course of their work, created them, or involved stakeholders in generating them. Turning an ethnographic gaze onto design's cultures will produce a deeper understanding of how designs are constituted and the various actors involved in this.

A third contribution that follows from the previous two is that the practice orientation de-centers the designer as the main agent in designing. This may not make sense to researchers who want to focus precisely on the designers and their expertise. However, the practice orientation can support a richer, more nuanced understanding of what goes on during design activity, and indeed supports the development of new kinds of professional expertises. In fact, the de-centering of the designer has been well underway for two decades in fields which draw extensively on the social sciences, such as Participatory Design and Computer Supported Cooperative Work (e.g. Ehn 1988; Suchman 1994; Hartswood et al. 2002). What this paper offers is a synthesis of this literature with research in design studies, a potentially deep vein for rethinking fields such as product and industrial design, visual communication, and craft, not just digital designing.

SOME IMPLICATIONS

For design research and practice, the practice-theoretical approach means that designers no longer have to make arguments about why stakeholders or end-users should be at the center of design. In this approach, they already are. In the practice approach, design is understood to be relational and it cannot be conceived of without the practices within which designing and designs are constituted. Further, stakeholders are co-designers and designers are another kind of stakeholder. Extending the view of practices as constituting designs through a nexus of minds, bodies, objects, structure, process, agency, and knowledge challenges the claims of some designers (e.g. Brown 2009) that designing is human-centered. Schön's (1983) description of how the materials "speak back" during designing already makes a move in this direction. Barad's (2007) post-humanism and Harman's (2009) object-oriented metaphysics offer alternatives that design researchers should explore further.

Methodologically, the practice orientation raises questions about research design, methods, and the boundaries set within a study. If studying a design process, what methods are appropriate for de-centering the human designers? Social scientists, in particular those studying science and technology, have developed an array of powerful methods that often involve following the objects (e.g. Latour 1987) or studying mundane things such as infrastructure (e.g. Star 1999). Several other questions come into view. If studying a designed thing, at what point in time does it make sense to start and stop, to examine its effects in practice? Which current and potential future users, customers, and other stakeholders in which specific cultures should be studied in order to understand a particular design?

Finally, for educators introducing approaches, methods, and tools from design within management education, the research presented here raises questions about the ease with which designers' expertise can be exported elsewhere. The adoption of design thinking into management education, for example, in the form of tools and methods separated from the culture of design, may not have the desired results. Practices associated with professional designers that involve visual and performative methods and attend to the aesthetic dimensions of organization life, for example, are part of an educational tradition in which challenging established categories is institutionally rewarded. In contrast, management education rooted in the social sciences and engineering knowledge may not welcome such approaches despite frequent claims that it should adapt (e.g. Huff and Huff 2001; Dunne and Martin 2006).

Finally, I describe some of the limitations of this study. First, while the concepts introduced here as a relational pair are suggestive, they have not been fully elaborated or tested. To what extent they provide a basis for discussing design in projects, organizations, communities, and other contexts requires further research. Secondly, they rest on an experimental ontology and epistemology in which the world is understood as co-constituted relationally, rather than a realist or constructivist approach (Schatzki et al. 2001; Latour 2005; Barad 2007; Harman 2009; Latour et al. 2011). While this serves the purposes of an exploratory essay such as this one, this analysis may not be fruitful for other research aims.

CONCLUSION

This paper has explored theories of practice to see how they might support a deeper understanding of design activity and designers' expertise. Practice theories see the locus of the social not at the level of individuals and their minds, or in organizations and groups and their norms but as a nexus of minds, bodies, things, institutions, knowledge and processes, structure and agency. For practice theorists, these elements are woven together into routines and structures that together co-constitute the sociomaterial world. The paper's contribution is to propose a new pair of concepts to describe and analyze design activity that acknowledge the work done by many actors in constituting designs relationally in practice. I have argued that this helps us rethink design thinking and avoid some of the problems that have emerged in previous literature. Using a practice approach re-conceives of design activity as linking both what designers do, know, and say, with what end-users and other stakeholders do, know, and say, acknowledging the materials and objects that are part of these activities and at the same time attending to the discursive practices that make possible particular ways of doing, knowing, and saying, but exclude others.

ACKNOWLEDGMENTS

Versions of this paper were presented at the European Academy of Management conference, Liverpool, May 2009, and at the Centre for Research on Socio-Cultural Change conference, Manchester, September 2009 in a panel I co-organized with Laurene Vaughan and Nina Wakeford. The paper was improved with feedback from the editor and anonymous reviewers and through discussions with Simon Blyth, Kees Dorst, Tomas Farchi, Anne-Laure Fayard, Philip Hill, Guy Julier, Noortje Marres, Steve New, Tim Schwanen, Nina Wakeford, and Cameron Tonkinwise.

NOTES

1. There are of course similarities with Paul du Gay et al.'s description of the Sony Walkman (1997), Stuart Hall's ([1977] 1992) discussion of the production, circulation, distribution, consumption, and reproduction of media, and Appadurai's (1986) object biographies. But here I synthesize these related endeavors into a formulation that focuses in particular on the relation between designers' work and designed things and the practices in which they are realized.
2. This research was supported by an award from the Designing for the 21st Century initiative of the UK Arts and Humanities Research Council and the Engineering and Physical Sciences Research Council.

REFERENCES

Appadurai, A. (ed.). 1986. *The Social Life of Things: Commodities in Cultural Perspective*. Cambridge, UK: Cambridge University Press.

Balsamo, A. 2011. *Designing Culture: The Technological Imagination at Work*. Durham, NC: Duke University Press.

Barad, K. 2007. *Meeting the Universe Half-way: Quantum Physics and the Entanglement of Matter and Meaning*. Durham, NC: Duke University Press.

Barley, S.R. and G. Kunda. 2001. "Bringing Work Back In." *Organization Science*, 12(1): 76–95.

Bate, P. and G. Robert. 2007. *Bringing User Experience to Healthcare Improvement: The Concepts, Methods and Practices of Experience Based Design*. Oxford: Radcliffe.

Bauer, R. and W. Eagan. 2008. "Design Thinking: Epistemic Plurality in Management and Organization." *Aesthesis*, 2(3): 64–74.

Boland, R. and F. Collopy. 2004. "Design Matters for Management." In R. Boland and F. Collopy (eds), *Managing as Designing*, pp. 3–18. Stanford, CA: Stanford University Press.

Botero, A., K.-H. Kommonen, and S. Marttila. 2010. "Expanding Design Space: Design-in-use Activities and Strategies." Paper presented at the Design Research Society, Montreal. Available online: http://www.designresearchsociety.org/docs-procs/ DRS2010/PDF/018.pdf (accessed November 16, 2011).

Bourdieu, P. 1977. *Outline of a Theory of Practice*. Translated by Richard Nice. Cambridge, UK: Cambridge University Press.

Brown, J.S. and P. Duguid. 2001. "Knowledge and Organization: A Social Practice Perspective." *Organization Science*, 12(2): 198–213.

Brown. T. 2009. *Change by Design: How Design Thinking Transforms Organizations and Inspires Innovation*. New York: Harper Collins.

Bucciarelli, L. 1994. *Designing Engineers*. Cambridge, MA: MIT Press.

Carlile, P. 2002. "A Pragmatic View of Knowledge and Boundaries: Boundary Objects in New Product Development." *Organization Science*, 13(4): 442–55.

Cross, N. 2004. "Expertise in Design: An Overview." *Design Studies*, 25(5): 427–41.

Cross, N. 2006. *Designerly Ways of Knowing*. Berlin: Springer.

Dougherty, D. 2004. "Organizing Practices in Services: Capturing Practice Based Knowledge for Innovation." *Strategic Organization*, 2(1): 35–64.

Du Gay, P., S. Hall, L. Janes, H. Mackay, and K. Negus. 1997. *Doing Cultural Studies: The Story of the Sony Walkman*. Thousand Oaks, CA: Sage.

Dunne, D. and R. Martin. 2006. "Design Thinking and How It Will Change Management Education: An Interview and Discussion." *Academy of Management Learning and Education*, 5(4): 512–23.

Ehn, P. 1988. *Work-oriented Design of Computer Artifacts*. Hillsdale, NJ: Lawrence Erlbaum Associates.

Ehn, P. 2008. "Participation in Design Things." In *Proceedings of the Tenth Anniversary Conference on Participatory Design 2008 (PDC '08)*. Indiana University, Indianapolis, IN, USA, pp. 92–101.

Ewenstein, B. and J. Whyte. 2009. "Knowledge Practices in Design: The Role of Visual Representations as 'Epistemic Objects.'" *Organization Studies*, 30(7): 7–30.

Florida, R. 2002. *The Rise of the Creative Class: And How It's Transforming Work, Leisure, Community and Everyday Life*. New York: Basic Books.

Fry, T. 2007. "Redirective Practice: An Elaboration." *Design Philosophy Papers*, 1.

Fry, T. 2009. *Design Futuring: Sustainability, Ethics and New Practice*. Oxford: Berg.

Garud, R., S. Jain, and P. Tuertscher. 2008. "Incomplete by Design and Designing for Incompleteness." *Organization Studies*, 29(3): 351–71.

Gell, A. 1998. *Art and Agency: An Anthropological Theory*. Oxford: Oxford University Press.

Giddens, A. 1984. *The Constitution of Society*. Cambridge, UK: Polity.

Hall, S. [1977] 1992. "Encoding/decoding." In S. Hall, D. Hobson, A. Lowe, and P. Willis (eds), *Culture, Media, Language: Working Papers in Cultural Studies, 1972–79*, pp. 117–27. London: Taylor and Francis.

Harman, G. 2009. *Prince of Networks: Bruno Latour and Metaphysics*. Melbourne: Repress.

Harman, G. 2010. *Towards Speculative Realism: Essays and Lectures*. London: Zero Books.

Hartswood, M., R. Procter, R. Slack, A. Voss, M. Büscher, and M. Rouncefield. 2002. "Co-realisation: Towards a Principled Synthesis of Ethnomethodology and Participatory Design." *Scandinavian Journal of Information Systems*, 14(2): 9–30.

Henderson, K. 1999. *Online and on Paper: Visual Representations, Visual Culture, and Computer Graphics in Design Engineering*. Cambridge, MA: MIT Press.

Huff, A. and J.O. Huff. 2001. "Re-focusing the Business School Agenda." *British Journal of Management*, 12, S49–S54.

Hutchins, E. 1995. *Cognition in the Wild*. Cambridge, MA: MIT Press.

Ingram, J., E. Shove, and M. Watson. 2007. "Products and Practices: Selected Concepts from Science and Technology Studies and from Social Theories of Consumption and Practice." *Design Issues*, 23(2): 3–16.

Julier, G. 2008. *The Culture of Design*. 2nd edition. London: Sage.

Kimbell, L. 2009. "The Turn to Service Design." In G. Julier and L. Moor (eds), *Design and Creativity: Policy, Management and Practice*, pp. 157–73. Oxford: Berg.

Kimbell, L. 2011. "Rethinking Design Thinking." *Design and Culture*, 3(3): 285–306.

Knorr Cetina, K. 2001. "Objectual Practice." In T.R. Schatzki, K. Knorr Cetina, and E. von Savigny (eds), *The Practice Turn in Contemporary Theory*, pp. 175–88. London: Routledge.

Krippendorff, K. 2006. *The Semantic Turn: A New Foundation for Design*. Boca Raton, FL: CRC Press.

Lash, S. and J. Urry. 1994. *Economies of Signs and Space*. London: Sage.

Latour, B. 1987. *Science in Action*. Cambridge, MA: Harvard University Press.

Latour, B. 2005. *Reassembling the Social: An Introduction to Actor-network-theory*. Oxford: Oxford University Press.

Latour, B., G. Harman, and P. Erdelyi. 2011. *The Prince and the Wolf: Latour and Harman at the LSE*. London: Zero Books.

Lawson, B. and K. Dorst. 2009. *Design Expertise*. Oxford: Architectural Press.

Margolin, V. 2002. *The Politics of the Artificial*. Chicago, IL: The University of Chicago Press.

Martin, R. 2009. *The Design of Business*: *Why Design Thinking Is the Next Competitive Advantage*. Cambridge, MA: Harvard Business Press.

Miller, D. 2010. *Stuff*. Cambridge, UK: Polity Press.

Nixon, S. and P. Du Gay. 2002. "Who Needs Cultural Intermediaries?" *Cultural Studies*, 16(4): 495–500.

Orlikowski, W. 2000. "Using Technology and Constituting Structures: A Practice Lens for Studying Technology in Organizations." *Organization Science*, 11(4): 404–42.

Østerlund, C. and P. Carlile. 2005. "Relations in Practice: Sorting Through Practice Theories on Knowledge Sharing in Complex Organizations." *The Information Society*, 21(2): 91–107.

Ravasi, D. and V. Rindova. 2008. "Symbolic Value Creation." In D. Barry and H. Hansen (eds), *The Sage Handbook of New Approaches in Management and Organization*, pp. 270–84. London: Sage.

Reckwitz, A. 2002. "Towards a Theory of Social Practices: A Development in Culturalist Theorizing." *European Journal of Social Theory*, 5(2): 243–63.

Schatzki, T.R. 2001. "Practice Theory." In T.R. Schatzki, K. Knorr Cetina, and E. von Savigny (eds), *The Practice Turn in Contemporary Theory*, pp. 10–23. London: Routledge.

Schatzki, T.R., K. Knorr Cetina, and E. von Savigny (eds). 2001. *The Practice Turn in Contemporary Theory*. London: Routledge.

Schön, D. 1983. *The Reflective Practitioner*. New York: Basic Books.

Schön, D. 1988. "Designing: Rules, Types and Worlds." *Design Studies*, 9(3): 181–90.

Shove, E. and M. Pantzar. 2005. "Consumers, Producers and Practices: Understanding the Invention and Reinvention of Nordic Walking." *Journal of Consumer Culture*, 5(1): 43–64.

Shove, E. 2011. "How the Social Sciences Can Help Climate Change Policy. An Extraordinary Lecture and Accompanying Exhibition." Performed by members of the social change climate change working party at the British Library, London, January 17, 2011. Available online: http://www.lancs.ac.uk/staff/shove/lecture/ filmedlecture.htm (accessed January 15, 2011).

Shove, E., M. Watson, M. Hand, and J. Ingram. 2007. *The Design of Everyday Life*. Oxford: Berg.

Simon, H. 1996. *The Sciences of the Artificial*. 3rd edition. Cambridge, MA: MIT Press.

Star, S.L. 1999. "The Ethnography of Infrastructure." *American Behavioral Scientist*, 43(3): 377–91.

Suchman, L. 1987. *Plans and Situated Actions*. Cambridge, UK: Cambridge University Press.

Suchman, L. 1994. "Working Relations of Technology Production and Use." *Computer Supported Cooperative Work*, 2(1): 21–39.

Suchman, L. 2003. "Located Accountabilities in Technology Production." Centre for Science Studies, Lancaster University, UK. Available online: http://www.comp.lancs.ac.uk/sociology/ papers/ Suchman-Located-Accountabilities.pdf (accessed June 16, 2011).

Verganti. R. 2009. *Design-driven Innovation: Changing the Rules by Radically Innovating What Things Mean*. Cambridge, MA: Harvard Business Press.

Walters, H. 2011. "Design Thinking Won't Save You." Blog post. Available online: http://helenwalters. wordpress.com/2011/03/21/ design-thinking-wont-save-you/ (accessed July 19, 2011).

Warde, A. 2005. "Consumption and Theories of Practice." *Journal of Consumer Culture*, 5(2): 131–53.

Whittington, R. 1996. "Strategy as Practice." *Long Range Planning*, 29(5): 731–5.

Yaneva, A. 2005. "Scaling Up and Down: Extraction Trials in Architectural Design." *Social Studies of Science*, 35(6): 867–94.

CHAPTER TWENTY NINE

Design Things and Design Thinking: Contemporary Participatory Design Challenges

ERLING BJÖGVINSSON, PELLE EHN, AND PER-ANDERS HILLGREN

© Erling Bjögvinsson, Pelle Ehn, Per-Anders Hillgren / Design Issues / MIT Press, 2012

INTRODUCTION

Design thinking has become a central issue in contemporary design discourse and rhetoric, and for good reason. With the design thinking practice of world leading design and innovation firm IDEO, and with the application of these principles to successful design education at prestigious d.school, the Institute of Design at Stanford University, and not least with the publication of *Change by Design*, in which IDEO chief executive Tim Brown elaborates on the firm's ideas about design thinking,[1] the design community is challenged to think beyond both the omnipotent designer and the obsession with products, objects, and things. Instead, what is suggested is: (1) that designers should be more involved in the big picture of socially innovative design, beyond the economic bottom line; (2) that design is a collaborative effort where the design process is spread among diverse participating stakeholders and competences; and (3) that ideas have to be envisioned, "prototyped," and explored in a hands-on way, tried out early in the design process in ways characterized by human-centeredness, empathy, and optimism.

To us this perspective sounds like good old Participatory Design, although we have to admit it has a better articulated and more appealing rhetoric. As active researchers in the field of Participatory Design for many decades, we fully embrace this design thinking orientation. However, we also hold that, given design thinking's many similarities to Participatory Design today, some of the latter's challenges also might be relevant to contemporary design thinking.

In this paper we put forth both some practical-political and some theoretical-conceptual challenges and dilemmas in engaging in design for change. We do so using the background of our own idiosyncratic encounters with the field and our view on how Participatory Design as a design practice and theoretical field has emerged and evolved since the early 1970s.[2]

In this paper, we argue that a fundamental challenge for designers and the design community is to move from designing "things" (objects) to designing Things (socio-material assemblies). We also argue that this movement involves not only the challenges of engaging stakeholders as designers in the design process, as in "traditional" Participatory Design (i.e., envisioning "use before actual use," for example, through prototyping), but also the challenges of designing beyond the specific project and toward future stakeholders as designers (i.e., supporting ways to "design after design" in a specific project). We see this movement as one from "projecting" to one of "infrastructuring" design activities. As further reflections on these challenges, we discuss our ongoing "infrastructuring" engagement in Malmö Living Labs as one in which we design "Things" for social innovation. We conclude by returning to design thinking and exploring the further challenges to infrastructuring and to open "design Things."

DESIGNING: FROM "THINGS" TO THINGS

As background, we suggest the need to revisit, and partly reverse, the etymological history of "things," as well as the political history and the value base of Participatory Design. The etymology of the English word "thing" reveals a journey from the meaning of a social and political assembly, taking place at a certain time and at a certain place, to a meaning of an object, an entity of matter. Originally, "Things" go back to the governing assemblies in ancient Nordic and Germanic societies. These pre-Christian Things were assemblies, rituals, and places where disputes were resolved and political decisions made. The prerequisite for understanding this journey from things as material object and back to Things as socio-material assemblies is that if we live in total agreement, we do not need to gather to resolve disputes— because none exist. Instead, the need for a common place where conflicts can be negotiated is motivated by a diversity of perspectives, concerns, and interests.

Our starting point in this paper is participation in Things—these kinds of socio-material assemblies that Bruno Latour so strikingly has characterized as collectives of humans and non-humans.[3] We argue that this shift of meaning in the word "thing" is of interest when reflecting on how we as designers work, live, and act in a public space of design—a space that permits a heterogeneity of perspectives among actors who engage in attempts to align their conflicting objects of design. How can we gather and collaborate in and around *design Things*—Things that are modifying the space of interactions and performance and that may be explored as socio-material frames for controversies, opening up new ways of thinking and behaving, being ready for unexpected use.[4]

Participatory Design, seen as design of Things, has its roots in the movements toward democratization of work places in the Scandinavian countries. In the 1970s participation and joint decision-making became important factors in relation to workplaces and the introduction of new technology. Early Participatory Design projects addressed new production tools, changes in production planning, management control, work organization, and division of labor from users' shop floor perspective.[5]

Participatory Design started from the simple standpoint that those affected by a design should have a say in the design process. This perspective reflects the then-controversial political conviction that controversy rather than consensus should be expected around an emerging object of design. In this situation, Participatory Design sided with resource-weak stakeholders (typically local trade unions) and developed project strategies for their effective and legitimate participation in design. A less controversial complementary motive for Participatory Design was the potential to ensure that existing skills could be made a resource in the design process. Hence, one might say that two types of values strategically guided Participatory Design. One is the social and rational idea of democracy as a value that leads to considerations of conditions that enable proper and legitimate user participation—what we refer to here as "staging" and "infrastructuring" *design Things*. The other value might be described as the idea affirming the importance of making participants' *tacit knowledge* come into play in the design process—not just their formal and explicit competencies, but those practical and diverse skills that are fundamental to the making of things as *objects* or *artifacts*.[6]

Hence, Participatory Design, as it emerged in the 1970s, might theoretically and practically be seen as a "modern" example of Things (or rather "thinging," as Heidegger would call it). Latour has called for a thing philosophy or object-oriented politics.[7] His explicit references to object-oriented programming are interesting, not least because a key actor in the early formation of Participatory Design in Scandinavia, Kristen Nygaard, also was one of the inventors of object-oriented programming. For our purposes, however, we focus on participation in *design Things* and on strategies for "infrastructuring" them. Included in this focus is the design of objects as "matters of concerns." So *design Things* are in focus when inquiring into the "agency" not only of designers and users, but also of non-human "actants," such as objects, artifacts, and design devices. How do they get things done their way? How are design and use related? How do design projects and design processes align human and non-human resources to move the object of design forward? How might designers participate in these Things and position themselves in the "collectives of humans and non-humans?"

As the paper evolves, two "thinging" approaches emerge. In the first, Participatory Design is characterized as an approach to involve users in the design and, as suggested by Redström, to encounter in the design process use-before-use.[8] In such a "traditional" approach, Participatory Design is seen as a way to meet the challenges of anticipating or envisioning use before actual use, as it takes place in people's lifeworlds. A complementary position suggests deferring some design and participation until after the design project, opening up the possibility of use as design, or design-after-design.[9] This approach means design as "infrastructuring," addressing the challenge of design as ongoing and as anticipation or envisioning of potential design that takes place in use after design in a specific project.

THINGING: FROM "PROJECTING" TO "INFRASTRUCTURING"

The *project* is the socio-material Thing that is the major form of alignment of design activities. A project is the common form for aligning resources (people and technology) in all larger design endeavors. Projects are Things that have objectives, time lines, deliverables, and more. In practice, resources that must be aligned in a design project might include project briefs, prototypes, sketches, ethnographies and other field material, buildings, devices, project reports, "users," engineers, architects, designers, researchers, and other stakeholders.

Projects often are designed to go through a number of consecutive stages of gradual refinement. They typically have names like "analysis," "design," "construction" and "implementation." However, the shortcomings of such an approach are well-known and many: the top-down perspective hindering adaptation to changing conditions, the hierarchical structure adverting "legitimate" participation, the rigidity of specifications. Hence, the call for user involvement and Participatory Design approaches.

Rather than thinking of a project as a design Thing consisting of the four phases of analysis, design, construction, and implementation, a Thing approach would see this as a collective of humans and non-humans and might rather look to the performative "staging" of it. Inspired by Pedersen, we could then consider these questions:[10] *How do we construct the initial object of design for a project? How do we align the participants around a shared, though problematic or even controversial, object of concern? How do we set the stage for a design Thing?* As work proceeds, *how can the involved practices be made reportable* (e.g., fieldwork, ethnographies, direct participation)? *How can the object of design be made manipulatable*, enrolling the participating non-human actors represented in forms that can be experienced (e.g., sketches, models, prototypes, and games)? *How are the objects of design and matters of concern made into public Things and opened to controversies among participants, both in the project and outside it* (e.g., negotiations, workshops, exhibitions, public debate)?

However, as Klaus Krippendorff has pointed out, projects are only part, or a specific form, of alignments in the life cycle of a device, and every object of design eventually has to become part of already existing ecologies of devices, in people's already ongoing lifeworlds.[11] Hence, both the beginning and end of a designed device is open and hardly ever constrained to the limits of the project. This openness is principally interesting because it emphasizes the importance of understanding how design in a project is related to user/stakeholder appropriation, be it as adoption or redesign, and how users make it part of their lifeworld and evolving ecologies of devices. Hence, strategies and tactics of design *for* use must also be open for appropriation *in* use, after a specific project is finished, and consider this appropriation as a potential, specific kind of design.

PARTICIPATORY DESIGN THINGS AND USE BEFORE USE

Early attempts to conceptualize Participatory Design were made by referring to Wittgenstein and the language-game philosophy.[12] Design was seen as meaningful participation in intertwined language-games of design and use (professional designers and professional users); whereas, performative design artifacts, such as mock-ups, prototypes, and design games, could act as boundary objects binding the different language-games together.[13]

With this conceptualization followed the specific design challenge of setting the stage for another specific design language game—one that has a family resemblance with (professional) language-games of different stakeholders, especially users (lay-designers) and (professional) designers. Thus, in the language of this paper, this staging meant literally assembling socio-material *design Things*, with potentially controversial design objects and matters of concern. The focus thus shifted to *socio-material Things as assemblies* rather than being on *things as objects*.

This shift led to recommendations and practices for a design process based on the (work) practices of legitimate but resource-weak stakeholders (i.e., actual or potential "end-users"). Work ethnographies and other ways to focus on the users' understanding became central. So did engaging in participative design activities, such as participative future workshops.[14] But the most significant shift was the replacement of systems descriptions with engaging hands-on design devices, like mock-ups and prototypes and design games that helped maintain a family resemblance with the users' everyday practice and that supported creative, skillful participation and performance in the design process. A decisive shift in design approach occurred when user participation as design-by-doing and design-by-playing became ways to envision use-before-use.[15] The shift came on the heels of a breakdown in communication between designers and users (lay designers) in using more traditional design methods. These methods did not make sense to all participants.

There are striking similarities here between how we started to use design-by-doing and design-by-playing design artifacts in participatory projects in the early 1980s (e.g., supporting graphic workers and their unions in shaping new technology and work organization in newspaper production) and the focus on prototyping and role-playing as creative tools in contemporary design thinking.[16]

Note that this view on design Things as intertwined language-games, with its focus on the relation between designers and users, was developed in the societal context for, and discourse around, democratization of the workplace in Scandinavia in the 1970s. In practice, design Things did not stand alone. They were linked to other Things—especially to a formal "negotiation model" for design projects focusing on skills and work organization, intended to strengthen the voice of workers and their local trade unions in negotiations with management and in controversies around the design and introduction of new technologies at the workplace.[17]

What, then, is the role of non-human "participants," such as design devices in the form of prototypes, mock-ups, design games, models, and sketches in design Things? In project work, a strong focus is placed on "representations" of the object of design. Traditionally, these representations are thought of as gradually more refined descriptions of the designed object-to-be. The suggestion here instead is to focus on these devices as material "presenters" of the evolving object of design supporting communication or participation in the design process. This evolving object of design is potentially binding different stakeholders together, and it clearly also has a performative dimension. The "presenters" of the object of design, of course, have to be elected and enrolled by the other participants, but once engaged, they are active participants in a design Thing as a collective of humans and non-humans.

We might also view these "presenters" as boundary objects in participatory design Things.[18] They stabilize the design Thing and allow some transference and commonality across the boundaries of language-games, but they also acknowledge that different stakeholders might at the same time hold very different views. Hence, in any design process, when establishing heterogeneous design Things with multiple stakeholders, considering how such boundary objects can be identified and enrolled would be important, as would being aware of the diverse meanings that these "presenters" might carry in relation to the different stakeholders.

With this view of Participatory Design as participative, entangled design Things that align language-games with heterogeneous matters of concern, and of design objects or devices both as "presenters" for the evolving object of design and as boundary objects for binding these heterogeneous language-games together, we now look to the challenges of this participative approach.

INFRASTRUCTURING THINGS AND DESIGN AFTER DESIGN

One limitation of participatory design Things as we've conceptualized them is the focus on projects supporting identifiable users. Basically, the design process described is laid out to support such users' interests, and the products or services designed are to be supportive of these interests as well. Critics have accurately pointed out that there are stakeholders other than immediate users and that people appropriate designs in unforeseen ways. Envisioned use is hardly the same as actual use, no matter how much participation has occurred in the design process.

Do the idea of Participatory Design and the strategies of envisioning "use before use" have to be given up altogether then? What can designers do, and how are these design actions related to unforeseen users' appropriation of the object of design into their lifeworlds? How can users in their everyday activities understood as a kind of design activity, be inspired by and "enact" the traces, obstacles, objects, and potentially public Things left by the professional designers? These design Things are different from those played and performed by designers in a project, but nevertheless, they are design Things (in use). We are not suggesting, of course, that all appropriation in use can or should be understood as design Things. However, we do recommend opening up design approaches in a design project to explicitly support this kind of appropriation in use after the specific design project.

In such an approach, both professional designers and potential users are seen as designers, much as in "traditional," project-bound Participatory Design; but rather than participating in design Things as synchronous entangled language-games, they are participating in design Things separated in time and space. Rather than focusing on involving users in the design process, focus shifts toward seeing every use situation as a potential design situation, as suggested for example by Fischer and Sharff.[19] So there is design during a project, but there is also design in use. There is design (in use) after design (in the design project).

Hence, in design Things carried out in a project, (professional) designers have to acknowledge that design Things potentially will go on in use, and they eventually might also have entirely new stakeholders. Hence, in design Things, the crucial perspective at project time is to open up for new design Things in later use. This shift in focus moves from design Things that aim at useful products and services, to design Things that support good environments for future design Things at use time. Shifting from traditional design for use Things to ongoing design for design Things, we seem confronted not only with design Things that engage multiple stakeholders and presenters, but also a chain of one design Thing after another. So the move is toward design Things (at project time) designing potential boundary-objects (infrastructure) that can be supportive of future design Things (at use time). However, the relations between these design Things, rather than being clear-cut, form a web of interwoven language games over time.

Star and Ruhleder have called such mediation infrastructuring, identifying it as more of a "when" than a "what."[20] An infrastructure (e.g., railroad tracks, cables, or the Internet) reaches beyond the single event (temporal) and the site event (spatial); it does not need to be reinvented every time; and it is embedded into other socio-material structures. However, the infrastructure also is accessible only by participation in specific practices. Hence, infrastructure, or rather *infrastructuring*, means aligning socio-material public Things; it is relational and becomes infrastructure in the relationships between design Things at project time and (multiple, potentially controversial) design Things in use. This infrastructure is shaped over extended timeframes, not only by professional designers, but also by users as mediators and designers who "infrastructure" in ways never envisioned at project time. Infrastructuring entangles and intertwines activities at project time (e.g., selection, design, development, deployment, and enactment) with everyday professional activities at use time (e.g., mediation, interpretation, and articulation), as well as with further design in use (e.g., adaptation, appropriation, tailoring, re-design, and maintenance).[21]

An infrastructuring strategy, according to architect Stan Allen, must pay attention to how existing infrastructures condition use, but in doing so, it also must deliberately design indeterminacy and incompleteness into the infrastructure, leaving unoccupied slots and space free for unanticipated events and performances yet to be.[22] Such strategies for opening up controversial Things serve as a kind of "event architecture," where the focus is on designing "architecture-events" rather than "architecture-objects," asserted Tschumi.[23] Here, the infrastructure supports multiple and heterogeneous, often controversial, design Things in use (rather than homogenous and unitary ones).

With an infrastructuring design approach at project time, then, perhaps one should try to develop the very object of design as public Things that potentially, by the appropriation and enactment by its users, can lead to new objects that in turn can make their way into the users' lifeworlds and already existing ecologies of objects. But this vision cannot be approached as design from nowhere. As we have mentioned, Participatory Design once grew out of a concern about how design could support resource-weak groups when information technology was introduced to the workplace. The designer in this case was clearly positioned in the midst of controversies regarding how the design was implemented in use. Continuing Participatory Design into design as infrastructuring, design-for-design, and design-in-use, the same guiding values—once advocated to counter a hierarchical and formalistic design process characterized by dominance—may prove useful. Dominance, hierarchy, and formalisms are certainly ways in which many social, technical, and spatial infrastructures can be characterized. Hence, the rational idea of democracy and legitimate participation might, in design as infrastructuring, lead to a focus on support for the emergence of design Things as "agonistic public spaces." As Mouffe argues, the goal of democratic politics is to empower a multiplicity of voices in the struggle for hegemony and to find "constitutions" that help transform antagonism into agonism, moving from conflict between enemies to constructive controversies among "adversaries"—those who have opposing matters of concern but who also accept other views as "legitimate."[24] These activities are full of passion, imagination, and engagement. As such, they are more like creative design activities than rational decision-making processes. We must then also pay special attention, as Star points out, to those "marginalized by standardized networks" or infrastructures.[25] These "creative design activities" cannot be performed in any universal sense as "design from nowhere," but, as Haraway puts it, only as "politics and epistemologies of location, positioning, and situating," where partiality rather than universality is the condition that allows users to be heard and to be understood in making "rational knowledge claims."[26] This is what Suchman has called the "local accountability" of researchers and designers.[27]

In this perspective, design becomes a question, not so much about the new or about innovative products, but, according to Barry, more about everyday practice in particular sites and locations.[28] This is a practice committed to the work of envisioning emerging landscapes of design through which social and material transformations take place, landscapes shaped by the opening up of questions and possibilities.

As we understand it, these challenges also relate to the design-thinking vision of designers engaging in design thinking and the bigger picture design, for example, to IDEO projects on design for social impact. In a European tradition, these challenges have been addressed as design for social innovation. Social innovations can be products or services just like any innovation, but they can also be a principle, an idea, a piece of legislation, a social movement, or an intervention—or some combination of these innovative possibilities. The key aspect is their capacity to simultaneously meet social needs and create new social relations. The Young Foundation in the United Kingdom has been a major player in developing the social innovation perspective in theory and practice.[29] Italian designer and researcher Ezio Manzini and the international group of people around him have been primary drivers in spreading such design practices.[30] Here, new ideas emerge from a variety of actors directly involved in the problem to be addressed: end users, grass roots designers, technicians and entrepreneurs, local institutions, and civil society organizations. From this perspective, design is no longer just a tool for the development of functional, innovative consumer products but is increasingly seen as a process for radical change—for developing services, systems, and environments that support more sustainable lifestyles and consumption habits. A foundational concept for Manzini and his colleagues is "collaborative services:" The role of the designer is initially to support the development of new concepts and later to make them attainable so they can result in "social" enterprises.[31]

Approaches to social innovation are in line with the ideas of Participatory Design and design as infrastructuring, and with the corresponding guiding values put forth in this paper. Social innovation offers challenging ways for designers to deal with both Participatory Design and infrastructuring design Things.

In the next section, we elaborate on the challenges of infrastructuring design Things, based on our own experiences.

EXPLORING INFRASTRUCTURING
DESIGN THINGS IN PRACTICE

Our experiences related to social innovation infrastructuring of design Things have come through the Malmö Living Labs project, which started in 2007 as a small-scale laboratory to explore how subcultures could be enhanced with new media.[32] The project may be characterized as providing venues for open-ended, prototypical practices, or arenas for communication and negotiations.[33] In practice, this environment has required that we build trust and long term relationships with the various lab partners, and as a result, we have avoided having clearly predefined projects and project constellations. Instead, our aim has been to create working relations that allow for various constellations to develop and for different possibilities to be explored. Our role in such an open-ended design situation has been to conduct continuous match-making processes, where partners co-develop future possibilities and try them out in real settings. Given that grassroots organizations and cultural producers are typically more resource-weak than the design, media, and IT companies, we pay special attention to foregrounding concerns and issues these partners face and to how they match up with matters the company partners face.

The starting point for our infrastructuring process was the arts and performance center, INKONST, which hosts a variety of non-governmental organizations (NGOs) and stakeholders that run activities and events related to film, performance, theatre, concerts, and music clubs. Although we have set up experiments with several of these stakeholders, for the purposes of this paper, we concentrate on RGRA, a grassroots hip-hop community (aka The Face and Voice of the Street), whose members are first- and second-generation immigrants living in the suburbs of Malmö. In hindsight, we can see how RGRA has been involved in a number of design Things: Now we see that what started out as broad, open-ended explorations has resulted in various constellations of projects in which RGRA youngsters and design researchers have collaborated with media companies, mobile phone software developers, mobile game developers, public transport companies, Swedish public television and radio, and city of Malmö departments. Several constellations have grown out of everyday issues: exploring how RGRA could engage in street journalism through mobile video broadcasting, dealing with dilemmas such as how professional media and grassroots media can collaborate, and looking at how to mediate a talent competition aimed at letting people in different parts of the city and enjoying and participating in different musical traditions meet and interact. Another strand of matters of concerns has centered on how RGRA might have a more visible and legitimate presence in the urban environment.

A FIRST NETWORK OF WORKING RELATIONS
EMERGING INTO A THING

During the open-ended infrastructuring process, several Things have emerged from the bottom up as one Thing led to another. Thus far, two of them have grown into more traditional research projects with more clearly defined project goals. The first concerned how RGRA could create new channels to distribute music produced by its members. The Thing's starting point was an early workshop between the Labs' designers and RGRA, where ideas emerged that RGRA could set up Bluetooth poles at strategic places or that Bluetooth senders could be put on buses, transforming the bus company into a media provider. (Many youngsters in Malmö spend up to two hours a day on a bus commuting back and forth to school.)

The interaction design company Do-Fi, which specializes in developing Bluetooth services, saw potential in the idea and agreed to participate in setting up a first round of experiments, as did two of our research colleagues at the university with special competence in place-centric computing. Skånetrafiken, a company in charge of the public transport in the region, and Veolia, which is contracted to operate many of Malmö's bus routes, also agreed to participate and to give access to the buses. The experiments indicated that the buses could become a new space for RGRA to distribute the music of its members and thus become more visible. The bus company saw new commuter services geared toward teenagers, which could potentially diminish vandalism. Do-Fi saw the potential of developing a new product and new services in collaboration with the company, Epsilon Embedded Systems. The researchers saw the potential of developing a new research project focusing on place-specific media. The group consisting of all of these stakeholders was granted research funding to develop a portable, low-cost media hub.

In one sense, the Bluetooth bus undertaking can be seen as just another experiment—but that view does not tell the whole story. This undertaking was also a Thing. The experiment revealed not only the possibility of aligning different matters of concern, but also controversies and conflicting matters of concerns. One controversy concerned the constellation of partners. RGRA members had split emotions and varying opinions about whether they should collaborate with Veolia because the international branch of the company at that time was engaged in building transportation infrastructure in East Jerusalem, on what is perceived by many Arabs to be Israeli-occupied Palestinian territory. At the same time, they saw that they could gain financially by participating and could benefit from having access to the network of actors. RGRA decided to participate on the condition that RGRA's and Veolia's logos would not appear next to each other in any press material. RGRA, foremost, was collaborating with the researchers and the interaction design company and only indirectly was working with Veolia. The bus experiment also generated debates around immaterial property rights: Who could apply for patents, and who should gain financially if a new form for Bluetooth push technology was developed? It also raised questions about what type of (media) space the interior of the bus could be. Could it be transformed into a more public and inclusive space, or is it to remain an exclusive space leased out only to commercial actors, as is the case today?

EXPANDING THE NETWORK OF WORKING RELATIONS INTO A NEW THING

RGRA members' experience of being to a large degree invisible in the urban environment parallels their feeling that their neighborhoods are largely unknown by people living in other parts of the city. (A common view is that their neighborhoods are dangerous.)

One approach suggested by the group's members to handle this lack of connection or visibility is to construct "tourist" routes in their suburbs and guide people through the areas. To investigate this issue, a new Thing emerged, this time assembling RGRA, Do-Fi and researchers with the company Ozma Game Design, and the city of Malmö. The strategy was to see how the mobile game platform UrbLove, developed by Ozma, could be used to create new experiences of RGRA neighborhoods. Using the platform, young people can explore urban environments by solving "text"-quizzes related to specific places. Combining Ozma's gaming platform with Do-Fi's Bluetooth technology seemed fruitful because players would be given the capability to download media files at specific spots. An initial experiment in which youngsters from RGRA helped to develop a game path in their neighborhood was conducted. They selected places, made questions, and provided locally produced music files available for Bluetooth download, the lyrics of which related to the game.

A trial game played by other youngsters showed (1) that they found gaming to be an interesting approach to learning about unknown urban environments, (2) that the game created a spontaneous interaction between the players and the locals, and (3) that developing a game engine with which the youngsters could easily make their own game paths was needed. The most important issue addressed in this Thing concerned which areas of the city are worth exposing in a positive light. The actors in this Thing applied for and received research money to explore how an open game engine could be developed and used to bridge urban barriers. This example illustrates how design Things also develops into specific projects (that then later may become part of new design Things).

In general, our experiences emphasize the challenging yet constructive ways in which unifying participation and infrastructuring can extend beyond the traditional design project and into new kinds of design Things. When reflecting on the shift from our previous experience of "projecting" to "infrastructuring," we see our strategy has changed in several ways to allow for working with infrastructuring for ongoing Thinging, or design-after-design. First, we have worked on creating ongoing working relationships or new forms of infrastructuring practice(s) so that heterogeneous partners can bring forth the issues or possibilities they want to explore and see if their vision or issue makes sense and matches with other partners' concerns. This approach has meant creating loose agreements and work practices on how to approach the unknown. This aspect of our work has been central because we live in a fluid society where access to a rich network of actors and resources is central—particular for providing the connections that those who are resource-weak tend to lack. It also has meant focusing on how specific issues and possibilities can be handled by creating ongoing infrastructuring processes, without predetermined sets of partners, that require reoccurring Things rather than a final solution. Our goal is to ensure that (1) these processes set precedents in ways that allow those participating to set up their own infrastructuring processes and Things, and (2) the objects designed allow for design-after-design and have at least elements of Thinging. In RGRA's case, the aim has been to create conditions that allow ongoing design of Things and infrastructuring to happen. At this time, RGRA members do not construct any objects on their own, although the aim is that they will. However, in both of the cases described, we have seen Things go beyond a specific project into more sustainable and long-term learning and working relationships. The relationship between the company Do-Fi and RGRA has, for example, gradually emerged into a self-sustaining collaboration. During the past two years, they have collaborated on several experiments within the framework of Malmö Living Labs. Their complementary competencies have been mutually recognized as valuable resources. They now are planning to form a company together.

Such Living Lab experiences bring to light the challenges that proponents of Design Thinking need to address. Although we agree with the basic tenets of Design Thinking, we argue that, to become a sustainable endeavor, it needs to go beyond projecting and be seen as ongoing infrastructuring for Thinging. Our experiences also show that those of us who take up the challenge of design-for-design need to consider how it can be done beyond making products that can be configured at use-time—in other words, how we as designers can develop practices that are always already ready for ongoing changes. This challenge is one we also bring with us as we seek to take our Living Labs infrastructuring design Things experience one step further.

THINGS THAT MATTER?

During the past years, we have been able to scale up our Living Labs design Things engagement. To maintain our close working relationships and the trust built among our partners, we have decided to grow three small collaborating labs, rather than one large lab. The city of Malmö is characterized by multi-ethnicity, cultural production, youth culture, and new media industry. These aspects also lead to the rationale behind the content orientation and cultural and geographic position for the three collaborating living labs innovation milieus: "The Stage," "The Neighborhood," and "The Factory." Although they differ in orientation and geographic location, these three living labs are all founded on some shared ideas and values. They are all based on user-driven design and innovation activities, growing out of social movements. They also are planned as open innovation social and technical platforms, integrated with the broader innovation systems in the city and region. From this position, they invite collaboration between people, companies, public agencies, cultural organizations, and NGOs, thus opening the borders and aligning potentially conflicting matters of concerns between users driving innovation, business incubators, new business models, research and education. Finally, although not driven by it, these environments all explore the potential of new media for co-creation and social innovation. As such, they support the collaboration between amateurs and professionals in collaborative cross-media productions. They use social media in co-creation projects leading to new services and products, and when applicable, they use new media co-creation strategies, such as open source, open content, do-it-yourself, etc.

Emerging design Things include a multiethnic group of women with a broad range of language skills organizing a collaborative service through which they provide meals for a large group of arriving refugee orphans, urban planning initiatives by citizens using new tools and participative processes, and the implementation of a creative commons business model that supports independent movie makers in financing and distributing their productions.

This infrastructuring of design Things might seem a long way from designers' participating in projects with typographers and machinists who are struggling to democratize the workplace in the 1970s. However, in our view the basic design approach and values represent a continuation of that movement, and the progression results in ways to seriously engage in controversial design Things—ways that seem to converge with, but also challenge, contemporary design thinking.

In the early development of Participatory Design, proponents envisioned a new role for the designer in setting the stage for collaborative design Things at project time. In this paper, we have further elaborated on the designer's role in supporting future appropriation—as a kind of design at use time, as ongoing infrastructuring design Things.

We opened the paper with reference to Bruno Latour's view on things as socio-material assemblies and collectives of humans and non-humans and his quest for a thing philosophy. As a final note, we bookend this paper with the position of pragmatist philosopher John Dewey on controversial Things and the public—that in fact the public is characterized by heterogeneity and conflict.[34] Designing for, by, and with stakeholders may be challenging enough where common social objectives are already established, institutionalized, or at least seen as reasonably within reach. These social communities are supported by relatively stable infrastructures. The really demanding challenge is to design where no such consensus seems to be within view, where no social community exists. Such political communities are characterized by heterogeneity and difference with no shared object of design. They are in need of platforms or infrastructures, "agonistic" public spaces—not necessarily to solve conflict, but to constructively deal with disagreements. In such heterogeneous design Things public controversial matters can unfold as actors engage in alignments of their conflicting objects of design. Design thinking that wants to make a difference cannot ignore the challenge of passionate engagement in controversial design Things.

© 2012 MIT. Previously published in *Design Issues*: Volume 28, Number 3, Summer 2012.

NOTES

1. Tim Brown, *Change by Design: How Design Thinking Transforms Organizations and Inspires Innovation* (New York: Harper Collins Press, 2009).
2. See, e.g., Erling Björgvinsson, *Socio-Material Mediations: Learning, Knowing, and Self-Produced Media Within Healthcare*, PhD Dissertation Series 2007–03 (Karlskrona: Blekinge Institute of Technology, 2007); Pelle Ehn, *Work-Oriented Design of Computer Artifacts: Arbetslivscentrum* (Hillsdale, NJ: Lawrence Erlbaum Associates, 1988); and Per-Anders Hillgren, *Ready-Made-Media-Actions: Lokal Produktion och Användning av Audiovisuella Medier inom Hälso-och Sjukvården* (*Ready-Made-Media-Actions: Local Production and Use of Audiovisual Media within Healthcare*) (Karlskrona: Blekinge Institute of Technology, 2006).
3. Bruno Latour, *Pandora's Hope: Essays on the Reality of Science Studies* (Cambridge, MA: Harvard University Press, 1999).
4. This frame or structure is also used for the book *Design Things* by Thomas Binder, Pelle Ehn, Giorgio de Michelis, Per Linde, Giulio Jacucci, and Ina Wagner (Cambridge, MA: MIT Press, 2011), in which we explore socio-material foundations for contemporary design from a pragmatic perspective. Ideas in this paper are dealt with in much more detail in the book.
5. Ehn, *Work-Oriented Design of Computer Artifacts*.

6. Ibid.

7. Bruno Latour, "From Realpolitik to Dingpolitik or How to Make Things Public" in Bruno Latour and Peter Weibel, eds., "Making Things Public: Atmospheres of Democracy" in *Catalogue of the Exhibition at ZKM—Center for Art and Media—Karlsruhe, 20/03-30/10 2005* (Cambridge, MA: The MIT Press, 2005), 4–31.

8. Johan Redström, "Re:definitions of Use," *Design Studies* 29, no. 4 (2008): 410–23.

9. Ibid.

10. Jens Pedersen, "Protocols of Research and Design" (PhD thesis, Copenhagen IT University, 2007).

11. See Klaus Krippendorf, *The Semantic Turn: A New Foundation for Design* (Boca Raton, FL: Taylor & Francis Group, 2006).

12. Ludwig Wittgenstein, *Philosophical Investigations* (Oxford: Basil Blackwell, 1953).

13. See Ehn, *Work-Oriented Design of Computer Artifacts*; see also Susan L. Star, "The Structure of Ill-Structured Solutions: Boundary Objects and Heterogeneous Distributed Problem Solving," in *Distributed Artificial Intelligence 2*, Les Gasser and Michael Huhns, eds. (San Francisco: Morgan Kaufman, 1989), 37–54.

14. Robert Junk and Norbert R. Müllert, *Zukunftswerkstätten: Wege zur Wiederbelebung der Demokratie* (Future workshops: How to Create Desirable Futures) (Hamburg: Hoffmann und Campe, 1981).

15. See Pelle Ehn and Morten Kyng, "Cardboard Computers," in *Design at Work: Cooperative Design of Computer Systems*, Joan Greenbaum and Morten Kyng, eds. (Hillsdale, NJ: Lawrence Erlbaum Associates, 1991), 169–96, and Pelle Ehn and Dan Sjögren, "From System Description to Script for Action in Design at Work: Cooperative Design of Computer Systems," in *Design at Work: Cooperative Design of Computer Systems*, 241–68.

16. Ehn, *Work-Oriented Design of Computer Artifacts*.

17. Pelle Ehn and Åke Sandberg, *Företagstyrning och Löntagarmakt* (Management Control and Labor Power) (Falköping: Prisma, 1978).

18. Star, "The Structure of Ill-Structured Solutions," 37–54.

19. Gerhard Fischer and Eric Scharff, "Meta-Design—Design for Designers," in *Proceedings of the 3rd Conference on Designing Interactive Systems* (DIS 2000), D. Boyarski and W. Kellogg, eds. (New York: ACM, 2000), 396–405.

20. See Susan L. Star and Karen Ruhleder, "Steps Toward an Ecology of Infrastructure: Design and Access for Large Information Spaces," *Information System Research* 7, no. 1 (1996): 111–34; see also Susan L. Star and Geoffrey C. Bowker, "How to Infrastructure," in *The Handbook of New Media*, Leah A. Lievrouw and Sonia M. Livingstone, eds. (London: Sage Publications, 2002), 151–62.

21. See Helen Karasti, Karen S. Baker and Florence Millerand, "Infrastructure Time: Long-term Matters in Collaborative Development" *Computer Supported Cooperative Work*, 19 (Berlin: SpringerLink, 2010), 377–405; Michael Twidale and Ingbert Floyd, "Infrastructures from the Bottom-Up and the Top-Down: Can They Meet in the Middle?" in Proceedings of the Tenth Anniversary Conference on Participatory Design (2008) (Bloomington: Indiana University Press, 2008), 238–24; and Volkmar Pipek and Volker Wulf, "Infrastructuring: Toward an Integrated Perspective on the Design and Use of Information Technology," *Journal of the Association for Information Systems 10*, no. 5 (2009): 447–73.

22. Stan Allen, Diana Agrest, and Saul Ostrow, *Practice: Architecture, Technology and Representation* (London: Routledge, 2000).

23. Bernard Tschumi, *Event Cities (Praxis)* (Cambridge, MA: MIT Press, 1994).

24. Chantal Mouffe, *The Democratic Paradox* (London: Verso, 2000).

25. Susan Star, "Power, Technology and the Phenomenology of Conventions: On Being Allergic to Onions," in *A Sociology of Monsters: Essays on Power, Technology and Domination*, John Law, ed. (London: Routledge, 1991).

26. Donna Haraway, "Situated Knowledges: The Science Question in Feminism and the Privilege of Partial Perspective," *Feminist Studies 14*, no. 2 (1988): 589.

27. Lucy Suchman, "Located Accountabilities in Technology Production," *Scandinavian Journal of Information Systems 14*, no. 2 (2002): 91–105.

28. Andrew Barry, *Political Machines: Governing a Technological Society* (London: Athlone, 2001).

29. See Robin Murray, Julie Caulier-Grice, and Geoff Mulgan, *The Open Book of Social Innovation* (London: The Young Foundation, 2010).

30. See François Jégou and Ezio Manzini, *Collaborative Services: Social Innovation and Design for Sustainability* (Milan: PoliDesign, 2008).

31. Ibid.

32. Malmö Living Labs is a program within Medea, a co-production and collaborative media initiative at Malmö University, Sweden (www.medea.se). Malmö Living Labs is sponsored by Vinnova, the Swedish Knowledge Foundation, and by the European Union Regional Development Fund.

33. See Björgvinsson, *Socio-Material Mediations*; Hillgren, *Ready-Made-Media-Actions*; Malmö New Media Living Lab, www.malmolivinglab.se (accessed February 23, 2012) and Erling Björgvinsson, "Open-Ended Participatory Design as Prototypical Practice," *CoDesign 4*, no. 2 (June 2008): 85–99.

34. John Dewey, *The Public and Its Problems* (New York: Henry Holt and Company, 1927); Noortje Marres, "Issues Spark a Public into Being," in *Making Things Public: Atmospheres of Democracy*, Bruno Latour and Peter Weibel, eds. (Cambridge, MA: The MIT Press, 2005), 208–17.

CHAPTER THIRTY

From Design Culture to Design Activism

GUY JULIER

ABSTRACT

Design culture has emerged as a broadly applied term in the past decade. Analytically, we can take it to describe the networking of the domains of design, production, and consumption within which questions of value, circulation, and practice reside. The reflexive promotion of design cultures and the enrollment of subjects and objects into its cause are taken to be of particular importance within neoliberalism. Since design cultures are networks, issues of their density and scale and the speed and strength of their interactions are of interest. Design activism has emerged as a movement, partly in response to the recent crises of neoliberalism. However, it is not necessarily independent of mainstream design culture. Instead, it picks up and runs with some of its key themes, including intensification, co-articulation, temporality, and territorialization.

Keywords: neoliberalism, relationality, value, ethical surplus, appropriation

Saturday January 28, 2012. I am walking through Clerkenwell, London, where the UK's most intensive concentration of design and media firms is to be found. Celebrated for its accompanying trendy bars and cafes, small art galleries, and loft-living, this once marginal area of the capital now provides a blueprint for other creative quarters that have sprung up in the UK's towns and cities. My first destination is a meeting of the Design History Society at the Women's Library, University of East London. Here I report on the Design Activism and Social Change conference we held. Much comment is made on the surge of historical interest in the radical design movements of the 1970s. I then head further eastwards to Bethnal Green—another zone of gradual gentrification. I join the inaugural UK meeting of Occupy Design. Called together at short notice through social media, students, academics, and junior designers huddle in a chilly warehouse. The workshop is in full swing as design activists discuss what Occupy Design can do in response to the social injustices that the economic crisis has exposed. The next time I am in Bethnal Green will be to hear a talk about how social design and design activism can help with public-sector service delivery. It feels like early days, still.

The debt crises in Europe, the foreclosures and unemployment in the US, bailouts of banks, the dramatic rise of commodity prices, climate change getting faster than predicted, the Arab Spring, Iraq and Afghanistan, massive migration piling pressure on urban infra-structures, the drug cartels in northern Mexico—they all produce a sense of a world in turmoil. And yet the structures and processes of neoliberalism that have come to dominate the majority of our planet through the last thirty years seem to rumble on. The culture of mainstream commercial design has developed through this period to support and promote neoliberalism. However, in more recent years design activism has emerged as a movement that contests it and searches for alternative models of practice. How do mainstream design culture and design activism exist side-by-side, however uncomfortably? Despite their different registers, what might they have in common?

The title of this article implies, in the words "from" and "to," that design culture and design activism occupy separate timeframes and that they are placed in sequence. Certainly one of my aims is to argue that these concepts can be viewed historically. Briefly, for now, I take a period of "(high) design culture" to coincide with the dominant epoch of neoliberalism, dating roughly from 1980 to 2008. While one might naturally refer to the design culture of other historical periods, these particular years have produced a specific set of qualities in its operation that include an increased intensification of the dynamics between design production and consumption and that I elaborate on further below. This neoliberalism/design culture period is bookended by two phases where more self-consciously radical possibilities for design arise, one of these coming in the 1970s with the second emerging from about 2005. This doesn't mean to say that one predates or postdates the other. Rather, I am describing a kind of "shadow period" that has existed during the formation of neoliberalism as a central tenet of political economy in the 1970s and, equally, during its crisis since 2008 where important design activist practices have also emerged.

Just as neoliberalism as the dominant economic mode of Western capitalism was very much under development from the early 1970s (when some of the most radical design thinking was also taking shape), so much of what we might understand as contemporary design activism has developed within and from the recent contexts of neoliberalism. The chief focus of this article takes into account these historical periods but, moreover, is concerned with the relationships between these concepts—their "to-ing" and "fro-ing."

Neoliberalism itself is a relatively recent term. The idea of economic practice distinct from classical liberalism can be traced back to the 1920s. It isn't until the 1970s that it gained traction in state policy. As a term in common usage, however, it has only circulated widely in the last decade (Peck et al. 2009). Put most bluntly and briefly, neoliberalism is typified by the following features:

- the deregulation of markets and the privileging of market forces, free of state intervention;
- the privatization of state-owned enterprises;
- the foregrounding of financial interests over others (e.g. communitarian, civic, social, environmental, etc.);
- an emphasis on competitiveness and on individual, entrepreneurial practices.

By extension, therefore, the relationship of design culture and design activism to neoliberalism must be understood. This means attempting to grasp how design works within, and takes advantage of, neoliberalism's structures, institutions, and resources. As such, pinpointing design's ideological and economic features and activities in this system comes to the fore.

Academic study in design, to date, has been remarkably devoid of considerations of political economy, particularly in terms of its theorization. One exception is Heskett (2008), who provides a generalistic survey of economic theories, design, and value creation. Another is Bryson and Rusten (2011), who focus on firms, individuals, and national policies in producing competitive advantage through design. Their aims, though, are not to provide a politicized view. The social and economic structures within and for which design functions and its relationship to the workings of power and capital are accepted as standard. Conversely, Fry (2010) develops a strident critique of politics and unsustainability from a design point of view; but he does not elaborate on how the economies act to produce unsustainability or how his proposals impact economic practices and political economy in a broader sense.

The point here is not to berate past authors but to establish that this article is written in an ill-defined and underdeveloped field. However, other fields can be drawn from. Needless to say, then, the work of Latour (e.g. 2005) and colleagues in actor-network theory (ANT) and science and technology studies (STS) has helped me consolidate a concept of design culture. Their understanding of social practices involving the networking of human and non-human actors is a useful starting point and has also been developed in relation to design by Fallan (2008), Yaneva (2009), Kimbell (2011, 2012), and Wilkie (2011). However, Hall's more nuanced discussion of "articulations" (1985) is also useful to developing a theoretical analysis of design culture. Recent work that develops the related notion of "practice theory" (e.g. Shove et al. 2012) usefully draws design more into this frame of STS and ANT. That said, I think there is still somewhere to go within this thinking with regards to considering the qualities and aesthetic experience of design things.

In recent years there has been a turn in sociology to the economic, itself partly stemming from actor-network theory. This is useful in bridging these slippery concepts of design culture and neoliberalism. Georg Simmel's 1907 text, *The Philosophy of Money*, has been reconsidered, particularly in the context of his discussions of value. Simmel drew attention to value's relational aspect—that it depends on understandings and interactions between actors (Canto Milà 2005). A design culture also involves enrollment into shared sets of understandings, knowledge, and outlooks that also engender value and its circulation. Studies of the stock market and financialization that draw on ANT are also useful (e.g. Knorr Cetina and Bruegger 2000; Mackenzie 2009) in highlighting the contingencies of people and objects within a system. Finally, a revindication of the notion of territory in human geography helps to (literally) ground considerations of design culture, design activism, and neoliberalism (e.g. Massey 2004; Painter 2010). This paper picks up on the lacuna of studies in design and political economy, and through drawing on some of the insights that have come from ANT and recent economic sociology, develops some themes that might also help us understand the relationships of design culture and design activism.

There is an asymmetry here. The term "design culture" suggests a state of being—something that is the result of actions. "Design activism" implies intention—an enthusiasm to act on a situation. Elsewhere (Julier 2006), I have distinguished between "Design Culture" (upper case) and "design culture" (lower case). The former was proposed as an academic field of inquiry to explore the relationships of contemporary design practice, production, and consumption. The latter usage, which this article foregrounds, still embraces these three considerations but is a descriptive term used in a variety of contexts, from the design studio to localities to the nation, but also in different scales of commercial design practice. Design cultures are made up of active agents, but their concatenation itself also has agency, albeit that this agency is often less explicitly declared. Thus, a design culture is largely produced through circumstances. It is reactive. Design activism is a movement that is more self-consciously and more knowingly responsive to circumstances. It is politicized.

"Design activism" is a relatively recent term. As we shall see, in the context of this article, my chief focus is on activist design, work that functions both in a utilitarian and a politicizing sense. This contrasts with activities and artifacts, such as writing manifestos or designing political posters, whose sole purpose is changing attitudes. Rather, I take design activism to include the development of new processes and artifacts, where their starting points are overtly social, environmental, and/or political issues, but where they also intervene functionally in these. Designers, professional and otherwise, curators, critics, and historians are still experimenting with alternative modes of practice and representation to the dominant narrative of design culture. Indeed, to return to the question of periodization, design activism in its various forms is arguably the first recognizably international movement in design since the radical design era of the 1970s. What came between as recognizable groupings—such as post-punk graphics—were stylistic tendencies.

This article begins by examining the relationships of design culture and neoliberalism. I firstly account for the rise of design culture within the processes of neoliberalism that privilege deregulation, marketization, privatization, and financialization. In particular, I am interested in how neoliberalism, and design culture, relies on systems of relationality while also constantly being future-orientated. As part of this, design culture draws on, leverages, or appropriates what exists on its edges—a tactic that is more general to neoliberalism as well. I then argue that, while the rise of design activism legitimately contests this, this is not to say that it will replace design culture wholesale. Nor will neoliberalism give way to a postneoliberal world. The flexibility of neoliberalism and design culture ensures their predominance. Nonetheless, neoliberalism and design culture themselves contain strategies and features that are open to (re)appropriation by design activism. Thus, ultimately, while this article focuses more on the traffic from design culture to design activism, there may also be an emergent dependency between the two.

The examples I draw on are illustrative and certainly not exhaustive. My primary geopolitical focus is on European and North American conceptions and practices. Further study, particularly outside these, may contest, modify, or provide alternative accounts to my claims.

DESIGN CULTURE AND NEOLIBERALISM

Harvey (2005) points out that it is more accurate to see neoliberalism as "a theory of political economic practices," rather than a complete political ideology. Indeed, neoliberalism has been deployed across a range of political frameworks (witness, for example, its vigorous application within Pinochet's dictatorship in Chile from 1973). Thus, neoliberalism is slippery. Indeed, just as designers "dodge and weave" to find new marketplaces for their skills, creating new needs and desires, so neoliberalism is constantly on the move, finding new territories and combinations. Neoliberalism, like design, is a process of change more than an endpoint.

So how, despite this sense of constant dynamic and change, are design culture and neoliberalism aligned?

To start with, we might understand the rise of design over the last thirty years as one of the fruits of neoliberalism. Deregulation of markets and the running down of state controls ultimately lead to new consumer goods and their repackaging, new shopping malls and media products. Privatization of welfare provision leads to a range of service providers with logos, leaflets, and websites. The privileging of financial flows, including the stock market, makes for company annual reports and new product strategies to be designed. Intellectual property rights, including design patents, ensure corporate differentiation and dominance over markets. Individual and corporate entrepreneurialism rest on design and innovation—and therefore a "creative class"—to ensure this differentiation in the marketplace.

Design culture is thus both a product and description of the wider social and economic processes of this design turn within neoliberalism. A well-trodden explanation of this turn is that this is part of a shift from organized to disorganized capitalism, from Fordist to post-Fordist systems, and from classical liberalism to neoliberalism. This has resulted in the growth of the importance of cultural goods and the more refined management of the interface between producer and consumer (Offe 1985; Lash and Urry 1987, 1994). As more producers enter freely into markets, so they have to find more ways of differentiating themselves and attracting our attention. This leads to design's role in the so-called "aestheticization of everyday life," where greater attention is paid to the formal presentation of goods and services, both in their production and consumption (Featherstone 1991).

But let us drill a bit deeper into the qualities that design culture embraces. If we are to view the concept of design culture as including the relationalities between designers, producers, and consumers, then we should also analyze and question the strength, scale, speed, and density of the exchanges between them.

To identify a design culture is to highlight the "fit" between its constituent parts (Bell and Jayne 2003). This is dependent on an ease of interchange between production, consumption, and the work of designers, as well as tacit or explicit understandings of how design objects function to carry value within, symbolize, facilitate, or guide interchanges (Julier 2006). The speed and frequency of interchanges between their elements work to legitimate and confer value on design cultures. By the same token, the neoliberal period has produced a voracious appetite for speed of delivery, coined with the new economy's mantra of "better, faster, cheaper." So, for example, products that rely on fast turnarounds between customer feedback, redesign, manufacture, and bringing to market (e.g. Zara or Benetton clothing) produce one kind of design culture. Here the apparent responsiveness to consumer demand on the part of designers and producers, or consumers' engagement with that brand, suggest a shared understanding as to their general qualities and ways of working.

Design cultures are also resolutely territorial. By this, I mean not just geographical, but also intellectual, territory. With regards to the former, for instance, the dense packing of designers, studios, design shops, and trendy restaurants to define "creative quarters" fulfills urban cultural strategies in signifying and promoting the presence of innovative knowledge economies for a global marketplace (e.g. Koskinen 2005; Vickery 2011). With regards to the latter, for example, intellectual property rights, design registrations, patents, or trademarks define and protect, through law, the commercial territory. These territories may therefore be distributed across a global market or concentrated into an urban regeneration strategy; they mark out a space through their intensification. Just as neoliberalism purportedly "frees up" the constraints of economic boundaries, so design cultures move to occupy and develop themselves at various scales within this.

Design cultures also include fixed assets, such as buildings, equipment, communication networks, or primary material resources, but these are also lashed together with human practices. These human practices might include "forms of bodily activities, forms of mental activities … a background knowledge in the form of understanding, know-how, states of emotion and motivational knowledge" (Reckwitz 2002: 249). The constellation of these human and non-human features may be described in order to territorialize a design culture.

The description of such articulations, or, indeed, *articulating* various assets, itself becomes a promotional trope. An articulation occurs when two things work together. This coming together is dependent on spatial and temporal circumstances—being in the right place at the right time—and therefore "is a linkage which is not necessary, determined, absolute and essential for all time" (Hall 1996: 141; Featherstone 2011). Articulation is therefore seen as being dynamic in that it is subject to change and even ephemeral. It is also seen to be productive in that the coming together of elements makes for new understandings and practices. Therefore there is a double meaning in this term "articulation," for it expresses both linking and description. Design exhibitions or magazine articles devoted to national or local design often assemble purviews of their objects or spaces but also their policies, educational resources, consumer practices, and tastes. For example, the jacket blurb from the book accompanying the Victoria & Albert Museum's 2012 exhibition on British design proclaims it as a "stunning record of Britain's rich design culture" (Breward and Wood 2012). However, it is not just these representational devices that articulate and promote a design culture. The concept circulates and is enacted through the objects and people themselves. A design culture comes into being as it is performed and as its constituent parts come together.

More specifically to government policy and commercial concerns, the measurement and valorization of the design industry has also developed and confronted the problems of measuring and auditing it (Julier and Moor 2009). The latter has involved "mapping documents" that attempt to quantify numbers of designers, contribution to Gross Domestic Product, "value-added" properties in terms of extra employment or turnover created, and so on. But they also include the measurement of more material assets, such as the existence of design schools or cultural centers that make up the fixed infrastructures of design cultures (e.g. British Council 2007).

These surveys find parallel challenges in how design consultancies valorize their work for clients (Dorland 2009; Julier 2010). What do you charge your clients for creativity, particularly when you don't know how successful an input will be? How do you calculate this against your fixed costs (e.g. office rental, materials, or equipment)? How much do you pay your enthusiastic, talented junior designers who put in many extra hours of work?

These quandaries exist for design, but reflect wider challenges of valorization in the neoliberal system. This is because this is not just an issue of articulating and quantifying material and immaterial assets. Branding and design are concerned with temporalities in that, like the finance and shares market, they relate to the future as a source of value (Lash and Lury in Julier 2009). It is also to do with the future orientation of creative work in particular and the neoliberal economy in general.

If the objects of design cultures include not only things, environments, visual communication, and digital platforms, but also knowledge, skill, information, and their carriers, both human and non-human, then these also move and change. Design cultures are therefore in a constant dynamic state. In order to further capture this temporal sense, it is perhaps worth thinking in terms of design culture as being continually engaged in producing future value. Design culture is future-directed, in an ongoing state of becoming, and its value is accounted for in terms of the relationship of input and output (Thrift 2008). Thus, it is stable in the way a design culture seeks elements of consensus in order to thrive and function, but also dynamic in the way it is constituted to produce novel and destabilizing scenarios (Slater 2002).

This sense of *in potentia* resonates with the wider conditions of neoliberalism. If a key feature of the era of neoliberalism has been the privileging of its financial institutions— merchant banking, the stock exchange, the International Monetary Fund—then underlying this has been a constant search for sources of future value. Banks, pension funds, stockbrokers, and private investors look for places to put their money where it will reap the biggest returns, pitting the risk of failure against potential large returns. Likewise, much of design is configured to either signal or unlock future value. How much might be spent on it is calculated, again, against what it might provide in terms of such things as new customers, secure brand loyalty, repeat visits, or, particularly in the built environment, the rise of land values.

Brand valuation assesses the reputational assets of products or services by, for example, how well they are known, how are they thought of, what loyalty they command. By turning qualitative information into quantitative data, value is calculated (Lindemann 2010; Moor and Lury 2011). This exposes the fact that a brand's value is less dependent on the fixed resources of a corporation than on the enthusiasm of its customers. (Needless to say, this is why they ask us to "follow [them] on Facebook or Twitter.") Drawing from the work of Lazzarato (1997), Arvidsson (2005) calls this enthusiasm "ethical surplus." He argues that brands work to muster "leftover" interest among the public that might otherwise be applied elsewhere. Ethical surplus is to be found in the values of sharing and respect that do not necessarily exist at the core of economic practices. You can go to work and do the job without hanging out with your colleagues or being a "team-player." You can consume products without being interested in their brand characteristics or chatting with your friends about them. But these social practices enrich and augment the economic sphere. The value of a thing depends on leveraging interest outside itself.

We can pin this observation back into the workings of the design industry and design culture itself. Needless to say, designers are also implicated in devising strategies to engage enthusiasm and loyalty among consumers. Again, this is about potential value—how the work of consumers down the line can add to the product. Furthermore, and extending, feedback loops from consumers (e.g. through brand websites and social media), and even where they directly engage in production (e.g. through Open Source systems), contribute to this. Arvidsson (2008) identifies this as a part of the developing socialization of capital (people, and groups of people, are seen as a resource), which is mobilized through cultural practices.

And what of those hardworking (and playing?) junior designers? Does their sociality also function as capital? This is certainly how Angela McRobbie (2002) sees them: their value as workers is dependent on a long-hours culture, precarious employment patterns and a willingness to engage beyond the nine-to-five day in "network sociality" (e.g. going to bars, exhibition openings, and design events to widen and consolidate professional contacts). They lend their ethical surplus to the business of design. In their flexibility, creative workers have been mobilized as a vanguard of some of the labor conditions of neoliberalism.

Design's heterogeneity, born of a lack of professional norms and a breadth of application and reception, sees to its flexibility. Just as neoliberalism strategically takes advantage of calamities and crises (Klein 2007), so new specialisms in design have continually emerged in response to them by dint of opportunism. Designers are adept at reinventing themselves for their clients by thinking through new ways of attracting their attention, accounting for their services. As cultural intermediaries, theirs is the work of "needs production" (Bourdieu 1984). Furthermore, they are able to re-scale their operations. Through the neoliberal period, designers have become progressively "lighter" in their operations. Freelancing has continued to dominate the industry; capital costs remain very low. This flexibility is matched by a resilience to withstand a long-hours culture as clients continue to drive down billings and expect designers to turn round more projects faster (British Design Innovation 2007).

Neoliberalism "operates amongst its others." It "invariably exists in an essentially parasitical relationship with those extant social formations with which it has an antagonistic relationship" (Peck et al. 2009: 104). By this, Peck and colleagues were referring to neoliberalism as an ongoing process of transforming and restructuring (e.g. privatizing state welfare provision, lifting trade barriers, deregulating labor). This may be seen on a global scale in terms of its search for new territories to operate in (e.g. the Far East or Arab nations).

We might also see neoliberalism as a continual process of renewing (or, indeed, redesigning) itself. This is done by drawing its "others" into its own workings. Within this paradigm and with reference back to creative work and design culture, we can cite the classic appropriation of the marginality of cultural production into the mainstream or, otherwise, the marketization of the tortured artist, as so brilliantly described by Frith and Horne (1987). But this doesn't always have to be the case....

DESIGN ACTIVISM, NEOLIBERALISM, AND POSTNEOLIBERALISM

What if designers have reached a tipping point? What if some creative workers are no longer willing to lend their "ethical surplus" out?

A recent in-depth inquiry into UK designers reveals profound dissatisfaction with working conditions in their industry. The Design Industry Voices 2011 report draws on a survey of 496 people working in design and digital media agencies and presents statistics to demonstrate that work in the design industry is not necessarily a happy place. Fewer opportunities for professional development, greater client expectations for less money, and more frequent use of unpaid interns are reported. But the sentiment with regards to dissatisfaction is best summed up by the following observation from a design agency director:

> "Whereas before candidates might have been happy to work hard on pitches into the evening on the hope that they will be rewarded later down the line with a bonus or time off in lieu [they] are now rejecting companies who are known to work their staff hard unless they get assurances in writing that they will be rewarded in some way for their hard work." (Cited in Design Industry Voices 2011: 2)

It may seem odd that candidates for design jobs are taking such a strident line in what is broadly a recession-hit industry. In a small way, this example suggests a limited politicization of designers. It may be that the downturn for the creative industries in some parts of the world has provoked reconsideration, providing an opportunity for designers to take stock of their conditions and motivations.

Beyond a realization of the straightforward exploitation of their own "ethical surplus," designers share a broader set of tumultuous political and economic circumstances in the West that may bring about politicization and a search for alternative models of everyday practice. These circumstances include the following:

- a superpower and its allies entrenched in protracted and expensive conflict far from its own territories;
- this conflict and previous state-expenditure commitments causing unprecedented high levels of national debt;
- economic recession leading to wage stagnation, particularly for the middle classes;

- the rapidly rising price of oil and other commodities causing high inflation and therefore a huge loss of expendable outcome;
- resulting political unrest that includes a turn away from party politics to issue-based concerns;
- a growing awareness of the connectivity of everyday concerns to global ones, particularly in relation to environmental issues.

All of these circumstances may also be cited within the early 1970s. And it is leading up to and through that period that a panoply of radical thinking in design emerged. It gave us the radical design of Italians—groups like Superstudio, Archizoom, and UFO, who theorized the idea of a possible network society where information systems would provide alternative structures for consumer culture. The early 1970s gave us "community architecture," wherein end-users of planning and building would have an active role in specifying form, itself pre-figuring co-creation and participatory design. The year 1972 saw the publication of key seminal books that influenced design thinking, such as Victor Papanek's *Design for the Real World*.

Permaculture, another invention of the early 1970s, developed design and planning models for low-energy-input food and sustainable food production. The appropriate technology movement also emerged in this era.

Whilst the 1970s and our contemporary period in the West share quite similar geopolitical features, our experience of and response to them will be distinct. The world is a different place. Rather, I want to make the somewhat obvious point that design activist impulses to develop new ways of working coincide with geopolitical, economic, and environmental crises.

To turn more to contemporary design activism, it is perhaps more precise to view it as a broad movement that partially overlaps with a range of practices, including social design, community design, participatory design, and critical design. As such, it ranges across all sectors of design and beyond to some practices in architecture, art, landscape architecture, and planning.

As one might expect, there is a time lag between design activism's actual happening and being brought into consciousness through its articulation. Recent publications have placed it variously in the frameworks of the production of artifacts within social movements, as a shift in the aims and methodologies of design, or as an iterative set of political contestations (Thorpe 2008; Fuad-Luke 2009; DiSalvo 2012). But here I wish to place the emphasis of design activism on its entanglements with the *realpolitik* of its actions. By this, my chief concern is not to produce further "wish lists" for design activists or report on experiments undertaken in the safety of the academic studio. Rather, I am drawing on observations of attempts to embed design activism into everyday life through its intervention with real people in real places. This is in part drawn from my own practice (see Julier 2011; Unsworth et al. 2011).

The pragmatic gesture of design activism that goes beyond manifestos or declarations is underlined by Markussen (2013: 38), who argues that, in design activism, "The design act is not a boycott, strike, protest, demonstration, or some other political act, but lends its power of resistance from being precisely a *designerly* way of intervening into people's lives" (2013: 38). As it involves the development of artifacts that exist in real time and space, it is situated within everyday contexts and processes of social and economic life. As intervention, it moves within the challenges of pre-existing circumstances, while also attempting to reorientate these. In this way, design activism also operates amongst its others. It exploits certain conditions of neoliberalism, to recycle and reprogram them.

Meanwhile, though, for many of the world's junior designers, their exploitation will continue, as will neoliberalism. One only has to look to the BRIC countries (Brazil, Russia, India, and China) to see how neoliberalism and GDP growth continues apace. Where neoliberalism thrives, so will design cultures. But even for those countries in long-term recession or merely bumping along, combined with all the other global challenges mentioned, a turn to a postneoliberal environment where power relations, the role of capital, and care for the environment are radically different is, I'm afraid to say, unlikely.

Neoliberalism is flexible. It is adept at exploiting crises. It is willing to reschedule and displace crises, for example, with the successive state bailouts of financial institutions. Even if, as an intellectual project, neoliberalism is dead, it may well be entering its "zombie period," where it continues to function, its institutions and power still intact. A growth model of economics mostly still dominates, globally (Peck et al. 2009). However, as an aside, one must keep in view geopolitical contexts, such as parts of South America, that offer alternatives to neoliberal modes (see Kennedy and Tilly 2008; Escobar 2010).

Elsewhere, there may be more dovetailing between design culture and design activism. Design activism may invoke a postneoliberal way of doing political economy while also existing in a predominantly neoliberal framework. Neoliberalism is here to stay in some form or other. But as design culture, understood here as an expression of neoliberalism, is made up of an assemblage of mainstream and marginal practices, so design activism can interweave with and exploit the conditions of neoliberalism.

FROM DESIGN CULTURE TO DESIGN ACTIVISM

Design culture and design activism exist in relationship to one other. In this final section, I wish to pick up four themes that exist both within mainstream design culture and design activism. These have been laced into the earlier section on "Design Culture and Neoliberalism." But here I want to be explicit in their usage. These are:

- intensification—which describes here a density of designerly intervention;
- co-articulation—which describes the marrying up of concerns or practices in a way that strengthens both;
- temporality—which describes the way that speed, slowness, or even open-endedness may be dealt with;
- territorialization—which describes the scale through which responsibility is conceived.

Neoliberalism includes the competition of monopolies. Competitiveness is not just between products or services for market share, but between brands, underpinned by intellectual property rights. Brands work through difference based on knowledge that is constructed relationally through multiple sites (Lury 2004). Each brand is singular in that while it may deliver a product that is relatively undifferentiated, in its performance (for example, petrol is just petrol), its way of operating, its way of interfacing with other clients or customers, its "instruction manuals," if you like, are distinct from those competing brands. Thus, designers are frequently involved in the design of "meta-data" (Sutton 2009). This means that they don't necessarily always design the end-product; rather, codes or guidelines are created that are subsequently applied by someone else. More ordinarily, the corporate identity, brand, or franchise manual is what the designer develops, itself to be rolled out and implemented by others. Equally, one could argue that the designer is always working with individual artifacts (through, for example, prototypes, drawings, or specifications) that are subsequently serially reproduced. They are fashioning singularities. Commerce turns these singularities, or intensities, into extensities through their circulation (Lash 2010).

Intellectual property is therefore at the core of this, and it is here that those intensities are tightly defined and protected by law. For example, in 2012, Apple Inc. was awarded $1 billion in damages against Samsung for a variety of patent infringements. Samsung's response was summed up in their words, "It is unfortunate that patent law can be manipulated to give one company a monopoly over rectangles with rounded corners" (Samsung cited by Arthur 2012). This comments on the pursuit of the use of intellectual property rights to maintain monopoly through design patent. The case also illustrates ways by which design is mobilized and intensified in this process. And in doing so, the designer is involved in the engineering of affect (Thrift 2004).

This emphasis on the affective in design can be taken a few steps further so that the cognitive and embodied engagement with material becomes a way of transforming outlooks. Two examples of urban design activism illustrate this. Heads Together's grassing over of a residential street in the city of Leeds in the UK was a tool to open up the imagination of neighborhood inhabitants and provoke a debate about what the street could be there for (Julier 2009). Similarly, Santiago Cirugeda's placing of skips in the streets of Seville and turning them into play objects questions and challenges ideas of public space and the street through their actual use (Markussen 2013).

It is therefore in this realm of affect that design activism picks up on and reuses mainstream design culture's tactic of **intensification**. Forms make political statements, but they also engage bodily dispositions and human emotions. The difference, however, is that this process in various forms of design culture seeks to engender enthusiasms and exploit ethical surplus for its own ends (for example, to maintain brand loyalty or a creative quarter). Leading on from Markussen (2013), within design activism, it is hoped that this intensification has a direct effect to produce new forms of cognition and practice and also politicizes.

The projects cited above slightly pre-date what I have identified as our current era of design activism. They feature attempts to disrupt the divisions between "above" and "below the line" design. They materially engage both end-users and policymakers at the same time through the affective domain. They are singularities, but ones whose ideas and applications may be rolled out further. They also try to create new relationships and marry interests by engaging existing, but untapped, interests, political concerns, everyday preoccupations, and ethical surplus. They seek a wider, systemic level of intervention than the mere delivery of discreet public services. Here, the design—its material outcome—gives focus to wider concerns that might be articulated in general, rhetorical terms: "I'm worried about the ways that private cars create pollution and global warming"; "There should be more possibilities for the community to meet"; and so on. But it also provides something through which these concerns can be acted on and thought through more.

This is where design works in a process of **co-articulation**. Here, objects function as a "materialization of participation" (Marres 2011: 516); they facilitate a performative engagement in public life without disembedding from the everyday. Users do not have to go "out there" to demonstrate their concerns. Instead, the (activist) object is something through which these concerns are looped within everyday practice. Again, within design culture, objects (such as the trendy bar in a creative quarter like Clerkenwell) can signify a creative quarter, but they are also enrolled into the functioning of that particular design culture, as are their users. Equally, using an iPhone enrolls you into the culture of Apple products. These are self-serving to their specific articulations. The design-activist object also enrolls, but toward ends outside itself, such as communitarian concerns for the environment. We have seen how the speed of exchange within design cultures works to valorize and legitimate them. This notion may include slow as well as fast and is also to be found in activist approaches. Examples include, here, *Città slow* or the Transition Towns movement (Parkins and Craig 2006; Hopkins 2008). However, we may also see **temporality** functioning in other ways.

In the two urban design activism examples cited, rather than seeing the lifetime of a project as being determined by client commission, through development to delivery, the activist is working in a more open-ended way that goes beyond the materialization of the design. Here, the designer works with and alongside the user and other interests. Implementation also involves a series of re-designs that doesn't necessarily mean that the design reaches an optimum point. Philosophically, of course, this has resonances with the notion of "wicked problems" (Rittel and Webber 1973). The designer remains embedded with their public and that responsibility becomes a shared one, and one that gives space for the designer to usefully contribute their expertise while engaging users in taking on and continuing to develop results.

The temporal regimes in mainstream design culture are not discreet or closed off. They do not necessarily seek resolution. In the first instance, this is implicit in the notion of "unfinished objects" that has been developed by Knorr Cetina (2001). Within design culture, the object is not singular. Rather, it exists in a variety of forms, either, for example, in the work of the designer as sketches, prototypes, and updates, or, more broadly, in the public sphere, for example as upgrades, repackagings, or a variety of media formats. In this way, it is subject to continual repositioning, heterogeneous modalities of encounter, different levels of learning, and so on. Furthermore, since we are describing complex networks of actors that are relationally configured and themselves in constant change, so the object is subject to constant transformations, either literally or in its meaning. The designer is working within this instability. The design activist is, too, but in order to redirect it.

Equally, we have seen how neoliberalism encourages the unlocking of future sources of value and how design cultures work within this. Likewise, a similar dynamic is at work in design activism. Much of the rhetoric in design and social innovation is directed at tapping into underused resources and freeing up their potential (Manzini and Jégou 2005; Unsworth et al. 2011). Thus, there is also a future orientation in design activism.

The overall ideological drive and language of neoliberalism is replete with aims toward the facilitation of the free global flow of capital and goods, the bringing down of barriers to this, and the speeding up of this movement. Neoliberalism mythologizes the idea of the world as a frictionless, unbounded space. In reality, neoliberalism is relentlessly territorialized. While capital has no sense of place, it is nonetheless moved from place to place, and, indeed, the places it is moved from or to is itself a territory that is marked out by material features and cultural practices (Escobar 2001; Mackenzie 2009).

Indeed, to step back from the global, financialist focus, one may regard, as Massey (2004) has, this territorializing as a "Russian doll effect" that starts at the home. The home provides the primary locus of financial calculations that is deeply entwined with the material. It is in itself a design culture in that the edifice itself, and its decor and contents, as formulated by its actor-inhabitants, are value-producing. Decisions are made that reconcile available money, taste, and future value.

But this is just a starting point of a series of scales that neoliberalism and design cultures act on. Neighborhood planning and design guides, city master plans and economic strategies, national fiscal strategies, and pan-national trading agreements all establish bounded spaces where exchange takes place within and between these scales. Design may be mobilized to mark these boundaries and identities, for example through place-branding and iconic architecture. In policy and planning, the language of capital is loosely attached to design to underline and promote its value, as in, for instance, "cultural capital" or "creative clusters." Design is framed both as an asset to a location and as part of the mechanisms that facilitate trade and the movement of capital between places. Thus, design culture functions in association with a variety of territorial scales.

Design activism may borrow from this "Russian doll effect" of territorialization to assert itself within these "geographies of responsibility," albeit with a different sense of responsibility (Massey 2004). For example, Rosenberg (2011) shows how home improvement aligns a culture of design with neoliberal ideals of asset creation. To return full circle to the notion of co-articulation, the design activist might find ways to reframe this object-subject relationship in order to align the home with other concerns such as climate change (see Marres 2012). Equally, the Transition Towns movement (see www.transitionnetwork.org), with its focus on relocalization, looks to intensify the local systems of exchange, thereby consolidating neighborhoods, their cohesion, resilience, and responsiveness to climate change, and the challenges of a post-carbon economy.

CONCLUSION

The scope of this article is wide. It engages with a process of neo-liberalism that has been under development for forty years and ranges across much of the world. It attempts to elaborate on "design culture"—a broadly used term—and design activism, a movement that is still in emergence. This feels necessary as a contribution to a better conceptual understanding of design culture and design activism, however introductory my arguments are. Space hasn't allowed for more in-depth discussion of the examples cited or expansion into or testing through others.

The contemporary crisis of neoliberalism does not signal a rupture and immediate shift to postneoliberalism. Parallels have been drawn with the fall of the Berlin Wall in 1989 (Peck et al. 2009). But the events of 1989 were largely unforeseen by those on the outside. A crisis of what became neoliberalism, by contrast, was calculated and foreseen even at its birth and then immediately before the financial crisis of 2008 (e.g. Meadows et al. 1972, 2004). Just as neoliberalism engages continuous calculation of its quantitative and qualitative mechanisms and assets, so calculation has revealed its limits, greed, untruths, and violence (e.g. Dorling et al. 2008).

While design activism responds to such knowledge, it has also been spurred on by individuals and groups who want to work in different ways to mainstream commerce. This has necessarily taken them into engagement with neoliberal effects, for instance by working within and between the fragmented and privatized elements of public-sector delivery. Thus, design activism adopts and reuses many of the tropes to be found in mainstream design culture.

As a system of networks or articulations, design cultures are made up of constellations of human and non-human features. The density of these and the scales on which they work configure them. The speed and strength of their relationships also mark out their qualities. Design cultures *are*. They come about and have been formed within neoliberal frameworks. Design activism *acts on them*. It enters into the networks of design culture (and neoliberalism) and looks to produce other futures.

Neoliberalism and design culture are engaged in continual leveraging of assets outside themselves—theirs is the work of transformation. Likewise, design activism looks to mobilize underused assets, leverage enthusiasms, and generally look for future sources of value. This is done through persuasion but, crucially, through everyday practice as well. The objects of design culture and design activism are affective; designers provide intensifications that give materiality. Through this, they orientate life in various directions. It is up to us to decide which direction we wish to enroll in.

REFERENCES

Arthur, Charles. 2012. "Apple Awarded More Than $1bn in Samsung Patent Infringement Trial." *The Guardian* (August 25). Available online: www.guardian.co.uk (accessed August 30, 2012).

Arvidsson, Adam. 2005. "Brands: A Critical Perspective." *Journal of Consumer Culture*, 5(2): 235–58.

Arvidsson, Adam. 2008. "The Ethical Economy of Customer Coproduction." *Journal of Macromarketing*, 28(4): 326–38.

Bell, David and Mark Jayne. 2003. "'Design-led' Urban Regeneration: A Critical Perspective." *Local Economy*, 18(2): 121–34.

Bourdieu, Pierre. 1984. *Distinction: A Social Critique of the Judgement of Taste*. Trans. Richard Nice. Cambridge, MA: Harvard University Press.

Breward, Christopher and Ghislaine Wood. 2012. *British Design from 1948: Innovation in the Modern Age*. London: V&A Publications.

British Council. 2007. *Mapping of Creative Industries in Albania*. Albania: British Council.

British Design Innovation. 2007. *The British Design Industry Valuation Survey 2006 to 2007*. Brighton: BDI.

Bryson, John and Grete Rusten. 2011. *Design Economies and the Changing World Economy: Innovation, Production and Competitiveness*. Abingdon: Routledge.

Canto Milà, Natália. 2005. *A Sociological Theory of Value: Georg Simmel's Sociological Relationism*. New Jersey: Transaction Publishers.

Design Industry Voices. 2011. "Design Industry Voices 2011: How It Feels to Work in British Digital and Design Agencies Right Now." Available online: www.designindustryvoices.com (accessed August 27, 2012).

DiSalvo, Carl. 2012. *Adversarial Design*. Massachusetts: MIT Press.

Dorland, AnneMarie. 2009. "Routinized Labour in the Design Studio." In G. Julier and L. Moor (eds), *Design and Creativity: Policy, Management and Practice*. Oxford: Berg.

Dorling, D., M. Newman, and A. Barford. A. 2008. *The Atlas of the Real World: Mapping the Way We Live*. London: Thames & Hudson.

Escobar, Arturo. 2001. "Culture Sits in Places: Reflections on Globalism and Subaltern Strategies of Localization." *Political Geography*, 20(2): 139–74.

Escobar, Arturo. 2010. "Latin America at a Crossroads: Alternative Modernizations, Post-liberalism, or Post-development?" *Cultural Studies*, 24(1): 1–65.

Fallan, Kjetil. 2008. "Architecture in Action – Traveling with Actor-Network Theory in the Land of Architectural Research." *Architectural Theory Review*, 13(1): 80–96.

Featherstone, David. 2011. "On Assemblage and Articulation." *Area*, 43(2): 139–42.

Featherstone, Mike. 1991. *Consumer Culture and Postmodernism*. London: Sage.

Frith, Simon and Howard Horne. 1987. *Art into Pop*. London: Routledge.

Fry, Tony. 2010. *Design as Politics*. Oxford: Berg.

Fuad-Luke, Alastair. 2009. *Design Activism: Beautiful Strangeness for a Sustainable World*. London: Earthscan.

Hall, Stuart. 1985. "Signification, Representation, Ideology: Althusser and the Post-Structuralist Debates." *Critical Studies in Mass Communication*, 2(2): 91–114.

Hall, Stuart. 1996. "On Postmodernism and Articulation." In D. Morley and K.-H. Chen (eds), *Stuart Hall: Critical Dialogues in Cultural Studies*, pp. 131–50. London: Routledge.

Harvey, David. 2005. *A Brief History of Neoliberalism*. Oxford: Oxford University Press.

Heskett, John. 2008. "Creating Economic Value by Design." *International Journal of Design*, 3(1): 71–84.

Hopkins, Rob. 2008. *The Transition Handbook: From Oil Dependency to Local Resilience*. Totnes: Green Books.

Julier, Guy. 2006. "From Visual Culture to Design Culture." *Design Issues*, 22(1): 64–76.

Julier, Guy. 2009. "Value, Relationality and Unfinished Objects: Guy Julier Interview with Scott Lash and Celia Lury." *Design and Culture*, 1(1): 93–113.

Julier, Guy. 2010. "Playing the System: Design Consultancies, Professionalisation and Value." In B. Townley and N. Beech (eds), *Managing Creativity: Exploring the Paradox*, pp. 237–59. Cambridge: Cambridge University Press.

Julier, Guy. 2011. "Political Economies of Design Activism and the Public Sector." Paper presented at NORDES 2011: Making Design Matter conference, Aalto University, Helsinki, Finland. Available online: http://ocs.sfu.ca/nordes.

Julier, Guy and Liz Moor (eds). 2009. *Design and Creativity: Policy, Management and Practice.* Oxford: Berg.

Kennedy, Marie and Chris Tilly. 2008. "Making Sense of Latin America's 'Third Left.'" *New Politics*, 11(4): 11–16.

Kimbell, Lucy. 2011. "Rethinking Design Thinking: Part 1." *Design and Culture*, 3(3): 285–306.

Kimbell, Lucy. 2012. "Rethinking Design Thinking: Part 2." *Design and Culture*, 4(2): 129–48.

Klein, Naomi. 2007. *Shock Doctrine: The Rise of Disaster Capitalism.* New York: Metropolitan Books.

Knorr Cetina, Karin. 2001. "Objectual Practice." In T.R. Schatzki, K. Knorr Cetina, and E. von Savigny (eds), *The Practice Turn in Contemporary Theory.* London and New York: Routledge.

Knorr Cetina, Karin and Urs Bruegger. 2000. "The Market as an Object of Attachment: Exploring Postsocial Relations in Financial Markets." *Canadian Journal of Sociology*, 25(2): 141–68.

Koskinen, Ilpo. 2005. "Semiotic Neighborhoods." *Design Issues*, 21(2): 13–27.

Lash, Scott. 2010. *Intensive Culture: Social Theory, Religion and Contemporary Capitalism.* London: Sage.

Lash, Scott and John Urry. 1987. *The End of Organized Capitalism.* London: Polity. London: Sage.

Lash, Scott and John Urry. 1994. *Economies of Signs and Spaces.* London: Sage.

Latour, Bruno. 2005. *Reassembling the Social: An Introduction to Actor-Network Theory.* Oxford: Oxford University Press.

Lazzarato, Maurizio. 1997. *Lavoro immateriale.* Verona: Ombre Corte.

Lindemann, Jan. 2010. *The Economy of Brands.* London: Palgrave Macmillan.

Lury, Celia. 2004. *Brands: The Logos of a Global Economy.* Abingdon: Routledge.

Mackenzie, Don. 2009. *Material Markets: How Economic Agents are Constructed.* Oxford: Oxford University Press.

Manzini, Ezio and François Jégou. 2005. *Sustainable Everyday: Scenarios of Urban Life.* Milan: Edizione Ambiente.

Markussen, Thomas. 2013. "The Disruptive Aesthetics of Design Activism: Enacting Design between Art and Politics." *Design Issues*, 29(1): 38–50.

Marres, Noortje. 2011. "The Costs of Public Involvement: Everyday Devices of Carbon Accounting and the Materialization of Participation." *Economy and Society*, 40(4): 510–33.

Marres, Noortje. 2012. *Material Participation: Technology, the Environment and Everyday Publics.* Basingstoke: Palgrave Macmillan.

Massey, Doreen. 2004. "Geographies of Responsibility." *Geografiska Annaler*, 86(1): 5–18.

McRobbie, Angela. 2002. "Clubs to Companies: Notes on the Decline of Political Culture in Speeded Up Creative Worlds." *Cultural Studies*, 16(4): 516–31.

Meadows, D.H., D.L. Meadows, and J. Randers. 2004. *Limits to Growth: The 30-year Update.* London: Earthscan.

Meadows, D.H., D.L. Meadows, J. Randers, and W.W. Behrens. 1972. *The Limits to Growth: A Report for the Club of Rome's Project on the Predicament of Mankind.* New York: Universe Books.

Moor, Liz and Celia Lury. 2011. "Making and Measuring Value: Comparison, Singularity and Agency in Brand Valuation Practice." *Journal of Cultural Economy*, 4(4): 439–54.

Offe, Claus. 1985. *Disorganized Capitalism.* Oxford: Polity.

Painter, Joe. 2010. "Rethinking Territory." *Antipode: A Radical Journal of* Geography, 42(5): 1090–1118.

Parkins, Wendy and Geoffrey Craig. 2006. *Slow Living.* Oxford: Berg.

Peck, J., N. Theodore, and N. Brenner. 2009. "Postneoliberalism and Its Malcontents." *Antipode: A Radical Journal of Geography*, 41(6): 94–116.

Reckwitz, Andreas. 2002. "Toward a Theory of Social Practices: A Development in Culturalist Theorizing." *European Journal of Social Theory*, 5(2): 243–63.

Rittel, Horst and Martin Webber. 1973. "Dilemmas in a General Theory of Planning." *Policy Sciences*, 4(2): 155–69.

Rosenberg, Buck. 2011. "Home Improvement: Domestic Taste, DIY, and the Property Market." *Home Cultures*, 8(1): 5–24.

Shove, E., M. Pantzar, and M. Watson. 2012. *The Dynamics of Social Practice: Everyday Life and How It Changes*. London: Sage.

Slater, Don. 2002. "Markets, Materiality and the 'New Economy.'" In J.S. Metcalfe and A. Warde (eds), *Market Relations and the Competitive Process*. Manchester: Manchester University Press.

Sutton, Damian. 2009. "Cinema by Design: Hollywood as Network Neighbourhood." In G. Julier and L. Moor (eds), *Design and Creativity: Policy, Management and Practice*, pp. 174–90. Oxford: Berg.

Thorpe, Ann. 2008. "Design as Activism: A Conceptual Tool." Conference paper presented at Changing the Change, Turin.

Thrift, Nigel. 2004. "Intensities of Feeling: Towards a Spatial Politics of Affect." *Geografiska Annaler*, 86B(1): 57–78.

Thrift, Nigel. 2008. *Non-representational Theory*. Abingdon: Routledge.

Unsworth, R., I. Bauman, S. Ball, P. Chatterton, A. Goldring, K. Hill, and G. Julier. 2011. "Building Resilience and Wellbeing in the Margins within the City: Changing Perceptions, Making Connections, Realising Potential, Plugging Resources Leaks." *City*, 15(2): 181–203.

Vickery, Jonathan. 2011. "Beyond the Creative City: Cultural Policy in an Age of Scarcity." Available online: www.made.org.uk (accessed August 26, 2012).

Wilkie, Alex. 2011. "Regimes of Design, Logics of Users." *Athenea Digital*, 11(1): 317–34.

Yaneva, Albena. 2009. "Making the Social Hold: Towards an Actor-Network Theory of Design." *Design and Culture*, 1(3): 273–88.

CHAPTER THIRTY ONE

Decolonizing Design Innovation: Design Anthropology, Critical Anthropology, and Indigenous Knowledge

ELIZABETH (DORI) TUNSTALL

This chapter proposes the methodology of design anthropology as an answer to how one might create decolonized processes of design and anthropological engagement. I first set out the contexts for the need for decolonized anthropology and design innovation (for instance, the use of design principles and frameworks to generate new or improved business outcomes). I then go on to explore what design anthropology is, its intellectual foundations and its principles, and to describe the first phase of the Aboriginal Smart Art project as a case study of its principles in practice.

THE CONTEXT FOR DECOLONIZATION

In 1991, Faye Harrison published the edited volume, *Decolonizing Anthropology*, in which she and a group of "Third World peoples and their allies" sought: "To encourage more anthropologists to accept the challenge of working to free the study of humankind from the prevailing forces of global inequality and dehumanization and to locate it firmly in the complex struggle for genuine transformation" (Harrison 2010: 10).

In 1991, I had taken my first anthropology course at Bryn Mawr College in the United States. There I learned that the founding fathers of physical anthropology did not think I had the cranial capacity to even be in my class because I was an African American and thus of low intelligence. In spite of that first encounter with anthropology, I stuck with it because there was something powerful about a field devoted to investigating the expanding notions of what it means to be human. But the classical anthropological framing of my peoples, Africans and African Americans, as objects of anthropological inquiry required that I take seriously anthropology's role in the project of colonialism, and also the role of design innovation in continuing projects of neocolonialism and imperialism.

The phrase "handmaiden of colonialism" to describe anthropology is attributed to anthropologist Claude Lévi-Strauss (Asad 1973). The *Stanford Encyclopedia of Philosophy* (Kohn 2011) defines *colonialism* as "a broad concept that refers to the project of European political domination from the sixteenth to the twentieth centuries that ended with the national liberation movements of the 1960s." It distinguishes colonialism from imperialism: with colonialism theoretically aligned with settlement and direct control and imperialism aligned with economic exploitation and indirect control. A wide range of anthropologists in the 1960s and 1970s began to directly address anthropology's implication in colonialism and imperialism. While the review of this literature is outside the scope of this chapter (see Uddin 2005 and Restrepo and Escobar 2005 for two exhaustive accounts), the points of criticism leveled against anthropology can be summarized as:

- classification of peoples, such that it overdetermined their characters and undermined their own self-definitions (Deloria Jr. 1988 [1969]; Hall 1992; Said 1978; Smith 1999);

- framing or representation of peoples as reduced "others" and outside the pale of time, civilization, and rationality (Fabian 1983; Smith 1999; Wolf 1982);

- evaluation of peoples in a hierarchy with European Caucasians in the top position of humanity and others ranked at various levels of subhumanness (Blakey 2010; Smith 1999); and

- lack of utility of its outputs, in the form of text-based ethnographies or films, for improving the quality of life of the peoples engaged as its anthropological objects/ subjects (Deloria Jr. 1988 [1969]; Smith 1999; Tax 1975).

These four kinds of critique represent the hallmarks of colonial, imperialist, and neocolonial anthropology for many indigenous, minority, migrant, and other marginalized communities who have been "coded into the Western system of knowledge" (Smith 1999: 43). What does this have to do with design innovation and design anthropology? As I stated earlier, my personal engagement with the field of anthropology has been about trying to create a space for a decolonized anthropology in light of the discipline's history. It has now also become about securing a space for decolonized design innovation practices.

The Oslo Manual defines *innovation* as "the implementation of a new or significantly improved product (good or service) or process, a new marketing method, or a new organizational method in business practices, workplace organization, or external relations" (OECD 2005: 6). Embedded in this definition of innovation, which I argue is hegemonic in the field, are three assumptive paradigms as it relates to culture. First, individual elites or companies generate innovation (Brown and Ulijn 2004; Jostingmeier and Boeddrich 2005; Light 2008). There is a growing discussion of grassroots innovation that links sustainable consumption with community action (Seyfang and Smith 2007), but it represents only an emergent thread in the innovation discourse. Second, innovation promotes modernist values. Spanish philosopher Rosa Maria Rodriguez Magda (2004) states how innovation was "the very driving force of modernity," which sought to replace old ways of knowing. Third, innovation benefits individual companies, individual entrepreneurs and inventors, or the undifferentiated masses of society. Design innovation, even within the social sector, reflects the modernist agenda of OECD definitions of innovation.

In 2010, on his *Fast Company* blog, Bruce Nussbaum posed a question to the design community that had never been broached so directly: "Is humanitarian design the new imperialism?" The article raised provocative questions about the ethics of humanitarian design projects such as Project H, Acumen Fund's Water Project in India, and One Laptop Per Child: "Are designers the new anthropologists or missionaries, come to poke into village life, *understand* it and make it better—their *modern* way?" (Nussbaum 2010a: 1). The response from diverse sectors of the design community was swift as those such as Emily Pilloton of Project H (2010) dismissed Nussbaum's article as a gross oversimplification of their on-the-ground-work with communities. Niti Bhan, the only commentator whose non-Western voice in the debate was promoted in the Design Observer round up (Editors 2010), reminded people *from the* OECD *world* that, to paraphrase, mutual respect, reciprocity, and political history and reality were not acknowledged in the issues raised. How could it be otherwise? Who are the generators, what are the underlying values, and who are the beneficiaries of innovation remain the issues for design innovation as a subset of the innovation discourse. Nussbaum's two follow-up articles partly opened up these issues. The first one raised the specter of the "unintended consequences" of humanitarian design by probing the underlying values and the true beneficiaries of design innovations in the social sector (Nussbaum 2010b). The second one provocatively opened the issue of the origins of innovation by showing how humanitarian designers forge relationships with local elites (Nussbaum 2010c). This focus on local elites is important because it is they who determine, not those from the OECD world, whether design innovation is the handmaiden of colonialism or imperialism today. What is it that they say? What might be their critiques of design innovation?

Surprising, in the major academic journals on design (for example *Design Issues* and *Design Studies*), there is limited discussion by Asian, African, Middle Eastern, or Latin American scholars of design and imperialism or colonialism. Main critiques of imperialism and colonialism are written by Caucasian scholars in ex-colonial peripheries of Australia (Fry 1989) and South Africa (Van Eaden 2004). Exceptions are found in the 1989 *Design Issues* special issue on "Design in Asia and Australia" with the contributions of Shou Zhi Wang (1989) on modern Chinese design and Rajeshwari Ghose (1989) on design and development in Asia, with a focus on India. Ghose's article in particular outlines a critique of design and development's ideological biases in how it classifies, represents, models, and evaluates the Indian nation and people. She states:

"No wonder then that neither of the terms design nor development have natural equivalents in most of the Asian linguistic traditions, for they carry with them all the ideological underpinnings of First World associations, aspirations, and debates. This realization and, more recently, the deep dissatisfaction that has followed this realization, both from an ideological/cultural as well as a pragmatic point of view, has led to some very serious soul searching among the thinking designers of Asia in recent years." (1989: 39)

Outside of academic journals, one finds strong critical voices on design and development in blogs and conference presentations by design scholars and practitioners such as Arvind Lodaya, M. P. Ranjan, and Niti Bhan of India, Ravi Naidoo of South Africa, Adelia Borges of Brazil, and Benny Ding Leong of China. Their points of critique are similar to those against anthropology in terms of how hegemonic discourses of design and innovation:

- classify traditional craft as distinct from modern design, excluding the histories and practices of design innovation among Third World peoples (and their allies especially in regards to their responses to colonialism, imperialism, and neo-colonialism) (Borges 2007; Ghose 1989; Lodaya 2003; Ranjan and Ranjan 2005);
- frame design thinking as a progressive narrative of global salvation that ignores the alternative ways of thinking and knowing of Third World peoples and their allies (Leong and Clark 2003; Lodaya 2007);
- evaluate European, Euro-American, and Japanese design and innovation as the top of the design innovation hierarchy (Jepchumba 2009; Leong and Clark 2003; Lodaya 2006; Ranjan 2006); and
- the lack of outputs because many design innovations are prototypes that have not been fully implemented, and thus have limited positive impact on communities.

A high-profile example of how design innovation can act in an imperialist way is the IDEO and the Rockefeller Foundation's Design for Social Impact initiative. The next section will briefly introduce the project and how it relates to the points of critique outlined previously.

THE IMPERIALISM OF DESIGN

In 2008, the Rockefeller Foundation invited IDEO, a global design consultancy, to explore how "design and how the design industry can play a larger role in the social sector" (IDEO and Rockefeller Foundation 2008a: 5). The first outcomes of this study were the *Design for Social Impact How-to Guide* (2008a) and the *Design for Social Impact Workbook* (2008b). Both texts seek to demonstrate how design thinking as a human-centered design process can contribute to "transformation change in communities" (IDEO and Rockefeller Foundation 2008a: 2). Although the initiative is focused on communities, it follows the hegemonic paradigm of innovation in terms of its framing of who generates innovation, its underlying values, and who benefits.

In the Design for Social Impact initiative, Western design companies generate innovation, which places them at the top of the design innovation process. The texts are "intended for design companies of any size or type," to guide them so that they can sell their services to nongovernmental organizations (NGOs) and start-ups that operate in the social innovation sector, mostly in India and South Africa (IDEO and Rockefeller Foundation 2008a: 4). Through a content analysis of the photographic images, illustrations, and texts of the *Design for Social Impact How-to Guide*, I found that Western design companies are represented as active agents who guide, serve, embed, build, pay, and staff (the design processes). On the other hand, Indian and African institutions are represented as those to be passively guided and directed or to serve as sabbatical hosts, sites for capacity building, philanthropic tourist destinations, and support staff for projects (IDEO and Rockefeller Foundation 2008a). Why does it matter that Indian and African (not to mention Chinese, Brazilian, Mexican, and other non-OECD nations) design companies are not also the audiences for the *How-to-Guide*? Ghose discusses how Asian design is directly tied to issues of "technology/design transfers from the First World, as well as problems associated with adapting new or changing technology to diverse economic, social, cultural, and political conditions" (1989: 32). By framing non-Western design companies outside of the discourse of *Design for Social Impact*, the IDEO document positions Western design companies in a unique hierarchical position enabling them to guide non-Western institutions on how to solve problems. This elides the history of non-Western design innovation in which designers in India and Africa have creatively responded to the challenges posed to their communities, often in connection with processes of imperialism, colonialism, and neocolonialism.

In the Design for Social Impact initiative, values of design thinking draw from a progressive narrative of global salvation that ignores non-Western ways of thinking rooted in craft practices that predate yet live alongside modern manufacturing techniques. The general absence of Indian, African, Asian, Middle Eastern, or any other non-Western knowledge, with the exception of C. K. Prahalad, in the over twenty bibliographic and Internet resources at the end of the *How-to Guide* reflects the disregard for local knowledge and the intention to supplant it with Western design thinking as the dominant methodology (IDEO and Rockefeller Foundation 2008a). In a World Bank Institute article entitled "Design Thinking for Social Innovation: IDE," Tim Brown and Jocelyn Wyatt describe the specific contributions of design thinking to social challenges. "As an approach, design thinking taps into capacities we all have but that are overlooked by more conventional problem-solving practices … [It] relies on our ability to be intuitive, to recognize patterns, to construct ideas that have emotional meaning as well as being functional, and to express ourselves in media other than words or symbols" (2010: 30). Brown and Wyatt (2010) posit design thinking as an alternative to linear, rational, and conventional approaches to problem solving. In its human-centered approach, design thinking is said to respect local knowledge through its processes of gathering user needs and codesigning through iterative prototyping. Yet postcolonial and feminist critiques of Western models of linear and rationalist thinking have been well established since the 1960s and predate IDEO's design thinking. In fact, design thinking sounds similar to what Rajeshwari Ghose expressed in the late 1980s as the task of Asian designers: "Here too [Asian] designers have the dual task of documenting and understanding ethnicity and regional cultures, for understanding them is the essential first step to evolving a medium of visual communication and restoring local confidence in an age when traditional institutions are crumbling fast and benefits of industrialization are yet to trickle down" (1989: 40–41).

While design thinking represents an advance in Western business thought, what does it mean to bring design thinking to places that already have their own indigenous forms of thinking also critical of linear and rational models? Saki Mafundiwa raises this issue in his description of the epiphany that inspired him to create ZIVA, the Zimbabwe Institute for Vigital Arts:

"These were Afrikan-trained designers—unlike me, an Afrikan trained in the west. Soon I realized that force-feeding Afrikans design principles born in Europe, principles that were the product of the European experience, just doesn't work … Afrikans have their own palettes that have no kinship with the principles of color devised by such schools of thought as the Bauhaus. Why do we ignore those? The rest of the world would love to understand this Afrikan sense of color! Tapestries woven by "unschooled" craftspeople grace some of the world's major museums and private collections—stunning testimonials to the Afrikan creative genius." (Jepchumba 2009: sec. 1, par. 10)

Saki's efforts to train his Afrikan students in Afrikan ways of knowing expose how, notwithstanding the good intentions by IDEO, bringing design thinking and other nonnative principles to India, Africa, or China, for example, risks becoming another form of cultural imperialism that destabilizes and undermines indigenous approaches coming out of other creative traditions. To this last point, Rajeshwari Ghose makes an important statement: "If design is perceived as an ancient activity that has gone on for several centuries rather than as a brand new profession, then our whole perception of what constitutes Asian design begins to change and, thenceforth, issues pertaining to Asian design assume different forms" (1989: 36).

In the Design for Social Impact initiative introduced earlier, the main beneficiaries of innovation are the participating companies and individuals as well as general society, while community benefits are limited by the lack of sustainable implementation of design prototypes. As outlined in the *How-to Guide*, each strategic approach is evaluated against its "benefit to the company" and "social impact" (IDEO and Rockefeller Foundation 2008a: 41). The benefits to the company are all clearly enunciated through the listing of what happens to each strategy when it works (for the company), both pros and cons. Although they define *social impact* as the "capacity of this type of work to create positive social change on communities and individuals," it is represented only as a graphical circle without descriptions of what that social impact might be (IDEO and Rockefeller Foundation 2008a: 41). More important, the Design for Social Impact initiative explicitly seeks to transfer the resources of philanthropic foundations and local NGOs to Western design companies. The extent to which this places the initiative in direct competition with local design companies means that while its intentions may be good, it outcomes are likely imperialistic. It resembles what Linda Smith refers to as the new wave of imperialist processes that "enter with goodwill in their front pocket and patents in their back pocket" (1999: 24). Thus, IDEO's Design for Social Impact initiative demonstrates how even a design innovation project with good intentions can be implicated in continuing practices of imperialism. While IDEO is a good company representing *good* people-centered design processes, it fails to respect the value systems of those communities it seeks to help. Design anthropology is proposed as a methodology that can reframe both anthropology and design innovation as decolonized practices of cultural engagement.

DESIGN ANTHROPOLOGY: A DECOLONIZED METHODOLOGY

Over the last seven years, I have defined, promoted, and taught design anthropology as a field that seeks to understand how the processes and artifacts of design help to define what it means to be human and that focuses on how design translates values into tangible experiences (Tunstall 2006, 2007, 2008a,b). I am proposing design anthropology as a methodology rather than a method, because what is at stake for me are the principles and rules for regulating the disciplines of design and anthropology to avoid neocolonization and imperialism. By *decolonized*, I refer to the status of being "self-governing or independent" (Dictionary.com 2011). Thus, what I mean by a *decolonized methodology* is a system of methods, principles, and rules free from the biases of the last five centuries of colonization and imperialism, and that thus contributes to the self-definition and self-determination of those formerly colonized. I seek to argue that design anthropology has great potential to become a decolonized methodology for engaging with social issues.

This, of course, is not the only definition of design anthropology. Sperschneider, Kjaersgaard, and Peterson define it as the bricolage of "making sense of what is there with remaking what is there to something new" (2001:1). The University of Aberdeen in its Masters of Science (Design Anthropology) program defines it as "a novel and exciting interface where the speculative imagination of possible futures meets the comparative study of human ways of living and knowing" (Leach 2011: sec. 1). Joachim Halse suggests that design anthropology is a provocation "that portrays the culture of use in terms of the culture of design" (2008: 31). Paula Gray defines it as "ethnographically-informed design of new products, services and systems for consumers and businesses" (2010:1). Two aspects of my definition of design anthropology distinguish it from others. The first is that my definition is not just about the application of anthropological theories and methods toward the better design of products, services, and systems. As I have stated elsewhere, "It allows for the possibility of saying stop to the design process" when the ethics of engagement are questioned (Tunstall 2008a: 28). The second is that "the outcomes of design anthropology include statements providing some deeper understanding of human nature as well as designed communications, products, and experiences" (Tunstall 2008b: sec. 1, par. 2). My definition of design anthropology draws from core sets of theoretical perspectives—the critical anthropology of "Third World peoples and their allies," indigenous and Scandinavian traditions of cooperative/participatory design, and indigenous, critical, feminist, ontological, and phenomenological knowledge traditions. In the following sections, I address how this particular methodological positioning impacts the principles of design anthropology.

PRINCIPLES OF DECOLONIZED UNDERSTANDINGS OF VALUE SYSTEMS AND CULTURES

In an article written for *Adobe Think Tank*, I argued that "Design anthropology does not place separate emphasis on values, or design, or experience, which are the domains of philosophy, academic design research, and psychology, respectively. Rather, design anthropology focuses on the interconnecting threads among all three, requiring hybrid practices" (Tunstall 2008b: sec. 5, par. 2). As a methodology, I propose a design anthropology that adheres to a set of seven principles regarding how one understands and positively impacts on (1) human value systems; (2) the processes and artifacts of designing in making value systems tangible; and (3) the aligning of people's experiences with the values they prefer—all under conditions of unequal power relations. Fredrik Barth has been critical of how anthropologists have used the term *values* without creating an "explicit theory and analysis of values" (1993: 31). I utilize the term *values* in my explanation of design anthropology because it highlights the different perspective that anthropologists have brought in their engagement with the design industries (Tunstall 2006) and it states what is at stake in processes of decolonization (Smith 1999: 74). In the edited volume, *Design Anthropology: Object Culture in the 21st Century*, Maria Bezaitis and Rick Robinson (2011) of E-Lab/Sapient argue that user research needs to get back to its emphasis on values as opposed to just being seen as valuable to industry. Thus, Bezaitis and Robinson contrast two of the three ways of talking about values noted by David Graeber. They promote what Graeber describes as values in the sociological sense "of what is ultimately good, proper, or desirable in human life" (Graeber 2001: 2) as opposed to the economic sense of measurement. What I have found most powerful about the role of anthropology in design is how it reveals the struggle over value systems as people seek to create meaning in their lives and pass them on to future generations. In this I share Barth's notion that studying values in and of themselves is not "a productive strategy … but [as part of social action] directs our attention to an area where collective institutions and representations articulate with individual behaviours" (1993: 44). Here Ton Otto's (2006) work about values and norms is illustrative. As the struggle over values affects people's identities, it also directly affects their ability to pass on those values to future generations. The collective creation of meaning and passing on to future generations is what can be defined as *culture*. As a decolonized methodology, design anthropology draws upon the concept of value systems, which can become cultures through consensus and transmission into the future, expressed in Cuban anthropologist Fernando Ortiz's theory of transculturation:

> "I am of the opinion that the word transculturation better expresses the different phases of the process of transition from one culture to another because it does not consist merely in acquiring another culture (acculturation)… but the process also necessarily involves the

loss or uprooting of a previous culture (deculturation) … and it carries the idea of new cultural phenomena (neoculturation)." (1995 [1945]: 102–103)

The theory of transculturation helps to define three key principles I believe should guide the praxis of design anthropology when it comes to understanding and having positive impact on value systems:

- Value systems and cultures have to be accepted as dynamic, not static. Each generation goes through the process of negotiating the elements that make up its value systems and cultures.

- One needs to recognize the mutual borrowing that happens among value systems and cultures and to seek to mitigate or eliminate the unequal circumstances in which that borrowing takes place.

- One must look simultaneously at what is expressed as that to be gained, lost, and created new in the recombination of value systems and cultures by a group of people.

Adhering to these three principles addresses what Faye Harrison describes as the project of decolonizing anthropology by "demystifying hegemonic ideologies and producing/ co-producing forms of knowledge that can be useful and potentially liberating for the world's dispossessed and oppressed" (2010: 8). The Aboriginal Smart Art project on which I am working provides an example of these principles in action.

THE ABORIGINAL SMART ART PROJECT

In 2011, Colin McKinnon Dodd of the Yamatji Aboriginal cultural group and the founder of the Aboriginal Artists Development Fund (AADF) asked me to conduct a project that would use technology to support Australian Aboriginal arts. The Koorie Heritage Trust, the peak Aboriginal institution in Victoria State, agreed to partner with the AADF and Swinburne University on a project focused on how indigenous knowledge belonging to Australian Aboriginal cultures can be used to create social, technological, and business innovations in the Victorian Aboriginal Art market that increase the holistic sustainability of Australian Aboriginal art-making communities. The project completed the first of three phases, focused on researching cultural values and codesigning innovation scenarios, in May 2012. This is to be followed by the implementation and then the roll-out and evaluation phases. The project's main aim embodies design anthropology's first principle by accepting the dynamic character of Australian Aboriginal culture. Lynnette Russell (2001) in her book *Savage Imaginings* discusses the way mainstream Australian society constructs Aboriginal culture as monolithic, located in the ancient past, and thus inauthentic if engaged with modernity. The Aboriginal Smart Art (ASA) project frames cultural diversity and hybridity as part of the dynamic nature of Aboriginal cultures. The contemporary living values of Australian Aboriginal storytelling and *their Dreamtime* (in other words lore guiding the interconnections between all things in the past and present) are not seen as anathema to modern technologies. The ASA project draws on the growing literature on Aboriginal communities and digital technologies that demonstrates the tremendous variability of intergenerational responses to technology in Aboriginal cultures (McCallum and Papandrea 2009; Samaras 2005; Verran and Christie 2007). As exemplified in the 2010 AIATSIS symposium on Information Technologies and Indigenous Communities, indigenous communities have been increasingly using information and communication technologies to support (1) cultural mapping, managing, and archiving; (2) cultural innovation, transmission, and communication; and (3) language revitalization (AIAT-SIS 2010). The Aboriginal Smart Art project extends these digital practices into the Aboriginal art market, thus also embodying the second principle of the design anthropology.

The borrowing of digital technologies by Aboriginal communities and the borrowing of indigenous visual representations by dealers, buyers, and viewers in the Aboriginal art market represents the mutual borrowing of cultures and values under unequal circumstances. For the Aboriginal Smart Art project, the main challenge is the commodification of Aboriginal artworks and exploitation of Aboriginal artists. Paraphrasing anthropologist Arjun Appadurai (2005: 34), I understand commodification as a process in which things are exchanged with minimal formation of social bonds and groups. The media's highlighting of the continued exploitation of Aboriginal artists by unscrupulous brokers, dealers, and gallery owners led to the development of the Indigenous Art Code in 2007. Yet the exploitation in the Aboriginal art market continues as manifested by the artwork being seen as objects for sale without connection to the artists, their families and communities, and the land. The Aboriginal Smart Art project seeks to eliminate the exploitation and commodification of Aboriginal artists by codesigning innovative technologies, business, and service models to embed story into Aboriginal artwork. People are less likely to exploit another person with whom they have established deep bonds through knowledge of the deeper meanings of the artwork to the artists and their communities. Artists are less likely to sell a painting on the roadside if it also carries story and ceremony for their future generations. The project seeks to use the values associated with Aboriginal storytelling to reduce the unequal circumstances of Aboriginal artists' participation in the Western art market by mainstreaming those values such that they change the business model for the market.

The Aboriginal Smart Art project embodies the third principle of design anthropology by examining what is gained, lost, and created new by embedding story in Aboriginal art. Through the interviews with artists, art coordinators, gallery owners, wholesalers, and technical experts, the Aboriginal Smart Art team of researchers, students, and client partners learned about Aboriginal communities' loss of revenue, cultural practices including storytelling, and identity caused by the exploitation of Aboriginal artists and their communities as a continuation of imperialism. The team learned what communities felt they did or did not have to gain from using the technologies to record the story of art making and how it differed for urban and rural artists. Yet the team learned what could be created new by bringing Aboriginal storytelling values and Western technological values together, which was represented through three design concepts with related business models and technological requirements. The 1D concept demonstrates the students' understanding that communities are the first point of authenticating Aboriginal artists' use of specific motifs in the art and stories. The students explored how available technologies in Aboriginal communities such as smartphones could capture the art and story-making processes to be stored in a general database and embedded in the artwork itself through RFID chips and GPS image tracking. At the point of sale, viewers and buyers can access the story through a smartphone application.

PRINCIPLES FOR DECOLONIZED DESIGN INNOVATION

The *design* of *design anthropology* is theoretically indebted to two areas of design theory and practice. The first is the design thinking exemplified in the works of such indigenous/Third World scholar/practitioners as Indian M. P. Ranjan, Zimbabwean Saki Mafundikwa, and Native Hawaiian Herman Pi'ikea Clark. M. P. Ranjan clearly articulates a view of designing to which design anthropology seeks to speak directly:

"Here we are proposing that the design action takes into account the structure of society along with their macro aspirations, their histories and cultural preferences as a starting point and from here build imaginative approaches for products, services and systems that would include the meta-system, the infrastructure, the hardware, the software and the processware to ensure a perfect fit to the circumstances and requirements of the particular situation." (2011: sec. 1, par. 4)

The approaches advocated by these and other Third World scholars provide alternatives to the classifications and representations that see design primarily as a modern Western phenomenon by showing the long history of making in these communities. This provides another principle for design anthropology:

One should seek to eliminate false distinctions between art, craft, and design in order to better recognize all culturally important forms of making as a way in which people make value systems tangible to themselves and others.

The second area of design thinking and practice is the Scandinavian cooperative and participatory design (Bødker, Ehn, Sjögren and Sundblad 2000; Buur and Bagger 1999). The results of the 1980s Utopia project as described by Bødker et al. inform design anthropology's focus on "staging active design exercises such as the organisational tool-box and use of mock-ups and prototypes as a way to involve end users in design" (2000: 3). The work of Jacob Buur's SPIRE research group has advanced these ideas to define the praxis of participatory innovation. The principle that it provides to design anthropology is:

Researchers and designers ought to create processes that enable respectful dialogue and relational interactions such that everyone is able to contribute their expertise equally to the process of designing and those contributions are properly recognized and remunerated.

These two principles can be glossed as ensuring processes of inclusion into the formation of design concepts, prototypes, and implementation such that the benefit of designing originates and ends with the groups involved, especially the most vulnerable group members. Here the Aboriginal Smart Art project again proves illustrative.

By seeking to embed the values of Aboriginal ways of visual culture as storytelling into a design project, the Aboriginal Smart Art project collapsed the distinctions between art, design, and craft (the fourth principle of design anthropology). Herman Pi'ikea Clark states that by creating the concept of art "no other pre-industrial society or culture in the world established a disassociated category for aesthetic objects as did Western European society" (2006: 3). While still using the term *art*, the Aboriginal Smart Art project attempts to transform aesthetic objects back to what Clark describes as their preindustrial roles as repositories, transmitters, and vehicles in the exploration and construction of knowledge (2006: 4). Aligning with the fifth principle of design anthropology, the project's two presentations and scenario codesign workshop created inclusive interactive forums in which Aboriginal artists, art coordinators, art collectors, business, technology, and design experts could contribute their knowledge to inform multiple scenarios for how the Aboriginal Smart Art processes might work. For the mid-semester presentations of learning from secondary research, the team used writing on sticky notes and directly on display banner posters to facilitate discussions of further directions for research to inform scenario planning. The scenario mapping and evaluation workshop demonstrated to the student team, the participating client, and the technical experts how complex and diverse were the possible solutions to the project's challenges. In the final semester presentation, participants, including Aboriginal artists, helped select which one of the three concepts the group will continue developing in phase two of the project. This process of inclusion will continue throughout phases two and three of the project.

PRINCIPLES FOR DECOLONIZED RESPECT FOR EXPERIENCES

Design anthropology, as I define it, comes directly out of my experiences of being an African American woman who has been trained in critical anthropology and applied that knowledge to the contexts of professional design and design education. It speaks to the heart of the atrocities of Western colonialism and imperialism, mainly the disrespect and disregard for the experiences of other people. Design anthropology enacts the critique of positionality and power articulated by Third World scholars, indigenous scholars, and second and third wave feminists by reframing the problem areas of social impact as within the value systems of imperialism. The design anthropology principle that emerges from this perspective is:

> Projects should use design processes and artifacts to work with groups to shift hegemonic value systems that are detrimental to the holistic well-being of vulnerable groups, dominant groups, and their extended environments.

Last, design anthropology requires that individuals and groups move beyond having empathy to acting with compassion. In an essay for the tenth anniversary of the ICOGRADA Design Education Manifesto, I combine Richard Sennett's (2003) definition of *respect* with Herbert Simon's (1969) definition of *design* to provide a definition of *respectful design* as "the creation of preferred courses of action based on the intrinsic worth of all human, animal, mineral, fauna and flora and the treatment of them with dignity and regard" (Tunstall 2011: 133). The acceptance of the intrinsic worth of everything and the treatment of them with dignity and regard characterizes compassion, which is a higher virtue than empathetic shared feelings advocated in design thinking. Design anthropology's final principle seeks a commitment to compassion from its students, scholars, and practitioners:

> The ultimate criteria for success of any design anthropological engagements are the recognized creation of conditions of compassion among the participants in a project and in harmony with their wider environments.

This may seem utopian, but it ensures that design anthropology understands its purpose as part of a spiritual system, not just an economic and social system. These last two principles require a longer time frame and greater scope for the praxis of design anthropology in order to build case studies. Yet at least anecdotally as I give presentations around the world, I am finding a shift already taking place in the ultimate purpose of design innovation and anthropology that closely aligns with these sentiments. Thus, I expect it will only be five years or so before we have these clear case studies.

CONCLUSION

By proposing design anthropology as a decolonized methodology, I return to where I began with Faye Harrison to advocate for design anthropology that frees its two parent fields from "the prevailing forces of global inequality and dehumanization and to locate it firmly in the complex struggle for genuine transformation" (2010: 10). Design innovation and anthropology have much that they can contribute to fighting global inequality, but first it should adhere to clear principles of respectful engagement with people's values, the translation of them through processes of inclusive codesign, and the evaluation of their effects on people's experiences from the perspective of the most vulnerable. The seven principles of design anthropology can assist in the evaluation of one's cultural interactions to ensure that one is avoiding the four imperialistic outcomes that others have critiqued in both anthropology and design innovation theories and practices. Having established these principles, I seek to focus on the implementation of design anthropology as a decolonized methodology through my projects and those of my allies and students. For what is needed now are clear case studies that demonstrate the creation of conditions of compassion as the true goal of any design anthropology engagement.

REFERENCES

IATSIS (2010), *Program of 2010 Information Technologies and Indigenous Communities Research Symposium*, AIATSIS, Canberra, July 13–16. Available at: www.aiatsis.gov.au/research/docs/iticPrelimProg.pdf. Accessed June 10, 2012.

Appadurai, A. (2005), "Commodities and the Politics of Value," in M. M. Ertman and J. C. Williams (eds.), *Rethinking Commodification: Cases and Readings in Law and Culture*, New York: New York University Press, 34–44.

Asad, T. (ed.) (1973), *Anthropology and the Colonial Encounter*, Ithaca, NY: Ithaca Press.

Barth, F. (1993), "Are Values Real? The Enigma of Naturalism in the Anthropological Imputation of Values," in M. Hechter, L. Nadel, and R. Michod (eds.), *The Origin of Values*, Hawthorn, NY: Aldine de Gruyter, 31–46.

Bezaitis, M. and Robinson, R. (2011), "Valuable to Values: How 'User Research' ought to Change," in A. Clarke (ed.), *Design Anthropology: Object Culture in the 21st Century*, New York: Springer Wien, 184–201.

Blakey, M. (2010), "Man, Nature, White and Other," in F. Harrison (ed.), *Decolonizing Anthropology*, 3rd ed., Arlington, VA: Association for Black Anthropologists, American Anthropological Association, 16–24.

Bødker, S., Ehn, P., Sjögren, D., and Sundblad, Y. (2000), "Co-operative Design: Perspectives on 20 Years with 'the Scandinavian Design Model,'" Stockholm, Sweden: Centre for User Oriented IT Design (CID), CID-104, 1–9. Available at: http://cid.nada.kth.se/pdf/cid_104.pdf. Accessed May 6, 2012.

Borges, A. (2007), *Design for a World of Solidarity*. Available at: www.adeliaborges.com/wp-content/uploads/2011/02/12–17–2007-forming-ideas-design- solidario1.pdf. Accessed May 10, 2012.

Brown, T. and Ulijn, J. (2004), *Innovation, Entrepreneurship and Culture: The Interaction between Technology, Progress, and Economic Growth*, Cheltenham, UK: Edward Elgar Publishing.

Brown, T. and Wyatt, J. (2010), "Design Thinking for Social Innovation: IDE," *World Bank Institute, beta*, July 12. Available at: http://wbi.worldbank.org/ wbi/devoutreach/article/366/design-thinking-social-innovation-ideo. Accessed March 27, 2011.

Buur, J. and Bagger, K. (1999), "Replacing Usability with User Dialogue," *Communications of the ACM*, 42(5): 63–66.

Clark, H. P. (2006), "E Kûkulu Kauhale O Limaloa: Kanaka Maoli Education through Visual Studies," Paper presented at the (2006) Imaginative Education Research Symposium, Vancouver, B.C., Canada: Imaginative Education Research Group. Available at:www.ierg.net/confs/viewabstract. php?id=254&cf=3. Accessed October 6, 2012.

Deloria Jr., V. (1988 [1969]), *Custer Died for Your Sins: An Indian Manifesto*, Oklahoma City: University of Oklahoma Press.

Dictionary.com Unabridged (2011), "Decolonised." Available at: http://dictionary. reference.com/browse/decolonised. Accessed November 14, 2011.

Dictionary.com Unabridged (2011), "Methodology." Available at: http://dictionary. reference.com/browse/methodology. Accessed November 14, 2011.

Editors (2010), "Humanitarian Design vs. Design Imperialism: Debate Summary," *Design Observer/Change Observer*, July 16. Available at: http:// changeobserver.designobserver.com/feature/humanitarian-design-vs- design-imperialism-debate-summary/14498/. Accessed March 15, 2011.

Fabian, J. (1983), *Time and the Other: How Anthropology Makes Its Object*, New York: Columbia University Press.

Fry, T. (1989), "A Geography of Power: Design History and Marginality," *Design Issues*, 6(1): 15–30.

Ghose, R. (1989), "Design, Development, Culture, and Cultural Legacies in Asia," *Design Issues*, 6(1): 31–48.

Graeber, D. (2001), *Toward an Anthropological Theory of Value*, New York: Palgrave.

Gray, P. (2010), "Business Anthropology and the Culture of Product Managers," *AIPMM Product Management Library of Knowledge*, August 8. Available at: www.aipmm.com/html/newsletter/archives/000437.php. Accessed May 6, 2012.

Hall, S. (1992), "The West and the Rest," in S. Hall and B. Gielben (eds.), *Formations of Modernity*, Cambridge, UK: Polity Press and Open University, 276–320.

Halse, J. (2008), *Design Anthropology: Borderland Experiments with Participation, Performance and Situated Intervention*, Doctoral dissertation, IT University, Copenhagen.

Harrison, F. (2010), "Anthropology as an Agent of Transformation," in F. Harrison (ed.), *Decolonizing Anthropology: Moving Further toward an Anthropology for Liberation*, third edition, Arlington, VA: Association of Black Anthropologists, American Anthropological Association, 1–14.

IDEO and Rockefeller Foundation (2008a), *Design for Social Impact How-to Guide*. New York, NY: IDEO and Rockefeller Foundation.

IDEO and Rockefeller Foundation (2008b), *Design for Social Impact: Workbook*. New York, NY: IDEO and Rockefeller Foundation.

Jepchumba (2009), "Saki Mafundikwa," *African Digital Art*, September. Available at: www.africandigitalart.com/2009/09/saki-mafundikwa/. Accessed October 6, 2012.

Jostingmeier, B. and Boeddrich, H. J. (eds.) (2005), *Cross-Cultural Innovation: Results of the 8th European Conference on Creativity and Innovation*, Wiesbaden, Germany: DUV.

Kohn, M. (2011), "Colonialism," *The Stanford Encyclopedia of Philosophy*, Fall. Available at: http://plato.stanford.edu/archives/fall2011/entries/colonialism/. Accessed October 6, 2012.

Leach, J. (2011), "MSc Design Anthropology," Department of Anthropology, University of Aberdeen. Available at: www.abdn.ac.uk/anthropology/postgrad/ MScdesignanthropology.php. Accessed October 6, 2012.

Leong, B. D. and Clark, H. (2003), "Culture-based Knowledge towards New Design Thinking and Practice—A Dialogue," *Design Issues*, 19(3): 48–58.

Light, P. (2008), *The Search for Social Entrepreneurship*, Washington, DC: Brookings Institute Press.

Lodaya, A. (2002), "Reality Check," *Lodaya.Webs.Com*. Available at: http:// lodaya.webs.com/paper_rchk.htm. Accessed March 29, 2011.

Lodaya, A. (2003), "The Crisis of Traditional Craft in India," *Lodaya.Webs.Com*. Available at: http://lodaya.webs.com/paper_craft.htm. Accessed May 10, 2012.

Lodaya, A. (2006), "Conserving Culture as a Strategy for Sustainability," *Lodaya.Webs.Com*. Available at: http://lodaya.webs.com/paper_ccss.htm. Accessed May 10, 2012.

Lodaya, A. (2007), "Catching up; Letting go," *Lodaya.Webs.Com*. Available at: http://lodaya.webs.com/paper_culg.htm. Accessed May 10, 2012.

Magda, R. M. R. (2004), "Transmodernidad," Barcelona: Anthropos. Available at: http://transmoderntheory.blogspot.com/2008/12/globalization-as-transmodern-totality.html. Accessed October 15, 2010.

McCallum, K. and Papandrea, F. (2009), "Community Business: The Internet in Remote Australian Indigenous Communities," *New Media & Society*, 11(7): 1230–1251.

Nussbaum, B. (2010a), "Is Humanitarian Design the New Imperialism?" *Co.Design*, July 7. Available at: www.fastcodesign.com/1661859/is-humanitarian-design-the-new-imperialism. Accessed March 27, 2011.

Nussbaum, B. (2010b), "Do-gooder Design and Imperialism, Round 3: Nussbaum Responds," *Co. Design*, July 13. Available at: www.fastcodesign.com/1661894/do-gooder-design-and-imperialism-round-3-nussbaum- responds. Accessed March 27, 2011.

Nussbaum, B. (2010c), "Should Humanitarians Press on, if Locals Resist?" *Co.Design*, August 3. Available at: www.fastcodesign.com/1662021/nussbaum-should-humanitarians-press-on-if-locals-resist. Accessed March 27, 2011.

OECD and Eurostat (2005), *Oslo Manual: Guidelines for Collected and Interpreting Innovation Data*, third edition, Oslo: OECD.

Ortiz, F. (1995 [1945]), *Cuban Counterpoint: Tobacco and Sugar*, Durham, NC: Duke University Press.

Otto, T. (2006), "Concerns, Norms and Social Action," *Folk*, 46/47: 143–157.

Pilloton, E. (2010), "Are Humanitarian Designers Imperialists? Project H Responds," *Co.Design*, July 12. Available at: www.fastcodesign.com/1661885/are-humanitarian-designers-imperialists-project-h-responds. Accessed March 27, 2011.

Ranjan, A. and Ranjan, M. P. (eds.) (2005), *Handmade in India*, New Delhi: National Institute of Design (NID), Ahmedabad, Council of Handicraft Development Corporations (COHANDS), New Delhi Development Commissioner (Handicrafts), New Delhi, and Mapin Publishing Pvt. Ltd.

Ranjan, M. P. (ed.) (2006),"Giving Back to Society: Towards a Post-mining Era," *IDSA Annual Conference*, September 17–20, Austin, TX.

Ranjan, M. P. (2011), "Design for Good Governance: A Call for Change, *Design for India Blog*, August 11. Available at: http://design-for-india.blogspot.com/2011/08/design-for-good-governance-call-for.html. Accessed November 14, 2011.

Restrepo, E. and Escobar, A. (2005), "Other Anthropologies and Anthropology Otherwise: Steps to a World Anthropologies Framework," *Critique of Anthropology*, 25(2): 99–129.

Russell, L. (2001), *Savage Imaginings*, Melbourne: Australian Scholarly Publishing.

Said, E. (1978), *Orientalism*, New York: Vintage Books.

Samaras, K. (2005), "Indigenous Australians and the 'Digital Divide,'" *Libri*, 55: 84–95.

Sennett, R. (2003), *Respect: The Formation of Character in an Age of Inequality*, New York: Norton.

Seyfang, G. and Smith, A. (2007), "Grassroots Innovation for Sustainable Development," *Environmental Politics*, 16(4): 584–603.

Simon, H. (1969), *The Sciences of the Artificial*, Cambridge, MA: MIT Press.

Smith, L. T. (1999), *Decolonizing Methodologies: Research and Indigenous Peoples*, London/Dunedin: Zed Books and University of Otago Press.

Sperschnieder, W., Kjaersgaard, M., and Petersen, G. (2001), "Design Anthropology—When Opposites Attract," First Danish HCI Research Symposium, PB-555, University of Aarhus: SIGCHI Denmark and Human Machine Interaction. Available at: www.daimi.au.dk/PB/555/PB-555.pdf. Accessed October 6, 2012.

Tax, S. (1975), "Action Anthropology," *Current Anthropology*, 16(4): 514–517.

Tunstall, E. (2006), "The Yin Yang of Ethnographic Praxis in Industry," in Ethnographic Praxis in Industry Conference Proceedings, Portland, OR, Berkeley: National Association for the Practice of Anthropology/University of California Press, 125–137.

Tunstall, E. (2007), "Yin Yang of Design and Anthropology," Unpublished paper presented at NEXT: *AIGA 2007 Annual Conference*. Denver, Colorado.

Tunstall, E. (2008a), "Design and Anthropological Theory: Trans-disciplinary Intersections in Ethical Design Praxis," in *Proceedings of the 96th Annual Conference of the College Arts Association* [CD], Dallas, TX: College Arts Association.

Tunstall, E. (2008b) "Design Anthropology: What Does It Mean to Your Design Practice?" *Adobe Design Center Think Tank*, May 13. Available at: www.adobe.com/designcenter/thinktank/tt_tunstall.html. Accessed August 5, 2008.

Tunstall, E. (2011), "Respectful Design: a Proposed Journey of Design Education" in Bennett, A. and Vulpinari, O. (eds.) ICOGRADA Education Manifesto 2011, Montreal: ICOGRADA.

Uddin, N. (2005), "Facts and Fantasy of Knowledge Retrospective of Ethnography for the Future of Anthropology," *Pakistan Journal of Social Science*, 3(7): 978–985.

Van Eeden, J. (2004), "The Colonial Gaze: Imperialism, Myths, and South African Popular Culture," *Design Issues*, 20(2): 18–33.

Verran, H. and Christie, M. (2007), "Using/designing Digital Technologies of Representation in Aboriginal Australian Knowledge Practices," *Human Technology*, 3(2): 214–227.

Wang, S. Z. (1989), "Chinese Modern Design: A Retrospective," *Design Issues*, 6(1): 49–78.

Wolf, E. (1982), *Europe and the People without History*, Berkeley: University of California Press.

CHAPTER THIRTY TWO

Social Design and Neocolonialism

CINNAMON JANZER AND LAUREN WEINSTEIN

ABSTRACT

This article examines the current field of social design: its claims, practices, and methodologies. Findings discovered through qualitative research illuminate the current application of social design practices and offer critique around their use in the social sphere. This article argues that designers must be sensitive to a variety of complex social and cultural cues and structures or they risk contributing to, or practicing, design neocolonialism. The article offers two key theoretical suggestions to further the emerging field's progress. First, social design must shift its focus from one that is human-centered to one that is situation-centered. Second, it is imperative that social design develops a shared framework for understanding, executing, and evaluating its initiatives and interventions. Additionally, this article introduces a matrix to serve as an early iteration of a shared framework.

Keywords: social design, design colonialism, human-centered design, design thinking, design methodology, framework, matrix

REFRAMING AN EMERGING PRACTICE

Social design is, in its broadest sense, the use of design to address, and ultimately solve, social problems. Currently, social design practice runs the gamut from policy development to Information Communication Technology (ICT) systems design and much in between. In addition to "social design," a number of different terms are used to refer to this type of work, including but not limited to: design for social innovation, design for social change, creative change-making, co-design, participatory design, interaction design, service design, empathetic design, and human-centered design. As the meaning and terminology of social design itself has yet to be concretely understood or collectively accepted (Kimbell 2011: 288), this article will use "social design" to capture all facets of design applied to the social realm with the intent of addressing and/or solving social problems.

In designing social situations, as social design aims to do, a different set of processes and research methodologies must be used than those employed in designing objects. If social designers want to create social change and solve social issues, they must first understand that solutions cultivated from afar must be considered subordinate to the beliefs, knowledge, and perspectives of the people affected by said issues.

As designers enter the social realm—and shift from designing objects to designing social change—the need for capable and ethical social practice must be acknowledged and developed. The field of social design must adopt new, more appropriate practices and modify—even disregard if necessary—methods that are unsuitable for designing situations. Social design must reorient its theoretical philosophy away from traditional human-centered priorities (which tend to be object centric) and shift instead towards new situation-centered (social centric) priorities.[1]

In order to cultivate a practice with a situation-centered focus, a complex, multidimensional understanding of people and their environments is essential. As Brazilian educator Paulo Freire wrote in *Pedagogy of the Oppressed*:

> One cannot expect positive results from an educational or political action program which fails to respect the particular view of the world held by the people. Such a program constitutes cultural invasion, good intentions notwithstanding. (Freire 2005: 95)

A holistic understanding is essential for the sustainability and efficacy of social design initiatives.[2] Designs must prioritize community ownership and inclusive participation to ensure that the sustainability of a project's future is embraced by the end user. Design work applied within the social realm must be collaborative, culturally relevant, socially applicable, and empowering rather than imposing and removed. Relevant stakeholders and communities must be given a highly regarded and considered voice, otherwise designers and their projects run the risk of being ineffective, at least and negatively impactful, at worst.

Edward Said stated in *Orientalism* that, "ideas, cultures, and histories cannot seriously be understood or studied without their force, or more precisely their configurations of power, also being studied" (Said 1979: 5). Those intent on changing elements of situations, or entire situations, must cultivate a thorough understanding of a situation's various underlying social factors—its economy, sociopolitical context(s), the views of its various constituents, and its history—what Said refers to as "force" (ibid.). As social design stands now, a Said-like understanding is absent from theory and practice.

Situation-centered design must hold the same concentrated, end-user prioritization that human-centered design does. However, the "end-user" in situation-centered design is social milieu: comprised of many, often varied, "end-users" as well as the delicate systems and structures in which these "users" interact. A shift in such thinking would serve as an acknowledgment of the complexity of the very social spaces this form of design aims to occupy. Inexorably, social change encompasses and affects much more than human interaction with an object.

Our systems' challenges and their root causes must be considered and ultimately redesigned, to yield positive impact. As sociologist Allan Johnson suggests:

> People of course, will have to change in order for systems to change, but the most important point is that changing people isn't enough. The solution also has to include entire systems, such as capitalism, whose paths of least resistance shape how we feel, think, and behave as individuals, how we see ourselves and one another. (Johnson 2005: 38)

Many social design interventions actively seek to participate in this redesign. If social design strives to positively reshape the social realm, then the social design study, practice, and practitioners must consider, and be able to consider, the macro and micro political, economic, and cultural systems that contribute to the issues and ills that social design seeks to change.

SOCIAL DESIGN: METHODOLOGIES AND PRACTICES

There are two primary and ubiquitous methodological tools employed within social design: design thinking and human-centered design. The concept of design thinking was introduced by several mid-century design theorists including Peter Rowe and Nigel Cross in their books *Design Thinking* and *Designerly Ways of Knowing*, respectively. Recently, however, design thinking has become popularized in the social design world after IDEO CEO Tim Brown wrote an article on the topic in *Harvard Business Review* (Brown 2008). Brown (2009) subsequently authored a book on the same subject titled *Change by Design*. Within social design, design thinking is considered to be an effective method for conceiving of and producing innovative solutions to social problems (Kimbell 2011: 292). Design thinking purportedly has a diverse range of functions such as a cognitive style, a general theory and practice of design, and an approach towards organization management (Kimbell 2012: 141).

Similarly, within the world of social design, human-centered design (HCD) is considered to be a process that transitions innovative ideas from cerebral concept to "actionable" reality; ideas relating to social change are particularly included (IDEO 2009: 4). HCD has been deployed and popularized through publications like IDEO's "HCD Toolkit," frog's "Collective Action Toolkit," the American Institute of Graphic Arts' "Ethnography Primer," and Helsinki Design Lab's "Design Ethnography Fieldguide."

Social design practice operates on the notion that design-based creative processes, such as design thinking and human-centered design, can and should be used to generate (presumably useful) solutions to social change problems, and therefore social change itself. Both human-centered design and design thinking have been given significant credit and credibility within the world of social design—they are continually relied upon as processes that can produce "new solutions for the world" (ibid.: 6) and that yield innovative, empathetic, user-centric results. However, the designers employing these practices are "not always working in close collaboration with public service specialists" (Kimbell 2011: 286), or the very actors within the domains they seek to improve.

SOCIAL DESIGN "LITE"

Human-centered design and design thinking are applicable methods for designing products that will be used or consumed by humans. However, social design is now functioning in a different environment—the social—which is a multidimensional, complex, and delicate space, whose expansive and nuanced nature is no longer adequately covered by "human-centered." The problem with employing object-centered methodologies to work that is based in the social is that the latter remains an immaterial space; it consists of intangibles, like Michel Foucault's "always-already" pervasive power structures (Foucault 1979: 82). Object-centered practices are suited for use in creating tangible objects but, logically enough, are less suitable for creating social change, which is often largely intangible.[3]

While the practices and materials of HCD and design thinking do allude to potentially relevant methodologies, they have been adopted in problematically diluted or "lite," iterations. These augmentations render potentially relevant practices insufficient for use within the social because they remove the critical facets that make these methods useful in the first place.

Design thinking and HCD quite problematically lack the credible, unbiased, qualitative and quantitative support necessary to back up the bold claims surrounding their efficacy when applied to the social.[4] For example, ethnography is a fundamental tool in anthropological and sociological research, leveraging in-depth relationship with the community or communities that the ethnographer is involved in, and these relationships continue over long periods of time—years, even decades. Such rigorous forms of ethnography are excluded from HCD and design thinking materials and processes. The ubiquitously perceived value and pervasive use of design thinking and HCD within social design is problematic because, with the most key and robust components of social science practice missing, design thinking and HCD remain too fundamentally callow for application within the social realm.

The weaknesses of design thinking and HCD, specifically with respect to their usefulness as processes that solve problems surrounding social change, can be summarized in three ways:

1. Research is deemphasized, devalued, and simplified. The necessary context required to inform effective problem definition and relevant concepts is removed.

2. There is no emphasis on ensuring or checking that solutions are appropriate, informed by context, or that issues are thoroughly understood prior to the design and implementation of solutions.

3. The agenda of the designer and freedom of creativity are prioritized over more paramount components such as end-user empowerment and a deep understanding of the end-user's worldviews.

If design-based social change is going to be effective and lasting, it must not be dependent upon the designer; rather, it must be rooted in empowerment. If social issues are to be addressed, processes must start with a solid foundation of in-depth, contextual research as exemplified by practices within relevant social science fields such as anthropology and sociology.

THE SOCIAL SCIENCES' CONTRIBUTION TO AN EMERGING PRACTICE

In the vein of social science fields, a shared framework for theory and practice must be developed and implemented as social design progresses. It is imperative that this framework facilitates an understanding of the differences between situation-centered and object-centered design work. One size does not fit all in terms of approach—what is useful for creating an object is likely not useful for creating social change. Therefore, it is critical that practitioners become equipped to identify the best and most suitable project-specific practices, which might often be a mix of multiple, relevant methods.

The process of selecting appropriate method or methods must begin by first understanding, then considering, the differences in scope and capability amongst the menu of methodologies available to social design. Without understanding why certain approaches are more appropriate for certain applications, different methodologies can be misappropriated and ineffectively applied—as is certainly the case with design thinking and HCD. To more appropriately incorporate and differentiate the necessary perspectives and methodologies of the social sciences when designing social change, the authors have developed a diagrammatic matrix. This matrix functions as an initial iteration of a pedagogical framework for understanding the widely varying audiences, attributes, and research needs of social design, so often missing in education and practice. The variety of different foci among social design projects warrants and requires the use of various methodologies dependent on the context in which they are operating. This matrix is used to differentiate between the various spheres of operation, which can then inform context-specific decisions around relevant and appropriate research method selection. Using this matrix as a guide towards relevant implementation approaches,

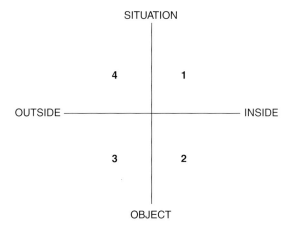

FIGURE 32.1 A Social Design Action Matrix. © Cinnamon Janzer and Lauren Weinstein 2014

designers can differentiate research needs based on the type, context, and scope of a particular project.

As seen in Figure 32.1, the social design matrix has two axes. The y-axis represents the spectrum of design intervention, ranging from situations to objects, from intangible to tangible. These binaries address the current social design trend to move beyond object-centered design and into situation-centered design. The x-axis represents the spectrum of the designer's solidarity with a given community in which they seek to work. To articulate the x-axis binaries, the words *outside* and *inside* are used.[5] An outside perspective refers to an intervention in which designers are not embedded in the community for whom they are designing. Outside perspective projects are characterized by "parachute" designs where solutions are proposed for, and even implemented within, communities from which the designer is heavily, or even completely removed. Conversely, an inside perspective refers to a context in which designers have developed a strong sense of solidarity with the community being addressed. Inside perspectives demonstrate a high level of earned trust from the community.

Using this matrix, social designers can better understand the various forms of their practice through a series of case studies, which have been identified for each quadrant in order to illustrate their different characteristics, namely their parameters, specific functionalities, and purposes. As seen in Table 32.1, useful and context-appropriate research methods are also provided to guide work within each quadrant.[6]

QUADRANT ONE, TRANSFORMATIVE SOCIAL CHANGE: DESIGNING A SITUATION WITH AN INSIDE PERSPECTIVE

Transformative social change values holism and considers the multiple systems at play within a particular situation, including but not limited to: people, culture, values, environments, history, power dynamics, socioeconomics, and future impact (Nelson and Prilleltensky 2010). Transformational social change often occurs on multiple levels (ibid.), and desired outcomes of such interventions often include increasing competency, independence, self-sufficiency, and access to resources (ibid.). Quadrant one encompasses projects in which designers cultivate an inside perspective; characterized by actions such as working with, living with, having first-hand experience with, or studying the social groups and societal contexts associated with the initiative for an extended period of time. Work conducted in this quadrant requires that the designer achieves a high level of trust from the community, has completed intensive and relevant research, and has developed a thorough understanding of all relevant complex social issues and systems—whether this is a task designers take on themselves or they solve by adding relevant members to their team. The designers working in this space dedicate a serious amount of commitment to the (often long term) creation, implementation, and evaluation of the project.

Case Study: Bicycles Against Poverty

Bicycles Against Poverty (BAP) began as a student project undertaken by an interdisciplinary team of young thinkers, spearheaded by Muyambi Muyambi, a civil engineer from Uganda

Table 32.1 Selected Appropriate Research Methods Organized by Matrix Quadrant

Quadrant	1	2	3	4
Approach Objective	Gather extensive situational and social understanding. Develop honest relationships.	Gather extensive research on the end-user, beneficiary, and their use experience.	Gather creative, innovative ideas.	Research methods not suggested, as work in this quadrant is not recommended.
Possible Research Methods and Approaches	Ethnographic Research, Participant Observation, Literature Review, Case Studies, Interviews, Problem Driven Iterative Adaption, Preliminary Desktop Research, Surveys, Social Work Intervention Process, Community Organizing Invention Process, Praxis Model, Participatory Action Research.	Human-Centered Design, Design Thinking, Probes, Diaries, Design Ethnography, Case Studies, User Personas, User Testing, Desirability Testing, Experience Sampling, Generative Research, Participatory Design Research, Interviews, Picture Cards, Surveys and Questionnaires.	Design Thinking, Creative Processes Collage, Thinking Wrong, Design Charette, Image Boards, Role Playing.	As the priority in quadrant four projects is one's own beliefs derived from personal experience, research is usually less often embraced. It is not suggested that projects operate with quadrant four perspectives. No methods are recommended.

and college-educated in the United States ("Muyambi Muyambi '12" 2009). Many of the students included in the original development group now hold professional positions within the BAP nonprofit, exhibiting a high level of commitment to the cause and organization (Bicycles Against Poverty [n.d.]). BAP collaborated with local community partners and earned a Community Organization status from the government in order to cultivate trust between the organization and the community (ibid.). Consequently, the community welcomes BAP's efforts and plays an active role in informing the organization's progress and outcomes (ibid.).

BAP's purpose is to alleviate poverty through fostering self-sufficiency by increasing access to resources rather than simply providing the resources themselves. Understanding that bicycles can serve as a vehicle for access to water, jobs, healthcare, and ultimately self-empowerment, BAP designed a system for making bikes a reachable option for people in Ugandan villages through micro finance lending for bike ownership (ibid.). However, the nonprofit's work extends beyond providing opportunities for bike access in northern Uganda. BAP believes that, for the system to work effectively, a holistic set of strategies should be incorporated including bike repair seminars, entrepreneurship technical training, money management workshops, and mechanisms for community feedback (ibid.). BAP's understanding of cultural specifics, level of continued commitment to the cause, and effort to design a holistic and multidimensional system for social change exemplify a quadrant one initiative.

QUADRANT TWO, HUMAN-CENTERED DESIGN: DESIGNING AN OBJECT WITH AN INSIDE PERSPECTIVE

Quadrant two encompasses projects and interventions aiming to design objects with a heavy emphasis on the end-user. Designers working on these projects employ inside perspectives, have a deep understanding of the end-user, or even incorporate the user throughout the design process. Work in this quadrant uses traditional human-centered design processes and methodologies; it is a space where designers prioritize and understand the end-user with the intent of designing relevant objects. Efforts in this space can positively contribute to social change through object design.

Case Study: NeoNurture: The "Car Parts" Incubator

Design That Matters sought to address the fact that a lack of hospitable environments for newborns in developing countries contributes to 1.8 million infant deaths yearly (NeoNature [n.d.]). To address this they designed NeoNurture: The "Car Parts" Incubator, a device used to reduce newborn deaths caused by a lack of warmth post delivery. The design team developed the concept through finding answers to critical, culturally relevant questions about sustainability, use, and maintenance to make their product successful in the context in which it was to be deployed (ibid.). Research guided their decision to design an incubator out of used and discarded car parts, an abundant resource in the developing countries in which they were working. The result was an affordable, accessible, and sustainable option for a sanitary incubator that can be used in rural areas and repaired by anyone who knows how to repair a car. NeoNurture contrasts with conventional incubators, which are financially inaccessible and impossible to be repaired by the populations most affected by this phenomenon (ibid.).

NeoNurture is characteristic of a quadrant two inside perspective because it used human-centered design to create a culturally relevant and viable object. Both the project and design exhibit an informed point of view, cultivated through interviews, qualitative data, quantitative data, first-hand cultural experience, and observations (ibid.).

QUADRANT THREE, TRADITIONAL DESIGN: DESIGNING AN OBJECT WITH AN OUTSIDE PERSPECTIVE

Quadrant three also encompasses projects aiming to design objects as well, however, designers working on these projects are characterized by employing an outside perspective. Work in this space may have socially focused content, but the social groups addressed are not intensively studied or included by the designer and are not necessarily represented and reflected in the design process or outcome. The designer is not embedded in the community the design addresses and, therefore, the target community has less trust in and interaction with the designer, if any.

Social design work in this space often manifests in two ways. The first is that organizations interested in bringing awareness to a certain issue hire a designer and provide them with relevant content. Second, particularly inspired designers feel inclined to practice or contribute to socially focused work on their own accord. This quadrant aligns with strategic consultant David Berman's message in *do good design*:

> But rather than sharing our cycles of style, consumption, and chemical addictions, designers can use their professional power, persuasive skills, and wisdom to help distribute ideas that the world really needs: health information, conflict resolution, tolerance, technology, freedom of the press, freedom of speech, human rights, democracy... (Berman 2009: 39).

Case Study: War Child Campaign Designed by John St.

War Child "works with children all over the world to reduce the effects of poverty, provide an education, and to defend and promote child rights" through awareness efforts and nine international projects (War Child [n.d.]). As a not-for-profit project, the Toronto-based design firm John St. designed print, film, and social media elements for a War Child campaign (John St. [n.d]). The campaign was designed to promote awareness around, and raise funds for, child soldiers. The campaign received much attention and several accolades, particularly for its mock child soldier camp held in North America. John St.'s work brought an important issue to public attention, using their talents and power of persuasion as a design agency to assist a charity organization in their efforts to better inform public thought and opinion.

As John St. was not embedded in the community of child soldiers which the campaign addressed and received information from the non-profit with which it partnered rather than cultivating the information for its campaign itself, John St., in this example, exemplifies an outside perspective. However, it is noteworthy to mention that design projects such as these do contribute in an impactful way to cultivating social change. These types of projects are important and accessible avenues for designers with socially focused intentions who want to work within the social realm and contribute to positive social change, but perhaps may be without the available amount of commitment and expertise required of projects in quadrants one and two.[7]

QUADRANT FOUR, DESIGN NEOCOLONIALISM: DESIGNING A SITUATION WITH AN OUTSIDE PERSPECTIVE

Quadrant four encompasses projects that, like quadrant one, aim to design situations. However, the designers in this space employ an outside perspective. Due to these inherent contradictions, quadrant four becomes a very precarious space in which to work; the outside perspective that defines this quadrant does not allow for the necessary components of effective situation design (such as trust and deep understanding) to exist. An outside perspective means that problem definitions and their solutions are identified and created in isolation from the addressed community and their particular social context(s); therefore, interventions in this space often exhibit a disconnect between the people involved and the social phenomena addressed. Consequently, there is a very high risk of cultural bias (Lasky 2013: 12) and what the authors define as deign neocolonialism in this quadrant.

Neocolonialism is defined as "is the continued exercise of political or economic influence over a society in the absence of formal political control" (Ritter 2007). Further distilled, neocolonialism can be understood as influence over a population, community, or society in the absence of direct, obvious or formal control. History shows that instances of neocolonialism can provide tangential social "benefits," such as the creation of schools. However, we must question the cost of such tangential "benefits." For example, if schools are developed as a result of neocolonialism, it is likely that the curriculum will be influenced, either partially or completely, by the culturally enforced educational ideals of the implementer, not those of the people being "served." Despite laudable intentions or seemingly beneficial outcomes, negative impacts at the communities' expense often result. Providing education that doesn't include a communities' culture, norms, or values serves to erase community and replace it with a "neocolony" of the creator. These negative impacts are why neocolonialism is a force for change that is fundamentally imposing rather than empowering.

Design projects that fall into quadrant four are considered design neocolonialism. Unfortunately, contemporary social design initiatives often operate in this quadrant. While designers likely do not actively seek to impose their values or ideas on others, "influence happens organically." (Altbach 2013). Seeking to create social change while employing an outside perspective is incredibly problematic and morally flawed; such approaches do not facilitate or create culturally sensitive, empowering, or lasting (and therefore successful) social change. Projects that do not understand, consider, or respect user's values, socioeconomic contexts, or the inherent agency end-users rightfully should have over their own situations are neocolonial in nature and are characteristic of quadrant four initiatives.

Case Study: One Laptop Per Child

One Laptop Per Child (OLPC) is a nonprofit organization working to provide rugged, low cost laptops to children in developing countries. The OLPC initiative's mission is to "empower the world's poorest children through education" (One Laptop Per Child [n.d.]). The OLPC initiative is a quadrant four project because it illustrates employing an outside perspective in an effort to change a situational context; OLPC highlights the dangers associated with quadrant four initiatives. Although a physical laptop is the design vehicle, the aim of the project is to improve education and increase information access through a situation-centered design. The laptop was developed in isolation from the end-using communities and employed via "almost in every way, a traditional top down" approach (Nussbaum 2007). The project has been described as a "parachute" effort where "cultural disconnects kept kids from benefitting from the machines" ("Peru's One Laptop Per Child" 2012).

Aiming to "transform communities" through education and information access is a situational context that requires a deep understanding of the existing education system, context(s) surrounding information access, cultural values, and political landscape(s) (One Laptop Per Child [n.d.]). Because the project was exclusive of these necessary elements which would have provided the OLPC creators with the insight to make their product culturally relevant, the laptop was subsequently not embraced or by or useful to the communities it sought to serve. Unfortunately, OLPC exemplifies the design neocolonialism that occurs frequently when designers attempt to change situations they do not sufficiently understand, or are not able to know if they sufficiently understand.

CONCLUSIONS AND LIMITATIONS

Social design has forged, somewhat haphazardly, into a new space where the design of social systems has become an equal opportunity focus for a variety of design disciplines. Without first considering processes, methodologies, frameworks, ethics, and foundations for the field, the freedom and dynamism currently present within social design is weakening the legitimacy and effectiveness of the field. Continuing this mode of practice can and does contribute to causing harm and negatively impacting populations in an attempt to make social change.

Since addressing all aspects requiring improvement within the social design field (or developing a comprehensive critique of social design practice) is beyond the scope of this article, this work is primarily research and pre-design focused. The authors do not argue that the suggestions previously discussed are a panacea for the issues surrounding social design. To the contrary, it is believed that these ideas will need further refinement with time via collaborative dialogue and constructive augmentation among social design educators, practitioners, and students.

The bias of the authors is rooted firmly in social science and grassroots development perspectives—a view is held that there are certain paramount traditions within the social sciences (such as rigorous research and comprehensive problem definition) which social design will need to adopt and adapt to as it continues to merge design and the social. However, the fact that social design is a developing field can be a potential strength, if approached thoughtfully. Social design has the opportunity to learn from the history and mistakes that fields like anthropology (playing a hand in colonialism) have made and avoid repeating them. Social design can also benefit immensely from the increasing populations of good-intentioned practitioners who are passionate about and committed to this sector of design work. The growing social design community shows promise of ambition, talent, and laudable aspirations on top of a desire to address our ever-increasing list of social challenges. That said, social change is no small feat. If social design seeks to educate students or provide practitioners with tools to create transformative change, social design must become rooted in a strong, well-developed, socially focused foundation.

NOTES

1. The term "situation-centered" was co-conceived by the authors and Victor Margolin, phone conversation, March 14, 2013.
2. Although not all design interventions should be sustained.
3. The authors do not claim that object design can't provide useful tools as elements of a situational design, or that there cannot be tangible indicators, but rather that object-focused philosophy is not appropriate for designing and understanding situations.
4. There are no citations of references listed to support this claim made in the HCD Toolkit or on the HCD Connect website as accessed January 4, 2014.
5. Myra Margolin, Community Psychologist, in discussion with the authors, April 1, 2014.
6. The authors suggest that most social design projects would benefit from the use of quadrant one research methods and approaches, not that they are limited for use within quadrant one initiatives. Any quadrant could strengthen its rigor and efficacy through use of quadrant one methodologies.
7. While John St. may have been familiar to the target audience, both War Child and John St. developed this campaign in isolation from the child soldier community. Because the purpose of the campaign was to improve the lives of child soldiers, a population from which both War Child and John St. were highly removed, this project falls in quadrant three.

REFERENCES

Altbach, Philip G. 2013. "MOOCs as Neocolonialism: Who Controls Knowledge?" *The Chronicle of Higher Education*. Posted December 4, 2013. Available online: http://chronicle.com/blogs/worldwise/moocs-s-neocolonialism-who-controls-knowledge/33431 (accessed March 29, 2014).

Berman, David B. 2009. *Do good design*. Berkeley, CA: New Riders in Association with AIGA Press.

Bicycles Against Poverty. n.d. Available online: http://www.bicyclesagainstpoverty.org (accessed April 9, 2013).

Brown, Tim. 2008. "Design Thinking." *Harvard Business Review*. Last modified June 2008. Available online: http://hbr.org/2008/06/design-thinking/ar/1 (accessed February 23, 2013).

Brown, Tim. 2009. *Change by Design*. New York: Harper Collins Publishers.

"Colonialism." *Stanford Encyclopedia of Philosophy*. First published May 9, 2006, revised April 10, 2012. Available online: http://plato.stanford.edu/entries/colonialism/ (accessed April 12, 2013).

Foucault, Michel. 1979. *The History of Sexuality, Volume 1: An Introduction*. London: Pantheon Allen Lane.

Freire, Paulo. 2005. *The Pedagogy of the Oppressed*. New York: Continuum International Publishing Group.

IDEO. 2009. "Human-Centered Design Toolkit." San Francisco, CA. Available online: http://www.ideo.com/work/human-centered-design-toolkit (accessed March 5, 2013).

Johnson, Allan G. 2005. "What Can We Do? Becoming Part of the Solution." In Susan J. Ferguson (ed.), *Mapping the Social Landscape: Readings in Sociology* [1988]. Boston, MA: McGraw Hill.

John St. n.d. Available online: http://www.johnst.com (accessed April 10, 2013).

Kimbell, Lucy. 2011. "Design Thinking Part I" *Design and Culture*, 3 (3): 285–306.

Kimbell, Lucy. 2012. "Design Thinking Part II" *Design and Culture*, 4 (2): 129–148.

Lasky, Julie. 2013. "Design and Social Impact". White Paper. The Smithsonian's Cooper-Hewitt, National Design Museum, the National Endowment for the Arts, and the Lemelson Foundation, New York.

Margolin, Myra. 2013. Community Psychologist, in discussion with authors, April 1.

Margolin, Victor. 2013. Design Historian, phone conversation with authors, March 14.

"Muyambi Muyambi '12." 2009. Bucknell University. Posted January 15. Available online: http://www.bucknell.edu/x47404.xml (accessed April 9, 2013).

Nelson, Geoffrey and Isaac Prilleltensky. 2010. *Community Psychology: In Pursuit of Liberation and Well Being*, 2nd ed. New York: Palgrave Macmillan.

"NeoNurture: The 'Car Parts' Incubator." n.d. Design that Matters. Available online: http://designthatmatters.org/portfolio/projects/incubator/ (accessed April 9, 2013).

Nussbaum, Bruce. 2007. "It's Time to Call One Laptop Per Child a Failure." *Bloomberg Businessweek*. Posted September 24. Available online: http://www.businessweek.com/innovate/NussbaumOnDesign/archives/2007/09/its_time_to_cal.html (accessed April 13, 2013).

One Laptop Per Child. n.d. Available online: http://one.laptop.org (accessed April 13, 2013).

"Peru's One Laptop Per Child Policy Comes with a Big Cost." 2012. News.com.au. Posted July 4. Available online: http://www.news.com.au/world-news/free-laptops-came-with-big-cost/story-fndir2ev-1226416238064 (accessed April 12, 2013).

Ritzer, George (ed.). 2007. "Blackwell Reference Online." *Blackwell Encyclopedia of Sociology*. Oxford: Blackwell Publishing. Available online: http://blackwellreference.com/public/book.html?id=g9781405124331_yr2013_9781405124331 (accessed March 29, 2014).

Said, Edward. 1979. *Orientalism*. New York: Vintage.

"Social Design." 2014. MICA MA Social Design. Last modified 2014. Available online: http://www.mica.edu/programs_of_study/graduate_programs/social_design_(ma).html (accessed March 29, 2014).

War Child. n.d. Available online: http://old.warchild.canst.com/work (accessed April 10, 2013).

CHAPTER THIRTY THREE

Futuristic Gizmos, Conservative Ideals: On Speculative Anachronistic Design

PEDRO J. S. VIEIRA DE OLIVEIRA AND LUIZA PRADO DE O. MARTINS

Speculative design is going through a troubled adolescence. Roughly fifteen years after interaction design duo Dunne and Raby first started talking about "critical design", the field seems to have grown up a bit too spoiled and self-centered. Being a fairly young approach to product and interaction design, it seems to have reached a tipping point of confusion, rebellion, contrasting opinions and confrontations. Presently, from practitioners to theorists there seems to be little consensus about what the field is able to offer—and whether it is of any use at all. In this article we hope to pinpoint some reasons why this is so, while at the same time offering not possible, plausible or probable but *preferable* developments for the field.[1]

Before introducing what we consider to be *truly* critical about speculative and critical design (from here on referred to as simply SCD), context is paramount. SCD made its first appearance as "critical design" in the late 1990s in the corridors and studios of the Royal College of Art (RCA) in London. It envisioned design as a tool for critique, and aimed to explore the metaphysical possibilities of the designed object in order to "provide new experiences of everyday life, new poetic dimensions" (Dunne 2005, p. 20). Even though the idea in itself was not new—with other practitioners already undertaking similar endeavours without necessarily defining them as "critical design"—this was perhaps the first time that criticality was proposed as a deliberate attitude to product and interaction design, "a position more than a method" (Dunne and Raby 2008, p. 265; 2013, p. 34). In the following years speculative proposals became a strong driving force and a trademark of the Design Interactions programme at the RCA—under the direction of Dunne—and a few other schools in northern Europe. Across the Atlantic, practitioners and authors such as Julian Bleecker and Bruce Sterling, as well as curators such as MoMA's Paola Antonelli, began taking interest in these new perspectives on design; in the U.S. the discipline was rebranded as "design fiction"—though it maintained most of critical design's core goals.[2]

Despite the growing number of practitioners and the interest that this approach has garnered in the design community since its inception, the discourse in the field has remained suspiciously static. In *Hertzian Tales* (2005), Dunne passionately argued for an exploration of the metaphysical possibilities of the designed object, focusing on its potential as embodied critique, political statement or activist provocation. His proposal rejected design as a discipline exclusively focused on servicing the industry, though it was equally careful not to align itself with Marxist ideals (ibid., p. 83). Distancing its speculative proposals from "market-led agendas" (Auger 2013, p. 32) emerged as the motto of Design Interactions' output, with a good number of the programme's alumni becoming mainstream references for what speculative design is able to achieve. Their projects follow a clear path of dreaming about the uncanny implications of tricky subjects such as birth,[3] death and social anxieties,[4] only to name a few. Yet, they are predominantly expressed through aesthetics of consumerism, still contained within a clear neoliberal framework. Fifteen years on, the field seems to have taken this fear of left-wing ideals at heart.

This reluctance in cutting its ties with the industry might be the effect of a narrow view of design's agency in everyday life. Whereas Dunne and Raby's famous *A/B Manifesto* (2013, vii) makes sure to differentiate their approach as directed towards "citizens" rather than "consumers", the authors reinforce in their most recent publication (*Speculative Everything*, 2013) that it is basically through *what people buy* that futures are brought into existence. In other words, a shopping window packed with near-futures, ready to be chosen and consumed (Dunne and Raby 2013, p. 37, 49, 161; Tonkinwise 2014; Kiem 2014). Furthermore, for Dunne and Raby, the political sphere of critical design ends where the design profession ceases its responsibility, that is, at the moment a consumer product (or a prototype thereof as "critical design") comes into being (2013, p. 161). Yet contrary to what they affirm, we argue that designers are as politically responsible and accountable for their practice as for their actions as citizens; there is no separation between one role and the other. When this simple assumption is taken into consideration, it becomes clear that the art gallery is not the most appropriate space for these "provocations" and discussions to take place—it needs to penetrate public discourse beyond the "art and design exhibition" setting in order to become an instrument of the political (Fry 2011; DiSalvo 2012; Keshavarz and Mazé 2013).

It is precisely because SCD's—and the debates they aim to incite—rarely leave these specific environments that they stall. The field's preoccupations are directed towards little more than an alleged "lack of poetic dimensions" in our relationship with designed objects (Dunne 2005, p. 20). SCD is made *by*, *for* and *through* the eyes of the Western—and typically northern European and/or US-American—intellectual middle classes; the vast majority of work currently available in the field has concentrated its efforts on envisioning near futures that deal with issues that seem much more tangible to their own privileged audience. Projects that clearly reflect the fear of losing first-world privileges in a bleak dystopian future abound, while practitioners seem to be blissfully unaware (or perhaps unwilling to acknowledge) the existence of different realities.[5] This myopic vision of the world has led the field to limit itself to superficial concerns, and stunted the development of its once-ambitious political aspirations.

Clear examples of these problems can be found in the visual discourse of SCD: the near-futures envisioned by the great majority of projects seem devoid of people of colour, who rarely (if ever) make an appearance in clean, perfectly squared, aseptic worlds. Couples depicted in these scenarios seem to be consistently heterosexual and bound by traditional notions of marriage and monogamy. There are no power structures made visible that divide the wealthy and the poor, or the colonialist and the colonised. Poverty still happens *somewhere else,* while the bourgeois SCD subject copes with catastrophe through consuming sleek, elegant, futuristic, white-cubed and white-boxed gizmos.[6] Gender seems to be an immutable, black-and-white truth, clearly defined between men and women, with virtually no space for trans⁎ and queer identities (let alone queer and trans⁎ voices speaking for themselves).[7] Between these narrow depictions of reality and whitewashed formulations of near-future scenarios, SCD seems to be curiously apathetic and apolitical for a field that strives to be a critical response to mainstream perceptions of what design is, and what it should and could do. In truth, the only message that this apathy can convey is that society is fine as it is.

The question is then whether it is possible to expand from these superficial concerns and provide more thoughtful perceptions and analyses of the world. While the majority of criticism towards the field remains highly sceptical (and perhaps rightfully so), we still believe SCD can be transformed into a strong political agent. For this to happen, however, it needs to be tested, spread out, modified, re-appropriated, bastardized. SCD's hesitation in acknowledging its problematic stances on issues such as sexism, classism or colonialism, to name a few, need to be called out. Projects promoting and perpetuating oppression should not be tolerated, and those not willing to second-guess their own decisions need to be held accountable for their political decisions. Assuming that the [white, cisgendered, male, European, etc.] gaze is "neutral" or "universal" is not only narrow-minded, but also profoundly reactionary.

Many of the problems we have highlighted within SCD stem from the tenuous grasp that the field seems to have of the humanities and social sciences. In its ambition for envisioning how technology reflects social change, it assumes a very shallow perspective towards what these social shifts mean; it avoids going deeper into how even our core moral, cultural, even religious values might—or should—change. While SCD seems to spare no effort to investigate and fathom scientific research and futuristic technologies, only a small fraction of that effort seems to be directed towards questioning culture and society beyond well-established power structures and normativities. This is, perhaps, the most defining trait of a teenaged field: the ironically anachronistic nature of a practice that creates futuristic gizmos for profoundly conservative moral values. In order to overcome this, we believe designers have to look beyond given socio-economical and political structures and inquire *how* and *why* our societies got there in the first place. One way to do so is to get closer to research in the critique of science, feminist and queer theories, sound studies and other scholarship that dare to question the hierarchies of privilege that constitute the world as we know it today. More than that, SCD should offer a helping hand towards making these tricky questions visible and tangible to the public discourse, well beyond exclusionary spaces such as academia, museums and art galleries. This needs to be done without fearing a dialogue with the so-called "mass culture" or "mainstream" so often neglected and avoided through the use of purposefully cryptic language.

While the issues highlighted in this article are not the only ones worthy of the field's attention, demanding meaningful engagement and thorough research from a community largely stemming from—or with connections to—academia is hardly asking too much. Such an attitude will not only prevent projects from incurring in the same basic mistakes pinpointed here and henceforth failing to address their aspirations, but will also offer some diversity beyond self-indulgent, narrow-minded perspectives. From the moment SCD researchers and practitioners start keeping these issues in mind and start holding themselves accountable for their political decisions, the field might finally start fulfilling its promises of critique. Until then, it will remain confined to a vicious circle of navel-gazing and self-appraisal.

© Luiza Prado de O. Martins and Pedro J. S. Vieira de Oliveira. This paper is an expanded and revised version of both "Questioning the 'critical' in speculative and critical design" and "Cheat-sheet for a non- (or less-) colonialist speculative design" and previously published in Laranjo, F. (Ed.) *Modes of Criticism 1 – Critical, Uncritical, Post-critical*. London: Modes of Criticism, 2015. Republished with kind permission from Pedro J. S. Vieira de Oliveira and Luiza Prado de O. Martins.

NOTES

1. We are referencing physicist Joseph Voros' *Futures Cone* (2003), recurrently employed by speculative and critical designers to position their projects (as seen in Dunne and Raby's *Speculative Everything* (2013, p.5), for example).
2. It is unclear who coined "design fiction"—although science fiction author Bruce Sterling is commonly credited. Dunne and Raby (2013, p.100) remark that even though similar in nature, design fictions are "rarely critical of technological progress and border on celebration rather than questioning." For a comprehensive account of design fiction, refer to Bleecker (2009) and Sterling (2009).
3. Ai Hasegawa's project *I Wanna Deliver a Dolphin* explores the possibility of humans birthing other animals: http://aihasegawa.info/?works=i-wanna-deliver-a-dolphin (Accessed October 14, 2014).
4. Auger Loizeau explore "the harnessing of our chemical potential after biological death through the application of a microbial fuel cell, harvesting its electrical potential in a dry cell battery" in their "Afterlife" project: http://www.auger-loizeau.com/index.php?id=9 (Accessed October 14, 2014). Sputniko's project "Crowbot Jenny" dreams of trans-species communication as a solitary girl's way of connecting with other living things: http://sputniko.com/2011/08/crowbot-jenny-2011/ (Accessed October 14, 2014). Auger Loizeau also explore social anxieties in their project "Social Telepresence": http://www.auger-loizeau.com/index.php?id=11 (Accessed October 14, 2014).
5. Michael Burton and Michiko Nitta's "Republic of Salivation" suggests a dystopian future in which citizens are fed rationed meals by the government. The designers seem to be unaware that this is already a reality for many countries in the developing world. Its inclusion in MoMA's "Design and Violence" online curating platform ignited a long debate on the validity of SCD and served as the

starting point for this and other essays. The thread is available at http://designandviolence.moma.org/republic-of-salivation-michael-burton-and-michiko-nitta/ (Accessed October 10, 2014).

6. As Tony Fry remarks, "[f]or the privileged, defuturing often happens under an aura of elegance" (2011, p.27).

7. Whereas Sputniko's "Menstruation Machine" attempts to tackle the subject of transsexuality and queerness, it still employs rather questionable terminology and representation of queer identities (cf. Prado de O. Martins 2014).

REFERENCES

Auger, J., 2013. "Speculative design: crafting the speculation". *Digital Creativity*, 24(1), pp.11–35.

Bleecker, J., 2009. "Design Fiction: A Short Essay on Design, Science, Fact and Fiction". *Near Future Laboratory*. Available at: http://nearfuturelaboratory.com/2009/03/17/design-fiction-a-short-essay-on-design-science-fact-and-fiction/ [Accessed October 10, 2014].

DiSalvo, C., 2012. "Spectacles and Tropes: Speculative Design and Contemporary Food Cultures". *The Fibreculture Journal*, (20), pp.109–122.

Dunne, A., 2005. *Hertzian Tales: Electronic Products, Aesthetic Experience, and Critical Design*, The MIT Press.

Dunne, A. & Raby, F., 2008. "Fictional Functions and Functional Fictions". In C. Freyer, S. Noel, & E. Rucki, eds. *Digital by Design: Crafting Technology for Products and Environments*. Thames & Hudson, pp.264–267.

Dunne, A. & Raby, F., 2013. *Speculative Everything: Design, Fiction, and Social Dreaming*, Cambridge, Massachusetts; London: The MIT Press.

Fry, T., 2011. *Design as Politics*, New York: Bloomsbury Academic.

Keshavarz, M. & Mazé, R., 2013. "Design and dissensus: framing and staging participation in design research". *DPP: Design Philosophy Papers*, (1). Available at: http://desphilosophy.com/dpp/dpp_journal/paper1/dpp_paper1.html [Accessed October 10, 2014].

Kiem, M., 2014. "When the most radical thing you could do is just stop". *Medium*. Available at: https://medium.com/@mattkiem/when-the-most-radical-thing-you-could-do-is-just-stop-1be32db783c5 [Accessed October 10, 2014].

Prado de O. Martins, L., 2014. "Privilege and Oppression: Towards a Feminist Speculative Design". In Design Research Society Conference. Umeå Institute of Design. Available at: http://www.academia.edu/7778734/Privilege_and_Oppression_Towards_a_Feminist_Speculative_Design [Accessed October 14, 2014].

Sterling, B., 2009. "Design fiction". *Interactions*, 16(3), pp.20–24.

Tonkinwise, C., 2014. How We Future—Review of Dunne & Raby "Speculative Everything" (Unpublished Draft). Available at: https://www.academia.edu/7710031/DRAFT_-_How_We_Future_-_Review_of_Dunne_and_Raby_Speculative_Everything_ [Accessed October 10, 2014].

Voros, J., 2003. "A generic foresight process framework". *Foresight*, 5(3), pp.10–21.

CHAPTER THIRTY FOUR

Privilege and Oppression: Towards a Feminist Speculative Design

LUIZA PRADO DE O. MARTINS

© Luiza Prado de O. Martins, 2014

ABSTRACT

Though critical and speculative design have been increasingly relevant in discussing the social and cultural role of design, there has been a distinct lack of both theory and praxis aimed at questioning gender oppression. Departing from an intersectional feminist analysis of the influences and origins of speculative and critical design, this essay questions the underlying privilege that has been hindering the discussion on gender within the discipline and its role in propagating oppression; it then goes on to propose the concept of a "feminist speculative design" as an approach aimed at questioning the complex relationships between gender, technology and social and cultural oppression.

Keywords: speculative design; gender studies; feminism; intersectionality

During the past few decades there has been a fundamental shift in the way we understand design and its cultural relevance. From ipads to smartphones, from automatic hoovers to intelligent fridges, we now have increasingly complex objects governing essential parts of our lives. In this world, where objects mediate most of our experiences, design has been gaining increasing significance—highlighting the necessity for research on the roles that designed objects have within society.

This increased interest in the sociological and cultural aspects of design has been a fundamental catalyst for the development of design research and its many related fields—from research through, for or about design (Frankel and Racine 2010) to constructive design research (Koskinen *et al.* 2011). Prominent among these ever-evolving fields are speculative and critical design, two closely related approaches to design practice (Auger 2013) that, usually departing from prosaic observations of our everyday interactions with technology, aim to provoke insightful analyses of the profound impact that designed objects have on our lives (Dunne 1999; Dunne and Raby 2001). This essay focuses specifically on these two approaches, questioning their shortcomings from an intersectional feminist perspective; it challenges speculative and critical design's aspirations to sociological critique within the larger framework of diverse oppressions in capitalist, heteronormative, sexist, racist and classist societies. Though a deeper understanding of how the politics of oppression influence human relationships with technology is essential to the development of a field that aims to be critical, projects mentioning these oppressions are astoundingly rare. This flaw may be associated with the fact that speculative and critical design have been, up until now, practiced and theorised largely within the privileged walls of costly universities in developed countries (Prado de O. Martins and Vieira de Oliveira 2014).

The primary focus of this essay is how gender is portrayed and approached in speculative and critical design practices—an analysis that cannot be disengaged from the portrayals of other forms of oppression. Thus, the previously mentioned intersectional feminist perspective advocated here stems from two key beliefs: that taking up an apolitical position means complying with and contributing to the *status quo,* and that oppressions (of gender, race or class, among others) cannot be understood separately. Hence the importance of not only a feminist perspective, but a feminist perspective firmly grounded in the idea of intersectionality (Crenshaw 1989): as a strategy for understanding how "oppression cannot be reduced to one fundamental type, and that oppressions work together in producing injustice." (Collins 2000 p. 18). The essay thus proposes the idea of a "feminist speculative design" as a strategic approach to addressing issues of systemic gender violence and discrimination within speculative and critical design practices.

ON SEMANTICS AND SCD

Design's peculiar, fluid position as a discipline capable of benefiting from both humanistic and scientific knowledge has long been one of its most distinctive traits. This innate ability for combining distinct fields of knowledge has recently led to increased interest in developing theoretical discourse that supports design as a method of research in its own right. As part of this, speculative and critical design—the two approaches to design research and practice this text takes interest on—have been gaining momentum as strategies to think critically about the essential role of objects within society. Anthony Dunne, who first coined the term 'critical design' defines it as an approach to design practice that "uses speculative design proposals to challenge narrow assumptions, preconceptions and givens about the role products play in everyday life" (Dunne and Raby 2008, p. 265). By challenging pre-established ideas, critical design works in the unstable, murky territory that is the intersection of politics and culture;

Dunne and Raby (2008, p. 265) go on to state that "[s]ome relatives are: activism, cautionary tales, conceptual design, contestable futures, design fictions, interrogative design, radical design, satire, social fiction, speculative design." Auger (2013, p. 11) discusses the semantics of some of these relatives, highlighting that "[t]here is much overlap between these practices, the differences are subtle and based primarily on geographical or contextual usage". He goes on to argue that most of these terms are detrimental, acting to "dislocate the object from everyday life, exposing their fictional or academic status" (*ibid*, p. 12). As such, he writes that "the choice of 'speculative' is preferable as it suggests a direct correlation between 'here and now' and existence of the design concept" (*ibid*). Though Auger's argument is sound, this essay uses the term 'speculative and critical design' for the sake of drawing a clear parallel between critical theory and speculative design as a starting point for discussing the problematic stance of a discipline that aims to be critical and yet ignores essential facets of our relationship with designed objects. For the sake of practicality and style the term will be referred to as 'SCD'.

CRITICAL THEORY AND CRITICAL DESIGN

Critical theory, a western school of thought first originated in the early 20th century, has had a profound impact in contemporary knowledge. In its initial proposition, critical theory was aimed at "emancipation and enlightenment, at making agents aware of hidden coercion, thereby freeing them from that coercion and putting them in a position to determine where their true interests lie" (Geuss 1981, pp. 55–56); it asserts that "the world should be understood, not by accepting unthinkingly the teachings of authorities such as the Church, but through individual reasoning." (Sengers *et al.*) Critical theory argues for critique as both part of the fabric of the world and an agent of change capable of altering the weave of this very fabric; as such, its influence in a wide range of fields in contemporary thought—from queer theory (Turner 2000) to critical architecture (Fraser 2005)—comes as no surprise. SCD is no exception to critical theory's wide-ranging impact: Dunne's original formulation seems to be profoundly influenced by the work developed at the Frankfurt School (the birthplace of critical theory), mentioned directly and indirectly (by referencing its main theorists) in several instances throughout *Hertzian Tales* (Dunne [1999] 2008, pp. 36; 83; 94; 96; 98). Dunne argues for designed objects as means of inciting a critical perception—sociological, psychological, cultural or otherwise—of the man-made world. The parallel to critical theory is quite clear: objects are designed as embodied critical discourse—and their very existence has the potential to change the world they are part of. Curiously, Dunne and Raby (2010) have tried to distance themselves from the Frankfurt School and from critical theory; Bardzell and Bardzell (2013, p. 02), however, point out:

> "[T]heir formulation of critical design has unmistakable affinities with [critical theory] Their language "illusion of choice," "passivity," "reinforces the status quo," "easy pleasure and conformist values," and "fuelled by the capitalist system" bear the unmistakable stamp of the Frankfurt view of ideology."

The relationship between critical theory and SCD is further explored by Bardzell *et al.* (2012) and Bowen (2010). By borrowing critical theory's approach to social and cultural change, however, SCD risks to incur in the very same mistakes for which critical theory has already been criticised: "promoting elitist views of a 'better world' that society should aspire towards" (Bowen 2010, p. 04). This tendency to elitism, well documented in the writings of critical theorists such as Horkheimer and Adorno,[1] seems to affect Dunne's ([1999] 2008, p. 94, my emphasis) work as well:

> "[...] this approach falls foul of a central contradiction of radical work, as Adorno demonstrated in his contrasting of modern classical music and popular jazz. *Because a mainstream film has to be immediately graspable by a broad audience, the fact of achieving this diminishes its critical potential.*"

Granted, any author undertaking the task of offering a critical view of the world incurs in the risk of sounding and acting in a patronizing, classist manner. Ignoring issues of race, class or gender when looking from a place of privilege is surprisingly easy, for that is the case with privilege: it is privilege precisely because "the very processes that confer privilege to one group and not another group are often invisible to those on whom that privilege is conferred" (Kimmel 2003, p. 04). Geuss (1981, p. 82) writes that most criticism on the Frankfurt School was aimed at the fact that it proposed a critical perspective on society "not because of the suffering it imposes on some oppressed group but because it fails to satisfy the neurasthenic sensibilities of a cultural elite". Pointedly, Bowen (2010, p. 04) asks of both SCD and critical theory "a 'better world' according to who?" (*sic*).

Dunne's elitist views seem to be shared by colleagues in the field, as demonstrated in a comment thread on MoMA's website for the "Design and Violence" exhibition.[2] The blog post, written by John Thackara, starts with a discussion on Burton Nitta's project "Republic of Salivation."[3] The discussion in the comment section rapidly evolved to a criticism of SCD's self- centered, privileged understanding of the world—a criticism promptly responded by designer James Auger with the question "What is this obsession with class systems? The UK may have its financial problems but most of us stopped obsessing about these divides in the distant past."[4] This patronising, classist and self-centered attitude within SCD may be explained by its history as a discipline theorised within the safe confines of developed, European countries and practiced largely by a privileged and mostly white, male, middle class crowd. Exceptions to SCD's narrow understanding of privilege politics are rather rare, though notable. Superflux, a studio founded by designer Anab Jain is one such exception, undertaking a string of admirable collaborative projects with small communities in Jain's native India.[5] The bottom-up empowerment of communities seems to be one of the trademarks of Superflux's projects, in stark contrast to the paternalist stance so common in SCD. Royal College of Art alum Sputniko is one of the few practitioners in SCD who overtly tackles issues of gender, though sometimes still under a definitely questionable perspective, as evidenced by her "Menstruation Machine" project.[6] Sputniko describes the project's video as featuring "a Japanese transvestite boy Takashi, who one day chooses to wear 'Menstruation' in an attempt to biologically dress up as a female, being unsatisfied by just aesthetically appearing female."

Though the project might have promoted the discussion of a few issues related to gender, its very description shows the lack of a basic understanding of gender and queer theory. Mistakes such as the use of a derogatory term—transvestite—to refer to the character Takashi[7,8]; the uncritical use of the concept of "biologically dressing up" as a gender—an affirmation that unwittingly hints to the heated discussions on biological essentialism versus anti-essentialism that have since decades divided theorists and activists in the feminist movement (Stone 2004); or the very portrayal of a gender-nonconforming person (by a cissexual woman, nonetheless) for shock value highlight the project's problematic approach to gender identity.

Though many discussions on the future of SCD have appeared recently, many of them seem to ignore these problems entirely (Antonelli 2011, Stevenson-Keating 2011); resistance to SCD's privileged ways is, however, bubbling: in February 2014 the aforementioned discussion on MoMA's Design and Violence website spawned several response articles (Prado de O. Martins and Vieira de Oliveira 2014; Revell 2014; Kiem 2014). Though SCD's future seems to be mostly that of white, European, cissexual, heterosexual people, this reality might be rapidly changing—a change of attitude that might just help build a more equal future.

INTERSECTIONAL FEMINISM AND SPECULATIVE DESIGN

This section of the essay introduces a central concept to its proposed discussion: intersectional feminism. The term "intersectionality" is generally considered to have been first coined by Kimberlé Crenshaw (1989) though the concept was not new—having already been advanced by others (McCall 2005). Intersectionality refers to the manner in which several different types of oppression can intersect and interact, defining one's social position. A European transgender woman is, for instance, the subject of different types of oppression in comparison to a Latin American disabled woman. The objective of taking these distinct forms of oppression into account is not to compare them; comparing the sufferings that individuals derive from the oppressions to which they are subjected is as useless as it is sordid, for the manner in which we experience oppression can be as subjective as it can be factual. Rather, taking the intersectional character of oppression into account is necessary in order to develop a better understanding of the way one navigates the world through the way in which these oppressions interact with each other.

Though much has been written about intersectionality, it does not, as of 2014, constitute a discipline in a by itself; rather, it is considered a theoretical stance, an approach to feminist activism: most researchers "use the term 'intersectional approach' to refer to the research application of these concepts" (Berger and Guidroz 2009, p. 01). Its importance to the development of a solid and inclusive academic discourse in the analysis of inequality is unquestionable; McCall (2005) claims that "[o]ne could even say that intersectionality is the most important theoretical contribution that women's studies, in conjunction with related fields, has made so far."

As mentioned in the previous section, SCD has long suffered from a blindly patronising and privileged perspective on technology. This is not exclusive to SCD either: design, as a product of a patriarchal, classist and racist society, is a discipline where the contribution of women has seldom been recognized throughout its history. Buckley (1999, p. 109) writes:

> "[...] the few women who make it into the literature of design are accounted for within the framework of patriarchy: they are either defined by their gender as designers or users of feminine products, or they are subsumed under the name of their husband, lover, father or brother."

This historical silencing of women in design does not limit itself to its women practitioners either: Buckley (*ibid.*) goes on to state that "women's needs as consumers/users often remain unaddressed". In the past few years this stance seems, fortunately, to be changing, with design taking a keen interest in the needs of minorities. Efforts in this direction have been made by Buchmüller (2013) in design research, Bardzell in HCI (Bardzell and Bardzell 2001; Bardzell 2010) and Rothschild in design and architecture history (1999), for instance. The creation of the International Gender Design Network by Uta Brandes and Simone Douglas[9]; the development of new fields such as inclusive design (Imrie and Hall 2001; Clarkson *et al.* 2003), of projects like Tom Bieling's Mobile Lorm Glove at the Design Research Lab[10] or Marcelo and Andréa Júdice's work at Vila Rosário (Koskinen *et al.* pp. 70–73) are all testimonies to a newfound understanding of design's role in propagating and counteracting oppression. SCD, however, remains a field where such initiatives still seem to remain few and far between.

Understanding privilege is essential in order to build a theoretical discourse capable of truly overcoming injustice. The problem lies in how difficult it is for the privileged to understand their own privilege, for privilege exists precisely because it is invisible to those who benefit from it. A white, heterosexual man will never know the hardships through which others have to go through. He will never be afraid of being raped while walking home alone at night; he will never be afraid of not being hired for a job because of his skin color, he will never be afraid to introduce a same-sex partner to his family. These privileges work silently for the benefit of those who fit into the narrow standards of an excludent society, and to the disadvantage of those who do not. When SCD ignores these issues it complies with oppression and works for a future of inequality.

The recent wave of unnecessarily gendered products—such as the Bic for Her Pen,[11] the Powerful Yogurt[12] or the new, gender-segregated Kinder Surprise[13]—doesn't help design culture either. The misguided marketing strategies behind these products are fueled by packaging and product designers eager to associate genders to colors, shapes and stereotypes. Dunne and Raby (2001, p. 58) claim that "[...] all design is ideological, the design process is informed by values based on a specific world view, or way of seeing and understanding reality". If all design is ideological, what kind of ideology are we, as designers, propagating to the world when we participate in the development of such products? By designing a world for exclusion and discrimination "[t]he systems and artefacts produced by technoscience" are able to provide "the material foundations for gender inequality" (Kirkup 2000, p. XIII).

As much as design can be a tool for oppression, it can also be an effective agent for social change. SCD, as previously mentioned, tries to do this by using artefacts in order to incite critical thought; the full accomplishment of this goal, however, seems to be hindered by the issues of privilege previously discussed on this essay. Curiously, while SCD's roots in critical theory may be a reason for its virtually nonexistent concern for issues such as gender or class (Fraser 1985; Fleming 1989), both feminist theory and intersectionality also take inspiration from critical theory. These disciplines have, however, gone a step further by building their own inclusive paradigms based on the initial propositions of critical theory, like queer theory (Turner 2000) or critical race theory (Collins 2000).

Intersectional feminism aims to empower those that are subjected to discrimination by understanding oppression as a highly individualized, unique experience; similarly SCD questions traditional notions of the user as a mere average number and as a mere receptacle to the actions defined by the designer, in a clear hierarchy of power. Instead, SCD proposes the notion of "[…] user as protagonist by embodying unusual psychological needs and desires […]". Addressing issues of gender discrimination through an intersectional perspective is, thus, an essential strategy to further develop SCD's original project.

FEMINIST SPECULATIVE DESIGN: METHODOLOGIES AND DISCUSSION

As part of an ongoing PhD on body extensions and the politics of designed artefacts, this essay aims to propose an intersectional feminist approach to SCD; it intends to point out the problematic position of a discipline that, despite its very valid aspiration to question our relationships with designed objects, focuses this critique on a purely aesthetic level. This essay therefore proposes the concept of a "feminist speculative design" as a potential strategy that might help addressing these questions. Feminist speculative design would be, first and foremost, an approach to SCD aimed at inciting critical thought on how electronic objects might propagate gender oppression under an intersectional perspective. Though it may seem at first a broad term, the word "feminist" is herein used as a bold political statement as to feminist speculative design's goals, proudly aligning this approach with those that have been derided, silenced and dismissed throughout history. This feminist approach to speculative design would allow for a better understanding of the interaction between the various facets of oppression related to the use of designed objects as part of our—in Cross' (1982) unsurprising choice of words—"man-made world".

Whereas the beneficial influence that an intersectional feminist perspective could have on SCD is clear, the profitable contributions that SCD could bring to the further development of intersectional feminist discourse need to be equally discussed. Being disciplines rooted mainly in the humanities, with strong ties to sociology, philosophy and political sciences, feminist and women's studies have a long tradition of textual research outcomes. This confines most of the production of knowledge in the field within the academic realm of books, papers and journals. The issues at hand are, however, much more tangible than this would suggest; oppression is a real, daily experience, capable of provoking serious consequences on the lives of those it affects. Although this is not to say that the academic production of knowledge in the field is not relevant to the lives of those affected by discrimination, rendering ideas of intersectionality and feminism inaccessible or difficult to understand defeats the very purpose of these approaches. Collins (2000, VII) writes in the introduction to Black Feminist Thought:

"I could not write a book about Black women's ideas that the vast majority of African-American women could not read and understand. Theory of all types is often presented as being so abstract that it can be appreciated only by a select few."

A book written in an accessible manner, free of unnecessary academicisms or extravagant wordiness might be a good start, but there are certainly other strategies that could help develop intersectional feminist discourse. McCall (2005) claims that "there has been little discussion of how to study intersectionality, that is, of its methodology." Intersectionality is a difficult subject, for it sets out to analyse the issue of oppression by taking into account the several axes that compose one's identity instead of compartmentalising these axes into separate groups. This leads to a complex net of possible paths for research that could only possibly be managed through an interdisciplinary approach to the problems at hand. McCall goes on to argue that "[t]he pressing issue then is to overcome the disciplinary boundaries based on the use of different methods in order to embrace multiple approaches to the study of intersectionality".

Feminist critical design could thus represent a very beneficial approach to intersectional feminist research: technology, artefacts and the "man-made world" with which design occupies itself are, after all, both results and propagators of "matrixes of domination" (Collins 2000, p. 18). The study of systemic inequalities cannot ignore the profound influence that the new behaviors and rituals created or modified by the ubiquity of electronic artefacts have in gender roles. From revenge-porn websites that publish unauthorized nudes complete with the victims' home addresses[14] to hackers who install malicious programs on women's computers in order to spy on them through their webcams,[15] the concerns that women have to face when using technology are entirely different from those of men.[16] Though a few scholars have been developing research on how technology intersects with gender oppression (Kirkup 2000; Du Preez 2009; Balsamo 1995), most of the outcome has been purely textual: there is a distinct lack of tangible, non-theoretical perspectives in the field.

Feminist speculative design would focus on using artefacts to provoke reflection on the privileges that give undue advantage to one part of the population while oppressing another. Recently, the Swiss women's organization Zürcher Frauenzentrale created a media campaign in order to raise awareness to the issue of wage gap where men using an ATM received 20% less than their desired sum[17] that could be used as an interesting inspiration for feminist speculative design projects. Objects discussing issues of gender-related Internet privacy, questioning meritocracy, addressing gender-based violence or deconstructing the male gaze (Mulvey 1997) might also be some of the many possible paths for feminist speculative design projects. The spontaneously dystopian nature of SCD is particularly suited for approaching such issues: feminist speculative design could focus on questioning the already dystopian nature of the present for minorities, and ask how their futures would be like; through the poetic, subjective and abstract dimensions of the designed artefact, it would challenge observers to question their own roles in maintaining social injustice.

Overcoming the academic nature of feminist theory and the elitism of SCD poses a challenge that is inextricably associated with whether design can truly provoke social change. Embodying critique in a physical artefact may indeed be an interesting strategy from the perspective of feminist theory; the question as to how these objects are presented, however, remains. In order to remain faithful to the essential premises of feminist speculative design, it would be essential to avoid presenting these artefacts merely within academic settings, galleries or museums. Feminist speculative design projects would, ideally, take up a life of their own; they would need to be shared, commented upon, questioned and criticised in order to be culturally relevant. Representation, another highly problematic issue in SCD, would also need to be carefully addressed through an intersectional perspective: if a video or a photo series on a future scenario only depicts white, European, middle class people, what does that say about the future of minorities?

Granted, changing a society is not an easy nor brief task, for structures of oppression are deeply ingrained into everything that surrounds us—from language to architecture. Departing from the premise that a designed object can be capable of generating resounding and immediate change within society would be naive at best. Change does, however, come in small steps; it happens first in our insular realities to only later become palpable. Design alone is not capable of changing society; nonetheless, as both a product and a producer of societal values it could trigger visible cultural shifts when approached with an interdisciplinary and critical stance. Artefacts that question oppression are able to produce small waves of change; it is these small changes that feminist speculative design would concern itself with, for they are what could later grow into a tangible shifts in society.

While feminist speculative design would certainly not be the only possible path into developing a truly critical discourse within design, it has the potential to be an effective one. Whereas words might be difficult to assimilate—especially words that incite us to leave our comfort zones—experiences are far more effective tools for provoking estrangement, discomfort and, ultimately, reflection. The mediation of electronic objects on our daily interactions with other individuals is built around a skeleton of complex hierarchies of power; it is the bone structure under the attractive and glossy skin of technology that feminist speculative design could expose, reflect upon and, hopefully, alter.

NOTES

1. "[...] under the conditions of later capitalism and the impotence of the workers before the authoritarian state's apparatus of oppression, truth has sought refuge among small groups of admirable men." (Horkheimer [1937] 1972, pp. 237–238).

    "The consumers are the workers and employees, the farmers and lower middle class. Capitalist production so confines them, body and soul, that they fall helpless victims to what is offered them." (Adorno and Horkheimer 1997, p. 133)

"The general intellectual level of the great masses is rapidly declining." (Horkheimer [1937] 1972, p. 238)

2. http://designandviolence.moma.org/republic-of-salivation-michael-burton-and-michiko-nitta/ (Accessed March 10, 2014).

3. http://www.burtonnitta.co.uk/repubicofsalivation.html (Accessed March 10, 2014).

4. http://designandviolence.moma.org/republic-of-salivation-michael-burton-and-michiko-nitta/ (Accessed March 10, 2014).

5. http://superflux.in/work/lilorann (Accessed March 11, 2014).

6. http://sputniko.com/2011/08/menstruation-machine-takashis-take-2010/ (Accessed March 11, 2014).

7. https://www.glaad.org/reference/transgender (Accessed February 26, 2014).

8. http://www.nlgja.org/files/NLGJAStylebook0712.pdf (Accessed February 26, 2014).

9. http://igdn.blogspot.com/ (Accessed March 10, 2014).

10. http://www.design-research-lab.org/?projects=mobile-lorm-glove (Accessed March 10, 2014).

11. http://www.bicworld.com/us/products/details/420/ (Accessed November 5, 2013).

12. http://powerful.yt/ (Accessed November 5, 2013).

13. http://www.independent.co.uk/news/uk/home-news/kinder-surprise-in-stereotyping-row-over-pink-and-blue-eggs-8747331.html (Accessed November 5, 2013).

14. http://gawker.com/5961208/revenge+porn-troll-hunter-moore-wants-to-publish-your-nudes-alongside-directions-to-your-house (Accessed November 5, 2013).

15. http://arstechnica.com/tech-policy/2013/03/rat-breeders-meet-the-men-who-spy-on-women-through-their-webcams/ (Accessed November 5, 2013).

16. http://www.theguardian.com/lifeandstyle/womens-blog/2013/nov/08/online-abuse-women-free-speech (Accessed November 8, 2013).

17. http://www.huffingtonpost.com/2013/04/11/equal-pay-day-commercial-prank-from-zurich-womens-center_n_3060740.html (Accessed November 5, 2013).

REFERENCES

Adorno, T.W. & Horkheimer, M., 1997. *Dialectic of Enlightenment*, Verso.

Antonelli, P., 2011. States of Design 04: Critical Design. *Domus*, 949 (July/August 2011). Available at: https://www.domusweb.it/en/design/2011/08/31/states-of-design-04-critical-design.html [Accessed November 8, 2013].

Antonelli, P. & Museum of Modern Art, eds., 2005. *Safe design takes on risk; [on the occasion of the exhibition "SAFE: Design Takes On Risk", The Museum of Modern Art, New York, October 16, 2005–January 2, 2006*, New York, NY: Museum of Modern Art.

Auger, J., 2013. Speculative design: crafting the speculation. *Digital Creativity*, 24(1), pp. 11–35.

Bardzell, J. & Bardzell, S., 2013. What is "Critical" About Critical Design? In *Proceedings of the SIGCHI Conference on Human Factors in Computing Systems*. CHI '13. New York, NY, USA: ACM, pp. 3297–3306. Available at: http://doi.acm.org/10.1145/2470654.2466451 [Accessed March 9, 2014].

Bardzell, S. et al., 2012. Critical Design and Critical Theory: The Challenge of Designing for Provocation. In *Proceedings of the Designing Interactive Systems Conference*. DIS '12. New York, NY, USA: ACM, pp. 288–297. Available at: http://doi.acm.org/10.1145/2317956.2318001 [Accessed March 10, 2014].

Bardzell, S., 2010. Feminist HCI: Taking Stock and Outlining an Agenda for Design. In *Proceedings of the SIGCHI Conference on Human Factors in Computing Systems*. CHI '10. New York, NY,

USA: ACM, pp. 1301–1310. Available at: http://doi.acm.org/10.1145/1753326.1753521 [Accessed March 17, 2014].

Bardzell, S. & Bardzell, J., 2011. Towards a Feminist HCI Methodology: Social Science, Feminism, and HCI. In *Proceedings of the SIGCHI Conference on Human Factors in Computing Systems*. CHI '11. New York, NY, USA: ACM, pp. 675–684. Available at: http://doi.acm.org/10.1145/1978942.1979041 [Accessed March 17, 2014].

Berger, M.T. & Guidroz, K., 2009. *The intersectional approach transforming the academy through race, class, and gender*, Chapel Hill: University of North Carolina Press.

Bowen, S., 2010. Critical Theory and Participatory Design. In *Proceedings of the SIGCHI Conference on Human Factors in Computing Systems*. CHI '10. Atlanta, Georgia, USA: ACM.

Buckley, C., 1999. Made in Patriarchy: Theories of Women and Design—A Reworking. In J. Rothschild & A. Cheng, eds. *Design and feminism: re-visioning spaces, places, and everyday things*. New Brunswick, N.J.: Rutgers University Press.

Clarkson, J. et al., 2003. *Inclusive Design: Design for the Whole Population*, Springer.

Collins, P., 2000. *Black Feminist Thought: Knowledge, Consciousness, and the Politics of Empowerment* Rev. 10th anniversary ed.; 2nd ed., New York: Routledge.

Crenshaw, K., 1991. Demarginalizing the Intersection of Race and Sex: A Black Feminist Critique of Antidiscrimination Doctrine, Feminist Theory, and Antiracist Politics. In K. Bartlett & R. Kennedy, eds. *Feminist legal theory: readings in law and gender*. Boulder: Westview Press.

Cross, N., 2006. Designerly Ways of Knowing. In *Designerly Ways of Knowing*. Springer London, pp. 1–13. Available at: http://link.springer.com/chapter/10.1007/1-84628-301-9_1 [Accessed November 8, 2013].

Dunne, A., 2008. *Hertzian tales: electronic products, aesthetic experience, and critical design*, Cambridge, Mass.; London: MIT.

Dunne, A. & Raby, F., 2001. *Design Noir: The Secret Life of Electronic Objects*, first edition, Birkhäuser.

Dunne, A. & Raby, F., 2008. Fictional Functions and Functional Fictions. In C. Freyer, S. Noel, & E. Rucki, eds. *Digital by Design: Crafting Technology for Products and Environments*. Thames & Hudson, pp. 264–267.

Dunne, A. and Raby, F., 2010. Dreaming objects. *Science Poems—Foundations*. Available at: http://files.ok-do.eu/Science-Poems.pdf [Accessed February 26, 2014].

Fleming, M., 1989. The Gender of Critical Theory. *Cultural Critique*, (13), p. 119.

Fraser, M., 2005. The cultural context of critical architecture. *The Journal of Architecture*, 10(3), pp. 317–322.

Fraser, N., 1985. What's Critical about Critical Theory? The Case of Habermas and Gender. *New German Critique*, (35), p. 97.

Gaver, W., 2012. What Should We Expect from Research Through Design? In *Proceedings of the SIGCHI Conference on Human Factors in Computing Systems*. CHI '12. New York, NY, USA: ACM, pp. 937–946.

Geuss, R., 1981. *The Idea of a Critical Theory: Habermas and the Frankfurt School*, Cambridge University Press.

Held, D., 1980. *Introduction to Critical Theory: Horkheimer to Habermas*, University of California Press.

Horkheimer, M., 1972. Traditional and Critical Theory. In *Critical Theory: Selected Essays*. Continuum.

Imrie, R. & Hall, P., 2001. *Inclusive design: designing and developing accessible environments*, New York: Spon Press.

Kiem, M., When the most radical thing you could do is just stop. *Medium*. Available at: https://medium.com/@mattkiem [Accessed March 17, 2014].

Kimmel, M.S., 2003. Towards a Pedagogy of the Oppressor. In M. S. Kimmel & A. L. Ferber, eds. *Privilege: A Reader*. Westview Press.

Kirkup, G., 2000. *The gendered cyborg: a reader*, London; New York: Routledge in association with the Open University.

Koskinen, I.K. et al., 2011. *Design research through practice from the lab, field, and showroom*, Waltham, MA: Morgan Kaufmann.

McCall, L., 2005. The Complexity of Intersectionality. *Signs*, 30(3), pp. 1771–1800.

Mulvey, L., 1997. Visual Pleasure and Narrative Cinema. In *Feminisms: An Anthology of Literary Theory and Criticism*. Rutgers University Press.

Oudshoorn, N., Rommes, E. & Stienstra, M., 2004. Configuring the User as Everybody: Gender and Design Cultures in Information and Communication Technologies. *Science, Technology & Human Values*, 29(1), pp. 30–63.

Prado de O. Martins, L. & Vieira de Oliveira, P.J.S., Questioning the "critical" in Speculative & Critical Design. *Medium*. Available at: https://medium.com/designing-the-future/5a355cac2ca4 [Accessed March 8, 2014].

Du Preez, A., 2009. *Gendered bodies and new technologies: rethinking embodiment in a cyber-era*, Newcastle upon Tyne: Cambridge Scholars.

Revell, T., Designed conflict territories. *openDemocracy*. Available at: http://www.opendemocracy.net/opensecurity/tobias-revell/designed-conflict-territories [Accessed March 17, 2014].

Rothschild, J. & Cheng, A., 1999. *Design and feminism: re-visioning spaces, places, and everyday things*, New Brunswick, N.J.: Rutgers University Press.

Serano, J., 2007. *Whipping girl: a transsexual woman on sexism and the scapegoating of femininity*, Emeryville, CA: Seal Press.

Stevenson-Keating, P., 2011. A Critique on the Critical | Studio PSK. Available at: http://pstevensonkeating.co.uk/a-critique-on-the-critical [Accessed November 8, 2013].

Stone, A., 2004. Essentialism and Anti-Essentialism in Feminist Philosophy. *Journal of Moral Philosophy*, 1(2), pp. 135–153.

Thackara, J., Republic of Salivation (Michael Burton and Michiko Nitta). *Design and Violence*. Available at: http://designandviolence.moma.org/republic-of-salivation-michael-burton-and-michiko-nitta/ [Accessed March 10, 2014].

Turner, W.B., 2000. *A Genealogy of Queer Theory*, Temple University Press.

CHAPTER THIRTY FIVE

Is Sustainable Innovation an Oxymoron?

ELIZABETH B.-N. SANDERS

© 2015 Elizabeth B.-N. Sanders

ABSTRACT

We face significant economic, environmental and social challenges today. Even "radical innovation" is not enough to address the challenges of wicked problems. Design innovation can help to address these challenges and ensure sustainable futures, but only if we open up the design process to everyone. Design-led innovation is not likely to support sustainable futures unless it is co-design-led innovation. Co-designing puts tools for creativity and communication in the hands of the people who will be served through design, giving all of us the means to collectively make sense of the future. Sustainable innovation is not an oxymoron.

INTRODUCTION

The pattern of the last 50 years can be seen clearly now, particularly in the United States. Consumerism had been growing since the 1960s and has resulted in many unsustainable products and practices flooding the landscape. Today many consumers are not aware of or are confused about the negative environmental impacts of their behavior. Consumerism has also led to a preoccupation in the business sector with innovation at all costs. Companies seek "radical innovation" (Verganti, 2009) in order to stay ahead of the competition.

A countermovement to this pattern of increasing consumption has recently become evident. First, the recession has made it abruptly and abundantly clear that continuous conspicuous consumption can no longer be maintained. And at the same time we see that many people, especially young people, are seeking ways to be economically, environmentally and socially responsible. Organizations are also making efforts to think and behave sustainably.

Can radical innovation be sustainable? Can radical innovation be socially responsible? Or is "sustainable innovation" an oxymoron? I will argue that innovation from a consumer-led perspective cannot be sustainable but innovation that is driven from a human-centered perspective can be sustainable. Taking a human-centered perspective requires a long view of the design development process and the use of collective creativity to explore what shape the future will take. Collective creativity refers to acts of creativity that are experienced jointly by two or more (and sometimes even crowds of) people.

THE DESIGN PROCESS IS CHANGING

Where does design fit into this picture? The shape of the design development process has changed over the last ten years with the emergence and growth of a very large front end as shown in Figure 35.1. The large front end is often referred to as the "fuzzy front end" because of its messy and chaotic nature. The fuzzy front end is made up of the many activities that take place in order to inform and inspire the exploration of open-ended questions. In the fuzzy front end, there is no clear path on how to proceed and there may be many divergent paths to explore before any questions can be answered. It is often not known whether the deliverable of this process will be a product, a service, an interface, or something else like a building. The goals of this exploration are to define the fundamental problems, identify opportunities for design and to determine what should *not* be designed. Design teams that are open to discovering what *not* to design can make very important contributions toward sustainable futures!

It also happens that today designers are being increasingly called upon to join, and sometimes to lead, teams that are tasked with very large challenges and problems to solve. These problems are often referred to as "wicked problems". What does this mean? In 1973, Rittel and Webber compared wicked problems to relatively tame problems, i.e., problems that could be solved. "Wicked problems are difficult or impossible to solve because of incomplete,

Fuzzy front end   Gap   Traditional design development process

FIGURE 35.1 The shape of the design development process has changed with the growth of a large front end

contradictory, and changing requirements that are often difficult to recognize. Moreover, because of complex interdependencies, the effort to solve one aspect of a wicked problem may reveal or create other problems" (Rittel and Webber, 1973). Working in the fuzzy front end of the design development process on wicked problems is a new and growing territory for designers and design teams.

As the front end of the design development process has been growing, so, too, has the gap between the front end and the back end. This so-called gap is the subject of discussion today, both by design practitioners and by design educators. There are actually two gaps. The first is the *gap between the designer and the user*. This gap happens when designers design stuff that people don't need, don't want, don't like or can't figure out how to use. Designers are well aware that they are designing for others, but they often lack the means to do this well. Most designers today acknowledge that they cannot know exactly what the "user" would say or do. Applied social scientists and other types of researchers have come into the picture to provide information and insight about people. They often serve as the representative or advocate for the "user". This has helped to narrow the gap to some extent. For example, ethnography has been recognized as providing knowledge about people, context and experience that can be useful in the design process.

But with the entry of the researchers into the design landscape, there is now even more talk about the *gap between researchers and designers*. The gap can be the source of conflict, misunderstandings and lack of respect. The gap is due to differences between people from a range of disciplines with their specialized skill sets, languages and mindsets. So while the fuzzy front end provides the context for design exploration, it also introduces gaps and barriers relating to the expertise of the people who are working together there.

Who are the real experts when we talk about designing and innovating for future experience? I will argue that the real experts are the people we are attempting to serve through the design process, not the designers, researchers, engineers and business people. With this shift in mindset, we can invite future "users" into the fuzzy front end of the design process and move toward designing *with* them, not just *for* them. A shared participatory mindset can break down the disciplinary and/or cultural boundaries. And when we add the appropriate environment and materials to support and provoke collective creativity (Sanders, 2013), we have a design space that supports the exploration of new ideas, even in wicked problem situations.

NEW ROLES FOR DESIGNERS AND THE PEOPLE THAT THEY SERVE

The move from *designing for* to *designing with* requires dramatic changes in the roles that people play. These changes relate to both designers and to those served by design. Figure 35.2 shows how these roles and relationships have changed over time.

Starting at the bottom of the diagram where the time is the recent past, we see that designers served industry while people played the roles of customers and consumers. Moving up the timeline, user-centered design is a pivotal point where the attention shifts toward the

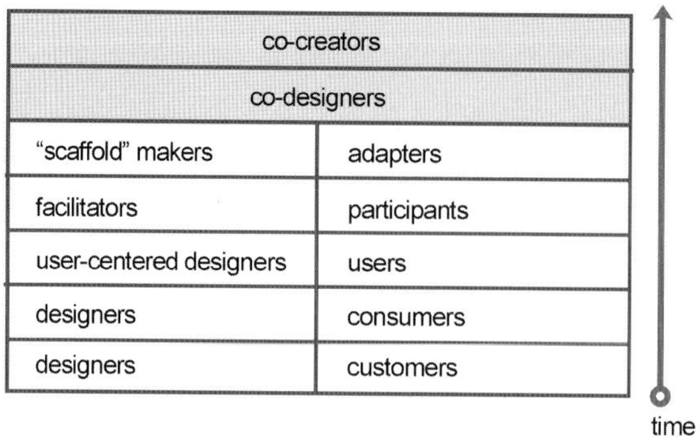

co-creators	
co-designers	
"scaffold" makers	adapters
facilitators	participants
user-centered designers	users
designers	consumers
designers	customers

FIGURE 35.2 The roles that designers play (in the left column) and the roles that people play (in the right-column) have been changing over time

future users but the mindset is still one of designing for them. The top four rows describe the various role relationships characteristic of the designing with mindset. Here we can see that designers change in their role to become facilitators of the co-designing process and the future users become participants in that process. It is at this stage that designers learn how to facilitate the creativity of non-designers. Moving up the timeline, designers are also exploring how to make scaffolds that others can use to support and provoke their own creativity (Sanders, 2002). In the top two rows, their roles blend together to the extent that is often difficult to tell who is who. In these situations the designer may play the activist role and serve mainly to catalyze the process of collective creativity for the people being served by design.

It is important to note that all the role-defined relationships shown in Figure 35.2 are important and relevant today. Design needs to serve both industry and the people. In fact, the proliferation of role relationships and the different objectives for designing are causing a radical rethinking and remaking of design curricula at the university level. We need to give students experience in both designing for people and designing with people so that they can decide for themselves what kind of designer they will become.

WHAT ARE THE SPACES OF CO-CREATION?

The stages on which design takes place are different today from the stages of the just recent past. Design is not just about visualization and the application of individual creativity anymore.

The problems that designers are being invited to help solve cannot be addressed by the individual, no matter how smart or creative they are. The situation is far too complex. We face significant challenges in that the problems are wicked and the new landscapes of design are fuzzy. The only way we will be able to address the important challenges we face today is to do so collectively. Collective creativity can lead to relevant and sustainable innovation.

What does it look like to be at the fuzzy front end of the design development process where the problems are wicked? Figure 35.3 shows a conceptual representation of nested design spaces as a framework for navigation (inspired by Lerdahl, E. 2001).

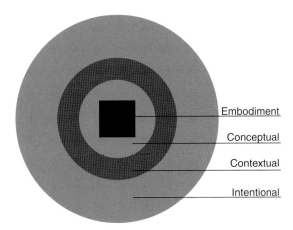

FIGURE 35.3 A framework for navigating the fuzzy front end of the design development process where the problems are wicked and the landscape is fuzzy

The *embodiment* of the idea (e.g., the resulting artifact, activity or experience) is shown at the core. This is the ultimate deliverable of design. Embodiment can take on many different forms depending on what the goal is and how the challenge is approached. For example, the embodiment might be the output of one of the traditional design disciplines (e.g., product, communication, space or system, etc.) or the myriad of forms that are emerging from the new landscapes of design (e.g., service design, social design, design fiction, etc.).

The *conceptual design space* surrounds the core. It consists of all the territory that has been or will be navigated in design exploration. The conceptual design space in nested within the *contextual design space* that is described by the larger and constantly changing domains relevant to design development including: use and ownership, environments of use, manufacturing constraints and opportunities, distribution patterns and processes, sales and marketing, etc.

The contextual design space is nested within the *intentional design space* which sits in the speculative future. It is here that we figure out what makes sense in the future. The intentional design space affords the solving of wicked problems and the identification of latent opportunities. For example, the exploration here might address issues such as:

- how can we improve people's lives?
- what is meaningful to people?
- what do people value?
- what do people desire?
- what will people find to be useful in the future?

The intentional design space points toward the future. Design embodiments that emerge from an exploration of intentional design space include organizational transformation, behavior change, and/or social transformation. Figure 35.4 shows that the fuzzy front end of design sits in the intentional design space.

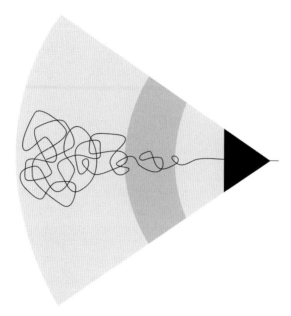

FIGURE 35.4 The fuzzy front end of design sits in the intentional design space

As we move from embodiment to concept to context and to intention, the space gets fuzzier and more complex. New tools for imagining, visualizing and communicating will be needed to navigate in the larger design spaces. We need tools for both two- and three-dimensional imagination and expression. We also need tools for four-dimensional (i.e., designing over time) imagination and expression in order to enact and reflect upon future scenarios of use.

Each larger design space requires more different types of people to be working together. We need a collective lens to make sense of what we see so that we can act from many simultaneous perspectives. If we work collectively in the fuzzy front end, we can get a very long view that will give us a far greater chance of achieving relevant and sustainable innovation.

HOW DO WE PRACTICE CO-CREATION?

How can we work collectively in the fuzzy front end? The participatory prototyping cycle (PPC) is a model for co-creation in design (Sanders, 2013). It invites all relevant stakeholders into the design process and supplies them with tools, methods and activities that they can use without having education or experience as designers. The PPC combines making, telling and enacting and uses each activity to fuel the next. For example, making is a skill that many adults do not necessarily feel comfortable using these days. Telling and enacting, on the other hand, are skills that everyone has familiarity with, especially when conducted in inviting environments. By putting making together with telling and enacting, we can empower people who are not skilled in making to externalize their ideas and feelings about the future.

The participatory prototyping cycle (PPC) is a framework for action in design. Prototyping unfolds as an iterative loop of making, telling and enacting in the future design domains.

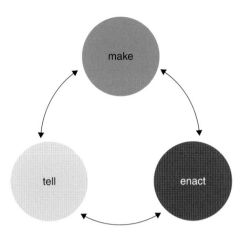

FIGURE 35.5 The participatory prototyping cycle (PPC) is a framework for action and a model for co-creation in design

A unique characteristic of the PPC model is its emphasis on the cyclic and iterative relationship between making, telling and enacting. You can enter the PPC at any point, i.e., by *making* things, or *telling* stories about the future or *enacting* future experiences. And from each entry point, you can move in any direction.

In making, we use our hands to embody ideas in the form of physical artifacts. The nature of the artifact changes from early to later stages in the design process. Artifacts made early in the process are likely to describe experiences while artifacts made later in the process are more likely to resemble the objects and/or spaces. Telling is a verbal description about future scenarios of use. We might tell a story about the future or describe a future artifact. But this can be difficult for people who don't have verbal access to their own tacit knowledge. Enacting refers to the use of the body in the environment to express ideas about future experience. We also call this pretending. Acting and performance can also be considered forms of enactment that are particularly useful later in the design process. There has been some interest lately in various forms of enactment as a design tool (e.g., Burns et al., 1995; Suri and Buchenau, 2000; Oulasvirta et al., 2003; Buxton, 2007; Simsarian, 2003; Diaz et al., 2009) and some of this work has been done collaboratively with end-users and other stakeholders.

HOW DOES THE PPC WORK IN THE DESIGN DEVELOPMENT PROCESS?

How does the PPC work in the design development process? Think of the PPC as a generative seed moving and tumbling across all phases of the design process over time. (See Figure 35.6.) The leading activity (i.e., making, telling or enacting) will vary by phase, influenced by team composition and project type.

In the fuzzy front end, enactment is the lead activity because the focus is on exploring and understanding experience (i.e., past, present and future experience). Enacting is the ideal

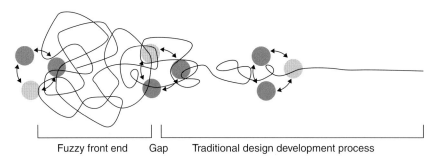

Fuzzy front end   Gap   Traditional design development process

FIGURE 35.6 The participatory prototyping cycle in action

medium for this. The earliest forms of enactment can be best described as 'pretending'. Later forms of enactment might include improvisation and performance. Enacting can be done alone, but the results are far more evocative and provocative when done collaboratively. Enacting will be further synergized when followed by making and telling activities.

Making is the PPC mode that is in the lead across the gap. The purpose here is to explore and visualize ideas in order to figure out what future situations make sense. The various forms of making give shape to the future, with enacting and telling being ways to enrich and extend future artifacts. The earliest forms of making include maps, timelines and collages. Later forms of making include props, Velcro-models and really rough prototypes. The traditional forms of prototyping such as sketching and model making appear much later in the design development process.

Telling is the PPC mode that is in the lead later in the design process. The purpose of telling is to keep the idea alive and evolving. The earliest types of telling come in the form of stories. Later forms of telling include descriptions of the artifacts that are imagined. Even later forms of telling include presentations and selling events. If a participatory process has been used throughout the design process, the primary activities will be telling or sharing since buy-in to the idea by future users and other stakeholders is likely to already have occurred. On the other hand, if a participatory process has not been used, the primary activity can better be described as selling since those who will be affected by the design may still need to be convinced that the idea is good.

The chart in Figure 35.7 compares the activities and artifacts that emerge in the use of the participatory prototyping cycle over time. The iterative use of the PPC throughout the process can help to bridge the gap between the fuzzy front end and the design development process.

IN CONCLUSION: WHERE ARE WE GOING?

We face significant economic, environmental and social challenges today. Design innovation can help, but only if we open up the design process to everyone. Most of us come to the table with our own disciplinary tools, methods and mindsets, but participation from people

	Fuzzy front end	Gap	Design development process
Making	Maps Collages Timelines	Very rough models Velcro-models Props	Sketches Mockups Models Prototypes
Telling	Sharing dreams Telling stories	Sharing thoughts Presenting ideas	Presenting the concept Selling the idea
Enacting	Pretending Role playing	Improvising Scenario building	Performing Presenting

FIGURE 35.7 Making, telling and enacting take on different forms in the fuzzy front end, the gap and in the design development process

across many disciplines is necessary. Radical innovation, with its focus on the individual designer, is not enough to address the challenges of wicked problems. Design-led innovation needs to be *co-design-led* to address sustainable futures. Participatory prototyping that starts in the fuzzy front end of the design development process can result in innovation that is sustainable.

Younger people are more open toward participatory practices than are older people. The Millennials, in particular, are often wonderful students and practitioners of co-designing since their worldview places high value on participation and collaboration. Co-designing will flourish in the future as more young people take on increasingly more influential positions within organizations and communities. Sustainable innovation is not an oxymoron.

© 2015 Elizabeth B.-N. Sanders. Previously published in *Changing Paradigms: Designing for a Sustainable Future*, 1st Cumulus Think Tank Publication, December 2015, Aalto University School of Arts, Design and Architecture, Finland, pages 296–301. Republished with kind permission from Elizabeth B.-N. Sanders.

REFERENCES

Burns, C., Dishman, E., Johnson, B. and Verplank, B. (1995) '"Informance': Min(d)ing future contexts for scenario-based interaction design', *BayCHI*, Palo Alto.

Buxton, B. (2007) *Sketching User Experiences: Getting the Design Right and the Right Design*, Morgan Kaufmann Publishers, San Francisco.

Diaz, L., Reunanen, M. and Salmi, A. (2009) 'Role playing and collaborative scenario design development'. *International Conference on Engineering Design*, ICED '09, Stanford University.

Lerdahl, E. (2001) *Staging for Creative Collaboration in Design Teams: Models, Tools And Methods*. PhD Dissertation. Norwegian University of Science and Technology, Department of Product Design Engineering, Trondheim, Norway.

Ouslasvirta, A., Kurvinen, E. and Kankainen, T. (2003) 'Understanding contexts by being there: Case studies in bodystorming'. *Personal Ubiquitous Computing*. Springer-Verlag, London.

Rittel, H. and Webber, M. (1973) Dilemmas in a general theory of planning, pp. 155–169, *Policy Sciences*, Vol. 4, Elsevier Scientific Publishing Company, Inc., Amsterdam.

Sanders, E.B.-N. (2002) Scaffolds for experiencing in the new design space. In *Information Design*, Institute for Information Design Japan (Editors), IID.J, Graphic-Sha Publishing Co., Ltd. (In Japanese).

Sanders, E.B.-N. (2013) Prototyping for the design spaces of the future. In Valentine, L. (Editor) *Prototype: Design and Craft in the 21st Century*, Bloomsbury.

Sanders, L. (2013) New spaces, places and materials for co-designing sustainable futures. *Emily Carr University of Art + Design, Design Research Journal*, Issue 04, Spring.

Simsarian, K.T. (2003) 'Take it to the next stage: The roles of role playing in the design process'. *CHI 2003: New Horizons*.

Suri, J.F. and Buchenau, M. (2000) 'Experience prototyping', *Symposium on Designing Interactive Systems, Proceedings of the Conference on Designing Interactive Systems: Processes, Practices, Methods, and Techniques*, pp. 424–433.

Verganti, R. (2009) *Design-Driven Innovation: Changing the Rules of Competition by Radically Innovating what Things Mean*, Harvard Business School Publishing Corp.

CHAPTER THIRTY SIX

Social Innovation and Design: Enabling, Replicating and Synergizing

EZIO MANZINI

Give a man a fish and you feed him for a day.
Teach a man to fish and you feed him for a lifetime.

Tao Te Ching

INTRODUCTION

Worldwide, contemporary society is facing new problems in everyday life. A growing number of people are using their capabilities and existing assets to invent new and sustainable ways of living and doing. Even though these inventions, as a whole, are still far from being considered mainstream, a new world is emerging: a sustainable world, an alternative to the still dominant one.

Is this interpretation a consistent one? Or is this emerging new world only wishful thinking? Or, on the contrary, it is a concrete possibility: something that is not yet a reality, but that could become real if the necessary moves were taken?

To aid in the development of this process, this chapter will propose a journey that, starting from an introduction to the notion of social innovation, focalizes some strategies *to empower, replicate and synergize* the most promising cases. It concludes by outlining, within this framework, what *design* can do to conceive and enhance such cases.

SOCIAL INNOVATION

Once we start to observe society in search of social inventions, a variety of interesting examples appear: groups of families who decide to share services to reduce economic and environmental costs, but also to create new forms of neighborhoods (*co-housing* and a variety of forms of *sharing* and *mutual-help* within a residential building or neighborhood); new forms of exchange and barter (*local exchange trading systems*, LETS, and *Time Banks*); services where elderly and young people help each other and, at the same time, promote a new idea of welfare (*collaborative social services*); neighborhood gardens set-up and managed by citizens who, by doing so, improve the quality of the city and of the social fabric (*guerrilla gardens, community gardens, green roofs*); systems of mobility alternative to individual cars (*car sharing, car pooling, the rediscovery of the possibilities offered by bicycles*), fair and direct trade between producers and consumers (*fair trade initiatives*). The list could continue touching every area of daily life and emerging everywhere in the world (To read more about social innovation cases, navigate the website of Young Foundation, Social Innovation Exchange, NESTA and DESIS).

The first and most evident common characteristic of these initiatives is that they are sociotechnical changes emerging from the creative re-combination of existing assets (*from social capital to historical heritage, from traditional craftsmanship to accessible advanced technology*), which aim to achieve socially recognized goals in a new way. The second one is that they are forms of innovation driven by social demands rather than by the market and/or autonomous techno-scientific research, and generated more by the actors involved than by specialists. We can name them, as a whole, social innovation (Mulgan, 2006; Murray, Caulier-Grice, Mulgan, 2010). More precisely: bottom-up social innovation towards sustainability (Jégou, Manzini, 2008).

Promising Cases

Looking at such cases of social innovation we can observe that they challenge traditional ways of doing things and introduce new, different and more sustainable behavior. Of course, each one of them should be analyzed in detail (to assess their effective environmental and social sustainability more accurately). However, we can easily recognize their coherence with some of the fundamental guidelines for sustainability.

First of all, many of them have an unprecedented capacity to bring individual interests into line with social and environmental ones (for example to reinforce social fabric) and generate new and more sustainable ideas of wellbeing, where greater value is given to the quality of the social and physical context, a caring attitude, a slower pace in life, collaborative actions, new forms of community and new ideas of locality (Manzini, Jégou, 2003).

Furthermore, achieving this wellbeing appears to be coherent with major guidelines for environmental sustainability, such as: positive attitudes towards sharing spaces and goods; a preference for biological, regional and seasonal food; a tendency toward the regeneration of local networks and finally, and most importantly, coherence with an economic model that could be less transport intensive and more capable of integrating renewable energies and eco-efficient systems (Vezzoli, Manzini, 2008).

Precisely because these cases suggest solutions that merge personal interests with social and environmental ones, they should be considered as promising cases: initiatives where, in different ways and for different reasons, people have been able to steer their expectations and individual behavior towards more sustainable ways of living and producing (Jégou, Manzini, 2008).

Creative Communities

Behind each promising case of social innovation are groups of people who have been able to imagine, develop and manage them. A first glance shows that they have some fundamental traits in common: they are all groups of people who cooperatively invent, enhance and manage innovative solutions. And they do so by recombining what already exists, without waiting for a general change in the system (in economy, institutions, large infrastructures etc.). For this reason, these groups of people can be defined as creative communities: people who cooperatively invent, enhance and manage innovative solutions for new ways of living (Meroni, 2007).

A second characteristic is that they have developed out of problems posed by everyday contemporary life such as: how can we overcome the isolation that an exasperated individualism has brought and brings in its wake? How can we organize daily functions if the family and neighborhood that no longer provide the support they traditionally offered? How can we respond to the demand for natural food and healthy living conditions when living in a global metropolis? How can we support local production without being trampled on by the power of the mighty apparatus of global trade?

Creative communities generate solutions able to answer all these questions. Questions that are as day-to-day as they are radical. Questions to which the dominant production and consumption system, in spite of its overwhelming offer of products and services, is unable to give an answer and, above all, is unable to give an adequate answer from the point of view of sustainability. We can therefore state that creative communities apply their creativity and take a different perspective on mainstream models of thinking. In doing so they, consciously or unconsciously, become concrete steps towards sustainability.

A third commonality is that creative communities result from an original combination of *demands and opportunities*. Here the demands are always posed by problems of contemporary everyday life, and the opportunities arise from different combinations of two basic elements: the existence (or at least the memory) of *traditions* and the possibility of using (in an appropriate way) an existing set of technologies (*in the form of products, services and infrastructures*) (Rheingold, 2002; Bauwens, 2007; Leadbeater, 2008).

Collaborative Organizations

Creative communities are living entities that evolve over time. A closer observation shows that the promising cases they generate can be seen as organizations at different stages of development. In fact, when they consolidate into mature organizations, creative communities become a new kind of organization: *collaborative organizations* that, in practical terms, can operate as social services, responsible enterprises or user associations (Jégou, Manzini, 2008).

- **Collaborative services** are a particular kind of services where final users are actively involved and assume the role of service co-designer and co-producers. Some examples are: houses where elderly people of different ages live in a resource-sharing community suited to their diverse needs and lifestyles; services that facilitate house sharing between elderly and young people, where students find cheap, family-style accommodation, while giving lonely but independent elderly people help, companionship and financial support; self-organized nurseries for small groups of infants, making best use of existing resources such as parents' capabilities (social resource) and houses (physical resource).

- **Collaborative enterprises** are entrepreneurial production and service initiatives that enhance new models of locally-based activities by encouraging direct relationships with users and consumers who, in this case too, become co-producers. Examples are: farms that help clients to experience the value of biodiversity in the food chain; local enterprises that teach people how to reuse old and used materials; shops where people exchange used sporting goods; housing companies that renovate houses for more collaborative ways of living.

- **Collaborative associations** are groups of people who collaboratively solve problems or expose new possibilities (and who, again, become co-producers of the results). Some examples in this category are: groups of residents who transform an abandoned lot into a shared neighborhood garden; groups of people who love cooking and who use their skills to cook for a larger group, dining together in one of the members' houses; groups of people who exchange mutual help in terms of time and skills; groups of elderly people and teachers who organize vegetable gardens for children in elementary schools.

Creative communities and the collaborative organizations they may generate are important for us not only because they are sociologically interesting (although they do reflect a significant aspect of contemporary societies) or because they can generate potentially profitable niche-markets for new businesses (even though this opportunity too could and should be explored). They are important because they are "prototypes" of sustainable ways of living that can be implemented as viable solutions to urgent modern-day problems. And therefore they have the possibility to spread and to support sustainable lifestyles for a large number of people.

Scaling-Up

Creative communities and collaborative organizations have been introduced here as bottom-up initiatives: actions "from the bottom" that give rise to promising cases of social innovations. However, a closer observation of their evolution from the initial idea towards more mature forms of organization indicates that their possibility of long-term existence, and often even of their start-up, depends on complex mechanisms, and that the initiative taken directly by the people concerned (bottom-up interaction) is often supported by information exchanges with other similar organizations (peer-to-peer interaction) and by different kinds of intervention from institutions, civic organizations or companies (top-down interaction).

For instance, a micro-nursery exists thanks to the active participation of the mothers and fathers involved. However, it may have been started by looking at the experiences of other groups (and eventually interacting with some of them) and it may be backed up by specific top-down initiatives and enabling tools, e.g. a guide-book indicating, step by step, the procedure to be followed in starting up and managing it; local authority support in assessment (to guarantee its conformity to established standards); the support of a centralized service (in case of educational or medical problems that cannot be solved within the nursery itself). These examples, like many other similar ones, tell us that *creative communities and collaborative services should be considered as bottom-up initiatives not because everything happens at grassroots level, but because the precondition for their existence is the active involvement of people directly interested.*

Consequently their starting up, their daily life and their possible improvement usually emerge out of a complex interplay between bottom-up, top-down and peer-to-peer interactions (which differ from case to case). It is exactly on this basis that we can assume that, even if the creativity and collaborative actions that are the necessary building blocks of every creative community and collaborative organization cannot be planned, something can be done to make their existence more probable and their diffusion potential higher. Therefore, the challenge now is: How to consolidate and scale-up promising cases of social innovation while trying to maintain the relational qualities of the original initiative? That is, how to increase their social and economic impact without dramatically increasing in size? A careful observation of the on-going initiatives indicates that this possibility concretely exists. In fact, if in the past century, consolidating and scaling-up small and local initiatives meant inevitably growing in dimension and bureaucratic structures. Today however, in the age of networks, there are additional possibilities. Here, two main, and complementary, design strategies are presented: (1) To consolidate promising cases enabling the active participation of a larger group of people (from "social heroes" to several "active people") and to spread the best ideas *replicating* them in other contexts (from few to many) and (2) to integrate different small projects into a larger program synergizing them (from local to regional).

ENABLING AND REPLICATING

The evolution from the original inventions and working prototypes towards lasting and effective collaborative organizations asks for both, a *favorable environment* aiming at creating for them tolerant norms and positive economic and socio-cultural habitat, and *enabling solutions* conceived to transform the original inventions into more accessible ones.

Favorable Environment

We have already stated that creative communities and collaborative organizations are living entities and that they depend on the quality of their environment. At the same time, they are brand new entities with (very often) a contradictory relationship with the same contexts in which they have appeared, that can be hostile or favorable to their existence and development.

The most favorable environment for creative communities and collaborative organizations is characterized by a high degree of tolerance. Since the promising cases at issue here are by definition forms of organization that radically differ from the norm, fostering them means accepting something that will probably not fit in with existing norms and regulations. Consequently the tolerance required for them to thrive must be expressed at different levels, i.e. in social, economical, political and administrative terms.

But the tolerance we are referring to here is not a natural gift. It depends on a wide range of choices done by different social actors, in different moments and dealing with different topics. In other words, to improve a context's capacity to tolerate creative communities *new governance tools* are needed. These tools must be capable of generating a favorable social, political and administrative context and, therefore, facilitate the regeneration of specific contextual traditions or foster an appropriate technological infrastructure, to cultivate new talents (skills and abilities). How can this be done? Obviously, there is no single, simple answer to this question. However, some particular opportunities are appearing. In particular, the diffusion of the new organizational models emerging from the Internet can become the enabling technology to facilitate the shift from the present rigid, hierarchical governance models to the flexible, open, horizontal ones needed to support creative communities and collaborative services. Finally, the existence of entrepreneurs capable of recognizing business potentials generated by social innovation is another component of an environment favorable to social innovation. In fact, when they exist, a very interesting virtuous cycle may appear: new business ideas and new technologies can support social innovation, and vice versa. This represents a positive loop, in which social innovation triggers new businesses and technological innovations, can promote a new and sustainable, economy.

In my view, the clearest example of this positive loop is the one created, in the last two decades, in the food and agriculture field. Its result has been the present broad recognition of the new value and viability of new food networks based on local and seasonal food. This new model is challenging, worldwide, the dominant unsustainable agro-industrial one. It must be added that this radical, positive innovation has been triggered and supported by movements (such as the Slow Food one) operating on both the practical side, with the farmers and the consumers/co-producers, and on the cultural and political ones, with opinion leaders and policy makers (Petrini, 2007; Petrini, 2010).

Enabling Solutions

Generating a new idea, creatively adapting and managing an existing one or even simply actively participating in an on-going venture often calls for a huge commitment in terms of time and personal dedication. Although this almost heroic aspect is one of the most fascinating characteristics of these initiatives, it is also an objective limit to their long-term existence and to the possibility of being replicated and adopted by many. So this appears to be the major limit to the diffusion of collaborative organizations: the limited number of people capable and willing to cross the threshold of commitment required to become one of their promoters, or even just an active participant. In fact, it has been verified that these initiatives, with their mix of practical results and socializing effects, appear very attractive to many people, but, in practice, for the majority of them, simply require too much attention and time, i.e., they call for too large an investment of the very resources that today are, or are perceived to be, the scarcest ones. To overcome these problems, collaborative organizations need to become more *accessible* (reducing the threshold we mentioned before), more *effective* (increasing the ratio between results and required individual and social efforts) and more attractive (enhancing people motivation to be active). In order to facilitate the positive evolution of the original ideas, a new generation of product-service systems, the enabling solutions, has to be conceived and developed.

For example: the intention of a group of parents to start up a micro-nursery could be facilitated by an enabling solution that includes, not only a step by step procedure indicating what must be done, but also a system of guarantees that certify to the suitability of the parent organizer and the house, and health and educational support for problems that cannot be solved within the nursery itself. Similarly: a solidarity purchasing group could be supported by special software designed to manage shopping and guarantee relationships with producers; a co-housing project could be facilitated by a system that puts potential participants in touch, helps find suitable buildings or building plots, and that helps overcome any administrative and financial difficulties. What these examples tell us is that, case by case, new product-service systems can be thought up which, starting from the capabilities of organizers, can supply support at the weak points, integrating the knowledge and abilities that prove to be missing.

Given the diversity of the organizations to which enabling solutions should be applied, each one of them will require specific features. Nevertheless, some very general guidelines can be outlined. For instance it will be necessary: to promote communication strategies that provide the required knowledge; to support individual capabilities in order to make the organization accessible to a larger group of people; to develop service and business models that match the economic and/or cultural interests of potential participants; to reduce the amount of time and space required, and increase flexibility; to facilitate community building; and so on (Cottam, Leadbeater, 2004; Manzini, 2010).

On these bases, we can propose the following definition of the new product-service systems: *enabling solutions are product-service systems* (Halen, Vezzoli, C., & Wimmer, 2005) *providing cognitive, technical and organizational instruments so as to enable individuals and/ or communities to achieve a result, using their skills and abilities to the best advantage and, at the same time, to regenerate the quality of living contexts, in which they reside* (Jégou, Manzini, 2008). In practical terms, enabling solutions can include:

- **Digital platforms** to connect people and to make it easier for collaborative organizations to function smoothly (such as: customized and intelligent booking and ordering systems, tracking and tracing technologies; fluid payment systems);
- **Flexible spaces** that can be used by communities for mixed public-private functions (and as incubators for the collaborative organizations start-up phase);
- **Logistic services** to support the new producer-consumer networks;
- **Citizens' agencies**, acting as catalysts for new grassroots initiatives, but also as facilitators for existing ones to grow, multiply and flourish;

- **Information services,** for example, to deliver specific advice when new procedures and/or new technologies have to be integrated;
- **Co-design methodologies,** to conceive and develop a way to collaborate all the previously indicated artifacts.

Replication Strategies

Until now, the diffusion of *collaborative organizations* took place spontaneously and at a relatively slow pace. Here we will discuss whether and how this movement could be accelerated by appropriate actions. That is, by applying some forms of the replication strategy.

Looking to what has been done until now in different fields of activities, we can easily discover that several kinds of replication strategies have been already proposed and developed to scale-up services, businesses and social enterprises. Even though operating in different contexts and moved by motivations, these existing replication strategies present interesting similarities and offer useful experiences. In particular, we will consider three of them: *franchising*, mainly used in commercial activities; *formats*, with reference to the entertainment industry, and *toolkits*, which is used in several application fields where the do-it-yourself approach has been adopted.

The first two replication strategies, *franchising* and *formats*, have different characters and, normally, they have been applied for commercial and business-oriented initiatives. Nevertheless, they can give an idea on how to deal with enabling the existence of small-scale enterprises (the case of franchising) and on how to actualize ideas and organizations in different contexts (the case of formats). Of course, a TV program idea is normally very far from collaborative organizations, and a commercial business under the umbrella of a big brand is even further. However, these experiences indicate that the discussion on how to enable a large number of collaborative organizations to transform a solution idea into operative programs must not start from zero.

Finally, we can consider a replication strategy based on toolkits. It is clear that the notion of toolkit could be very interesting in the discussion on how to replicate promising collaborative organizations.

A *toolkit* normally consists of a set of tangible and intangible instruments conceived and produced to make a specific task easier (and, therefore, feasible also for non-expert people).

Today, tools and toolkits are (mainly) conceived for individual self-help. In order to support collaborative organizations, these traditional "individualistic" toolkits must evolve and become community-oriented ones: sets of tools conceived to empower groups of people. That is, to help them in being active and building, in an easier and more effective way, some commonly recognized values. If and when this evolution takes place, the toolkit idea converges with an enabling solution. In short: toolkits become enabling solutions conceived to make a collaborative organization idea more easily replicable in several different contexts.

SYNERGIZING

The *synergizing strategy* consists in developing local projects and coordinating and systemizing them at a larger territorial scale (neighborhoods, cities, regions) and/or in relation to larger complex systems (healthcare, education, administration, and so on).

When a territorial system is concerned (it could be a urban regeneration program, a regional food network promotion, a community-based development), a synergizing strategy permits to improve its overall social, economic and environmental quality thanks to a development process triggered by a set of synergic self-standing local initiatives. Similarly, when the challenge is transforming a complex organization (could it be a public administration, an healthcare or a school system), the process can be prepared, started and oriented launching a number of local initiatives to mobilize the whole organization and promote its transition towards a more effective one.

To better understand what this expression refers to, let's consider, as an example, the *Nutrire Milano* project: an on going initiative promoted and developed in Milano by Slow Food, Politecnico di Milano, Facoltà di Scienze Gastronomiche and several other local partners (Meroni, Someone, Trapani, 2009). This project aims at regenerating the Milanese peri-urban agriculture (that is the agriculture near the city) and, at the same time, offering organic and local food opportunities to citizens. To do that implies promoting radically new relationships between the countryside and the city. That is, to create brand-new networks of farmers and citizens based on direct relationships and mutual support.

The process started from the recognition of available (social, cultural and economic) local resources and of existing best practices. Moving from there, a strategy developed considering the emerging trends towards a new possible synergy between cities and their countryside (such as the ones towards 0-mile food and proximity tourism). On this basis, a shared and socially recognized vision has been built: the vision of a rural-urban area where agriculture flourishes feeding the city and, at the same time, offering citizens opportunities for a multiplicity of farming and nature related activities.

To enhance this vision the program is articulated in local projects, which are several self-standing projects, each of them supporting, in different ways, some farmer activities and *framework* actions including in-depth context analysis, scenario co-creations, communication, promotion and coordination of different individual local projects. It is remarkable that in a large project like this (a 5-year project involving a very wide regional area), thanks to its adaptability and scalability, a first concrete result has been obtained in less than one year since its launch (it has been a very successful farmers market initiative). It can be added that two new initiatives will be realized in the next two years and that several others are progressing and will be implemented in the future (keeping in account the very concrete experiences of the first three ones).

Acupunctural Planning

As it has been said, the previous example represents a growing group of large-scale projects.[1] These projects are very diverse and context-specific. Nevertheless, they present four common characters: (1) all of them aim at sustainable social changes at the regional scale; (2) all of them express the explicit intention to achieve these results activating high level of citizen participation and (3) all of them have been started and are driven by some specific *design initiatives* (that is, they have been—explicitly or implicitly—led by design, i.e. by design agency and/or design schools) (Manzini, Rizzo, 2011).

These large-scale projects present a similar architecture: Multiple local projects are promoted and synergized by one *framework*. Where local projects are self-standing initiatives, highly rooted in the local specificities and capable to use at best some existing physical and social resources. And where *framework projects* are design and communication initiatives including *scenarios* (to give different local projects a common direction), *strategies* (to indicate how to implement scenarios) and specific supporting activities (to systemize the local projects, to empower them and to communicate the overall project) (Manzini, Jégou, Meroni, 2009).

Given its specific nature, the synergizing strategy permits to conceive and develop large-scale programs that, thanks to its same nature, are extremely flexible, scalable and adaptable in time. A strategy that is particularly adapt to be implemented in turbulent times (as the ones we currently live in) and when *territorial systems* or *large organizations* are involved. For this same reason, it can also be defined as *planning by projects* or, adopting as a metaphor the practice of the traditional Chinese medicine—*acupunctural planning* generating changes in large and complex systems operating with well-defined initiatives on some of their "sensible nodes" (Meroni, 2008; Jégou, 2010).

DESIGN FOR SOCIAL INNOVATION

Today, creative communities and collaborative organizations constitute a constellation of small initiatives mainly promoted by active local communities. Nevertheless, as we have seen, an attentive observation indicates that, if *favorable conditions* are created, these small, local social inventions and their working prototypes can be scaled-up and consolidate, replicate and integrate with larger programs and generate great sustainable changes. In other words, we have seen that, if the *original social invention can be generated on the bases of pure intuitions, to make these initiatives more effective and replicable a design approach is required* (Brown, Wyatt, 2010; Manzini, 2009).

It comes that scaling-up social innovation is a particular kind of design process: a design process in which those who "design" are very diverse social actors (including "ordinary citizens"), and in which a new field of activities emerges for the "design experts". We will refer to it with the term: *design for social innovation*, and intend: *"whatever expert design can do to trigger and support social innovation"* (here, the term "expert design" refers to the whole design community, including, as we will see later, whoever is using design knowledge in an expert way: from professional designers to researchers and theorists, from design schools to design journals and publishers).

Creative People and Design Experts

Given the previous very general definition, let's consider what it means in practical terms. We can take, as examples, two well-known solution ideas; *co-housing* (family living nearby, sharing some residential services and collaborating in facing some everyday life problems) and *car-pooling* (people using the same car in order to share the journey expenses and reduce the traffic). They are examples of social innovation we can find in Europe and worldwide. Of course, other and very diverse examples could be chosen. But these ones seem quite clear and sufficiently well known to be effectively used for our discussion.

Both co-housing and car-pooling have been started by "ordinary citizens" capable of imagining something new, that is, something radically different from the mainstream way of thinking and doing. In fact: the co-housers formulated a concept of housing based on an original mix of private and community spaces and services; the car-poolers had the idea of using private cars as a quasi-public service (and to become, as car owners, quasi-public drivers). Further to this, all of them have been able to move from these visions to reality, setting up the appropriate processes and becoming active agents in the delivery of the imagined results. Now, given that to imagine something that does not exist yet and to make it happen is, by definition, a design activity, it results that these co-housing and car-pooling solutions are, by all means, the results of successful design processes.

These specific observations can be generalized saying that, as anticipated, all the social innovation processes are design processes. And all the involved actors, adopting a design approach, are (consciously or not) designers.

Given that, the question is: if all the social innovation actors—"ordinary people" included—are de-facto designers, what is the role of the design experts and their design community? To make a long story short, we could say that the design experts' role is to use their expertise (that is, their specific design knowledge and skills) to empower the other social actors' design capabilities.

Design Knowledge

The previous statement asks for some explanations. The starting point is the observation that adopting a design approach corresponds to the use of basic human capability (that is, a capability that every human being has). This potential human capability, as every other capability, from creativity to music sensitivity, can be cultivated or not. In particular, it can be applied in a naïve way or in an expert way. And here we are with the specific issue raised by our original observation: the human capability to adopt a design approach can be applied inventing, or re-inventing, what to do—from zero. Or, it can build on existing knowledge (previous experiences, appropriate methods and skills, cultivated sensitivities). This specific knowledge, to which we can refer with the term *design knowledge*, is what design experts, and in general the whole design community, can bring to social innovation.

It comes, in conclusion, that design for social innovation is what the design experts can do to trigger and support more effective co-design processes.

Let's return to the co-housing example. In Milano, some years ago, the DESIS Lab of the Politecnico di Milano developed, with other partners, an enabling system dedicated to groups of people willing to realize co-housing initiatives. This system included a digital platform (to create a large community of interest regarding co-housing). Several specific services were also included to help potential co-housers in the co-housing realization process: from the search for suitable areas to the co-housers' group building, and from real estate experts' services to the specific technical expertise needed in the co-design of shareable services and spaces. Parallel to that, a communication strategy (to make the co-housing advantages more evident and attractive) was developed. The first result of these design initiatives was the creation of a dedicated company (Cohousing.it) which is still promoting several cohousing initiatives in Milano. The second, and probably most important result was that this experience generated a design knowledge that, successively, has been adopted and further developed, by the Fondazione Housing Sociale (Social Housing Foundation)—an important institution dedicated to the support of the social housing in Italy. The Fondazione Housing Sociale now integrates the notion of *collaborative housing* in its programs and utilizes several design ideas and tools coming from the previous co-housing experience.

By generalizing this specific experience, we can say that if it is true that cases like these have historically and frequently been started by ordinary, but highly committed people. To last in time and to spread, they had to be reinforced by appropriate top-down interventions. It is in this delicate interplay between bottom-up and top-down initiatives that design for social innovation can play a major role.

The mainstream way of doing it is, for design experts, to facilitate existing cases of social innovation, helping them to become more effective, accessible, pleasurable and, potentially, replicable. But designers can also act as activists, triggering, or even initiating, new collaborative organizations (replicating good ideas or starting-up brand new ones). In parallel to this, as we have seen in the previous paragraph, design experts can also promote large systemic changes synergizing a variety of local initiatives and developing specifically conceived *framework projects*. Finally, they can feed the social conversations with *scenarios* and *proposals*, aiming at building shared visions of the future.

A New Design Field

Traditionally, designers were asked to recognize technological innovation and translate it into socially acceptable products and services. This activity, of course, remains valid. But now, to support social innovation, something else has to be done. The bridge between technology and society has to be trodden in the opposite direction too. In fact, to promote social innovation, design experts must use their design skills and competences to recognize promising cases when and where they take places and to reinforce them. That is, to make them more visible and to support their scaling-up conceiving and developing sets of "appropriate technologies" (i.e. specifically designed products, services and communication programs). Doing that, a new field of design activities (design for social innovation) appears.

This new field of design activities doesn't create a brand new design discipline. What it does do is to ask for new approaches, sensibilities and tools that can be transversal to, and impact on, all the (traditional and new) design cultures and practices: from product design to service design, from communication to interior design, from interaction design to strategic design. Nevertheless, dealing with design for social innovation, two of these design disciplines are particularly relevant: service design (to conceive and develop solution ideas considering the quality of these interactions) and strategic design (to promote and support partnerships between the different involved actors). It comes that, to promote and support social innovation, all the design skills, capabilities are to be used, blending them in different ways, case by case. But in all of the design skills and capabilities are to be used, some strategic and service design components will be included.

Finally, it has to be underlined that design for social innovation requires also, and maybe most of all, a different idea of the designers' role and position among other social actors involved. Traditionally, designers have been seen, and have seen themselves, as the only creative members of the interdisciplinary design processes. Dealing with social innovation this clear distinction blurs, and they become professional designers among many non-professional ones. But, as it has been previously anticipated, even if this distinction blurs, it does not mean that design experts' role is becoming less important. On the contrary, in this new context, design experts may have a lot to do in bringing very specific design competences in these co-design processes. That is, they become a particular kind of process triggers and facilitators who use specific design skills to empower the other actors' capability to be, themselves, good designers (Thackara, 2005; Manzini, 2009; Manzini, Rizzo, 2011).

Empowering People's Capabilities

If designers must learn how to work with other non-professional designers, an important step to be done is to redefine the profile of the people for whom and with whom they—the design experts—design: to look at the "final users" for their capabilities, rather than their needs. That is, to consider them neither as consumers nor as passive users, but as active subjects, endowed with resources and, if the conditions are right, ready to put them into play.

This approach, that can be defined as the *capability approach*, per se, is not new: more than 2,500 years ago Lao Tzu's wrote: *"Give a man a fish and you feed him for a day. Teach a man to fish and you feed him for a lifetime"* (Tao Te Ching). It means that, to give people long-lasting well-being we must make it possible for them to deal with problems themselves. And, to do so, they may need access to appropriate knowledge and tools. Moving to the present, we can find Amartya Sen who says that what determines well-being is neither goods nor their characteristics, it is "the possibility of doing things with those goods and characteristics ..." (Nussbaum, Sen, 1993). In fact, it is this possibility that enables people to approach their own ideas of well-being and feel able to "be" what they wish to be and "do" what they wish to do. And this is what design can do: to focus on people's capabilities and to conceive and develop the solutions to increase them.

Coming back to our main topic, design for social innovation, we can state that Sen's capability approach could (and should) offer a solid theoretical basis. By adopting it, the fundamental question of what to design and how, could have a very simple but challenging answer: *design to expand the capabilities of people to lead the kind of lives they value. And to do it in a sustainable way.*

NOTE

1. For instance, we can quote the ones that have been collected and analysed in the framework of an international research program on the role of design in defining, shaping and implementing social innovation initiatives: the SEE-Sustainable Everyday Explorations research, within the PERL European project. These projects are: Nutrire Milano (Italy), Dott 07—Designs Of The Time (UK); Chongming Sustainable Community (China); Amplify (USA); Malmo Living Lab (Sweden).

REFERENCES AND FURTHER READING

Bauwens, M. (2007). *Peer to Peer and Human Evolution*. Foundation for P2P Alternatives, p2pfoundation.net.

Brown, T. & Wyatt, J. (2010). "Design Thinking for Social Innovation." *Stanford Social Innovation Review*, Winter 2010.

Cottam, H. & Leadbeater, C. (2004). "Health. Co-creating Services." Design Council—RED unit, London, UK.

Halen, C., Vezzoli, C., & Wimmer, R. (2005). *Methodology for Product Service System Innovation*. The Netherlands: Koninklijke Van Gorcum.

Jégou, F. (2010). "Social innovations and regional acupuncture towards sustainability" in Zhuangshi, Beijing.

Jégou, F. & Manzini, E. (2003). *Sustainable Everyday*, Edizioni Ambiente, Milano.

Jégou, F. & Manzini, E. (2008). "Collaborative services social innovation and design for sustainability." Polidesign. Milano.

Leadbeater, C. (2008). *We-Think*. Profile Books, London.

Manzini, E. (2009). "New Design Knowledge." *Design Studies*, 301.

Manzini, E. (2010). "Small, Local, Open and Connected: Design Research Topics in the Age of Networks and Sustainability" in *Journal of Design Strategies*, Volume 4, No. 1, Spring.

Manzini, E. (2011). SLOC, The Emerging Scenario of Small, Local, Open and Connected, in Stephan Harding, ed., *Grow Small Think Beautiful* (Edinburgh, Floris Books).

Manzini, E., Jégou, F. & Meroni, A. (2009). *Design orienting scenarios: Generating new shared visions of sustainable product service systems*. UNEP in Design for Sustainability.

Manzini E. & Rizzo F. (2011). "Small Projects/Large Changes: Participatory Design as an Open Participated Process", *CoDesign*, Vol. 7, No 3–4, 199–215.

Meroni A. (2007). *Creative communities: People inventing sustainable ways of living*. Polidesign, Milano.

Meroni, A., Simeone, G. & Trapani, P. (2009). "Envisioning sustainable urban countryside: Service Design as Contribute to the Rururban Planning" in *Cumulus Working Papers—St. Etienne*, edited by Justyna Maciak, Camille Vilain and Josyane Franc, University of Art and Design Helsinki.

Mulgan, J. (2006). *Social innovation. What it is, Why it Matters, How it Can Be Accelerated*. Basingstoke Press, London.

Murray, R., Caulier-Grice, J. & Mulgan, G. (2010). *The Open Book of Social Innovation*. NESTA Innovating Public Services, London.

Nussbaum, M. & Sen, A. (1993) *The Quality of Life*. Clarendon Press, Oxford.

Petrini, C. (2007). *Slow Food Nation. Why Our Food Should Be Good, Clean and Fair*. Rizzoli, Milano.

Petrini, C. (2010). *Terra Madre. Forging a New Network of Sustainable Food Communities*. Chelsea Green Publishing Company, London, UK.

Rheingold, H. (2002). *Smart Mobs: The Next Social Revolution*. Basic Books, New York.

Rifkin, J. (2010). *The Age of Empathy*. Penguin Group Inc., USA.

Thackara, J. (2005). *In the Bubble: Designing in a Complex World*. The MIT Press, London, UK.

Vezzoli, C., Manzini, E. (2008). *Design for Environmental Sustainability*. Springer-Verlag, London.

CHAPTER THIRTY SEVEN

Global Methods, Local Designs

AHMED ANSARI

© 2017 Ahmed Ansari

1. EPISTEME, METHOD, TOOLKIT

Within the current landscape of toolkits, frameworks, literature, and conferences that fall under a constellation of related projects like design for social innovation, design for social impact, humanitarian design, design humanism, or social design (I will stick to the short "social design" here), two words from its lexicon and the discourses around them have been instrumental in its rapid global adoption and success: "design methods" and "design thinking." No toolkit, book, lecture, or workshop opens without a fresh definition or homage to these two terms; one cannot, presumably, practice social design *without* defining them.

It may seem a little odd that these two words are given such disproportionate due: Isn't any form of practice without thought or some kind of methodology impossible? And yet, this is precisely the critique that the first generation of the Design Methods movement, developed in the 1960s and 1970s with the explicit aim of externalizing and formalizing the design process, provided. John Chris Jones, in his foundational work, *Design Methods*, devoted the first third of his book to an analysis of why "traditional," or craft-centered, as he framed them, ways of designing were insufficient in dealing with the complexity of modern design problems:

> Craftsmen do not, and often cannot, draw their works and neither can they give adequate reasons for the decisions they take … the form of a craft product is modified by countless failures and successes in a process of trial-and-error over many centuries. (Jones, 1970, p. 19)

This framing of traditional design as lacking deliberation, planning, and complexity led to Jones advocating for the need for designers to "externalize the design process" in the form of explicit methodological structures, also demystifying what had hitherto been considered as a largely black boxed process, and opening it up so that other stakeholders could be involved, albeit only as observers and commentators, in the design process (in an interesting parallel, these changes were happening at around the same time as similar moves toward conceptualizing the "knowledge worker" and organizational and processual management were happening in the management sciences (Drucker, 1959).

The history of Design Methods has been troubled: key figures such as Christopher Alexander and John Chris Jones later distanced themselves from it, mostly due to what they feared was the tendency of designers to rely dogmatically on methods to the exclusion of developing flexibility and sensitivity in their work, ironically, especially when dealing with projects with rising levels of complexity. In particular, there was a realization that at the very least, the uncritical formalization of methods and methodologies did not add anything to the way designers had designed traditionally—in a telling interview in 1971, Christopher Alexander excoriated the design profession for having turned methods into rote processes to solve a diversity of problems:

> Whenever something doesn't help me make better designs, I get rid of it, fast. What I am most anxious to convey to you, and to the people who read this interview, is the idea that if that is your motive, then what you do will always make sense, and you get somewhere— but if your motive ever degenerates, and has only to do with method, for its own sake, then it will become desiccated, dried up, and senseless. (Cross, 1984, p. 316)

Subsequent generations of thinkers on design began to turn to the analysis of specific aspects of creative problem solving as observed in the processes of expert practitioners in order to propose better, more flexible models of what designerly activity was. This led to the emergence of the term "design thinking," from Nigel Cross with his designerly ways of knowing based around design codes and object languages (Cross, 1982), to Donald Schön's observation of design as reflective practice, constituted as a dialectic between the designer and his materials (Schön, 1983), to Horst Rittel's view of design as a process of argumentation (Rittel, 1988). Cross, tracing the history of the Methods Movement and its practice of design as science down to Schön and arguing for design as an interdisciplinary practice uniquely concerned with the artificial world, concluded that in order to establish design practice as embodying its own epistemologies "we must avoid swamping our design research with different cultures imported either from the sciences or the arts" (Cross, 2001, p. 55).

It is worth noting, therefore, that "design methods" and "design thinking" emerged initially as diametrically opposed concepts: one prescribed an approach modelling itself along the formalized, rules, and procedures based epistemological structures of the sciences, the other sought to claim an approach peculiar to design and the arts, rooted in pattern sensing, reflexivity, intuitively and experientially informed judgment, rhetoric and discourse, etcetera. It is also worth noting that there was a distinction, albeit a subtle one, that the thinking or episteme of design practice was something that found its articulation in, but importantly, *was not reducible to*, its methodologies and processes. However, today, it seems that both methods and thinking have undergone a definitional synthesis, enjoying a joint heyday within contemporary professional practice, particularly as design practice moved out of the realm of design agencies and consultancies to become a principal instrument of humanitarian organizations seeking to employ designerly practices in their own repertoire. This synthesis or alignment becomes especially visible in that exemplar of social design practice, the *methods toolkit*.

The basic anatomy of the social design toolkit, if we begin to dissect it, is formed thus:

1. there is a portion devoted to framing the problem from the perspective of the principal stakeholders who will, presumably, be empowered through using the toolkit;

2. a definition of design thinking specific to that toolkit—this usually provides a proposition, sometimes relying on an appeal by ethos or logos for why a designerly, rather than an engineering or sociological approach, is necessary, and a description of the design process and the methods employed, and then the methods themselves, with details of when, where, and how to use them—this is the epistemic justification for why the design thinking process will work.

As examples, let's take two popular kits, IDEO's Design Thinking for Educators Toolkit, and Nesta's Development Impact and You Toolkit. Breaking them down, we find that both toolkits devote several pages to framing what it is that their stakeholders want to accomplish—IDEO does this by throwing questions that they presume teachers often ask themselves, for example, "How might my classroom be redesigned to better meet my students' needs?" (IDEO, 2011, p. 2), while Nesta has statements that map a plan of action onto a particular goal, for example, "I want to develop a clear plan on how to grow my idea into something bigger" (Nesta, 2014, p. 5).

Additionally, there is always a page or two clearly outlining what design thinking is. In the case of IDEO's toolkit, "Design thinking is a mind-set. Design thinking is about believing we can make a difference, and having an intentional process in order to get to new, relevant solutions that create positive impact" (IDEO, 2011, p. 11). Internalizing this mind-set, the toolkit assures its readers, key to which is being human-centered, collaborative, optimistic, and lean, is the gateway to understanding that "the design process is what puts Design Thinking into action. It's a structured approach to generating and evolving ideas. It has five phases that help navigate the development from identifying a design challenge to finding and building a solution" (IDEO, 2011, p. 14). In Nesta's case, the fact that the approach is methodological is proof in-itself: "The tools are not coming out of thin air. Many of them are well documented and have been widely used in other sectors. In that sense this toolkit is standing on the shoulders of giants" (IDEO, 2011, p. 11), followed by a page showing a matrix where a single method is neatly mapped onto each possible permutation of stakeholder plan and goal.

It becomes immediately evident from the examples given above that it is curious how design thinking and methods were both inverted and divorced from their historical definitions when brought into the realm of the social: from being that which was intended to as bringing more self-reflexivity and rigor into designers own processes, they now serve as part of prepackaged, formulaic, self-contained packages intended less for the designer than for an intended audience of stakeholders "closer" to the problem space. As we've seen, this idea that designing can be reduced to a set of tools, employable by anyone, runs counter to the critiques of methods-driven design posed by the very people that advocated for those methods in the first place!

The existence of the toolkit, therefore, opens up an interesting ontological challenge to what design *is*: is it a form of practice, structured, yes, and with its own tools and frameworks, but *dependent* on its own sensibilities and attunements, and rich in a form of knowledge that is partly inarticulate, contingent, and built through experience, separate from the knowledge that the sciences and the humanities exhibit? Or is it a form of practice that can retain its adaptability and attention to detail even after being reduced to pure methodologies and tools, and one that does not need the unique training, the eyes and hands, of designers?

Moreover, looking at the peculiar rhetorical strategies employed and the structure of the toolkits, it seems that the toolkit is something not just simply trying to empower stakeholders but to actively convince them of its own power as a means of giving them agency and control over their situations. However, the way that this takes place is through the construction of a tautology: design thinking will get you results, since it has proven to be innovative time and again within professional design practice, but for it to get you results you must believe in it and the values it espouses. These values are precisely those that, incidentally, as Naomi Klein points out, neoliberal "disaster capitalism" prizes: a results-focused, action-oriented, attitude, tighter coupling between corporate institutions, aid agencies, and local polities, and an approach that is less interested in poverty reduction or systemic overhaul than in encouraging industrial development, technological innovation, and entry and participation in the global market, etcetera (Klein, 2007). Additionally, the toolkit requires its users, much like the design establishments that designed it, to believe in the modern promise that technology and technological innovation hold universal solutions to local problems entrenched in complex social, political, economic, environmental, and cultural histories. In sum, design thinking through the toolkit, to put a Latourian spin on it, turns back on itself and becomes oddly scientistic: like scientism, it requires an almost absolute faith in its own logic and authority (Latour, 2013).

There is a third dimension to the claim that toolkits make, and this is the crux of the critique offered in this essay: that their particular claims to knowledge and ways of doing things are *universal*, usable by anyone anywhere. This is done through the deployment of rhetorical strategies based on two additional logics: one of *simultaneous inclusion and exclusion*. On the one hand, they attempt to universalize by extending themselves to include cultures outside of the Anglo-European sphere. For example, Frog Design's Collective Action Toolkit states:

> Frog set out to prove the (design) practice is universal by creating the Collective Action Toolkit, a set of resources and activities to help people accomplish tangible outcomes through a set of guided, nonlinear collaboration activities … It is currently available in English, Chinese and Spanish, with more languages to come. The kit is a demonstration of Frog's commitment to social action and goal to make design thinking universal. (Frog, 2013)

However, this inclusiveness is limited to a mere translation of the content into a language other than English—there is no attempt to include or engage with the knowledge of other regions, cultures, and communities. In fact, by not even referencing sociocultural differences in favor of advocating methodologies based on a singular, seemingly universal logic, one can argue that the toolkit employs a strategy of erasure or exclusion.

These claims to universality can and need, we believe, to be questioned. It is worth asking: What does happen when the universal toolkit with its universally applicable forms of knowledge is translated and exported to other countries? Whose hands does it end up in? How is it used? How does it transform the creative economy? How does it transform the nature of design practice and pedagogy? How does it transform the social and political dimensions of local practice? Which discourses, and the people who advocate them, does it raise, and which discourses and polities does it suppress?

Questions like these have been raised before in earlier debates around the politics of social design as the movement was gaining steam, perhaps most notably in Bruce Nussbaum's fiery critiques of the work of Project H and other design firms that sought to do global humanitarian work as a form of new neoliberal imperialism (the rebuttals to Nussbaum and the subsequent debates that followed were archived and are available on Design Observer's website). Toward the end of the debate, Nussbaum argued that social design, in privileging and imposing its own values and ways of doing things, ignored the voices and knowledge of local communities of experts:

What do you do when the local elites are good guys who simply don't want you doing good in their country for historic reasons? What do you do if they are highly educated, speak your language, go to the same conferences, belong to the same "global elite culture," and still don't want you proposing solutions to their country's problems just because? Do you ignore them, work around them, argue that your mission is of a higher order than nationalism? Do you ask what they are doing to help the poor in their country? And finally, what do you when those local elites who question your presence are design elites—just like you. I'm not sure, but I believe that the reaction to humanitarian design that I saw in Asia was from this group of local design elites. They are a growing, powerful force in India, China, Brazil, and elsewhere—and we need to know what they think. What they really think. (Nussbaum, July 30, 2010)

So, what do they really think?

2. ARRIVING METHODS, RETREATING POLITICS

On arriving back in Karachi after spending two years away in the United States in 2013, I returned to find the landscape of design practice rapidly changing. In the span of two years: a start-up culture was beginning to establish itself with both local governments and private investors developing incubators and accelerators, the first of which was Plan 9 in Lahore, set up in 2012 by the Punjab Information Technology Board under the leadership of Umar Saif; erstwhile traditional engineering, computer science, and business schools had invested in social innovation spaces, like the newly established IT University's Innovations for Poverty Alleviation Lab (IPAL) and LUMS' Social Innovation Lab (SIL), albeit these tended to vary in terms of their roles, with IPAL acting as a working extension of the Ministry of IT, while the SIL acts as an incubator for the business school; and both local and international

NGOs like the Pakistan Innovation Foundation, the British Council, and the Acumen Fund had launched annual programs focused on encouraging local entrepreneurship, supported with foreign funding from institutions like the UK's Department for International Development. A word barely known in 2011, "design thinking" now dominated the discourse around social innovation, picked up by the humanitarian-corporate complex on the basis of its promise to deliver solutions to long-standing infrastructural problems.

Most of these new discourses, practices, initiatives, and institutions did not evolve organically out of the reflexive concerns of practitioners or academics, or through external, macro-level pressures. Therefore, when I say that they "arrived," they really did appear *de novo*, like in the classical Greek myth of Athena springing from the head of Zeus, fully formed and divorced from their origins, histories, and debates in the Anglo-European world. They arrived, as they did in other parts of the world, as vehicles for championing and pushing a particular model of development that tied all too well into both the Pakistani state's agenda of projecting the appearance of a prosperous, developing economy to boost trade and foreign investment, and into the local humanitarian sector's proclivity to be seen as effective in a global context.

The political economy of the creative industries and design education had both remained relatively unchanged and stable since Partition. There were a few design schools in the major cities, producing graduates in a handful of design disciplines, communication, textile, and fashion design being the most common—industrial design programs were a late and rare development, and interaction or service design programs were almost entirely absent. Graduate programs in design too were a rarity—there were, and are still none in Karachi and only a handful in Lahore. Influences on the institutional structure and curricula of local undergraduate programs came from a synthesis of sources: as an inheritance from British colonial rule, influences from late-nineteenth-century British commercial art education, which themselves drew from German philosophies that emphasized aesthetics over utility (Khan, 2015); through developments in Indian design education, the Bauhaus and its foundation program (Bilgrami, 2016); and through a tight coupling with the professional sector, from which faculty were drawn, as well as the craft and artisanal industries (Bilgrami, 1990). It is important to note that design studies has been completely absent in local academia—in its place, design students took art history classes, although some programs have begun to supplement these with liberal arts courses. Until very recently, the concept of research occupied a marginal position in design programs—at most, it had a cursory place in the student's life in their very last year at school, where a literature review or a field survey was expected as part of their graduating thesis.

In practice, which academia was mostly structured to service, the outlets for design practice were constrained to the advertising agencies and local design firms that competed for local and multinational clients, in the fashion and textile sector, which was a major and incredibly active source of revenue for the economy, contributing to about 8.5 percent of the country's GDP and in the entertainment industries. Even the smartphone revolution of the late 2000s had not substantially changed the nature of practice: while advertising agencies had dedicated teams to web and mobile content design, their major source of revenue, and subsequently focus, was through consulting and television advertising, while smaller digital advertising hotshops with an exclusive focus on developing digital content had just started to appear. Again, design thinking and research, if they were relegated to the margins in academia, were almost entirely absent in mainstream industry—in their place, brand and media strategy, usually undertaken by business executives and based on analyses of market trends, was what agencies brought as part of their knowledge capital to give value to clients. This was the general climate at the time when the sudden explosion of new forms of design practice and discourse happened.

In the two years that I was in Karachi, strongly advocating for the introduction of design studies and for research to take a more central role in the curricula of local programs, I found that the general design community was surprisingly critical and cautious of the changes happening and for a good reason. Art and design programs in Pakistan have generally seen themselves as safeguarding and preserving traditional practice, culture, and craft, and there has always been a close relationship between design practice and local artisanship. Most faculty have side practices where they work closely with artisans and craftsmen, to whom a surprisingly substantial amount of the design process is delegated, especially with respect to translating sketches into materials and workable forms. In Pakistan, formally uneducated but incredibly skilled technicians and craftsmen occupy a special and quite irreplaceable place as knowledge workers of a particular order—they know exactly how a print design is to be translated so that it prints perfectly, and they understand the technical processes of metalworking, carpentry, etcetera in order to translate a blueprint into a highly finished product. This is also why product and industrial design have been slow to embrace CAD softwares—the lack of sophisticated, automated production machinery and the ready availability of an expert technical class meant that for the longest time, one could simply hire human labor to do what machines were not available for.

Similarly, and until recently, there was very little in the way of conceiving design practice as involving socio-technical problem solving, let alone problem framing. Historically, the emphasis has been on meaning and sense-making, with design as a form of cultural production. This reflects the fact that in established schools like the National College of Arts, the boundaries between fine art and design departments have been fluid, with faculty often teaching in both—for example, the painter Zahoor ul Ikhlaq was also well known as an iconic identity designer, while the advertiser Imran Mir was also a prolific sculptor and painter. Moreover, this also comes from certain vested class dynamics: until recently, the design community was small, and mostly consisted of well-educated and travelled, modern middle to upper-middle class people with the requisite sensibilities, tastes, and aspirations of upward mobility. Additionally, there has been little historical collaboration between the creative disciplines and others in Pakistan, with the arts, sciences and humanities having enjoyed completely separate domains. Again, we can see this in the fact that, also until the last half-decade, with the exception of the large provincial public universities, the most common model in higher education was that of the specialized trade school. Business schools, art schools, science and engineering polytechnics, etcetera dominated the academic landscape, and in fact, the most successful and highly prestigious schools all belonged to this model. Thus, having been a profession that has always shared social and cultural capital with the vastly more internationally recognized and considerably wealthier fine art community, and with the way that the creative community in general, being small and tightly knit, has always been hierarchized, with career advancement heavily contingent on senior patronage, it can also be argued that the Pakistani design community is also wary of what it sees as the democratization of design with outsider groups belonging to outsider disciplines now intruding into what used to be exclusive social, cultural, and professional space.

Then there is also a certain history of the creative disciplines playing a political role in the country; painters, sculptors, and graphic designers, alongside writers, poets, and performing artists, could often get away with scathing critiques of government and society where other disciplines could not. Because of the real lack of space for public critical expression in cities like Karachi, especially in recent times, a certain amount of social and cultural distance between the artist or designer and the conservative public, as well as the removal of the artist from the work of public art, has allowed for collectives like the Tentative Collective or Awami Art Collective to see the public projects that they do as a reclamation of public space, from where they can launch critiques of globalization, market neoliberalism, and state sponsored violence. This sensibility was coupled, very importantly, with a certain definition of creative practice as having an inherent social dimension. Again, we can tie this to class dynamics, a certain class-based humanitarian outlook based on, the one hand, considerable class privilege, and on the other, the recognition that the labor of the creative elite (and hence their social and cultural capital) relied extensively on the labor of working class artisans. Many of the classes that I took as a student, and that I found myself teaching alongside my colleagues later on, where classes that had, from the outset, an outward engagement with some local community, and it was a part of the culture of most institutions where students were told that in addition to aspiring to get gainful professional employment, they were expected to dedicate some of their time to social projects. Thus, no hard separation between design as social practice and as professional practice existed; for a great many practitioners, both went hand in hand, even if the output was limited in scope and didn't really orient itself to solving large scale, systemic infrastructural issues, lacking the class interests necessary to create systemic change in a country with a history of decades of piecemeal progress hard won by dedicated working or middle class activists, and destroyed by misguided political agendas, change of rule, or even assassinations (the murder of the social activist Parveen Rehman, director of the Orangi Pilot Project (OPP) in May 2013 is a particularly tragic example). There are exceptions to this, of course: the architect Arif Hasan and his Urban Resource Centre have been significantly involved in both the OPP and leading the fight for land rights, studying the development of Karachi and other urban centers for decades.

This traditional economy of design practice has been disrupted with the arrival and popularization of design thinking and methods as the handmaidens of neoliberal models of development championed by an ascendant technocracy. Local artists and designers are very critical of initiatives like the Punjab Safe Pani Company, or the Orange Metro (Yusuf, 2015) and other major development (Chaudhri, 2016) projects, which they see as primarily politically motivated, with politicians funding massive development projects to get re-elected and invite foreign investment, using social design as due process' in order to appease foreign and local donors, and in the process often using violence to get rid of undesirable actors. By association then, the introduction and dissemination of design thinking in the social sector has therefore come to be associated as a tool for the state to maintain the status quo, rather than for radical structural reform. What is perhaps most interesting in these shifts is that one form of class power, that belonging to a niche, somewhat elitist group, has been displaced by another form of class power, that of corporations, bureaucrats, and professionals that don't belong to the creative class at all.

3. EPISTEMOLOGICAL ASPHYXIATION AND COUNTERING ASPHYXIATION

With our analysis of the situation above, we can now see how the claims of design thinking, exemplified in the form of the materialized methods toolkit, are not what they claim to be when they come into contact with local practitioners: they displace the economy of labor and challenge the skill and of design practitioners and craft artisans; they bring in value systems and support agendas of development that are destructive to local economy and environment; and they transform the definitions and the scope of social design practice, excluding the very people who were advocates for and engaged in the practice.

That last observation is a concern that I would now like to focus on. In rapidly becoming the de-facto way of practicing social design, in alienating and crowding out existing voices in design practice, design thinking will effectively stymie the organic development of alternatives to neoliberal development through the displacement of different ways of seeing and interpreting the world. What it becomes, in other words, is a vehicle for advancing the politico-economic, but in particular, intellectual hegemony of what academics like Ramon Grosfoguel (borrowing the term from Immanuel Wallerstein) term "the modern world-system" (Wallerstein, 1974):

> Following Peruvian Sociologist Aníbal Quijano, we could conceptualize the present world−system as a historical−structural heterogeneous totality with a specific power matrix, which he calls a 'colonial power matrix' ('patrón de poder colonial'). This matrix affects all dimensions of social existence such as sexuality, authority, subjectivity and labour. (Grosfoguel, 2015)

According to decolonial theorists like Grosfoguel, Walter Mignolo, Anibal Quijano, etcetera, coloniality, which is the logic underlying global Western hegemony, did not end with the departure of the colonial powers in the first half of the twentieth century. Instead, a new global order that institutionalized Anglo-European hegemony cemented itself after the Second World War, stabilizing new "haves" and "have-nots" in the order of nations, creating new flows and distributions of resources and labor, and establishing new political and economic criterion for the newly freed ex-colonies to abide by if they wanted a stake in the global market. However, Anglo-European hegemony goes much deeper than political and economic coercion and control—far more subtle and problematic is the fact that Western knowledge and its systems of production and dissemination are reproduced almost unchallenged in the developing world. Knowledge and its generation are located as part of a geo-politics:

> By setting the scenario in terms of geo- and body-politics I am starting and departing from already familiar notions of "situated knowledges." Sure, all knowledges are situated and every knowledge is constructed. But that is just the beginning. The question is: who, when, why is constructing knowledges?. (Mignolo, 2009)

Coloniality, is therefore, epistemological—one can ask the question: why, with its own situatedness, its embeddedness, in a cultural and social history, in environments different from any in the West, does Pakistani academia and industry rely on knowledge, in both its sense as content and as framing the interpretation of world, that originates in the West? Why must it rely on definitions of development, growth, and progress that orient themselves to ends that model themselves after Anglo-European social institutions? Why must workers in the social sector in the Global South come to understand, know, and design for local problems and challenges in frames predetermined by discourses set in the Global North?

Epistemological colonialism has another aspect—it reproduces by marginalizing extant professional communities of practice and thus hampering the ability of the discipline to grow and change to accommodate new areas of practice by prefiguring those spaces to receive only certain forms of practice and thought. Thus, voices calling for alternative forms of practice, or in trying to derive new forms of practice from old are crowded out as standardized methods and methodologies become the de-facto way of designing and making. This was certainly the case that I observed and that local critics of development in Pakistan have stressed for years:

> As a result of the culture of globalisation and structural adjustment conditionalities, there are proposals for the privatization of public sector utilities and land assets. In some cities the process has already taken place. There are indications that this process is detrimental to the interests of the poor and disadvantaged groups and there is civil society pressure to prevent privatization and to reverse it where it has taken place. (Hasan, accessed 2017)

Moreover, epistemological colonialism also engenders a kind of uncritical acceptance of Western tools and techniques without a nuanced understanding of what the circumstances of their creation were, or what they were originally designed to tackle. This leads to the lack of adaptation in deploying methods and methodologies when applied into very specific contexts with specific problems, challenges, and opportunities. As development theorists like Aminur Rahman point out, even the assertions of internationally lauded schemes that have claimed success elsewhere, like the microfinancing schemes of the Grameen Bank, can be analyzed piecemeal to reveal that in effect, they either ignore and perpetuate existing cultural and social problems, or create entirely new ones in new contexts (Rahman, 2008). Contrary to the assumptions of design toolkits, methodologies, and frameworks, the shape of development everywhere is not homogenous—in all of the workshops I conducted with incubators, startups and NGOs over two years, there was a persistent tendency among both donor agencies and incubatees to treat the methods as due process rather than as crucial to really understanding and modelling systems, this was because there was little investment in any goals outside of developing a product or service which was justified in being deployed because it had been shown to work elsewhere.

To sum, therefore, design thinking thus becomes a means of extending the "colonial matrix of power," what decolonial thinkers like Mignolo and Anibal Quijano have identified as the global Western hegemony over systems of economy, sovereign authority, subjectivity, and knowledge under the rubric of growth and development—it becomes a way of thinking that suppresses and marginalizes local knowledge, thought, and expertise.

What is to be done in the face of this globalized flattening of knowledge and practice? One way is to stress that local practices cannot be divorced from a dedicated politics that stresses an "ecology of difference" (Escobar, 2008). Such a decolonial practice of design would be rooted in the need to imagine alternate institutional arrangements and address systemic inequalities and biases, to be politically active and critical, and to be concerned with the preservation of traditional forms of life while extending them as alternatives to globalization-as-colonialism. So far, little offered in current design literature points toward such a practice, with the exception of the practice of ontological design developed by Tony Fry and outlined most recently in *Design in the Borderlands* (2014) coedited with Eleni Kalantidou, one of the few works that acknowledges how practices of design developed in the Global North are exported to the Global South, extending Anglo-European ways of thinking and being as well as affirming political and economic power.

Locally, one can begin to trace the beginnings of emergent, parallel design practices, as local designers and design schools are working toward the recovery of a design tradition from Muslim and Indian subcontinental heritage by locating practices usually associated with design thinking today within a larger history of making artifacts and environments, and by experimenting with marrying vernacular forms, philosophies, and understandings with new materials and methods (e.g., the work shown last year at the Dubai Design Week by the design studio Coalesce). Local publications on design and culture like the anthology "Mazaar Bazaar" have focused on the links between design as a practice deeply tied to spirituality and faith, something that the rationalist, secular Anglo-European tradition has tended to de-emphasize (Zaidi, 2009). Very recent initiatives like the Anti-Art University that are actively pursuing decolonial agendas seek to problematize and contest academic institutions that chose to turn inwards and depoliticize themselves as the space for political engagement gradually shrunk in the post-9/11 era:

> Policed by Rangers and surrounded by barriers, our art institutions today display their investment in reproducing and subjecting their student bodies to the daily humiliations and disciplining of hegemonic power structures and relations ... we seek then, in the Karachi Art Anti University, not to build structures or walls, but a refuge. To build what Fred Moten and Stefano Harney call "the fugitive public"—to flee the halls and corridors of institutionalized education and instead occupy and claim street and public space in the city as sites of study. (Tentative Collective, 2015)

And lastly, there have been cautious moves to integrate research through design into the fabric of several local programs while not necessarily following the prescribed methodologies of imported social design practice, as well as toward developing more graduate programs.

And so, coming back full circle, one can conclude that what we need are not toolkits, nor their "universal" definitions of design thinking or their processes, but new, diverse philosophies and frameworks that are tied to local knowledge and practice, informed by local politics and ethics—perhaps what we need are methods developed locally and drawing from local ways of interpreting the world and how designers act within it. Great challenges remain: the lack of government support for the arts and humanities; the instrumentalization of education by bureaucratic structures; and the endangered status of social workers, artists, and designers alike as it becomes ever more difficult to express views and undertake work that runs counter to entrenched political interests in an increasingly violent country. There is also the problem of escaping the orbit of a history of design as an elitist practice deeply intertwined with the politics of class and social hierarchy. As more and more design programs emerge and cater to students from more diverse socioeconomic backgrounds, the field is slowly becoming more and more democratized. Yet, the emergence of a truly decolonial practice of design, one that does not necessarily rely purely on foreign universal claims to knowledge and of where value lies, and at the same time is well equipped to deal with the unique problems of the Global South—designing for scales unimaginable in the Global North, rampant illiteracy and a largely oral culture, and basic infrastructural problems in even the largest cities—has yet to be seen.

And yet, as the country's situation becomes ever more urgent and dire, both old and new academics and practitioners have been galvanized to begin searching for new ways to design. It is still early days, but there is hope that the discipline matures so that local designers do not have to rely on foreign exports of knowledge, and where the social sector can rely on the expertise of locally trained designers. Maybe one day, as modern developmental paradigms prove insufficient in tackling growing crises like climate change, population displacement, rising religious fascism, and political instability, it will be methods and frameworks developed in conditions of adversity and resiliency and drawing from the immense wealth of local knowledge from the Global South that will find their way to the Global North to learn from.

© 2017 Ahmed Ansari. This revised paper was initially published as "Politics & Method" in Laranjo, F., Ed. (2016) *Modes of Criticism 2 – Critique of Method*. London: Modes of Criticism. Republished with kind permission from Ahmed Ansari.

REFERENCES

Bilgrami, N. (1990), *Sindh jo ajrak*, Department of Culture and Tourism, Government of Sindh.

Bilgrami, N. (2016), "The History of IVS," IVS website. http://indusvalley.edu.pk/web/about-ivs/our-history/history-of-ivs/.

Chaudhri, Y. (2016), "Anxious Public Space (A Preface)," *The Herald*. https://herald.dawn.com/news/1153271/anxious-public-space-a-preface.

Cross, N. (1982), "Designerly Ways of Knowing," *Design Studies*, 3 (4): 221–7.

Cross, N. (1984), *Developments in Design Methodology*. New York: John Wiley & Sons.

Cross, N. (2001), "Designerly Ways of Knowing: Design Discipline versus Design Science." *Design Issues* 17 (3): 49–55.

Drucker, P. F. (2011), *Landmarks of Tomorrow: A Report on the New*, New York: Harper & Sons.

Escobar, Arturo. (2008), *Territories of Difference: Place, Movements, Life, Redes*. Durham, NC: Duke University Press.

Frog Design (2013), "Frog Collective Action Toolkit." http://www.frogdesign.com/work/frog-collective-action-toolkit.html.

Grosfoguel, R. (2015), "Transmodernity, Border Thinking, and Global Coloniality," *Nous* 13, (9).

Hasan, A. (n.d.), "How Can This Be Changed?" http://arifhasan.org/articles/how-this-can-be-changed.

IDEO, "Design Thinking for Educators Toolkit," https://www.ideo.com/news/second-edition-of-the-design-thinking-for-educators-toolkit.

Jones, J. C. (1970), *Design Methods*, New York: John Wiley & Sons.

Kalantidou, E., and T. Fry (eds.) (2014), *Design in the Borderlands*, London: Routledge.

Khan, Hussain Ahmad. (2015), "Tracing the Genealogy of Art Instruction in Colonial Lahore: German Philosophy, Design Pedagogy and Nineteenth-Century England," *Journal of the Research Society of Pakistan*, 52 (2).

Klein, Naomi (2007), *The Shock Doctrine: The Rise of Disaster Capitalism*, New York: Macmillan.

LaPiere, R. T. (1965), *Social Change*, New York: McGraw-Hill.

Latour, B. (2013), *An Inquiry into Modes of Existence*, Cambridge, MA: Harvard University Press.

Mignolo, Walter D. (2009), "Epistemic Disobedience, Independent Thought and Decolonial Freedom." *Theory, Culture & Society*, 26 (7–8): 159–81.

Nesta, "Development Impact & You Toolkit," https://diytoolkit.org/download-diy-toolkit/.

Nussbaum, B. (2010), "Should Humanitarians Press on, if Locals Resist?" *Fast Company*, http://www.fastcodesign.com/1662021/nussbaum-should-humanitarians-press-on-if-locals-resist.

Rahman, A. (2008), *Women and Microcredit in Rural Bangladesh: An Anthropological Study of Grameen Bank Lending*, Boulder, CO: Westview Press.

Rittel, H. W. (1988), *The Reasoning of Designers*, delivered at the International Congress on Planning and Design Theory, Boston, IGP: Stuttgart.

Schön, D. A. (1983), *The Reflective Practitioner: How Professionals Think in Action*, New York: Basic Books.

Tentative Collective (2015), "Pedagogy of the City," *Dawn* Sunday Magazine. http://www.dawn.com/news/1197318.

Wallerstein, I. (1974), *The Modern World-System 1: Capitalist Agriculture and the Origins of the European World-Economy in the Sixteenth Century*, US: Academic Press.

Yusuf, A. (2015), "Development: Inanimate Faces," *Dawn*, Dawn.com. https://www.dawn.com/news/1219398.

Zaidi, Saima. (2009), *Mazaar, Bazaar: Design and Visual Culture in Pakistan*, Oxford, UK: Oxford University Press [in cooperation with] Prince Claus Fund Library.

CHAPTER THIRTY EIGHT

The Emerging Transition Design Approach

TERRY IRWIN

© Terry Irwin, 2018

ABSTRACT

This paper outlines an emerging Transition Design approach for addressing "wicked" problems (such as climate change, loss of biodiversity, crime, poverty, pollution, etc.) and catalysing societal transitions toward more sustainable and desirable futures. Wicked problems are "systems problems" that exist within large, socio-technical systems and therefore require new problem-solving approaches. The Transition Design Framework brings together an evolving body of practices that can be used to: **1.** visualize and "map" complex problems and their interconnections and interdependencies; **2.** situate them within large, spatio-temporal contexts; **3.** identify and bridge stakeholder conflicts and leverage alignments; **4.** facilitate stakeholders in the co-creation of visions of desirable futures; **5.** identify leverage points in the large problem system in which to situate design interventions. Rather than a fixed, templatised process, the Transition Design Framework provides a logic for bringing together an evolving set of practices relevant to designing for systems level change. This paper reports on how this approach is being tested on a community based project that was informed by classroom based coursework.

Keywords: Transition design; wicked problems; socio-technical transitions; sustainable design

THE NEED FOR A NEW DESIGN-LED APPROACH

A new, design-led approach is needed to address the complex, wicked problems confronting societies in the 21st century (Hughes & Steffen, 2013; Jensen, 2017) and to seed and catalyse societal transitions toward more sustainable and desirable long-term futures (Porritt,

2013, pp 274–276). Problems such as climate change, water security, poverty, crime, forced migration, and loss of biodiversity are "systems problems" and challenging for several reasons: **1)** they involve multiple stakeholders with conflicting agendas (Dentoni & Bitzer, 2015, p 68); **2)** straddle disciplinary boundaries; **3)** are ill defined and stakeholders rarely share an understanding of the problem; **4)** the problem is continually changing and evolving; **5)** problems exist at multiple levels of scale and are interdependent and interconnected; **6)** any intervention (attempted solution) in one part of the system, ramifies elsewhere in unpredictable ways; **7)** interventions take a long time to evaluate, and problems, a long time to resolve (Rittel & Webber, 1973, Buchanan, 1995; Coyne 2005; Irwin, 2011a, 2011b, 2015).

Traditional design approaches (that were characterized by linear processes and de-contextualized problem frames, whose objective was the swift realization of predictable and profitable solutions) were inadequate for addressing this class of problem (Irwin, 2011b, p 235; Sanders & Stappers, 2008, p 10; Norman & Stappers, 2016). Areas of design focus such service design, experience design, design for social innovation, deep design, metadesign and various ecological and sustainable design processes take a more systematic approach in addressing complex problems. However, they still tend to frame problems within relatively narrow spatio-temporal contexts and do not offer a comprehensive approach for identifying *all* stakeholders and addressing their conflicts. A more holistic approach is needed to address problems that will take dozens of years or even decades to resolve.

A new, design-led approach should:

- Enable stakeholders to arrive at a shared definition of the problem and an understanding of its complexities and interdependencies
- Identify stakeholder concerns, relations, expectations and beliefs and factor them into both problem frames and designed interventions in order to leverage collective stakeholder intelligence (Forrester, Swartling & Lonsdale, 2008; GPPAC, 2015, p 4)
- Provide a process for stakeholders to transcend their differences in the present by co-creating visions of a shared and desirable long-term future (visioning)
- Frame wicked problems within radically large spatio-temporal context
- Provide stakeholders and interdisciplinary teams with a palette of tools and methodologies useful in resolving wicked problems and seeding/catalysing systems-level change
- Provide a rationale for "intervening" in complex systems and "solutioning" over long periods of time (dozens of years or even decades) vs. creating short-term, one-off solutions

THE IMPORTANCE OF STAKEHOLDER INVOLVEMENT IN WICKED PROBLEM RESOLUTION AND SYSTEMS TRANSITIONS

Wicked problems and socio-technical systems transitions are challenging because of the high degrees of social complexity which permeate them. Social issues form the roots of many wicked problems, yet often go unseen and unaddressed by traditional problem-solving approaches. Identifying these social roots and involving *all* affected stakeholders (Carlsson-Kanyama, Drebord, Moll, & Padovan, 2008; Baur, Elteren, Nierse & Abma, 2010; Simon & Rychard, 2005) is crucial in resolving wicked problems and designing for systems-level change. User- and human-centred design approaches seldom have the objective to identify *all* affected stakeholder groups and surface their concerns. Rather, these processes identify "key" groups and privilege the concerns of some over others (for example the concerns of the group commissioning a project, perceived target audiences or those of higher socio-economic rank).

Because the distribution of power among stakeholders is almost always unequal (Bauer et al., 2010, p 233; Lawhon & Murphy, 2011), if one or two groups are in the position to frame (define) the problem, their needs and concerns will be privileged over those of others. Although traditional design-led approaches consider user preferences and motivations, they seldom examine the individual and collective stakeholder beliefs, assumptions and cultural norms that have contributed to the problem. Social factors such as practices and behaviours are underpinned by beliefs, assumptions (Niedderer, Cain, Lockton, Ludden, Marckrill & Morris, 2014; Ajzen, 1985; 1991) and cultural norms, and *must* be taken into consideration when framing the problem and designing "systems interventions" (solutions) aimed at its resolution (Incropera, 2016, p 15).

Transition Design draws on approaches from the social sciences to understand the social roots of wicked problems and places stakeholder concerns and co-design/collaboration at the heart of the problem-solving process. We use the term "stakeholder" to refer to anyone who has a stake or interest in a specific issue or is affected by a particular problem. The importance of engaging stakeholders in the problem-solving process is well known, particularly in the areas of policy and governance, environmental issues, backcasting and conflict resolution (Grimble & Wellard, 1997, p 173; Bohling, 2011, p 4; Quist & Vergragt, 2006, p 1028; Carlsson-Kanyama, et al., 2008, pp 34–35; Global Partnership for the Prevention of Armed Conflict, 2015, p 4), but it has yet to be integrated into most traditional design-led approaches.

An Australian Public Service policy report noted that "a key conclusion of much of the literature about wicked policy problems is that effectively engaging the full range of stakeholders in the search for solutions is crucial" (2007, p 27). There are many well established methods for engaging stakeholders in relation to complex problem solving, for example: Multi-stakeholder Governance (Helmerich & Malets, 2011), Multi-Stakeholder Processes (MSPs) (Global Partnership for the Prevention of Armed Conflict, 2015) and Stakeholder Analysis (SA) (Grimble & Wellard, 1997).

Participatory Action Research (PAR) (Cornwall & Jewkes 1995; Chatterton, Fuller & Routledge, 2007), focuses upon knowledge for action (p 1667), and is "aimed at social transformation rather than to use a set of tools aimed at the 'production of knowledge' and the 'solving' of 'local' problems" (Chatterton, Fuller and Routledge, 2007, p 218). The Global Partnership for the Prevention of Armed Conflict list the following benefits of multi-stakeholder engagement (MSP) (2015, p 23):

1. The involvement of more actors provides a broader range of expertise and perspectives. This means problems can be **analyzed better**, based upon several different viewpoints.

2. Such analyses can lead to a more **comprehensive strategy** to address complex conflict situations.

3. MSPS provide the opportunity for greater understanding of different stakeholders' capacities, roles and limitations, thus contributing to **better coordination** of interventions.

4. MSPS can help organizations **pool and share resources**, including skills, funding, staff time, and logistical or administrative resources.

5. The involvement of multiple stakeholders can be conducive to public outreach and awareness raising at different levels simultaneously, increasing the reach from grassroots to policy mobilization. In this way, they have potential for **multiplier effect** when the key messages of the process are communicated to the participant's respective constituencies.

6. MSP can contribute to building **trust** among diverse stakeholders, and enable relationships that can outlast the process itself.

7. They can provide a platform for much needed **capacity building** among practitioners at different levels.

8. Sharing skills and knowledge can enable participants to see problems in a new way, which is also conducive to **innovation**.

Transition Design argues that stakeholder relations can be seen as the "connective tissue" within a wicked problem, and failure to address these concerns and complex relations, are barriers to problem resolution. Conversely, because stakeholder relations permeate the problem (system), they also have the potential to be leveraged in designing interventions aimed at its resolution (Reed, Graves, Dandy, … Stringer, 2009).

THE TRANSITION DESIGN FRAMEWORK AND PHASED APPROACH

A Transition Design approach for addressing wicked problems and catalysing systems-level change is emerging. We call it an "approach" rather than a "process" because this work will require a variety of tools and methodologies, used in different ways—no single, prescribed process would be effective in all circumstances. The approach described in this paper emerged out of workshops conducted with the city of Ojai, California to frame their water shortage as a Transition Design problem (Irwin, 2017) and was informed by coursework in the design program at Carnegie Mellon University and short courses taught in 2016, 2017 in the UK and Spain. Two key components have emerged: A framework that provides logic for bringing together knowledge and practices outside the design disciplines, and a three-phased approach for applying them to design interventions. It should be stressed that this approach is still in nascent form and is offered here as an invitation to other researchers and practitioners to provide feedback, critique and engagement with the objective of co-constituting a new area of design focus aimed at systems-level change (Figure 38.1).

The Transition Design Framework

The Transition Design Framework provides a logic for bringing together a variety of practices (knowledge and skillsets outside the design disciplines), situated within four mutually-influencing,

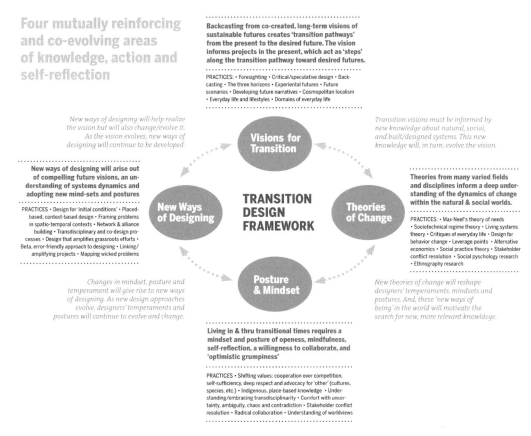

FIGURE 38.1 The Transition Design Framework brings together a body of practices in four key areas useful in designing for systems-level change.

Source: T. Irwin.

co-evolving areas that are relevant to seeding and catalysing systems-level change: Vision (because we need to have clear visions of what we want to transition toward), Theories of Change (because we need a variety of theories and methodologies that explain the dynamics of change within complex systems), Mindset and Posture (because we will need to develop postures of open, collaboration and self-reflection in order to undertake this work), and New Ways of Designing (which will arise out of the previous three areas). Each of these four areas contains a variety of practices that can evolve and change, and which together, form a "palette" from which practitioners and researchers can configure situation-appropriate designed interventions.

The Transition Design Phased Approach

Practices from the framework can be applied within three phases: Re-Framing the Present and Future; Designing Interventions; Waiting and Observing. Rather than a process, these phases suggest the types of action (or inaction) that should be considered when designing for systems-level change.

1. REFRAMING: THE PRESENT AND FUTURE

In this phase, stakeholders "reframe" the problem in the present and envision a long-term future in which it has been resolved. Whether it is acknowledged or not each stakeholder affected by a wicked problem has an implicit or explicit vision of the future associated with it (Rawolle, Schultheiss, Strasser, & Kehr 2016, p 1). Sociologist George Lakoff describes frames as "mental structures that shape the way we see the world" (2004, pp xi–xii). These structures and cognitive models are influenced by metaphors, norms, mass media, political movements, personal history, etc. and each stakeholder group brings with them, their limited understanding of the problem (the problem frame) as well as their fears, expectations and beliefs with them, all of which are influenced by individual and collective "frames".

Mapping the Problem in the Present

In this step, stakeholder groups collaborate to visually map the wicked problem, identifying as many relationships within it as possible. This process is intended to: **1.** Enable stakeholders to achieve a shared definition of the problem; **2.** Provide stakeholders with an understanding and appreciation of the complexities of the problem; **3.** Develop an appreciation of the limited perspective and knowledge base of each stakeholder group (i.e. no single stakeholder group can solve the problem); **4.** Enable stakeholders to adopt collaborative (as opposed to confrontational) postures which aid in transcending differences; **5.** Position stakeholder workshop participants as representatives (within their wider community group) of a diversity of stakeholder perspectives; **6.** Create a visual artefact (problem map) that can be continually updated and validated through qualitative research and informal feedback, to serve as a rallying point for community education, action and awareness.

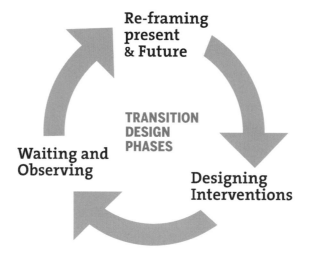

FIGURE 38.2 The emerging Transition Design approach suggests three phases comprised of reframing the problem and its context in the present and future, designing interventions, then observing how the system responds. These broad phases accommodate a variety of practices and processes tailored to specific problems and contexts.

Source: T. Irwin.

The 2007 report by The Australian Public Service Commission stressed the importance of achieving a shared understanding of the problem among stakeholders: "it can be extremely difficult to make any headway on an acceptable solution to the wicked problem if stakeholders cannot agree on what the problem is. Achieving a shared understanding of the dimensions of the problem and different perspectives among external stakeholders who can contribute to a full understanding and comprehensive response to the issue is crucial (p 27)." How problems are framed determines how they will be understood and acted upon. Bardwell (1991, pp 604–605) argues that people solve problems based upon mental models (cognitive maps) assembled over the course of their lives and draw on these subconsciously when encountering new situations. Therefore, people frame new problems in old ways reflecting existing values, assumptions "profoundly impacting upon the quality of solutions." Because addressing wicked problems will be a new experience for most people, it is imperative that old frames and cognitive models are set aside, in order to reframe the problem using the group intelligence of stakeholders themselves.

An important part of the Ojai problem mapping process involved identifying as many inter- connections and lines of relationship as possible between factors/causes. The types of relationships found within a wicked problem such as a water shortage include: **interdependencies** (between the social issue of residents' lack of awareness/ignorance of the water shortage and the political issue of a lack of support for developing new policies restricting water use), **causal relationships** (the economic issue of businesses promoting tourism and development is causally related to the environmental issue of the depletion of local water reserves and the environmental issue of the decline of ecosystem health due to the increased demand for water), **conflictual relationships** (the economic issue of increased tourism is at odds with the social issue of residents facing a water shortage while tourists in the hotels are not compelled to conserve) **or affinities** (between the political issue of the need to pass new laws limiting water use and alignment with the environmental issue of conservationists' desire to protect the integrity of local water sources) and relationships that **feedback** on each other (the economic issue of marketing to increase tourism increases the popularity of Ojai as a destination, which results in more people, using more water, which exacerbates the water shortage—a positive feedback loop). These relationships comprise *the dynamics within wicked problems* often go unaddressed by traditional design approaches.

Asking stakeholder groups to map the problem together accomplished several things: **1.** Participants discovered facets of the problem they were unaware of, which challenged what they believed to be "true"; **2.** The process fostered empathy for the way the water shortage affected other stakeholder groups; **3.** Transformed a potentially "confrontational" meeting among opposing stakeholder groups into a co-creation process with elements of discovery and "play". And, it prepared them for the following step which looks more closely at the relations between groups.

Mapping Stakeholder Concerns & Relations

Failure to consider stakeholder concerns, fears, hopes and desires related to the problem can be a barrier to problem resolution. As yet, there is no design-led process aimed at identifying these concerns and integrating them into problem frames and designed interventions.

However, in other fields there are many well documented approaches, including Needs-Fears Mapping (Wageningen University, 2017), Conflict Analysis Tools (Mason and Rychard, 2005), and Multi-Stakeholder Processes (Hemmati, 2002), to name a few. These delve more deeply into understanding stakeholder differences, mindsets and relations than traditional design processes (such as actor and stakeholder mapping which often privilege the consultant/expert designer's or client's point of view), and offer collaborative processes for resolving conflicts and facilitating more meaningful collaboration and understanding.

What these approaches lack is a design-led component leading to tangible action and material results. For example, designed interactions, communications and artefacts can educate, clarify and facilitate new behaviours and outcomes and permeate socio-technical systems. Transition Design aspires to integrate these stakeholder conflict resolution methods as a strategy for addressing wicked problems.

In the Ojai workshops, stakeholder groups listed both their fears/concerns and hopes/desires related to the regional water shortage and were asked to identify and label relations among groups. Tape was used to connect points of opposition (red) and points of affinity and alignment (green) to which they added notes explaining the nature of the connection. This informal and rather "boisterous" process interjected an element of discovery, surprise and "play" into what would ordinarily have been a tense and potentially confrontational debate among diverse stakeholder groups about how to solve the problem. The results showed several red lines of stark oppositions (instances in which one stakeholder group's greatest fear is another's fondest wish) but these were identified in a spirit of discovery and friendly competition to see how many connections could be identified. Dialog between opposing groups was collegial, even light hearted and stakeholders were surprised at the number of lines of affinity among groups, which became points of positive speculation and discussion.

A final discussion around the large, sprawling map of concerns, fears, hopes and desires focused on how red lines of opposition could be resolved, and lines of affinity leveraged. This shifted the focus from debating differences to conversations about how to resolve them. More research to validate this approach is planned; however early signs show it has the potential to spark dialog among stakeholders with opposing agendas and move them toward collaboration in areas of common interests and objectives. In a final, self-reflective exercise, groups examined the cultural norms, beliefs and assumptions (held by their stakeholder group) that may have contributed to the water shortage. This is challenging work, because few of us are skilled in examining our own worldviews and mind-sets (Lent, 2017; Clarke, 2002; Woodhouse, 1996; Kearney, 1984; Kuhn, 1962) as the roots of a wicked problem. Once stakeholder groups identified their cultural norms, beliefs and assumptions connected to the problem, they were asked: "if by 2050, the problem has been resolved, how would cultural norms, beliefs and assumptions have changed?"

At the conclusion of the exercise, each stakeholder group had two sets of contrasting beliefs, assumptions and norms: one set for 2017 (that had contributed to the problem) and a second "future" set from 2050 (that would inform its resolution via the re-conception of lifestyles and place- based solutions). As an example, one group articulated their 2017 beliefs as "we believe that water is something to be bought and sold, because there will always be enough of it." This contrasted with their set of 2050 beliefs: "water is precious and sacred—it is part of 'the commons' and everyone has a right to enough. To waste it is seen as a criminal offense." This exercise, while challenging, marked a distinct change in tone in the workshop. Participants appeared to slow down and became more speculative, even contemplative. Encouraging participants to adopt this new posture (which relates to the Mindset & Posture area of the Transition Design Framework) prepared participants for the following step.

Future Visioning

Transition Design aspires to draw on a range of foresighting techniques that enable stakeholders to co-create compelling visions of long-term, lifestyle-based futures in which the problem has been resolved and many stakeholder fears/concerns addressed and hopes/desires fulfilled. These visions help stakeholders transcend present-day differences and they act as both a "magnet" that pulls communities toward co-envisioned, desirable futures, and a compass which guides the design of systems interventions in the present.

The intersection of foresight studies and design has given rise to several new areas of theory, research and practice including Design Fiction (Lindley & Coulton, 2016; Sterling, 2005), Speculative/ Critical Design (Dunne & Raby, 2013) and Experiential Futures (Candy & Dunagan, 2017; Candy & Kornet, 2017) that are concerned with envisioning and prototyping both *possible* and *preferable* futures. Candy and Dunagan (2017, p 3) note that "experiential futures [are able to] catalyse high quality engagement, insight, and action to shape change, using whatever means fits the situation" and seek to provide individuals and groups with glimpses of a future that resonates more deeply than other modalities.

New tools and approaches for enabling stakeholders to co-create compelling visions of long-term, desirable futures are needed. Stakeholder groups in the Ojai workshops undertook an exercise called "Snapshots from 2050" to develop lifestyle-based narratives of Ojai in 2050, in which the water shortage had been resolved. Groups were provided with relevant examples of "day-in-the-life" narratives to ensure they remained focused on *the holistic process of envisioning/ reconceiving entire lifestyles*, vs. the dominant, reductionist approach of *envisioning discipline-based solutions*. Groups were provided with narrative word/image "templates" and prompted with questions such as: "what would the resolution of the problem make possible for your stakeholder group?"; "what might you be able to do/accomplish that you currently cannot?"; "in what ways would your everyday life (practices, surroundings, profession, home life) look different or be better if the water shortage were resolved?"

Groups used their previously articulated 2050 beliefs, assumptions and cultural norms as the springboard for the futuring exercise. They were asked to consider how their 2050 "worldview" might inform new practices, behaviours and designed interactions, and how artefacts would be part of their narrative. Participants also referenced their earlier lists of fears/concerns and hopes/desires, and speculate about how they would have been resolved or fulfilled in the future, and as a way to develop more concrete examples for the day-in-the-life narratives. In a final group critique, groups reprised the exercise of drawing green lines of affinity and red lines of opposition between the different narratives. The results showed many green lines due to the striking similarities among the visions, and few red lines of opposition. Our hypothesis (which can only be borne out through additional, extensive research with more groups) is that the "space" participants enter into when envisioning a desired, common future, enables them to transcend opposition and conflict in the present and focus on affinities and similarities in a commonly envisioned, hypothetical future.

Backcasting

Backcasting (Robinson, 1982; Dreborg, 1996) has been successfully used to address long-term, complex societal issues that involve multiple stakeholder groups (Carlesson-Kanyama, et al., 2008; Quist & Vergragt, 2006). It begins with defining a desirable future then "backcasting" to the present to create a "transition pathway" along which projects, initiatives and programs are positioned as initial "steps" in a longer transition. It differs from forecasting in approach. Forecasting extrapolates current trends (based in dominant paradigms out of which the problem arose) into the future, whereas backcasting attempts to define preferable futures, analyse their consequences, and determine the conditions necessary for them to materialize. Robinson (1982) notes "the major distinguishing characteristic of backcasting analysis is a concern, not with what futures are likely to happen, but with how desirable futures can be attained. It is thus normative, involving working backwards from a particular desirable future end-point to the present, in order to determine the physical feasibility of that future and what policy measures would be required to reach that point" (p 337). Transition Design proposes backcasting as a collaborative activity in which stakeholder groups leverage their visions of desirable futures to inform tangible, consensus-based action in the present.

Due to time limitations, Ojai workshop participants did not delve deeply into this process. Groups were asked to create a transition pathway from the present to their 2050 vision and use post-it notes to speculate on what projects, initiatives, and milestones would be necessary (between the present and 2050) to achieve the vision. This technique draws on the approaches used by Porritt (2013), Carlesson-Kanyama et al. (2008), and Sharpe (2013) in using backcasting to envision a process of societal transition.

Workshop organizers observed that participants were highly challenged when asked to think in long horizons of time and struggled with the exercise. Further research must be undertaken to evolve the backcasting process for Transition Design, and it is likely that a variety of approaches can be employed and combined in different ways (including the STEEP and Three Horizons tools).

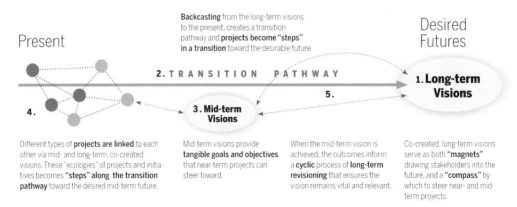

FIGURE 38.3 Backcasting from a co-created future vision creates a "transition pathway" along which new and existing projects can be connected and situated as "steps" in a long transition toward the desired future.

Source: T. Irwin, G. Kossoff, C. Tonkinwise.

Irwin, Tonkinwise, and Kossoff (2015) have proposed an iterative and cyclical process, shown in Figure 38.3 for backcasting and visioning as the slow process of problem resolution and societal transitions unfold. This process ensures that long-term thinking becomes common and that future visions do not become "fixed" and static, but rather, are in a continual process of evolution and change, based upon feedback and outputs from present and near-term projects (steps in the transition).

2. DESIGNING INTERVENTIONS

Phase 2 situates both the problem map and the future vision within a large, spatio-temporal context (Figure 38.4). It also draws on tools and approaches from the Transition Design Framework to develop interventions for problem resolution and systems transition. Most design-led approaches situate problems within small, manageable problem frames and contexts in order to arrive at swift, profitable solutions. We argue that wicked problem resolution requires myriad interventions at multiple levels within extremely large spatio-temporal

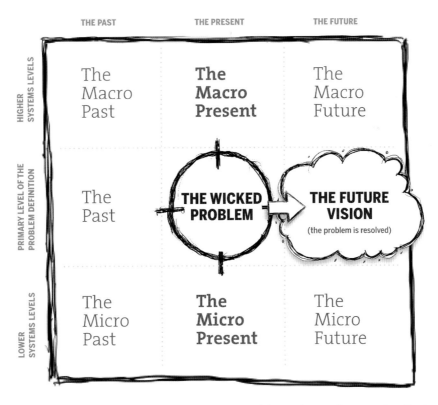

FIGURE 38.4 Transition Design draws upon the concept of the Multi-Level Perspective (Geels, 2006) to situate both the wicked problem and a future, lifestyle-based vision in a large, spatio-temporal context. This large context is explored in order to identify the most promising points of "intervention" lie within this large context.

Source: T. Irwin.

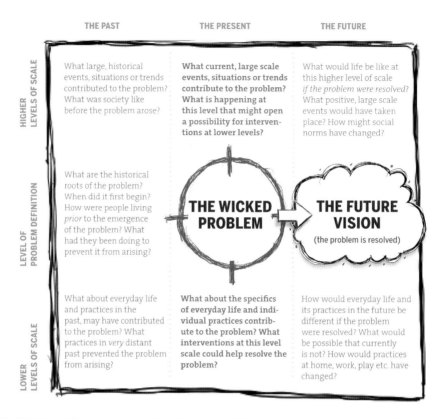

FIGURE 38.5 Specific questions can be asked at each level in the past, present and future in order to guide research and bring a higher level of fidelity to the future vision.
Source: T. Irwin.

contexts (over long periods of time). Wicked problems exist at multiple levels of scale and *always* have their roots in the past because it takes years, decades, or even longer for problems to become wicked. It is necessary to look at both higher *and* lower systems levels to understand the problem's ramifications and consequences in the present, and look to the past in order to understand the problem's root causes and evolution.

In essence, phase two of the transition design process involves *looking up and down systems levels in space, and backward and forward in time* in order to contextualize and address wicked problems—both dimensions play a role in devising interventions (Figures 38.4 & 38.5). Exploring this large context helps us: **1.** understand the **present**-day ramifications and consequences of wicked problems (looking up and down systems levels); **2.** Understand how wicked problems evolved and identify their root causes (in the **past**); **3.** Know where to situate interventions aimed at transitioning the system (problem and context) toward the preferred **future**.

Many of the practices listed in the Transition Design Framework (Figure 38.1) will prove useful in the design of systems interventions (both in wicked problem resolution and initiating systems transitions). Due to the limited length of this paper, only six have been listed in

Figure 38.6 with an overview of the practice, its relevance to Transition Design and references where more information can be found.

Tools & Practices for Designing Systems Interventions

PRACTICE	WHAT IT IS	WHAT IT IS USEFUL FOR	REFERENCES
MLP The Muli-Level Perspective	Conceptual framework used to investigate **how large socio-technical systems transition** over long periods of time. Describes 3 distinct systems levels in which events unfold, infrastructure and artifacts arise, and webs of interaction occur.	Useful in exploring large, spatio-temporal contexts; identifying the **historical roots** of complex problem(s) and "entrenched"/intractable areas within a large system; **reveals opportunities for disruptions** (designed interventions); provides large enough context to reveal connections between multiple wicked problems.	Geels, 2006 Irwin, Tonkinwise & Kossoff, 2015 Gaziulusoy & Brezet, 2015 Grin, Rotmans & Schot, 2010 Rotmans & Kemp, 2003 Tiist & Murray, 1993
Max-Neef's Theory of Needs	Proposes that **needs are ontological, non-hierarchical, finite and universal**, but how they are satisfied is limitless and specific to culture, place, gender, age, and era. **"Poverties"** of unmet needs are the root of many problems.	Can be **integrated into problem frames** to ascertain if the proposed solution is meeting genuine needs (in sustainable ways) or whether it might be undermining the ability to meet other needs. Can be used as an approach to **socially and environmentally responsible design**. Useful in designing systems interventions at mezzo and micro levels.	Max-Neef, 1991 Irwin, 2011 a, p.50 Kossoff, 2011, p.130
Social Practice Theory	Considers the entire **ecology** of elements that are involved in practices: **materials, competencies and meanings**. Used as a strategy for sustainability, it looks particularly at how practices arise and then become inertial.	Can be used at the **micro-systems level** to understand how people's practices contribute to wicked problems and systems entrenchment. Because practices are so ubiquitous, they can be used as a **leverage point for change** within complex systems like wicked problems and socio-technical systems.	Shove & Walker, 2010 Shove et. al., 2012 Kossoff, Tonkinwise & Irwin, 2015 Scott et al., 2011 Kuijer & De Jong, 2011 Bourdieu, 1997 Giddens, 1984
Design for Behavior Change	Focuses on people's **attitudes, behaviors, motivations** and understandings to leverage psychological principles in the design of products and services that can **influence users' behavior for social benefit**.	Understanding how individuals' and groups' beliefs, attitudes and **behaviors contribute to both wicked problems** and systems inertia or entrenchment can become a strategy for systems-level change. Useful in combination with social practice theory in examing the social interactions and interdependencies found within large, socio-technical systems and wicked problems.	Lockton et. al, 2013 Jana, 2010 Abraham & Michie, 2008
Domains of Everyday Life & Lifestyles	Everyday life and lifestyles refer to the way in which individuals, communities and societies meet their needs. The Domains Framework proposes that **everyday life is comprised of nested systems levels** in which particular types of needs are best satisfied: The household, the neighborhood, the city, the region, the planet.	Can be used as a **more appropriate context** within which to conceive sustainable solutions and design interventions and catalyze systems-level change. Solutions can be intentionally situated in a particular domain of everyday life to become **more effective systems interventions**. Long-term visions are more powerful when developed within the context of everyday life and lifestyles.	Lefebvre, 1991 Debord, 2002 SPREAD, 2012 a, b, c Kossoff, 2011 de Certeau, 1984
Social Pathways Matrix The Winterhouse Institute	A model developed by design educators to **map the territories in which designers now work**. The matrix shows the **scale of engagement and the range of expertise** required of types of projects and their impact.	Can be used as a **guide in designing interventions** in large, spatio-temporal systems. The tool can inventory existing and proposed interventions in order to ensure that interventions are situated at multiple levels in the system (wicked problem) and over multiple time horizons.	Winterhouse, 2017 Irwin, 2015 Amatullo, 2016

FIGURE 38.6 The practices above are listed in the Transition Framework and can be especially useful in designing systems interventions within large, spatio-temporal contexts.
Source: T. Irwin.

Linking and Amplifying Projects

Many one-off projects and initiatives are often developed to address wicked problems like a water shortage; however, Transition Design argues that these are unlikely to resolve the problem, or catalyse systems-level change. A new design-led approach must provide a rationale for linking efforts together, over time, for greater traction and 'leverage; (Meadows, 1999). Linking new *and* existing projects (from multiple sectors, including service design and social innovation) to each other *and* long-term visions of co-created, desirable futures is a key Transition Design strategy (Figure 38.3).

Amplifying projects (Manzini, 2015, pp 123–124; Penin, 2010; Amplifying Creative Communities, 2010) refers to the need to look for what is already working at the grassroots level in order to support and "amplify" these efforts. This will call for decidedly different mindsets and postures—that of the non-expert, who approaches a new situation in a posture of empathy and sensitivity to "emergent solutions". The expert designer mindset that aims to "fix what is wrong" through superior specialist knowledge, whereas the transition designer "looks for what is right" within local, indigenous efforts already underway.

3. WAITING AND OBSERVING (MINDSET & POSTURE)

In order to seed and catalyse change in complex systems and resolve wicked problems, multiple interventions, at multiple levels of scale over multiple time horizons will be required. Working with and *within* large, slow moving systems will involve periods of activity and intervention counter-balanced by intervals of observation and reflection in *order to understand how the system has responded to the perturbation*. This contrasts with traditional, design-led approaches, characterized by fast-paced, linear processes whose objective is clear, predictable, conclusive results (solutions).

Complex systems with large social components (lots of people interacting with each other) display properties of self-organization, including "the spontaneous emergence of new structures and new forms of behaviour" (Capra, 1996, p 85). Because these systems are self-organizing, the ways in which they react to perturbations from their environment (designed interventions) are internal and self-determined; i.e. their response cannot be predicted. This is an extremely important principle that, if properly understood, should radically transform traditional design process. The context for these interventions—socio-technical systems and social organizations—will rarely respond to an intervention the way we think it will, and the more complex the system, the more unpredictable its response. This principle of self-organization is why so many meticulously designed solutions fail. Instead of thinking in terms of "designing solutions", transition designers must think in terms of "solutioning" at multiple levels of scale, over long periods of time. Or, as Wheatley and Kellner-Rogers have said, we must learn to "tinker" things into existence (1996, p 10).

This extremely important part of the Transition Design approach will be highly controversial because it challenges the dominant socio-technical, economic and political paradigms out of which most wicked problems have arisen. These paradigms are based upon a style of thinking that has been widely critiqued and described in turn as "mechanistic", "reductionist" and "de-contextualized" (Author 2011b, p 254; Capra 1996; Capra & Luisi, 2014; Scott, 1998; Toulmin, 1990; Mumford, 1971; Berman, 1981). Sociologist George Ritzer argues that this style of thinking dominates 21st century society via business models characterized by efficiency, calculability, predictability and control (Ritzer, 2004, pp 12–15). Transition Design argues that these same characteristics are found in traditional problem-solving processes and are—ironically—one of the root causes of wicked problems (Irwin 2011b, p 235).

Designing for systems-level change will require fundamentally different mindsets and postures (Irwin 2015, p 236) and will be slow, patient work with "emergent outcomes." It will also challenge dominant paradigms that demand fast, concrete, predictable and profitable results. Orr (2002) makes an important distinction between fast and slow knowledge, arguing that "the twentieth century is the age of fast knowledge driven by rapid technological change and the rise of the global economy. This has undermined communities, cultures, and religions that once slowed the rate of change and filtered the appropriate knowledge from the cacophony of new information" (p 36). The aim of slow knowledge is resilience, harmony and the preservation of patterns that connect (p 39) and will challenge transition designers to adopt a slower pace and the ability to think in longer horizons of time. Stewart Brand of the Long Now Foundation asks "how do we make long-term thinking automatic and common instead of difficult and rare?" (Brand, 1999, p 2). Similarly, the "seventh generation" principle from the Great Law of Iroquois Confederacy required its citizens to make crucial decisions with the welfare and preservation of the 7th future generation in mind (Loew, 2014). This type of long-term thinking, along with an understanding of the longer, slower cycles that govern the natural world, *must* underpin a Transition Design approach.

The Transition Design approach can be compared with Chinese acupuncture. An acupuncturist will closely observe the patient for a period of time in order to understand the imbalances or blocks in the system (body) and then place needles along specific meridians in order to shift energy (this is similar to a practitioner designing systems interventions). After placing the needles, he/she will *always* wait and observe how the body (system) responds. Sometimes several weeks might go by before another treatment is recommended. The practitioner places needles based upon his/her experience and a "working hypothesis" that a certain response is *probable*, however a good practitioner will wait to see how a specific individual responds (based upon their own physiology, psychology, lifestyle, etc.) before intervening again. Designing interventions for socio-technical systems will require a similar approach in which periods of action and intervention are punctuated by periods of observation and reflection *in order to understand how the system is responding*. This process will be at odds with 21st century expectations for quick, conclusive, profitable and quantifiable results. For this reason, the transition designer will also need to develop compelling arguments and narratives about the (long-term) value and benefits of the process itself.

CONCLUSION

This paper has outlined an emerging, design-led approach for addressing complex, wicked problems and catalysing societal transitions toward more sustainable futures (Figure 38.7A–C). It emphasizes the need to engage *all* stakeholders (human and non-human) affected by the problem in order to create a shared problem definition and understanding of the oppositions and alignments among them. A framework or "guide" for situating problems within large, spatio-temporal contexts is proposed. This framework can be used to understand root causes and consequences and identify leverage points for interventions aimed at transitioning the system along a transition pathway toward a co-envisioned future.

PHASE ONE	PRACTICES USED IN OJAI
Reframing: Past and Present Reframing the present in order to arrive at a shared understanding of the problem. Reframing the future through the co-creation of visions of where we want to go.	**1. Mapping the Problem** Stakeholders collaborate to create a shared understanding of the problem, its complexity and interconnections and inter-dependencies. **2. Mapping stakeholder concerns and relations** Stakeholders identify their fears/concerns, hopes/desires and their beliefs, assumptions and cultural norms that have contributed to the problem. **3. Developing visions of the future** Stakeholders co-create lifestyle-based visions of a shared, desirable future in which the problem has been resolved and their needs met. **4. Backcasting to create transition pathways** Stakeholders backcast from the vision to create a transition pathway to the present. Projects and initiatives will become steps toward the desired future.

FIGURE 38.7 (A)–(C) An overview of the emerging Transition Design approach is presented using several of the practices included in the Framework. These can be configured differently and appropriately for different problems and situations.

Source: T. Irwin.

PHASE TWO	USEFUL APPROACHES
Designing Interventions Situating the problem map and future vision within a large, spatio-temporal context. Identifying consequences and root causes at multiple levels of scale in order to design interventions aimed at resolving the problem, and catalyzing system transition.	• **Multi-Level Perspective** The problem is situated within its socio-technical context in order to identify its historic roots and opportunities for interventions at multiple levels of spatio-temporal scale. • **The Domains of Everyday Life/Lifestyles** Interventions are developed within the context of re-conceived lifestyles and everyday life. • **Max-Neef's Theory of Needs** The satisfaction of genuine needs (as opposed to wants/desires) is a strategy for designing more effective interventions. • **Social Practice Theory & Design for Behavior Change** Individual and collective practices and behavior are seen as both causes of wicked problems as well as leverage point for change. • **Winterhouse Social Pathways Matrix** A useful tool for planning interventions at mutiple levels of scale over multiple horizons of time. • **Linking and Amplifying** Existing and new projects/initiatives (many of which arise at the grassroots level) are linked together and amplified to catalyze systems-level change.

FIGURE 38.7 *continued . . .*

PHASE THREE	USEFUL APPROACHES
Waiting & Observing Periods of activity and intervention are counterbalanced by periods of observations and contemplation which requires new mindsets and postures. **3**	• **Patience and restraint** Instead of rushing to completion with the expectation of clear, measurable results, the designer takes up a posture of patient observation and waiting. The designer resists the pressure of coming to quick conclusions about the results of interventions. • **Slow knowlege/long time horizons** The designer understands the slower cycles that characterize ecosystems and design with these slower cycles in mind. They frame interventions within long time horizons and know that outcomes may take dozens of years or decades. • **Design with living systems principles** Designers have a deep appreciation of living systems principles such as self-organization, emergence, sensitivity to initial conditions and feedback and integrate this understanding into their process. • **Speculation vs. certainty** The designer understands that the outcomes of interventions cannot be predicted, and therefore postures of certainty must be replaced by speculation and spontaneity.

FIGURE 38.7 *continued* . . .

Transition Design aspires to become a flexible, integrated approach that makes design-led tools and approaches available to transdisciplinary teams working on transition-related projects and initiatives. Still in its nascent phase, it will require researchers and practitioners from many disciplines and a diversity of cultural perspectives working together to constitute a broadly applicable, transdisciplinary process. This paper is presented as an invitation for critique, speculation and a roadmap for further research.

© Terry Irwin 2018. Previously published in proceedings of DRS 2018 "Design as a Catalyst for Change", University of Limerick, June 25–28, 2018. A longer version of this paper was published in the *Journal of Cuadernos del Centro de Estudios en Diseño y Comunicación* of Universidad de Palermo 2017. Republished with kind permission from Terry Irwin.

REFERENCES

Abraham, C., & Michie, S. (2008). A taxonomy of behavior change techniques used in interventions. In *Health Psychology*, 27 (3), 379–387. doi.org/10.1037/0278-6133.27.3.379

Ajzen I. (1985). From intentions to actions: A theory of planned behaviour. In Kuhl J. & Beckman, J. (Eds.) *Action-control: From Cognition to Behaviour*. Heidelberg, Germany: Springer.

Ajzen I. (1991). The theory of planned behaviour. In *Organizational Behaviour and Human Decision Processes*, 50, 179–211.

Amatullo, M. (Ed.). (2016). *LEAP Dialogues: Career Pathways in Design for Social Innovation*. Pasadena, CA: Designmatters at Art Center College of Design.

Amplifying Creative Communities (2010). Retrieved from Parsons DESIS Lab website: http://www.amplifyingcreativecommunities.org/#p1b

Australian Public Service Commission. (2007). *Tackling Wicked Problems: A Public Policy Perspective*. Commonwealth of Australia.

Bardwell, L. (1991). Problem-Framing: A Perspective on Environmental Problem-Solving. In *Environmental Management*, 15, 603–612.

Baur, V., Elteren, A., Nierse, C. & Abma, T. (2010). Dealing with Distrust and Power Dynamics: Asymmetric Relations Among Stakeholders in Responsive Evaluation. In *Evaluation*, 16, 233–248.

Berman, M. (1981). *The Reenchantment of the World*. Ithaca, NY: Cornell University Press.

Bohling, K. (2011). *The Multi-Stakeholder Approach in the United Nations: Unprecedented Perhaps, but not Unexpected*. Presented at Transnational Private Regulation in the Areas of Health, Environment, Social and Labor Rights. Retrieved from Technische Universitat Munchen, Lehrstuhl fur Wald- und Umweltpolitik website: https://www.wup.wi.tum.de/fileadmin/w00beh/www/Files/Boehling_TransReg_2011.pdf

Bourdieu, P. (1997). *Outline of a Theory of Practice*. Cambridge: Cambridge University Press.

Brand, S. (1999). *The Clock of the Long Now: Time and Responsibility*. New York: Basic.

Buchanan, R. (1995). Wicked problems in design thinking. In Margolin, V. and Buchanan, R. (Eds.) *The Idea of Design*. Cambridge, MA: MIT Press.

Candy, S., & Dunagan, J. (2017). Designing an Experiential Scenario: The People Who Vanished. In *Futures*, 86, 136–153. doi:10.1016/j.futures.2016.05.006.

Candy, S. & Kornet, K. (2017). A Field Guide to Ethnographic Experiential Futures. In *Journal of Futures Studies*, June issue. DOI: 10.13140/RG.2.2.30623.97448.

Capra, F. (1996). *The Web of Life: A New Scientific Understanding of Living Systems*. New York, NY: Anchor Books.

Capra, F. & Luisi, L. (2014). *The Systems View of Life: A Unifying Vision*. Cambridge, UK: Cambridge University Press.

Carlsson-Kanyama, A., Dreborg, K., Moll, H., & Padovan, D. (2008). Participative Backcasting: A Tool for Involving Stakeholders in Local Sustainability Planning. In *Futures*, 40, pp 34–46.

Chatterton, P., Fuller, D., & Routledge, P. (2007). Relating Action to Activism: Theoretical and Methodological Reflections. In Kindon, S., Pain, R. & Kesby, M. (Eds.), *Participatory Action Research Approaches and Methods: Connecting People, Participation and Place*. London: Routledge.

Clarke, M. (2002). *In Search of Human Nature*. New York: Routledge.

Cornwall, A. & Jewkes, R. (1995). What is Participatory Research? In *Social Science & Medicine*, 41, pp 1667–1676.

Coyne, R. (2005). Wicked Problems Revisited. In *Design Studies*, 26, pp 5–17.

Debord, G. (2002). Perspectives for Alterations in Everyday Life. In Highmore, B. (Ed.), *The Everyday Life Reader*. London: Routledge.

Dentoni, D. & Bitzer, V. (2015). The Role of Universities in Dealing with Global Wicked Problems Through Multi- Stakeholder Initiatives. *Journal of Cleaner Production*, 106, pp 68–78.

de Certeau, M. (1984). *The Practice of Everyday Life*. Berkeley: University of California Press.

Dreborg, K. (1996). Essence of Backcasting. *Futures*, 28, pp 813–828. Great Britain: Elsevier Science Ltd.

Dunne, A. & Raby, F. (2013). *Speculative Everything: Design Fiction and Social Dreaming*. Cambridge MA: MIT Press.

Forrester, J., Swartling, A. & Lonsdale, K. (2008). *Stakeholder Engagement and the Work of SEI: An Empirical Study*. Stockholm, Sweden: Stockholm Environment Institute.

Gaziulusoy, I. & Brezet, H. (2015). Design for System Innovations and Transitions: A Conceptual Framework Integrating Insights from Sustainability Science and Theories of System Innovations and Transitions. In *Journal of Cleaner Production*, 108, pp 558–568.

Geels, F. (2006). Major System Change Through Stepwise Reconfiguration: A Multi-Level Analysis of the Transformation of American Factory Production. In *Technology in Society*, 28, pp 445–476.

Giddens, A. (1984). *The Constitution of Society*. Cambridge, UK: Polity Press.

Global Partnership for the Prevention of Armed Conflict (GPPAC). (2015). *Multi-Stakeholder Processes for Conflict Prevention & Peacebuilding: A Manual*. GPPAC.

Grimble, R. & Wellard, K. (1997). Stakeholder Methodologies in Natural Resource Management: A Review of Principles, Contexts, Experiences and Opportunities. In *Agricultural Systems*, 55, pp 173–193.

Grin, J., Rotmans, J. & Schot, J. (2010). Conceptual Framework for Analysing Transitions. In *Transition to Sustainable Development: New Directions in the Study of Long Term Transformative Change*. New York: Routledge.

Helmerich, N. & Malets, O. (2011). *The Multi-Stakeholder Approach in the United Nations: Unprecedented Perhaps, But not Unexpected*. Presented at Transnational Private Regulation in the Areas of Health, Environment, Social and Labor Rights conference. Retrieved from the Technische Universitat Munchen website: https://www.wup.wi.tum.de/fileadmin/w00beh/www/Files/Boehling_TransReg_2011.pdf

Hemmati, M. (2002). *Multi-stakeholder Processes for Governance and Sustainability: Beyond Deadlock and Conflict*. Earthscan Publications, London.

Hughes, L. & Steffen, W. (2013). *The Critical Decade: Climate Change Science, Risks and Responses*. Australia: Climate Commission Secretariat.

Incropera, F. (2016). *Climate change: a wicked problem: complexity and uncertainty at the intersection of science, economic, politics and human behaviour*. New York, US: Cambridge University Press.

Irwin, T. (2011a). Design for a Sustainable Future. In Hershauer, J., Basile, G. & McNall, S. (Eds.), *The Business of Sustainability: Trends, Policies, Practices and Stories of Success*, pp 41–60. Santa Barbara, CA: Praeger.

Irwin, T. (2011b). Wicked Problems and the Relationship Triad. In Harding, S. (Ed.), *Grow Small, Think Beautiful*. Edinburgh: Floris Books.

Irwin, T. (2015). Transition Design: A Proposal for a New Area of Design Practice, Study and Research. In *Design and Culture Journal*, 7, 229–246.

Irwin, T. Tonkinwise, C. & Kossoff, G. (2015). *Transition Design: An Educational Framework for Advancing the Study and Design of Sustainable Transitions*. Presented at the STRN Conference, University of Sussex. Available on Academia.edu: https://www.academia.edu/15283122/

Transition_Design_An_Educational_Framework_for_Advancing_the_Study_and_Design_of_
Sustainable_Transitions_presented_at_the_STRN_conference_2015_Sussex_

Irwin, T. (2017). *Mapping Ojai's Water Shortage: A Workshop*. Unpublished report, retrieved from Academia.edu website: https://www.academia.edu/30968737/Mapping_Ojais_Water_Shortage_The_First_Workshop_January_2017

Jana, R. (2010, March). IDEO's Tim Brown on Using Design to Change Behavior. *The Harvard Business Review*. Retrieved from https://hbr.org/2010/03/design-to-change-behavior-tips

Jensen, L (Ed.). (2017). The Sustainable Development Goals Report 2017. New York, NY: United Nations.

Kearney, M. (1984). *Worldview*. Novator: Chandler & Sharp

Kossoff, G. (2011). Holism and the Reconstruction of Everyday Life: A Framework for Transition to a Sustainable Society. In Harding, S. (Ed.), *Grow Small, Think Beautiful*. Edinburgh: Floris Books.

Kossoff, G., Tonkinwise, C. & Irwin, T. (2015). *The Importance of Everyday Life and Lifestyles as a Leverage Point for Sustainability Transitions*. Presented at the STRN Conference, University of Sussex. Available on Academia.edu: https://www.academia.edu/15403946/Transition_Design_The_Importance_of_Everyday_Life_and_Lifestyles_as_a_Leverage_Point_for_Sustainability_Transitions_presented_at_the_STRN_Conference_2015_Sussex_

Kuhn, T. (1962). *The Structure of Scientific Revolutions*. Chicago: University of Chicago Press.

Kuijer, L. & De Jong, A. (2011). Practice Theory and Human-Centered Design: A Sustainable Bathing Example. In *Proceedings Nordic Design Research Conference* (NORDES). Helsinki: Aalto University.

Lakoff, G. (2004). *Don't Think of an Elephant! Know your Values and Frame the Debate*. White River Junction, VT: Chelsea Green.

Lawhon, M. & Murphy, T. (2011). Socio-technical regimes and sustainability transitions: Insights from political ecology. In *Progress in Human Geography*, 36, 354–378.

Lent, J. (2017, May). *A House on Shaky Ground: Eight Structural Flaws of the Western Worldview*. Retrieved from Tikkun website: http://www.tikkun.org/nextgen/a-house-on-shaky-ground-eight-structural-flaws-of- the-western-worldview.

Lefebvre, H. (1991). *Critique of Everyday Life: Foundations for a Sociology of the Everyday, Vol. 1*. London: Verso.

Lindley, J. & Coulton, P. (2016). *Pushing the Limits of Design Fiction: The Case For Fictional Research Papers*. Proceedings of the 2016 CHI Conference on Human Factors in Computing Systems. CHI '16. New York, NY, USA: ACM: 4032–4043. doi:10.1145/2858036.2858446

Loew, P. (2014). *Seventh Generation Earth Ethics*. Madison, WI: Wisconsin Historical Society Press.

Lockton, D., Harrison, D., Cain, R., Stanton, N., & Jennings, P. (2013). Exploring Problem-Framing Through Behavioral Heuristics. In *International Journal of Design*, 7, 37–53.

Manzini, E. (2015). *Design, When Everybody Designs: An Introduction to Design for Social Innovation*. Cambridge, MA: MIT Press.

Mason, S. & Rychard, S. (2005). *Conflict Analysis Tools*. Swiss Agency for Development and Cooperation, SDC. Retrieved from the SDC website: http://www.css.ethz.ch/content/dam/ethz/special- interest/gess/cis/center-for-securities-studies/pdfs/Conflict-Analysis-Tools.pdf

Max-Neef, M. (1991). *Human Scale Development: Conception, Application and Further Reflections*. New York, NY: Apex. Retrieved from http://www.wtf.tw/ref/max-neef.pdf.

Meadows, D. (1999). *Leverage Points: Places to Intervene in a System*. Hartland, VT: The Sustainability Institute.

Mumford, L. (1971). *The Myth of the Machine: Pentagon of Power*. London: Secker & Warburg.

Niedderer, K., Cain, R., Lockton, D., Ludden, G., Mackrill, J., & Morris, A. (2014). *Creating Sustainable Innovation through Design for Behaviour Change: A Full Report*. London, UK: The Arts & Humanities Research Council.

Norman, D. & Stappers, P. (2016). DesignX: Complex Sociotechnical Systems. In *She Ji: The Journal of Design, Economics and Innovation*, 1, pp 83–106. https://doi.org/10.1016/j.sheji.2016.01.002

Orr, D. (2002). *The Nature of Design: Ecology, Culture and Human Intension*. New York, NY: Oxford University Press.

Penin, L. (2010). *Amplifying Creative Communities in New York City*. Cumulus Proceedings, Cumulus Shanghai Conference. Retrieved from: https://s3.amazonaws. com/academia.edu.documents/30857482/Cumulus_Proceedings_Shanghai.pdf?AWSA ccessKeyId=AKIAIWOWYYGZ2Y53UL3A&Expires=1503862148&Signature=q4n PD9Alh53zTYwlpwyIKq3rRI c%3D&response-content disposition=inline%3B%20 filename%3D2010_Designing_sustainable_sanitation_th.pdf#page=447

Porritt, J. (2013). *The World We Made: Alex McKay's Story from 2050*. New York: Phaidon.

Quist, J. & Vergragt, P. (2006). Past and Future of Backcasting: The Shift to Stakeholder Participation and a Proposal for a Methodological Framework. In *Futures*, 38, pp 1027–1045.

Rawolle, M., Schultheiss, O., Strasser, A. & Kehr, H. 2016. The Motivating Power of Visionary Images: Effects on Motivation, Affect and Behavior. In *Journal of Personality*, December.

Reed, M., Graves, A., Dandy, N.,…Stringer, C. (2009). Who's in and Why? A Typology of Stakeholder Analysis Methods for Natural Resource Management. In *Journal of Environmental Management*, 90, pp 1933–1949.

Rittel, H. & Webber, M. (1973). Dilemmas in a General Theory of Planning. In *Policy Sciences*, 4, 155–169.

Ritzer, G. (2004). *The McDonaldization of Society*. Thousand Oaks, CA: Pine Forge Press.

Robinson, J. (1982). Energy Backcasting: A Proposed Method of Policy Analysis. In *Energy Policy*, 10, 337–344.

Rotmans, J. & Kemp, R. (2003). *Managing Societal Transitions: Dilemmas and Uncertainties: The Dutch Energy Case Study*. Report from an OECD Workshop on the Benefits of Climate Policy: Improving Information for Policy Makers. Retrieved from http://www.oecd.org/ netherlands/2483769.pdf

Sanders, E. & Stappers, P. (2008). Co-Creation and the New Landscapes of Design. In *Co.Design*, 4, pp 5–18. DOI: 10.1080/15710880701875068.

Scott, K., Bakker, C., & Quist, J. (2011). Designing Change by Living Change. In *Design Studies Journal*, 33, 279–297.

Scott, J. (1998). *Seeing Like a State*. New Haven, CT: Yale University Press.

Sharpe, B. (2013). *Three Horizons: The Patterning of Hope*. Axminster, UK: Triarchy Press.

Shove, E., Walker, G. (2010). Governing Transitions in the Sustainability of Everyday Life. In *Research Policy*, 39, 471–476.

Shove, E., Pantzar, M., & Watson, M. (2012). *The Dynamics of Social Practice: Everyday Life and How it Changes*. London, UK: Sage Publications.

Simon M. & Rychard, S. (2005). *Conflict Analysis Tools*. Retrieved from the Swiss Agency for Development and Cooperation (SDC) website http://www.css.ethz.ch/content/dam/ethz/ special-interest/gess/cis/center- for-securities-studies/pdfs/Conflict-Analysis-Tools.pdf

SPREAD. (2012a). *Sustainable Lifestyles: Today's Facts & Tomorrow's Trends*. Report funded by the European Union's Seventh Framework Programme. Retrieved from http://www.sustainable-lifestyles.eu/fileadmin/images/content/D1.1_Baseline_Report.pdf

SPREAD. (2012b). *EU Sustainable Lifestyles Roadmap and Action Plan 2050*. Report funded by the European Union's Seventh Framework Programme. Retrieved from http://www.sustainable-lifestyles.eu/fileadmin/images/content/Roadmap.pdf

SPREAD. (2012c). *Scenarios for Sustainable Lifestyles 2050: From Global Champions to Local Loops*. Report funded by the European Union's Seventh Framework Programme. Retrieved from http:// www.sustainable- lifestyles.eu/fileadmin/images/content/ D4.1_FourFutureScenarios.pdf

Sterling, B. (2005). *Shaping Things*. Cambridge, MA: The MIT Press.

Trist, E. & Murray, H., (Eds.). (1993). *The Social Engagement of Social Science, Vol. 2, The Socio-Technical Perspective*. Philadelphia, PA: University of Pennsylvania Press.

Toulmin, S. (1990). *Cosmopolis*. New York: The Free Press.

Wageningen University. (2017). *Needs-Fears Mapping*. Retrieved 8.26.17 from Wageningen University website: http://www.managingforimpact.org/tool/needs-fears-mapping

Wheatley, M. & Kellner-Rogers, M. (1996). *A Simpler Way*. San Francisco, CA: Berrett-Koehler Publishers.

Winterhouse Institute. (2017). Social Design Pathways. Retrieved from http://winterhouseinstitute.squarespace.com/pathways/

Woodhouse, M. (1996). *Paradigm Wars: Worldviews for a New Age*. Berkeley: Frog.

CONTRIBUTORS

Ahmed Ansari is a PhD candidate in Design Studies at Carnegie Mellon University. His current work looks at the analysis of modernity, and the development of a decolonial design studies and South Asian philosophy of technology.

Erling Björgvinsson is PARSE Professor of Design at the School of Design and Craft, Faculty of Fine Arts, Gothenburg University. His central topic of research is participatory politics in design and art, in particular in relation to urban spaces and the interaction between public institutions and citizens.

Michael Braungart is a chemist and the founder of the Environmental Protection Encouragement Agency (EPEA) in Hamburg, Germany. He lectures at universities, businesses, and institutions around the world on critical new concepts for ecological chemistry and materials flow management. He is the coauthor of *Cradle to Cradle: Remaking the Way We Make Things* (2002), and its follow up, *The Upcycle: Beyond Sustainability-Designing for Abundance* (2013).

Richard Buchanan is Professor of Design and Innovation at Case Western Reserve University and former head of the School of Design at Carnegie Mellon University. Professor Buchanan is coeditor of *Design Issues*, published by the MIT Press. He received his AB and PhD from the University of Chicago. Buchanan is also Chair Professor of Design, Strategy, and Entrepreneurship in the College of Design and Innovation at Tongji University in Shanghai, China.

Alison J. Clarke is a design historian and a trained social anthropologist. She joined the University of Applied Arts Vienna as a full professor having previously held a senior faculty post at the Royal College of Art, London. In 2010, she was appointed Director of the Victor J. Papanek Foundation heading the biennial symposia in contemporary design theory.

Nigel Cross is Emeritus Professor of Design Studies, the Open University, UK, where he pioneered distance education in design. His research interests are principally in understanding the nature of design thinking and the development of design skill from novice to expert. His books include *Designerly Ways of Knowing* (Springer/Birkhauser, 2006/2007) and *Design Thinking: Understanding How Designers Think and Work* (Berg, 2011).

Clive Dilnot was Professor of Design Studies at the Parsons School of Design, New York until 2017. His recent work includes *Design and The Question of History* (2015); *A John Heskett Reader: Design History Economics* (ed.) (2016); and *Design and the Creation of Value* (ed.) (2017). He is currently working on a four-volume series of essays on thinking design: *On History; On Acting; On Knowledge; On Configuration* (2019–20) and on an extended essay *The Sense of the Artificial*.

Anthony Dunne is Professor of Design and Emerging Technology at Parsons, The New School for Design, and a partner in the design studio Dunne & Raby. Between 2005 and 2015, he was professor and head of the Design Interactions program at the Royal College of Art in London. His work with Fiona Raby uses design as a medium to stimulate discussion and debate among designers, industry and the public about the social, cultural and ethical implications of existing and emerging technologies.

Pelle Ehn is Professor Emeritus, School of Arts and Communication at Malmö University, Sweden. He is a researcher, designer, and activist who is passionately engaged with issues of design, democracy and participation. He has cowritten books and articles including *Work-Oriented Design of Computer Artifacts* (1988), *Manifesto for a Digital Bauhaus* (1998), *Design Things* (2011), *Making Futures* (2014), and *Learning in PD as I found it* (1970–2015) (2017).

Kate Fletcher is Research Professor at Centre for Sustainable Fashion, University of the Arts London, UK where she explores design for sustainability in fashion.

Jorge Frascara is Professor Emeritus and former chairman, Art and Design, University of Alberta; Honorary Professor, Emily Carr University; Fellow, Graphic Designers of Canada; Former President of Ico-D; Advisor, Doctorate in Design, IUAV University of Venice, and Board Member of *Visible Language, Design Issues* and *Information Design Journal*. He has published ten books and more than ninety articles and received honors from eight countries for his socially oriented practice and promotion of communication design.

Ken Garland is a British graphic designer, photographer, writer, and educator. He studied design at London's Central School of Arts and Crafts in the early 1950s and has made a significant contribution to the development of graphic design since the mid-twentieth century. In 1962, he formed the prolific design studio Ken Garland & Associates (until 2009) in Camden, London, where he continues to live and work today.

John Heskett (1937–2014) was a pioneering British-born writer and lecturer. He served as Chair Professor of Design at the School of Design, Hong Kong Polytechnic University, after serving fifteen years as Professor of Design at the Institute of Design, Illinois Institute of Technology in Chicago. His research was foundational for the study of industrial design, and his research into the relationship between design, policy and economic value is still a regular reference-point for academics and students alike.

Per-Anders Hillgren is an Associate Professor in Design and Social Innovation at the School of Art and Communication and coordinates the research network Alternative Future Making at Malmö University. He holds a PhD in interaction design and a MSc in fine arts and is passionate about exploring opportunities for how to democratize innovation.

Andrew Howard is a graphic designer, teacher, curator, and design writer living and working in Porto, Portugal since 1993. He has specialized over the years (both in the UK and in Portugal) in design work for cultural and educational organizations and institutions. Much of his design work in recent years has been devoted to editorial and exhibition design. He devised and is currently course leader of the MA in Communication Design at *Escola Superior de Artes e Design* (ESAD) in Matosinhos.

Terry Irwin is Professor and Head of the School of Design at Carnegie Mellon University. She has been a design practitioner for more than forty years and was a founding partner of the international design firm MetaDesign. Her research focus is in Transition Design and how principles from living systems and Goethe's approach to understanding natural phenomena can inform more responsible and sustainable design approaches.

Cinnamon Janzer is an independent journalist who covers travel, culture, and social justice. Her work has been published in outlets like *National Geographic*, *Fast Company*, the *Washington Post*, *Pacific Standard*, *New York Magazine*, and more. You can read more about her and see selections of her work at www.cinnamon-janzer.com.

Guy Julier is the author of *Economies of Design* (2017) and *The Culture of Design* (3rd revised edition, 2014). He is currently Professor of Design Culture at the University of Brighton. As Professor of Design at Leeds Metropolitan University (2001–10), he founded DesignLeeds, a cross-disciplinary research and consultancy unit specializing in social design. With Lucy Kimbell, he has led projects to develop thinking and methods in social design.

Lucy Kimbell is the Director of the Innovation Insights Hub and Professor of Contemporary Design Practices at University of the Arts London. She is an experienced researcher, postgraduate educator, and design consultant, and has spent much of her career on design's fringes, intersecting with other disciplines and contexts including management and policy.

Kalle Lasn is the cofounder, copublisher, and art director of Adbusters. Adbusters is a not-for-profit media foundation that publishes *Adbusters* Magazine six times per year with a global circulation. The magazine concerns itself with the erosion of our physical and cultural environments by commercial forces. *Adbusters* documents and discusses the urgent issues of our global economy and culture while providing literary and insightful activist commentary.

Ezio Manzini is currently President of the DESIS Network, Distinguished Professor of Design for Social Innovation at Elisava Design School and Engineering, Barcelona; Honorary Professor at the Politecnico di Milano, and Guest Professor at Tongji University (Shanghai) and Jiangnan University (Wuxi). Recent publications include: *Design, When Everybody Designs: An Introduction to Design for Social Innovation*, MIT Press (2015) and *The Politics of Everyday (Designing in Dark Times)*, Bloomsbury Academic (2019).

Sylvia Margolin worked as Professor of Social Work at Governors State University after receiving a PhD in Social Work from the University of Illinois and teaching as an adjunct at the University of Chicago. She taught a variety of courses to master's degree students. Her publications include a book, *Complete Group Counseling Program for Children of Divorce*, and a number of articles.

Victor Margolin is Professor Emeritus of Design History at the University of Illinois at Chicago, USA. He is a founding editor and now coeditor of the academic design journal *Design Issues*. His many books include: *The Designed World: Images, Objects, Environments*; *The Politics of the Artificial: Essays on Design*; *Design Discourse: History, Theory, Criticism*; *Discovering Design: Explorations in Design Studies*. He has been awarded a Lifetime Achievement Award by Cumulus and the Design Research Society.

Katherine McCoy cochaired Cranbrook Academy of Art's Design Department for twenty-four years. She was a senior lecturer at Illinois Institute of Technology's Institute of Design in Chicago and a Distinguished Visiting Professor at the Royal College of Art. Honors include the AIGA medal, elected member of the Alliance Graphique Internationale, an Honorary Doctorate from Kansas City Art Institute, and with her husband Michael, the Smithsonian Design Museum's first Design Mind Award.

William McDonough is an architect and a globally recognized leader in sustainable design development. He was the inaugural chair of the World Economic Forum's Meta-Council on the Circular Economy and currently serves on the Forum's Global Future Council on the Future of Environment and Natural Resource Security. For more than forty years, McDonough has defined the principles of the sustainability movement. He is the coauthor of *Cradle to Cradle: Remaking the Way We Make Things* (2002), and its follow up, *The Upcycle: Beyond Sustainability-Designing for Abundance* (2013).

Victor J. Papanek (1923–1998) was a philosopher of design and author of the seminal publication *Design for the Real World: Human Ecology and Social Change* (1971). In the course of his career as both a professor and a working designer, Papanek applied the principles of socially responsible design in collaborative projects with concerns such as UNESCO and the World Health Organization. He consistently strove to use design as a force for the improvement of life quality in developing countries and peripheral communities in Europe and in the United States.

Luiza Prado de O. Martins is a Brazilian researcher and artist. Her work looks into questions of gender, technology, and the body. She is one-half of the artistic research duo A Parede and holds a PhD in Design Research from the University of the Arts Berlin.

Elizabeth Resnick is Professor Emerita, former chair of Graphic Design and current part-time faculty at Massachusetts College of Art and Design, Boston. She is the editor of *The Social Design Reader*, Bloomsbury Visual Arts (2019). Her previous publications include *Developing Citizen Designers*, Bloomsbury Academic (2016); *Design for Communication: Conceptual Graphic Design Basics*, John Wiley & Sons Publishers (2003); and *Graphic Design: A Problem-Solving Approach to Visual Communication*, Prentice-Hall Publications (1984).

Elizabeth Sanders is the founder of MakeTools, LLC, where she explores new spaces in the emerging design landscapes. As a practitioner, she introduced many of the methods being used today to drive design from a human-centered perspective. She has practiced participatory design research within and between all the design disciplines. Her current research focuses on codesign processes for innovation, intervention, and transdisciplinary collaboration.

Daniela Sangiorgi is an Associate Professor in the Design Department at Politecnico di Milano. As one of the first researchers investigating the area of Service Design, she worked in the Lancaster University Imagination research group from 2009 to 2015. Her research focuses on the role of design in the development of services with a particular focus on public sector innovation and within the service science debate.

Ann Thorpe teaches sustainable design at several universities in and around London, England. She has published a number of papers and two books, *The Designers Atlas of Sustainability* and *Architecture and Design versus Consumerism*. Her work examines design's role in sustainable consumption, activism, and innovation, particularly moving from reformist to transformative policies.

Cameron Tonkinwise is Professor of Interdisciplinary Design at University of Technology Sydney. He was previously the Director of Design Studies at Carnegie Mellon University and the cochair of the Tischman Environment and Design Center at The New School. With colleagues at Carnegie Mellon University, he has been developing Transition Design, a collection of techniques for design-enabled multi-stage change toward more sustainable futures.

Jan van Toorn maintains a practice in communication design in Amsterdam (the Netherlands). He taught for many years at various academies and universities, including the Gerrit Rietveld Academy (the Netherlands) and the Rhode Island School of Design (the United States), and was the director of the Jan van Eyck Academy (the Netherlands, 1991–1998).

Elizabeth (Dori) Tunstall is a design anthropologist and design educator who works at the intersections of critical theory, culture, and design. She holds a PhD in Anthropology from Stanford University and a BA in Anthropology from Bryn Mawr College. She currently serves as Dean of Design at Ontario College of Art and Design University, the first black and black female dean of a faculty of design.

Pedro J. S. Vieira de Oliveira is an artist and researcher in sound studies. He holds a PhD (currently Dr. des) in Design Research from the University of Arts Berlin and is currently lecturer in Cultural Studies at the Heinrich-Heine Universität Düsseldorf. He is the other half of the artistic research duo "A Parede" and one-eighth of the "Decolonising Design" group.

Lauren Weinstein is a multidisciplinary designer working at the intersection of social change and codesign who holds an MA in Social Design and a BA in Sociology. She is currently a principal at The Australian Centre for Social Innovation. Lauren has codesigned and implemented services, systems, and policy that build social and economic prosperity across North America, Central America, Africa, Southeast Asia, and Australia.

Nigel Whitely (1953–2010) was Professor and Head of the Art Department at Lancaster University in the UK. He published a number of scholarly books on design, consumerism, architecture, and art. In 1993, Whiteley published *Design for Society*. The book examines British and European approaches to the ethics of design within the context of a consumer-driven society.

FURTHER READINGS

The texts listed below were acquired to be included in this reader. Space limitations precluded publishing all the articles selected for this volume. As such, I encourage all readers to acquire these materials. Texts are available in public and university libraries, on-line, or by contacting the author(s) directly.

Abdulla, D. (2014), "A Manifesto of Change or Design Imperialism? A Look at the Purpose of the Social Design Practice," paper presented at the *5th STS Italia Conference: A Matter of Design: Making Society through Science and Technology*, Milan, 12–14 June 2014.

Abdulla, D., A. Ansari, E. Canli, M. Keshavarz, M. Kiem, P. Oliveira, L. Prado, and T. Schultz (2016), "Decolonising Design." http://www.decolonisingdesign.com/statements/2016/editorial/ (accessed August 31, 2018).

Bonsiepe, G. (2006), "Design and Democracy," *Design Issues*, 22 (2): pp. 27–34.

Boylston, S. (2017), "Graphic Design and the Anthropocene: An Argument for More Sustainable Design Thinking—And Thus a More Sustainable World," *Print* Magazine Fall 2017.

Bruinsma, M. (2001), "The Long March" Typotheque [Internet blog]. https://www. typotheque.com/articles/the_long_march (accessed February 23, 2014).

Bruinsma, M. (2015), "The Utrecht Manifesto." http://www.utrechtmanifest.nl/utrecht-manifest-5/het-utrechts-manifest/ (accessed August 31, 2018).

Burdett, S. (2004), "The Rise of Responsible Graphic Design." http://fnewsmagazine.com/2004-mar/current/2004-mar/pages/p18.html (accessed August 31, 2018).

Casey, V. (2007), "Designer's Dilemma: Changing the Way We Think about Design to Better Tackle the Challenges of Climate Change." https://www.readingdesign.org/the-designers-dilemma/ (accessed August 31, 2018).

Chapman, J., and N. Gant (2009), "The Sustainable Design Context," in *Designers, Visionaries and Other Stories: A Collection of Sustainable Design Essays*, London: Earthscan Taylor & Francis/Routledge, pp. 3–5.

Cross, N. (2011), "Design Ability," in *Design Thinking: Understanding How Designers Think and Work*, Oxford and New York: Berg Publishers, pp. 3–30.

de Bretteville, S. L. (1974), "A Reexamination of Some Aspects of the Design Arts from the Perspective of a Woman Designer," in E. Kamarck (ed.), *Arts in Society: Women and the Arts* (Spring–Summer), Madison, Wisconsin: University of Wisconsin, pp. 114–123.

DiSalvo, C. (2010), "Design, Democracy and Agonistic Pluralism," in D. Durling (ed.), *Design and Complexity. Proceedings of the Design Research Society Conference*, 7–9 July, Montreal (Quebec), Canada: Université de Montréal.

Dorst, K. (2015), "Frame Creation and Design in the Expanded Field," *She Ji: Journal of Design, Economics, and Innovation*, 1 (1): pp 22–33.

Ehn, P. (2008), "Participation in Design Things," in the *Proceedings of the Tenth Anniversary Conference on Participatory Design 2008*, Bloomington, Indiana, pp 92–101.

Evans, D., and T. Jackson (2008), "Sustainable Consumption: Perspectives from Social and Cultural Theory," *RESOLVE Working paper*. http://resolve.sustainablelifestyles.ac.uk/sites/default/files/RESOLVE_WP_05-08.pdf (accessed August 31, 2018).

Fenn, T., and J. Hobbs (2015), "Wicked Ethics in Design," in 7th International DEFSA Conference Proceedings, Design Education Forum of South Africa. https://www.researchgate.net/publication/301534312_Wicked_Ethics_in_Design (accessed August 31, 2018).

Fuad-Luke, A. (2015), "Design Activism's Teleological Freedoms as a Means to Transform Our Habitus," in A. Fuad-Luke, A. Hirscher, and K. Moebus (eds.), *Agents of Alternatives: Re-designing Our Realities*, Berlin, Germany: Agents of Alternatives, pp. 281–94.

Holmlid, S. (2009), "Participative, Co-operative, Emancipatory: From Participatory Design to Service Design," in *Dethinking Service, Rethinking Design, First Nordic Conference on Service Design and Service Innovation*, Oslo, Norway, 24–26 November .

Howard, A. (2000), "Design Beyond Commodification," *Eye*, 10 (38), Winter 2000.

Icograda (2000), "Oullim Manifesto 2000." http://www.ico-d.org/resources/design-education-manifesto (accessed August 31, 2018).

Icograda (2011), "Icograda Design Education Manifesto 2011." http://www.ico-d.org/resources/design-education-manifesto (accessed August 31, 2018).

Kimbell, L. (2011), "Designing for Service as One Way of Designing Services," *International Journal of Design*, 5 (2): pp 41–52.

Koskinen, I., and G. Hush (2016), "Utopian, Molecular and Sociological Social Design," *International Journal of Design*, 10 (1): pp 65–71.

Krippendorff, K. (1997), "A Trajectory of Artificiality and New Principles of Design for the Information Age," in K. Krippendorff (ed.), *Design in the Age of Information: A Report to the National Science Foundation (NSF)*, Raleigh, NC: School of Design, North Carolina State University, pp. 91–6. Retrieved from http://repository.upenn.edu/asc_papers/95.

Lasn, K. (1998), "The People vs The Corporate Cool Machine," *Adbusters* (23) (Autumn).

Lasn, K. (2000), "The New Activism (Fire in the Belly)," in *Culture Jam: The Uncooling of America*, New York: Quill Publishing, pp. 111–21.

Manzini, E. (1994), "Design, Environment and Social Quality: From 'Existenzminimum' to 'Quality Maximum,'" *Design Issues*, 10 (1): pp 37–43 (Spring).

Margolin, V. (2005), "The Citizen Designer," in M. Bierut, W. Drenttel, and S. Heller (2006). *Looking Closer 5: Critical Writings on Graphic Design*, New York: Allworth Press.

Margolin, V. (2007), "Design, the Future and the Human Spirit," *Design Issues*, 23 (3): pp. 4–15 (Summer).

McCoy, K. (1994), "Graphic Design in a Multicultural World," in *How* Magazine 10.24.1994, and reprinted in A. Bennett (ed.), *Design Studies: Theory and Research in Graphic Design*, New York: Princeton Architectural Press, 2006, pp. 200–5.

McCoy, K. (1998), "Education in an Adolescent Profession," in Steven Heller (ed.), *The Education of a Designer*, New York: Allworth Press, pp. 3–12.

McCoy, K. (2002), "Greening Communications: Cultural Sustainability," *High Ground Design*, Colorado: Buena Vista.

Mitrovic, I., and O. Suran, eds. (2016), "Introduction to Speculative Design Practice," in *Introduction to Speculative Design Practice—Eutropia: A Case Study*, Split: Ministry of Culture of the Republic of Croatia & Croatian Designers Association. http://interakcije.net/2015/05/12/introduction-to-speculative-design-practice-eutropia-a-case-study/ (accessed August 31, 2018).

Mouffee, C. (2007), "Artistic Activism and Agonistic Spaces," *Art and Research: A Journal of Ideas, Contexts and Methods*, 1 (2): pp 1–5 (Summer).

Oswald, D. (2016), "From Ethics to Politics: If Design is Problem Solving, What Then Are the Problems?" in the *Proceedings of the 18th International Conference on Engineering and Production Design Education*, 2016, published by the IED and Design Society.

Schwarz, M., and J. Elffers (2010), *Sustainism Is the New Modernism: A Cultural Manifesto for the Sustainist Era*, New York: D.A.P./Distributed Art Publishers.

Schwarz, M., and D. Krabbendam (2013), "Social Design in the Era of Sustainism," in Michiel Schwarz and Diana Krabbendam (eds.), *Sustainist Design Guide**, Amsterdam, The Netherlands: BIS Publishers, pp. 11–20.

Thorpe, A. (2010), "Defining Design Activism." http://designactivism.net/wp-content/uploads/2011/05/Thorpe-definingdesignactivism.pdf (accessed August 31, 2018).

Tonkinwise, C. (2015), "Design for Transitions—From and to What?" https://digitalcommons.risd.edu/critical_futures_symposium_articles/5 (accessed August 31, 2018).

Tonkinwise, C. (2015), "Just Design: Being Dogmatic about Defining Speculative Critical Design Future Fiction," *Medium* blog. https://medium.com/@camerontw/just-design-b1f97cb3996f (accessed August 31, 2018).

van Toorn, J. (2004), "Communication Design: A Social Practice," in *Design's Delight*, Rotterdam, The Netherlands: 010 Publishers, pp. 51–63.

INDEX

AADF. *see* Aboriginal Artists Development Fund (AADF)

A/B Manifesto 376

Aboriginal Artists Development Fund (AADF) 353–6

Aboriginal Smart Art project. *see* Aboriginal Artists Development Fund (AADF)

action research 263–4, 272n1

active citizens 264–6

actor-network theory (ANT) 329

Acumen Fund 422

acupunctural planning 411–12

Adams, Robin 286

Adbusters magazine 185

Adobe Think Tank 352

Adorned in Dreams: Fashion and Modernity (Wilson) 147

Adorno, Theodor W. 69

AgeLab 205

Agenda 21: The Earth Summit Strategy to Save Our Planet 23

AHRC. *see* Arts and Humanities Research Council (AHRC)

Aid as Imperialism (Hyter) 33

AIGA Journal 185

Alexander, Christopher 35, 81, 282, 418

Allen, Stan 317

Alperovitz, Gar 25

Alpine Architecture (Taut) 20

Alstyne, Greg Van 19

American Institute of Graphic Arts 363

American Revolution 112

amplifying projects 443

Anderson, Laurel 260

Anglo-European hegemony 425–6

Ansari, Ahmed 194, 417

Anscombe, Isabelle 146

ANT. *see* actor-network theory (ANT)

Ant Farm 21

Anti-Art University 427

Antonelli, Paola 376

Appadurai, Arjun 307, 354

Appleton, Jay 90

Archer, Bruce 68, 73

Archeworks 206

Archigram 21, 181

Architects for Humanity 25

"The Architecture of Public and Private Life" (essay) 146

Architecture without Architects 34

Archizoom 21, 279

Are Clothes Modern 34

Arizona State University's Center for Services Leadership 260

Arnstein, S. R. 267

artful integrations 298

articulation 332

Arts and Crafts movement 111, 278

Arts and Humanities Research Council (AHRC) 5, 9, 18

Art-Union article of 1848 113

Arvidsson, Adam 334
ASA. *see* Aboriginal Artists Development Fund
    (AADF)
Ashley, Laura 150
Association for Consumer Research 272n1
Attfield, Judy 146, 153
Auger, James 383–4
Australian Communication Research Institute 211
Australian Public Service Commission 433, 437
Awami Art Collective 424

backcasting 440, *440*
Baldwin, Jay 242
Banded Workshops 111
BAP. *see Bicycles Against Poverty* (BAP)
Barad, Karen 296, 298, 304–5
Bardwell, Lisa V. 437
Bardzell, Jeffrey 383–4, 386
Bardzell, Shaowen 383–4, 386
Barth, Fredrik 352
Barthes, Roland 171
Bate, Paul 268
Baudrillard, Jean 176
Bauer, Robert 285–6
Bauhaus manifesto of 1919 (Gropius) 20
Benn, Anthony Wedgwood 40
Benn, Caroline Wedgwood 40
Bentley, Tom 264
Berlin Wall 341
Berman, David 369
Berry, Wendell 114
Beyond the Limit 219
Bezaitis, Maria 352
Bhamra, T. A. 245
Bhan, Niti 347–8
Bicycles Against Poverty (BAP) 366–8
Bieling, Tom 386
Billingsley, K. 261
Björgvinsson, Erling 190, 311
Black Feminist Thought 388
Blake, William 110, 218
Bleecker, Julian 376
Blueprint magazine 45
Boland, Dick 296
Boltanski, L. 279
bookish culture 121, 132n14
Borges, Adelia 348
Botero, A. 301
Boulton, Matthew 104–6
Bowen, S. 384

Boys, Jos 157–8
Brand, Stewart 445
Brandes, Uta 386
Brandt, Marianne 21
Braungart, Michael 187, 217, 245
Breuer, Marcel 21
British Council 422
Brown, Tim 189, 284–6, 349, 363
Bruce, Margaret 151, 156–7
Bryn Mawr College 346
Bryson, John 329
Buchanan, Richard 43, 117, 283, 287
Buchmüller, S. 386
Buckley, Cheryl 147, 386
Buckminster-Fuller, Richard 6
Buck-Morss, Susan 69
Bunyan, John 110
Burdick, Anne 168
Burnette, Charles H. 283
Burns, Colin 257–8, 261
Burton, Michael 378n5
Business Council for Sustainable Development 221
Buur, Jacob 355

California Institute of the Arts 201
Candy, Stuart 439
capability approach 415
capitalism, and creative class 279–80
Carlesson-Kanyama, A. 440
Carlile, Paul 298
Carson, Rachel 33, 187, 218, 242
categories and placements 123–4
'Cathedral of Socialism' 20
Cavanagh, Sue 161–2
Cellnet 180
Cetina, Knorr 339
Chandler, Alfred 112
*Change by Design: How Design Thinking Transforms
    Organizations and Inspires Innovation* (Brown)
    284, 311
Changing Course 221
Chaplin, Charlie 54
Chapman, Jonathan 247–8
Chiapello, È. 279
Chochinov, Allan 11
Churchman, C. West 134n37
Città slow 339
Clark, Herman Pi'ikea 355–6
Clarke, Alison J. 6, 31
Club of Rome 219

Club of Rome's Limits to Growth (Carson) 242
Coca Cola 148
Cockburn, Cynthia 151–2
co-creation
    practice 398–9
    spaces 396–8
co-designing 401
Colburn, Theo 221
Cole, Henry 107–8
Colin McKinnon Dodd 353
collaborative associations 406
collaborative enterprises 406
collaborative housing 414
collaborative organizations 405–6
collaborative services 260, 406
Collective Action Toolkit 420
"Collective Action Toolkit" 363
Collins, Patricia Hill 388
Collopy, Fred 296
colonialism, defined as 346
coloniality 426
colonial power matrix 425
communication design 121, 125, 210–11
communication theory 123
Communist Manifesto 109
community centred approach 266
Computer Supported Cooperative Work 305
conceptual design space 397
Conference on Design Methods of 1962 281
conflict analysis tools 438
connective tissue 434
consciousness-raising/conscientization 264
contextual design space 397
Cooper-Hewitt National Design Museum 19
Cornwall, Andrea 266
Corporate Social Responsibility 234
Cottam, Hilary 257–8, 260, 261, 265
Coughlin, Joseph 205
countering asphyxiation 425–8
Counter Spy Shop 180
Cowan, Ruth Schwartz 153
Cowan's More Work for Mother: The Ironies of Household Technology from the Open Hearth to the Microwave (Schwartz Cowan) 145
craft culture 103
Craig, John 268–70
Cranbrook Academy of Art 167, 171
creative class, and capitalism 279–80
Creative Commons 28
creative communities 405

creative quarters 332
Creative Review 157
"Creatures of Habit? The Art of Behavioral Change" report 244
crèche provision 161–2
Crenshaw, Kimberlé 385
critical design. *see* speculative and critical design (SCD)
critical theory 383–5
critical thinking 82
Cross, Nigel 41–2, 73, 283, 363, 387, 418
"Crowbot Jenny" 378n4
Csikszentmihalyi, Mihaly 246, 249
cultural impact *vs.* operational impact 210
cultural interpreter, designer as 278–9
The Culture Industry: Enlightenment as Mass Deception 35
culture of design. *see* design culture
Cumulus 25

Davidoff, Leonore 146
Davidson, Caroline 145
de O. Martins, L.P. 192–3, 375, 381, 385
de Oliveira, P.J.S.V. 192–3, 375, 385
Decoding Advertisements (Williamson) 145
decolonized design innovation
    Aboriginal Artists Development Fund (AADF) 353–5
    context for 345–8
    design anthropology 351–2
    imperialism of 348–51
    overview 345
    principles for 355–6
    respect for experiences 356–7
    value systems and cultures 352–3
decolonized methodology 351–2
Decolonizing Anthropology (Harrison) 345
dematerialization, of design 209–15
Democratic National Convention 138
Department for International Development 422
design, as reflexive practice 175–8
design activism. *see also* design culture
    description 337–40
    overview 327–31
    and postneoliberalism 335–7
"Design and Gender" essay 146
design anthropology 351–2
design-as-practice 299–300, 302–3
Design Council 248, 272, 284
design culture. *see also* design activism

description 337–40
and design thinking 286–9
and feminist perspectives 157–8
and neoliberalism 331–5
overview 327–31
and postneoliberalism 335–7
design dematerialization 209–15
design education
criteria 76–7
description 75–6
design processes 78–81
design products 81–2
intrinsic value of 82–3
overview 73–5
ways of knowing 78
designer, as cultural interpreter 278–9
Designerly Ways of Knowing (Cross) 363
Designers Without Borders 25
"Design Ethnography Fieldguide" 363
design fiction 378n2
"design for behavior change" approach 245
design for children 158–60
Design for Social Impact 348–50
Design for Social Impact How-to Guide 348
Design for Social Impact Workbook 348
design for social innovation 412–15
Design for Society (Whiteley) 44, 242
Design for the Real World (Papanek) 6, 18–19, 32–3
design genres 179–80
Design Industry Voices 2011 335
design innovation, defined as 347
Design Innovation Group 156
design-in-practice 300–2
Design in the Borderlands (Fry) 427
Design Issues 17, 347
design knowledge 413–14
design-led approach 431–2
design methods/design thinking 417–28
Design Methods (Jones) 417
Design Noir: The Secret Life of Electronic Objects (Dunne) 46
Design Observer 347
The Design of Business 285
design processes 78–81, 394–5
design products 81–2
Design Research Lab 386
design-society relationships 63–70
design theory, and wicked problems 125–9
design things. *see also* design thinking
description 312–13

infrastructuring things 316–18
overview 311–12
participatory design things 314–16
projecting to infrastructuring 313–14
working relations 320–2
design thinking **281**. *see also* design things
challenges 280–1
creative class and capitalism 279–80
de-politicizing managerial practice 284–6
description 280, 295–7
and design-as-practice 299–300, 302–3
and design cultures 286–9
designer as cultural interpreter 278–9
and design-in-practice 300–2
fragmented core 282–4
overview 277, 295
Design Thinking for Educators Toolkit 419
Design Thinking Research Symposium 281
Design Thinking (Rowe) 282, 363
DESIS Network 24, 25, 413
Developing Citizen Designers (Resnick) xv
Development Impact 419
Dewberry, Emma 247
Dewey, John 118–20, 128–9, 135n42, 283, 287, 323
Dilnot, Clive 32, 41, 63
disaster capitalism 420
DMG Newsletter 134n33
Doblin, Jay 133n24
doctrine of placements 120–4, 133n23
Do-Fi company 320–1
Dorst, Kees 283
DOTT07 programme 267, 270, 272n2
Douglas, Mary 65, 81–2
Douglas, Simone 386
downcycling 222–4
Dresser, Christopher 107
Dumanoski, Dianne 221
Dunne, Anthony 179, 375–6, 382–4, 386, 456
Dymaxion World Map 22

Eagan, Ward 285–6
Earl of Warwick 105
Earth Charter 23
"The Earthly Paradise" (poem) 111
EBD. *see* experience-based-design (EBD)
eco-design 242, 245
Ecodesign: A Promising Approach to Sustainable Production and Consumption 242
eco-efficiency 221, 225–8

Ecological Design 242
ecological humanism 242
edugraphology 57–62
Eginton, Francis 105
Eginton, John 105
Ehn, Pelle 190, 269, 301, 311
Ehrlich, Anne 219
Ehrlich, Paul 219
E-Lab/Sapient 352
Emigre 185
enabling solutions 408–10
enacting future experiences 399–400, *401*
end-of-pipe solutions 224
Engineering and Physical Sciences Research Council 307
Engine Service Design group 260
Environmental Defense 218
environmental destruction 227
environmental policy 243–5
epistemological asphyxiation 425–8
Epsilon Embedded Systems 320
Eternally Yours Foundation 247
ethical surplus 334–5
"Ethnography Primer" 363
Experience and Nature (Dewey) 119
experience-based-design (EBD) 261
Eye magazine 185

Fair Trade 231
Falk, John H. 89
Fallan, Kjetil 329
FAN. see Feminist Arts News (FAN)
Fast Company 347
favorable environment 407–8
The Female Eunuch (Greer) 145
Feminist Arts News (FAN) 146–7
Feminist Design Collective 146
feminist perspectives
    alternative criteria 160–1
    culture of design 157–8
    design for children 158–60
    gender stereotyping 148–51
    and man's world 155–6
    overview 145–7
    socio-spatial perspectives 161–3
    style and gender 153–5
    symptoms/causes 164–5
    and tacit knowledge 155
    women as providers 152–3
    women as users 151–2

feminist speculative design 387–9
Figes, Eva 145
Finnish Funding Agency for Technology and Innovation 259
First Things First manifesto 21, 39–40, 167, 185
Fisch, Richard 261
Fitch, Rodney 157–8
Flaxman, John 106
Fletcher, Kate 187–8, 229, 247
Florida, Richard 279
Fondazione Housing Sociale 414
Ford, Henry 220
Forrester, Jay 22
Foucault, Michel 364
Fox School of Business 284
fragmented core, design 282–4
Frankfurt School 383–4
Frascara, Jorge 186, 209
Freire, Paulo 362
Frith, Simon 335
Fry, Tony 296, 304, 329, 378n6, 427
Fuad-Luke, Alastair 247
Fuller, Buckminster, R. 21–2, 24, 39, 54, 242
Fund, Acumen 347
Futures Cone (Voros) 378n1
fuzzy front end 394–5, 399

Gablik, Suzi 141
Garland, Ken 21, 39–40, 45, 47, 49, 167, 170, 185
gender
    stereotyping 148–51
    and style 153–5
General Motors 113
German Werkbund 111
Geuss, Raymond 384
Ghose, Rajeshwari 347–8, 350
Gide, André 93
Godwin, William 217
Goggin, Philip 247
Golembiewsky, R. T. 261
Goodall, Phil 146, 151, 153, 160, 162
Good Society 27–8
Gorz, André 35
Gotham Green 26
governments, and social design 14
Graeber, David 352
Grameen Bank 426
The Grand Domestic Revolution: A History of Feminist Designs for American Houses, Neighbourhoods and Cities (Hayden) 146

graphic design 172
   education 59
graph theory 134n32
Gray, Paula 351
Greater London Council 146, 161
The Great Exhibition of All the Nations 106–8
Great Law of Iroquois Confederacy 445
Greer, Germaine 145
Gropius, Walter 7, 20–1, 24, 34, 35, 131n3
Grosfoguel, Ramon 425
gross domestic product 333, 337
Guardian newspaper 40
Guattari, Félix 176
Guide to EcoReDesign 242

Hackwood, William 106
Haines, Douglas 167
Hall, Catherine 146
Hall, Edward 90
Hall, Stuart 169, 307, 329
Halse, Joachim 351
"handmaiden of colonialism" 346
Harary, Frank 134n32
Harman, Graham 305
Harrison, Andrew 82
Harrison, Faye 345, 353
Hartswood, Mark 296
Harvard Business Review 279, 284, 363
Harvey, David 331
Hasan, Arif 424
Hasegawa, Ai 378n3
Hatchuel, A. 290n3
Haug, Wolfgang 33
Hayden, Dolores 146
HCD. *see* human-centered design (HCD)
"HCD Toolkit" 363
"Hello Again" exhibition 242
Helsinki Design Lab 363
Hertzian Tales (Dunne) 46, 376, 383
Heskett, John 43, 101, 329
The Hidden Dimension (Hall) 90
Hillgren, Per-Anders 190, 311
Hippie Modernism 33
Hiroshi Shinohara 115
H&M 233
Hochschule für Gestaltung (HfG) Ulm 125, 131n2
Horkheimer, Max 34
Horne, Howard 335
Housewife (Oakley) 145
Howard, Andrew 167, 185

Howells, J. 259
'How Public Design?' 25
human-centered design (HCD) 210, 363–4
Hyter, Teresa 33

ICOGRADA Design Education Manifesto 356
ICSID. *see* International Council of Societies of
   Industrial Design (ICSID)
ICT. *see* Information Communication Technology
   (ICT)
IDEO 284, 285, 318, 348–9, 419
Ikea 161
Ikhlaq, Zahoor ul 423
ill-structured problem 136n48
imperialism, of decolonized design innovation
   348–51
"Improving Well-being through Transformative
   Service" 260
indeterminacy 126
Indigenous Art Code 354
industrial design 155
industrialization and design 101–15
Industrial Revolution 43, 101–2, 129, 201, 217,
   225
Information Communication Technology (ICT) 361
Information Technologies and Indigenous
   Communities 354
INKONST 319
Innovations for Poverty Alleviation Lab (IPAL) 421
intellectual property 338
intentional design space 397
International Council of Societies of Industrial
   Design (ICSID) 19, 25
International Encyclopedia of Unified Science 131n7
International Gender Design Network 386
International Monetary Fund 23, 333
intersectional feminism 385–7
IPAL. *see* Innovations for Poverty Alleviation Lab
   (IPAL)
irrelevant design 212
Irwin, Terry 196, 431
Isherwood, Baron 65, 81–2

Jackson, Tim 241, 250
Jacobs, Jane 224–5
Jain, Anab 384
Janzer, Cinnamon 18, 192, 361
Johnson & Johnson 221
Jones, J. C. 71n6, 81, 282, 417–18
Júdice, Andréa 386

Julier, Guy 191, 278, 327
Junginger, Sabine 262

Kalantidou, Eleni 427
Kalman, Tibor 185
Kaplan, Rachel 90
Kaplan, Stephen 90
Keedy, Jeffery 171
Kefauver, Estes 50
Kelley, David 285
Kellner-Rogers, M. 444
Kelly, Owen 169
Kent City Council 260
Kimbell, Lucy 189–90, 277, 295, 329
Kinder Surprise 386
King, Martin Luther 138
Kirkham, Pat 146
Klein, Naomi 420
Koolhaas, Rem 177
Kornet, Kelly 439
Kossoff, Gideon 196, 441
Kotler, Philip 136n54
Krippendorff, Klaus 314
Kuhn, Thomas 133n26
Kuilman, Dingeman 168, 171
Kurgan, Laura 5

Ladner, Sam 284
Lam, William M. C. 90
Lasn, Kalle 185, 199–200
Latour, Bruno 10, 13, 312–13, 323, 329
Lawson, Bryan 78, 283
Lawton, M. Powell 204–5
Lazzarato, Maurizio 334
Leadbeater, Charles 260, 265
LEED 244
Legionnaires' Disease 92
Leigh Star concept 269
Leong, Benny Ding 348
Leopold, Aldo 218
Levin, P. H. 80
Lévi-Strauss, Claude 346
Levy, Amir 262
Lewin, Kurt 263
Lewis, Jenny 156–7
Lilienfeld, Robert 220
Lilley, Debra 245
The Limits to Growth 22, 219
Living in a Man-Made World (Roberts) 146
Lodaya, Arvind 348

Loizeau, Auger 378n4
Long Now Foundation 445
Lotus Notes software 298

McCall. Leslie 385, 388
McCoy, Katherine 44, 137
McDonough, William 186, 217, 245
McLuhan, Marshall 35
McPeck, John E. 82
McQuiston, Liz 146, 156
McRobbie, Angela 334
Maddox, Eva L. 206
Magda, Rosa Maria Rodriguez 347
Mahatma Gandhi 109
Making Space: Women and the Man-Made
    Environment 146
making things 399–400, 401
Malmö Living Labs 190, 312, 319–21, 325n32
Malos, Ellen 145
Malthus, Thomas 187, 217–19
Maniates, Michael 243
Manzini, Ezio 4, 9, 15, 24, 133n24, 194, 248, 269,
    318, 403
Mapping Social Design Practice and Research
    project 9
Margolin, Myra 372n5
Margolin, Sylvia 17, 186, 201, 251
Margolin, Victor 5–6, 17, 186, 201, 251, 296
Markussen, Thomas 336, 338
Marsh, George Perkins 218
Martin, Roger 284–6
Martin, Rosy 151, 154, 161, 164
Marx, Karl 109
Maslow, Abraham 91
Massey, Doreen 340
Massive Change 18–19
material objects 121–2
Matlow, Erica 160
Mau, Bruce 18
Max-Neef, Manfred 237
May, Ernst 21
Mazaar Bazaar 427
Meadows, Dennis 219
Meadows, Donella 219
mediation infrastructuring 317
"Menstruation Machine" project 378n7, 384
Meroni, Anna 266, 269
Merton, Jubal 103
metaphoric appreciation 82
Methods Movement 418

methods toolkit. *see* design methods/design thinking
Meulman, Neils 168, 171
Meyer, Hannes 21
Mick, David Glen 272n1
Mignolo, Walter D. 425
Millennium Development Goals 23
Miller, Daniel 246
Millett, Kate 145
Mills, C. Wright 53
MindLab 25–6
Mir, Imran 423
Mobile Lorm Glove 386
Mobile Moments: A Collection of Tales for the '90s
     180
Modernism 140
modern world-system 425
Monsanto 221
Morris, William 6, 20, 22, 24, 39, 109, 111, 114,
     278
Mouffe, Chantel 317
MSPs. *see* multi-stakeholder processes (MSPs)
Muir, John 218
multi-stakeholder processes (MSPs) 433–4, 438
Mumford, Lewis 51, 113
Murdoch, George 97
Muyambi, Muyambi 366–7
Myers, John Peterson 221
Myrdal, Gunnar 29n16

Naidoo, Ravi 348
National College of Arts 423
National Endowment 138
National Health Service 301
Natural Resources Defense Council 218
needs-fears mapping 438
negotiation model 315
neocolonialism 197n13
     Bicycles Against Poverty (BAP) 366–8
     description 361–3
     human-centered design (HCD) 364
     methodologies and practices 363
     NeoNurture: The "Car Parts" Incubator 368
     One Laptop Per Child (OLPC) 370–1
     and transformative social change 366–8
     War Child 369
neoliberalism 197n11
     and design culture 331–5
     and postneoliberalism 335–7
NeoNurture: The "Car Parts" Incubator 368
neoteric arts 136n55
Nesta 419

Netherlands Design Institute 181
Neutra, Richard 34
New Economy movement 25, 30n23
New Left 138
News from Nowhere (Morris) 111
New World 218
NGOs. *see* nongovernmental organizations (NGOs)
Niedderer, Kristina 248
Nitta, Burton 384
Nitta, Michiko 378n5
"non-dimensional images" 133n28
nongovernmental organizations (NGOs) 319,
     349
Nussbaum, Bruce 192, 289, 347, 421
Nutrire Milano project 411
Nygaard, Kristen 313

Oakley, Ann 145, 152
Ojai workshops 438–9
Old Testament 109
OLPC. *see* One Laptop Per Child (OLPC)
One Laptop Per Child (OLPC) 347, 370–1
Open Welfare 265
Operating Manual for Spaceship Earth (Fuller) 22
operational impact *vs.* cultural impact 210
OPP. *see* Orangi Pilot Project (OPP)
Orange Metro 424
Orangi Pilot Project (OPP) 424
organisational transformation 262
Orientalism (Said) 362
Orlikowski, Wanda 296, 298, 300
Orr, David W. 445
Ortiz, Fernando 352
The Oslo Manual 347
Østerlund, Carsten 298
Otto, Ton 352
Our Common Future 23, 220
Our Stolen Future 221
Owen, Robert 108
oxymorons 122, 193, 197n16
Ozma Game Design 321

Pakistan Innovation Foundation 422
Pantzar, Mika 297
Panzer Division 213
Papanek, Victor 3, 6, 14, 18–19, 32–5, 39, 41–2,
     87, 201, 204, 242, 336
PAR. *see* Participatory Action Research (PAR)
paradigmatic change 262
Participatory Action Research (PAR) 433
participatory design things 314–16

participatory prototyping cycle (PPC) 398–400, 399, 400
Patriarchal Attitudes (Figes) 145
Paxton, Joseph 106
Peccei, Aurelio 22
Peck, Jamie 334
Pedagogy of the Oppressed (Freire) 362
Peters, Richard S. 76–7
The Philosophy of Money (Simmel) 329
Pilloton, Emily 347
placements and categories 123–4
Plan 9, 421
'Plug-In City' project 34
The Pluralist Commonwealth 25
Politecnico di Milano 413
The Politics of Housework (Malos) 145
Polyani, Karl 35
Popay, J. 267
Popper, Karl 134n36
Population: The First Essay (Malthus) 217
The Population Bomb (Ehrlich) 219
The Population Explosion (Ehrlich) 219
Porritt, Jonathon 440
postneoliberalism, and design culture 335–7
postwar American art 141
Poynor, Rick 39, 168
PPC. *see* participatory prototyping cycle (PPC)
Prius hybrid automobile 245
privilege and oppression
  critical theory and critical design 383–5
  feminist speculative design 387–9
  intersectional feminism and speculative design 385–7
  overview 381–2
  on semantics and SCD 382–3
Project H 347, 421
promising cases 404–5
psychology, and sustainable consumption 245–9
Punjab Information Technology Board 421
Punjab Safe Pani Company 424

Quijano, Anibal 427

Raby, Fiona 375–6, 383, 386
Ranjan, M. P. 348, 355
Rathje, William 220
Reckwitz, Andreas 296, 299
The Red Desert (film) 54
Redgrave, Richard 107
Red House 20
reduction 221–2

The Reenchantment of Art 141
Rehman, Parveen 424
"Re-Materialize" exhibition 242
Renaissance 117
replication strategies 410
"Republic of Salivation" 378n5, 384
The Revolution of Everyday Life (Vaneigem) 171
RGRA 319–21
The Rich Nations and the Poor Nations (Ward) 22
Rifkin, Jeremy 27
Rio Earth Summit (1992) 23, 220
Rittel, Horst 125–7, 134n34, 134n36, 135n41, 339, 418
Ritzer, George 444
Robert, Glenn 268
Roberts, Marion 146
Robinson, J. 440
Robinson, Rick 352
Rochberg-Halton, Eugene 249
Rockefeller Foundation 4, 348
Rogers, Richard 132n20
Rohe, Mies Van der 35
Rope Pump for Burkina Faso (van Tijen) 19
Rose, Gillian 68
Rosenberg, Buck 340
Rotman School of Management 284
Rowe, Peter 105, 282, 288, 363
Royal College of Art (RCA) 40, 75, 77, 84, 375, 384
Ruegg, Ruedi 132n22
Ruhleder, Karen 317, 318
Rural Studio 25
Ruskin, John 109, 111, 114
Russell, Lynnette 353
Russian doll effect 340
Russian Revolution 21
Rusten, Grete 329
Rylander, A. 280, 283, 287
Ryle, Gilbert 77
Ryn, Sim Van der 242

SA. *see* Stakeholder Analysis (SA)
Said, Edward 362
Saïd Business School 284
Saif, Umar 421
Saki Mafundiwa 350, 355
Salt, Titus 108
Samsung 338
Sanders, Elizabeth 193, 393
Sangiorgi, Daniela 188–9, 257, 262
Savage Imaginings (Russell) 353

SCD. *see* speculative and critical design (SCD)

Schatzki, Theodore 296, 299

Schmidheiney, Stephan 221

Schön, Donald 283, 305, 418

Schumacher, E. F. 33, 114, 219

Schwartz, Ruth 145

science and technology studies (STS) 329

The Sciences of the Artificial (Simon) 131n12,
    136n49, 282, 290n3

Scope of Total Architecture 131n3

"seat-of-the-pants" design 87

semantics and SCD 382–3

Sen, Amartya 415

Sennett, Richard 356

services, design for 13–14

Sexual Politics (Millett) 145

Shapiro, Robert 220

Sharpe, Bill 440

Shove, Elizabeth 288, 296, 297

Sierra Club 218

SIL. *see* Social Innovation Lab (SIL)

The Silent Language (Hall) 90

Silent Spring (Carson) 33, 218–19, 242

Simmel, Georg 329

Simon, Herbert 120, 128, 131n12, 135n37,
    136n49, 286, 290n3, 356

situation-centered design 18, 361–2, 365, 370,
    372n1

Skidmore, P. 268–70

Skills Share Day 267

Sloan, Alfred P. 113

slow design 247

*Small is Beautiful: A Study of Economics as If People
    Mattered* (Schumacher) 33, 219

Smith, Adam 104

Smith, Kenwin K. 262

social design and neocolonialism
    description 361–3
    human-centered design 364
    methodologies and practices 363
    NeoNurture: The "Car Parts" Incubator 368
    One Laptop Per Child (OLPC) 370–1
    overview 361
    and transformative social change 366
    War Child 369

social design toolkit 419

Social Impact Design Summit 4

social innovation
    acupunctural planning 411–12
    collaborative organizations 405–6
    creative communities 405

design for 412–15
    design knowledge 413–14
    enabling solutions 408–10
    favorable environment 407–8
    overview 403
    promising cases 404–5
    replication strategies 410
    scaling-up 406–7
    synergizing strategy 411–12

Social Innovation Lab (SIL) 261, 421

Socialist League 20

social model, of design 201–6

social workers 203–4

Society of Arts competition 107

sociology, and sustainable consumption 249–51

socio-spatial design 161–3

'soft' styling 154

Sottsass, Ettore 34

South Kensington Museum 107

Spaceship Earth (Ward) 22

speculative and critical design (SCD) 375, 382–9

Sperschnieder, Werner 351

SPIRE research group 355

Sputniko 384

Stam, Mart 21

Stam, Robert 177

Stanford Encyclopedia of Philosophy (Kohn) 346

Stanford Social Innovation Review 284

Star, Susan L. 317, 318

Sterling, Bruce 376

story telling 399–400, *401*

Strauss, Carolyn F. 247

Strong, Maurice 220

STS. *see* science and technology studies (STS)

Stubbs, George 106

Sturt, George 103

style, and gender 153–5

Suchman, Lucy 288, 296, 302

Sullivan, Louis 58

Summum Bonum 93

Superflux 384

Super Satisfiers project 237–8

Superstudio 21, 279

sustainable consumption, and design
    environmental policy 243–5
    overview 241
    psychology 245–9
    sociology 249–51
    timeline 241–3

sustainable fashion
    description 230–1

Local project 234–5
and nature 231–4
Nine Lives project 236–7
No Wash project 236
overview 229–30
Super Satisfiers project 237–8
Updatable project 235
5 Ways 234–8
sustainable innovation
    co-creation practice 398–9
    co-creation spaces 396–8
    design process 394–5
    overview 393–4
    participatory prototyping cycle (PPC) 398–400
    roles for designers 395–6, 396
symbolic resources 176, 249
synergizing strategy 411–12
Systems of Survival 224

tacit knowledge 155, 159
Tang, T. 245
Tassinari, Virginia 27
Taut, Bruno 20–1
telling stories 399–400, *401*
Tentative Collective 424
Thackara, John 384, 415
thinkpublic 261, 267
Third Industrial Revolution 28
Third International Conference on Indoor Air
    Quality and Climate 92
Third World 171, 355–6
Thoreau, Henry David 187, 218
Thorpe, Ann 188, 241
3M 221
Tigerman, Stanley 206
timeline, and sustainable consumption 241–3
Tonkinwise, Cameron 9, 196, 441
Toorn, Jan van 45, 175
Toscani, Oliviero 170–1
Trachtenberg, Alan 113
transformational change 261–3
transformation design 196n5
    active citizens 264–6
    building infrastructures and enabling platforms
        268–9
    capacities and project partnerships 266–7
    and community centred approach 266
    description 260–1
    enhancing imagination and hope 269–70
    overview 257–9
    practices and principles 263–4

redistributing power 267–8
success and impact 270–1
transformational change 261–3
transformative services 259–60
transformative services 259–60
transformative social change 366–8
transition design 435, 441
    design-led approach 431–2
    overview 431
    and phased approach 434–47
    stakeholder involvement 432–4
Transition Towns movement 339–40
The Truth Phone 180
Tschumi, Bernard 317
Tunstall, Elizabeth (Dori) 191, 197n12, 345, 351

UK Arts and Humanities Research Council 307
Unimark International 138
United Nations Conference on Environment and
    Development 23
Unto this Last 109
Urban Resource Centre 424
UrbLove 321
*Use Less Stuff: Environmental Solutions for Who We
    Really Are* (Lilienfeld and Rathje) 220
US Green Building Council 244
utopian thought 20–2

value systems and cultures 352–3
Vaneigem, Raoul 171
Vanstone, Chris 257–8, 261
van Tijen, Reinder 19
Velde, Henry van de 20
Vickers, Geoffrey 27
Victoria & Albert Museum 332
*A View from the Interior: Feminism, Women and
    Design* (Attfield and Kirkham) 146
Vila Rosário 386
Voros, Joseph 378n1

Walker, Sam Bass 112
Walker, Stuart 247
Wall Street economy 25
Wang, Shou Zhi 347
War Child 369
Ward, Barbara 22, 29n16
Water Project 347
Watt, James 105
Watzlawick, Paul 261
WDS. *see* Women's Design Service (WDS)
Weakland, John H. 261

The Wealth of Nations (Smith) 104
Weatherhead School of Management 284
Wedgwood, Josiah 105–6
Weinstein, Lauren 18, 192, 361
WEN. *see* Women's Environmental Network (WEN)
Wheatley, Margaret J. 444
The Wheelwright's Shop (Sturt) 103
Whitehead, A. N. 75
Whiteley, Nigel 44, 145, 242
wicked problems 394, 431
    and design theory 125–9
    doctrine of placements 120–4
    and intentional operations 118–20
    stakeholder involvement in 432–4
    and technology 129–30
"Wicked Problems in Design Thinking" 283
Wilderness Society 218
Wilkie, Alex 329
Williamson, Judith 145
Wilsdon, James 264
Wilson, Elizabeth 147
Winhall, Jennie 257–8, 261
Winterhouse First Symposium on Design Education and Social Change 4
Woman's Touch: Women in Design from 1860 to the Present Day (Anscombe) 146
A Woman's Work is Never Done: A History of Housework in the British Isles 1650–1950 (Davidson) 145
women
    design (*see* feminist perspectives)

    as providers 152–3
    as users 151–2
Women in Design—A Contemporary View (McQuiston) 146, 156
Women's Design Service (WDS) 146, 162
Women's Environmental Network (WEN) 146
Wordsworth, William 218
World Bank 23
World Bank Institute 349
World Commission on Environment and Development 23, 220
World Design Science Decade 22
World Resources Inventory 22
World War I 139
World Wildlife Federation 218
Wright, Frank Lloyd 113
Wright, Joseph 106
Wright, Lloyd 58
Wurtman, Richard 89
Wyatt, Jocelyn 349

Yamatji Aboriginal cultural group 353
Yaneva, Albena 329
You Toolkit 419

The Zero Marginal Cost Society (Rifkin) 28
Zero Waste initiative 26
Zimbabwe Institute for Vigital Arts (ZIVA) 350
ZIVA. *see* Zimbabwe Institute for Vigital Arts (ZIVA)
Zürcher Frauenzentrale 388